XPM
SINCE 1999

Contents

R-NET

180

CHAPTER 7

Daily Life

204

CHAPTER 8

Kids

220
CHAPTER 9
Education

248
CHAPTER 10
Health Care and the Medical System

264
CHAPTER 11
Things to Do in Your Free Time

About The Holland Handbook

24TH EDITION

Welcome, expat, to the Netherlands! We are proud to present you this twenty-fourth edition of *The Holland Handbook*, which we hope will prove to be as good a friend to you during your stay in the Netherlands as it has been to numerous other expats over the past twenty-three years.

This book has been compiled for a very mixed group of readers who have one thing in common and that is that they want to find their way in the Netherlands: the expat employee, the expat partner, foreign entrepreneurs, and the many foreign students who come to the Netherlands to train or study. Also for those involved in expatriate affairs who want to keep abreast of the latest developments in their various areas of interest, this book has proven to be a very welcome source of information. Last but not least, this book is a wonderful reminder, including beautiful photographs, of life in the Netherlands for those who are moving on to their next posting – or back home.

The Holland Handbook is the result of the enthusiastic efforts of more than 20 authors, organizations and proofreaders of various nationalities and with very different backgrounds. Most of them are specialists who work for international companies and organizations and who have an impressive amount of know-how when it comes to providing expatriates with information.

The diversity of the editorial team makes reading this book a journey in itself. You will find technical information on practical subjects interspersed with personal experiences, background information and columns – all written in each contributor's personal style. With so many topics to cover, *The Holland Handbook* may at times take an unexpected turn – however, as this book is primarily meant as a reference book and not as a book to be read in one go, you can simply select the topic you want to read up on, even if you only have a few minutes to spare.

Though *The Holland Handbook* contains a wealth of information, we do not have the illusion that it is at all complete. It is meant as an introduction, or orientation if you will, into the various subjects that can be of interest to you. By referring you to the relevant literature, addresses and websites, we have provided you with as many sources of additional and/or more in-depth information as we can think of. Undoubtedly, we have forgotten a few subjects, websites or books. If you feel that we have left out something that should not have been missed, we would greatly appreciate it if you let us know about this, for instance by sending an e-mail to editor@xpat.nl.

Bert van Essen and Gerjan de Waard, Publishers

www.facebook.com/XPatMedia

Art, music, architecture, folklore, foods and dress, our roles and relationships, body language, gestures, greetings and partings, all weave together to form a rich cultural diversity. Every culture is the outcome of centuries of social interaction, a shared history, religious norms and experience – however, it is only when we are among people of a different culture that we really become aware of how much we are the product of those shared elements ourselves. It is just as important to realize that the majority of the people in our host culture are also not aware of how their shared background influences their own behavior – and of how unfamiliar and uncomfortable this behavior may be for us (or perhaps, how reassuringly similar!). When attempting to understand and survive in another culture, there are many areas in which we need to pause and consider how our own culture and the host culture differ. This takes time, patience, and some sense of adventure. The first step in achieving this is realizing that neither way of living is wrong or right – it's just... different.

INTRODUCTION

A New Life in the Netherlands

Adapting to a New Country and a New Culture

BY DIANE LEMIEUX

So you decided to come live in the Netherlands. You may have been tantalized by the idea of exploring old-world Europe with its architecture and museums. Or maybe it was the possibility of viewing kilometers of flower beds and sand dunes from the seat of a bicycle that attracted you to this country. Perhaps the adventure of undertaking something new, something different is what tipped the balance for you. Whatever it was that made you say yes to a move to the Netherlands, here you are and the country is just outside your door, waiting to be discovered.

But now, instead of having time to visit, like a tourist on an extended trip, you are faced with the task of undertaking all of life's daily chores in an entirely new environment. Whereas at home you did most of these things without thinking, you must now spend time and energy discovering where to buy milk and how to pay the phone bill. The climate is different, you need to get used to the types of products that you can and cannot find at your local grocers', and you have to orient yourself using street signs and product labels you do not understand. You suddenly discover that English is used far less than you had expected, and that Dutch is far harder to learn than you had hoped.

This is the process of adaptation, of creating a new home in this foreign country. Eventually you will be settled in a new house, and will have established routines that make life seem more normal; you will have identified a favorite grocery store or market, know where to purchase your home-language newspaper, and may even have discovered a favorite café for your usual Sunday morning breakfasts. This book will help you with this process of adapting to this country you have adopted, however briefly, as your home.

But this book also has a different focus; to describe the culture of the people who live here, as well as the practicalities of life in the Netherlands. The word 'culture' as it is used here is not about the artistic and historic expressions of culture you find in museums. It is about everyday behavior, the glue that binds communities, the norms and values that regulate social life. Like all cultures, the Dutch culture is expressed through language, through social structures and habits, through the way people communicate with each other. This culture is subtle and you will discover it slowly over time, as you increasingly deal with the 'locals'. It is something you will piece together as you interact with your neighbors, as you watch your colleagues at work, from the way you are treated in the shops or when taking the train.

The Dutch, of course, are not explicitly aware of their culture, just as we are not aware of our own. It is only because we are here as foreigners, observing another culture, that we become aware of the differences between the way members of the host culture react, and our own expectations of how one 'should' act. We came, expecting certain patterns of behavior from our hosts: the stereotypes typify the Dutch as being tolerant, frugal and hardworking. From the stories of the red light district you may expect a very liberal society and, knowing of the reputation the country as a leader in graphic design and architecture, you may expect an innovative attitude to life and work. And yet you will also find conservative attitudes and behaviors.

Dutch society is a highly complex, multi-cultural mix of historic and modern influences, whose daily practice and social behavior may not live up to the values and etiquette that you are accustomed to. Your daily chores bring you into a series of intercultural encounters with the Dutch which sometimes leave you wondering 'what just happened?' It is this process of accumulated 'incidents' that we call 'culture shock' and that is blamed for much of the strife associated with expatriate living.

It is popularly understood that culture shock is a process, containing a set of phases which will all pass, eventually leading you to return to your normal, happy state as a well-adjusted individual. What is not often explained is that culture shock is experienced differently by every individual, depending on their own culture, attitudes, expectations, and previous international experience. Furthermore, moments of frustration and anger may occur at any time during a stay in a foreign country and are a normal part of adjustment. However, culture shock is also a process which can be controlled and minimized.

The advice given by most intercultural or adaptation specialists is to get to know your host culture. Understanding the underlying reasons for the behavior of the Dutch helps to see them as individuals and not as a global 'them'. The Holland Handbook has been written by both Dutch individuals and expatriates with years of experience in living with and explaining the Dutch to foreigners. They describe the historic and cultural aspects that influence the behavior you observe, making it more comprehensible and logical. You don't have to like everything about the Dutch culture or adapt to every aspect of it either. But with a bit of understanding and good will, you will most probably come to find at least a few friends in this society, people who will make the experience of having lived in the Netherlands a memorable one.

You Have Arrived in the Netherlands

BY HAN VAN DER HORST

What does it mean to be in the Netherlands? You crawl ahead on the highway behind laboring windshield wipers, watching the ragged horizon of apartment buildings go by as the gray clouds are chased along by a strong south-western wind. Due to the 2020 and 2021 Covid restrictions, there was a period of quiet on the highways, but now that the epidemic appears to be under control, traffic jams have come back with a vengeance, with 8.8 million cars in the Netherlands (954,000 of which are fully electric or hybrid). Should the government – in connection with the pandemic – once again ask the people to work from home as much as possible, then the highway system of the country could easily handle the number of cars. However, under normal circumstances, there are hundreds of kilometers of traffic jams at the beginning and end of the day. Sometimes, this almost leads to actual chaos, but generally speaking this can be avoided.

As the slowly moving traffic jams come to another halt, you have the chance to focus on your fellow drivers. Your first conclusion is obvious: you are in a wealthy country. This is evident from the newness of the cars and the number of traffic jams. Meanwhile, as you will surely notice, the government is working hard at widening the highways, or laying new ones – a cause of considerable temporary inconvenience. This has been going on for quite some time. Towards the end of 2015, for instance, it opened an addition to the A4, which connects The Hague and Rotterdam, thanks to which these two cities – which are only 20 kilometers apart – are now linked by two highways instead of one. Not that this put an end to the traffic jams around Rotterdam, the second largest city of the Netherlands. The new tunnel underneath the Nieuwe Waterweg (New Waterway), west of Rotterdam will hopefully be ready in 2024 and the bottlenecks around Utrecht were tackled in 2021. Also the A2 – the start of the Route de Soleil to the Mediterranean Sea – has been improved in a number of places.

This traffic situation has revived an age-old discussion; the levying of a traffic jam toll – a dynamic toll such as they have in Singapore that makes drivers pay to make use of the highways. Whereby they pay more during rush hour and much less, for instance, at night. In return, the road tax that everyone owes would be reduced, or abolished. ICT would make this all possible, but – so the opponents insisted – there are many objections: the average employee, for example, has no choice but to travel during rush hour – should they be 'punished' for this? For a while, this became a moot point, when Covid-19 reared its ugly head. ICT allowed many employees to work from home and, from one day to the next, the traffic jams were over. Until the government decided, in the summer and early fall of 2021, to lift the restrictions, at which point they came back with a vengeance. Did this mean that putting a price on the use of the highways was the only remedy? Should employees – epidemic or no – be encouraged to work from home? Perhaps a combination of the two? More and more Dutch people are willing to answer this question with a 'yes' – however, no decisions have been made. If the government were to stop creating new roads, this would free up € 2 billion, which the government could put to good use on something else, such as measures aimed at the reduction of the emission of CO_2. Not to mention the introduction of the self-driving car – no longer something from science fiction. *So many heads, so many opinions*, the Dutch say. There seems to be no in in sight to discussion of the road toll. Rutte's (fallen) fourth Cabinet had been hoping to introduce it by 2030, whereby it would charge seven to eight cents per kilometer.

Stuck among the traffic are many trucks, which are well-kept and loaded with valuable goods. These goods are seldom raw materials, but rather finished industrial goods. The prominent phone numbers and e-mail addresses that can be found on the sides of the trucks are testimony to the fact that this country has a good network of electronic communication, and that the electronic highway is fully operational. You can't see this from behind your steering wheel, but these past years the chances that the trucks are carrying products that have been manufactured in the Netherlands are small. Already at the start of this century, the Dutch government decided that this country is a post-industrial services economy. The throughput of goods – entering and leaving the country through harbors such as Rotterdam as well as the airports – has become an important sector of the Dutch industry. At the same time, the Netherlands is among the top four food exporters in the world, not to mention being a top exporter of plants and flowers.

You will see countless Eastern European URLs on the sides of trucks bearing Eastern European license plates (from Poland, Hungary, Slovenia and Rumania): the wages and taxes in these countries are lower, so that these transportation companies can offer their services at lower rates, forcing more and more Dutch transportation companies to move their business to Eastern Europe. A similar step to what the shipping companies ended up doing during the second half of the previous century when their ships started bearing Panamanian and Liberian flags. Some of these changes are contributing to an increasing undercurrent of nationalism and anti-EU sentiments among the Dutch, as membership of the EU is allowing other transportation companies to offer their services at cheaper rates, leading to unfair competition. More and more measures are being taken to ensure that the competition on the road does not become dangerous. For instance, for some time already, all drivers are required to have a computer in their truck that registers exactly how long they drive; if their breaks are too short, they are fined heavily. Another measure forces drivers to sleep in a hotel and not in their truck.

Coming back to the nation's wealth: there is an apparent contradiction to the perceived wealth, if you look around you. The cars are far from luxurious. You are surrounded by middle-class cars, and you can see how strongly the Asian market is represented in the European car market as, during the past few years, the Dutch have embraced smaller, more economic cars – due to the crisis and the accompanying tight pockets, but also thanks to the temporary introduction of fiscal measures aimed at stimulating the purchase of environmentally friendly cars. Where are the Rolls Royces, Daimlers, Aston Martins and Ferraris? In the Netherlands, if you want to see one of these cars, you will have to visit a dealer's showroom. On the road, the most expensive cars you will see are the standard Mercedes, Audis, Land Rovers, Volvos and BMWs. And, should you actually spot a Rolls Royce trying to make its way through traffic, you will notice that it does not really command any respect. To the contrary. It will even seem as if the owners of the middle-class cars think it inappropriate for such a showpiece to be on the road and will want to prove, by the way they drive, that they are worth just as much as the fellow in the Rolls. This is even more so among the younger generation. To millennials, a car is something to get from point A to point B and not a status symbol or an expression of your personality – as was sometimes the case for their parents. Many don't even bother to obtain a driver's license as they are not planning on spending their days in a traffic jam, just to be unable to find a parking spot upon reaching their destination. They prefer public transportation, (electric) bicycles and rental cars. Why buy a car, if you only plan to use it occasionally? This is supported by the numbers; the Netherlands has 23.5 million bicycles – much more than its number of inhabitants. Approximately 6 million of these are electric, and an end to this upward trend is not in sight.

The overall picture, however, becomes quite different when you look at the distribution of wealth. The wealthiest 10% of the population owns more than half (61%) of the total wealth in the Netherlands – in fact, one-third of this belongs the top 2% of this group – while the bottom 60% owns approximately 1% of the nation's total wealth. In 2017, the Dutch became richer – by 53 billion dollars – but almost half of this went to the wealthiest 1% of the Dutch. This trend is further strengthened by something that has been typical of western economies for the last couple of decades; though the economy might grow, the wages don't keep up. This is the case for the Netherlands too. At first sight, the numbers seem to negate this conclusion. During the first quarter of 2023, the average wage increase was 5%, almost twice that of the previous year. This hadn't happened in 40 years. However, this was counterbalanced by a sizeable inflation in the euro countries, as a consequence fo which – at best – the people's purchasing power remained equal. The good news is that there are still a lot of job openings. In the final quarter of 2022, the employee shortage proved a difficult issue in several sectors – for instance, at Schiphol Airport, where a shortage of luggage handlers and security personnel led to delays and even cancelations. In this case, this opened the door to negotiations that resulted in a 33% wage increase. It also became clear that approximately 50% of employees are looking for a new job that will allow them to better combine their professional and private lives – as a consequence of which the number of fixed employment contracts has been decreasing since 2008, while the number of people working in self-employment, with no personnel (the so-called ZZP-ers), who are treated by the law as entrepreneurs, has grown substantially. This shortage of employees became even more acute as the year 2022 progressed. The Dutch NS railway company saw itself forced to reduce the number of rides by 10%, because there were not enough conductors and train drivers. For the same reason, a lot of projects were delayed, and people were confronted with long waiting lists, particularly also in health care. We will be getting back to this elsewhere in this Holland Handbook.

Yet, the Dutch wouldn't be the Dutch if they thought this concentration of wealth in the bank accounts of just a few was alright, and they have been pleading for a rise in wealth tax.

When Europe exited the lockdown halfway 2021, this almost immediately led to a boom that compensated for the economic decline of 2020. Statistics published by the Dutch Central Bureau for Statistics showed that the growth had primarily been given an impetus by consumers who embarked on a spending spree after they had been forced to hold on to their money during the lockdown. Also the government contributed to this boom, with the large-scale purchase of vaccines, masks, and Covid tests. An increased demand led to large increases in prices of raw materials – in particular in the energy market, where Asian countries had been able to get their hands on huge tankers full of natural gas in the Middle East. Oil and gas prices shot up so fast that the government had to introduce a considerable reduction in taxes on natural gas, in order to avoid that too many families would be faced with financial difficulties. The consumers were confronted with higher prices in a variety of areas. Inflation went up to approximately 3%. This had not happened since 2002.

In retrospect, these days were easy compared to what 2022 was to bring. The war between Russia and Ukraine drove energy prices even further up. The EU member states tried to punish the Russian economy with increasingly heavier sanctions. Russia, in turn, became less and less inclined to deliver oil and gas to Europe, to the point that, towards the end of the summer, nothing more was coming in from the east. Europe tried to close this gap by buying oil and gas on a large scale from the United States and the Middle East. They succeeded quite well in creating a supply for the winter, but it proved far from cheap. By August 2022, it had become very clear that not only lower, but also middle, income households would be experiencing severe financial problems unless the government subsidized their bills. And that is exactly what happened. During the final months of 2022, all Dutch households received an amount of € 180 (twice even) to help cover increased household expenses, while 2023 saw the introduction of a variety of subsidies. The maximum rate for the first 1,000 cubic meters of gas was set at € 1.45 per cubic meter, and for the first 2,900 kWh of electricity the maximum rate was € 0.40. Whoever used more would have to pay the market price for the excess. Furthermore, a one-time so-called energy supplement of € 1,300 was made available to households with a minimum income. This way the government helped avoid widespread debt among the country's citizens, which would have resulted in their having their utilities shut off. In reality, the price increase in the energy market was not as bad – nor did it not last as long as anticipated. Over the course of 2023, they went back down to below the ceiling that the government had determined.

Not only energy prices went up in 2022. The same happened to the price of basic necessities and luxury articles. In September, inflation, compared to the same month of the previous year, had gone up a whopping 17%. The last time this had happened had been decades ago. Only senior citizens with personal memories of the stagflation of the 1970s were in a position to compare the current conditions with those of back then. The European Central Bank saw itself forced to raise interest rates.

In 2021, Klaas Knot, President of the Nederlandsche Bank, expressed his concern about the housing market. Thanks to the efforts of the European Central Bank to artificially keep interest rates at a minimum, mortgage burdens were at an all-time low. The demand for housing went up to where it had been before the crisis of 2008. The increase in prices – initially limited to the larger cities – had spread across the country. And, despite the heavy economic downturn in 2020, house prices continued to be on the rise to the point where, in the second quarter of 2021, they had gone up an average of 28% compared to the previous year. Then, over the course of 2022, the housing bubble started to lose air as mortgage interest rates went up, reducing the demand for houses. Houses were on the market longer and fewer and fewer people bid more than the asking price, sometimes even under it – for instance, based on the argument that the house was not well insulated, which could reduce the price by up to € 50,000. Still – primarily due to a shortage of houses – buying a home in the Netherlands remains expensive and the dip in house prices has come to a halt. In fact, many houses are put on the market at a minimum price, meaning that the house goes to the highest bidder, while the average house price has gone up from € 500,000 in 2022, to € 544,000 in the third quarter of 2023. In some cases, the concept of the highest bidder even applies to rental homes; the one offering to pay the highest rent gets to move in. In the bigger cities, only members of the upper middle class can afford a reasonable home. For police officers, nurses or teachers this remains unattainable.

In 2022, the economy also took a turn that no one had anticipated. The economic boom – partially triggered by expenditures that had been postponed during the lockdown – gave rise to a shortage of raw materials and parts across the world. For instance, the production of cars was upset by a shortage of chips. At the same time, a rapid increase in economic activities led to a rise in energy prices, which – due to the war between Russia and Ukraine – became quite acute. This led to a level of inflation within Europe that it had not seen in decades. An underlying factor could also be the billions that governments across the world had brought into circulation in order to support citizens and companies during the Covid crisis. The Netherlands was hit hard by inflation, particularly the low income and lower middle-income classes. The number of people visiting food banks doubled and in the educational sector an increasing call was heard for school breakfasts as a growing number of children were coming to the classrooms on empty stomachs. The government came to the conclusion that the country was becoming poorer. Extra supplements for those receiving a benefit as well as measures in order to make energy bills – up to a certain level of consumption – affordable were introduced in order to soften the blow. A few economists criticized this approach, calling it a stopgap, saying that the only thing that would really help would be an increase in wages, benefits and pension payments. They pointed to Belgium, where employee wages are automatically corrected for inflation. Opponents, however, feared that this would give rise to a wage / price spiral that would ultimately make it impossible to manage inflation. The people and the government looked towards 2023 with concern.

In practice, all was not as bad as it seemed it would be. Over the course of 2023 inflation gradually went down. This largely had to do with decreasing energy prices. The prices for basic necessities were less favorable; the effect of this was reflected in the purchases made by the Dutch consumers towards the end of 2023. The expectation was that there would be a turnover of €15.6 billion, 730 million more than in 2022, but it turned out that fewer articles were bought than in the previous year. Any increase in profit was solely due to inflation.

In 2023, wages went up an average of 7%. Towards the end of the year, the unions in certain sectors submitted new wage demands aimed at raising them up to 15%. The employers responded negatively as this was bound to impact their earnings. Though, as mentioned earlier, the luggage handlers of Schiphol Airport did manage to negotiate a raise of 33%. Not that there was any other option; they would have been happy to vote with their feet and leave the job.

This all took place while the Dutch economy ended up in a light recession that nonetheless appeared to constitute no reason for concern. There is still a shortage of employees, leading – among others – to the need for shorter prison sentences or the use of ankle cuffs. Not because of a lack of prison cells but because of a lack of guards.

There is one sector of the economy that we haven't talked about here yet, though it involves dozens of billions of euros. This is the trade in, as well as production, import, export, and re-export of drugs. Since the '70s of the previous century, the Netherlands has acquired an international name when it comes to its tolerance of this aspect of society. For almost half a century now, the sale of cannabis products to consumers has been possible and has become an important source of tourism to the Netherlands; a place where you can visit the so-called coffee shops and legally buy your joints, or your blocks of hash. The idea was behind this that this would facilitate keeping an eye on the soft drug market. The consumption of drugs – particularly cocaine and pills that increase feelings of euphoria when partying – has seen a huge increase. Young people use them on a large scale, in fact it has become part of life among societally successful hipsters – though drugs such as speed, cocaine, and heroin remain illegal. The same goes for synthetic drugs such as XTC, and designer drugs, which remain on the list of forbidden narcotics.

The Netherlands is a warehouse of international renown. Huge volumes of goods come through the Dutch harbors and airports, making it easy to hide drugs among them. The outcome of this is a huge increase in the drugs trade and production in the Netherlands, which is in the hands of criminal gangs that often have international ties with especially South America and Asia. These gangs have become increasingly violent; they fight out their conflicts with weapons, often in public. Assassination attempts on competitors are part of this business model.

Immediately after becoming Minister of Justice and Security, Dilan Yesilgöz started a war on drugs. And with success. In the year 2023, authorities managed to confiscate 239,702 kilos of drugs with a street value of € 2.2 billion. This did not impact the prices on the street, however, which gives you an idea of how many drugs manage to enter the country under the radar. Those who criticize the Netherlands, call it a narco state, especially after drugs criminals started assassinating unaccommodating actors in legitimate society, such as the lawyer Derk Wiersum and the famous criminal reporter Peter R. De Vries. A new phenomenon entered the scene in the years 2022 and 2023: the placing of – light – bombs in front of houses and companies belonging to people who 'required' intimidation. The culprits were often young people who received an attractive remuneration and didn't know who had really given the order. Young kids from disadvantaged neighborhoods were often recruited to take the drugs out of the shipping containers and to deliver them to consumers. This led to the creation of an intricate network of criminal youth, who lead a short and dangerous life. The thought that the war on drugs has been lost anyway and that one might as well therefore go ahead and legalize it, however, has little support in politics. It is also worth mentioning that – though they remain illegal here, as mentioned earlier – the Netherlands is world's largest producer of XTC, while it also produces synthetic drugs. The government is hunting down these laboratories which often dump their waste in nature areas. The same effort is to is being put into finding weed farms, as the trade in soft drugs via coffee shops is allowed but the cultivation of cannabis is not. Not a day goes by without the storming of an attic or a remote office housing a weed farm. And yet again this only represents a fraction of what there is.

Urbanized Center

The Randstad, in the provinces of North Holland, South Holland and Utrecht, is strongly urbanized. There are no real metropolises with millions of people in Holland. The largest city, Amsterdam, does not have more than about 918,000 inhabitants. Still, the Netherlands is a highly urbanized country. Every few kilometers, there is an exit to one, two or three municipalities that have a couple of thousand to not many more than 100,000 inhabitants. These cities and towns all have their own character and are all equally picturesque. In the urban areas, you will find neither hovels nor palaces. What you will find are primarily middle-class houses. Even Wassenaar, Aerdenhout or Rozendaal, the Dutch equivalents of Miami Beach and Beverly Hills, look comparatively modest. There is an undeniable air of wealth, but none of the glitter of excessive opulence.

The cities of the Randstad – Rotterdam, Delft, The Hague, Leiden Haarlem, Amsterdam, Hilversum, Utrecht, Gouda and Dordrecht – form an almost continuous circle or half-moon. The Dutch call this a 'rand', or 'edge', hence the name Randstad. In the middle of this lies a green area, with small and medium-sized villages. Together with the Southeastern area of Brabant (Eindhoven), this area is the country's economic powerhouse, where the majority of companies are located, money is made and culture is generated.

You will also not find harbors filled with expensive yachts. This is big business in the Netherlands, but mostly for foreign consumers. Those who buy a pleasure yacht in the Netherlands will have a hard time finding a spot for it, as the harbors are all full. Not with luxurious three-masters and a regular crew, however, but rather with motor and sail boats of all shapes and sizes. And should there be one that sticks out above the rest, chances are it is flying a foreign flag. You would almost think that socialism reigns here, even more so than in the countries of the former East Bloc. A conclusion several conservative as well as liberal bloggers would be happy to support. However, economic statistics show the opposite. When it comes to per capita income, the Netherlands is securely situated towards the top of the European Union. After all, the wage system is pretty balanced and there are no extreme differences.

When it comes to wealth, the situation is different. There are approximately 317,000 millionaires and 50 billionaires (who jointly add up to approximately 110 billion) in the Netherlands and one in three households has at least € 100,000 in a bank account. The rest has to make due with less. Often much less. Towards the end of 2023, 726,000 households were faced with debts. Without even taking into account debts that have been incurred despite government support for the various sectors as a consequence of the Covid crisis. Should you run into a Dutchman who complains about the taxes and how the middle class is suffering, ask him to show you the numbers. Whereby it must be noted that the crisis did contribute to poverty. In 2023, 830,000 lived in poverty – on a population of 17.8 million. Princess Laurentien, the socially-engaged wife of the King's youngest brother Constantijn, is involved with their plight and – with the help of the government – runs the Missing Chapter Foundation, which invests in projects aimed at combating poverty among children. In the Netherlands, someone who has less than € 1,550 to spend a month, is considered poor. Couples who have no children are considered poor if they have less than € 1,330. Does this sound like plenty to you? Most Dutch people have high fixed expenses, so that only a modest amount, in the range of € 30-60, remains a week, for food and clothes. The Covid crisis itself did not contributed significantly to the number of poor people. This is largely thanks to the support given by the government to companies impacted by the crisis. As a consequence, the number of bankruptcies remained below average. An end to this support came in October 2021, while the government also started to collect taxes that had been deferred in connection with the lockdowns.

The Netherlands
WADDEN ISLANDS
WADDEN SEA
Leeuwarden
Groningen
Assen
Den Helder
IJSSELMEER
Emmen
NORTH SEA
Alkmaar
Hoorn
Lelystad
Zwolle
Haarlem
Amsterdam
Almere
Hengelo
Leiden
Amersfoort
Apeldoorn
Enschede
Den Haag
(The Hague)
Utrecht
Zoetermeer
Gouda
Delft
Rotterdam
Arnhem
Nijmegen
's-Hertogenbosch
GERMANY
Breda
Tilburg
Middelburg
Eindhoven
Venlo
Duisburg
Essen
Antwerp
Düsseldorf
Mönchengladbach
BELGIUM
Highway
Road
Airport
Main City
Brussels
Cologne
Heerlen
Maastricht
Luik
Aachen

They Must Be Giants

BY STEVEN STUPP

One of my first observations about the Netherlands was how tall the Dutch are. Actually, tall doesn't do them justice. They are really tall. Damn tall. I am not used to thinking of myself as short; I'm above the average, adult-male height in my native land. But after a few introductions, where I looked up and found myself staring the person in the throat, the point hit home.

According to the statisticians, the Dutch are currently the tallest people in the world. The average height for men is 6 foot, 0.4 inches (1.84 meters); the women come in at a respectable 5 foot, 7.2 inches (1.70 meters). Cold averages, however, don't convey the entire picture. Connoisseurs of numbers know to look at the tails of a distribution. There are quite a few Dutch men, and even a few women, who are over seven feet tall (2.10 meters). This poses some interesting problems. For example, they are taller than the height of many doorways in the Netherlands; I have no doubt that the risk of accidental concussions is now a painful reality. On the other hand, size does offer some advantages: the Dutch are already a volleyball powerhouse, and if basketball ever catches on in the somehow misnamed Low Countries, they'll give the Michael Jordans of this world a run for their money.

What is truly remarkable is that the Dutch are getting taller. While the average height in all first-world countries increased dramatically over the last century, this growth spurt has slowed down of late and seems to be leveling off. The increase in the average height of the Dutch, however, shows no sign of abating. In the last decade alone, the average height of 18 to 39-year-old men and women has increased by 0.9 inches (2.3 centimeters) and almost 0.7 inches (1.7 centimeters), respectively. It is in this context that height has taken on an interesting significance in Dutch society. Enhancing one's stature has become surprisingly important. Techniques range from the large hats Dutch policewomen wear – it makes them appear taller – to surgery.

The Dutch are often critical – and rightly so – of cosmetic surgery, such as face-lifts, tummy-tucks and breast implants. That stated, every once in a while a particularly short Dutch man or woman (typically, shorter than five feet tall or some 1.5 meters) undergoes a fairly radical surgery called the Ilizarov procedure, in which a patient's femurs are broken and the bone ends are separated using a metal frame. Over time, the bones grow together and fuse, thereby increasing the patient's height. Aside from the pain and the risk of infection, there is nothing fundamentally wrong with the procedure and the patients usually seem pleased with the results. A similar technique is used in other countries, but it is reserved for cases of exceptional dwarfism. What defines that, I suppose, is a question of perspective.

Male tourists will encounter this quote-unquote difference in perspective the first time they go into a public bathroom. The urinals are mounted sufficiently high on the walls to make it almost impossible to use them, unless you stand on your tiptoes. Unfortunately, there are no boxes or phone books in the bathrooms to level the porcelain playing field and to give foreigners a much-needed leg up! As a consequence, I always enjoy the look of shock on the faces of many male visitors in the Netherlands as they return from the *wc* (the Dutch phrase for toilet).

An exchange I once had with a Dutch friend is also illustrative. She was reading a Dutch magazine when I suddenly heard "Tsk, tsk, tsk, tsk, tsk." (A sound the Dutch like to make. In this case it conveyed sympathy.) "That's terrible," she said. I asked her what was wrong. "There's a letter here from a mother whose daughter is only twelve years old and is already 183," she replied. That seemed unremarkable, so I asked, "Pounds or kilograms?" A bewildered look crossed her face and her head recoiled in shock. It took a few seconds for what I had said to sink in. Finally, she blurted out, "No, centimeters!" (While there is nothing inherently wrong with being very tall, the Dutch mother was concerned that her daughter might be teased or could encounter other social problems.)

That conversation also emphasizes the fact that, no matter how hard you try, you remain a product of your country of origin. People in many countries (in particular, Americans), even if they don't have the problem personally, are obsessed with weight. The Dutch are plagued by their size, although they seem to deal with their affliction better than most. As an aside, the Dutch still don't really have a weight problem. While there are overweight people in the Netherlands (the overall trend mirrors that found in other countries), obesity is less prevalent, and frankly, is never carried to the extremes that occur in places like the United States. How is this possible? Simple: they don't eat as much and what they do eat contains a lot less sugar and fat. If anything, some of the Dutch have the opposite problem with regard to weight. I know a few Dutch women, and even a few men, who are not anorexic, but do have an odd problem: they can't gain weight. They eat lots of junk food and still can't gain weight. What do you say to someone who tells you, with complete sincerity, that they have always wanted to know what it feels like to go on a diet? Welcome to a different world.

Aside from the general improvement in the standard of living over the last half-century and the more even distribution of wealth in Dutch society, the best explanation I've come across for the remarkable growth spurt in the Netherlands is their diet. Specifically, the infant diet. In a laudable program, the government-subsidized *Consultatiebureau* provides regular advice to parents about their children's health and nutrition through four years of age. The objective is to improve the well-being of newborns. It has been an admirable success. The hypothesized impact on the height of the general population is apparently unintended. Alternatively, in a new twist to the age-old, survival of the fittest argument, a few British colleagues once proposed a theory over a couple of beers in a pub. "It's all a simple matter of natural selection," they said. "How's that?" I asked. To which they answered: "What with all of those floods, only the tall could survive."

Steven Stupp is the American author of the book *Beneden de zeespiegel* (literally translated: Underneath the Sea Level). He resided in the Netherlands for several years, and in this book he tells us, with characteristic dry humor, about the cultural shock of living here, while sharing what he got to know about the country and her inhabitants.

The windmills of your mind are not playing tricks on you. You have (or your Significant Other has) accepted that job in the Netherlands. The dust, created by the whirlwind consequences of this decision, has started to settle and you are beginning to wonder what type of country you have come to. Having read about culture shock in the preceding introduction, you now know that the best step towards familiarizing yourself with this new culture is knowing more about it. First off, relax in the knowledge that the Netherlands has one of the highest standards of living in the world. But what about their government and politics, economy, the climate, and their religion? This chapter will tell you about how history and living below sea level helped shape the politics of this nation.

CHAPTER 1

The Netherlands in a Nutshell

CONTRIBUTING AUTHORS STEPHANIE DIJKSTRA AND HAN VAN DER HORST

HISTORY AND ITS INFLUENCE ON THE DUTCH OF TODAY

In the Middle Ages, there were many countships and the occasional duchies on the territory of the Netherlands, which for the larger part coincide with the current provinces. By way of a long historic process, the King of Spain inherited all of these in the second half of the 16th century. However, his hands were tied by the many privileges that the cities and rural districts had acquired in the time of the counts and dukes. These had to do with autonomy and other regulations, as a result of which the King was obligated to appoint the local governors from a predetermined select group of persons, recommended by prominent local families.

Philip II's intention was to end these privileges. For his day and age, he was a modern ruler who believed in a powerful central authority that maintained the same procedures everywhere, and who based his decisions on the ethical and ideological principles of one sole religion, that of the Roman Catholic Church. However, in the Netherlands, there was much sympathy for Protestantism, especially that of John Calvin.

Philip II's ideas were therefore not met with much enthusiasm. There was a successful uprising – in which a central role was played by William of Orange, the patriarch of the Dutch royal family. William of Orange was a stadtholder – a representative of the king – in several of these countships, including Holland, and he found he could not agree with the loss of the existing privileges nor with the persecution of the Protestants, which was a central element in the royal politics.

The uprising against Philip II resulted in the Republic of the Seven United Netherlands, in which the old privileges and local autonomy remained of central importance. This republic could be seen as a union of states, something like the European Union, in which the independent states worked together closely without relinquishing their sovereignty. In this system, no one could muster enough power to conquer a position of dominance in this republic and, if one was too much of a braggart or made too much of a show of wealth and power, one only succeeded in creating enemies. A politically high-ranking position could only be based on influence and not on power. Even the stadtholders, who were always recruited from the House of William of Orange – and who managed to make their position a hereditary one – were unable to acquire very much power. Though they might have had the authority vested in them by Philip II, this was subject to the many constraints that also came with the system of privileges and old rights.

To get something done in the old Republic required the formation of coalitions with others, while also making sure to not unnecessarily offend one's opponents. Central conditions to being successful were: respect for others, a modest life style, a willingness to listen and the capacity to restrain oneself. Calvinism, the source of this philosophy, was embraced in a liberal way by a majority of the elite, and was very influential.

The Netherlands is no longer a union of states, but instead a democratic state whose unity is symbolized by the King – a descendant of William of Orange's older brother Jan. However, the mentality of the Dutch has remained the same. Even though Dutch society has become strongly secularized, it is still greatly influenced by Calvinistic philosophies. Still evident today is the strong Protestant work ethic characterized by overtones of moderation in all aspects of life, decision-making by consensus, and the stymieing of individualism. The Netherlands is a country in which ostentatiousness and boastfulness are akin to sinfulness, and where orderliness and cleanliness are next to godliness. Showing off your wealth is still considered equal to showing a lack of respect, and secretiveness is looked upon with suspicion – hence the open curtains after dark, serving a triple purpose: to demonstrate a lack of ostentatiousness, the evidence of orderliness and to show that there are no secrets. The Protestant work ethic is further reflected in the way in which the country is run, a system generally referred to as the 'Poldermodel'.

POLDERMODEL

A piece of land that is completely surrounded by a dike for the purpose of protecting it against high waters is called a polder in Dutch. You can find them in all shapes and sizes. The largest in the Netherlands, Flevoland (large enough to have become the Netherlands' youngest province), measures 48,000 hectares. The management of such a polder requires a tight cooperation between the users. The smallest mistake can result in disaster, as a dike is only as strong as its weakest point.

Life behind the dikes has influenced the Dutch culture. It might be going too far to say that it is solely responsible for making the Dutch a democratic people, however, it is clear that they are partial to detailed agreements, to which they must strictly adhere – for all are responsible for 'their part of the dike'. Foreigners never fail to notice the large degree of organization and planning in Dutch society.

This coming together to reach a consensus, this give and take in the various areas, all characterize Dutch society and Dutch poli-

The Netherlands Without Dikes

The Netherlands literally means Low Lands: 40% of this nation's land lies below sea level. Dunes, dikes, dams and delta works protect us against the water of the sea and the rivers. Without these barriers, the Netherlands would become largely immersed under water.

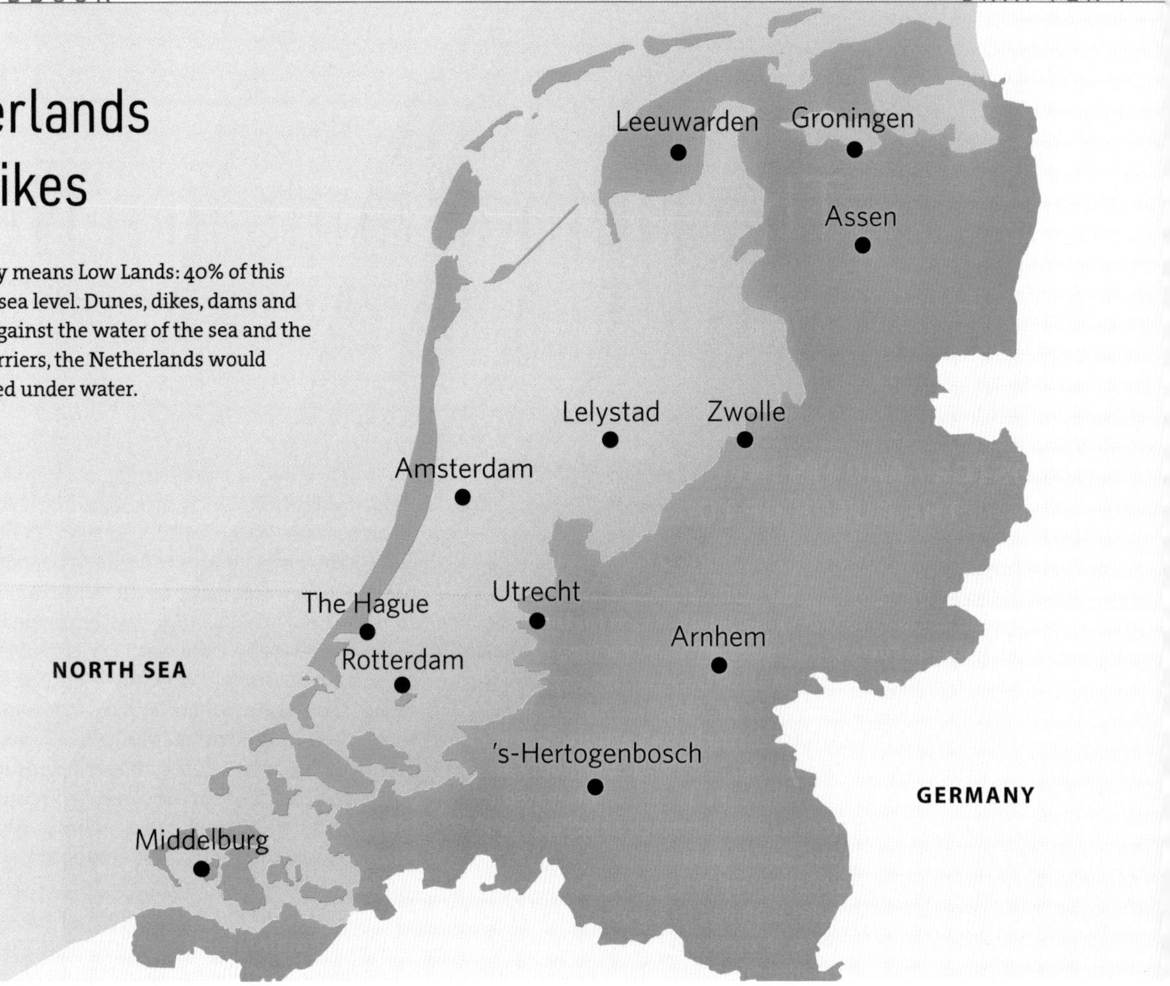

tics. It has resulted in, for instance, the downward adjustment of wage demands, the tolerance of drugs and the legalization of prostitution. This attitude can be summarized in a 'new' word, invented by the British press in 1997: poldermodel.

This poldermodel has not been consistently popular, however. During the first years of the 21st century, the Dutch themselves started to become less enthusiastic about it – led by the suddenly very popular newcomer Pim Fortuyn, who appeared almost as if out of nowhere in the political arena, but was shot to death on May 6, 2002, before he could truly embark on a political career. Fortuyn and his followers were of the opinion that all this poldermodel-consulting and searching for consensus only distracted people from the real problems in society and was keeping them from making important decisions that were long overdue. The economic recession, the increasing unemployment, and the reduction in income of the average Dutch citizen further fed the criticism of the poldermodel, and the subsequent Cabinets, led by CDA-Christian Democrat Jan Peter Balkenende, were strongly influenced by this train of thought. However, only 10 years later, setting aside Dutch nature in favor of a different approach proved to be harder than initially anticipated and the Dutch re-embraced their old tradition of consultation and detailed agreements.

THE DUTCH POLITICAL SYSTEM IN BRIEF

THE GOVERNMENT

The Dutch government is what one calls a 'monarchical government', meaning that it is not only comprised of the ministers and the state secretaries, but also the monarch, King Willem-Alexander. Another term for describing this is: a constitutional monarchy with a parliamentary system, whereby the constitution has determined how the powers are divided between the monarch and the other institutions of the government. For instance, the Parliament has been given certain rights allowing it to check the power of the government (listed further on in this chapter). Notably, the ministers are accountable to Parliament, and not to the King. In fact, since 1848, the person of the king is inviolable. The ministers are responsible for everything he does or says. This puts him in a delicate position; the King, the Queen and their princesses cannot make any public statements without consulting with the Prime Minister first.

THE CABINET

The Cabinet is made up of the country's ministers and state secretaries and its responsibilities are: preparing and implementing legislation, overseeing the local government, carrying out the day-to-day business of government and maintaining international relations. The observant follower of Dutch politics will notice that the number of ministers tends to change from one Cabinet to the next. This can be due to the introduction of a new post that resorts under an existing ministry, but that is considered sufficiently important under the current circumstances to warrant its own minister. Sometimes, the reason behind the addition to, or reduction in, the number of ministers or state secretaries is merely a political one. The numeric distribution of the members of the Cabinet must reflect the representation of the coalition partners in the Parliament as closely as it can. Otherwise, one of the coalition partners might feel sold short, which could eventually lead to the fall of the Cabinet.

The complete Cabinet includes three Ministers Plenipotentiary from the Caribbean; they are from Aruba, Curaçao and Sint Maarten, respectively. Though these three islands have their own government, they are part of the Kingdom of the Netherlands – for instance, defense and foreign policy are the responsibility of continental Netherlands. Three other islands – Bonaire, St. Eustatius and Saba – are considered special municipalities.

In the United Kingdom, ministers are also members of the Parliament. This is not the case in the Netherlands; any adult citizen can be requested to become minister. It is a position that comes with a salary, and one remains minister as long as one has the confidence of the majority of the Dutch Parliament.

THE PARLIAMENT

The Netherlands has a representative democracy and its Parliament (*Staten Generaal*) is made up of two chambers: the Upper House (*Eerste Kamer,* or First Chamber – which is how it will be referred to in The Holland Handbook, as this is closest to how the Dutch refer to it), whose 75 members are elected by the members of the provincial councils; and the Lower House (*Tweede Kamer,* or Second Chamber – once again; which is how it will be referred to in *The Holland Handbook*), whose 150 members are elected directly by the people.

The two Houses of Parliament have been given four rights: the right to set a budget; the right of interpellation; the right to put questions before the ministers and state secretaries; and the right of inquiry. The First Chamber focuses primarily on the passing of legislation, while the Second Chamber has been given two further rights: the right of amendment and the right to propose legislation.

Until 1917, the Netherlands made use of the district system for elections. This was then replaced by proportional representation, making the country, province or municipality one single borough. And then there is the quota; if you divide the total number of votes collected by the number of seats in the representative body, you have a quota. In order to win a seat, you must attain this quota. For instance, the Second Chamber has 150 seats; in order to win a seat, one has to have won 1/150 of all votes. In this system, voters vote for a party that submits a list of candidates. It is possible, however, to vote for a particular candidate. Though this will always count as a vote for the party, those who receive more than 25% of the party's quota for a seat are guaranteed a seat in the Parliament. The other seats are divided according to the order in which the party candidates appear on the list. For a while, Prime Minister Mark Rutte proposed reducing the number of parliamentary members to 100, so as to cut costs. However, this requires an amendment to the Constitution. And it takes time – while furthermore requiring a two-thirds majority in Parliament. After a while, Rutte changed his mind, as several of his ministers resigned out of sheer fatigue. Sadder and wiser, he realized that Cabinet ministers and representatives have huge workloads and the reducing their numbers would be good populism, but bad politics.

The elections for the Second Chamber (by the people) and the First Chamber (by the members of the Provincial States) do not take place simultaneously. In fact, they are separated by a number of years. The government has to be supported by both Chambers. This means that if the opposition has the majority in the First Chamber, this can make things complicated. In order to remain in the saddle, the government then regularly has to make concessions to the opposition. This was the case during the last two Rutte Cabinets – though it must be said that Rutte was always clever enough to work things out. Also the new Cabinet is not expected to have a fixed majority in the First Chamber.

THE ROLE OF THE BIGGER POLITICAL PARTIES – NEW AND OLD

The Dutch Second Chamber of Parliament is elected by proportional representation. Traditionally, the three most established parties were the PvdA (or Labor Party), a social democratic party that has its roots in the trade union movement; the CDA (Christian Democrats), a merger of three confessional parties that bases its

Concern About the Impending Switch in the Netherlands

The Netherlands is at the doorstep of a complete reconstruction. It has signed all the international agreements aimed at bringing climate change to a halt – and, in order to achieve this, the emission of CO_2 will have to be drastically reduced. At the climate conference in Glasgow, Prime Minister Rutte demanded actions instead of words. "Action, action, action" he cried, as if he were the leader of a union. When talking to a Dutch audience, the Prime Minister is usually more moderate. Then, his mantra is mostly "doable and affordable", words that rhyme in the Dutch language. In the Netherlands, only the extreme right parties consistently oppose the proposed climate measures. Their leaders deny that there is a problem or insist that it is not anthropogenic. The severe negative impact that Covid had on the economy does not seem likely to change this. To the contrary, prominent economists are recommending making these reforms an integral part of the recovery policies that will be put in place after the pandemic fades away.

This will have drastic consequences for the set-up of the country and presumably also for its residents' daily lives. Before 2050, the Netherlands will have to have stopped using coal, oil and natural gas and will have to have switched entirely to solar, wind and perhaps even tidal energy, as well as geothermal energy. And the more controversial source: nuclear energy. Particularly on the right-hand side of the political spectrum, parties do not want to exclude this option. They argue that nuclear power plants are much safer than they were in the previous century and that their CO_2 emission is zero, while sun and wind will not be able to meet energy demands. On the other hand, the construction of these plants takes a lot of time and money, while there still isn't a good solution for the processing of their waste.

As a consequence of the plans, the majority of homes will have to undergo drastic renovations. Transportation will have to be electric, and ships maybe too, while air transportation will have to be reduced, unless someone designs airplanes that do not use fossil fuels – which is highly unlikely. The same goes for companies and public institutions. By 2030, the first step down this path will have to have been taken. By then, the sale of cars that run on fossil fuel will be prohibited in the Netherlands. In Glasgow, the Netherlands joined a number of countries who aim to have a fully electric freight traffic system by 2040.

The proposals have generated several plans that have caused great alarm among the citizens. For instance, forbidding the sales of gasoline and diesel-run cars by 2030 would have drastic consequences for the value of the national car supply and would hit the consumers' wallets hard. At the moment, electric cars are only affordable for those who have a sizable income, even taking into account the subsidies granted by the government. Hope is now pinned on Chinese producers, who are aiming high with the development of much cheaper alternatives to the current supply. This hope is threatened by the fact that within the European Union people are lobbying zealously for high import duties, as the Chinese cars are affordable thanks to government support in China – which the European industry sees as unfair competition. These developments will force the European producers to at least try to do them one better, though the industry is still busy trying to play catch-up in the market of electric cars. Incidentally, in the period between January through August 2023 only 35,690 new electric cars were sold, while there are also very few second-hand cars available. As long as this is the case, the average Dutch citizen is not likely to settle behind the wheel of an electric car.

Cars are only one side of the story. In order to reduce the emission of CO_2 in the Netherlands, a revolution will have to take place when it comes to how the Dutch heat their houses. Most of them use natural gas. The government aims to phase out this fossil fuel by 2050. The houses will have to make a switch to district heating – leftover heat from industrial processes – as well as clean electricity such as solar and wind energy, or geothermal heating. Furthermore, the great majority of homes in the Netherlands will have to be better insulated. However, it is unclear how the necessary renovation of the houses would be funded, should the Netherlands stop making use of natural gas. The idea was proposed that loans could be made available to help stimulate an increase in the sustainability of homes, which could then be funded through the savings made on energy expenses –

which were sure to go down once the houses were snugly insulated and making use of a heat pump installation that was connected to the central city warming system that processes residual heat from industrial processes. Or, alternately, the people could sell the land their house stood on, and then lease it back from the municipality. Indeed, the sale of solar panels is experiencing a boost, partially thanks to special measures. Unfortunately, the electricity network is becoming over-extended, and it will be impossible to meet the demands of a further increase in the use of electricity as long as capacity is not greatly expanded upon. The fact that this could cost a lot of money is not considered to be the problem so much as the amount of time it would take. This has fed societal criticism on these changes.

These ideas have been causing quite some unrest among the people and populist leaders Geert Wilders and Thierry Baudet have turned this into political capital, by denying the existence of global warming and talking about 'climate insanity' and a half-baked elite that is trying to financially ruin the regular people and in particular the middle classes. At the same time, they say that a small country like the Netherlands would have little impact on this global issue, while the other countries are not doing anything at all – which is a huge, albeit widely-ascribed-to, lie.

Another question is whether the plans are even practical. The Dutch construction industry is already having trouble keeping up with the demand for new houses, due to a serious lack of personnel. Many masons and other construction workers were fired after the 2008 crisis and, having learned their lesson, found a new trade with no plans of going back into construction. Also the installation technology sector does not have enough people to supply the country with new heating installations, leading to long waiting lists and high prices. The Covid crisis we have just come out of has also made this scarcity in what the Dutch call 'hands' (in this case; construction workers, plumbers, etc.) even more urgent.

All these plans were upset by the energy crisis of 2022. On top of the quickly rising prices of oil and especially gas due to an increase in demand during the post-Covid boom came the consequences of the war between Russia and Ukraine, which upset the supply of energy. In June 2022, Rob Jetten, D66 minister for the energy transition, saw himself forced to give permission to the coal-fired power plants to go full steam ahead despite their excessive emission of CO_2. Otherwise, a part of the Netherlands would have ended up without electricity. In the Eemhaven harbor of Groningen, space was created for supertankers that brought in liquid natural gas.

At the start of 2023, the quickly rising prices of gas and electricity still threatened to create grave financial problems for millions of Dutch people: despite the measures introduced by the government to provide support, a large proportion of the people's income still went to heating, lighting, and the use of household appliances and computers, thereby reducing the amount of money available for a better insulation of the homes, or the purchase of solar panels and heat exchangers. Though, towards the end of 2023 friend and foe agreed that Jetten had managed the crisis well, nonetheless consumers on average now pay twice as much for energy as they did before the Covid crisis and this is going to become an important issue, being as how the energy transition will require substantial investments in the people's homes.

ideas on religious principles; and the VVD (Liberals). In the '80s of the previous century, the largest parties – CDA and PvdA – would generally always garner 40 to 50 seats in Parliament. In the 21st century, the Dutch voters have become more diverse, thanks in part due to the rise of populist politicians.

This hegemony of the three big parties led to great predictability in Dutch politics, until the country was awakened from its slumber by the flamboyant personality of Pim Fortuyn. Fortuyn openly expressed his distaste of the Islam and argued for a halt to immigration. At the same time, he was openly gay and did not hide the fact that he enjoyed life – and being driven around in a Daimler by a chauffeur. This combination appealed to the electorate. He canalized discontent towards his party by simply ignoring the taboo on anti-immigration rhetoric and introducing scapegoat politics in the Netherlands; for every societal failure a scapegoat was identified. According to Fortuyn, these were the migrants on the one hand and the so-called elite on the other hand. They held the reins and didn't give one whit for the needs of the ordinary man. His view of the world had similarities with those of Donald Trump, who also profited from a similar type of discontent.

On May 6, 2022, two days before the parliamentary elections, Pim Fortuyn was shot to death by a lost and fanatical environmental activist. He was the country's second politician to meet this fate. The first had been the nation's father; William of Orange, in 1584. The murder of Fortuyn still feels traumatic to the nation. In the elections, his party won a significant majority but, without its flamboyant leader, soon fell apart into squabbling factions. The dissatisfied electorate, however, was still there and went in search of a new rescuer. This shrunk the pond in which the traditional middle parties could fish; instead of 40 to 50 seats, they were lucky if they obtained 20 to 30. In practice, this meant that often more than two or three parties were required to create a majority coalition in Parliament. Prime Minister Rutte's last two Cabinets were made up of four parties; the VVD, the CDA, the D66 and the ChristenUnie, a small, strict Christian party that, with its five seats, was necessary to create a majority. This led to extended Cabinet formations, as it takes four parties more time to come to an agreement than three. This is certainly the case in the Netherlands, which has a habit of drawing up very detailed government agendas. At the same time, this precision was also a recipe for disaster, as governing is not only looking ahead but also dealing with unforeseen circumstances – which can lead to the demise of certain standpoints with which the coalition parties accentuate their profile, as well as to the loss of the detailed content and relevance of the government's program in the light of changed circumstances.

Over the past two decades, more and more new politicians have entered the scene and have tried to take over Fortuyn's legacy; that of the discontented electorate that was looking for a populist savior. Of these, only Geert Wilders still stands. Initially a member of the VVD, he left the party in 2004 when it became evident that his anti-Islamist standpoints conflicted with those of the party, which considers itself liberal. Wilders subsequently started the Partij voor de Vrijheid (PVV, or Party for Freedom) of which he was the only member, meaning he was free of any criticism from within his constituency and that he was personally in charge of appointing candidates for political functions. During the 2006 elections he obtained nine seats; in 2010, 24; in 2012, 15; in 2017, 20; and in 2021, 17. On the one hand these are strong fluctua-

Fossil Energy

The plans to phase out fossil energy have nothing to do with the problems in the northern province of Groningen, which is where most of the country's natural gas is sourced. Extraction started in the '60s. Since 2010, the area has regularly been hit by earthquakes, albeit mild ones that remain below 4 on the Richter scale. There have been no human casualties, but houses and other buildings have suffered severe damage. Though the owners have been promised compensation, the actual payment thereof has been hindered by political conflict and treacly procedures. Consequently, the population of this area has lost much of its faith in the government. And, though the government decided to close down the extraction of gas in Groningen as quickly as possible, it took them a long time to communicate a deadline – which, according to many cynical Groningers, was another clear message. Whereby it should be noted that the Netherlands can import all the gas it wants, from, for instance, Norway, the U.S. or the Middle East. The way this issue is still being dealt with is sure to lead to an increasingly serious scandal that will take years to untangle. By the time 2022 came around, only a small group of Groningers had received compensation or assistance in making their homes more earthquake-proof. In fact, they did not receive a whole lot more than pretty words. And symbolic actions. For instance, the negotiators for the new Cabinet moved their meeting place to the provincial government offices of Groningen at the start of November 2021. More or less at the same time, the Ministry of Economic Affairs and Climate announced that the country might have to extract more gas from the Groningen fields, if international gas prices continued to be so high.

The 2022 energy crisis led to a call from other parts of the country to nonetheless continue extracting gas from the Groningen gas fields. The suggestion was made to share half the gross yield with those who were negatively impacted by this decision, as a type of indemnity, but this suggestion was not widely supported and the government – time and again – was able to stick to the plans to close the fields, unless circumstances became too extreme. What constitutes too extreme? For instance, if hospitals were to experience a loss of power. Finally, in 2023, a definitive end was put to the extraction of gas in Groningen.

In 2018, the Dutch economy was faced with another problem. The country had reached international agreements on the reduction of the emission of nitrogen, as an excess of this gas had been causing unwelcome changes in the flora and fauna of the national parks. These agreements threatened to impose considerable limitations on a number of economic activities, as a consequence of which the Dutch government introduced the so-called PAS (Program for the Tackling of Nitrogen), which basically aimed at *not* tackling the emission of this gas. It promised companies the option of obtaining (construction) permits, in return for the promise that nitrogen emissions would be limited. On May 30, 2019, the Council of State put an end to this trick after environmental activists, led by environment veteran and chemist Johan Vollenbroek, brought a case before it. As a consequence, the government could not extend a great many permits for many projects and many sectors, as the emission of nitrogen was still too high. One consequence was that, despite there being a shortage of houses, construction came to a halt in many places. Minister of Agriculture Carola Schouten came down strong on the farmers too, as they were considered responsible for half the nitrogen emissions.

Just before the Covid crisis, furious farmers rode their tractors to various locations in the country, but particularly to the government offices in The Hague, to express their anger. A new action committee, the Farmers Defense Force, took an aggressive stance when communicating with the government. Among the farmers, confidence in the politics of the Ministry of Agriculture and Fishery sank to new depths. A solution is still not in sight. In the meantime, the support for the BBB party (the Farmer's Civil Movement party that you could read about earlier) has reached new heights – particularly at the expense of the CDA, which, until not too long ago, was the one that most farmers, as their fathers and grandfathers before them, felt best represented their interests.

For a while, Covid interrupted this threatening conflict between the agricultural sector and the government. In 2022, however, it returned with a vengeance. Minister Christianne van der Wal (VVD) published a plan based on the judicial ruling to strongly reduce the emission of nitrogen in agriculture. Many livestock farmers feared that this would lead to a severe reduction in their income, if not the need to close operations. The government set aside € 25 billion for purposes of compensation and buyouts.

Things led to great anger among the Dutch livestock farmers, and Agractie and the Farmers Defense Force organized intense protests across the country. They occupied intersections and sent processions of tractors to The Hague to demonstrate there, even appearing before Van der Wal's house in the evening. Their symbol was an upside-down Dutch flag that you can still see dotting the countryside in some places. Parliamentary member Caroline van der Plas and the BBB (BoerBurgerBeweging) successfully took it upon themselves to be the parliamentary representatives of this uprising. Many noticed that the police were noticeably mild when confronting these farmers, while environmental demonstrators who similarly occupy an intersection are often made to lie on the ground and are taken away. In 2023, a new organization arose; Extinction Rebellion – which arranged spectacular protests. For instance, they blocked the A12 – the main traffic artery into The Hague – every week, whereby the die-hards had no compunction about gluing themselves to the asphalt. It required a lot of effort from the police to remove the peaceful demonstrators. As of September 9, these demonstrations started to take place on a daily basis, though they were suspended when the Second Chamber passed a motion aimed at quickly reducing the granting of fossil fuel subsidies – though they didn't really rightly carry this label; they were tax rebates for large industrial consumers who otherwise would be at a disadvantage in the international competitive field. Environmental activists are upset with the fact that consumers and smaller companies are faced with increasingly high taxes on their energy consumption, while the large companies enjoy rebates. Extinction Rebellion enjoyed a lot of support, which became clear during a demonstration that had been organized on the huge Museumplein in Amsterdam, attended by 75,000 supporters who had come to see media phenomenon Greta Thunberg. When she pro-

claimed her support for the Palestinians in Gaza, this led to some upheaval and this taking of a position in an international political conflict has not borne out well for Extinction Rebellion.

Back to 2022: eventually things got so out of hand that Prime Minister Rutte asked a political veteran, Johan Remkes, to help calm things down. The savvy Remkes was not new to this game. In a number of meetings with the people involved, he managed to get the government and the representatives of the farmers to sit around the table together. At the same time, he came up with a recommendation that really did not differ much from the government plans, but had been formulated in a more friendly way and was full of criticism of the Cabinet, without actually criticizing the plans themselves. This served to, for the meantime, defuse the situation. The matter was also overshadowed by the rise in energy prices, which also had a severe impact on agriculture.

But that was not the end of it all. In the summer of 2022, environmental activist Johan Vollenbroek again took to the courts to object against certain exceptions to the nitrogen decision that were being made for construction activities. He won again and thereby managed to stop construction of the Porthos Project on the Tweede Maasvlakte (part of Rotterdam harbor). Whereby it should be noted that this was a factory that was being created specifically for the large-scale storage of CO_2. In other words, once again an environmental activist had succeeded in putting a stop to a project that was essential for reaching the Dutch environmental goals. Vollenbroek's victory has now created extra delays for other large construction projects in the country that had been based on the ability to benefit from these (now forbidden) exceptions. Incidentally the projects that have come to a standstill will be continued once they meet the stricter environmental criteria. Still: a delay is bad enough and has had consequences for the Dutch housing shortage. The ambition to have built a million new houses within 10 years already seemed very ambitious, now it is certainly unattainable.

In 2020 and 2021, the thought of generating nuclear energy entered the arena as an alternative to fossil fuels. The underlying thought was that, without nuclear energy, the country will not be able to reduce the emission of CO_2 on time. The long-suffering Groningers were also informed of the fact that their province might become the location for new nuclear plant, should the country decide to expand its generation of energy extraction to this controversial form of generating energy. At the moment, the Netherlands has but one, small and outdated, nuclear plant located in Borssele, Zeeland. For decades, this form of generating energy has been a taboo. The reason: no one knew what to do with the radioactive waste and there was the fear that if something goes wrong, it goes seriously wrong.

Now it is particularly the right-wing politicians who are willing to set aside this objection. They state that modern nuclear plants generate a lot less radioactive waste than the old plants did. Furthermore, they say, it would be easy to build a series of smaller installations, in keeping with the modern requirements, and to do this affordably. As the Dutch say, a lot of water will have to run through the Rhine and the Meuse before a consensus will be reached in the Netherlands when it comes to nuclear energy – be this either positive or negative. An additional problem is that the right and the extreme right have the tendency to make nuclear energy the new best idea, while the left continues to embrace the taboo approach. Consequently, the debate is more a political-tactical one than a scientific one. Nonetheless, it does appear now that the Netherlands will become home to two new nuclear reactors. One of them will be close to Borssele and no notable protest has come from its inhabitants. Even Minister Rob Jetten is taking a carefully positive stance.

And finally: the use of hydrogen as a source of energy is still in its infancy. Somewhere in Groningen, there is one single pump for cars that run on hydrogen energy. This, however, is going to change; investments are in the pipeline. King Willem-Alexander has announced that he will be directing particular focus to hydrogen. In a monarchist country such as this one, this type of endorsement carries weight.

tions, on the other hand they represent admirable stability. Wilders continues to profile himself through sharp and aggressive anti-Islam rhetoric, particularly aimed at Muslims from Morocco. He wants to ban the Koran and close Islamic schools and houses of prayer. He is also of the opinion that the Netherlands must leave the European Union and that the climate problem is a hoax. He presents himself as a defender of health care and of a pension that would start paying out at the age of 65, which could be financed using funds that would be released by abolishing development aid and art subsidies, and by closing the border to refugees. Wilders also expects the Netherlands to experience an economic boom if only it were to leave the EU and the euro. He and his Hungarian wife live in safe houses. The 2023 elections brought Wilders the largest victory of his career; he won an additional 20 seats and became the leader of a party of 37 members. We will be going into this further on. First we will look at the coloring of the political landscape of the Netherlands.

Since approximately 2016, Geert Wilders' PVV has had to deal with a competitor for the favors of the far right, the Forum voor Democratie (Forum for Democracy, or FVD). This is the brainchild of Thierry Baudet, who caused a stir with his Ph.D. thesis, in which he defended the nation state and spoke out against multilateralism and the European Union. Baudet considers himself a defender of western civilization and is of the opinion that western culture experienced a decline in the 20th century. He is in favor of using education – and in particular history – to revive a sense of pride in the Dutch nation. He wants to give the executive more power and wants to introduce binding referendums so that the government can appeal to the people directly. The party is against immigration, but does not take this as far as Wilders and the PVV, with their call for banning the Koran and closing all mosques.

In 2017, to everyone's surprise, Baudet's party won two parliamentary seats. In the polls, the support for the Forum voor Democratie started to grow quickly. The first real test was in March 2019, during the elections for the Provincial States. Baudet's party came out the largest – which sounds more impressive than it really is, as the Dutch political landscape is so divided that this came down to 15% of the votes. (The outcome of this election has consequences for national politics, as mentioned earlier, as it is the members of the Provincial States who elect the 75 members of the Upper House, or the Dutch Senate.) The 13 senators of the FvD robbed Prime Minister Rutte's party of its majority in the Senate, which meant that he had to seek support for his policies among the parties in the opposition. In the 2021 elections for the Second Chamber, the PVV went from 20 to 18 seats and the FvD up from two to eight, and JA21, a spin-off of the FvD, obtained three seats. Meanwhile, the FvD parliamentary members distinguished themselves by misbehaving during debates, and making statements that opponents could easily link to fascism and national socialism. In the fall of 2022, Baudet shared in an interview that in the background, the world was being ruled by lizard people. In the 2023 elections, it retained only three seats; JA21 only one. The party is starting to look like a sect. Despite its defeat in the elections, the FvD has more than 60,000 members and Baudet and his followers are creating their own society, with schools, (social) networks, meetings, educational institutes, and even parties.

The traditionally powerful parties of the Netherlands, the Christian Democratic CDA and the social democratic PvdA have incurred severe losses in the 20th century. In the 2017 elections, the PvdA was punished for its four-year coalition with the VVD, led by Rutte, and retained only eight seats. For the 2023 elections they decided to collaborate with the more radical competitor GroenLinks – which brought them 24 seats. The CDA was left with five seats and currently has little impact as a political factor.

As noted earlier, there are also several other parties, whose popularity waxes and wanes in accordance with the political climate in the country, and some of which last only a few years, while others have been around for decades. An example of the latter is the D66, a progressive liberal party that was founded in 1966 and which has fruitlessly been campaigning for the introduction of the district system and the election of mayors. Having gone from three to 12 seats between 2006 and 2010, the party went to 24 seats in the 2021 elections, after apparently regaining the confidence of the voters, yet it was once again left with nine seats in the November 2023 elections. In the meantime, the party has presented itself – in Parliament as well as in the government – as a champion of an active climate policy, as well as of improvements in education and more accommodation for refugees. The leader of this party, Sigrid Kaag, became the object of very personal attacks from the far-right corner. This had to do with the fact that, before she entered Dutch politics, she had negotiated in Syria for years on behalf of the United Nations. Furthermore, she was married to a prominent, retired Palestinian politician. Wilders did not hesitate to place a shroud of national betrayal over her; in debates, he openly called her a witch, to which Baudet added the accusation of being a spy for a foreign country. When he did this, the entire government protested by leaving the meeting of the Second Chamber. In disgust, Minister Kaag decided she would leave Dutch politics as soon as the outgoing 4th Rutte Cabinet made way for the new government.

THE SMALLER PARTIES

The Staatkundige Gereformeerde Partij, or SGP, which has had two or three seats in the Parliament since 1920, is part of national folklore. Its constituents are among the most orthodox protestants of the country and many of them still reject television and consider the taking out of insurance as an unlawful way of escaping God's hand. Until recently, the SGP also still rejected female suffrage. For a while, the party and its principles were under fire, as some of its views were considered inappropriately close to Muslim fundamentalism – a globally hot topic. Now, its members appear to be loosening up somewhat; its parliamentary members even routinely participate in political TV programs – something that until the turn of the century would have been seen as akin to consorting with the devil. In 2023, the leader of the party, Kees van der Staaij, received a standing ovation from his fellow parliamentarians after 25 years of membership. He is well respected thanks to his demeanor, style and experience with constitutional law. Van der Staaij is a member of the Old Reformed Churches, the most fundamentalist of all Protestant groups in the Netherlands.

GroenLinks started out as a merger of several parties that represented a combination of greens, pacifists and communists. Its focus is on environmental issues. In the 2017 elections, it grew to 14 seats, thanks to its new young leader Jesse Klaver, who has been compared in the media to both Obama and Kennedy, but went back down to 8 in the 2021 elections. In the 2023 elections, he relinquished his podium to his fellow parliamentary member Frans Timmermans, political leader of the PvdA and former member of the European Commission for Environmental and Climate Affairs.

The ChristenUnie was founded in 2000, and is a merger of two rather fundamentalist protestant parties. It wants to balance the tendency towards materialism and individualism, by focusing on a joint responsibility within society for each other, and would like to see the return of Sunday as a day of rest. It is a culturally conservative party that rejects abortion and legal prostitution. It is a stable party with active constituents, that nonetheless never manages to acquire more than five or six seats. The 2023 elections brought it three seats.

The Netherlands is the only country in the world with a Party for the Animals; Partij voor de Dieren. Its parliamentary members focus on supporting animal rights, fighting the inhumane treatment of animals in the bio-industry, and creating an ecologically based policy. Increasingly, it is becoming a movement that represents environmentally conscious voters who see the climate challenges and the decreasing biodiversity as a danger to the continued existence of the human race. The party won six seats in the 2021 elections, but internal struggles cost it two seats in the 2023 elections.

NEW PARTIES

In 2021, half-Irish Caroline van der Plas – who rode a tractor into the Second Chamber complex – joined the Parliament as the only representative of a new party called BoerBurgerBeweging (BBB, or Farmer Citizen Movement). This party had been set up in 2019 by agrarians who felt threatened by the climate and environmental measures. Large agro-industrial companies generously pledged financial support. Van der Plas is a former agricultural journalist, who knows how to get attention and is often to be found in the media, where she uses strong words to express her dissatisfaction with a variety of topics. In the Second Chamber, she has presented herself as a no-nonsense homemaker who is not impressed by show-offs and is not afraid to use her sharp tongue if someone treats her condescendingly. This made her seem like a promising candidate for Fortuyn's electoral legacy and, at the start of 2023, her party was doing very well in the polls – especially since the spectacular farmers' demonstrations of 2022, protesting the Cabinet's decision to limit agricultural production in connection with this sector's huge emission of nitrogen. In fact, in the March 2023 provincial states elections, the BBB came out on top as the country's largest party, while Wilders and the PVV scored badly. The party managed to place representatives in almost all provincial governments, which led to the need for negotiations and concessions. This proved a bit much for many of her constituents, while others went in search of a better representative. Their vote for BBB and Caroline van der Plas had really been a second choice anyway, as their first choice, Pieter Omtzigt, had not been a candidate in the provincial elections.

Omtzigt is a special phenomenon in Dutch politics. His roots lie in Catholic Twente, an area close to the German border in the province of Overijssel. His career is anything but provincial. He is a brilliant econometrician and for a long time he taught at an Italian university. Yet he chose to go into politics; in 2003, he became a parliamentarian for the CDA. However, as he proved to be too independent, placing more stock on facts and hard statistics than on political opportunism, the leaders of the party wanted to get rid of him after four years and placed him at the bottom of the list, where he theoretically could not be voted into Parliament. Thanks to preferential votes, however, he was nonetheless able to remain in Parliament. Through tireless investigation, he revealed a political scandal as a consequence of which 40,000 taxpayers were undeservedly almost driven to financial ruin, thanks to alleged fraud with subsidies for child care. The party and the governments tried to make Omtzigt "come to his senses" – to use the words of party leader Wopke Hoekstra – but to no avail. During the most recent membership elections, he was almost even voted party leader. Shortly afterwards, Omtzigt – partly due to the efforts of the members of his party to thwart his initiatives – ended up with a burn-out. For months, he stayed away from the government offices in The Hague and eventually left the party to become an independent member of Parliament. Since then, he has regularly embarrassed ministers with probing questions that require a greater knowledge and financial know-how than they have. Omtzigt has also persistently warned against a threatening impoverization of large sections of the population, and has calculated that a thorough overhaul of the pension system would have disastrous consequences, with which the aforementioned scandal would pale in comparison.

With his well-argued speeches, Omtzigt got the attention of the media. Polls indicated that he would be able to count on 27 seats if he were to create a party – but for a long time, he was not ready for this. He wrote a political pamphlet in which he diagnosed the many ills of the Netherlands, called *Nieuw Sociaal Contract* (New Social Contract). His premise is that a large proportion of the country's citizens has lost confidence in politics and the government, and with good reason. Which is why a new social contract is due, in which the government is to be responsible for a certain level of financial security, a home, health care, education, etc. For instance, the shortage of homes needs to be dealt with. At the same time, the position of citizens in their dealings and conflicts with the government should be made stronger – for instance, there should be a constitutional court that holds laws against the constitution. Though it may seem like one, the New Social Contract is not a leftist pamphlet. In the remedies Omtzigt proposes, you can recognize a lot of the social learnings of the Roman Catholic Church, such as a rejection of individualism, and the idea that people can only flourish as part of society.

Only in August 2023, did Omtzigt decide to take his chances on creating a new party that, like his pamphlet, would bear the name Nieuw Sociaal Contract (New Social Contract). He drew up a list of candidates that included a lot of experienced politicians with a CDA background, as well as a number of intellectuals. His program – which was only completed a few weeks before the November 22 elections – elaborated upon his pamphlet. The right to a certain level of security for the people was central in his propaganda. Omtzigt did this quietly, rejecting demagoguery; he emphasized that it would take at least ten years to correct the mistakes of the past decade. He was rewarded with 20 seats.

A party on the other end of the spectrum, DENK, represents the interests of foreign nationals and immigrants and is of the opinion that Dutch society is marked by institutional racism. It has been formed by two dissident PvdA parliamentary members with a Turkish background. They separated from the socialist party and their primary supporters are Turkish Muslims. Many consider DENK to be a prime example of the populist parties that are currently in the Dutch Parliament. In 2017 and in 2021, it won three seats, while DENK also participated in a number of municipal elections with quite some success. It was able to contribute one to three members in a number of municipalities – and that is not so bad at all for a party with a limited constituency. In the November 2023 elections, they held on to their position.

There is also another new party that focuses on ethnic minorities in the Netherlands, called BIJ1. It is strongly Caribbean in nature, though it explicitly states that is for anyone who wants an inclusive society. BIJ1 is greatly motivated by the Black Lives Matter movement in the U.S. and the need for awareness of the existence of white privilege. In 2021, the leader of this party, former TV presenter Sylvana Simons, managed to obtain a seat in the Second

The Former Prime Minister

Mark Rutte did not play a role in the November 2023 elections; to the surprise of many, he announced shortly after the fall of his fourth Cabinet that he was leaving politics. He has been traveling around since then and he even did a stab at negotiating in the conflict between Israel and Hamas. In the meantime, he has made it known that he is available for a new position: Secretary General of the NATO. Mark Rutte's departure constitutes an end to 13 years of being Prime Minister, while also a great number of very experienced politicians have left, led by Sigrid Kaag, of D66. When the new Parliament was sworn in on December 6, 2023, 80 of the 150 members were newcomers. The outcome of the parliamentary elections of November 2023 took everyone by surprise. After the votes had been counted, it turned out that the existing political establishment had lost all popularity. The electorate mercilessly held the parties – the VVD, the CDA, the D66, and the ChristenUnie – that had been in the last two Rutte Cabinets to account; the group retained only 41 of the 150 seats, leaving the VVD as the only player of significance with 24 seats.

Was this also to be considered a rejection of Rutte? It would seem that way. As political leader of the VVD, he had been Prime Minister since 2010, leading four Cabinets. This made him the longest-sitting Prime Minister in the history of the Netherlands. He achieved this due to two personality traits: he was pragmatic and at the same time a control freak. One of his best-known sayings was: "If you are looking for a vision, you should go see an optician". It was his habit to insist on thoroughly worked-out government programs. The fact that this sometimes took months, and then another couple of months, was considered to be a lesser evil. Every Monday morning, he would get together with the leaders of the coalition parties and together they would painstakingly prepare, for each party, what they would say in Parliament on each topic. This way, everything was precooked, as the Dutch say, which removed every element of surprise from political debates – as Rutte does not like surprises or developments that he himself has not set in motion. The opposition consistently ran into a brick wall created by this disciplined majority. Anyone who wanted to be contrary was set aside by Rutte. His first Cabinet was 'tolerated' by Wilders and the PVV, meaning that though they did not provide any ministers, they would provide support in case of important votes within the Second Chamber. In 2012, the economic situation had become so bad that the existing government program had to be set aside. To this purpose, Rutte conferred with his coalition partners and Wilders. After approximately ten days, Wilders suddenly left the negotiations and withdrew his support. As of that moment, Rutte refused to ever work again with the PVV. A standpoint he made clear time and again.

When Rutte became Prime Minister, the credit crisis was quickly approaching its apex. The Rutte Cabinets all opted for a policy of austerity in order to be able to cut its coat according to its cloth. Collective provisions were severely reduced and a number of tasks, particularly regarding care for the elderly and children with problems, were transferred to municipalities – as these were considered to be closer to the people, supposedly facilitating their ability to provide tailor-made and cheaper care. In anticipation of these measures, budget cuts were made in the provisions for youth and elderly care. As a consequence, care for the youth came under huge pressure, sometimes leading to the placement of innocent teenagers in juvenile prison due to a lack of institutions providing adolescent psychiatric help, subjecting these teenagers to the same regime as criminal inmates, while the decision to close all elderly care homes forced the elderly to stay in their own home, even when this was not practical. Furthermore, the Ministry of Housing and Spatial Care was abolished as it was assumed that the housing market would find its own balance. In practice, this led to a quickly growing shortage of homes, while purchase and rental prices went up by leaps and bounds, leading to an increase in the number of homeless people.

Another issue that did not reflect well on the government was the child care subsidy scandal exposed by Pieter Omztigt: in the Netherlands, parents with a low income receive subsidy in order to help pay for child care. Should their income exceed a certain threshold thanks to an improvement in their financial position, the entire amount has to be paid back even if this improvement only boils down to a couple of euros. The tax authorities proved merciless in this situation. Furthermore, sometimes innocent mistakes were made on the complicated request forms, but were nonetheless seen as punishable fraud. Aside from having to pay back what they had received, the accused were also subjected to substantial fines and no option for staggered payments. This led to the financial ruin of tens of thousands of families. It also became clear that suspects were identified using algorithms that had a racist basis; there were almost no white people among the victims. In the end, the scandal grew to such dimensions that the government had no other choice than to tender its resignation. In practice, they stayed on as the outgoing Cabinet. In 2023, to add insult to injury, it became clear that a large majority of the victims of the subsidy scandal had still not received sufficient indemnification, while it became clear that many of them had seen their children placed out of home by the state, as they were purportedly not able to adequately take care of them themselves.

And let's not forget the Covid epidemic, with its strict measures of lockdowns, curfews and the closing of the schools, which, in general, the Dutch population followed. Despite the unpopularity of many of the measures, in the 2021 elections – when the epidemic was still far from over – Rutte's coalition once again attained a majority. Over time, however, it became clear that the participating coalition parties had grown apart and it took ten months to form a new Cabinet. From the outset it was clear that there was a lot of disagreement within the coalition and that there would plenty of challenges, while there were considerable problems that had received less attention during the pandemic than they deserved. For instance, it was clear that conquering the climate crisis would require a complete overhaul of the Netherlands.

The Run-Up to the 2023 Elections

Thanks to the subsidy on energy prices, 2023 remained an economically and socially stable year for consumers. Nonetheless, right from the start of Rutte's 4th Cabinet, election polls indicated that people were increasingly becoming dissatisfied. It had been a long time since confidence in politics had been so low and more and more people were subscribing to the idea that the Netherlands had hit a rut in the road it had taken. The one who was poking the bear, Pieter Omtzigt, acquired political gain with his focus on his New Social Contract. In the meantime, the Cabinet was forced to deal with more and more challenges that seemed impossible to resolve. Despite the housing shortage, the construction of new houses was going slowly due to strict nitrogen rules for construction permits. A shortage of employees in many sectors led to delays and waiting lists. The health care sector had to cope with more and more practical problems. A typical example of this situation was the solar panel factory that couldn't connect to the electricity network – as it was 'full' – forcing it to make use of diesel generators.

Against this background, drug criminals were becoming increasingly assertive, committing, among others, the aforementioned murders of the lawyer Derk Wiersum and criminal investigator / reporter Peter R. de Vries. Though there was no hard evidence of this, it was suspected that the organization of a well-known criminal who was standing trial was trying to interfere in the proceedings. The fact that Crown Princess Amalia needed special protection under these circumstances also did not help stimulate the people's confidence in politics.

Another issue was the provision of shelter for asylum seekers. During Covid, the number of asylum seekers had gone down and, based on the just-in-time principle, cuts had been made in shelters and personnel. Now that the stream of incoming asylum seekers was growing, the reception center in Ter Apel was the site of unheard-of scenes: people had to sleep on chairs in bathing areas and waiting rooms and, during the summer, on the grass outside the buildings. State Secretary of Asylum Affairs Eric van de Burg (VVD) had to do all that he could to pass a law that obligated municipalities to receive a commensurate number of asylum seekers. This proved hard, as the local government bodies tried to pass responsibility for these decisions on to others.

A second factor in all of this was the fact that a lack of personnel meant that the procedure for these asylum seekers experienced long delays. The investigation and interrogation procedures took months and all this time, the asylum seekers were not only stuck in the procedure but also in the shelter. Right-wing politicians blamed this on the fact that rejected asylum seekers had the right of appeal and, not only that, were assigned a lawyer to that purpose. To be fair, the state was just as guilty of consistently starting an appeal procedure when the courts found in favor of an asylum seeker.

The situation was made worse by the fact that whoever was granted political asylum, was not easily able to find a home. Many of the locals were convinced that asylum seekers were given priority when it came to the assignment of social housing and that the waiting lists for the local population could go up to more than ten years – in a country that at the time had 40,000 homeless people. Populist politicians used this to their advantage: they demanded a total stop to the admission of asylum seekers. The whole right-wing side of politics partially supported the sentiment. Rutte repeatedly promised that he would slow the stream of asylum seekers. The people in the Netherlands were shocked to hear that 403,108 people had immigrated into the Netherlands in 2022. The fact that most of these came from other EU member states to do work that the local population couldn't or wouldn't do was a detail that was seldom shared. And also not the fact that most of the immigrants were refugees from Ukraine. The number of asylum seekers was only 49,000, yet they were a central topic in the societal and political debate. Within the Cabinet, this topic generated more and more friction; D66 and the ChristenUnie were in favor of opening the doors, CDA and VVD were opposed to it – egged on by their constituents. In the end, Rutte decided to force the issue. In the negotiations on the asylum policy, the VVD came up with a proposal to limit the possibilities for family reunification. This had to do with the following: one can only request asylum in a member state of the EU within that member state itself, but not for another member state. But a visa with which to enter the country is seldom granted, causing people to have to cross the border illegally. This led to the phenomenon of rickety boats full of asylum seekers on the Mediterranean Sea. For asylum seekers, whether they be real or economic refugees, coming to the EU is a dangerous mission to which you will not soon subject your wife and children. For this reason, families often sent a father or an adult brother ahead. Once this person had requested political asylum, their direct family could also request asylum and enter the Netherlands via official channels. This is what the VVD was proposing to make more complicated, among others through a lengthy procedure. The left-liberal ministers of the D66 were as unhappy with this as those of the ChristenUnie, a party that places great stock in the concept of a core family. In reality, the whole issue regarded a group of maybe a few hundred people a year, but this led to the demise of Rutte's Cabinet.

In July 2023, a surprising successor to Mark Rutte presented herself: Minister of Justice Dilan Yesilgöz, herself a refugee with a Kurdish background who nonetheless strongly supported limiting the ability of those who suffered the same fate to come into the country. Dilan Yesilgöz has a way with words and seemed the perfect successor to Mark Rutte in the VVD: a woman, a person with a non-Dutch background and yet 'comfortably' right-wing. And that, those in the VVD party smirked, while the socialists had united themselves behind lily-white Frans Timmermans. Frans Timmermans had made a name for himself in Brussels as European Commissioner for Climate Action. In this capacity he had, for lack of a better word, shoved a big package of environmental and climate measures down the throat of an unwilling European Parliament and an equally unwilling European Council of Ministers. He give up this position to lead the PvdA in the Netherlands – which, among others, decided to work closely with the left-wing competitor GroenLinks in hopes that together they might be able to become the largest party, which would be a first step towards Frans Timmermans becoming Prime Minister. The party campaigned on a program in which environmental policy and combating poverty went hand-in-hand. He tried to shift the central theme of the elections towards the right, emphasizing the need for a certain level of security, the concept that Pieter Omtzigt had introduced in politics. Whereby it should be remarked that though Omtzigt also believed that combating poverty and administrative changes should be central, he had different

remedies in mind than Timmermans and his leftist blend – such as a lowering of the energy tax and drastically raising the minimum wage.

And so the VVD campaign strategy started to flail. At first, Timmermans and Omtzigt dominated during the debates while Yesilgöz and Wilders lost the initiative. Another person who was not doing well was Caroline van der Plas and her BBB, who lost support among the Dutch voters thanks to the participation of Omtzigt and would eventually have to make do with eight seats. This was a cold shower after the outcome of the Provincial States elections. Had the trend of those elections been continued, she would have been able to count on 24 seats in the Second Chamber, but in the end she had to make do with just those eight. Yet she remains a politician to take into account as, with 12 seats in the First Chamber, she has a lot of say. But we are moving ahead of ourselves.

Initially, the run-up to the elections had been a bit boring, but this changed when Dilan Yesilgöz announced that – under circumstances – she would be willing to work together with Wilders and his PVV. By doing this, according to the media, she cracked open the door. It was clear, for instance, that she wanted to work together with him in order to limit the stream of asylum seekers. This shook things up a bit. It immediately elevated Wilders to a factor of importance. And he cleverly made use of this by repeatedly saying that he was not opposed to making compromises. For instance, he was willing to put discriminatory measures against the Muslims – such as a ban on the Koran – on the back burner. He furthermore profited from the fact that though the BBB and Pieter Omtzigt's party had identified the influx of foreigners as a problem, they 'only' wanted to limit this influx to 15,000 or 50,000. This taught the voters that anyone who really wanted strict measures against asylum seekers would have to rely on Wilders. And then something unexpected happened, in another country. Hamas attacked Israel on October 7 – leading to a brutal war.

Traditionally, Dutch public opinion supports Israel, but it became clear that there was a lot of support for the Palestinians, who were seen as the victims of a genocidal war carried out by Israel. Sizeable pro-Palestinian demonstrations took place as well as sit-ins at large train stations. One could see thousands of people parading through the cities waving Palestinian flags. Reports on antisemitism increased. Generally speaking, the politicians did not make the war in Gaza into a central topic of the elections, yet it is still likely that the large pro-Palestine demonstrations influenced the atmosphere in the country. They might even have been able to give Wilders an electoral push, as the right-wing voters saw the pro-Palestinian movement as an alien element in Dutch society. They decided to make clear that they were voting for the PVV, as Wilders' support of Israel was not up for debate.

In the last week before the elections, Wilders succeeded in drawing a lot of attention to himself during the televised debates. He focused the spotlight on the asylum problem and placed responsibility for all societal issues on the immigration of particularly Muslims. At the same time, he scored well with a number of social demands, such as bringing the pensionable age back down to 65 and getting rid of the deductible in health care insurance. These types of measures could easily be paid for by getting rid of development aid and subsidies on art and culture.

The verdict came on November 22nd. The PVV won 20 seats, bringing it up to 37. Omtzigt's Nieuw Sociaal Contract (NSC) went from zero to 20 seats and also the PvdA / GroenLinks fared well: seven seats more, bringing it up to 24. This, however, came particularly at the expense of other left-wing competitors, such as the Socialist Party, the Partij voor de Dieren, and Volt. Dilan Yesilgöz's VVD had to make do with 24 seats. Sympathizers of the PVV claimed that the people had finally asked for a right-wing government and that it was time that they got one. A majority coalition could be formed with the PVV, the VVD, the BBB and NSC. However, there were two obstacles: Pieter Omtzigt was hesitant about working together with a party that supported unconstitutional ideas, such as forbidding Islamic schools and the Koran, and he also had his doubts about issues such as the introduction of an administrative detention without the interference of a judge. It was hard to forget proclamations made by Wilders regarding a fake Parliament headed by himself, or the thought of the land being ruled by D66 judges.

As leader of the largest party, Wilders was allowed to appoint the person who would advise on how best to form a Cabinet. His first choice, Gom van Strien, PVV-member in the First Chamber, was forced to withdraw after only a day when it turned out he was involved in a fraud case. Wilders then chose Ronald Plasterk, who had been Minister of Education and of Internal Affairs for the PvdA at the start of this century, and who had taken a political turn to the right, as was clear from the weekly populist column that he published in the conservative Telegraaf newspaper. Plasterk opened talks with the leaders of the political parties in order to come up with a proposal. From his statements it became clear that it was important to him to remove in any obstacles to working together with Wilders and the PVV. Yesilgöz came with a surprising opening move. She stated that she felt it wasn't fitting for the VVD to join the Cabinet after incurring such a loss in the elections. She was, however, willing to tolerate a Cabinet with other parties and to not bring it to a fall – as long as it supported a policy that was favorable to the VVD. One thing was clear: Pieter Omtzigt's 20 seats were essential for any type of combination – right or left, as it was theoretically possible that the PVV might be exchanged for a combination of PvdA / Groenlinks and D66. Particularly as it was Omtzigt's party that had little faith in Wilders' constitutional ideas. All in all, it promised to be a long and tortuous formation. And the question remained how the new Parliament would position itself towards the outgoing Rutte Cabinet that was to continue to run the country, though within the boundaries set by the parliamentary majority.

This did not work out well: in preparation for the elections, the politicians had barely spoken of the international situation, such as the wars in Ukraine and Gaza. Yet these situations did threaten the safety of the Netherlands. In the fall of 2023, the Netherlands pledged € 2 billion of support to Ukraine and supplied a number of F16 airplanes. Geert Wilders, however, is vehemently opposed to financial and military support for Ukraine. Should he become Prime Minister as leader of the largest party, then he could, together with his Hungarian kindred spirit Orban, block all aid from the EU. Plus there was the matter of his rejection of the climate issues as a hoax and his plans to bring a referendum on Nexit – or the leaving of the Netherlands of the European Union. Even though he controls only a quarter of the Second Chamber, it makes people uncomfortable.

It looks like 2024 will be a roller coaster year. Climate and environmental problems will require powerful policies. The Netherlands will have to declare a position on the war between Russia and Ukraine. It will push for a well-defined Middle East policy. And it will have to come up with a clear immigration policy. Pieter Omtzigt has already carefully wondered whether it is a good idea for the economic sectors – such as logistics, the agrarian sector or the meat sector – to be so dependent on foreign employees. Is this a good thing in the Netherlands? Do the benefits outweigh the problems? Should they stop teaching in the English language in the Dutch universities in order to stem the flow of foreign students – which now represent 40% of all students in the Netherlands? These are sensitive subjects that can give rise to a lot of controversy. The question arises whether the old system of the poldermodel is strong enough to accommodate the political polarization in this country in which one in four voters has elected the populist option.

Chamber. She proved something of a parliamentary natural, as she was able to clearly formulate and support her criticism on the Cabinet, in a way that was appreciated both on the left and on the right – though this was largely tongue-in-cheek. Due to health problems, Sylvana Simons decided not to pursue candidacy in the November 2023 elections and the party did not obtain enough votes for a seat in Parliament.

A final interesting newcomer in 2021 was the European party Volt, which is establishing itself in a growing number of member states of the EU. The aim of the party is to foster more European integration, in which federalization and democratization of the union of states is a central demand. Volt has an air about it of the progressive liberal spirit that is reminiscent of D66. The three Volt parliamentary members are young, enthusiastic and serious. It would appear that many of the progressive voters feel left out in the current political system and are therefore seriously considering supporting Volt in order to give new power to cosmopolitanism in its fight against the extreme nationalistic right-wing factions.

It is often remarked, in the Netherlands, that this large number of parties makes it difficult to create a stable government and results in endless debates. In practice, things have proven not to be so bad. Until now, various majority coalitions have been formed that, thanks to so-called fraction discipline (in the Netherlands, the members of a political group that are in Parliament – or some other administrative body – are referred to as a *fractie*, or 'fraction'), have managed to keep the government in the driver's seat. The amount of time that people are allowed to talk in the Second Chamber is divided fairly over the members, though it must be remarked that the leaders of the larger parties make ample use of speaking time that is actually assigned to other members of their parties, who then remain silent. This helps avoid that einzelgängers or mini parties frustrate and sabotage the democratic process with endless discourses.

FORMING A CABINET

Because there are so many political parties in the Netherlands, there are numerous coalition possibilities. Consequently, several months generally pass after the elections (in 2021, this was almost 10 months – who knows how long it will take after the 2023 elections), during which, after extensive deliberation, a Cabinet is formed with a program to which the majority of the members of Parliament can give their approval.

Does this mean that the Netherlands does not have a government in the interim? Of course not. After the Prime Minister tenders the resignation of the entire Cabinet, the King 'answers' by requesting the Cabinet to stay on until there is a new one. The incumbent ministers then continue to run the country – until the new Cabinet is formed. However, decisions that might lead to extensive discussions in Parliament are delayed until the new Cabinet is in power. A chamber majority places them under a 'controversial banner' and they are then taken off the agenda because they are part of the 'formation process'.

The so-called splintering of Dutch politics is making it increasingly difficult to form a Cabinet. As mentioned earlier, there used to be three large parties in Parliament; liberals, Christian Democrats and Social Democrats. Historically, the Christian Democrats positioned themselves in the middle and *de facto* determined with whom they would form a coalition; the liberals or the Social Democrats. During the first 15 years after the Second World War, they preferred to work together with the Social Democratic Party PvdA, after which they switched to coalitions with the VVD. During the '90s, this changed: the liberals and the Social Democrats together managed to relegate the Christian Democrats to the opposition for the first time in almost 90 years. They subsequently introduced a policy of reformation that included liberalization on all fronts, from the opening of stores on Sundays to the privatization of government services. After the turn of the century, the large traditional government parties started to crumble under the force of populism. The populists, however, failed to create stable parties and thereby contributed to an increased splintering of Dutch politics in which the largest party, the VVD, has proven unable to attain even 25% of the votes. These days, at least four political parties are needed to create a doable coalition with a majority in Parliament. This makes the formation of a Cabinet quite a challenge and it was only on January 10, 2022 (ten months later) that its members were sworn in by the King. Then, a mere 18 months later, on July 7, 2023, the Cabinet tendered its resignation – which, as reconstruction proved impossible, led to the need for new elections on November 22nd of that same year.

THE THREE LEVELS OF GOVERNMENT

The Netherlands not only has a central government, but also provincial and municipal governments and the water boards. The central government occupies itself with matters of national interest. The provincial governments concern themselves with social work, cultural affairs, environmental management, spatial planning, energy and sports. The municipal governments occupy themselves with traffic, housing, social services, health care, sports, culture, the water supply, public schooling and recreation. In 2013, the second Rutte Cabinet placed a number of care and social measures with the municipalities, based on the idea that local governments are closer to the people, making it easier to create tailor-made solutions of high quality. There are, however, a lot fewer funds available for this than the government had at its disposal for these same measures. Whichever way you look at it, the daily life of the citizens has become increasingly important to the municipalities – though this has not yet led to an increase in interest among the people for local politics. They are still more focused on 'The Hague' and the government. Even when voting in municipal elections, they tend to let themselves be led by their national political preferences, rather than any opinion on the quality of the local leaders. Though there is an increase in local parties, this seems to be fed by people who are worried about the influence of populists on a national level. The splintering of politics also exists on a municipal level, with 10-15 parties in the larger municipalities. The next municipal elections will be in 2026.

In order to help fund these activities, the provinces and municipalities receive government funding and levy their own local taxes. The municipalities are trying to make up for government-induced cuts in their funds by raising taxes, particularly on real estate. You can read more about the local taxes that may affect you on page 111. The last elections for the water boards took place in 2023, at the same time as the elections for the Provincial States, and of the 518 available seats, 118 (23%) went to the new BBB party. Ninety-one seats went to WaterNatuurlijk, while the Partij voor de Dieren, though it no longer has any seats in the Second Chamber, successfully grew from 17 to 37 seats.

VOTING AND STANDING FOR ELECTION AS A NON-DUTCH NATIONAL

Voting

If you are an EU citizen, you are allowed to vote in municipal elections under the same conditions as Dutch nationals. This means that you must be at least 18 years of age on the day of the election and you must be a resident of a particular municipality on the day on which the candidates are nominated. If you are a non-EU national, you may vote under the same conditions; however, you must also have been a legal resident of the Netherlands for a continuous period of at least five years. To vote for the water boards, you must be living in a 'watership', at least 18 years of age, and have Dutch/EU nationality or – if you are of another nationality – be a legal resident of the Netherlands. For more information on whether you can be considered a legal resident for voting purposes, you can call the Ministry of Home Affairs (see the end of the chapter).

If you are a member of consular or diplomatic staff, you are not allowed to vote in the Netherlands, nor is your spouse/partner or children (if they are members of your household).

If you are an EU citizen, and a resident of the Netherlands, you are allowed to vote in elections for the *European Parliament* provided you do not vote in the same election in your home country, are 18 years of age or older, and are not disqualified from voting in the Netherlands or your home country.

Only Dutch nationals may vote in elections for the Second Chamber of the Parliament (the members of the First Chamber are elected by the members of the Provincial States) and the Provincial States.

Standing for Election

You can stand for election to municipal councils under the same conditions as stated above for voting. The only difference is that you must satisfy these conditions not on the day of nomination, but on the day you are admitted to the municipal council. You can also stand for election in Dutch elections to the European Parliament, provided you do not stand for election elsewhere.

Only Dutch nationals may stand for election for the First and Second Chamber of the Parliament, as well as for the Provincial States.

ECONOMY

The Netherlands is in the world's top ten in export volume and ranks in the world's top twenty for GNP, even though, in terms of square kilometers, it is one of the smallest countries in the world. Though it is true that, in population density, it is on a par with countries such as India and Japan, nonetheless this only amounts to a population of 17.8 million.

GATEWAY TO EUROPE

The Netherlands owes its favorable ranking, among others, to its advanced transportation infrastructure, with, at its hub, both the port of Rotterdam (the largest European seaport in the world in terms of container activity) and Schiphol Airport (the busiest airport on the European mainland). Also the country's advanced telecom infrastructure and its extensive (hi-speed) railway network help support the Netherlands' position as 'the gateway to Europe'.

Traditionally, the Dutch economy has been one that other countries are eager to become a part of, which has been reflected by the huge investments made in the country's economy and companies over the years. This willingness to invest in the Dutch economy is largely due to the country's stable and flexible work environment (thanks to the poldermodel), its central geographic location, its well-educated multilingual work force and the amount of know-how available here.

Individuals, often enticed while traveling here to stay and find a job, are as motivated as companies are to settle in the Netherlands, particularly since the opening of the frontiers within the European Union. The Dutch government, recognizing the value of top-notch specialists who contribute to the knowledge pool and economy of the Netherlands, has also introduced a number of tax measures aimed at making it more attractive for non-Dutch nationals to come and work here (you can read more about this in chapter 5). Also the bureaucratic red tape has been simplified, reducing the number of hoops employers and employees have to jump through to obtain the necessary papers.

RANDSTAD

After Paris, London and Milan, the Randstad (the area including, and between, Amsterdam, The Hague, Rotterdam and Utrecht) is the largest economic urban area in the EU, measured in terms of gross domestic product. This is largely due to the strong presence of financial and commercial services; the motors of Dutch economy.

SECTORS

Though the economy of the Netherlands is relatively resilient, it is nonetheless dependent – as a country of trade – on the economic situation in the rest of the world. It might not drop as quickly as the overall economy, but it will not bounce back as quickly either, due to the relatively high costs of labor (wages and pension premiums). The most important sectors for the country – in terms of added value as well as employment – are trade, business services, transportation and storage, education and health care. Important trade commodities for the Netherlands are machinery and transportation equipment, followed by chemical and mineral products.

As the 'gateway to Europe', the Netherlands' most dominant sector is the services sector, accounting for approximately 80% of its work force. Another dominant sector is that of mineral extraction, particularly the production of natural gas – of which the Netherlands is the second largest producer on the European mainland. Other sectors that consistently contribute to the Dutch economy are the restaurant, trade, and repair services sector, and the health care and related services sector. A final important sector is the agricultural and food sector; it generates approximately 10% of the GNP; 75% of the agricultural produce is exported.

The Dutch economy benefits greatly from the fact that the world's largest chemical companies are based here, while the Netherlands is one of Europe's largest suppliers of high-tech goods for both the industrial and the consumer market. Rotterdam imports and refines huge amounts of crude oil that is shipped to the rest of western Europe. Thanks to these offshore installations and refineries, the Netherlands has many activities in the oil and gas industries, including a strong research and development technology and a specialized construction industry.

A major contributor to the Dutch GNP is trade: imports and exports from and to the Netherlands contribute to approximately

50% of the country's GNP – however, if re-export to other countries is included, it accounts for 90% of the Dutch GNP.

WELFARE

All in all, this makes the Netherlands a wealthy country, with a high per capita GDP boosted by social security measures guaranteeing a minimum income, health care and education.

COMPARING 2022 AND 2023

While economic growth amounted to 4.9% in 2021, it was 4.5% in 2022, according to the Dutch CBP (Centraal Planbureau). Nonetheless, economic growth in the Netherlands exceeded that of the surrounding countries or even the EU as a whole. Household consumption contributed to 50% of this growth, despite low consumer confidence and inflation, thanks to higher employment and higher wages. Another boost was given by the fact that certain sectors that had suffered during the Covid-19 pandemic – such as travel, transportation, hospitality and recreation – experienced a revival and contributed significantly to the country's economic growth. This was largely due to the opening of society, post-pandemic, and the resulting consumer expenditures in these sectors, as well as on clothing and shoes. Also industrial production experienced a boom, reaching its highest point ever in April 2022. The recreation, culture, sports and other services sector grew 34% over 2022, while the energy sector grew by 9.8%, the business services sector grew by 8.8%, and the trade, transportation and hospitality sector grew 7%. What tempered these positive developments in 2022 were inflation and the consequences of the war in Ukraine, which resulted in high energy prices which, together with warmer weather, led to a reduction in the use of natural gas.

Unemployment went down from 4.2% in 2021, to 3.5% in 2022, whereby all age groups experienced an increase in job opportunities, but particularly the age group 15-25. Inflation, due to the war in Ukraine and the post-pandemic economic recovery, came out at 10% – compared to 2.7% the year before and while it hadn't exceeded 4% (and seldom 2%) since 2001. Energy prices were, on average 114% higher than in 2021 – contributing 4.6 of the 10% of inflation – while food was 10.8% more expensive, and consumer goods and services; 5.1%. Coming back to imports and exports, whereby it was noted earlier that they account for 90% of the Dutch GNP, 2022 was the first year in which re-exports exceeded exports – by more than 50% – and almost 58% higher than the pre-Covid. This was largely due to the re-export of mineral fuels, whose prices had risen steeply, among others due to the war in Ukraine. Though the volume of refined oil products went up 0.2%, their export price went up almost 83%. Other re-export products included machinery and equipment, chemical products, manufactured products, and food & beverages. Fifty-five percent of the re-export went to Germany, Belgium, France, the U.K. and the U.S., whereby goods produced in the Netherlands constituted the biggest group in exports to the U.K., China and the U.S.

As things stood at the start of the fourth quarter, 2023 was a less rosy year, in terms of economy: in all three quarters, the economy had shrunk compared to the previous quarter. In the third quarter, investments went down 1.8%, exports 1.6% and imports 2.3% – among others, due to high interest rates and inflation (4.8% for 2023 and 3% expected for 2024). Demand for Dutch products went down, investments went down and rising interest rates pushed down house purchases and real estate investments. Government consumption went up, though, and the government is focusing on stimulating the economy, which it plans to continue doing into 2024. Contrary to 2022, the Netherlands is not doing as well as its neighboring countries – however, it is still looking alright thanks to its performance over the previous years. Though three successive quarters of a shrinking economy indicate a recession, the continued low unemployment rate (3.6%) and a predicted continued demand for employees serve to dampen this the conclusion.

For 2024, expectations are that the Dutch economy will grow 0.8%, inflation will go down to 3%, unemployment will remain in the neighborhood of 3.7%, and consumption will grow slowly. Foreign demand for Dutch products as well as imports will grow modestly, mortgage interest rates will go up, and the housing market will go down somewhat, in prices and in purchases – though it will stabilize over the year. In short, neither very exciting nor very distressing – time will tell.

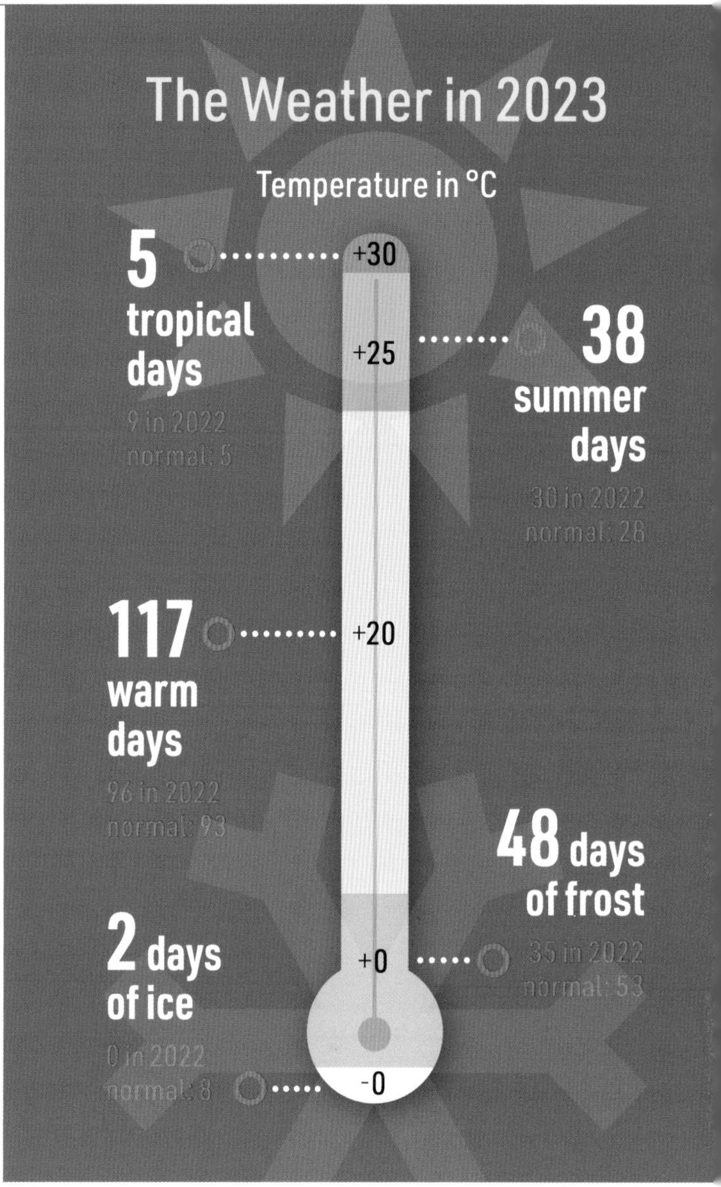

CLIMATE

BORING?

The Netherlands is not really known for its exciting seasons. Just about every season has its fair share of gray skies and precipitation that last weeks. Nonetheless, also this country has joined the rollercoaster ride of climate change. Indeed, the amount of rainfall has increased by 20% since 1950 – not necessarily because it rains more days, but simply because it rains more. On the other hand, the summers are dryer and periods of drought are more extended, with more extreme temperatures (expressed in tropical days). It is the other three seasons that are wetter, while the winters are milder, with 20 fewer days of frost, compared to 100 years ago. This means that the annual chances of the famed *Elfstedentocht* have gone down, from 25% to 10%, with the last one in fact having taken place 27 years ago. The seasons are also 'shifting'; plants bloom earlier, birds lay their eggs earlier, certain species of frogs are staying away, and there is a change in the type of caterpillars, spiders and crickets you will find in your backyard. Birds that tended to come to the Netherlands for the winter are staying in colder places, but then again, birds that used to fly elsewhere for summer are staying. Something similar, in fact, applies to tourists; those in search of snow are going elsewhere, while those who are in search of warmth are increasingly coming here – to the delight of the tourism industry.

WINTER

Let's take December. During the first two decades of the 21st century, the average temperature during the month of December was 4.4° C – while during the first 20 years of the 20th century, it was 3.2. Decembers just don't get very cold here; the coldest December of this century so far was in 2010, when the average temperature was -1.1° C, and the coldest December over the past 120 years was only 0.6° C colder, at -1.7° C in 1969. This doesn't mean that it never gets really cold; in the winter of 2011-2012, the temperature somewhere in Lelystad reached a frigid -22.9° C, while the country also has the occasional 'cold wave'... Of course, December is only the start of the winter, and perhaps January and February can tell us more about recent climate developments; during the first two decades of this century, January brought us an average temperature of 3.8° C and February brought us 4° C, while during the first two decades of the 20th century, these were 2 and 2.6° C, respectively.

In short, it can indeed be concluded that Dutch winters have been heating up over the course of the past 100 years. This is blamed on the uncommon strength of the western winds, which allow the warm temperatures of the seas (7° C) to influence the winter temperature, rather than the winds that come in from the north-east. In combination with the increase in precipitation, this amounts to an awful lot of rain, rather than snow. Hence the rather unexciting winters.

SUMMERS

And the summers? The Netherlands is known for its wishy-washy summers in two senses; warm and dry one year, cool and wet the next – or warm and dry this *week*, cool and wet the next. Whether or not you can pack up your tent and enjoy the local vacation spots depends entirely on your luck. A note: though seasons have been changing due to global change, the KNMI (Dutch Meteorological Institute) assures us that Dutch summers have been this brand of wishy-washy since before the Middle Ages. Albeit on a more modest level, without the heat waves of the last 10 or so years. What do the average temperatures tell us? Average temperatures from 1900 to 1920 were 14.9° C in June, 16.4° C in July and 16.0° C in August. From 2000 to 2020, the same months saw an average of 16.5° C, 18.4° C and 17.9° C. So, yes, average temperatures have gone up.

Perhaps the categories 'summer days' and 'tropical days' can tell us even more – and they do. There are more than twice as many summer days than around 1900 and four times as many tropical days. This is also reflected in the sales of air conditioners, particularly to consumers (offices generally already have temperature regulation) – with sales going up 50% and more in recent years. Not a bad thing, as they are considered to have a positive impact on the value of your home. in 2019, sales of air conditioners went up 30%, in 2020; another 50%. Though climate change is having an impact that is not always considered positive, the local population generally appreciates the extra days that they can sit out in the sun and are happy to install air conditioning to get through the sweltering nights!

2022/2023

The verdict is in: 2023 was the second-wettest year in recorded history with an average of 1,037 mm across the country – and that while we also had 39 days of no rain at all; another record. Let's take a look at the weather in 2023.

The first 18 days of winter – starting in December 2022 – were cold, but January and February were, on average 2° C warmer than normal. New Year's Eve was celebrated in practically spring conditions: around 16° C, after which the first ten days of the year hovered around 9° C, and with a few dips, the winter temperature remained higher than normal. As for precipitation: December was normal, January very wet (108 ml vs 68), and February very dry (20 ml, versus 56) – to make up for what we put up with in January it would seem. As for snow; the clouds brought us three days of snow – that was it – while they parted to brings us more than average sunshine in February. Spring saw a similar continuation of conditions: March was relatively mild, April was relatively cool, and May was 'normal' – in this case, average was simply average. As hinted at earlier: less average was the precipitation: normally, we see 148 ml of rainfall in spring, but the spring of 2023 doused us with a liberal 205 ml – in some places even 233 ml, just barely missing the top ten wet springs measured since 1906. Sunshine was average again, with only May treating us to 255 hours of sun instead of 225. The summer of 2023 was in the top-ten warmest summers since 1901; something you find hard to imagine if you realize that this means the average temperature this past summer was 18.4° C, compared to a 'normal' of 17.5° C. Sometimes we just can't resist referring to the Dutch Royal Weather Institute, which says that in July, we had one very warm period around the 7th – one whole day! And they call it a 'period'. Still, all kidding aside, if you look at the number of warm (>20° C), summer (>25° C) and tropical days (>30° C), it was a perfectly good summer, with 75, 30 and 3 of each, respectively. June was dry, July and August were wetter than average. Which brings us to the fall of 2023. In September, almost every day exceeded average temperatures, making it the second warmest September since 1901, while October was the sixth warmest October measured since 1901 – and also the wettest ever measured since 1906. And then November entered

with a bang; storm Ciarán, with gusts of up to 115 km/h was the messenger, telling us that winter was on its way. It was the time to look forward to the cozy, gezellige days of winter, with family holidays, perhaps a little skating, and mugs of hot chocolate.

RELIGION

Although modern Dutch society is very secular, 49% of the Dutch people identify with an organized religion or philosophical group, and you will see plenty of churches and other places of worship, while you will have ample opportunity to practice your own religion if you wish. You would be hard-put not to find a church, mosque or temple nearby where you can exercise your religious beliefs. The only hurdle you might face is the language, though the larger municipalities that have a more ethnically diverse population offer Christianity in a variety of languages – as you will soon learn on the Internet. This is even more so for Islam.

THE CHURCHES YOU SEE

Before the Protestant Reformation, Dutch people were almost exclusively Roman Catholic. The churches built were clearly Catholic in nature; full of altars, images and decoration.

The religious reforms of the 16th century took place in the Low Countries against a background of resistance against Spanish domination. The Spanish were militant Catholics, and their persecution of Protestant 'heretics' sharpened the economic and political conflict. It also sharpened the fury with which the Dutch reformers stripped their churches of all the trappings of the Catholic Church. All statues and decorations were removed, and altars were either removed or replaced by burial monuments for leading citizens. Only the pulpits were left standing. These more sober and democratically furnished interiors suited the beliefs of the Calvinists better. Today, most of the churches built before the Reformation are still Protestant and sober, having been stripped of their Catholic 'frills'. Only in the southern provinces, where Catholics accounted for a larger percentage of the population, did they succeed in regaining control of the old churches.

The people who remained Catholic after the Protestant Reformation were never systematically persecuted in the Netherlands, but they were discriminated against and hindered in the practice of their religion. For centuries they kept a low profile, getting together for services in hidden, or semi-hidden churches. They were called Papists (*Papen*), and even today you see traces of their neighborhoods reflected in the names of streets and towns. Only in the middle of the 19th century, with the start of the industrial revolution, did the Catholics have enough confidence and resources to start building their own large churches again. Most of these were built in neo-Gothic style. Their newer-looking, machine-made bricks distinguish them from the older churches.

Except for Maastricht and other cities in the south, nearly all large churches you see in Dutch city centers fall into one of these two categories: Protestant and dating from between the 13th and 16th centuries, or Catholic and dating from the 19th century. Churches that date from the 17th, 18th or 20th centuries were usually built on a modest scale.

DUTCH DENOMINATIONS

The southern provinces of Brabant and Limburg are predominantly Catholic, and the other provinces are predominantly Protestant. Of the Dutch people who nowadays claim church affiliation, there are more registered members of the Roman Catholic Church (24%, or 4.1 million) than of the Protestant Church (16%, or 2.7 million). However, only 17% of the Catholics go to church regularly, while 46.8% of the Protestants do; filling the Protestant churches with almost twice as many people.

PROTESTANTS

At the time of the Reformation, some Dutch Protestants followed the teachings of Martin Luther, but most followed the more radical John Calvin, of France. The main feature of Calvinism, in addition to its sobriety, was its belief in predestination – the belief that some people are destined for a place in heaven and others are not. These ideas have evolved, and different streams and communities have developed throughout the years.

The three main categories of Protestantism in the Netherlands today are *Nederlands Hervormd* (Dutch Reformed; 7%), *Protestantse Kerk in Nederland* (Protestant Church in the Netherlands; 6%, and *Gereformeerd* (Reformed; 3%). But there are other groups as well – Evangelical, Lutheran, Baptist, Apostolic, Pentecostal and many more. Approximately half a million Dutch people belong to what is kiddingly referred to by outsiders as 'the black stocking church'. This denomination adheres to radical cultural and social conservatism: they choose to interpret the Bible as literally as possible. Many of them are creationists and they fully believe that Sunday is the day of the Lord. They are also staunch objectors to matters such as abortion, gay marriage or female pastors. Contrary to other denominations, these groups suffer little apostasy or disinterest. Their constituents have their own political party that has three seats in Parliament – the Staatkundig Gereformeerde Partij – and their own newspaper, the *Reformatorisch Dagblad*. Their churches are also quite popular among the younger generation. The black stocking churches are flanked by the Pentecostal movement, which has been growing considerably of late.

CATHOLICS

In the 1960s and 1970s, the Dutch Catholic Church was extremely progressive. A series of conservative appointments by subsequent Popes has made it less so, but you can still find a full range of communities – at one end of the spectrum parishes still using the Latin liturgy, and at the other end parishes committed to the most modern ideas and practices – as well as Byzantine Catholic communities.

The progressiveness of the Catholic Church in the Netherlands went so far that already towards the end of the 1960s of the previous century, the Vatican felt it had interfere. Since then, the bishops that are nominated have consistently been conservative, while young priests – insofar as available – have proven quite traditional. This has alienated quite a few Catholics over the past 50 years, causing the need to close churches and merge parishes. There is now a great shortage of priests while, until approximately 1960, the Dutch Catholics sent armies of missionaries to all corners of the world. Now, their parishes can barely function without foreign priests.

A little-known group is the so-called Old Catholics; in 1723 – in protest against the concentration of power in Rome – they 'broke' with the city by choosing their own bishop. When, in 1870, the infallibility of the Pope was announced, many Old Catholics and others of similar conviction came together and, in 1889, formed the Union of Utrecht. The old Catholics do not practice celibacy and their priests may wed. Currently, the Old Catholic Church has approximately 5,800 members in 26 parishes in the Netherlands, however, worldwide there are over 500,000 members.

PHILOSOPHICAL GROUPS

As mentioned earlier, instead of being members of churches, some people in the Netherlands belong to groups that share a particular philosophical outlook on life. There are of course many of these, but the main ones that are also known outside the Netherlands are: Anthroposophists, Humanists, New Age and the Sufi Movement.

ISLAM

With approximately 872,000 (practicing) Muslims living in the Netherlands (5% of the population), Islam has become one of the country's main religions. Mosques have been built in most of the larger cities by communities of immigrants from Turkey, Morocco and Indonesia, and the Dutch public is gradually learning more about Islam – enough to make allowances for colleagues and pupils who are fasting for Ramadan, for example.

Though many believe that Islam is the fastest-growing religion in the Netherlands, that is not necessarily the case; the method of counting applied to the group of Muslims and the group of Christians is different. Only church-registered Christians are taken into account, versus all immigrants from Muslim-countries. If Christians (immigrants) were to be counted in the same manner, then this would prove to be the fastest-growing religious group. The prediction was once made that by the year 2020, Islam would be the second largest religion in the Netherlands, with 7% of the populace being Muslim, and only 10% Catholic. Looking at recent numbers, however, with Roman Catholics making up 20% of the population, Protestants 15%, and other religions / philosophical groups 6%, it is clear that these predictions did not actually pan out. The country still has 35% registered Christians, while also among Muslims, second and third generation 'immigrants' are becoming more secularized, even though – at the same time – Saudi Salafism, with its separation of the sexes and conservative views, has increased somewhat in popularity.

JUDAISM

Before and during the Second World War, when Hitler's anti-Semitism took hold in Europe, many Jews came to the Netherlands. Aside from the fact that there already was a large Jewish community in the Netherlands, this country had remained neutral during the First World War, and more importantly, had (has) a centuries-long tradition of religious tolerance. The Jews hoped that these factors would allow them to find a safe haven here – but unfortunately, history took a different turn. The Netherlands was occupied by the Germans during the war and could not be the safe haven the Jews had hoped for. In fact, only 13% of the Jewish population of the Netherlands, which had been at 140,000, survived the Second World War. This has since grown to a sizeable Jewish community, of around 35,000 members, of which the center is in Amsterdam, though synagogues can also be found in other cities.

OTHER RELIGIONS

Other religious affiliations that have active communities in the Netherlands include Hinduism, Buddhism and Baha'i. For addresses, check the end of this chapter.

YOU CAN'T FIND A COMMUNITY THAT PRACTICES YOUR RELIGION?

Try contacting the Netherlands Center for Foreigners (NCB or *Nederlands Centrum voor Buitenlanders*) in Utrecht, Amsterdam, Rotterdam, Leiden or Tilburg (www.ncbnet.nl).

Holland or the Netherlands?

Now there's a good question: why is this country sometimes referred to as Holland and sometimes as the Netherlands? The official name of the country you have come to live in is the Netherlands, or 'Low Lands'; a country where 60% of the people live below sea level.

Then why is this country so often referred to as Holland? The answer to this question lies in its history. A few centuries ago, the province of Holland (which included today's North and South Holland provinces) was economically the strongest of all the Dutch provinces, and the one from which virtually all foreign trade originated. Most of the Dutchmen whom foreign traders dealt with were Hollanders, literally from Holland. Hence, when talking about the Netherlands, this became the customary way of referring to the country and its people. Over the years, both names have come to be accepted, although the official name, of course, remains the Netherlands.

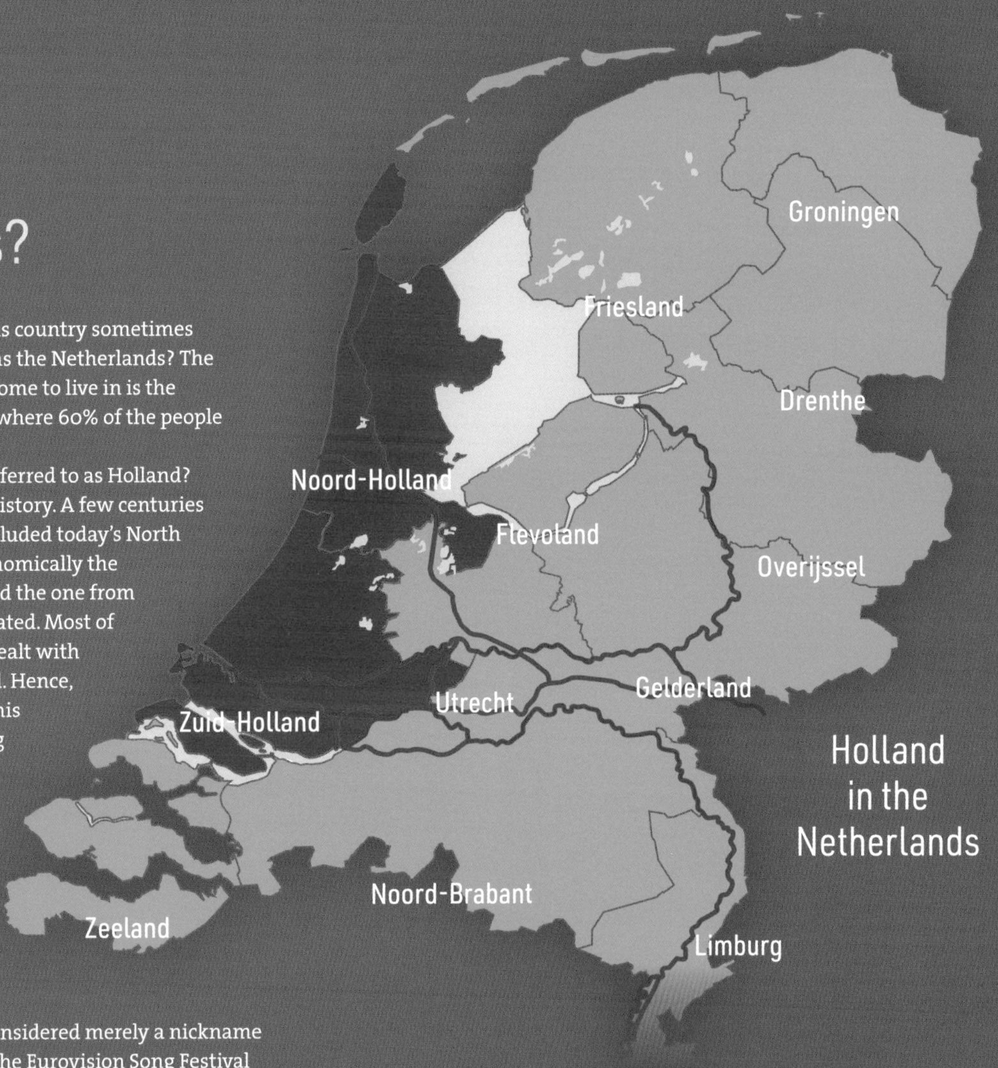

Holland in the Netherlands

OFFICIAL NAME CHANGE

On January 1 2020, the country changed all official references to itself to 'the Netherlands'. Holland is considered merely a nickname and not formal enough for matters as the Eurovision Song Festival – which it hosted in 2021, after it was postponed in 2020 due to Covid – or the Olympics. The aim is also to increase awareness among tourists that there is more to the country than just the two provinces that are home to the big cities of Amsterdam, Rotterdam and The Hague. Whether the official name change, which cost the country € 200,000, will actually have effect, remains to be seen; 'Holland' rolls much more smoothly from the tongue than tongue twister 'the Netherlands'.

SENSITIVITY

Though it is generally accepted that the Netherlands is referred to as Holland, those who are not from the provinces of North or South Holland do not like to be referred to as Hollanders, or to have their language referred to as *Hollands*. The other Dutch provinces are: Friesland, Groningen, Drenthe, Limburg, Utrecht, Gelderland, Overijssel, Noord-Brabant, Zeeland and Flevoland (the latter came into existence as recently as 1986 and consists entirely of reclaimed land), and they all have their own, distinct way of articulating the Dutch language.

RANDSTAD

Nowadays, it is of course – long since – no longer the case that the Holland provinces are the most advanced, though most businesses are still located in the provinces of North and South Holland and Utrecht – an area that is commonly referred to as the Randstad. The rest of the Netherlands is just as well-developed and houses many international businesses and expatriates, and the infrastructure (road, rail, water and telephone) is excellent, all across the country.

The Randstad

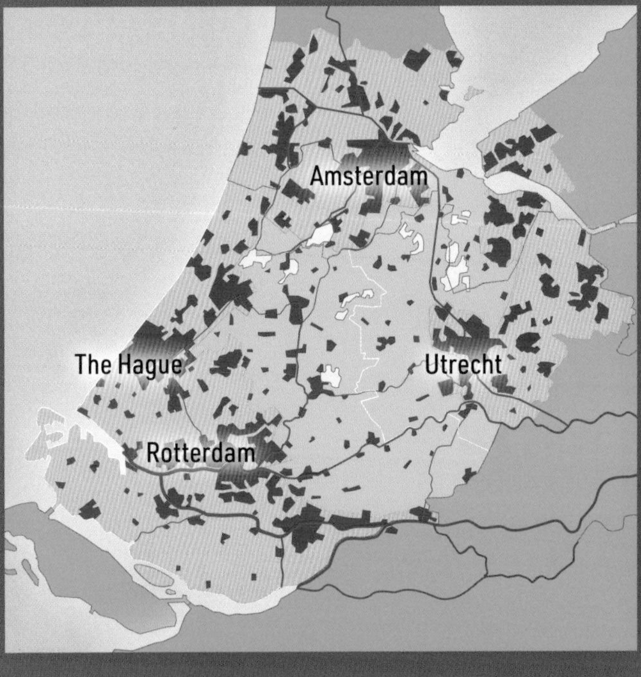

The Netherlands' North Sea coastline

642 KM

The coastline is longer (642 km) than its border with either Belgium (407 km) or Germany (556 km)

The total land surface area

33,948 KM² 21,218 MI²

This excludes all inland and territorial waters wider than 6 meters/ 20 feet. If all the water surface area is included, the Netherlands has an area of 41,526 km²/25,954 mi²

About **60%** of the population lives below sea level

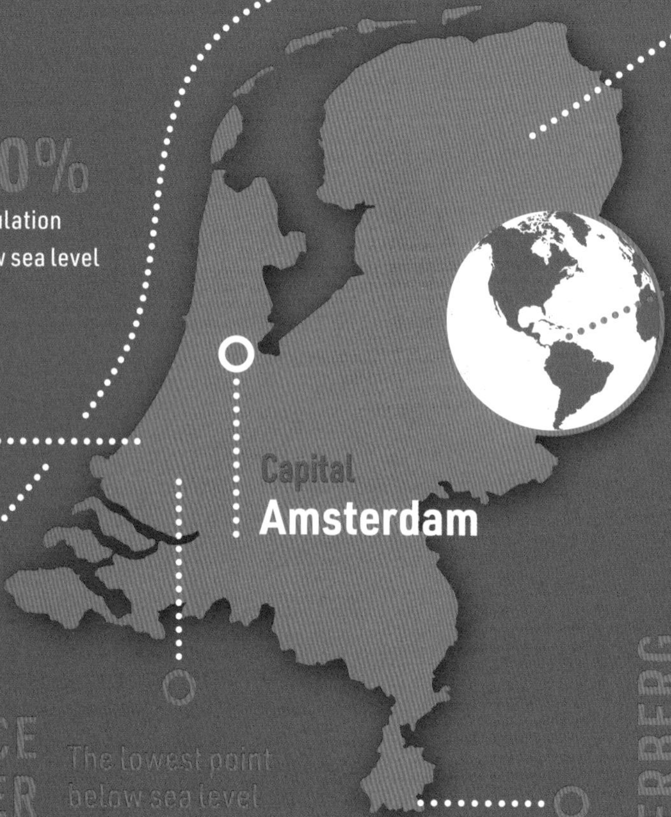

The Kingdom of the Netherlands also includes the countries of Aruba, Curaçao and Sint Maarten. Together with the three particular municipalities of Bonaire, St. Eustatius and Saba, they form the Caribbean part of the Kingdom

Seat of government
The Hague

Capital
Amsterdam

PRINCE ALEXANDER POLDER

The lowest point below sea level

6.76 METERS 22.18 FEET

The lowest point in the country is in the Prince Alexander Polder northeast of Rotterdam (Nieuwerkerk a/d IJssel)

VAALSERBERG

The highest point above sea level

321 METERS 1,053 FEET

The highest point in the Netherlands is the Vaalserberg in the province of Limburg

Population
17.9 MILLION

Migration background
26.4%

KING WILLEM ALEXANDER

Head of State

CONSTITUTIONAL MONARCHY

Type of State

8.3 MILLION

Number of households

Population growth
220,000
(2023)

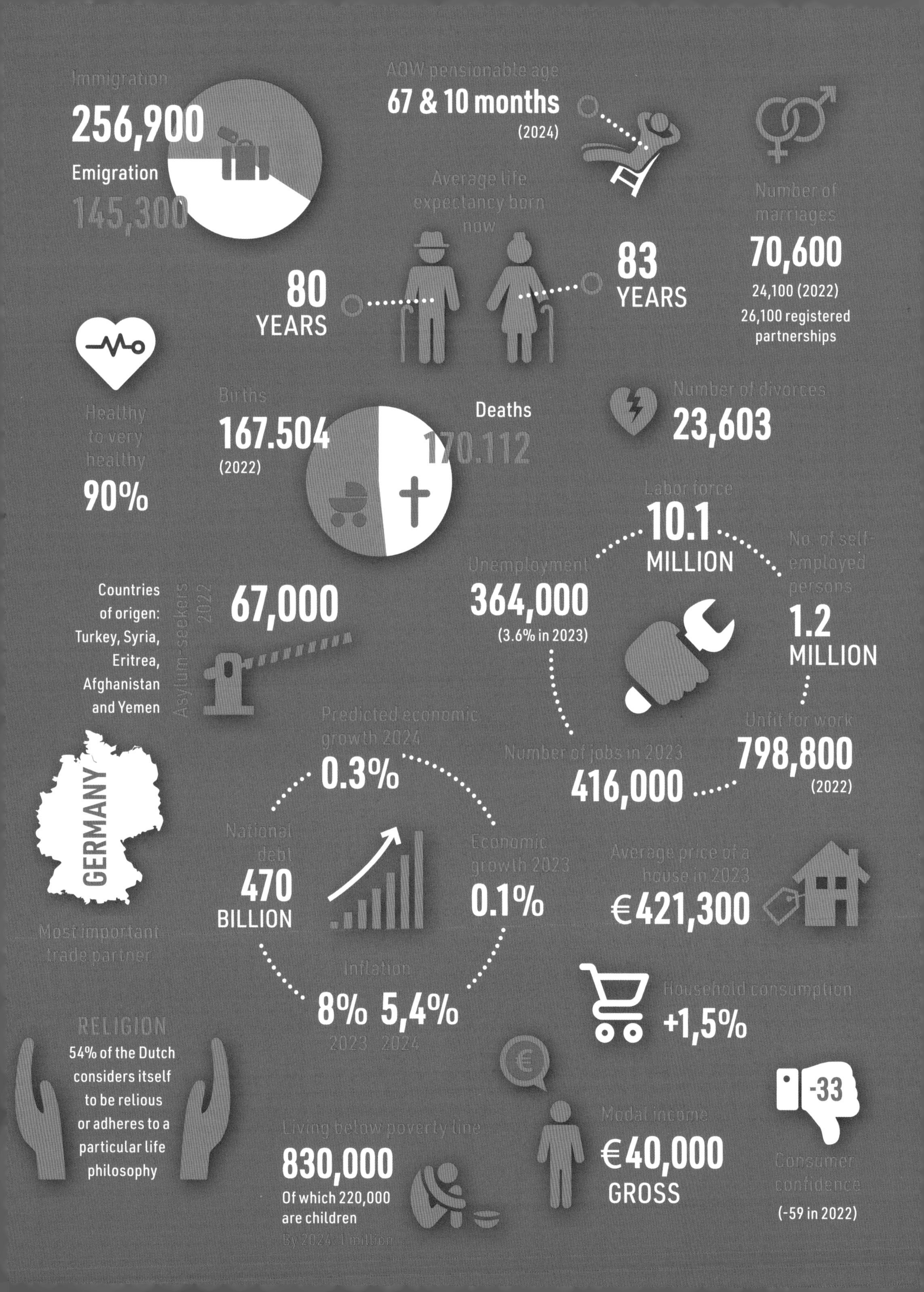
Immigration
256,900
Emigration
145,300
AOW pensionable age
67 & 10 months
(2024)
Average life expectancy born now
80
YEARS
83
YEARS
Number of marriages
70,600
24,100 (2022)
26,100 registered partnerships
Healthy to very healthy
90%
Births
167.504
(2022)
Deaths
170.112
Number of divorces
23,603
Labor force
10.1
MILLION
Unemployment
364,000
(3.6% in 2023)
No. of self-employed persons
1.2
MILLION
Countries of origen: Turkey, Syria, Eritrea, Afghanistan and Yemen
Asylum-seekers 2022
67,000
Predicted economic growth 2024
0.3%
Number of jobs in 2023
416,000
Unfit for work
798,800
(2022)
GERMANY
Most important trade partner
National debt
470
BILLION
Economic growth 2023
0.1%
Average price of a house in 2023
€421,300
Inflation
8% 5,4%
2023 2024
Household consumption
+1,5%
RELIGION
54% of the Dutch considers itself to be relious or adheres to a particular life philosophy
Living below poverty line
830,000
Of which 220,000 are children
By 2024: 1 million
Modal income
€40,000
GROSS
-33
Consumer confidence
(-59 in 2022)

References

CHAPTER 1

The Netherlands in a Nutshell

THE NETHERLANDS INFO FOR EXPATS
www.dutchnews.nl – English-language daily news from the Netherlands
www.dutchreview.com – News, culture and guides for expats in the Netherlands
www.expatica.com – News and community portal for expats in Europe
www.gogodutch.com – Biggest online platform for the Chinese language community In the Netherlands
www.holland.com – For useful and fun information on what's on in the Netherlands
www.iamexpat.nl – News, life style, housing, career and education in the Netherlands
www.internations.org – Events for expats in cities all over the Netherlands
www.NLtimes.nl – Dutch news in English
www.xpat.nl – Your guide to living, working and studying in the Netherlands

DUTCH GOVERNMENT
www.overheid.nl – access to the websites of the Dutch Government Departments and Ministries

THE DUTCH ECONOMY
Statistics Netherlands (CBS)
www.cbs.nl
De Nederlandsche Bank (DNB)
www.dnb.nl

WEATHER INFORMATION
www.buienradar.nl
www.knmi.nl
www.weeronline.nl
www.weerplaza.nl
www.weathernews.nl

Recommended Reading

LITTLE ORANGE HANDBOOK 2.0
The Netherlands for Newcomers
By Stephanie Dijkstra
Published by XPat Media
A practical guide and quick introduction to the Netherlands.
To order: www.hollandbooks.nl

THE DUTCH AND THEIR DELTA
Living Below Sea Level
By Jacob Vossestein
Published by XPat Media
The fascinating account of how the Dutch manage to live below sea level
To order: www.hollandbooks.nl

THE LOW SKY
By Han van der Horst
Published by Scriptum
The book that makes the Netherlands familiar
A detailed exploration of the reasons for desire of the Dutch for independence, their sense of respect and their business sense
www.scriptum.nl

DUTCH HISTORY IN A NUTSHELL
By Herman Beliën and Monique van Hoogstraten. Published by Prometeus
An outline of the history of the Netherlands in just over 100 pages.
www.hollandbooks.nl

THE UNDUTCHABLES 9.0
By Colin White and Laurie Boucke
Published XPat Media
A tongue-in-cheek observation of the Netherlands, its culture and its inhabitants.
www.undutchables.com
To order: www.hollandbooks.nl

THE AMERICAN NETHERLANDER – 25 YEARS OF EXPAT TALES
By Greg Shapiro
Published by XPat Media
Greg Shapiro celebrates 25 years in the Netherlands by revealing his hilariously clumsy assimilation into Dutch society.
To order: www.hollandbooks.nl

Places of worship

AFRIKAANSE GEREFORMEERDE KERK (SOUTH AFRICAN CHURCH)
Gruttersdreef 106, 7328 DN Apeldoorn
Tel.: 055 543 18 93

AMERICAN PROTESTANT CHURCH OF THE HAGUE
Esther de Boer van Rijklaan 20,
2597 TJ The Hague
Tel.: 070 324 44 90
www.apch.nl

ANGLICAN CHURCH – CHRIST CHURCH
Groenburgwal 42, 1011 HW Amsterdam
Tel.: 020 441 03 55
www.christchurch.nl

THE BAHA'I FAITH NATIONAL CENTRE
Riouwstraat 27, 2585 GR The Hague
Tel.: 070 517 80 24
www.bahai.nl

THE BLUE MOSQUE
Henri Dunantstraat 10 – 12, 1066 AX Amsterdam
Tel.: 020 223 53 30
www. blauwemoskee.nl

THE BLESSED TRINITY
Zaaiersweg 180, 1097 ST Amsterdam
Tel.: 020 465 27 11
www.blessedtrinity.nl

CHURCH OF CHRIST
De Gaarde 61, 2542 CH The Hague
Tel.: 070 329 73 80
www.gemeentevanchristus.nl/denhaag

CROSSROADS INTERNATIONAL CHURCH OF THE HAGUE
Bezuidenhoutseweg 249, 2594 AM The Hague
Tel.: 070 322 24 85
www.crossroadschurch.nl

ENGLISH REFORMED CHURCH AMSTERDAM
Begijnhof 48, 1012 WV Amsterdam
Tel.: 020 624 96 65
www.ercadam.nl

ENGLISH SPEAKING CATHOLIC CHURCH OF THE HAGUE – CHURCH OF OUR SAVIOUR
R. C. Parish
Bezuidenhoutseweg 157, 2594 AG The Hague
Tel.: 070 328 08 16
www.parish.nl

ENGLISH AND AMERICAN EPISCOPAL CHURCH OF ST. JOHN & ST. PHILIP
Ary van der Spuyweg 1, 2585 JA The Hague
Tel.: 070 355 53 59
www.stjohn-stphilip.org

THE ENGLISH CHURCH OF ST. JAMES
Koninklijke Marinelaan 53,
2251 BA Voorschoten
Tel.: 071 561 15 28
www.stjames.nl

ESSALAM MOSQUE
Vredesplein 7, 3074 SN Rotterdam
Tel.: 010 419 3666
www.essalamrotterdam.nl

HOLY TRINITY CHURCH
Van Hogendorpstraat 26, 3581 KE Utrecht
Tel.: 030 251 34 24
www.holytrinityutrecht.nl

HOPE INTERNATIONAL BAPTIST CHURCH
Schiedamse Vest 121, 3021 BH Rotterdam
Tel.: 010 888 90 46
www.hope-baptist-church.com

INTERNATIONAL CHURCH LEIDEN
Vijf Meilaan 137, 2344 VV Leiden
www. ichurchleiden.nl

INTERNATIONAL CHRISTIAN FELLOWSHIP ROTTERDAM
Carnissesingel 20, 3084 NA Rotterdam
www. icfrotterdam.nl

JEWISH COMMUNITY
Van der Boechhorststraat 26, 1081 BT Buiten-veldert, Amsterdam
Tel.: 020 646 00 46
www.nihs.nl

LIBERAL JEWISH COMMUNITY OF THE HAGUE
Prinsessegracht 26, 2514 AP The Hague
Tel.: 070 365 68 93
www.ljgdenhaag.nl

MOBARAK MOSQUE
Oostduinlaan 79, 2596 JJ The Hague
Tel.: 070 324 59 02
www.alislam.org

REFORMED COMMUNITY THE HAGUE
Diamanthorst 187, 2592 GD The Hague
Tel.: 070 385 87 07

TRINITY BAPTIST CHURCH
Bloemcamplaan 54, 2244 EE Wassenaar
Tel.: 070 517 80 24

TRINITY INTERNATIONAL CHURCH
Gruttolaan 23, 2261 ET Leidschendam
Tel.: 070 517 80 24
www.trinitychurch.nl

THE SCOTS INTERNATIONAL CHURCH ROTTERDAM
Schiedamsevest 121, 3021 BH Rotterdam
Tel.: 010 412 47 79
www.scotsintchurch.com

UNIVERSEL MURAD HASSIL SOEFI TEMPEL
Zuidduinseweg 7, 2225 JS Katwijk aan Zee
Tel.: 06 4265 1155
www. universel.nu

ST. MARY'S ANGLICAN EPISCOPAL CHURCH OF ROTTERDAM
Pieter de Hoochweg 133, 3024 BG Rotterdam
Tel.: 010 476 40 43
www.stmarys.nl

TRINITY CHURCH EINDHOVEN
Pensionaat Eikenburg, Aalsterweg 289,
5644 RE Eindhoven
Tel.: 040 244 81 49
www.trinitychurcheindhoven.org

ULI CAMII MOSQUE
Moskeeplein 89, 3531 BX Utrecht
Tel.: 030 294 3714
www.ulumoskee.nl

Now that you have learned more about the history of this country and its political system, economy and climate, you might be wondering about the people you are sharing this country with. What kind of people are the towering Dutch? What about their customs and etiquette, particular ways of celebrating holidays and special occasions, and their oh-so-challenging language? As this chapter helps you navigate through some of the canals of these riddles, you will realize that, in the end, the effort you put into rowing through uncharted territory will matter more than which way the wind is blowing.

CHAPTER 2

Social Life

CONTRIBUTING AUTHORS STEPHANIE DIJKSTRA, ARNOLD ENKLAAR AND BEN VAN DER HAVE

CUSTOMS AND ETIQUETTE

Before you put your proverbial foot in your proverbial mouth, here are some lessons picked up at the school of hard knocks, where the price of tuition is a lot higher than learning it here.

PERSONAL SOCIAL SPACE

Dutch social space is determined in great part, it is deemed, by the lack of physical space that is available in Holland. Granted, everything and everyone is very close together: Holland has one of the highest average population densities in the world; 522 inhabitants per km^2.

Theory has it that the Dutch compensate for this lack of physical space by making their personal social space bigger, so that they can better deal with the problems of living in such a crowded society.

Observe, for instance, the Dutch standing in line, if you can find one. They normally stand much closer together than Americans do. Americans tend to feel uncomfortable if you stand that close to them in line. American social connections, on the other hand, are much more intimate than Dutch social connections. While Americans interact with people with seeming informality and call everyone by his or her first name, Dutch interaction is generally stylized and formal. Calling a Dutch person by first name when you are not supposed to is like talking to an American with your nose three inches from his. You are invading his space and that makes him feel uncomfortable.

The extended Dutch social space is viewed by many foreigners as standoffishness, but to the Dutch it is just a way of coping with life in a shoebox. As long as you are polite enough to respect other people's social space, they will politely respect yours and tolerate almost anything you want to do – testimony to a nation dually praised and criticized for its tolerance – as long as you keep it inside your social and personal space and out of theirs.

GETTING A WORD IN EDGEWISE

Oddly enough, the amount of time that the Dutch pause at the end of a sentence to indicate that they have finished talking and that someone else can take a turn is a lot shorter than it is in English. Even when they speak English, the Dutch still use the same short 'change-speakers' pause to give others a chance to join the conversation. Until you get used to it, you may not get much said, because you may not recognize the shorter pause as a signal to say something, and thereby miss your turn, feeling like they're rudely cutting you off. The cue to change speakers is something that you normally perceive subconsciously, based on years of experience listening to other people talk. Just being aware that there is a difference between cultural modes is usually all you need to reset the length of time that you recognize as a change-speakers' cue, so that you can get a word in edgewise.

VISITING

Generally, the Dutch do not like company to stop by informally, if they just happen to be 'in the neighborhood'. If you know someone very well, you can call in the morning to ask if you can come by that evening, but normally you should call further in advance. The greater the social distance between you, the longer in advance you need to call. Grown children even call their parents – and vice versa – to see if it is all right to come by for a visit.

FASHIONABLY LATE

Conversely, do not invite Dutch acquaintances to 'drop by anytime'. Set a specific time and date, and specify what you intend to serve. "Come by next Tuesday at two for coffee" and they will be there at the stroke of two. 'Fashionably late' in Holland is waiting for the bell on the tower clock to finish ringing before you ring the doorbell.

COFFEE

Since the Dutch do not like 'surprise' company, the coffee will be ready to pour when you arrive. Yours should be too. An offer of coffee (or tea) is the absolute minimum expected when someone visits your home. Even the workmen who come to fix a leaky faucet will be offered a cup of coffee. Suffice it to say that there will also be cookies, or, if this is a special occasion like a birthday or anniversary, pastries. ALWAYS WAIT TO BE SERVED. It's considered very impolite to help yourself. Conversely, do not forget to offer your Dutch guests a second round of coffee, tea, or cookies; they will not help themselves.

A couple we know, who speak no Dutch, went to visit friends in Holland and when they came back, they were proud to announce that they had learned the Dutch word for 'Hello'. *Koffie?* he said with no accent at all, and he was right. The first thing any Dutch host(ess) says when someone comes into the house is not "Hello", but: "*Koffie?*" (Do you want a cup of coffee?).

HOSPITALITY GIFTS

A visit to someone's home invariably calls for a hospitality gift. Flowers, cookies, or candy are almost always appropriate. If you think that your host(ess) might be dieting or diabetic, take flowers. Flowers are quite inexpensive in Holland, as this is the world's largest flower exporter, and are a welcome present.

Dutch National Holidays and Main Festivities 2024

JANUARY 1
New Year's Day

FEBRUARY 11
Start Carnival

FEBRUARY 14
Valentine's Day

MARCH 29
Good Friday

MARCH 31
Easter Sunday

APRIL 1
Pasen Easter Monday

APRIL 27
Koningsdag
King's Birthday

MAY 1
Labor Day

MAY 4
Dodenherdenking
Commemoration of the Dead

MAY 5
Bevrijdingsdag
Liberation Day

MEI 9
Hemelvaartsdag
Ascension Day

MAY 12
Mother's Day

MAY 19
Pinksteren Whit Sunday

MAY 20
Tweede Pinksterdag
Whit Monday

JUNE 6
Father's Day

SEPTEMBER 17
Prinsjesdag
Opening of Parliament

OCTOBER 4
Dierendag
International Animal Day

DECEMBER 25
Christmas Day

DECEMBER 26
'Second Christmas Day'

New Year's Eve
DECEMBER 31

(Hint: buy flowers with the blooms still closed. Not only do they last longer, but fully open flowers have an aura of cheapness about them. The impression will either be that the florist took advantage of your being a foreigner and palmed them off on you, or you took advantage of their lower price to skimp on your hospitality gift.)

KISSING

The arrival ritual for good friends and family members at a Dutch home catches many foreigners by surprise. Ladies enter first to a round of three – the number is significant – kisses on the cheek (right-left-right) with each person there. The men follow, shaking hands with the other men and fashionably kissing all the ladies lightly on the cheek three times (right-left-right). As a foreigner you can get by with shaking hands instead of kissing.

Stating your name – both first and last or just first or last name only – as you greet someone is considered basic protocol. Understanding the name that they've just told you is another matter.

SPECIAL OCCASIONS – THE DUTCH WAY

BIRTHDAYS

Nearly all Dutch people celebrate all of their birthdays with great enthusiasm. On that day they can usually expect family and friends to visit them at home, or to telephone or send a birthday card. It is considered rather anti-social for a person to ignore his or her own birthday (*verjaardag*). Contrary to American custom, for example, where the birthday celebrant is catered to, the Dutch celebrant plans and hosts the festivities, inviting and catering to friends and family, most often at home. The custom in the workplace is to bring pastries for colleagues at work to enjoy over coffee. Likewise, children bring treats to school for all their classmates.

Birthday calendars (*verjaardagkalenders*), which are usually hung prominently in the bathroom, help people keep track of the dates on which they have to pay visits or send cards. A word of advice: don't overlook a Dutch person's birthday; such forgetfulness borders on insolence.

Curiously, it is customary to congratulate not only the person whose birthday it is, but also his or her relatives, friends and even neighbors. To say 'Congratulations (*Gefeliciteerd*!) on the birthday of your brother-in-law' would be quite normal. By the same token, don't be caught off guard if someone congratulates *you* whenever it's your spouse's or child's birthday. You'll now understand what you did to deserve the kudos!

TURNING FIFTY: 'ABRAHAM AND SARAH'

The 50th birthday is a milestone that the Dutch are particularly keen to celebrate. The person in question is then referred to as Abraham (for men) or Sarah (for women), a tradition that originates from a reference to the Bible where Jesus is explaining that Abraham had 'seen' the day on which Jesus would become the Messiah. Skeptics thought he meant that he had actually 'met' Abraham and sarcastically said: "Not yet 50 years of age, but already you have met Abraham!" Hence the tradition in the Netherlands that, when you reach the age of 50, you see Abraham or Sarah. A life-size doll, with a big sign hung from its neck indicating one or the other constituent, is often placed in front of the celebrant's house. Unlike some cultures that tend to hide or bury the aging process, the Dutch seem uncharacteristically proud of reaching a ripe old age. In their view, the more years the merrier.

WEDDINGS

The pre-wedding custom of a bridal shower is one that supposedly originated in Holland. It is said that the daughter of a miller wanted to marry a man her father didn't approve of, and he wouldn't provide her with a dowry. The villagers took pity on the girl and 'showered' her with gifts, enabling her to marry the man of her choice. If this is true, however, it is certainly one custom that left the Netherlands along with settlers to the New World, as it definitely does not exist in the Netherlands of today.

Strangely enough, a church ceremony alone does not constitute a legal marriage here. A civil ceremony, often conducted in the town hall by a local official, is required for a couple to be legally married (see more on page 131). As such, a Dutch wedding could easily consist of both a civil and a church wedding in one day. Following the ceremony, the celebrations may take place in three parts: a *receptie, diner*, and a *feest* (reception, dinner and party). Unusual as it may seem, it is quite common to invite different people to different parts of the celebrations. Family and very close friends may be invited to everything, whilst colleagues and neighbors may be invited to the *receptie* only.

WEDDING ANNIVERSARIES

Though not always customary, the Dutch will at times succumb to the temptation to celebrate a wedding anniversary with a large group of friends and family, usually on the 12 1/2, 25th or 50th anniversary. In such cases, the appropriate gifts are typically flowers, wine or a joint gift given by a group of friends, colleagues or relatives. Often you are approached in a letter by one of the children or a family friend, inviting you to sing a song, give a speech or contribute to a joint gift.

BIRTHS

That pink or blue balloon-decked stork in your neighbor's garden means that a new baby boy or girl has arrived. Friends, colleagues and relatives, even those that the parents may have long since forgotten, call to make an appointment, no less, to come and admire the little darling, and bring along a gift – usually a toy or some item of clothing. Visitors are served tea or coffee and *beschuit met muisjes*; rusks or crisp bread covered with sugared aniseeds (sweets resembling mice, or muisjes); pink for girls and blue for boys. (You can read more about this on page 208.)

GIFTS, CARDS AND PARTY ETIQUETTE

Dutch people routinely give each other gifts on various occasions. These include birthdays, visits to someone's home for a meal, and parties to celebrate weddings, anniversaries and graduations. Gifts are generally small and not lavish, unless they are for a family member. Bouquets of flowers, bottles of wine and boxes of chocolates are common gifts. In fact, a group of friends might even put their money together and buy what is considered a larger gift, such as a book, an expensive household item, or gift card.

A Dutch person generally presents a gift as soon as he sees the recipient, and the recipient generally opens the gift immediately. Not to do so would be considered impolite. Don't, however, expect effusive thanks, as the Dutch are not generally known for their ebullience. Over-enthusiasm can be viewed as pretentious behavior, or insincere.

Greeting cards are sent on many occasions. In addition to birthday cards, there are cards of congratulations for events such as passing exams, moving to a new home, and taking early retire-

ment. Millions of postcards are also sold, and not just to tourists. While people on holiday send postcards to family and friends back home, many Dutch people also send them just for fun.

DEATHS

When a member of the family passes away, the family sends out cards, usually with gray borders, announcing the death, and often place an obituary in the newspaper. When you hear about the death of a friend, or a dear one of a friend, it is greatly appreciated if you write a short note of condolence. If the friend is a close one, you can visit the family to pay your respects (do not do this unannounced) or give them a short phone call. The Dutch traditionally go to the funeral service (which is most often held in the funeral home and not in a church) and, depending on their close ties with the deceased, have a flower arrangement delivered by a florist, to be placed on the casket, to which a ribbon or card is attached with a few final words and the names of the sender(s). Sometimes, the announcement already states that the family does not wish to be disturbed before the funeral (*bezoek is niet gewenst* – we would prefer no visitors) or that the funeral will be held for only the immediate family (*de overledene wordt in besloten kring begraven*). Some families prefer that you donate money to a charity rather than give flowers, and the card will then suggest the charity of choice. After the funeral, a reception is held, where you will be given the opportunity to pay your condolences in person to the family.

TYPICAL DUTCH FESTIVITIES

CARNIVAL – FEBRUARY

Carnival, the Dutch either love it or hate it. Those who live *beneden de rivieren* (below the rivers, in other words in Noord-Brabant or Limburg) love it and celebrate it with a passion. Virtually all businesses close (except cafés and restaurants of course) in a three-day celebration of life, spring, beer and friendship, though in the province of Limburg there is an added element of poking fun at the government and politics. In the provinces *boven de rivieren* (above the rivers) the general attitude towards carnival is one of aloofness – adding to their reputation among the Southerners as a dour and 'un-fun' people – a gray dividing line that, some would say, smacks of a still Protestant-based north and a predominantly Catholic south.

Dutch carnival has the same origins as carnival in Rio (the period of excess preceding the period of self-deprivation of Lent) and is about as wild, though you must bear in mind of course, that it is celebrated by the 'cold-blooded' Dutch rather than the 'hot-blood-

ed' Brazilians, not to mention the general difference in temperature at that time of year! People get dressed up and go from café to café, singing songs, participating in parades and consuming large quantities of beer. There is no need to be afraid of this being a local festivity at which strangers are not accepted: strangers are welcome, and it is a great way to meet new people. Breda, Maastricht and 's Hertogenbosch are three of the major venues.

APRIL 27: KING'S (BIRTH)DAY – KONINGSDAG

Although not necessarily known to be royalists, the Dutch are extremely fond of their Royal Family. Throughout history, the Dutch Royal Family has been very popular and the Family's birthdays have been celebrated with enthusiasm. As of 1898, Queen Wilhelmina's 18th birthday, the holiday has been officially referred to as *koninginnedag* (literally Queen's Day). April 30th officially became *koninginnedag* when Queen Juliana changed the date to her own birthday. Queen Beatrix, whose birthday is actually on January 31st, left April 30th as the official day to celebrate her birthday as the weather would then (theoretically) be much better than at the end of January. As of 2014, the King celebrates his birthday – now called Koningsdag, or King's Day – on April 27.

You can celebrate the King's birthday either by visiting the town or city the King visits on this day – and witness traditional entertainment and games – or you can visit some of the bigger cities. Amsterdam, in particular, goes all out on this day, with a *vrijmarkt*; a free market that fills the streets in the center of Amsterdam with stands run by people aged 5 – 105, selling anything and everything. People from all across the world come to Amsterdam (including an annual influx of gays from San Francisco hyped on the suggestive nomenclature of old; *Queens'* Day) to enjoy this special atmosphere. Another option is to visit the traditional *koningsmarkt* (King's Market) of your own town, where the locals sell just about anything for a song, a great opportunity for bargain hunters and antique buffs – but be there early for the best values (6 A.M.)!

COMMEMORATING THE DEAD: MAY 4TH

More a day of national significance than of festivity, May 4th is initially the day on which the Dutch remember those who fell during the Second World War: soldiers, people in the Resistance and those who did not survive concentration camps in Europe as well as in Indonesia. Since 1961, it commemorates all war victims in the years since the start of the Second World War in general. Between 8 P.M. and 8:02 P.M., a two-minute silence is observed nationally. People stop whatever they are doing (often pulling their cars over to the side of the road) to remember those who did not make it through the war. Even local radio and television broadcasts are halted. In many municipalities, people come together for short ceremonies, particularly in The Hague, on the Waalsdorpervlakte, and in Amsterdam, on the Dam Square. Flags are hung half-mast throughout the country.

LIBERATION DAY: MAY 5TH

Following the sober day of May 4th, the Dutch celebrate their total liberation from the occupying forces in 1945 (some parts of the Netherlands had been liberated in November 1944) on Liberation Day, May 5th. Flags are hung full-mast and the streets take on a festive look. Because commemorating the dead and celebrating liberation deserve individual and equal attention, they have been set on different days. Unfortunately, this memorable day is not celebrated as extensively as it used to be: some businesses and most government offices are closed for the day (in keeping with the collective labor agreement), but most are not. However, there is always some celebration going on somewhere, while movies and documentaries about this period on TV provide you with the opportunity to learn a little bit about (recent) Dutch history, if you want.

TRICK OR TREATS – SINT MAARTEN

Increasingly, the trick or treats day of November 11 is being reintroduced. On this day, children (often accompanied by parents) come to your door, carrying lanterns and singing songs such as '*Sint Maarten, Sint Maarten, de koeien hebben staarten, de meisjes hebben rokjes aan, daar komt Sint Martinus aan*' (St. Martin, St. Martin, the cows have tails, the girls wear skirts, there comes St. Martin – who *knows* what the one has to do with the other). This day is a 'treats'-day – no tricks – the treats being anything from tangerines to cookies to candy. The children do not get dressed up for this occasion, either; it is a simple – though friendly and *gezellige* – neighborhood event. In some cities, due to the exposure to other cultures, rather than with Sint Maarten on November 11, children go trick or treating on October 31; Halloween.

SINTERKLAAS

You may have already met up with a typical Dutch personality called Sinterklaas, or St. Nicholas. You may too have observed that he has many similarities with that white-bearded, red-clothed man you tend to run into towards the end of December in other countries (as well as in the Netherlands). However, Sinterklaas has made considerably better arrangements for himself. Santa Claus may live on the North Pole, but Sinterklaas lives in the South of Spain. Santa Claus flies in from the North Pole on his sleigh, high through the freezing skies; Sinterklaas takes a leisurely cruise from the South of Spain to the Netherlands (hence the song: *Zie ginds komt de stoomboot uit Spanje weer aan* – or, 'Look, there comes the steamboat from Spain'). Santa Claus has to squeeze down and back up all those chimneys himself; Sinterklaas has a whole crew of helpers named Roet Pieten, or Soot Petes, to do that for him.

The phenomenon of Roet Piet's predecessor, Zwarte Piet, is an element that tends to surprise visiting foreigners. In this era of post-anti-apartheid and desegregation, what exactly did the Dutch think they're doing with black-face-painted helpers? Well, Sinterklaas's Zwarte / Roet Pieten actually represent the Moors of Spain; chased into the Sierra Nevada by the Catholic Spaniards in the 15th century, they apparently sought gainful employment in the services of St. Nicholas. As a matter of fact, and this is the God's honest truth, if you drive along the coast of Southern Spain, between Motril and Málaga, you run into a tiny little sign, pointing up a narrow winding road into the hills, saying San Nicolás.... Incidentally, there is no evidence whatsoever that the presence of Zwarte / Roet Piet at Sinterklaas' side has in any way influenced children's perception of people of another race – nonetheless, the decision was made to abolish the 'black' element, both in color and features, and replace it with a milder soot color and a variety of hairstyles. We refer you to page 64 for more on this topic.

December 6th is St. Nicholas's birthday (or as some claim, the anniversary of his death, the 5th being his birthday) when, according to legend, this 4th-century Saint gave gifts of gold to three poor girls for their dowries, a tradition the Netherlands emulates (children still receive chocolate coins around this time). Throughout the centuries, Sinterklaas has been considered the patron saint of children (as well as of traders). Consequently, on December 5th, he brings them gifts that are surreptitiously dropped off in a sack on the doorstep of each household. During the evening, families exchange gifts, and traditionally drink hot chocolate and eat *banketstaaf*, made of puff pastry and almond paste. On December 6th, as a birthday present to himself, some would say, Sinterklaas hightails it back to warm, sunny Spain for another 11 1/2 months.

Sinterklaas's birthday is not only a holiday for children; grown-ups like to participate in the fun by means of a gift (serious, silly or, often, homemade, called a *surprise*) with an accompanying poem that summarizes the receiver's past year, intermingled with surprising habits and silly mistakes – often in a slightly ridiculing tone. (Bear in mind that the Dutch love to tease and the more they make fun of you, the more they like you, although it has been known to happen that the unsuspecting receiver of such a lovingly and amusingly composed poem has rushed out of the room in tears.)

For more on Sinterklaas, see page 208.

CHRISTMAS DAY AND NEW YEAR'S EVE

Christmas Day itself is normally reserved for religious observances and family get-togethers (see more about this on page 208), increasingly combined with gifts. Likewise, the stroke of midnight on New Year's Eve signals that it's time to pay a quick visit to your neighbors with good wishes for the coming year. New Year's Day is a quiet continuation of the same. This all sounds rather tame and civilized, but don't worry; there are plenty of wild parties on New Year's Eve for those who care to go all out! Not to mention the millions of euros that are annually spent on fireworks – not by the municipalities, but by the people themselves – which create enough commotion to traumatize the more sensitive of souls...

THE DUTCH LANGUAGE

First off, be thankful that almost everyone speaks virtually fluent English in the Netherlands. The Dutch are enviable linguists who switch from one language to another with the greatest of ease. In the beginning, the Dutch think it's perfectly fine if you speak English, and they will respond in English. But don't be fooled into thinking that their own language is not so important to them. If, after a year or two, your Dutch is still non-existent or barely so, they will become considerably less tolerant. Thinking that you are not doing your best to accept their culture, they may hold this against you – either explicitly or implicitly.

Like it or not, you must realize that *you* are a guest in *their* country, not the other way around, and that, by right, you should learn your host's language if you're going to live here for any length of time.

WHY SHOULD YOU LEARN DUTCH?

Maybe you think: 'I'm only going to be in Holland for a few years, and everyone understands me at work – why should I make the effort to learn a language I am not going to need for the rest of my life?' Experience shows that you will not only feel more acclimated if you learn the language of your host culture, but that you will generally be more accepted and appreciated for having made the effort, especially with such an obscure and sufficiently difficult language.

Moreover, if you are the partner or spouse of an employee who has been placed in the Netherlands, your life is probably quite different. If you do not have a job, you run more of a risk of becoming isolated, particularly if you can't speak the local language. If you remain an outsider, you will miss out on the finer subtleties of the language and, therefore, the culture itself. In short, you will simply feel more comfortable with your life in Holland if you can understand what's going on around you. You'll quickly realize that having a command of the Dutch language will go a long way towards being able to decipher all those packages in the supermarket, for example, not to mention being able to read the local newspaper. Learning Dutch may, consequently, be of unexpected significance to both you and your children, though they will most likely pick up the language more easily through immersion in daily life, or what seems to adults as pure osmosis. Survival of the fittest is key to any expatriate experience, and language adaptation is no exception.

HOW DIFFICULT IS DUTCH?

Dutch is not an easy language for English speakers – we simply do not have the capacity for those throaty, guttural sounds on which Netherlandish children are weaned. Sentence structure is awkwardly reversed, and the Dutch seem to have imposed no limit on word length. (*Levensverzekeringsmaatschappijen*, translated as 'life insurance companies', and *projectontwikkelingsmaatschappijen*, meaning 'property development companies', at 32 and 34 letters each, are the two longest official words in the Dutch language, although there are even much longer unofficial, makeshift conglomerations of words used in everyday language.) If your native language is similar to Dutch, or you've studied a parallel language, you'll be one step ahead of the game.

THE FIRST STEPS

Decide whether you would prefer to follow an established course or take private lessons. The Netherlands has a national network of language institutes that offer courses in Dutch to foreigners (usually, these courses are referred to as NT2, *Nederlands als tweede taal* – Dutch as a second language). The local city or town hall will advise you as to where the nearest institute is, so that you can make an appointment. During an interview, they will probably ask you what type of school you went to at home, what diplomas you have, whether you interact with a lot of Dutch people, whether you have time to go to a school and to do homework, etc. They may also ask you to take a placement exam to determine what level you should pursue. Depending on your specific needs, the institute may suggest an intensive course for quicker immersion.

Caution: don't be tempted to buy a Dutch phrasebook, as these are generally geared to tourists and often don't accurately reflect common usage. Invest instead in a good Dutch dictionary and a basic 'Dutch for beginners' book to get you started.

Of primary importance is learning the numbers in Dutch, as you'll quickly discover that such everyday tasks as shopping and making appointments rely on this basic knowledge. Dutch numbers require some mental gymnastics – '21' is expressed as 'one and twenty', for example – so be prepared.

SOME PRELIMINARY WORDS OF ADVICE

- *Let everyone know that you don't (or hardly) speak any Dutch* Do this before the other overestimates your capacity to understand him or her, and starts off too quickly and with too complicated a vocabulary. Don't, however, insist on only English conversation as you'll never learn Dutch that way. Simply employ the following sentence if need be: *Ik wil Nederlands leren* (I want to learn Dutch). The reactions will vary. Some will turn up the volume, others will revert to a type of pidgin Dutch, as if talking to a child. Don't be offended; it's a natural reaction.
- *Do not be afraid to make mistakes* Many expatriates want to master Dutch as well as they do their native language – and it annoys them if they can't converse quickly. Though this is understandable, patience is of the essence. Fluency takes much time, and all that matters at first is basic communication.
- *Don't make it unnecessarily hard* Try to avoid difficult subjects at first. Keep your initial conversations simple.

Twelve Clues to Understanding the Dutch Mentality

BY BY ARNOLD ENKLAAR

At first sight, the Dutch appear to be like many other normal Europeans. But those of you who have lived here longer and have worked with the Dutch, will have found dramatic differences. In order to avoid irritation or surprises, it might be good to know a little more about the Dutch culture. In these paragraphs, you will find a short overview of the 12 principles or values that rule Dutch society, from politics, work, and school, to the most intimate parts of family life.

The first four values come straight from Christianity:

1 SALVATION You your sacrifices and efforts will be rewarded in the future
2 GUILT You are responsible for the good and bad things that are the consequences of your acts
3 LOVE THY NEIGHBOR You should be concerned about the welfare of others
4 TRUTH You should always tell the bare facts

In the first place, the Dutch, just as other people who live in Christian cultures, are strongly oriented towards the future. Progress and innovation are important issues. Secondly, they are always worrying whether they did things right or wrong. The degree of personal responsibility is high. Thirdly, the Dutch feel greatly involved with people who have troubles, or who are suffering – whether close to home or on the other side of the world. This is evident from the country's extensive social security system and its high budget for developmental aid. Fourthly, the Dutch put a lot of stock in the objective truth and the bare facts. They find it more important to tell someone else exactly what they think than to be polite.

The next five values follow from Protestantism:

5 WORK It is good to work
6 ORDER & TIDINESS You should be well-organized
7 UTILITY Everything you do, must have a purpose, you may not waste
8 RELIABILITY You must do what you promised
9 MODERATION You must exercise self-control, and must not overdo

The Dutch think that it is better to work than to idly sit by. The higher they are on the corporate ladder, the harder they work. They appreciate an organized life that is dictated by the clock and their agenda, and think that a house should be neat and clean. The Netherlands is a relatively clean and well-organized country, in which a lot of big and little rules tell you how to behave. Also abroad, the Dutch are known for their tightness. One thing is certain; they hate waste; of money, time or anything else. Don't be surprised if they ask you what purpose your proposal serves. Couldn't it be done more efficiently, or perhaps effectively? The Dutch are very literal about their agreements and promises; if you agree to do something, then you must actually do it, or they will conclude that you are unreliable. In daily life, the Dutch hate extremes and exaggeration, they applaud self-restraint and frown upon expressing strong emotions. Only under certain conditions (a soccer match, carnival, at a disco), do they ever let it rip.

All this may sound pretty familiar to people from other Christian or Protestant countries. But the difficult part is still to come. The last three principles are typically Dutch and explain why certain things are done differently here or are found to be different than they are in the surrounding countries.

10 CONSENSUS You should always try to compromise

The Dutch dislike conflict and aggression, and consistently strive for consensus and harmony, which they refer to affectionately as *gezelligheid*. They devote quite a bit of time to meetings and discussions, in order to make sure that all disagreements have been resolved. Instead of letting the democratic majority rule the minority, they prefer to find a solution that appeals to everyone; a compromise. A compromise that everyone will then stick to, for fear of conflict. This is often referred to as the 'poldermodel'. Consequently, the Netherlands has a relatively peaceful, non-violent society, in which strikes end rather quickly in compromise and the police apply a de-escalating approach to handling skirmishes.

So what was going on, these last couple of years, when so many Dutch gave heed to the calls of radical politicians such as Fortuyn and Wilders and started agitating harshly against immigrants in general and Muslims in particular? Precisely because the political elite had spent years ignoring certain problems and societal discontent, for fear of uncomfortable discussions, the proverbial camel's back had to break some day. And when this happens, also the goody-goody Dutch can become hostile and unreasonable. Luckily, the atmosphere is changing again, measures have been taken to deal with the problems and most Dutch have resumed their normal, peaceful and consensus-oriented attitude.

11 EQUALITY You should not think that you are better than anyone else

In the Netherlands, all hierarchy and differences in social status are carefully smoothed over and disguised. It is painful to give direct instructions to someone who is under you, such as your cleaning lady. You can't just say: "Daisy, clean up the kitchen and the bathroom!" To the Dutch, this is a brusque order against which they rebel immediately. Instead, they formulate it as a polite question: "Would you perhaps be willing to do the kitchen and the bathroom today?" It sounds like a suggestion, but to the Dutch, this already feels like giving / receiving an order. The Dutch do not apply politeness towards superiors, but rather reverse politeness towards inferiors. You must, at all cost, avoid the impression that you think you might be superior to the other (even if you are a minister or have won the Nobel prize). It is perfectly easy to manage the Dutch, provided you treat them as equals and disguise every instruction as a friendly request.

The Dutch are allergic to people who toot their own horn; they expect modesty and if you fail to act like a 'normal' person, you will be mowed down. You are not only not allowed to be openly proud of your achievements, the same applies to being proud of your country and your history. To many Dutch people, nationalism is a cardinal sin. This is not to say that the Dutch are not proud of their country; they just cannot say so openly.

12 SELF-DETERMINATION I will decide what I do – not my father, boss or government

The Dutch find it more important that people be allowed to make their own choices, than to tell them what to do. Their motto is: everyone should decide for themselves what to do, as long as what they do doesn't interfere with my life. This is the basis for Dutch tolerance: it is not so much that they understand people who think differently, as that they are pragmatic; if you leave me alone, I will leave you alone. This explains why the Dutch tolerate the use of soft drugs, abortion and euthanasia. It does not so much mean that they 'do' it, but rather that they feel that whether or not someone else does, is their personal choice and none of anyone's business. This explains why so many different lifestyles can coexist in such a small country, from extravagant gay people who marry, to black-clad orthodox protestants who go to church three times every Sunday.

Children are not so much raised to respect their elders or general moral principles – but to think for themselves and speak for themselves. Dutch employees are expected to demonstrate a high degree of responsibility and initiative. Do take into account therefore that all Dutch people, be they young or old, have an opinion on everything and want to be heard. After which they will call a meeting, to reach a compromise!

- *Don't pretend to understand* If the other person has already explained something twice and you still don't understand, the temptation is great to nod enthusiastically as if you get it. You do not want to appear stupid or impolite. However, it is best to admit defeat; have them repeat it again. Who knows what you will learn?
- *Absorb all day* As you hear Dutch in your daily activities, pay attention to what others are saying and how they say it. If you don't know the words, look them up for future reference and try to use them yourself. Attempt to read local or national newspapers and to decipher Dutch television. It's a great way to practice.

WHICH DUTCH?

Not all Dutch people speak the same Dutch language. There is a standard language: *Algemeen Beschaafd Nederlands* (ABN), which translates into the somewhat pompous-sounding 'General Civilized Dutch'. Well-educated Dutch people who live in the Randstad (the area around Amsterdam, The Hague, Rotterdam, Utrecht and everything in between) speak this, as it is the old dialect of the District of Holland, which was once the most powerful province. *Hollands* thus became the most widespread dialect and the basis for the standard language that is spoken by the Royal Family, the members of Parliament, teachers and preachers, and on radio and television.

The other regions in the Netherlands speak the same language, but the pronunciation can be quite different and hard to understand at first: there is *Zeeuws* (spoken in Zeeland), *Twents* (spoken in Twente – in the east), *Gronings* (spoken in Groningen), *Drents* (spoken in Drenthe), *Brabants* (spoken in Noord-Brabant) and *Limburgs* (spoken in Limburg) – and even within these dialects, there can be considerable variation. And then the people from the various cities all have their very distinct way of pronouncing the language as well. The Dutch can tell within a sentence whether someone is from The Hague, Amsterdam, Limburg or Groningen.

In Friesland, a province in the northwest of Holland, there is a wholly different language called 'Fries', or Frisian, which is spoken in addition to Dutch. Though perhaps many of the words used are the same – but pronounced differently – they also have a whole unique vocabulary. An interesting factoid to note is that Frisian is considered, historically, to be closer to the English language than Dutch is. Unless you're a die-hard linguist, however, it would be highly unlikely for you to need or want to learn this unique language unless, of course, you intend to live in that region for a lengthy period of time. Even then, Dutch would suffice, as everything is signposted in both languages there.

YOUR AIM

In the end, how far you progress with Dutch will depend on the amount of time you put into it, your ambition and your talents. You might attain the highest level: speaking with ease, making virtually no mistakes, understanding complicated speeches and articles and writing a nearly faultless proposal. Or maybe you will never get any further than a sort of tourist Dutch enabling you to at least carry on a semblance of a conversation. In a country where English is second nature, it will require some determination on your part to plunge hook, line and sinker into learning Dutch. Chances are you won't regret it.

The Royal Family

THE MEMBERS

The Dutch Royal Family and the 'Royal House' are not the same. Not every member of the Orange Nassau family is a member of the Royal House. The Royal Family is made up of the former Queen and her sisters, their spouses and their children, King Willem-Alexander, his brothers, their spouses and their children and grandchildren. Who becomes a member of the Royal House – and therefore could theoretically become the monarch – has been determined by law and consists of the Head of State King Willem-Alexander, his wife Queen Máxima, their children and their spouses and grandchildren, his mother (formerly Queen Beatrix), as well as his brother Prince Constantijn and his wife Princess Laurentien, and his aunt Princess Margriet and her husband Pieter van Vollenhoven.

Members of the Royal House who marry without the official approval of the Parliament, lose the right to succeed to the Throne – an issue that came to bear when Crown Prince Willem-Alexander announced his engagement in 2001 and again when and his late brother Johan Friso announced his engagement in 2003. Johan Friso as well as two of Queen Beatrix's sisters lost the right to the throne by marrying without this permission. Now that the oldest daughter, Princess Amalia, has reached the age of 18 and is therefore an adult, she will automatically take the throne should something happen to her father. Her great-grandmother Wilhelmina had become queen in 1898 at the age of 18. She had been 10 years old when her father King Willem III had died in 1890 and her mother, Queen Emma, in the meantime had become Regent – a task that she fulfilled both with fervor and discretion. Incidentally, should something happen to King Willem-Alexander in the short term, Amalia will postpone her inauguration. Instead, she would prefer that her mother take on the task of Head of State for a couple of years, as she herself feels that she is still too young and inexperienced to become queen. This can be read in a book written by the Dutch cabaret artist Claudia de Brey – based on a number of interviews she had with the Crown Princess. In another book on the topic of succession to the throne, written by political analyst Peter Rehwinkel, it was posed that the legislation surrounding the succession to the throne would not allow Amalia to enter into a same-sex marriage. The thought was that this would not yield a legitimate successor, as the couple would have to look for a donor outside the family. After all, this is what had been stated in the law permitting same-sex marriages, which the Netherlands had been the first in the world to pass. The government immediately announced that there was no reason whatsoever why a same-sex marriage would hinder the path to succession. "It only means we'll have two queens," Prime Minister Mark Rutte remarked. The outcome will be unusual. The title of the spouses of Queens Wilhelmina, Juliana and Beatrix had been 'prince consort'. Should Amalia marry someone of the same sex, this would make her spouse 'princess consort'. On the other hand: the spouse of the Dutch king is generally referred to as a queen, even though this is only an informal title. It sounds kind of nice: a country with two queens.

In 2022, Crown Princess Amalia was faced with a personal disappointment that at the same time had serious political connotations and that shed a negative light on security in the Netherlands. She had been looking forward to moving into a student home with a couple of friends in Amsterdam, where she would be following the Politics, Psychology, Law and Economics program. With this decision, she broke with the family tradition of studying at the University of Leiden, which had been gifted to the city in 1575 by William of Orange, the nation's father.

When it became known that Crown Princess Amalia was being threatened to such a degree that it would prove irresponsible for her to move to the center of Amsterdam, she was forced to go and live with her parents at the Huis den Bosch palace. From there, she travels, under heavy security, to the university in order to follow classes and participate in work groups. The nature and background of the threat have not been shared, but it is generally assumed that it has to do with drug cartels. They are trying to use this to scare off the government from starting too drastic a campaign against the trade and use of drugs. It is a bad sign that these cartels are powerful enough to limit a princess in her freedom of movement. Cynics are already referring to the Netherlands as a narco state, because of the huge production of synthetic drugs here and the fact that the harbor of Rotterdam is essential to the importation of cocaine into Europe.

POLITICAL POSITION

The King, together with the ministers, form the government. It was determined in 1848 that the ministers, and not the King, are responsible for acts of government. Laws that have been passed by the Parliament, and Royal Decrees, are signed by both the King (Queen) and the minister in question, lending them the authority of the Head of State and placing the responsibility for them with the minister.

Until 2012, after elections, the then-Queen, upon the recommendation of the Vice President of the Council of State, the Presidents of both Houses of the States-General, the presidents of the Parliamentary groups of the political parties and sometimes the Minister(s) of the State, appointed the so-called (in)formers (*formateurs* or *informateurs*) who were to form a new cabinet, based on the outcome of the election. In 2012, the Dutch Parliament decided that it was perfectly capable of appointing its own (in)formers. Consequently, the King no longer plays a role in the formation of the cabinet other than its swearing in – which is merely a ceremony.

Every year, on the third Tuesday of September, called *Prinsjesdag*, the King and members of his family ride in an historic carriage from the palace on the Noordeinde to the Binnenhof, where the government is housed. Here the King holds his famous speech, called the *Troonrede*, before the members of the First and Second Chamber, in which the government's policies for the coming year are set out. For two years in a row, the Covid pandemic made this tradition impossible. The King arrived, with his wife and children, in a limousine at The Hague's Jacob (or St. James) Church; a huge, Medieval construction. There, the parliamentary members could sit at a safe distance from each other. In connection with public health, the people were discouraged to come watch the royal cavalcade. This lent an element of somberness to the opening of the parliament.

Prinsjesdag is a popular outing for schools, but also for grown-ups and tourists, who come to The Hague to admire the beauty of the royal procession and taste a bit of the atmosphere of yesteryear. For several years now, the Royal couple has not used the traditional Golden coach. At first, this was because it was being subjected to a five-year restoration effort. The coach had been a gift from the people of Amsterdam to Queen Wilhelmina when she was crowned in 1898 and reflected the spirit of those days, with one side depicting how the colonies gratefully offered their riches to the

mother country in return for, among others, knowledge. Especially social justice warriors objected to this type of racist expression and wanted to see the coach relegated to a museum. Some even went so far as to claim that this is why its restoration took so long; at least, this way, the controversial illustration on its flank was kept out of sight. Also Queen Wilhelmina had not been a great fan of the coach, finding it too ostentatious for her taste. However, her royal household pointed out that she could not simply stuff it away in a dark corner, so that she found herself with no other option than to use it. In the meantime, the restoration has been completed. For now, the golden coach has been carefully put away in the Historical Museum of Amsterdam, accompanied by a whole bunch of historical (con)text. The general expectation is that is the King will happily leave the golden coach where it is. As is cleverly noted by its opponents, however; this way the disputed illustrations are seen by many more people than they would be on the two short annual outings through The Hague. The royal couple has started to use the glass coach from 1835, which according to friend and foe is much more refined than that gaudy contraption with which the city of Amsterdam had tried to please its queen.

In the early '50s of the previous century, Queen Juliana started a new tradition of Christmas speeches that were broadcast on the radio and television. In these speeches, she emphasized the unity of the country and the fact that the Dutch should look out for each other. She also commemorated national tragedies of the year in question, if there had been any, while she clearly expressed her religious devotion, without specifying her denomination. King Willem-Alexander has chosen to continue this tradition with passion and enthusiasm. In his speeches, he always tries to emphasize the unity and cohesion of the Dutch people – no exceptions made.

TRAGEDIES

These past years, the Royal Family has been hit by two tragedies. In 2009, there was an attempt on the lives of the members of the Royal Family on Queen's Day. Every year, on April 27, the members of the Family visit a municipality and participate in the festivities. In 2009, when it was still Queen's Day (and still on April 30), they visited Apeldoorn. After the festivities, they boarded a bus (in stereotypical Dutch fashion; let's not get too fancy) and were heading towards the Palace 't Loo when a Suzuki Swift drove into the crowds in an attempt to hit the bus. It crashed into a monument and the driver died later that day. Before lapsing into a coma, however, he told a police officer on the scene that he had wanted to hit the Royal Family. Seven onlookers had been killed. The Royal Family expressed their sympathy and the Queen gave an impassioned speech on the tragedy the next day.

The second tragedy took place in February of 2012, when, during their annual ski vacation in Lech, Austria – a place the Family has been visiting for decades and where they are considered honorary citizens – Prince Friso, the Queen's second son, was hit by an avalanche. Though he survived the incident, he remained in a coma until he passed away on August 12, 2013. The ceremony of his funeral was impressive, but in consultation with, and out of respect for, the Royal Family, the Dutch broadcasting companies only televised a few moments of it.

THE KING AND QUEEN

In 2010, Queen Beatrix celebrated her 30th anniversary as Queen of the Netherlands and speculation abounded as to whether or not she planned to abdicate. Finally, in 2013, on January 28, the Queen announced her plans to abdicate on April 30 of that year – the day on which she normally would have celebrated her birthday. The Dutch public expressed its appreciation of the pride and sense of duty of the Queen and agreed that she deserved some peace and quiet. She has been succeeded by King Willem-Alexander to universal acclaim. Willem-Alexander has had plenty of opportunity to practice for his royal position through his activities which focused on two main issues: sports, and water and its role in the Netherlands and the world. He was sorry to have to abdicate from the Olympic Committee as this cannot be combined with the position of Head of State. The same goes for his position of stimulator and Chairman of the Dutch water sector.

Almost from the beginning, the King's Argentinean wife Máxima has been involved in all sorts of activities aimed at integrating non-native Dutch women into Dutch society and – on a worldwide level – in initiatives providing micro-credit as an instrument of developmental aid. In 2009, the royal couple made a well-documented trip to the South Pole, where they – from the depths of a glacier – expressed their concern about the climate crisis. As Queen, she can continue these activities as she, contrary to husband, does not fulfill an official position – as determined by the Constitution of the Netherlands.

Just before he was crowned, Willem-Alexander announced that he planned to the position of monarch on his own, and not share the job with the new Queen – in keeping with the constitution. he also said that his demeanor would likely be less formal and majestic than that of his mother. Queen Beatrix had always been a somewhat stand-offish monarch, who adhered strictly to protocol. Only when she visited the victims of disasters to offer consolation and sympathy on behalf of the Dutch population, did this stand-offishness disappear. Willem-Alexander is far more jovial and Queen Máxima also contributes a certain Latin American savoir vivre to their public appearances. This already became clear during the inauguration. As the new Royal Family sailed down the IJ in Amsterdam, the new King moored his boat to visit the podium where world-famous DJ Armin van Buuren was playing. Queen/Princess Beatrix would have been more likely to visit the Nederland Dans Theater ballet, or a concert of classical music. After the inauguration, the royal couple visited various parts of the country, once again showing their more informal demeanor. The King also considers himself an ambassador of the Dutch economy and, like his grandfather Prince Bernhard, wishes to support the Dutch commerce by means of marketing activities – provided of course, that this does not damage his constitutional position as Head of State. During state visits, the King makes clear that he is committed to these issues – to the general appreciation of society and the business community. Towards the end of 2021, it was officially announced that His Majesty would be focusing on the introduction of hydrogen as an energy supply.

Meanwhile, Queen Máxima is also taking on a number of international issues in her own name. In most cases, these are not in name of the Netherlands, but of the United Nations. For instance, she is helping make credit facilities available to the poorest people in Indonesia. When doing this, she always stresses the importance of verified facts and numbers. This probably has to do with her past, working for the Deutsche Bank in New York. Máxima is also a member of the Dutch Committee for Entrepreneurialism, as well as honorary member of a number of boards – as befits a member of a royal dynasty.

At the start of 2016, Willem-Alexander had been king for 1,000 days – cause for reflection on his performance. The people's opinion was unanimously positive. In the eyes of the royalty watchers, the King is a nice guy, who – contrary to his somewhat formal and stiff mother, is quick to put his subjects at ease with a quip. On the other hand, he is definitely capable of displaying royal dignity when so required; during state visits and ceremonies. He visibly enjoys decorating brave soldiers who have put the lives of their comrades above their own in the line of duty. It is clear that speaking in public is something that the King does not necessarily enjoy, nonetheless his efforts are always rewarded.

Máxima still shines, albeit slightly more in the background now that her husband is wearing the crown. And of course, the King moves within the limits set by the Dutch constitution. The princesses are adorable – as they should be. It is already clear that Princess Amalia is aware of the responsibilities to which she will be called in the future. She reminds the Dutch of her grandmother, from whom she appears to be learning on a daily basis. Incidentally, nothing appears to indicate that she is dreading ascending to the throne. As noted earlier, she feels that she is as yet too young and inexperienced for the task. Also this is proof of how seriously she takes things.

The question arises: did the King learn a profession? In order to prepare for his position of monarch, he obtained a masters' degree in history at the university of Leiden – which was founded in 1574 by the nation's founding father William of Orange. His true passion, however, is airplanes. The King is an excellent pilot, who used to pilot KLM passenger planes under the pseudonym Willem van Buren (he is the Count of Buren). In 2016, a discussion arose regarding the replacement of the slowly aging Dutch government plane. Sharp observers noted that this would be a Boeing, as this is the plane in which the King has learned to fly. Apparently when making state visits, the King wants to sit in the cockpit himself. The Dutch think this is pretty cool.

Not so cool, in the eyes of the Dutch, is the King's income. Of course, if asked, the average Dutchman will tell you: "A president also costs money", yet nonetheless, a growing number of citizens feel that he is earning much too much. The King lives, rent-free, in various palaces, of which the upkeep is paid for by the taxpayers. Furthermore, he receives a constitutional salary € 1,086,000 (plus € 5,709,000 for expenses), while his wife earns € 431,000 (plus € 700,000 for expenses) per year. His mother, Princess Beatrix, has to 'make do' with € 600,000 (plus 1,200,000 for expenses), and Princess Amalia receives € 300,000 (and € 1,500,000). A great deal of their expenses are fixed – for instance, for gas, electricity, coaches, horses and cars. The other two princesses also receive approximately € 600,000 and € 400,000 to spend as they please. Aside from what their family capital generates, of course. In September 2020, Crown Princess Amalia announced that she felt uncomfortable about this payment and that she would rather not receive it that year – but this proved impossible to turn down as it was a constitutionally based payment. Nonetheless, her sentiment and effort were generally appreciated by the public. Since then, it has been agreed that her payment will be deposited in the country's coffers, until such time as they are really necessary to cover expenses related to being the first in line for the throne. As for her personal life: Crown Princess Amalia likes to go away over the weekend and the gossip mill has talked about boyfriends, but generally speaking the international gossip media is unable to get a peek into her private life.

Younger sister Alexia comes across as a bit more frivolous. Her parents have sent her to an elite boarding school in Wales; the United World College of the Atlantic. There she became immediate friends with the Spanish Princess Leonor. Thanks to the fact that her mother is Argentinian, Alexa speaks perfect Spanish. It is not always easy for both royal families to discipline their lively daughters. Little can be said, as yet, about Ariane, Willem-Alexander and Máxima's youngest daughter.

Prince Constantijn, The King's younger brother, is also someone who comes across as rather serious. He allows himself to be interviewed by young entrepreneurs and innovative startups that he likes to support. His 20-year-old daughter Eloise is more clearly present on social media; her vlogs are becoming increasingly popular. They present us the life of a well-brought-up, well-to-do girl with a lust for life.

At the moment, the family has only one black sheep. This would be Bernhard jr, son of Princess Margriet – Willem-Alexander's aunt. He is a flamboyant and adventurous businessman who is making a place for himself in Amsterdam real estate investment. He has a tendency to, as the Dutch say, 'approach he limits of the law', which has given him something of a reputation as a slumlord. Whether or not this is actually true, is not clear. Bernhard jr also invests in the Zandvoort Racing Circuit.

KING'S DAY, APRIL 27

By now, the Dutch are pretty much used to the new word; *Koningsdag*. It means King's Day and refers to His Majesty's birthday. Until King Willem-Alexander became King, it was called *Koninginnedag* – Queen's Day – a name it had had since 1890, when the nation's last king – Willem III – passed away. Since that day, there had only been women on the throne.

On Queen's Day, or Kings' Day, the Dutch show their affection for the throne. Almost every municipality has an 'Orange Association' of diehard monarchists who work together with the municipality to arrange a number of festivities that involve a lot of folklore and children's games. Wherever you go, you hear the thump of marching bands and other music. In Amsterdam, people come together to sell their secondhand items on the so-called Free Market (*Vrijmarkt*). This custom has spread across the nation the past 30 years to almost all municipalities, meaning that you will likely run into your neighbors' kids selling their old toys on that day, which they have spread out on an old rug on the street. They will be flanked by grown-ups who are selling old percolators and other household items for a song. Don't hesitate to encourage your children to join in and develop their marketing qualities. Or to display their musical talents for a pittance. Or to 'take to the streets' with your own obsolete household items. The Dutch will be sure to appreciate and applaud your initiative, taking into account the fact that you are an expatriate. *Koningsdag* is the nation's largest public party, even more widespread than carnival.

On her birthday, Queen Juliana used to stand on the steps of her palace and 'Orange Associations' from across the nation would parade by. Queen Beatrix would take a helicopter or royal bus (typical Dutch: a bus, rather than a cavalcade of limousines) to visit two municipalities. There, the local population would arrange traditional games and art forms, and the Royal Family would join in on the fun. Once, King Willem-Alexander, who was still Crown Prince at the time, found himself obligated to join in on a game of toilet bowl throwing.

After his inauguration, the King introduced a number of changes. He only visits one single municipality, and the idea is that this municipality presents things of which it is proud. As the visit is televised live, this is an opportunity for the municipality to intensively market itself. And this is precisely in line with how the new business-like King wishes to fulfill his position – for this is how he himself refers to it. In 2018, the King decided to celebrate his birthday in Groningen, which had been hit by earthquakes that had been caused by decades of extracting natural gas, in order to put the city in the spotlight.

Despite the fact that the King's birthday remains the largest 'street party' in the Netherlands, it can be said that support for monarchy is nonetheless waning. This can be attributed, among others, to a number of mistakes that the Royal Family has made. For instance, during the first lockdown in the year of 2020, the family announced that it would be traveling to their vacation home in Greece by plane. This public relations disaster was avoided in the nick of time, but Willem-Alexander and Máxima nonetheless made a televised appearance in order to apologize. The fact that the king had expressed that he would like to get a speed boat for his birthday, was another thing that did not go down well. Generally speaking, people have become more critical of this family's lifestyle of luxury, as well as of its members' high salaries and fiscal privileges.

Prinsjesdag 2022 brought something new. During their ride to the parliament and as he appeared on the balcony of the palace, Willem-Alexander was booed by a number of people in the public. From across the country, opponents to the Covid policy as well as antivaxxers had come to The Hague to make themselves heard. This did not happen again in 2023, but a poll showed that only 51% of the Dutch population supports the Royal Family. Confidence in King William-Alexander has gone down even more and only 38% of those polled have 'great confidence' in him and 21% has little to no confidence. The rest is in the middle.

These numbers are cause for concern for the monarchy. Without a doubt, the highly intelligent Crown Princess Amalia will be aware of this matter – though she is enthusiastic to become queen – as is her mentor, Grandmother Beatrix.

Asylum Policy and Migration

All the Rutte cabinets have been quite conservative when it comes to allowing migrants and asylum-seekers into the country, while citizens of other EU countries are free to settle in the Netherlands. Particularly citizens from Eastern European countries have made grateful use of this opportunity. Without their efforts, the horticulture, agriculture and (minor) construction sectors would not have been able to function over recent years. In 2020, when the most recent research was done on this topic, the Netherlands was home to 768,000 employees with a foreign passport, half of whom came from another EU country.

People from outside the EU only qualify for a residence permit if they are able to fill a position that cannot be filled by Dutch person or someone from another EU member state. Partners from non-EEA countries are only allowed to immigrate into the country if they have taken an assimilation course at the Dutch embassy abroad, and if the resident non-Dutch national can provide for both of them. In 2023 (through October), 256,900 immigrants from within and outside the EU settled in the Netherlands, while 145,300 residents left the country for good in search of greener pastures. Deducting emigration from immigration leaves a positive balance of approximately 110,700 a year. In especially conservative circles this is seen as a problem; at an immigration rate of what comes down to a provincial city every year, the country will become overpopulated in no time. Since the arrival of rightist populism, also the middle spectrum parties are voicing this sentiment in varying degrees. All Rutte cabinets have tried to hinder the arrival of newcomers, in keeping with a tradition that came about in the '90s of the previous century, as well as of refugees. Leftist parties, in particular, GroenLinks, ascribe to a more generous refugee policy.

Those who seek asylum in the Netherlands, are sent to IND reception centers. There they are subjected to a lengthy investigation into the background of their request for asylum and must submit sufficient proof of the fact that they risk persecution in their home country. The authorities that ask these questions are very strict and not quickly satisfied. They feel that experience has shown that it is wise to thoroughly check the truth behind the refugees' stories. If the request for asylum is denied, there is the option of bringing an appeal before the court, whereby the asylum-seeker can request the assistance of a specialized lawyer. In practice, this procedure can be time-consuming, as both refugees who have been denied asylum and the government always make use of this opportunity. It is commonly thought that a large majority of asylum-seekers are economic immigrants who are not professionally qualified and are only in search of a better life or social benefits. Prime Minister Rutte has invented the term "happiness seekers" for them.

The wave of refugees that arrived from Syria in 2015 caused a considerable increase in the number of asylum-seekers that came to the Netherlands. This created the need for the IND to increase the number of reception centers, which elicited sometimes aggressive reactions from the locals. However, the upheaval died down quickly and when the media visited the villages a year later, the general sentiment was that the 'feared' asylum-seekers were very friendly people. Nonetheless, the government felt it had learned a lesson and decided to close its borders as much as possible to newcomers. When migrants started to cross the Mediterranean by the hundreds in wobbly barges and rubber boats, the Netherlands felt less than inclined to help the southern EU states – in particular Italy and Greece – deal with them. The EU plan to pay Turkish president Erdogan for stopping the stream of refugees from Syria was partially inspired by Dutch politicians. Then-PvdA leader Diederik Samsom came up with the idea that, for every refugee who ended up in Greece and that it took in, Turkey could send a Syrian to the EU.

Halfway 2021, the number of asylum seekers rose so fast that the reception centers could not handle the influx. This was exacerbated by the fact that there are not enough homes in the Netherlands. Consequently, a lot of recognized refugees were forced to remain in the reception centers.

A special issue is the influx of refugees that was triggered by the quick victory of the Taliban in Afghanistan. In the past, Dutch occupying forces in Afghanistan had hired a lot of local staff; translators,

cooks, guards, etc. By the Taliban, these people were seen as traitors and were in acute danger. It was therefore logical that the Netherlands would offer these local allies a safe haven should the situation in Afghanistan become too threatening. This group, if you include their families, encompassed several thousands of people. The State Secretary for Alien Affairs took too long in deciding what to do, afraid as she was of criticism from the extreme right as well as her own VVD constituency. Subsequently, it became clear that the government was only willing to allow a few of these Afghan staff members to enter the country. This only changed when a parliamentary majority expressed their disapproval. The pro-western Afghan government had collapsed and the scenes at the airport, where thousands of Afghans were trying to flee to safety along with their western counterparts, were extremely chaotic. It became clear that communications between the Ministry of Foreign Affairs and the former Afghan staff members were insufficient and terse. The staff of the Dutch embassy in Kabul showed their true colors by fleeing to the airport in the middle of the night in order to continue working from there without even warning the local Afghan staff members. The Netherlands was only moderately successful in bringing their allies to safety, using, among others, two military airplanes, one of which broke down. In the end, at least 2,000 former staff members were left behind. The minister of foreign affairs, leader of the D66 political party, was forced to resign within weeks after accepting this position. She was forced to do this thanks to a widely supported motion of censure submitted in the Second Chamber.

It proved complicated to find a temporary place to stay for the Afghans who had been saved. They were placed in, among others, tent camps. The extreme right was bitterly opposed to the arrival of these Afghans and riots broke out close to one of the reception centers near the town of Harskamp in the Veluwe. However, the majority of the Dutch population is of the belief that leaving them behind would have constituted gross betrayal.

The summer of 2022 saw a new crisis. The number of asylum seekers – this time, from Ukraine – grew so quickly that the reception center in Ter Apel once again could not handle the influx. At first, the newcomers had to sleep on chairs in the waiting room – later there wasn't even space enough there, forcing them to sleep outside, in the open air. The COA, the Central Organization for the Reception of Asylum Seekers, was at a loss, partially due to a shortage of personnel. People brought in tents, but these were appropriated by the municipality as they were considered a fire hazard that furthermore made crowd control impossible.

Eric van der Berg (VVD), State Secretary for Asylum Affairs, did what he could to convince the municipalities in the Netherlands to take in more asylum seekers and receivers. This proved a tough nut to crack. All municipalities were dealing with a serious shortage of houses and particularly social housing (for people with low income) – largely due to measures taken by the Rutte cabinets, as a consequence of which it was no longer in government hands. Local people, looking to buy a home, did not take kindly to the fact that asylum seekers might rise to the top of the waiting list that they had spent years climbing. In those municipalities that did accept a new asylum seekers' center, the local population protested vehemently, fearing that it would no longer be safe for their daughters to go out unaccompanied. Finally, Van der Berg took drastic measures: a law was drafted that would force municipalities to accept asylum seekers and receivers. He was severely criticized by his own party and Prime Minister Rutte was forced to bring his own VVD party to order on this matter.

Around that same time, it became clear that the Dutch population would be approaching 18 million within no time. The 20 millionth Dutch resident is expected to enter the scene around 2040. This has fed into the notion "the Netherlands is full" and has triggered a desire to conduct a national debate on population policies, as the general opinion is that this increase in inhabitants can mostly be attributed to immigration. This was an issue that clearly on the agenda for the 2023 elections for the Second Chamber and appears to have had an important impact on the outcome, with Geert Wilders' PVV anti-immigration stance bringing in the majority of the votes. Meanwhile, there is the situation of the war in Israel. The IND (Immigration and Naturalization Services) has decided to pause any evaluation of asylum requests from Palestinians; this means they will be neither accepted nor rejected for the time being, which also means that they will not be able to bring in family members under the banner of family reunification.

The Definitive End of the Golden Century?

When the Dutch talk about the Golden Century, they generally mean the 17th century, the time of great painters such as Rembrandt and Vermeer, and of great victories at sea and spectacular expeditions. Recently however, as touched upon elsewhere in this chapter, some people have become critical of this label: after all, it was also a time of transatlantic slavery and colonialism, whereby the greatest amount of wealth ended up with the elites in the Western part of the country. Take for instance the luxurious homes along the canals of Amsterdam. No, the real Golden Century started with the reconstruction of the Netherlands after the Second World War. This was a period of general wealth, democratization and personal freedom. After a dip in the '70s and '80s, Internet and globalization brought new wealth. With the fall of communism, it seemed as if a period of peace and European unity had arrived, from which a nation of trade such as the Netherlands was sure to benefit.

The credit crisis in 2008 was a sobering moment – however, the world seemed to have recovered from the consequences approximately eight years down the road. The Netherlands was preparing for a new version of the roaring '20s.

Then Covid arrived. For the first time in a century, a huge epidemic upset something that hitherto had seemed impossible to disrupt; life in general. Along with the rest of the world, the Netherlands had no other recourse than to introduce medieval methods of isolation, quarantine, and a freezing of public life in order to limit the spread of the disease. It took a year for the first working vaccines to come onto the market and their usefulness furthermore proved to be limited, creating the need for boosters time and again.

Without the additional measures that the government introduced, the lockdowns would have led to a total collapse of the economy. The government avoided this by postponing taxation and by subsidizing companies and self-employed people on a large scale, allowing them to survive and to continue to pay their employees who were now often working from home. Still, a lot of entrepreneurs lost their (pension) reserves. They also accrued huge obligations towards the owners of the buildings who had temporarily lowered rental prices or frozen them. After the epidemic, companies and entrepreneurs were expected to use their newly generated income to pay off these debts. For instance, companies were given five years to pay their deferred taxes.

When last lockdown ended, consumers, who had had little opportunity to spend their money over the past two years, became spendthrifts and money rolled as never before. All did not go smoothly, however; Covid had deregulated worldwide distribution channels and many products were not available or only insufficiently so. Also another problem arose; a huge shortage of personnel. This had been predicted long ago; due to the aging of the Dutch population, more people were retiring than entering the labor market. It was inevitable that at some point this would lead to a structural shortage of people – or 'hands', as the Dutch like to say. This point arrived sooner than had been anticipated. Hospitals had been dealing with a shortage of personnel for quite some time, but now it was happening across the board and people who wanted to have construction done, found themselves on a waiting list. Etcetera.

What happens when there is a lot of money but not enough goods? Prices go up. Furthermore, in response to the credit crisis, the European Central Bank had brought an unprecedented amount of money into circulation. Initially, this primarily had consequences for the capital market, but in the second half of 2022, it impacted the entire economy. Consequently, a continent that for decades had lived on the edge of deflation was suddenly confronted with a devaluation of money of 10% and more. The Netherlands led the European countries in September 2022, with an inflation of more than 17%.

Just like the Fed had done before, the European Central Bank tried to turn the tide with the help of a hike in interest rates, but had to do this with care in order to not force the southern European debt countries into the same type of bankruptcy that it had managed to avoid in 2012, thanks to a spectacular lowering of interest rates – even to the point of introducing negative interest rates. The Dutch banks did not pass on the new interest rates to the savers. However, they did raise the mortgage interest rates, resulting in a cooling of the tight housing market. This was not necessarily to the advantage of buyers, as it would primarily lead to an increase in their living expenses.

In the summer of 2022, it became clear that the people in the Netherlands were dealing with a considerable loss of purchasing power and financial reserves. "We are all getting a little bit poorer," Minister of Finance Sigrid Kaag said consolingly. But who would call 15% 'a little bit'? Those at the lower end of the income spectrum as well as of the middle class generally found themselves unable to survive due to the increase in prices. The number of people visiting food banks doubled to 400,000. The percentage of officially poor people – approximately 10% – started to rise.

The unions began to stir and demanded an increase in wages that would have to compensate more or less for inflation, and, for the first time in years, the number of union members started to increase – and there were strikes at the Dutch railway company. The government then decided to approve a considerable increase in minimum wage. A number of economists warned that this type of wage / price spiral would exacerbate inflation, especially now that, thanks to energy subsidies, so much money was being pumped into society. The Dutch people just shrugged.

Yet, there was an undeniable reduction in general welfare. At the same time, younger people, due to a shortage of homes, could still barely find a place of their own. Waiting times, caused by a lack of personnel, led to frustrating waiting lists, while, in the fall of 2022, the government started to collect deferred taxes. At the same time, entrepreneurs were presented with extremely high energy bills as, once their existing energy contracts came to an end, they were confronted with market prices. Consumer confidence reached new depths. In particular, shops selling durable goods found that their customers were keeping a tight grip on their wallets.

The trend continued in 2023 with a continuously shrinking economy, decreasing house purchases and investments and increasing interest rates and inflation, as a consequence of which the Netherlands is not doing as well as its neighboring countries. Nonetheless, though three successive quarters of a shrinking economy indicate a recession, there is some good news as well: the continued low

unemployment rate and a predicted continued demand for employees are dampening the negative circumstances of the economy.

And it was under these circumstances that the Netherlands was also supposed to continue to make its supplies to Ukraine, which it incidentally happily continued to do and still does.

In the meantime, the importance of Europe – as a concept – and of European collaboration is growing, thanks to Russia's attack on Ukraine, which has generated a united response in the West. The NATO and the European Union are supporting the Ukraine in many ways – other than sending their own soldiers. The Netherlands is waging an economic war against Russia, which is partially responsible for the current inflation and, after a long period of reduced defense spending, the Netherlands – as have its allies – has made the switch to renewed weaponization. Admiral Rob Bauer, currently the highest military within the NATO, suggested in a TV interview that a transition is being made to a war economy, in which the production for the military forces is given priority over production for civilians.

This all is taking place in a world that seems to be saying goodbye to globalization. We see that China is working on becoming a heavily armed power bloc and is isolating itself economically. In the United States, a similar movement is taking place. This means that the European Union will be forced to form a third economic bloc that will compete against the other two. This might be the case, but it will certainly focus more on welfare than on the worldwide free trade of the past few decades.

All the pundits are warning of a heavy recession. Is this a precursor to the Iron Age that will follow the Golden Age of welfare after the Second World War? Will that which so many Dutch parents fear, come true; namely that their children will not be better off but worse off than they had been themselves? Chances of this are quite real.

Prostitution, Drugs and Euthanasia

High on the to-do list of every visitor to the Netherlands, right up there with the famed museums, is a walk on the wild side of seemingly sedate Dutch society: a tour of the red-light district in Amsterdam. The *wallen* ('the walls'), as that part of town is known, lives up to its billing. Everything you expect is there. Teeming crowds juxtaposing businessmen and tourists; prostitutes publicly ensconced in the windows of the numerous business establishments; the quote-unquote coffee shops that sell everything from Thai stick to space cakes – coffee definitely not being the specialty of the house.

POINT OF VIEW

After soaking in the sights for a few minutes, you may notice an unexpected aspect of human nature: the only thing that makes the goings-on into a spectacle is your point of view. Having spent some time in the Netherlands, you probably aren't surprised that everything is well-organized (the Dutch police even have an English-language how-to guide to help tourists safely explore the steamier side of the city); but you probably did not expect it to be 'dead normal', as the Dutch say. The only difference between the streets of the red-light district and other shopping districts in the city is the merchandise. While there are prostitutes and drugs in every large city, Dutch or otherwise, in the Netherlands both businesses are given an air of legitimacy that exceeds that found in most other countries. Like so many other visitors, you marvel at the tolerant Dutch in action.

CLICHÉS

Noting that the Dutch are tolerant, however, is not exactly a radical discovery. Social experiments in the Netherlands are sufficiently renowned that such comments are almost clichés. But there is more to this than just being open-minded. Most visitors are shocked when they learn that until recently prostitution was illegal and that the possession or sale of recreational drugs remains against the law. After one day in Amsterdam, it is hard to believe that any of this ever was a criminal offense – which, in a sense, is correct: even when illegal, these activities occurred and thrived with the tacit approval of the local community and the Dutch government.

TURNING A BLIND EYE

How does one reconcile the contradiction? Activities were or are illegal yet officially tolerated at the same time. The superficial answer, in a tradition that is centuries old, is that the laws in the Netherlands are intentionally enforced in a selective manner via a practice called *gedogen*, which means something like turning a blind eye. When it comes to social policy, the underlying motive is the Dutch are not just tolerant; they are incredible pragmatists.

TOLERANCE VS. ACCEPTANCE

Don't confuse Dutch realism with loose mores. As individuals, most are principled; a fair number are very religious. When asked, the overwhelming majority indicates that they don't use drugs or prostitutes, and the statistics bear this out. Remarkably, the Dutch make a distinction between their values and what they expect from others. While there is general agreement that recreational drugs and prostitution are social evils, there is also a strong consensus that they are going to occur whether they are illegal or not and that prosecution often results in social ails worse than the original malady. Thus, it is better to mitigate the negative aspects of these activities with regulation (what could be more Dutch than that?) than to drive them underground through futile attempts at eradication. That these vices were or are still technically illegal is mostly a reflection of the consensus-building that is implicit to Dutch public policy: it is one thing to passively accept certain activities as inevitable; it is another to actively endorse them. In short, there is a big difference between tolerance and acceptance.

A WORK IN PROGRESS

Sounds great. But how well do these Dutch approaches work? The answer depends on your priorities. In the case of prostitution, the public-health accomplishments are impressive. Thanks to access to medical care and routine testing, the physical well-being of most prostitutes and their clients is significantly better in the Netherlands than in many other countries. Unfortunately, rules only protect those who are a part of the system, and even then, only those who are able to understand and use them. In particular, many of the prostitutes are thought to be illegal immigrants, including an unknown number who were coerced into the trade and work in de facto slavery. Due to fear of reprisals or deportation, it is less likely that foreign prostitutes will contact the authorities for help if they need it. Recent attempts to expand government control by legalizing brothels may have made things worse: the added expense has driven some activity underground. While such problems are not unique to the Netherlands, the abuse of these individuals, in spite of the existing rules and regulations, is, to say the least, extremely troubling to the Dutch.

DRUG TOURISM

There are also some notable achievements associated with the recreational drug policies. While the drug business undoubtedly accentuates the petty theft that is prevalent in the Netherlands (Hey! Where's my bicycle?!?), the fears of critics have not come to pass. The streets of the country are not clogged with addicts; and while most Dutch teenagers go through a period of exploration, where some experiment with drugs, most move on: teenage and adult drug usage rates are relatively low. The biggest problems with Dutch drug policy are associated with foreigners, including a thriving business in drug tourism. Many of these visitors are the source of much of the drug-related theft and the less frequent acts of violence. Other countries in the European Union that have stricter drug policies have pressured the Dutch to modify their approach. To date the Dutch have largely resisted these demands. However, they have introduced a new regulation regarding the purchase of soft drugs in the so-called 'coffee shops'; you have to prove that you are a legal resident and older than the age of 18, by means of proof of registration with the municipality you live in and an ID, while, officially, tourists are banned from purchasing soft drugs at a coffee shop. However, the mayor of Amsterdam has already publicly stated that visitors will not be refused. See also page 185.

EUTHANASIA

New ground-breaking social policies, often controversial and influential, continue in the Netherlands. A recent example is the legalization of euthanasia. Legislative experiments in this regard date back more than two decades. The old law offered the usual subtle compromises, where euthanasia was technically illegal but physicians were rarely prosecuted. Once again, the fears of critics were largely unfounded: euthanasia was reserved as a treatment option of last resort (most were terminally ill cancer patients) and studies confirmed that there was no systematic abuse of the system. However, the same studies showed that the majority of euthanasia cases went unreported, presumably out of fear of prosecution. The new law attempts to correct these and other deficiencies. While the requirements are similar, oversight is now after the fact and a doctor's actions are now presumed legal unless there is evidence that the guidelines have been severely violated. As with some other recent Dutch experiments, the efficacy of the new law remains to be seen.

TOO PRAGMATIC?

All of this leads some to conclude that the Dutch are too pragmatic. The foreign press invariably carries stories that make you shake your head in wonder, such as the one about the Dutch parents who ran the coffee shop in their town: if their children were going to experiment with controlled substances, they felt better knowing who was selling them the drugs! Nonetheless, in spite of the occasional excesses and the remaining problems, rational social policies as well systematic and open education on sex, drugs as well as alcohol have successfully encouraged responsible behavior. As a consequence, most Dutch teenagers choose abstinence or practice safe sex, as evidenced by the low rates of sexually transmitted diseases, teen pregnancies and abortions. (Even dictionaries for Dutch tourists propagate the party line. When it comes to sex, the content is restricted to such useful phrases as 'Only with a condom' and 'Let's not take any chances'.)

While it may not be politically or culturally feasible for other countries to adopt these policies or approaches, one cannot help but admire what the Dutch have accomplished.

Zwarte Piet – Controversial Children's Friend

While all across the world Christmas decorations are being unpacked, they remain in their boxes for another couple of weeks in the Netherlands. Here, the shop windows are inhabited by two unusual figures: a bishop with a long white beard and his pal, a soot-faced servant, dressed up like a 16th-century nobleman, wearing poofy pants and a cap with a feather. These men are Sinterklaas (or Sint Nicolaas) and Roet Piet, previously known as Zwarte Piet. Sint Nicolaas rides a white horse; his servant transports himself on foot. And together, they visit almost every house in the Netherlands on December 5 to drop off bags of presents. Sometimes they hand them over personally – but most of the time they just bang on the windows and leave the bag by the door.

Sint and Piet arrive in the Netherlands halfway November, and are officially welcomed to each town and city by the local mayor. Every year, one of these official 'processions' is televised. Preceding this day, Dutch television brings us three weeks' worth of the Daily Sinterklaas News. Sinterklaas lives in Spain and travels to the Netherlands by ship, meeting all sorts of challenges along the way; for instance, he loses his book, in which he has noted which child gets which gifts. However, after a series of cliffhangers, he makes it just in time for his official entry into the country. And you might notice that there is more than one Roet Piet. By now, Sinterklaas is accompanied by hundreds of them, all of whom help the gift distribution company of Sinterklaas operate effectively.

During his procession through town, Sint Nicolaas tells the children that they can place their shoe by the chimney. In this shoe, they place bread and/or a carrot for his horse. And they place a cup of water next to it. All of this will be gone the next morning, as Sinterklaas and his helpers travel across the roofs, whereby Roet Piet goes down the chimney and leaves behind a gift, taking the carrots, bread and water back up for Sinterklaas' horse.

The big party however, as said earlier, is December 5. On this day, a bag of presents is produced that has surprises in it – also the Dutch call them, literally, 'surprises'; pronounced *surpreezes*. A large 'surprise' could contain only a very small present – such as a single candy. Many of these surprises have been made with a lot of dedication and hard work and have been given the shape of an animal or some other object. Often Sint and Piet have added a poem to the gift, in which the receiver is gently teased. It is of great essence that the no one be able to link the gift to the real giver.

December 6 marks the end of this period. Sinterklaas vanishes without a trace and the next day all store windows reflect the Christmas spirit while the newspapers carry one last-ditch headline: "Once again, Sinterklaas proved his generosity".

A few years ago, these festivities became quite controversial – because of the role of Zwarte Piet, who is now largely referred to as Roet (Soot) Piet. To the Dutch people of Caribbean heritage, this fairytale figure is a racist caricature. They associate Zwarte Piet with the transatlantic period of slavery, in which the Netherlands played a significant role. Approximately 15% of slaves on the Middle Passage were transported by Dutch ships. Most of them were brought to Suriname or the island of Curaçao before the coast of Venezuela, where they were sold on to other parts of Latin America and the Caribbean area. Currently, Curaçao is an autonomous part of the Kingdom of the Netherlands.

These opponents of Zwarte Piet received a lot of support from abroad. The Americans saw 'blackface' in him; part of their vaudeville tradition in which white people with partially blackened faces played clownesque roles. Since the '70s, blackface has been considered unacceptable.

In the fall of both 2013 and 2014, artist Quinsy Gario got a lot of publicity when he criticized Zwarte Piet. He bluntly called the Sinterklaas festivities racist, meant to undermine the position of black people. Only the complete eradication of Zwarte Piet would cleanse the festivities and make them suitable for the 21st century.

This brought about a storm of protest. Most Dutch parents had never seen anything evil in this important child benchmark of the year. And now they were being told that they were tolerating racist activities in their very own homes. In 2013, the Piet-ition, a special Facebook-page in support of the traditional Zwarte Piet created by a small advertising agency in Roosendaal, garnered more than two million likes. And not only that; Geert Wilders and his PVV immediately came to the defense of Zwarte Piet, making the children's friend a political issue. On the one side of the spectrum, he was portrayed as a symbol of racism while on the other side – the extreme right – he was elevated to the status of icon of authentic Dutch culture. The discussion in the media soon became venomous. Anyone who dared to say that Zwarte Piet was a symbol of white hegemony and white privilege was bound to be told by someone that he could pack his bags and get lost if he didn't like it here. Or, at the very least, that Zwarte Piet's face had become blackened by the soot in the chimney.

Quinsy Gario turned out to have solid supporters, not only among minorities, but also among the white majority. Together with these supporters, he created the pressure group Kick Out Zwarte Piet – which since protests the existence of Zwarte Piet every year. He himself has retired from the direct protests and has been replaced by a Ghanaian poet, Jerry Afriyie.

The traditional answer to any type of discussion of this nature in the Netherlands is, of course… compromise. Concessions were made in order to remove any dissatisfaction. The suggestion that Zwarte Piet could be given another color – say, a rainbow Piet – were immediately rejected, however, by the radical opponents of his very existence: the entire symbol of slavery had to be eradicated. The mayor of Amsterdam decreed that during Sinterklaas' procession through Amsterdam, the Zwarte Pieten were not to wear golden hoops in their ears.

At the same time, a trial took place. Opponents of the Zwarte Piet-phenomenon argued that the official arrival of Sinterklaas should be abolished, on the grounds that the racist nature of this event constituted a threat to certain ethnic groups. At first, a judge ruled that some people might indeed feel restricted in their freedom by the performance of Sinterklaas' black-faced helpers. The mayor of Amsterdam appealed this decision as he feared that the same arguments might be used by opponents of other manifestations, such as Gay Pride. The highest court for these types of cases, agreed with him. It decided that mayors should only focus on threats to the public order. This was a clever way of avoiding the issue of whether or not the existence of Zwarte Piet could be considered racist. In the fall of 2014, it became clear where this was all heading. On television, the Sinterklaas-News program for children showed an old factory in which candidates for the position of Zwarte Piet had to go down a chimney – after which they reemerged with black soot on their faces. The Zwarte Pieten who had already qualified for the position in previous year kept their blackened faces. And the soot-faced Pieten opened the possibility to other colors in the future – which were already present at a variety of Sinterklaas parades across the country.

It became clear that the controversy surrounding Zwarte Piet would probably rear its ugly head a couple of more times during the years to come. Particularly as there were so many angles to it. And also particularly because his opponents had decided to be principled and uncompromising on the issue. The fact that Zwarte Piet could be linked to racial practices and customs, also made it hard for his supporters to compromise: for, if they were to do this, they would implicitly be admitting that they had (subconsciously) been acting in a racist manner themselves. A concept that made them unwilling to make any concessions at all.

People wondered how this was all to end. Only one thing was beyond discussion: Zwarte Piet is to the Dutch, what the bullfights are to the Spaniards. Or, as critics of his appearance like to say, he has lost his innocence forever. By 2020, it seemed as if Zwarte Piet was on his way out. More and more municipalities decided that they would only subsidize the arrival of Sinterklaas if the Chimney Soot Piet variety was chosen. National television had already made this choice earlier on. In 2021, this new development continued. Insofar as Sinterklaas was allowed to officially arrive in the various municipalities – in connection with Covid measures – approximately 90% of the accompanying Piets were Chimney Soot Piets.

Linked to the battle against Zwarte Piet is the criticism on the traditional rendition of Dutch history. Strongly influenced by the Black Awareness Movement in the U.S., Dutch activists have taken it upon themselves to claim that Dutch society is riddled with 'white privilege'. With this, they not only refer to discrimination on the labor market (for which they is ample evidence), but also to the Dutch culture and generally accepted views in the Netherlands. These activists are demanding a re-writing of Dutch history – which is dominated by white prejudice. Traditional national heroes, almost without exception 17th-century seafarers, admirals and colonial pioneers, do not deserve their statues – to the contrary; they enriched themselves through criminal means. In Rotterdam, for instance, there was much ado when the Center for the Arts, Witte de With, decided it no longer wanted to be named after the fleet's master of 300 years ago, because he had worked for the Dutch West India Company, which had been active in the slave trade. Nonetheless, the institute chose a new name; Melly – after a work of art displayed on its outside wall. Supporters of this movement also wondered whether a number of streets and squares – which had been named after Witte de With and his pals, or others, named after South African Boer leaders, such as Paul Kruger or Jan Smuts – were not due for a renaming.

This led to a general sentiment of anger and sneering remarks. Opponents claimed that the Netherlands could not be compared to the U.S. and that 'white privilege' was just a nonsensical term used by blind ideologists. And then there is a third group that wonders how much the Dutch would really stand to gain if the white legend of patriotic excellence were to be replaced by a sinister myth of crime and culpability. By understanding the reality of the past, one can perhaps introduce changes – but understanding it is not the same as idealizing or judging it. It is also not something in between; it is something entirely different.

In the summer of 2020, the American Black Lives Matter protests found their way to the Netherlands. Demonstrations were held in various places and were attended by crowds of a size that took even the organizers by complete surprise. Apparently, there was greater dissatisfaction regarding racism and unequal treatment than had generally been assumed. The activists' criticism focused primarily on the white aspect of Dutch culture. This included, of course, Zwarte Piet. At the largest BLM demonstration in the Netherlands – on the Dam in Amsterdam – rapper Akwasi gave a rousing speech that culminated in the following threat: "If I run into a Zwarte Piet in November, I will personally kick him in the face." This brought him a conditional charge – as inciting and threatening violence is a punishable act in the Netherlands. On the other side of the spectrum, September saw a number of court cases against those who had harassed Clarice Gargard – a supporter of Black Lives Matter – on social media with death threats and racial epithets. A well-known Dutch saying makes things clear: similar monks should wear similar hoods – or, if something is (un)acceptable for one person, it's (un)acceptable for another.

Towards the end of 2022, the Kick Out Zwarte Piet group announced that it would be demonstrating in all municipalities in which Sinterklaas appeared with his black helper. To this end, it opened up a telephone line so that people could report any Zwarte Piet sightings. The aim was to forever rid the country of Zwarte Piets by the end of 2023. And this has been largely successful. A few towns clung to the phenomenon of a Black Piet, to the dismay of Kick Out Zwarte Piet, who came to protest – and who, in turn were confronted with the aggression of angry youngsters who supported Zwarte Piet and thereby unwittingly attached the label of hooligan to the whole concept.

A Colonial Past

Children have been heard to whisper: "Zwarte Piet? He doesn't exist, a real Piet only has soot smudges on his face". To conservative Dutch people this is a revolutionary stance – a point of view that newcomers might find hard to sympathize with, taking into account the country's history of colonization. It is a process that involves tradition, but also embarrassment and racism vs. what some hesitantly call 'wokeness'.

One might shrug at so much controversy and the debate about what many after all call a children's festivity. Yet the struggle around the concept of Zwarte Piet represents a much larger societal debate: who does the Dutch history belong to and who's going to shape the collective memory of society? The Netherlands is still largely a white country, but the number of fellow countrymen with roots in other cultures is increasing. In the larger cities, they are often more than half of the population. One could say that their ancestors have had a different experience from the local Dutch. The Dutch with a Caribbean background have developed an acute realization of what transatlantic slavery means to them and directly link this to the racism of today. Increasingly, and with more force, the last few decades have seen a demand that Dutch society as a whole take responsibility for this often glossed-over past. Also Dutch people with roots in the previous colony Dutch East India have joined this cry. What really happened there when it comes to exploitation and (mass) murder? Recent publications have taught us that the inter-Asian slave trade, carried out under the Dutch flag, was at least as bad as the Transatlantic slave trade. There there's even proof for the statement that the slave traders of the middle passage based their activities on the earlier experiences of the Dutch in Asia.

The decolonization of Indonesia was a painful process, during which the Dutch colonial authorities tried to maintain control of the country through violence. In the end, they sent 150,000 soldiers, most of them conscripted. Nowadays, the government recognizes that it let this led to colonial war in which the Dutch systematically committed war crimes. As touched upon in *Zwarte Piet – Controversial Children's Friend*, the question arises: what do you do now if you have a street named after General Spoor, a military leader of the Dutch during this horrible period, in your town or city?

On August 17, 1944, freedom fighters Sukarno and Hatta declared Indonesian independence. The Netherlands only recognized this in the 21st century. Until this time, they had held that the ceremony that had taken place on December 27, 1949, the so-called transition of sovereignty, had been the start of Indonesian independence. The fact that Indonesia – and the rest of the world – thought differently, made no difference.

An end to this mentality seems to be in sight. Over the past few years, several large companies – led by De Nederlandsche Bank – have requested that research be done into their history of slavery, by independent historians. King Willem-Alexander followed suit by opening the royal archives to these historians. It is more than clear that painful facts regarding the involvement of the Orange dynasty in the slave trade will be uncovered. Also municipalities and provinces are having this research carried out. This has already resulted in a number of publications that throw a different light on the history of the Netherlands.

Local authorities have seen the outcome as reason to officially apologize for this history of slavery. In 2023, also Prime Minister Rutte did this, while the King apologized at Keti Koti – the official day commemorating the abolition of slavery in the Caribbean area in 1863. This was valued by many slave descendants.

Yet this does not mean that the chapter can now be closed. People from the Caribbean are demanding indemnification, based on the fact that the descendants are still paying the price, particularly in the shape of discrimination and racism – which needs to be remedied. In discussions within the Netherlands, the term 'white privilege' has been heard. In recent years, the struggle has acquired a more cultural – rather than socio-economical – character. For instance, they are demanding the removal of statues of so-called prominent Dutch people, who – upon closer inspection – in fact were colonial criminals. Or they are demanding the introduction of new terminology, such as 'enslaved' rather than 'slave', as this word better expresses that no person is born an object of trade, but rather is made one. This word has been taken over by the media.

Seen in this light, the controversy surrounding Sinterklaas clearly symbolizes something greater: changes in how the Dutch view themselves. That this process is accompanied by heavy polemics and fierce confrontations, should come as no surprise.

Sinterklaas and Zwarte (Roet) Piet, a European Tradition

The Sinterklaas-festivities are not purely Dutch. He appears in a number of European countries, but is hardly a saint there. And nowhere does his existence have any implications for commercial enterprises, while here it constitutes a large portion of their sales.

In other parts of Europe, Saint Nicholas is a frightening figure whose hideous sight intimidates people, with the help of a black creature who is dressed like the devil – known in Germany and Austria as Krampus. Young children hide behind their mothers' skirts when he rattles his chains.

It isn't even always a children's festivity. There are towns in Switzerland in which young men from different neighborhoods battle each other, led by their own personal Sinterklaas. The ambulances and other health services are on the alert during these battles, but everyone is willing to make this sacrifice for this tradition. Despite the blood and violence.

On the Dutch Wadden Island of Ameland there is another ancient tradition. It clearly has its own fifty shades of grey, and outsiders (such as tourists) are strongly advised to leave the island around December 6, as infractions of these rules are not tolerated by anyone. First, in all the villages, the women and children are chased into their houses. The streets are ruled by Sunneklazen, the men of the villages who are dressed up as unrecognizable Sinterklaas-like appearances. They are armed with sticks. The houses in which the women are waiting, are unlocked. The men 'force' their way inside and make the women jump over their sticks and dance with them. If they do not obey, they are swatted on their shins. Sometimes, a woman will disguise herself as a man and mix with the male Sunneklazen. If they are caught, they are given a beating or made to sit on a pile of dung. The Amelanders are very close-lipped about this tradition, and both the men and women are fond of it. They are only moderately willing to explain it to outsiders and will simply not tolerate any criticism.

From this all, it is clear that Sinterklaas has his origins in very old, heathen traditions that could be thousands of years old. We know that missionaries converted Europe to Christianity approximately 1,500 years ago, implementing one of Pope Gregory the Great's instructions: to not eradicate any of the heathen traditions, but to give them a Christian flavor. For instance, cult places where the people had worshiped Freya, goddess of fertility, became places where Jesus's mother Maria was worshiped – which they remain to this day. Saint Nicholas is the Christian version of the German god Wodan. Why Nicholas and not someone else? He is the patron saint of merchants, fishermen and seamen – which basically just about covers all of the Netherlands.

Wodan rode his eight-legged horse Sleipnir along the heavens and used his one eye (the sun) to peer down the chimneys and into the houses of the Germans to ensure that they were making the right sacrifices. Sinterklaas riding his horse on the roofs can clearly be led back to this god, as can the bread and carrots by the chimney be led back to the sacrifices. Wodan was accompanied by a goblin-like fertility god, who is conceivably the origin of Krampus and Zwarte (now mostly referred to as Roet, meaning 'soot' – as in covered in soot from coming down the chimney) Piet. Particularly if you take into account the fact that Roet Piet not only carries a bag, but also a cane – former instruments of punishment.

In the 19th century, the Netherlands went through a large-scale civilization process. The builders of this nation created not only a liberal constitution, but also a national system of education, in which the national language and the nationally 'accepted' norms, values and traditions were taught. This included the tradition of Sinterklaas, but without the wild, heathen and Dionysian elements. In the western part of the Netherlands, the Sinterklaas festivities already represented a long-standing tradition of being a children's party in which the Saint handed out gifts and Roet (Zwarte) Piet 'threatened' the children with his cane – without really carrying out the threat. Something they did fear however – along with a sack of salt instead of gifts – was being carried off in the sack. Where to? Spain, as this is where legend had it that Sinterklaas lived, and where they would be put to work for a year, until Sinterklaas returned to the Netherlands.

An Amsterdam-bred teacher, Schenkman, canonized Sinterklaas somewhere around 1850 in a book of rhymes, in which the saint and his helper feature. The text makes no mention of the skin color or name of the helper. The illustrators were the ones who gave him a black complexion. In the first edition of Schenkman's book on Sinterklaas, Zwarte Piet – Black Piet, as he is called there – is dressed as an Ottoman prince, in the second edition, as a 16th-century page. He rode a horse, just like Sinterklaas. It is clear that he is not a slave, but rather a type of medieval squire. This is the "Zwarte" Piet that has evolved into the current jolly children's friend.

Opponents of Zwarte Piet claim that the black helper is some sort of racist symbol. Some go so far as to claim that Schenkman also meant him to be a slave – the Netherlands only abolished slavery in the colonies in 1863 – but this is highly unlikely. In Schenkman's social circle, slavery was very controversial. Nor do his appearance and position point to slavery.

This does not take away the fact that if your frame of reference is formed by a history of slavery, this might by be painfully triggered by Zwarte Piet's appearance, if it remains Black and not Soot. Which is invoked by his opponents as an argument for changing him or abolishing the Sinterklaas festivities altogether – nor does it sound completely unreasonable. On the other hand, the Netherlands has more than one tradition that is not understood, or at the very least, misunderstood, outside certain circles. If the concept of Piet helpers for Sinterklaas were to disappear because certain categories of the population found him offensive, this could also have consequences for other customs and festivities.

It would appear as if the purely black-faced Zwarte Pieten are slowly but surely on their way out. This is the consequence of how the Dutch authorities have taken their familiar path of compromise, introducing a soot-faced Piet, a Piet with no make-up at all, or a rainbow Piet – who acquired his color as the ship sailed underneath a rainbow, though this latter option has not proven very popular.

References

CHAPTER 2
Social Life

THE DUTCH ROYAL FAMILY
www.royal-house.nl

Support Organizations

ACCESS
ACCESS is a dynamic volunteer, not-for-profit organization serving the needs and interests of the international community by:

- providing information and guidance, free of charge,
- offering professional volunteering opportunities to accompanying partners, and through on-call Counsellors, childbirth preparation courses, and a training network of professionals.

The ACCESS website contains over 300 FAQS and answers. Questions can also be sent to helpdesk@access-nl.org or asked in person at one of the expat centres ACCESS works from (in Amsterdam, Amstelveen, The Hague or Utrecht).
Details of addresses and opening times on www.access-nl.org
Address: Lange Voorhout 12, 2514 ED The Hague
Tel.: 085 4000 338 – www.access-nl.org

OUTPOST THE NETHERLANDS
Outpost the Netherlands is part of Global Outpost Services which supports Shell's global mobility policy with over 35 locations worldwide. They support employees and partners/families before and during an assignment in all Shell locations across the Netherlands (The Hague, Rijswijk, Rotterdam, Amsterdam, Assen) and offer non-contractual support and practical information. Their job is to help Shell employees including their partners who are on an international assignment or returning to base to make informed decisions, connect with people on the ground and build networks.

SHELL HEADQUARTERS
Carel van Bylandtlaan 16, 2596 HR, The Hague
Tel.: 070 377 6530
www.netherlands.globaloutpostservices.com
E-mail: Outpost@shell.com

EXPATRIATE ARCHIVE CENTRE
The Expatriate Archive Centre welcomes contributions from retired, repatriated or current expatriates and their children.
Paramaribostraat 20, 2585 GN The Hague
Tel.: 070 427 20 14
www.xpatarchive.com

Expat Centers

IN AMSTERDAM
World Trade Center Amsterdam
I-Tower, ground floor (entrance via Zuidplein)
Strawinskylaan 1767, 1077 XX Amsterdam
Tel.: 020 254 7999
www.iamsterdam.com/en/in-amsterdam

EXPATS HAARLEM
Gedempte Raamgracht 32, 2011 WK Haarlem
Tel.: 023 576 32 36
www.expatshaarlem.nl

THE HAGUE INTERNATIONAL CENTRE
The Hague City Hall, Atrium
Spui 70, 2511 BT The Hague
Tel.: 070 353 50 43
E-mail: internationalcentre@denhaag.nl
www.thehagueinternationalcentre.nl

ROTTERDAM EXPAT CENTRE
Korte Hoogstraat 31, 3011 GK Rotterdam
Tel.: 010 790 01 90
www.rotterdamexpatcentre.nl

EXPAT CENTRE LEIDEN
Stationsweg 26, 2312 AV Leiden
Tel.: 071 516 60 05
www.expatcentreleiden.nl

HOLLAND EXPAT CENTER SOUTH
Vestdijk 27a, Eindhoven
Tel.: 040 238 67 77
Spoorlaan 81, Tilburg
Tel.: 040 238 67 77
Mozartlaan 35, Breda
Tel.: 076 560 7870
www.hollandexpatcenter.com

EXPAT CENTRE MAASTRICHT REGION
Mosae Forum 10, 6211 DW Maastricht
Tel.: 043 350 50 10
www.expatcentremaastrichtregion.nl

INTERNATIONAL WELCOME CENTER NORTH
Gedempte Zuiderdiep 98, 9711 HL Groningen
Tel.: 050 367 71 97 – www.iwcn.nl

EXPAT CENTER EAST NETHERLANDS
Industrieplein 2, 7553 LL Hengelo
Tel.: 074 250 33 25
www.expatcentereastnetherlands.nl

EXPATDESK NIJMEGEN
Oranjesingel 2, 6511 NS Nijmegen
Tel.: 024 357 25 77
www.expatdesknijmegen.nl

EXPAT CENTER UTRECHT
Utrecht City Hall
Stadsplateau 1, 3521 AZ Utrecht
Tel.: 030 286 00 00
www.utrecht.nl/expatcenter

EXPAT CENTER FOOD VALLEY
Akkermaalsbos 14, 6708 WB Wageningen
Tel.: 0317 482 609
www.expatcenterfoodvalley.com

Expat Fairs

IAMEXPAT FAIR
The biggest expat fair in the Netherlands organized in April in Amsterdam and In November In The Hague
www.iamexpatfair.nl

I AM NOT A TOURIST – EXPAT FAIR FOR INTERNATIONALS
www.expatfair.nl

FEEL AT HOME IN THE HAGUE
Event for the international community in the Hague region
www.feelathomeinthehague.com

Culture Training

ROYAL TROPICAL INSTITUTE (KIT)
Intercultural Management & Communication
Offers various group programs designed for foreign employees and their partners who are posted to the Netherlands.
Linnaeusstraat 35F, 1093 EE Amsterdam
Tel.: 020 568 83 19
www.interculturalprofessionals.nl

Recommended Reading

General

THE LITTLE ORANGE HANDBOOK 2.0
The Netherlands for Newcomers
Published by XPat Media
This book offers, compact, clear and to-the-point information on the Netherlands.
A practical and quick introduction to a country in which at times it is easy to get lost in a maze of rules, regulations and laws.
To order: www.hollandbooks.nl

THE UNDUTCHABLES 9.0
By Colin White and Laurie Boucke
Published XPat Media
A tongue-in-cheek observation of the Netherlands, its culture and its inhabitants.
www.undutchables.com
To order: www.hollandbooks.nl

THE LOW SKY, UNDERSTANDING THE DUTCH
By Han van der Horst
Published by Scriptum
The book that makes the Netherlands familiar.
A detailed exploration of the reasons for desire of the Dutch for independence, their sense of respect and their business sense
www.scriptum.nl

DEALING WITH THE DUTCH
By Jacob Vossestein
Published by LM Publishers
The cultural context of business and work in the Netherlands
To order: www.hollandbooks.nl

THE DUTCH AND THEIR DELTA
Living Below Sea Level
By Jacob Vossestein
Published by XPat Media
The fascinating account of how the Dutch manage to live below sea level
To order: www.hollandbooks.nl

THE AMERICAN NETHERLANDER – 25 YEARS OF EXPAT TALES
By Greg Shapiro
Published by XPat Media
Greg Shapiro celebrates 25 years in the Netherlands by revealing his hilariously clumsy assimilation into Dutch society.
To order: www.hollandbooks.nl

DISCOVERING THE DUTCH
By Emmeline Besamusca & Jaap Verheul
Published by Amsterdam University Press
This updated edition tackles the heart of the question of Dutch identity through a number of essential themes that span the culture, history and society of the Netherlands.
To order: www.hollandbooks.nl

STUFF DUTCH PEOPLE LIKE
By Colleen Geske
A study of all things orange. It investigates and highlights the idiosyncrasies of the Dutch culture and their uncanny ability to talk on a mobile phone, while carrying 2.5 children, 6 bags of groceries, a television set, and a mattress balanced on a gear-less bicycle,
www.stuffdutchpeoplelike.com

NEW VISIONS OF THE NETHERLANDS
By Martijn de Rooi
Photography: Jurjen Drenth
With 250 exceptional photographs, New Visions of the Netherlands provides a comprehensive image of the country most people know as Holland. www.dutchshop.nl or www.hollandbooks.nl

NL365 – A YEAR IN THE NETHERLANDS
Photography: Frans Lemmens
This extensive photobook is a feast for the eyes and an ode to a special and beautiful country.
www.franslemmens.com or
www.hollandbooks.nl

HOLLAND BOOKS
Features a wide range of books and travel guides on Holland: www.hollandbooks.nl

Cultural Transition

THE ART OF CROSSING CULTURES
By Craig Storti
Published by Intercultural Press
www.interculturalpress.com

THE PSYCHOLOGY OF CULTURE SHOCK
By Colleen Ward, Stephen Bochner, Adrian Furnham
Published by Routledge
www.routledge.com

CULTURESHOCK! NETHERLANDS
A survival guide to customs and etiquette
By Hunt Janin
Published by Marshall Cavendish Editions
www.marshallcavendish.com

A MOVEABLE MARRIAGE
Relocate your Relationship Without Breaking it
by Robin Pascoe
Published by Expatriate Press Ltd.
www.expatexpert.com

HOMEWARD BOUND
A Spouse's Guide to Repatriation
By Robin Pascoe
Published by Expatriate Press Ltd.
www.expatexpert.com

THE MOBILE LIFE – 2ND REVISED EDITION
Published by XPat Media
By Diane Lemieux & Anne Parker
Master the challenge of moving somewhere new – Also available as e-book
www.themobilelife.eu
www.hollandbooks.nl

Dutch Language

DUTCH FOR SELF-STUDY
By Hinke van Kampen
Published by Het Spectrum
This book and two cd-roms provide the basic structures of the Dutch language
www.spectrum.nl

DUTCH FOR DUMMIES
By Margreet Kwakernaak
Published John Whiley and Sons
Turn your Double Dutch into Fluent Dutch
www.bol.com

DUTCH LANGUAGE TRAINING
www.berlitz.com
www.britishschool.nl/languagecentre
www.directdutch.com
www.dnalanguages.nl
www.dutchindialogue.com
www.dutchforexpats.com
www.ita-talen.nl
www.kickstartschool.nl
www.kit.nl
www.koentact.nl
www.languageone.org
www.learndutch.org
www.lexicon.nl
www.linguarama.nl
www.nt2digitaal.nl
www.nederlandsalstweedetaal.nl
www.nedles.nl
www.pcilanguages.com
www.reginacoeli.nl
www.taalhuisamsterdam.nl
www.taalthuis.nl
www.taaltaal.nl
www.toptaal.com
www.volksuniversiteit.nl
www.volksuniversiteitamsterdam.nl

Many of you have come to the Netherlands as an expatriate – placed or transferred here by your employer – so that most of the important things have been taken care of for you. On the other hand, many of you have not come here with the full company support system behind you. If this is the case, there are a number of things you need to know before entering the job market, such as: the make-up of the Dutch employment market, finding a job here as an expatriate, Dutch labor law, the Dutch social security system, the possibilities of continuing the social insurance legislation of your country of origin in the Netherlands and how to go about setting up your own business. Going through this chapter will help you prepare for your ventures, by providing an overview of these topics as well as, on the reference page, the addresses, phone numbers and websites of those organizations that can help you along the way.

CHAPTER 3

Working in the Netherlands

CONTRIBUTING AUTHORS STEPHANIE DIJKSTRA, HAN VAN DER HORST, DOROTA KLOP, ARJAN ENNEMAN, NANNETTE RIPMEESTER AND LIANE VAN DE VRUGT

THE DUTCH EMPLOYMENT MARKET

The Netherlands is known for its tulips and windmills, but is far more diverse and pluralistic than you might expect. It offers job seekers from across the world endless possibilities and has plenty to offer foreign students as well. As everywhere else, the global pandemic also had its impact on the Dutch job market, in the sense that many more employers offer the option of working from home – or a hybrid job of partially working from home and partially from the office. Despite the looming recession, there are still talent shortages in all lines of work, and the vacancy rate (number of open vacancies against 1,000 jobs) was at a record level of 4.6% in November 2023. The flexible work culture in the Netherlands, supported by a strong educational structure, may have contributed to this quick post-pandemic labor market recovery. In the context of economy, it should be noted that the international orientation of the Dutch job market, with its two international mainports and its longstanding tradition as a nation of trade, make it vulnerable to global events, but also supports its rebound. Below, you will find information on the labor market of this small country with its international and impressively diverse job market.

THE LABOR MARKET SITUATION

The Dutch unemployment rate – at 3.7% in the third quarter of 2023 – is low for a country that historically relies on international trade. In the third quarter of 2023, the working population in the Netherlands amounted to roughly 10.1 million individuals, of whom 9.4 million were employed. In October 2023, the EU unemployment rate was 6.5%, versus 3.7% in the Netherlands. The global pandemic initially hit many sectors hard, but the recovery has also been speedy and despite the economic (and geopolitical) uncertainties, the Dutch job market offers many job opportunities, as we can see further on in this chapter.

Part-time employment in the Netherlands is relatively high; reports state that it constitutes more than 50% of the total Dutch labor force, or 4.7 million people. Though 517,000 of these part-time employees have indicated that they would like to work more hours, this desire to work more has not yet relaxed the tightness of the Dutch labor market. For the first time since the UWV (Employee Insurance Agency) started keeping track of the tension in the labor market, the labor market has been classified as "very tight"; meaning there are more vacancies – due to the popularity of part-time work, almost 32% of total job vacancies posted are for part-time employment – than job seekers to fill them. The number of vacancies has increased, and many job seekers have found work, yet there are staff shortages in almost all professions. The labor market achieved this status for the first time in mid-2021. In the third quarter of 2023, tension in the labor market decreased slightly, with fewer vacancies (-12,000) and more unemployed persons (+16,000) than the previous quarter.

Gender differences in employment participation have slowly been decreasing; over time, more women in the Netherlands have found the route to the job market – 69% of Dutch women have a job, compared to 77.7% of men. Women do work fewer hours than men though; 28 hours a week versus 36 hours a week – except in the 15-25 age category, where 76% of both genders work.

Though most people work directly for an employer, a considerable and growing number are self-employed; according to the Dutch Bureau of Statistics CBS, 16% of the Dutch labor force consists of people claiming to be self-employment (referred to as *Zelfstandige Zonder Personeel*, or *ZZP-ers*), which is approximately 1.6 million people – if you add to this the number of people working both in employment and for themselves, the numbers are even higher. The greatest increase in self-employment has been in construction, ICT and communications. Compared to other European countries, the level of self-employment in the Netherlands is quite high, particularly among younger people – and though it appears to be quite stable, it is always prone to fluctuation and remains hard to predict. The number of flexible contacts is also on the rise, again, especially among young people. In the third quarter of 2023, there were more than 2.7 million 'flex-workers' in the Netherlands, or 26.7% of the total workforce.

SECTORS

The resilience of the Dutch labor market became evident through its recovery after the impact of the Covid crisis: after a rapid decline of 30% in open vacancies and a sharp rise in unemployment figures, the situation is now completely different – with considerable shortages in most sectors. These shortages have given rise to problems at, for instance, Schiphol Airport and with the Dutch railways – with the greatest need being for engineers, electricians, machine workers, as well as health care workers and software developers.

THE DUTCH WORK FORCE

The education level of those working in the Netherlands has been rising steadily over the past decade; one in every three high school graduates continues their education at a research university or a university of applied sciences (you can read more about the distinction between these two in chapter 9). Moreover, according to a

report by Nuffic, 24% of the international students who studied in the Netherlands still live and work in the country five years after graduating.

Though traditionally the Netherlands was a country in which employees worked for the same employer their whole life, this changed dramatically during the '90s when, due to the flourishing economy, the age of job-hopping arrived. This development came to a halt again with the arrival of the economic crisis around 2008, when competition for jobs increased and employees opted to stay put. Nonetheless, the tendency to stay with one employer for life remains a thing of the past. In the next section, we will take a look at the gender aspect of the Dutch labor market.

EMANCIPATION?

The Netherlands is viewed by those abroad as an 'emancipated' country, where women share an equal standing with men. To a large degree this is true; in fact, many expats comment on how the Dutch women are the ones 'who wear the pants at home' – to use a Dutch expression. However, the workforce does not reflect this emancipation, particularly not in the full-time and/or highest paid job sectors. The cause for this can presumably be found in the fact that, aside from there being relatively little government support for child care, Dutch social values still dictate that women spend more time with their children.

Although Dutch society is egalitarian by nature, on average the more traditional role definition still holds true; men work full-time, women part-time, and the women play a greater part in the raising of the children. Based on a study conducted by the Central Bureau for Statistics, more women (especially with a higher education) expect that their career opportunities will be negatively affected once they have children. Indeed, over 45% of working women either reduce their working hours or stop working altogether after the birth of their first child. Men, interestingly, agree that becoming a parent has a more significant effect on women's career paths compared to theirs. That said, nonetheless, in reality the percentage of households in which the man is the sole earner and the woman does not work at all is only 20%. One could argue that it is not so much the 'glass ceiling' that keeps the women in the Dutch labor market from progressing up the career ladder, but that the 'sticky floor' plays a major role too, with women seeing a reduction of their income by 47% (2022) on average after their first child, which is referred to as the 'baby penalty'. For instance, the structures around child support make it difficult for parents to continue to work full-time. Unlike the situation in neighboring countries of the Netherlands, schools here end at quarter past three daily, and parents are expected to collect their children from school. Dutch day care centers, though open five days a week, prefer that parents bring their kids for a maximum of three days – as social convention dictates that leaving the children at a day care facility five days a week would burden the relationship between parent and child.

The most common earnings model in the Netherlands is the 'one-and-a-half-earner', with both partners working, but one of them half-time. In 2020, 36% of couples belonged to the high earning 'one-and-a-half-earners', with large differences based on education level of the woman; among higher-educated women, 52% belong to this group, whereas among lower-educated women, this is only 26%. Between 2003 and 2018, the average working week for mothers with young kids increased by 6.5 hours a week. The Netherlands has the highest share of women working part-time – 63% of total employment against 24% for men – and the largest difference between women and men. As a result, 1 out of 6 women does not have enough money to be economically independent, as their income is less than 70% of the net minimum wage. The Dutch government therefore wants to increase women's economic and financial independence and a positive development is that between 2013 and 2022, labor participation among women aged 45-55 went up from 76.2% to 82.1% and for those aged 55-65, from 49.3% to 63.5%.

The aim of the Dutch government – to have 65% of the women working at least 12 hours a week – is yet to be met, though the previous paragraph shows that numbers have clearly continued to rise while this issue remains on the political agenda. Consequently, to the dismay of expat women, few women are in the business's top echelons or among the top earners. Between 2008 and 2018, the percentage of women at the top increased from 4% to 15%, yet there are still considerably fewer women at the top in the Netherlands than in other countries. There has also been a steady increase among the number of women on management boards in recent years, the majority of which are non-executive managerial positions. The Dutch Female Board Index 2023 shows that, among newly appointed executives, the vast majority is still men (84%). While for non-executives, we last year saw – for the first time – a small majority (55%) of new female appointees, this year the majority of supervisory board positions went to men (53%). The 88 companies listed in the Netherlands in 2023 had 15.3% female executives and 39% female non-executives.

Notably, women are far better represented in the non-profit sector than they are in the business sector, which has been to their advantage, as the number of jobs available in health care, education and the public sector has been increasing over the past years. All in all, nonetheless, it can be said that Dutch women – reflective of the country's overall population average – generally enjoy a high standard of living and material satisfaction. As well as highlighting the very equitable distribution of wealth found in the Netherlands, this points to the general acknowledgement that these women – with their flexible attitude towards work – are an integral part of the country's solid financial structure.

DUTCH EMPLOYMENT LAW

DUTCH EMPLOYMENT LAW

As many of you will not have moved to the Netherlands on an expat contract governed by your home country laws, the rules that apply to those employed directly by a Dutch employer can be of great importance to you. Even expatriates, whose contract explicitly states that a foreign law applies to the employment relationship, will find that they are subject to mandatory rules of Dutch employment law and/or Dutch rules of public order by means of binding allocation rules of international private law. For this reason, we include an overview of the main issues contained in this law, whereby we will go into some of them in more detail further on in this chapter.

PROBATION PERIOD

TYPE OF CONTRACT	MAXIMUM DURATION OF PROBATION
Contract for less than 6 months	no probation period
Contract between 6 months and for 2 years	1 month
2-year or permanent contract	2 months

As you can see in above graph, for any temporary employment contract with a total duration of less than six months, a probation period is not permitted.

CHAIN CONTRACTS

If you enter into a series of more than three consecutive fixed-term contracts with the same employer (a 'chain' of contracts), the fourth employment contract is deemed to be a contract for an indefinite period of time, even if it is explicitly stated that it is a fixed-term contract. If you first work for an employer via an employment agency and then directly for this same employer, the first contract – through the employment agency – counts as the first contract of the chain of three. However, if there are more than six months between two of these contracts, this 'chain' is considered to have been 'broken' and the counting starts anew. Also if you have had a series of temporary contracts with the same employer that amount to a total of three years, then, if you are offered a new contract within six months of the last contract, this will be deemed a contract for an indefinite period of time, though an exception has been made for substitute teachers. Temporary work that can only be carried out nine months a year may only have an interruption that does not exceed three months; this must be included in the collective labor agreement.

MINIMUM/MAXIMUM / ZERO HOUR CONTRACT

If you work on call, there are two types of contracts you can enter into. One is the min/max contract: this offers you a guaranteed number of hours of work (and pay) as well as the possibility that your employer will call you in to work more hours, to a predetermined maximum. Every time you are called in, you receive a minimum of three hours' pay, if you have a contract for a maximum of 15 hours and the hours are not fixed. It offers you certain rights that all employees have, such as continued pay (70%) during illness, protection against dismissal, and the accrual of a holiday allowance, as well as the obligation on your side to show up if you are called in – provided you are given at least four days' notice that you will be expected. If your employer cancels less than four days in advance, they must pay you for this job. After the first 12 months have passed, your employer is obligated to offer you a contract for the average number of hours you worked over these 12 months.
There is also the 'nul-uren contract' (0 hours contract), which does not offer a minimum number of hours, but does require your employer to pay you at least three hours every time he calls you in. It can be for a limited or an unlimited period of time. If you have worked for this employer longer than six months, then you have a right to wages if, for instance, there is no work or your employer does not call you in though there *is* work.

TERMINATING AN EMPLOYMENT CONTRACT

There are two options for an employer who wishes to terminate an employment contract, depending on the reason for the termination. If the working relationship is damaged, the employer can only terminate the employment contract via the sub-district sector of the District Court (or Cantonal Court). In case of economic reasons or in case of illness of the employee, the employment contract can be terminated via the UWV (Employee Insurance Agency). A so-called transition compensation is due upon termination of the contract. See below. (See more on dismissal on page 78.)

NOTICE PERIOD

When terminating an employment contract, an employer must apply the following notice periods (these do not apply when the employment contract is dissolved by the courts):

LENGTH OF EMPLOYMENT PERIOD	NOTICE PERIOD
0 - 4 years	1 calendar month
5 - 9 years	2 calendar months
10 - 14 years	3 calendar months
> 15 years	4 calendar months

The above notice periods apply to contracts for an indefinite period of time. In the case of other contract forms, such as a temporary employment contract, the employer must notify the employee one month in advance of their intentions. For 'temp' contracts with a duration of fewer than six months, termination is/can be with immediate effect.

For an employee, the notice period is always one month, unless – either in the employment contract or in a separate written agreement – the employer and the employee agree upon a different notice period. Whereby it should be noted that any personally agreed-upon notice period for the employee is doubled for the employer (i.e. if an employee agrees to a two-month notice period at the beginning of their contract, the employer must agree to give four months' termination notice to said employee). Collective agreements can provide for different (and even equal) notice periods to be observed.

SEVERANCE PAYMENT

A severance payment can be granted either as a lump sum (known as a 'golden handshake'), or as a periodically paid supplement to the unemployment benefit (for more on this benefit, see page 84) or lower wages in the next job. In the case of collective dismissals or high-paid individuals, the payment is usually in the form of a lump sum. The taxation of the lump sum cannot be deferred; instead it is taxed at a rate that takes into account the total amount earned during that year. For a while, there was much upheaval about the severance payment of some high-paid senior managers, causing the Dutch government to rethink the dismissal process in the Netherlands, leading to a much lower *transitievergoeding*.

These past years, a number of changes have been introduced, making it possible to take into account the labor market perspective of the dismissed employee, the employee's behavior, and the financial situation of the employee and the employer. Also, short-term contracts are better covered by the new model; employers owe compensation if they terminate a permanent contract or a temporary contract.

Regardless of the termination route (UWV or District Court/ Cantonal Court), a severance payment (*transitievergoeding*) must be paid by the employer, to a maximum of € 94,000 (2024). For more information, see page 80, or consult www.rijksoverheid.nl/onderwerpen/ontslag/vraag-en-antwoord/hoe-hoog-is-de-transitievergoeding-als-ik-word-ontslagen.

WORKING THROUGH AN EMPLOYMENT AGENCY

The Netherlands, where the first temporary employment agencies started over 30 years ago, was also one of the first countries where these agencies were very successful. They still remain important players on the labor market, and currently the top agencies include Randstad Nederland, Adecco, and Manpower, but also MSPs, such as HeadFirst Group and Brainnet/Pro Unlimited.

There are two main Temporary Workers unions; the ABU and NBBU. These unions are governed by their own collective labor agreement (CAO), in which various regulations are given on (but not limited to), such subjects as:

- statutory number of vacation days
- holiday allowance
- national holidays
- salary statement specifications
- working overtime
- illness/sick pay
- the 'Phase system' and 'Chain system'.

Not all employment agencies have joined a Union for Temporary Workers, as membership is not obligatory. Nonetheless, all employment agencies must conform to the legally binding aspects of the Collective Agreement for Temporary Employees. This collective labor agreement applies to both the ABU and the NBBU. For more specific information, see website of the ABU, www.abu.nl.

FOREIGN TEMPS

(Some provisions of) the Collective Agreement for Temporary Employees (ABU Collective Agreement) apply/applies to all employment agencies, thus also to (foreign) employment agencies that place employees on the Dutch labor market from abroad. Keep in mind that nationals of the European Economic Area (EEA) can move to the Netherlands for work and enjoy the same conditions as Dutch nationals in areas such as access to housing, wages, and social security – among others.

MULTILINGUAL JOBS

When looking for employment in the Netherlands whereby you can work in your native language, you can either register with various specialized employment agencies (a listing of these can be found at the end of this chapter) or you can apply directly with companies where the business language is your native language. The job market for foreign staff encompasses a wide spectrum of professions including, but not limited to: administration, secretarial, IT, finance, marketing, support staff, sales, logistics, middle and senior management, etc.

After the UK, Germany and France, most 'multilingual' jobs are to be found in international call and shared service centers located in the Netherlands. There are over 150 of these multilingual service centers in the country, most of which are located in the Randstad region (the triangle between, and including, Utrecht, Rotterdam, The Hague, and Amsterdam). However, you will find more and more pan-European centers in Maastricht, Arnhem, and other cities, particularly near the border. Within these organizations, English is usually the business language.

Most Dutch people speak more than one foreign language to some extent (usually the Dutch rate their own language skills a lot higher than they actually should!), yet the international centers and companies have a preference for native speakers. Please do read the paragraph on *Protection Labor Market*, further on, however.

LANGUAGE

It is still pretty common for foreigners to live and work in the Netherlands for years without learning the language, however, we cannot emphasize enough the importance of learning Dutch; this will not only be beneficial within the workplace but also during your day-to-day endeavors in the Netherlands. Far too many foreigners make no effort to learn even the basics, but the Dutch always appreciate and respect those who make an effort to learn their language. Dutch is not the easiest language to learn, and it can be very difficult for those who live in the Randstad to find the opportunity to practice their Dutch language skills, as the helpful Dutch will almost invariably switch to English once they detect an accent. But please persevere; the effort will pay off in the end,

especially for those who plan on staying in the Netherlands for a longer period of time. The good thing about learning Dutch is that the Dutch do not have a problem with other people's grammatical mistakes – they still get the point you are trying to make. Do ask them to correct you though; otherwise, you will keep making the same mistakes!

PROTECTION LABOR MARKET

When applying for a work permit, beware of the stringent legal protection of the Dutch labor market, making it difficult for non-EU/EEA/Swiss nationals to receive such a permit (you can read more about this on page 129). If the job you are applying for meets the criteria for the so-called Highly Skilled Migrant Program, do note that the IND provides your prospective employer with a simplified application procedure, as the aim is to attract talent to the Netherlands and retain it here. Certain salary requirements apply – you can read more about this on page 130. For EU/EEA and Swiss nationals, freedom of movement applies, in keeping with the Freedom of Labor Act (Wet Arbeid Vreemdelingen, or WAV). This means that they do not need a work permit to work here. It also means that, when seeking to fill a job opening, employers in the Netherlands must prioritize not only Dutch applicants over foreign applicants, but also EU/EEA/Swiss applicants over non-EU/EEA/Swiss applicants. Being a native speaker of a particular language will no longer automatically qualify you, if the Dutch authorities are of the opinion that your prospective employer should be able to find a Dutch/EU/EEA/Swiss employee who can also speak your language.

Please also note that when faced with the choice, the employer, who will be the one applying for your work permit, might well choose an employee who does not need a work permit over you (if you do need one) – as the application process is a time-consuming one. This may seem unfair – yet is something you should realistically take into account. With any luck, new regulations, aimed at simplifying and shortening this procedure, will succeed in leveling this aspect of the playing field.

SALARIES

In general, you may be surprised at the salaries in the Netherlands compared to those in your country of origin. Salaries are always commensurate with the general cost of living and pay parity is generally only reached at very senior management levels. However, you will find that, in fact, the net wages are comparable as most expense compensations and some allowances are tax-exempt.

Furthermore, a statutory holiday allowance (minimum of 8% of a gross annual salary), paid in the month of May, is awarded to each individual, pro-rated to the number of months worked.

(COMPULSORY) HEALTH INSURANCE

All residents of the Netherlands who work and pay taxes in the Netherlands must arrange private health care insurance (there is sometimes the option of participating in a collective insurance arranged by the employer). This form of private insurance is known as *Zorgverzekering* (or 'care insurance'); for more information on insurances, see page 141.

HOW TO FIND A JOB

The world, which was still recovering from the Covid pandemic, was hit by the start of the war in Ukraine in 2022. This had a big impact on the economy. Looking at the Dutch labor market, companies and organizations were faced with shortages of qualified staff for several professions – a situation that continued through 2022 and 2023. The job market in 2023 was still tight; there were 122 vacancies per 100 job seekers in the second quarter, and 114 in the third. The CBS (Dutch Bureau for Statistics) has confirmed that, for already two years in a row, there have been more vacancies than job seekers, which is something that hasn't happened over the last 50 years.

Throughout 2023, the unemployment rate fluctuated, being as low as 3.4% in April, and as high as 3.7% in September 2023. In July 2022, the number of job openings hit an all-time record of 479,800, compared to 213,700 in January 2021. In the second quarter of 2023 the number was 416,800.

In general, despite the possible language barrier, the Dutch employment market still offers foreigners plenty of career opportunities. There is a demand for professionals and starting graduates in a number of industries and functional areas, such as: health care, engineering, ICT, Internet / social media, high-tech, technical positions, logistics, customer services, legal and tax professionals, interim managers, education and science.

It is for this reason that the Dutch government has introduced the Highly Skilled Migrant Program – a tax measure created to make working here attractive for high-earning professionals recruited abroad, as well as highly educated graduates from abroad who are searching for a first employment position in the Netherlands. You can read more about this on page 130 and 236. Having said this, the following sectors are still struggling and not hiring many new employees: banking, the government, NGOs, and non-profit organizations.

Currently, the length of the average job search is about two to four months, though for newly arrived internationals it can take up to six months.

Because the Dutch economy is very internationally oriented, the ability to speak English – fluently – is an important requirement when looking for a good job. However, this is primarily the case for commercial companies and less so for certain sectors, such as the health sector, non-profit organizations, NGOs, and governmental organizations. Remember also that it is not easy to find a part-time job of fewer than 30 hours a week (particularly if you don't speak Dutch).

THE FIRST STEP

There are four ways to find a job:

- through ads on the Internet (on jobsites, social media, the websites of the employers) and, to a lesser extent, in the printed press
- through employment and recruitment agencies
- by means of an open application
- by networking.

In principle, you should try all four and not limit yourself to one of these as, in the Netherlands, only half of the vacancies are published in the media/Internet or offered through agencies. This means that more than 50% of the vacancies are part of what we call the 'hidden job market', and are only visible to insiders. That is why it is very important that you approach employers directly (with an open application) and that you quickly start working on building your own network.

FINDING A JOB VIA THE INTERNET / JOBSITES

Most job seekers focus on the jobsites (see the list below), however there are a lot of jobs that are only published on the websites of the employers themselves. Therefore, we recommend that you make a list of top 30 organizations that you would like to work for, and that you visit their career page regularly. The most relevant jobsites are:

- www.careerjet.nl
- www.glassdoor.nl
- www.intermediair.nl (in Dutch)
- www.iamexpat.nl/career/jobs-netherlands
- www.jobbird.com (in Dutch)
- www.linkedin.com
- www.monsterboard.nl (in Dutch)
- www.nationalevacaturebank.nl (in Dutch)
- www.nl.indeed.com
- www.togetherabroad.nl (in English)
- www.toplanguagejobs.com
- https://vacatures.fd.nl (in Dutch).

NEWSPAPERS

About 95% of the jobs that are posted publicly are posted on the Internet and only 5% in the printed media. The best newspapers for jobs are the Saturday editions of the national and regional newspapers, for commercial and administrative / clerical jobs, and the free news-tabloids.

EMPLOYMENT AND RECRUITMENT AGENCIES

For those who do not have sufficient (job-specific) work experience, *uitzendbureaus* (employment or temp agencies) are a good first step, but be clear about the type of job you do and do not want. If you have more than three years' (specific) work experience, then you should also approach the specialized recruitment agencies. Currently, many companies are using temp agencies to help recruit employees for highly skilled jobs too. This offers them flexibility.

In certain industries, competition is still very high, and the employment agencies are getting a lot of applications and calls. Consequently, these agencies are *only* interested in candidates who fit the profiles for the vacancies they have open. If there is no match with a current job opening, they will put your CV in their database and might contact you in future should they have a fitting vacancy. Keep this in mind when composing your CV: they will want to see it first, before deciding whether or not to meet you in person. Beware that agencies are normally not interested in candidates who need a work permit to work in the Netherlands, unless you have a skill that is in high demand. If you need a work permit, your best chance is through contacting companies directly and not through an agency (you can read more about when you need a work permit and the complicated legal rules around obtaining one on page 129).

OPEN APPLICATIONS

Open applications are also a good way of finding a job, though possibly not the quickest. Especially small and medium-sized organizations appreciate the attention they receive and the willingness to take the initiative that you thus demonstrate. You should of course orient yourself on the organizational structure, the department and the positions. Be clear about what you want and what you have to offer. Furthermore, it is always advisable to address a specific person in your application, preferably the hiring manager or the human resources manager who is responsible for recruitment.

NETWORKING

In the country, where approximately 50% of the vacancies belong to the 'hidden' job market, networking can be your top strategy to find a suitable job, and, it is often the most successful one. There are two main ways you can network; online and offline. While in post-Covid times, online networking really took off, good old-fashioned face-to-face networking still remains the most effective but also the most time-consuming one. To start with, you should make an overview of networking opportunities (organizations related to your profession, expat networks, meet-ups, trade fairs, etc.), and decide which ones you want to visit.

Online networking is a great way to get to know people quickly and extend your professional network. Both LinkedIn and Facebook offer a great way to network. Especially LinkedIn has become embedded in Dutch culture and is used by many Dutch professionals, recruiters and employers. The most important thing to keep in mind is that you should clearly and concisely communicate what you are looking for and what you have to offer. Always keep in mind that networking is a two-way street so offer your help to others too.

TIPS FOR WRITING YOUR RESUME

A resume is called a 'curriculum vitae' (or cv) in Europe. In the Netherlands, employers prefer a concise cv (one or two pages) that has been tailor-made for the position you are applying for. Always start with your profile summary (three to four sentences which describe you as a professional, your core skills and what you are looking for), followed by your work experience. Arrange your experience in reverse chronological order, starting with the most recent experience. Do not forget to mention your achievements next to your responsibilities. Pay special attention to the job titles of the positions you held: is the job title the same in the Netherlands as in the country you are from? Do not forget to have your diplomas evaluated by the IDW (www.idw.nl, see the end of the chapter) so that your employer knows what the comparable Dutch diploma is. Also make clear if you have lived / worked / studied in more than one country, as today's employers are often specifically looking for employees who have international experience. Last but not least, clearly specify your language abilities and extra-curricular activities such as volunteering.

TIPS FOR WRITING A COVER LETTER

If it is explicitly stated that a cover letter is required, you need to submit one along with your cv. Express the reasons and your motivation for applying for this position. When writing a cover letter, relevancy is a key. Focus on the top three requirements mentioned in the job ad and explain how your past work experience matches those requirements. It goes without saying that it is important to know about the organization to which you are applying and to show enthusiasm both for the role and the organization. Mention also what you expect to contribute to the company. Use the same type of language used in the job description.
If you step for a moment into recruiter's or employer's shoes, you will realize that they receive dozens of applications a day. So, make sure you distinguish yourself through your cv, cover letter and (online) profiles: keep them concise and to-the-point.

TIPS FOR WRITING A LINKEDIN PROFILE

In recent years, LinkedIn has become not only an invaluable platform for connecting professionals with each other, but also a huge recruiting machine. To cut down on the recruiting costs related to advertising the job offers in traditional ways, many recruiters in the Netherlands (and worldwide) use LinkedIn as their top recruitment tool. To scout for talent, they not only rely on posting the jobs on LinkedIn, but also actively use LinkedIn to hunt for talent.

That's why it is crucial to have a complete LinkedIn profile. The most important sections are: your profile picture, headline, 'About' and 'Experience'. Make sure your profile picture is a professional one, write a strong headline that contains your role's name, key skills, industry. Be sure to write a compelling 'About' section that talks about who you are as a professional and what you have to offer. Last not least, complete the 'Experience' section with your responsibilities, achievements and skills. Also keep in mind the importance of keywords (Keywords section below).

KEYWORDS

Now that you have adapted your cv for a particular job; have you checked if the most important requirements are expressed, using the right keywords? What are keywords and why there is so much fuss about them? Keywords are words that describe requirements for a specific job, such as hard and soft skills, tasks, achievements, verbs, etc. Nowadays with the digitization of our world, before your cv is going to be read by a human, it first will be read by ATS – Applicant Tracking System. ATS scans your cv for the right keywords and if doesn't pass a certain number of those, it is not going to be selected, so no actual human being will see that you CAN do that job and invite you to a job interview.

Make sure your cv, cover letter and LinkedIn profile are optimized for the right keywords. How do you do it? Simply collect 7 – 10 job applications for a specific job and use a software such as jobscan.co to collect the relevant keywords, then just sprinkle those in your application.

E-LANCERS

The Internet has made it very easy to work from your own home (or wherever you are) and has led to the phenomenon of e-lancing. E-lancing allows you to work and still be there for your family, to take on that one essential job when on vacation and, in certain countries, being a self-employed e-lancer allows you to benefit from great reductions for tax purposes, allowing you to convert a considerably higher amount of your gross income into net income. This is certainly the case in the Netherlands; if you want to know more about setting up your own business, we refer you to page 86.

AI IN JOB SEARCH

Artificial intelligence has just made its entrance into the world and is definitely conquering the recruiting field too. On every step of the job search you can use helpful AI-powered tools. These will help you to write a cv, cover letter, check your application against the job offer, find relevant keywords and even update your LinkedIn profile. Always keep in mind not to just copy-paste whatever ChatGPT has written for you, but to use it as a tool to help you make a start and as a source of inspiration rather than the end product.

INTERNET ADDRESSES

You will find a selection of useful websites at the end of the chapter.

BSN: CITIZEN SERVICE NUMBER

Everyone who is employed legally must have a Citizen Service Number – or *burgerservicenummer*, widely referred to as BSN – for tax purposes. Without this number, your employer cannot properly pay out your salary for tax purposes or credit your contributions for your benefits, while you also need it to apply for the 30%-ruling. Also expat family members need to obtain a Citizen Service Number. They will need this number – and proof that they are staying here legally, such as a residence permit or a valid passport – to arrange their obligatory health insurance (you can read more about this on page 141). You also need a Citizen Service Number (BSN) when you register with temporary job agencies.

The Citizen Service Number is issued to those persons who in one or other way have to deal with government organizations (for instance, for tax matters, benefits, rent subsidy or educational purposes, to name a few). If you are going to reside in the Netherlands for longer than four months, you have the legal obligation to register with the municipality – BRP, or *Basis Registratie Personen* – within five days of your arrival. It may take some time to make an appointment so contact the municipality as soon as possible. You will then receive your personal Citizen Service Number straight away or within a few days, by mail.

If you are not a resident of the Netherlands or will be staying here fewer than four months, you do not have to register with the BRP. However, you can opt to register with the BRP voluntarily so that you are issued a *Citizen Service Number (BSN)*. You are then registered with the RNI, or Register for Non-Residents (*Register Niet Ingezetenen*). This can come in handy if you need to arrange tax-related matters, your pension, or benefits, such as the General Old Age Pension (AOW), if you live abroad.

If your stay here extends beyond the initially intended four months, you are de-registered with the RNI, and registered as a resident. Your *BSN* stays the same. In principle, you will have this *BSN* for the rest of your life, even if you move to another country.

DISMISSAL

In this part, we will provide you with more in-depth information on the unique dismissal system of this country. There are few countries where employees enjoy as much protection against dismissal as they do in the Netherlands.

Here a short overview of the rules and regulations governing this subject.

FIXED VS. INDEFINITE CONTRACT

When explaining the rules on dismissal, a distinction should be made between an employment agreement for a fixed period of time and an employment agreement for an indefinite period of time. An employment agreement for a fixed period of time ends automatically (under certain conditions) by operation of law upon expiration of the agreed-upon period. The fixed period does not necessarily refer to a particular date. It can also be linked to the occurrence of a particular objectively assessable circumstance. For instance; the completion of a project, or the return of a sick or pregnant employee (who was being replaced).

An employment contract for an indefinite period of time is terminated by either giving notice of termination or by a dissolution decision given by the court or the UWV (Employee Insurance Agency). You can read about both procedures in the following paragraphs.

Other ways to terminate an employment agreement for a fixed period of time or an employment agreement for an indefinite period of time are: by mutual consent, during the probationary period, or through summary dismissal for 'urgent cause'. Also these will be described in more detail in the following paragraphs.

THE WORK AND SECURITY ACT

On June 10, 2014, the Dutch Senate passed the Work and Security Act (Wet Werk en Zekerheid, WWZ). Below, you will find an overview of the rules it introduced.

Probationary Period

Employment contracts may not include a probationary period if the employment contract is entered into for a period of six months or less. Any probationary period agreed upon will be deemed null and void.

Non-Compete Clause

Non-compete clauses may not be included in employment contracts for a fixed period of time (regardless of the duration), unless the employer indicates in writing in the employment contract why compelling business or operational interests require such a clause. If no written reasons are given, the clause is void. These compelling business or operational interests must still exist when the clause takes effect, i.e. on the termination date of the employment contract.

These rules apply to all employment contracts entered into on or after January 1, 2015.

Notification Obligation

There is a notification obligation for employment contracts for a fixed period of time of six months or longer. No later than one month before the employment contract for a fixed period expires, the employer must notify the employee in writing whether or not the employment contract will be extended and, if so, on what terms. If the employer does not notify the employee at all, the employee is entitled to a compensation of one month's gross salary. If the employer fails to notify the employee about the termination or extension on time, the employee is entitled to pro rata compensation. The notification obligation does not apply to employment contracts that do not end on a specific calendar date (such as a project or the replacement of a sick employee), nor to temporary agency contracts containing an assignment clause (*uitzendbeding*).

The notification period for contracts for an indefinite period of time have been discussed earlier, under Dutch Employment Law – Notice Period.

The Obligation to Continue to Pay Salary

In the absence of work, the obligation to continue to pay salary can be excluded in writing during the first 26 weeks of the employment contract. After this initial 26-week period, only if a CAO (Collective Labor Agreement) applies, this period may be extended – but only for positions which by their nature involve occasional rather than permanent work.

Main Rule 'No Work, No Pay' Reversed?

The Act also provided for the deletion of the main rule 'no work, no pay' – as in, if the employee does not work, they will not get paid. At the same time the so-called risk rule, which was an exception to this main rule, was amended. According to this risk rule, an employee retains the right to pay if they have not been able to work due to a cause which should reasonably be for the account of the employer. Although the Minister explained that no major changes were envisaged, the majority is of the opinion that, by deleting the main rule, the burden of proof will be reversed to the employer: the employer will be obligated to pay salary if the employee does not perform any work, *unless* the employer can prove that this should reasonably be for the account of the employee. Examples of such a situation might be participating in a strike, not arriving at work on time or serving a prison sentence. This part of the Act entered into force on January 1, 2020.

The Chain Rule

As mentioned earlier, the so-called chain rule stipulates that employment contracts for a fixed period of time will be converted by operation of law into indefinite employment contracts at some point in time. The maximum period for successive employment contracts for a fixed period of time is three years. The maximum number of contracts that may be concluded within this period is three. For employment contracts to be considered successive, the permitted interval between them is six months. The Act limits the possibility of deviating from the chain rule by means of a CAO; only in the case of a temporary agency contract, or if the intrinsic nature of the business operations so requires, may the maximum period for successive temporary employment contracts be extended to four years and the maximum number of temporary contracts be increased to six.

Certain categories of employees are excluded, such as employees younger than 18 years of age who, on average, do not work for more than 12 hours, and other groups to be designated by the Minister.

DISMISSAL

The Act also provided for major changes in the rules for dismissal. The most important rules are set out below.

Imperative Dismissal Route

If an employer wants to dismiss an employee for business economic reasons or due to long-term incapacity for work, the employer must apply for a dismissal permit with the UWV. If the dismissal is based on other (personal) reasons, such as unsatisfactory performance or a damaged working relationship, the employer must go to the subdistrict sector of the District Court.

Training Obligation

The employer must enable employees to take training courses required to perform their work. This obligation plays an important role for both the UWV and the court when deciding whether an employee may be dismissed or not: if the employee can be reassigned to a different, suitable position, with or without training, or if this would be the more logical course of action, dismissal will be denied. Nor may an employee whose performance is unsatisfactory be dismissed if it turns out that their underperformance is the result of the employer not complying with this obligation.

Notice Period
The time taken for proceedings before the UWV or the subdistrict sector of the District Court may be fully subtracted from the notice period provided that at least a one-month notice period remains. The Court is not required to take the notice period into account in the event of a serious culpable act or omission by the employee.

Transitional Payment
An employee is entitled to a transitional payment (*transitievergoeding*) if the employer either terminates the employment contract, gives notice to terminate or does not renew it. The employee will also be entitled to a transitional payment if they themself dissolve, terminate or do not renew the employment contract due to a serious culpable act or omission by the employer.

An employee accrues a transitional payment of 1/3rd of the monthly salary per year, or a pro-rated part thereof. The maximum statutory transitional payment will be € 94,000 gross (2024) or – in some cases – one year's salary if it exceeds € 94,000, to a maximum of € 233,000. The employer and employee may agree on higher payments in the employment contract (golden parachutes).

In the event of a serious culpable act or omission by the employer, the court may grant an extra compensation (or 'fair payment') to the employee.

The transitional payment will not be due if the employer:
- is declared insolvent
- is granted a suspension of payments, or
- is subject to debt rescheduling.

A transitional payment does not need to be paid either if the employee:
- is not yet 18 years of age and works 12 hours per week or less
- has reached retirement age, or
- is guilty of a serious culpable act or omission.

Deduction of Transitional and Employability Costs
An employer may deduct so-called transitional and employability costs from the transitional payment. Transitional costs are costs incurred in connection with terminating or not extending an employment contract. They must aim to prevent or curtail unemployment, e.g. training and outplacement costs, as well as costs for observing a notice period that is longer than what is applicable between the parties, while the employee is free to look for another job. Employability costs are costs incurred during employment and that aim at increasing employability. Costs incurred for increasing possibilities for internal reassignment, or which are directly connected with the employee's current responsibilities, may not be deducted from the transitional payment, nor may employability costs be deducted if they were incurred more than five years prior to the termination date.

An employer may only deduct transitional and employability costs with the employee's consent. That consent is not required if arrangements are made in a CAO.

Appeal
The Act also introduced the possibility of filing an appeal (or even an appeal in cassation) against a dissolution decision of the subdistrict sector of the District Court. In addition, a decision made by the UWV is open to appeal. For instance, if the UWV does not grant a dismissal permit, an employer can still appeal to the subdistrict sector of the District Court to terminate the employment contract with the employee. Should the UWV have granted a dismissal permit, it is the employee who can appeal and claim reinstatement of their employment contract.

Any claims relating to termination of the employment contract must be filed in court by means of an application (*verzoekschrift*).

TERMINATION WITHOUT THE COURT OR THE UWV

Probationary Period
During and even before the start of the probation period, either party may terminate the employment contract with immediate effect without stating any reasons. A probationary period is only valid when it has been agreed upon in writing.

Termination by Mutual Consent or Agreement
An employment contract may only be terminated without the involvement of the UWV or the subdistrict sector of the District Court if:
- the employer gives notice to terminate and the employee gives their consent, or
- a settlement agreement has been reached.

When the settlement has been reached, the employee will have two weeks to reflect and to either retract their consent or dissolve the settlement agreement. The employer must notify the employee of this statutory period of reflection and retraction in writing. If the employer fails to inform the employee in writing of this right of reflection and retraction, the reflection period will be extended to three weeks.

If the employee retracts their consent or revokes the settlement agreement, the employer must follow the imperative dismissal route or try to reach a new settlement agreement. Special rules apply with respect to managing directors.

If a settlement agreement is entered into, the employer is not obligated to pay the statutory transitional payment. Parties are free to make their own arrangements regarding whether or not a severance payment is to be paid. The employee is, however, not likely to accept an amount that is lower than the transitional payment. Please note that, if the employer gives notice to terminate the employment agreement with the consent of the employee, they are still obligated to pay a transitional payment.

Urgent Cause
Sometimes, an urgent situation can arise in which either the employer or the employee cannot reasonably be expected to continue the employment relationship. If this situation has been caused by the employee, the employer is entitled to terminate the employment agreement without notice and with immediate effect, without following the imperative dismissal route. The Dutch Civil Code gives a number of examples of what constitutes an urgent cause, such as misleading or false statements, theft, fraud, breach of trust, gross negligence, etc.

The urgent cause must be sufficiently urgent to warrant immediate and irrevocable termination and must be communicated to the employee as soon as possible, stating the exact reasons for termination, preferably in writing. In general, a delay will be regarded as evidence that the cause was not that urgent.

If the court is of the opinion that the cause was not urgent enough to justify an immediate termination, it can declare the dismissal void. Since no prior approval of either the Court or the UWV was obtained, the employee will then in principle be entitled to receive their salary as of the date of the nullified termination until the employment agreement is properly terminated.

30%-RULING

Losing your job need not have consequences for the application of the 30%-ruling in the future; if you find a new employer within three months and all other conditions for application of the ruling are still met, you will be able to apply for the ruling again and benefit from it for the remainder of the applicable period.

IMPLEMENTATION DIRECTIVE TRANSPARENT AND PREDICTABLE EMPLOYMENT CONDITIONS

As of August 1, 2022, all employers must ensure clear and predictable employment conditions. This is based on the act called Implementation Directive Transparent and Predictable Employment Conditions, and follows from a European directive.

The background of this new law is to increase transparency when it comes to employment conditions. Its aim is to lead to a more predictable work pattern for employees who mainly work on a flexible basis. The Netherlands already partially complied with the European directive, but not on all points yet.

In summary, the main changes are the following:

Repayment of Study Costs Is Limited

Study cost clauses are now subject to stricter rules. In case of compulsory trainings, e.g. training that is mandatory according to the law or a CAO (collective labor agreement) – for example in the field of safety and maintaining professional knowledge – the related costs cannot be recovered by means of a study cost clause. It has furthermore been determined that the employee in question must be given the opportunity to follow the training during working hours. A study costs clause may, however, still be agreed upon for courses that are not mandatory.

Limited Prohibition of Ancillary Activities

As of August 1, 2022, an ancillary activities clause (*nevenwerkzaamhedenbeding*) may only be agreed upon if the employer can state objective justifications for invoking this clause. Objective justifications include, but are not limited to, the protection of confidential information, prevention of conflict of interest, health and safety, or violation of the Working Hours Act. The objective justification for this clause does not have to be included in the employment contract. The justification may also be given afterwards.

Request for a More Predictable Work Pattern

Employees who work flexible hours and have been employed for at least 26 weeks, are allowed to request a more predictable work pattern once a year, provided that the employer has work for them. Employers with 10 employees or more must provide a motivated response in writing to this request within one month – 'small' employers with fewer than 10 employees are given three months to do so. If the employer does not respond or does not respond within the required time frame, the work pattern will be adjusted in accordance with the employee's request.

Extension of Information Obligation

Employers are obligated to inform employees of the essential elements of their employment relationship. This ensures the transparency and predictability of the employment conditions of the employee. The Act has extended this information obligation to include, among others:

- duration and conditions of the probationary period
- working hours
- workplace(s)
- wage components (bonus and allowances)
- procedural aspects upon the termination of employment contract
- right to training
- (paid) leave arrangement(s).

In case of 'largely unpredictable working hours', employees receive information on the number of guaranteed paid hours and the pay for the work performed in addition to those hours, as well as the days and hours when the employee may be required to perform work.

Provision of Information

All information must be in writing, either by including this information in the employment contracts or by referring to an applicable personnel manual / handbook or CAO in which this information is included. Reference can also be made to the statutory regulations.

The employee can enforce compliance through the courts and claim compensation if the employer has not provided the required information or has not provided it in time, as a direct consequence of which the employee has suffered damages.

PENSION

One of the things you will want to arrange when you come to work in the Netherlands, is your old age pension. The easiest would be for you to be able to continue participating in your existing pension scheme back home (or your former country of employment). However, for this to be without negative tax consequences, your pension scheme must 'qualify'.

QUALIFYING PENSION SCHEME

In general, foreign (non-Netherlands) pension schemes do not 'qualify' for Dutch tax purposes. However, according to Dutch law, a foreign pension scheme can be approved by the Dutch tax authorities as a qualifying pension scheme if it meets the following conditions:

- you are working in the Netherlands on a temporary basis
- you and your employer jointly file a request with the Dutch tax authorities to have the scheme deemed a qualifying scheme
- your Dutch employer has granted pension rights / entitlements to you under the foreign pension scheme
- you were already participating in the foreign pension scheme before your assignment here
- the foreign pension scheme is a common pension scheme in its country of origin
- the foreign pension scheme meets several Dutch statutory conditions for qualifying pension schemes
- the pension fund or pension insurance company is a professional insurance company in accordance with Dutch tax law.

Pension contributions you pay to a qualifying pension scheme are deductible for Dutch tax purposes and the pension contributions paid by your employer are not considered taxable wages. The pension benefits you receive at a later date will be subject to wage tax. This is called the 'rule of reversal'. If you are participating in a pension scheme arranged by a Dutch employer, then in all likelihood, it is a qualifying pension scheme.

If you contribute to a pension scheme that does not qualify, your contributions are not tax-deductible, nor are your employer's contributions considered non-taxable income. The actual pension benefit payments, however, will be tax-free.

AFTER LEAVING THE NETHERLANDS

If you leave the Netherlands and have participated in a qualifying (Netherlands or approved foreign) pension scheme, the Dutch tax authorities will impose a so-called protective tax bill (*conserverende aanslag*) on your pension rights. You will, however, not have to pay this tax bill, unless you carry out what is referred to as a 'forbidden act', which could indicate that you have made improper use of your pension insurance. An example of such an act would be commuting the pension, selling it, or using it as security. If, after ten years, you have not done any of this, or if you move back to the Netherlands, then the protective tax bill is revoked and you will not have to pay it. The protective tax bill only relates to the pension premiums for which you enjoyed a tax benefit in the Netherlands.

Where your pension payments will be taxed, depends on the applicability and contents of a tax treaty on this matter at the time of payment.

SOCIAL SECURITY

TO WHOM IS IT APPLICABLE

Those who legally reside and/or work in the Netherlands are in principle subject to the Dutch social security system. This legislation is also important for their partners and/or other members of their families, unless they are exempt under EC Regulation 883/2004 or a bilateral social security treaty (both of which you will read about further on). There are two kinds of compulsory social insurance schemes in the Netherlands; one that is applicable to the population in general (national insurance schemes) and one that is applicable to employees only (employee insurance schemes).

NATIONAL INSURANCE SCHEMES

In principle, the national insurance schemes (*volksverzekeringen*) cover all persons living or working in the Netherlands. The schemes are as follows:

General Old Age Pensions Act (AOW)
Those who are covered by the AOW are entitled to an old age pension upon reaching a certain age, which for many years was the age of 65. A legislative proposal was passed that resulted in an incremental raising of the pensionable age to 66 years and 10 months by 2023. As of 2024, the pensionable age will – to a certain degree – depend on the average life expectancy. Future recipients of the AOW will be informed five years in advance as to when they can expect to receive it.

General Surviving Relatives Act (ANW)
Those who are covered by the General Surviving Relatives Act (ANW) are entitled to a widow's, widower's or 'dependent children' benefit. The deceased spouse, partner or parent must have been insured under the ANW at the date of their death.

The amount paid out on the basis of the benefit is a percentage of the legal minimum wage – however, the actual benefit can be less since the ANW survivor's benefit is income-dependent.

Long-Term Care Act (WLZ)
This act makes a provision for those who need intensive care or supervision 24/7. For instance, elderly persons with dementia, or persons with severe mental, physical or hearing/seeing disabilities. This includes treatment and nursing in recognized institutions and nursing homes, personal care and nursing, the supply of artificial appliances, medical care, and transportation to the place of supervision or treatment. In order to receive this care, the person must be approved for it. They are then issued a so-called WLZ-*indicatie*.

The Health Insurance Act (ZVW)
Everyone who legally resides in the Netherlands and is subject to the Dutch social security system is obligated to have health insurance, to be taken out with a 'private' health insurance

company. These companies are obligated to accept everyone for the standard package, irrespective of gender, age, or health. You can choose between two types of insurance policies, or a combination of these two:

- policy in kind (*natura*): the insurance company enters into several contracts with health care suppliers and pays the insurance companies' bills directly
- restitution policy (*restitutie*): the insurant chooses the health care supplier themself, and pays the bills themself, after which they are reimbursed by the insurance company.

You can also take out 'additional' health insurance, if you want to cover more than the standard medical care. However, there is no acceptance obligation for insurance companies in the case of additional insurance.

Child Benefit Act (AKW)
In principle, this benefit (*kinderbijslag*) is for children under the age of 18. The amount of the allowance depends on the age of the child and special rules apply to children aged 16 and 17.

CONTRIBUTIONS (PAYABLE TO TAX DEPARTMENT)

Contributions for the national insurance schemes are levied on income up to € 38,110 per year (to a maximum of appr. € 10,537), together with the income tax. The percentages are:

	EMPLOYER	EMPLOYEE
AOW	-	17.90%
ANW	-	0.10%
AKW	-	-
WLZ (formerly AWBZ)	-	9.65%
ZVW	6.57%	

Note: the income-dependent contribution for the zvw is levied on the employee, but compensated by the employer on a maximum income of € 71,624. Self-employed persons and retirees pay an income-dependent percentage of 5.32, which is not compensated.

The zvw (Health Insurance Act) is financed by means of a nominal premium per person of approximately € 1,800 on average per year (depending on the insurance company) and an income-dependent contribution. If you are an employee, your income-dependent contribution (5.32%) will be compensated by your employer. If you are self-employed or unemployed, you will receive no such compensation. Also if you receive an old-age pension or a benefit, you will pay an income-dependent contribution. Whether or not this is compensated, depends on your pension plan / social security institution. If your income lies below a certain level, you can request the government for financial assistance to help pay your insurance premiums (referred to as the *zorgtoeslag*). Children are covered by the basic insurance, free of charge, till the age of 18.

EMPLOYEE INSURANCE SCHEMES

In principle, anyone employed in the Netherlands is compulsorily insured under the employee insurance schemes (*werknemersverzekeringen*). If the total of any of the first three benefits and any other family income is less than the statutory social minimum income, the recipient is entitled to apply to the Social Security Institution for one, or all, of the supplements under the Supplemental Benefits Act (*Toeslagenwet*), which are paid out specifically to help finance rent, health care insurance premiums, daycare for the children of working parents, and general expenses related to having children.

The schemes are as follows:

Sickness Benefits Act (ZW) / WULBZ / WVLBZ
Pursuant to the WULBZ (*Wet Uitbreiding Loondoorbetalingsplicht bij Ziekte* – Continuation of Wage Payments during Sickness Act) and the WVLBZ (*Wet Verlenging Loondoorbetalingsplicht bij Ziekte* – Prolongation of Continuation of Wage Payments during Sickness Act), an employer is obligated to continue paying 70% (up to a maximum of 70% of € 274.44 gross per social security day – the so-called daily wage, for 2024) of the employee's salary during the first 104 weeks of sickness, provided the employee is subject to the Dutch social security system or has a contract that is governed by the Dutch civil code. Depending on the employer, this payment is capped or can even be 100% of the employee's last-earned salary.

The Sickness Benefits Act (ZW) will only provide a 'safety net' for certain categories of employees, such as employees who do not – or no longer – have an employer (for example temporary workers), and employees who have taken out a voluntary ZW-insurance. Sick pay is usually 70% of the daily wage and is paid out until the employee has been on sick leave for a maximum of 104 weeks.

Female employees are given at least 16 weeks' leave in the event of pregnancy, during which period a pregnancy benefit is paid out by the Social Security Institution (you can read more about this on page 209). The benefit is then 100% of the so-called daily wage, although in practice the employers often pay out the gap between this daily wage and their last-earned salary.

Work and Income According to Labor Capacity Act (WIA)
The WIA applies to all employees who have been disabled for work for more than 104 weeks. The aim of this act is to stimulate 'ability' for work and to make a clear distinction between long-term disability for work (no recovery within five years), temporary complete disability (80-100%) and partial disability for work (35-80%). Before an employee qualifies for the WIA-benefit, it will have to be determined whether both employer and employee have put enough effort into reintegrating the employee back into the labor process. In the case of complete and permanent disability, this will not be necessary, and the employee will have a right to an IVA-benefit (benefit for fully disabled persons), amounting to 75% of the most recent (maximum) daily wage. Those who are less than 80% but more than 35% disabled, have a right to the WGA-benefit (Reintegration Act Partially Disabled Persons). This benefit is at first a salary-related benefit, the duration of which depends on the employment history of the employee in question. At the end of this period, the employee receives either a supplementary allowance or a follow-up allowance. An employee who works and earns at least half of their residual earning capacity (*restverdiencapaciteit*) is entitled to 70% of their WIA monthly wage minus 70% of the amount the employee could earn, or the amount actually earned if they fulfilled 100% of their residual earning capacity. However, an employee who earns less than half their residual

earning capacity is entitled to a follow-up allowance of 70% of the legal minimum wage multiplied by a factor that is determined by the percentage of their occupational disability. In principle, the employee is entitled to one of these allowances until they reach retirement age.

Disability Insurance Act (WAO)
The WAO will continue to apply to employees who were already receiving the WAO-benefit on January 1, 2006. It entitles employees under the pensionable age to a benefit if they are still at least 15% unfit for work after 52 weeks of disability. The amount of the benefit depends on the kind of benefit, the degree of disability, the last-earned wage and the age of the employee.

Unemployment Insurance Act (WW)
The WW insures employees against the financial consequences of unemployment. There are a few requirements that they must meet to be entitled to a WW-benefit. they must:

- have been insured against unemployment, which is generally the case if they have worked in employment
- have been employed for a period of at least 26 weeks over the 36 weeks immediately prior to becoming unemployed ('week requirement')
- have worked at least 208 hours during 4 of the 5 preceding years ('year requirement')
- have worked an average of at least 10 hours a week and lost at least 5 of these hours (of fewer hours, but lost at least 50% of these hours)
- not to be held accountable for losing their job
- immediately be available for another paid job.

If only the first requirement is met, the employee will receive 75% of the last-earned wage (with a maximum of 75% of € 274.44 gross per social security day – i.e. the maximum daily wage for 2024) during the first two months. During the third month, they will receive 70% of the (maximum) daily wage. If both requirements are met, they will receive – in addition to this three-month benefit – a salary-related benefit of 70% of the (maximum) daily wage. The duration of the salary-related benefit depends on the employee's employment record, but can, in total, not exceed 24 months. This can be arranged differently in a collective labor agreement (CAO) and extended to 38 months.

CONTRIBUTIONS

	EMPLOYER	EMPLOYEE
WAO/WIA basis	6.18 (low) 7.54 (high)	-
WAO/WIA differentiated*		
WW general	2.64% (low) 7.64% (high)	-
WW differentiated*		-

* = these percentages vary per company

Contributions for the employee insurance schemes are levied on wages and salaries up to € 71,624.

Perhaps you have heard of it, perhaps you haven't: DigiD. DigiD is your digital identity, consisting of a username and password, which allows you to make use of the electronic services of several government institutions and organizations. Some organizations link your DigiD to the use of a so-called sms code; a code that is sent as a text message to your mobile phone, as an extra safety measure before you can go online to secure sites. You have to set this up on the DigiD website. You use the DigiD, for instance, to file your online tax return, arrange the Child Benefit, order municipal documents online, but also to make an appointment for your driver's exam or to obtain insight into year health care insurance expenditures, register at a university, etc. You are not required to have a DigiD, as most services can still be arranged by telephone or letter – it is merely a way of making it possible for you to take care of certain matters online.

To obtain your personal DigiD, you must make sure you are registered with the municipality you live in. Then you visit www.digid.nl, where you fill in your *burgerservicenummer* (see page 78), date of birth, postal code, house number, mobile phone number and e-mail address. Five days after you do this, you will receive your activation code by mail, which you must use within 20 days. This will allow you to make use of the DigiD app as well.

CONTRIBUTIONS (PAYABLE TO TAX DEPARTMENT)

The contributions for both the national insurance schemes and the employee insurance schemes are levied by the tax department, together with the wage tax.

'DOUBLE' SOCIAL INSURANCES

ANOTHER EU MEMBER STATE

Dutch Social Security
An employee who starts working in the Netherlands is, in principle, subject to the Dutch social security legislation. One of the exceptions to this main rule applies if they have been posted from another EU or EEA (European Economic Area) member state or Switzerland. In the following sections this exception will be discussed in more detail.

Period Shorter than Six Months
Special rules apply to non-residents who carry out work in the Netherlands for a period shorter than six months; they will under certain conditions not be subject to the employee insurance schemes. However, if the income earned in the Netherlands is subject to wage tax here, and the duties are in fact carried out in the Netherlands, they will nevertheless be subject to the national insurance schemes.

Continued Social Security
In May 1, 2010, EC Regulation 1408/71 was replaced by EC Regulation 883/2004.

It is important to note that the provisions of Regulation 1408/71 will continue to apply to non-EU nationals, as the new regulation will only apply to them once the EU Member States have agreed to enlarge the scope of application to this effect. The provisions of Regulation 883/2004, however, also apply to nationals of Norway, Iceland, Liechtenstein and Switzerland.

Assignments
Under Regulation 1408/71, the period during which an employee was eligible for the continuation of the social security scheme of their country of residence while they were on assignment abroad was equal to 12 months with the option of prolonging the secondment with another period of 12 months – provided the host country gave prior approval. Under Regulation 883/2004 this period has been extended to 24 months. This means that the application for a 24 month-assignment will no longer require the intervention of the social security authorities of the host country.

The main conditions for assignment remain unchanged, being:

- the employee is covered by the social security schemes of a member state
- the employee remains in the employment of the company that has assigned them
- the anticipated duration of the assignment does not exceed 24 months
- the employee is not assigned to replace another employee who has completed their maximum term of assignment
- the Dutch company to which the employee is temporarily assigned will not subsequently assign them to work for another company
- the employer usually carries out work on the territory of the assigning state.

If the above conditions are satisfied, the social security legislation of the first member state will remain applicable.

Simultaneous Employment
Under Regulation 883/2004, an employee will only be subject to the social security scheme of their country of residence, in a similar situation, provided they carry out a *substantial* part of their activities in the country of residence. 'Substantial' activities are defined as 25% or more of the working time, remuneration or turnover. This definition could change the social security situation of a number of mobile employees who are working in several countries and who are currently subject to the social security scheme of their country of residence.

In addition, under the new regime, the so-called 'Annex VII situations', whereby an employee may – by way of exception – be subject to two different social security schemes, has been abolished. Anyone who works as an employee as well as a self-employed person in several countries at the same time, will automatically be subject to the social security scheme of the state in which they work as an employee.

Benefits
Specific changes have also been introduced for a number of social security benefits. For instance, the exportation of unemployment benefits is now possible during a period of six months instead of the three months under Regulation 1408/71.

Exceptions
Both Regulations also contain a general exception (article 17 of EC Regulation 1408/71 and article 16 of EC Regulation 883/2004) that can be invoked in those cases in which it is in the interest of the employee to deviate from the mandatory allocation rules, for instance, when it is already clear beforehand that the duration of the assignment will exceed 24 (12) months. In the event of such a request, the two member states concerned will conduct negotiations and, if the request is granted, will reach an agreement. Requests to continue the application of the foreign social security legislation under this provision are generally granted when the anticipated duration of the assignment does not exceed five years. Extensions beyond the five-year period are only very exceptionally allowed.

Certificate
An A1 certificate is issued in order to make clear in which country social security contributions are to be paid. In order to actually receive medical care (ZVW or WLZ) in the Netherlands, in addition to the certificate, a European Health Insurance Card is needed. This is issued by the competent authorities abroad and enables the employee to register with a health insurance company in their country of residence. This is of particular importance if medical care cannot be delayed.

ANOTHER TREATY MEMBER STATE

Social Security Treaty
If a person is assigned from abroad to the Netherlands and the Netherlands has entered into a social security treaty with that other country, the applicable legislation will be determined in accordance with the allocation rules of this treaty. It should first be determined whether the person is covered by the scope of the treaty. For this to be the case, it is generally required that the employee is a national of one of the treaty states and/or was insured in one of the states before being assigned abroad.

Temporary Assignment
If the assignment is temporary, most treaties allow the continuation of the application of the legislation of the country from which the employee has been assigned.

Conditions
The conditions that must be satisfied may vary slightly from one treaty to another, but will generally comprise the following:

- before being assigned abroad, the employee was insured according to the social security legislation of the country from which they are being assigned
- the employment with the company in the country from which the person is assigned is continued.

Period
The period during which the posting is allowed to continue varies from 12 months to an unlimited period (depending on the treaty) and extension is sometimes possible (also depending on the treaty).

Certificate
It is advisable to apply for a certificate stating which legislation is applicable. In some treaty member states, having this certificate is one of the conditions for assigning an employee abroad.

General Rule
If the conditions are not satisfied, the general rule of the relevant treaty takes effect. In all treaties, the general rule is that the Dutch social security legislation is applicable if the work is carried out in the Netherlands. Nearly all treaties prevent the simultaneous applicability of the legislation of two countries.

A NON-TREATY MEMBER STATE
Exemption not Possible
If a person is assigned from a country with which the Netherlands has not entered into a social security treaty, it is – in general – not possible to obtain an exemption from the Dutch social insurances. As there is no applicable treaty, it is possible that the employee, pursuant to the applicable national social security laws, will have to participate in the social security systems of both countries. This may result both in double liability to pay contributions and double entitlement to benefits.

STARTING YOUR OWN COMPANY

Maybe you came to the Netherlands for the purpose of starting your own company. Or maybe you came here with your spouse / partner – who was assigned here by their employer – and want to generate an income of your own. In either case, you are considering setting up (your own) business in the Netherlands. What are some of the things you have to think of? And who can help you answer the many questions you will have? What diplomas do you need?

There are various organizations that you can turn to for help.

CHAMBERS OF COMMERCE
The Netherlands is divided into five regional Chambers of Commerce (Kamers van Koophandel) regions, with several Chambers of Commerce under them, which represent the economic interests of the businesses and entrepreneurs in their region. One of their main tasks is to register (practically) all companies based in the Netherlands, whether they are of Dutch or foreign origin. Public and private limited companies, cooperative societies, mutual guarantee associations, sole traders, partnerships and homeowners associations are obligated to register with the Chamber of Commerce of the district in which they are established, even if they do not carry out a business. Private persons who work on a free-lance basis and persons who carry out one of the professions specified on the professions list of the Chamber of Commerce, are also obligated to register. The purpose of this registration is to enable third parties to find information on a company – such as who is liable, who can make binding commitments; in other words, the legal structure of a company. The system has been proven to be reliable, transparent and up-to-date.

The Chamber of Commerce is a public institution and the information desk can provide you with information on how to start a business, which diplomas you need for your specific line of business, how to write a business plan to be able to finance your ideas and what (zoning) plans your municipality has within the area in which you want to establish your firm.

MKB-NEDERLAND
Another institution you can turn to for information is MKB-Nederland (Instituut voor Midden- en Kleinbedrijf), an organization that represents the interests of small and medium-sized companies. Various activities are initiated by this institute, aimed at offering its members relevant knowledge and expertise as well as at improving the general position of small and medium-sized companies. You will find its address and telephone number at the end of the chapter.

OTHER INSTITUTIONS
Other institutions that can offer you advice are banks and the national tax office. Both have information desks for people who plan to start their own business and can provide you with the information you need. And last, but not least, all major cities have a business desk at the town hall.

PROOF OF IDENTITY
When you start a business or are given authorization to take responsibility in a business, for example as a private entrepreneur or as director or partner, proof of identity will be required when registering with the trade register. At the counter of the Chamber of Commerce, valid proof of identity together with an original private bank statement or an original extract from the population register (not older than one month) should be presented.

The following documents are accepted as valid proof of identity:
- a valid travel document (Dutch or foreign passport, European identity card)
- a valid Dutch driver's license (a foreign driver's license will not be accepted)
- a residence permit issued by the Dutch aliens police
- a Dutch refugee passport
- a Dutch aliens passport.

SETTING UP ESTABLISHMENT
The Dutch policy of free enterprise entails that there are no specific restrictions for foreign companies who wish to start a business in the Netherlands, nor are there restrictions on the ownership of real estate or on the remission of capital and profits abroad.

There are various ways in which (foreign) companies can set up permanent establishment in the Netherlands. The Dutch legal system provides a framework with various options, which are described briefly in this section:
- branch office
- *eenmanszaak*: a 'one-man' business
- *maatschap*: partnership – business involving more than one person, usually used by accountants, doctors, etc.
- *vennootschap onder firma* (VOF): general or commercial partnership – business involving more than one person, under a common name, each severally liable

- *commanditaire vennootschap* (CV): limited partnership with managing and 'silent' partners
- *besloten vennootschap* (BV): private company with limited liability
- *naamloze vennootschap* (NV): (public) corporation.

BRANCH OFFICE

A foreign company does not require any prior approval from the Dutch authorities to establish a branch office in the Netherlands. It does have to file various details (i.e. name, trade name, objects, manager) and documents (i.e. articles of association) pertaining to the company and the branch office with the Chamber of Commerce. The local manager of the branch office does not have to be of Dutch nationality. Insofar as the obligation to publish the annual report and accounts also applies under the law of the country of formation of the foreign company, these should be filed with the Dutch Chamber of Commerce as well.

PARTNERSHIP

Under Dutch law it is possible to set up a partnership with two or more partners: the general partnership ('VOF' or *vennootschap onder firma*) and the limited partnership ('CV' or *commanditaire vennootschap*). The basic difference between these two forms of partnership is the partners' liabilities. A limited partnership has one or more managing partners (*beherende vennoten*) and one or more 'silent' partners (*commanditaire vennoten*). The liability of the 'silent' partners is limited to the amount of their capital contributions. Each partner in a general partnership is, in addition to the partnership itself, severally liable for the obligations of the company. Under Dutch law, a partnership is similar to a business under single proprietorship, except that there are two or more owners.

COMPANIES WITH LIMITED LIABILITY

In the Netherlands, corporate law defines two different types of companies with limited liability: the NV (*naamloze vennootschap*), which is a public company with limited liability, and the BV (*besloten vennootschap*), which is a private company with limited liability. The main differences between the two types of companies are:

- the shares in the NV can be either in bearer or in registered form; the shares in the BV are in registered form only
- the minimum issued and paid-up capital of the NV is € 45,000; there is no minimum capital for BVs
- the Articles of Association of a BV must include restrictions for the transfer of its shares; such restrictions are optional for the NV
- the legal limitations regarding the company's purchase of shares in its own capital and regarding financial assistance by the company are stricter for an NV than for a BV
- the BV form is particularly suitable for a wholly owned subsidiary, joint venture companies and family businesses. The NV is suitable for larger companies whose shares may be listed.

Ask your accountant, legal or financial advisor or the Chamber of Commerce about the legal and fiscal consequences of the above forms.

TAXES SELF-EMPLOYED PERSONS

If you run your own business you can be held liable for the following:

- wage tax
- income tax
- national insurance schemes (which includes contributions towards health insurance)
- employee insurance schemes (if you have employees)
- VAT (value added tax).

Self-employed persons who have only themselves to think of owe income tax, VAT, and must arrange their own medical insurance, for which they, as does everyone else, owe a fixed contribution and an income-dependent contribution. If their income (if they have a partner for tax purposes; together with their partner) lies below a certain level, they can apply for government assistance in paying for this insurance, called the *zorgtoeslag*. You can read more about this insurance on page 82 and on page 141. Enlisting the services of an accountant will help you benefit from the many deductions that apply to you.

VAT

Those who deliver services and goods in the Netherlands are obligated to charge their customers VAT (*Belasting Toegevoegde Waarde* or BTW), which they subsequently pay to the tax authorities. The general VAT rates are 21% and 9%. They owe this, no matter whether they (aim to) make a profit or not, the moment an invoice is sent out. To the delivery of goods and services outside the Netherlands, other rules apply.

However, the amount of VAT that you have paid to others who deliver their goods and services to you, can be deducted from the amount of VAT you owe. Those whose 'VAT income' does not exceed a certain amount enjoy a full or limited exemption from paying the amount due to the tax authorities.

The amount of VAT due should be reported on the *Aangifte omzetbelasting*, or Turnover Tax Return, on a regular basis (monthly, quarterly or yearly). This is done online, by means of the so-called electronic, or *elektronische*, Tax Return. The tax authorities issue you a username and a password to do this.

DBA

On February 2, 2016, the First Chamber adopted the Deregulation Labor Relations Assessment Law (Wet deregulering beoordeling arbeidsrelaties – DBA).

Although the DBA law has entered into force, its enforcement has been postponed. The tax authorities will only enforce this law in the case of so-called seriously malicious persons (*kwaadwillenden*), being persons who work with the intent to commit fraud or to swindle – involving cunning, forgery or conspiracy – and to create situations that lead to serious distortions of competition, economic or social disruption, or exploitation. As of July 1, 2018, this notion of serious malicious persons has been extended to include malicious persons who intentionally create or continue a situation of obvious false self-employment (*evidente schijnzelfstandigheid*). The Tax Authorities will then take action if the following three criteria are met:

- there is a (fictitious) employment relationship
- there is obvious false self-employment
- there is intentional false self-employment.

FINANCIAL AID AND DEDUCTIONS

The national tax office can tell you about the Tante Agaath-regulation, a scheme that makes it fiscally attractive for private persons to lend money to those who are setting up a business. Of course, you can approach a bank and see what they can do to help you, too.

When it comes to income tax, entrepreneurs enjoy an additional deduction, over and above the levy rebate that every taxpayer has a right to every year, of € 3,750 (2024), irrespective of the actual profits – though it may not exceed the profits (this will be reduced gradually, until it reaches € 900 in 2027). To this purpose you must prove that you spent at least 1,225 hours over the past tax year working for your own business (if your spouse works for the same company there are additional rules and possible deductions). Those who are starting up a new business (*startende ondernemers*) have a further deduction, subject to certain conditions, over the first few years of € 2,123. If you are disabled for work and start your own company, you enjoy a generous tax deduction during three of the first five years – subject to certain conditions that you can find on the website of the tax authorities. Furthermore, tax credits are available for investments made in cultural investment funds, green funds and socio-ethical funds.

DIPLOMAS / PERMITS

Depending on the type of business you want to start, there are a number of diplomas you might need. For most types of businesses, however, no diploma is required. Furthermore, some businesses are subject to a zoning plan, or require a building, environmental or establishment permit. Before you start your business, you must make sure you obtain the required permits and/or diplomas, for instance by contacting your municipality.

You can ask at the Chamber of Commerce as to what specific (type of) diploma you will need and how or where you can obtain this. If you have obtained a diploma in another country, this diploma can be evaluated by IDW (see the end of the chapter), to see whether it qualifies.

FREE-LANCING

There are two ways you can go about free-lancing; either as a self-employed person or through an intermediary agency. In the first case, you can read about some of the rules that apply to you in these paragraphs; in the latter case, you are, in principle, treated as an employee of the intermediary agency for tax purposes – you can read more about working for an employment agency in the first paragraphs of this chapter.

PERMITS AND CITIZEN SERVICE NUMBER

Note: Every natural person who wants to work in the Netherlands, whether in employment or self-employment, needs to comply with the Dutch entrance requirements set (if they apply to you – for instance, based on nationality) and must have a Citizen Service Number (*burgerservicenummer*); see page 78 (for Citizen Service Number) and page 127 (for permits). Note that you do not need a work permit to work here in self-employment.

At Work: Egalitarianism and Compromise

EGALITARIANISM

If you were to hear or read an interview with a Dutch captain of industry, you might be surprised to hear them downplay any central role they might have played in the company's success. they would declare themself a team player and would praise the creativity that is found throughout the company. They would accentuate the fact that all involved carried out the task as a team and that they would of course have accomplished nothing were it not for the energetic input and output of everyone. They would not sell themself as the genius with all the ideas but would describe themself as the coordinator, even if all involved realized deep in their hearts that, without their leadership, the stock value of the company would have long since plummeted.

This all has to do with the great appreciation that the Dutch have for egalitarianism, and their general resistance to being told what to do without any preliminary discussion. And of course, their undeniable need to seek compromise whenever possible. But that's not all. Their ingrained inclination to respect another person will not allow them to give out orders and commands. Conversely, the modern Dutchman likes to 'recognize themself' (their input) – as they put it – in any decision made. In other words, they expect to be involved in the decision-making. If ministers or CEOs choose to keep a low profile, then this is purely a matter of strategy and tact.

Foreigners who work with Dutch companies – either as a customer or as an employee – are often confused by this egalitarianism. They are amazed at the informality between those who occupy the various rungs on the corporate ladder. Secretaries are on a first-name basis with their bosses. There is little evidence of hierarchy. Even the managers' offices are soberly decorated and visitors are given a modest welcome. It is perfectly normal for the company CEO to stand in line for lunch with the other employees in the company cafeteria – with the visitor right next to him. This does not mean that this visitor is not an honored one, and it gives no indication whatsoever of whether this visit is appreciated. This will only become evident from the meetings themselves and the agreements reached.

COMPROMISE – OVERLEG

Those who work in the Netherlands are often under the impression that a lot of time is wasted on discussions and that these discussions all lead to nothing. There are often meetings, commonly named *overleg* (consultation, or deliberation), with documents, an agenda and a chairman. All those present have their say, after which their remarks are discussed. And all this can be done quite eloquently. At the end, everyone pulls out their *agenda* (calendar), to schedule the next meeting.

They who decide to skip an *overleg* because they have something more urgent to attend to, will soon learn that this is not a wise decision – even if their colleagues were to admit readily that there is much too much *overleg* going on. The interacting that takes place during such a meeting is very important for the general progress. They who do not appear are saying that they do not think that the subject is sufficiently important or, even worse, that they apparently do not take their colleagues seriously. Furthermore, they run the risk of missing essential information that may become evident during the meeting.

Those who are present during *overleg* show an interest in the problems of their colleagues. They supply suggestions, rather than amendments or commands, and thus declare themselves 'co-responsible'. The Dutch, in their final conclusions, like to use such metaphors as: 'we are all in one line'. Or even: 'our noses are pointing in the same direction again'. Ambitious beginners can also obtain useful information during an *overleg*: for instance, on what the pecking order is within the company.

As the Dutch only consider an idea to be partly theirs if they have been able to exercise influence on it and have been allowed to join the thinking process, it is advisable to take this into account when making plans. When you present a sharply chiseled decision, you will find that everyone has something to say about it and has questions to ask. This is why the Dutch will not be quick to present something as the only, the correct and the true solution. The advantage to this approach is that such an *overleg* will often lead to genuinely valuable suggestions for the improvement of certain aspects of a plan. As a result, the plan will be a joint approach and you will be able to count on everyone's cooperation.

This time-consuming and seemingly useless process of *overleg* helps colleagues become a team. The amount of time that is lost around the table is more than made up for in efficiency and input once everyone goes back to work. Statistics clearly show this. Dutch employees are among the world's leaders when it comes to work productivity.

HARMONIOUS RELATIONSHIPS

You will find this attitude not only on a smaller scale, but also on a larger scale. Dutch business life is generally characterized by harmonious relationships. This is evident from the works council that companies are obligated by law to have and that is elected from and by the employees. Though this council does not have a lot of authority and cannot do much more than advise management, management has the obligation to consult it in many situations, such as reorganizations or large investment plans. The relationship between employer organizations and unions is also very harmonious, therefore employees seldom go on strike in the Netherlands. The worst that could happen is that, in the case of wage negotiations, one of the parties involved leaves the negotiation table. Then, after a small concession has been made, the *overleg* will simply resume.

References

CHAPTER 3
Working in the Netherlands

Social Security

MINISTERIE VAN SOCIALE ZAKEN EN WERKGELEGENHEID
Ministry of Social Affairs and Employment
Anna van Hannoverstraat 4,
2595 BJ The Hague
Tel.: 070 333 44 44
www.rijksoverheid.nl

DE SOCIAAL ECONOMISCHE RAAD (SER)
The Social and Economic Council of the Netherlands
Bezuidenhoutseweg 60, 2594 AW The Hague
Tel.: 070 349 94 99
www.ser.nl

SOCIALE VERZEKERINGSBANK
Social Insurance Bank
Rhijnspoorplein 1, 1091 HG Amsterdam
Tel.: 020 656 52 01
www.svb.nl

UWV
www.uwv.nl

Immigration/Permits

IMMIGRATIE EN NATURALISATIE DIENST (IND)
Immigration and Naturalization Service
Tel.: 0900 123 45 61
www.ind.nl

MINISTERIE VAN BUITENLANDSE ZAKEN
Ministry of Foreign Affairs
Bezuidenhoutseweg 67, 2594 AC The Hague
Tel.: 070 348 64 86
www.government.nl/ministries/ministry-of-foreign-affairs

NEW IN THE NETHERLANDS
The official website of the Netherlands on immigration: www.government.nl/topics/new-in-the-netherlands

WORK PERMITS
www.workpermit.com/netherlands

Taxes

GENERAL
In Dutch, English and German:
www.belastingdienst.nl

INTERNATIONAL TAX OFFICE HEERLEN
Postal address: P.O. Box 2865, 6401 DJ Heerlen
Visiting address: Kloosterweg 22,
6412 CN Heerlen (by appointment only)
Tel.: 0800 05 43 (National telephone number)

DUTCH CUSTOMS (DOUANE)
P.O. Box 4486, 6401 CZ Heerlen
Tel.: 045 574 27 00
www.belastingdienst.nl and www.douane.nl

Business Organizations

BUSINESS.GOV.NL
Government support for entrepreneurs
Business.gov.nl is the go-to website for finding all the information you need on starting a business in the Netherlands
www.business.gov.nl

MKB-NEDERLAND
Institute for small and medium-sized companies
Brassersplein 1, 2612 CT Delft
Tel.: 015 219 12 12
www.mkb.nl

FENEDEX
Non-governmental export network
Raamweg 14, 2596 HL The Hague
Tel.: 070 330 56 00
www.fenedex.nl

Major Netherlands Chambers of Commerce

KAMER VAN KOOPHANDEL AMSTERDAM
Amsterdam Chamber of Commerce
De Ruyterkade 5, 1013 AA Amsterdam
Tel.: 020 531 40 00
Team International Trade Information
Tel.: 020 531 44 39
www.kvk.nl/english

KAMER VAN KOOPHANDEL ROTTERDAM
Rotterdam Chamber of Commerce
Blaak 40, 3000 AL Rotterdam
Tel.: 088 585 1585
www.kvk.nl/english

KAMER VAN KOOPHANDEL DEN HAAG
The Hague Chamber of Commerce
Koninginnegracht 13, 2514 AA The Hague
Tel.: 088 585 15 85
www.kvk.nl/english

KAMER VAN KOOPHANDEL UTRECHT
Utrecht Chamber of Commerce
Sint Jacobsstraat 300, 3511 BT Utrecht
Tel.: 088 585 1585
www.kvk.nl/english

KAMER VAN KOOPHANDEL EINDHOVEN
Eindhoven Chamber of Commerce
J. F. Kennedylaan 2, 5612 AB Eindhoven
Tel.: 088 585 1585
www.kvk.nl/english

KAMER VAN KOOPHANDEL GRONINGEN
Groningen Chamber of Commerce
Leonard Springerlaan 15, 9727 KB Groningen
Tel.: 088 585 1585
www.kvk.nl/english

International Chambers of Commerce

INT. CHAMBER OF COMMERCE (ICC)
Bezuidenhoutseweg 12, 2594 AV The Hague
www.iccwbo.org

AMERICAN CHAMBER OF COMMERCE IN THE NETHERLANDS
P.O. Box 15783, 1001 NG Amsterdam
Tel.: 020 7951840
www.amcham.nl

ITALIAN CHAMBER OF COMMERCE
De Ruyterkade 5, 1013 AA Amsterdam
Tel.: 020 751 33 63
www.italianchamber.nl

JAPANESE CHAMBER OF COMMERCE
World Trade Center 8-9, Strawinskylaan 935, 1077 XX Amsterdam
Tel.: 020 662 14 57
www.jcc-holland.nl

NETHERLANDS BRITISH CHAMBER OF COMMERCE
Benoordenhoutseweg 21-23,
2596 BA The Hague
Tel.: 070 205 56 56
www.nbcc.co.uk

NETHERLANDS CANADIAN CHAMBER OF COMMERCE
Wilhelminastraat 184 HS, 1054 WT Amsterdam
Tel.: 070 2210 555
www.nccc.trade

CHAMBER OF COMMERCE NETHERLANDS ISRAEL
www. israel-netherlands.com

NETHERLANDS GERMAN CHAMBER OF COMMERCE
Nassauplein 30, 2585 EC The Hague
Tel.: 070 311 41 36 – www.dnhk.org

NETHERLANDS FRANCE CHAMBER OF COMMERCE
Hogehilweg 16, 1101 CD Amsterdam
Tel.: 020 562 82 00
www.cfci.nl

NETHERLANDS SOUTH AFRICAN CHAMBER OF COMMERCE
Pr. Beatrixlaan 582, 2595 BM The Hague
Tel.: 070 347 07 81
www.sanec.org

World Trade Centers

World Trade Center Business Club:
www.wtcamsterdambusinessclub.com
World Trade Center Amsterdam:
www.wtcamsterdam.nl
World Trade Center Almere: www.wtcaa.nl
World Trade Center Schiphol Airport:
www.wtcschiphol.nl
World Trade Center Rotterdam:
www.wtcrotterdam.nl
World Trade Center The Hague:
www.wtcthehague.com

Regional Information Centers

AMSTERDAM IN BUSINESS
World Trade Center Amsterdam
I-Tower, ground floor (entrance via Zuidplein)
Strawinskylaan 1767
1077 XX Amsterdam
www.iamsterdam.com/en/business

AMSTERDAM AIRPORT AREA
P.O. Box 75700, 1118 ZT Schiphol Airport
Tel.: 020 405 47 77
E-mail: Info@aaarea.nl
www.aaarea.nl

THE HAGUE BUSINESS AGENCY
Prinses Margrietplantsoen 35,
2595 AM The Hague
Tel.: 070 311 55 55
www.businessagency.thehague.com

THE HAGUE INTERNATIONAL CENTRE
The Hague City Hall (Atrium) Spui 70,
2511 BT The Hague
Tel.: 070 353 50 43
www.thehagueinternationalcentre.nl

ROTTERDAM EXPAT CENTRE
Korte Hoogstraat 31, 3011 GK Rotterdam
Tel.: 010 790 01 90
www.rotterdamexpatcentre.nl

EXPAT CENTER LEIDEN
Stationsweg 41, 2312 AT Leiden
Tel.: 071 516 60 05
www.expatcenterleiden.nl

LEIDEN BIO SCIENCE PARK
Poortgebouw Noord
Rijnsburgerweg 10, 2333 AA Leiden
Tel.: 071 524 75 53
www.leidenbiosciencepark.nl

PROVINCE OF UTRECHT – INVEST UTRECHT
Archimedeslaan 6, 3584 BA Utrecht
Tel.: 030 258 90 12
www.investinutrecht.com

INTERNATIONAL WELCOME CENTRE UTRECHT REGION
Utrecht City Hall
Stadsplateau 1, second floor
3521 AZ Utrecht
Tel.: 030 286 58 20
www.welcome.utrechtregion.com/en

BOM FOREIGN INVESTMENTS
Goirlese Weg 15, 5026 PB Tilburg
Tel.: 088 831 11 20
www.foreigninvestments.eu

BRAINPORT DEVELOPMENT
Emmasingel 11, 5611 AZ Eindhoven
Tel.: 040 751 24 24
www.brainport.nl

HIGH TECH CAMPUS EINDHOVEN
High Tech Campus 1, The Strip,
5656 AE Eindhoven
Tel.: 040 230 55 00
www.hightechcampus.com

HOLLAND EXPATCENTER SOUTH
Vestdijk 27a, Eindhoven
Tel.: 040 238 67 77
Mosae Forum 10, Maastricht
Tel.: 043 350 50 10
Stadhuisplein 128, Tilburg
Tel.: 040 238 67 77
www.hollandexpatcenter.com

ONTWIKKELINGS MAATSCHAPPIJ OOST NEDERLAND NV
Meander 601, 8625 ME Arnhem
Tel.: 026 384 42 22
Hengelosestraat 585, 7521 AG Enschede
Tel.: 053 851 68 51

LIMBURGSE ONTWIKKELINGS MAATSCHAPPIJ (LIOF)
Boschstraat 766211 AX Maastricht
Tel.: 043 328 02 80 – www.liof.com

Trade and Investment

INVEST IN HOLLAND
Prinses Beatrixlaan 2, 2595 AL The Hague
Tel.: 088 602 80 60
www.investinholland.com

Business Clubs

THE AMSTERDAM AMERICAN BUSINESS CLUB
A professional networking organization for Dutch and American companies around Amsterdam
Keizersgracht 62-64, 1015 CS Amsterdam
Tel.: 020 520 75 34 – www.aabc.nl

CLUB OF AMSTERDAM
An independent, international, future-oriented think tank involved in channeling preferred futures
www.clubofamsterdam.com

COMMERCIAL ANGLO DUTCH SOCIETY
Provides an informal meeting point for Dutch and British professionals
http://cads-amsterdam.org

WTC THE HAGUE INTERNATIONAL BUSINESS CLUB
Prinses Margrietplantsoen 33,
2595 AM The Hague
Tel.: 070 304 36 65
www.wtcthehague.com

CONNECTING WOMEN (THE HAGUE)
A network of professional internationally aware women.
Koninginnegracht 28, 2514 AB The Hague
www.connectingwomen.nl

WOMEN'S BUSINESS INITIATIVE INTERNATIONAL
A community of entrepeneurial women.
Lange Voorhout 12, 2514 ED The Hague
www.womensbusinessinitiative.net

WOMEN'S INTERNATIONAL NETWORK (WIN)
The international networking association for professional women in the Netherlands
www.winconference.net

Volunteer Work

ACCESS ARE ALWAYS LOOKING FOR NEW VOLUNTEERS
Visit their website for information on the monthly Info Mornings
www.access-nl.org

Recruitment Agencies for Non-Dutch Nationals

ADAMS MULTILINGUAL RECRUITMENT
Amsterdam, tel.: 020 580 03 40
Rotterdam, tel.: 010 303 10 10
www.adamsrecruitment.com

BLUE LYNX EMPLOYMENT
Frederik Hendriklaan 85B, 2582 BV The Hague
Tel.: 070 311 78 22
www.bluelynx.com

YOUNGCAPITAL
Aquarius – Siriusdreef 12
2132 WT Hoofddorp
Tel.: 020 6531544
www.youngcapital.nl

MADISON PARKER INTERNATIONAL
Charlotte van Pallandtlaan 12-18,
2273 JJ Voorburg
Tel.: 070 387 59 11
www.madisonparker.nl

OCTAGON PROFESSIONALS
Prinses Margrietplantsoen 33,
2595 AM The Hague
Tel.: 070 324 93 00
www.octagon.nl

PROJOB
Van Baerlestraat 63-65, 1071 AR Amsterdam
Tel.: 020 573 83 83
www.projob.nl/en

UNDUTCHABLES RECRUITMENT AGENCY
Head Office, tel.: 020 345 51 04
Amsterdam, tel.: 020 623 13 00
Amstelveen, tel.: 020 445 97 38
The Hague, tel.: 070 711 83 00
Utrecht, tel.: 030 238 22 28
Eindhoven, tel.: 040 237 33 95
www.undutchables.nl

Job Searching Websites

- www.careerjet.nl
- www.glassdoor.nl
- www.intermediair.nl (in Dutch)
- www.iamexpat.nl/career/jobs-netherlands
- www.jobbird.com (in Dutch)
- www.linkedin.com
- www.monsterboard.nl (in Dutch)
- www.nationalevacaturebank.nl (in Dutch)
- www.nl.indeed.com
- www.togetherabroad.nl (in English)
- www.toplanguagejobs.com
- www.undutchables.nl
- https://vacatures.fd.nl (in Dutch)

Career Service

DOSO! COACHING & COUNSELING
Dorota Klop-Sowinska
Van Eeghenlaan 27, 1071 EN Amsterdam
Tel.: 06 13 253 655
E-mail: dorota@dosocoaching.com
www.dosocoaching.com

Recommended Reading

EMPLOYMENT IN THE NETHERLANDS
Published yearly by Loyens & Loeff
Conditions of employment, tax and social security aspects
Available on request by e-mail: info@loyensloeff.com
www.loyensloeff.com

CAREER JUMP!
By Dorota Klop-Sowinska
How to successfully change your professional path
www.careerjump.nl

THE ACCESS GUIDE/WORKING & UNEMPLOYMENT IN THE NETHERLANDS
This guide gives an overview of Dutch Employment Law and information on how to find a job
www.access-nl.org

LOOKING FOR WORK IN THE NETHERLANDS
By Nannette Ripmeester
Published yearly by Expertise in Labour Mobility
If you are looking for work in the Netherlands, this guide provides accurate and practical information on the job hunting process
www.labourmobility.com

A CAREER IN YOUR SUITCASE
By Jo Parfitt and Colleen Reichrath-Smith
A practical guide to creating meaningful work... anywhere
www.careerinyoursuitcase.com

LEGAL ASPECTS OF DOING BUSINESS IN THE NETHERLANDS
Published yearly by Loyens & Loeff
For entrepreneurs and their legal service providers who are or about to be engaged in business operations in the Netherlands
Available on request by e-mail: info@loyensloeff.com – www.loyensloeff.com

THE MOBILE LIFE – 2ND REVISED EDITION
Published by XPat Media
By Diane Lemieux & Anne Parker
Master the challenge of moving somewhere new – Also available as e-book
www.themobilelife.eu

Before buying or renting a house or apartment in the Netherlands, there are several things you should consider. This chapter offers you practical tips and useful information such as where to buy or rent, selecting an agent, and negotiating the deal. It also points out some of the consequences of your choice in terms of property taxes, waste collection taxes, sewerage taxes, etc., and the taxes (or related exemptions) in connection with the importation of your household goods.

CHAPTER 4

A Place to Live

CONTRIBUTING AUTHORS RICHARDO CRUZ FORTES, KAROLA GRÜNENBAUM, CONNIE MOSER, PATRICK ROVERS AND ANNETTE DE VREEDE

RENT OR BUY

HOUSING MARKET

During the Covid pandemic, the housing market experienced a boom. Then, in 2022, due to economic insecurity, inflation and increased interest rates, the price hike slowed down. In 2023, the housing market remained similar to 2022; though it became a bit tighter as there were more people looking for houses than houses being put on the market. Wages were rising and people were looking for freestanding houses or apartments rather than row or corner houses. Compared to the second quarter of 2023, prices were up 1.7% in the third quarter of 2023, but down 1.7% compared to the year before. House sales went up 7% for houses whose asking price exceeded € 500,000 and down 6% in the lower-priced market, and the average sales price in the third quarter of 2023 was € 422,000. The average asking price, however, went up from € 500,000 in 2022, to € 544,000 in the third quarter of 2023. Though there were certain regions in the Netherlands where prices went up more than 6%, this was not the case in the bigger cities, where is stayed between 0.5% and 1.6%. In 2023, approximately 45% of houses sold at (an average of 0.2%) more than the asking price – in 2022, 64% sold at 3% more than the asking price. At the start of the year, houses spent an average of 42 days on the market before being sold, but this steadily decreased to 33 days in the third quarter – which was still more than 25 days in 2022. The market for newly-built houses followed its own trajectory, however, and experienced a slump that it hasn't seen since 2014. In the apartment market, sales went up, though the number of apartments on the market continued to rise and their prices went down. In order to encourage young buyers looking for their first home to enter the market, the transfer tax on purchasing a home (to a maximum purchase price of € 510,000) has been reduced to 0% for those younger than 35. Other measures, such as a special *starterslening* (starter's loan), or the possibility for parents to guarantee mortgage payments or even offer a so-called family mortgage are meant to support younger people looking for their first home.

In order to protect the local market, municipalities are now allowed to reserve a percentage of (rental) homes for 'locals' in order to make it possible for them to stay in their hometown. This, as a consequence of the fact that many homeowners in the bigger cities have been cashing in on their more expensive homes and using this money to buy something bigger in the surrounding villages – thus pushing out the locals.

The rental market experienced a mixed development over 2023. More than 70% of all rentals go via housing corporations and rental prices went up by 0.1%, compared to 2.6% over 2022. The other portion of social housing saw an increase in rent of 3.7% compared to 2.8% in 2022, while in the free sector rental prices went up 4.5%, compared to 3.8% in 2022. As homeowners are not limited in how much they can raise the rent once they enter into a contract with a new renter, rental prices went up an average of 10.9% for new rental contracts, compared to 9.7% over 2022. The greatest increase was seen in the provinces of Friesland, Overijssel and Noord-Brabant, while – of the country's four largest cities – prices went up the most in The Hague and Utrecht. For a long time now, it has been noted that rental prices in the Netherlands are nonetheless reasonable, compared to other European countries. However, this sweeping statement can no longer be made, with Amsterdam coming in in first place (most expensive rental prices) Utrecht fifth, and Rotterdam eighth, and The Hague ninth – compared to cities such as Paris (fourth), Rome (third) and Lisbon (second, was first for a while).

FINDING A HOUSE

There is a considerable variety of properties to choose from, although much depends on where you want to live, the living space needed, and your budget. There is a good choice of rental properties in the so-called Randstad area, in the western part of the country (Amsterdam, The Hague / Wassenaar, Rotterdam and Utrecht), where most international companies are based. You can find a house for sale or for rent through contacts at international clubs, international schools and/or colleagues. Yet the best way to explore the market is by checking popular websites such as www.funda.nl (in Amsterdam; www.mva.nl), and www.pararius.com, or the lesser-known www.jaap.nl, or www.zah.nl.

Though you can go a long way on your own with the help of the Internet, it still remains advisable to contact an agent for the actual house-search and negotiation phase. Most expatriates have never lived in the Netherlands and are therefore not familiar with price ranges, local contracts, 'invisible' obligations, laws and customs. Using an agent, even though this is more expensive, will help you get a good impression of the living area, speed up the search for suitable accommodation, and get a better deal on the property. Another advantage to using an agent is that they have access to a computerized multiple-listing system which keeps them completely up-to-date on properties available in their district, though you should keep in mind that a listing real estate agent represents the seller or landlord and will not have your interests in mind. More on the real estate agent further on.

TO BUY OR TO RENT

Of course, there are a lot of benefits to buying a house. Apart from the fact that you own real estate of which the price may increase again, there is the advantage of a tax relief on the mortgage interest – it is tax-deductible if the house is your principal place of residence, provided you take out an annuity or straight line mortgage (starting 2015, new tax measures were introduced that reduced this benefit incrementally; from 40% in 2022, to 36.97% in 2024). In addition, a number of the costs related to the financing of the house are also tax-deductible. This means that some of the civil law notary's fees, the closing commission, and the fee for the appraisal of the house are all tax-deductible. Hence, if you are in the highest tax bracket of 52%, the net costs are 48%. (You can read more about the role of the civil law notary on page 138.)

Although at first sight it might seem an attractive option to buy a house, it is a decision that needs serious and careful consideration. A disadvantage when buying real estate in the Netherlands is that you have to pay approximately 6-7% of the purchase price as one-time buyers' expenses. These expenses consist of a transfer tax of 2% (first-time house buyers between the ages of 18 and 35 are exempt of this if the purchase price of the house does not exceed € 510,000), estate agent fees, civil law notary's fees, a fixed fee for the bank or broker (generally ranging from € 2,500 to € 5,000), fees for the structural surveyor (€ 400) and the financial appraiser (€ 800 to € 1,000), etc. In addition to this, homeowners must add the so-called deemed rental value (*eigenwoningforfait* – you can read more about this on page 104) to their taxable income, and pay taxes over this.

As a result, the break-even point between rent or buy usually occurs after a few years, assuming that housing prices remain constant. Bearing in mind that expatriates usually stay in the Netherlands for a relatively short period of time, this is an important issue to take into account. This risk makes buying a medium to long-term decision (three to five years) – though rising prices over recent years are making it more attractive to go ahead and buy instead of rent.

Of course, if you rent a house, you circumvent a lot of the problems and risks, but you also miss out on the possible benefits. And don't forget: rent can be (is) high in the Netherlands. You can read more about the tax consequences of renting, and having your rental costs reimbursed by your employer, on page 105.

CHECKLIST OF IMPORTANT ITEMS

If you decide to rent or to buy, make a checklist of items that are important to you and your family, and which will influence the location and style of the property. Discuss these with your agent. For example:

- proximity to work and the children's school
- (type of) public transportation
- school bus routes
- location of shopping centers / areas
- type of neighborhood
- type of house: period or modern
- when renting: is it fully-furnished – *gemeubileerd* (all furniture, fixtures and kitchen appliances provided) – or unfurnished (*ongemeubileerd*; fixtures, flooring, curtains, working kitchen and bathroom, and no furniture).

REAL ESTATE AGENT

As mentioned earlier, taking into account your likely lack of knowledge of national laws and regulations, you are advised to enlist the services of a real estate agent when looking for a house. Try to find a real estate agent in the city or town you want to buy in. Although some realtors work across a wider area, they may not always be aware of the specific ins and outs of a city, if they do not work there regularly. Issues such as bidding systems, zoning plans (*bestemmingsplan*), soil contamination and city council regulations are matters that are specific to each city. Any realtor has access to this information and should be able to inform you accordingly, yet local realtors – who know their contracts inside and out – are best equipped to advise you on these, as well as on building aspects and resolutive conditions.

Real estate agents charge a brokerage fee (*courtage*) for their services. This is usually between 1.5 to 2%, ex VAT, of the purchase price of the house, though with some realtors the percentage is negotiable. The fee depends on the specific services offered; some real estate agencies offer an expat service package. Though brokerage fees have gone up slightly, it is important to keep in mind that without the services of a realtor it is very likely that you, as a prospective buyer, will lose out on great deals, simply because you are not privy to the latest information, such as the latest listings of properties. Another matter that the realtor can help you out with, is finding a building expert (for instance, for the structural survey), an appraiser and a civil law notary – all of which will play an important role in the buying process.

If you have chosen to rent a property, there are several rental organizations available – which one you choose will depend on where you will be looking for property to rent. Check the resource pages at the end of the chapter.

You can usually find the right agent to suit your needs through word-of-mouth, via a Relocation Agency or via advertisements in publications or websites targeting expats. Basically every agent connected to the largest branch organization NVM has the same information available through the multiple listing system www.

funda.nl, but much depends on how well the agent uses this information and how they go about selecting the right properties according to the specifications of the lessee or buyer. Therefore, it is important that you feel you can trust your agent. It is practical and saves time and effort to use only one agent. However, if you are not satisfied, if you feel you are not seeing the right properties or that your agent does not understand your needs, get a different one.

AREAS

Most expatriates live in the Randstad, in the area including and in between Amsterdam, The Hague, Rotterdam and Utrecht. There are many pleasant residential areas near Amsterdam such as Amstelveen, Aerdenhout, Bloemendaal and Heemstede; in 't Gooi (between Amsterdam and Utrecht) which includes Bussum, Hilversum, Naarden, Huizen and Laren; near The Hague around Wassenaar, Voorschoten, Voorburg, Rijswijk and Oegstgeest; or in the residential areas of Rotterdam such as Kralingen and Hillegersberg. Of course, there are also many smaller villages where pleasant housing can be found – particularly now that expats are not being paid the attractive salaries they used to get. Especially Almere, Purmerend and Zaandam (around Amsterdam) are therefore quickly gaining in popularity.

YOU HAVE DECIDED TO RENT

TYPES OF RENTAL PROPERTIES

Different combinations are possible, depending on the landlord:

- Unfurnished (*Ongemeubileerd*). This offers the barest of necessities – namely, empty. Nothing much is included here; no carpeting, no curtains, often a minimum of or no appliances and no utilities. Generally speaking, this is not what expats are looking for, while they also don't qualify – in terms of income – for renting this type of property, as it is usually reserved for subsidized living.
- Semi-furnished or partly furnished (*Gestoffeerd*). Semi-furnished contains some furnishings and carpeting, a working bathroom and kitchen, light fixtures, and possibly a few appliances. Keep in mind to ask for a complete list of what is included. Utility inclusion or exclusion depends on the landlord.
- Fully furnished (*Gemeubileerd*). Everything has been taken care of and the apartment is ready to be moved into. It may contain any combination of furniture, appliances, curtains, light fixtures, carpets, cutlery and dishes, television, stereo equipment, kitchen appliances such as microwave, dishwasher, refrigerator, and sometimes even bed linens and blankets or duvets. Make sure to ask for a complete inventory list before agreeing to anything. If anything is missing, negotiate it before you sign the lease. Utilities might or might not be included.

THE RENTAL CONTRACT

Dutch law requires that all rental contracts be in the Dutch language. However, many rental contracts have been especially designed to meet the needs of expatriates, and include an English translation. A rental contract usually includes the following items:

- rent: the rent is payable one month in advance on the first of each month
- the term: a temporary rental contract is allowed for a maximum of 2 years; once it is extended – or not terminated on time – it becomes a contract for an indefinite period of time
- if you are renting a room (as a student) a temporary contract has a maximum duration of 5 years

- a deposit: a one-month deposit; however, some owners demand a 2 or 3-month deposit, especially in better locations and for higher-end housing
- an annual adjustment of the rent, based on increases in the cost of living, as determined by the Central Bureau of Statistics (CBS). This has averaged 2 to 3% over the past years
- user's costs, which are usually not included in the rent, i.e. utilities, municipal levies and garden maintenance
- the so-called diplomatic clause, which gives you the option of terminating the contract by giving two full calendar months' notice if you are transferred abroad (see the following paragraph) – this depends on the entry date of the diplomatic clause
- the brokerage fee, usually one month's rent (or a minimum of € 1,200, in many cases), excl. 21% VAT
- a clause on minor repairs: the law states exhaustively which minor repairs may be expected and borne by the lessee. If the costs exceed a certain amount, the location of the item that needs repair is hard to reach or if the repair requires specific technical knowledge, then the repair costs are to be borne by the owner
- a clause stating that the lessor is responsible for the yearly cleaning of the central heating system, water boilers, chimneys, gutters and draining pipes
- the obligation to return the property in the same condition, normal wear and tear excepted, at the end of the rental period – or else forfeit (a part of) the deposit.

In connection with repairs, you are advised to do a careful walk-through of the house or apartment you are planning on renting, during the check-in procedure, to verify damages and the need for repairs and improvements – and to determine who will be responsible for arranging and paying for these – before you sign on the dotted line. Every rental agreement has to come with a so-called condition report, which is mentioned in the contract. In order to avoid conflict, it is advisable to take pictures with a date on them, for your own records.

DIPLOMATIC CLAUSES IN RENTAL CONTRACTS

In principle, a rental contract is for a period of two years, after which it becomes a rental contract for an indefinite period of time (you can read more about this further on). However, a diplomatic clause can be included in the rental contract for the benefit of renter, ensuring that, even though the rental contract may not have expired, the property can be vacated after a notification term mutually agreed upon in advance. This has been created for those lessees who may want to take into account the possibility that they could be relocated by their employer – which would entail the need to move house before the end of the contract. There are various scenarios that come to mind – for instance, the parties may agree to this clause if the lessee is transferred to a place more than 50 (or 75) km from the actual residence. Or it may be subject to a stricter condition: the lessee must be transferred abroad before the expiration date of the agreement.

The lessor may want to include a diplomatic clause for themself, but this only covers the fact that they will be abroad temporarily – for a specific period, after which they want to be able to move back to their house and not have to be faced with rent protection for their lessee. They cannot use it to terminate the rental contract before it reaches the end of its term under other circumstances – which is why most landlords will not extend the rental contract beyond the initial two years. Also note that, despite the existence of this clause, they will still have to terminate the rental contract in writing.

CHECKING IN

When the contracts have been signed, and the rent and deposit have been paid into the account of the agent, the lessee will be handed the keys to the property. Ideally, the lessee will be checked in by the owner or their representative, assisted by their own agent. A checklist, including photographs, will be filled out regarding the condition of the house, the furniture, fixtures and fittings belonging to the house, the condition of the exterior / garden, and there will be a check of the inventory. This is signed – if the rental property is an apartment; along with the house rules. Once the copy of house rules is signed by the lessor, this is often sent by the realtor to the Committee of Homeowners, so that they know who is staying in the home. Many of these committees specifically forbid subleasing and demand that the lease be for at least one year, in order to avoid AirBnB-type situations. The house should be thoroughly cleaned, including the inside of kitchen and bathroom cabinets. The inspection report as well as the inventory list must be signed by lessee and lessor.

DEFECTS

If the space you have rented turns out to have defects, you can demand that the owner fix these unless:

- you yourself have caused this defect
- it entails a small repair that you can carry out (and pay for) yourself
- repair is impossible
- the repair costs are prohibitively high, and you cannot reasonably demand that the lessor pay these
- your rental contract has other provisions.

A defect is defined as: a failure to meet that which you might reasonably have expected and that hinders your enjoyment of the property. This could be construction issues, bad maintenance, mold, or pests – but is not limited to this list. More on hidden defects can be found on page 100.

TERMINATING THE RENTAL CONTRACT

To avoid anxiety and unnecessary costs later, you will need to inform (remind) your landlord well in advance as to what date the contract for your apartment will expire and when you will be leaving. This should be done by way of a registered letter and by email. Depending on your rental contract, there is a notice period to be given before the expiration of the tenancy of:

- at least one calendar month in case the lessee terminates
- at least three months + one month for every year the property has been rented to the lessee with a maximum of six months in case the lessor terminates the contract
- the period specified in the diplomatic clause of the contract.

Currently, many rental contracts are for a period of two years. As the end of this period approaches, for the contract to indeed be terminated, the lessor has to notify you of the fact that the contract will be terminated – and do this between three to one months before the 24 months come to an end, followed by two written

Redoing Your Home

Few people have bought a house of which they thought: 'Yup, *precisely* the way I wanted it,' and left everything the way it was. On the other hand, few people are as notorious for clearing out all but the outside walls and rebuilding from scratch as the Dutch are. Likely, you are somewhere in the middle. Note: when you buy a house, you can arrange a 'construction loan' – be sure to ask your mortgage advisor for more information.

CONTRACTOR – AANNEMER

Should you wish to redo your house (change a wall or two, put in a new bathroom or kitchen, build a fireplace), the person you are looking for is a contractor. Contractors can be found online under the name *aannemers*. There you will find probably at least 100 to choose from – which does not make the choice any easier. A safe bet would be to opt for a contractor who is listed with BouwGarant. Those listed with BouwGarant must meet strict requirements, and can be found on www.bouwgarant.nl, after entering your town / city on the home page, and then clicking on Een *aannemer zoeken*. Otherwise, ask around and see whom others recommend. Be sure to invite a few *aannemers*, as prices can vary considerably, not to mention compatibility: chances are, these people will be running around in your house for weeks, if not months. To certain home improvements, a reduced VAT rate of 9% applies – including, but not limited to, painting, insulation and wall-papering. Additional conditions apply, such as the age of the home and the purpose to which it is used. There are also certain costs that are tax-deductible; be sure to explore this with your contractor and/or tax consultant.

OVERSEEING THE PROJECT

The contractor could be a one-man operation or a company (*bouwbedrijf*) ranging in size from two people to several dozen skilled employees. They are responsible for purchasing all the necessary supplies (*bouwmaterialen*) and overseeing the installation of the project, making sure that all of the skilled personnel (a contractor has qualified plumbers, electricians, carpenters, etc. on their payroll) complete their portions of the project at the right moment during the process. They also make sure that the materials used are up to code and meet current safety requirements.

PAPERWORK

All necessary paperwork can also be handled by your contractor. It is best to leave the requesting of building permits and the execution of building plans and blueprints in their hands. Not only do they have ample experience in dealing with the bureaucracy inherent in securing permission, it tends to go much faster than if you attempt to do it yourself.

MONUMENTS

An important matter in this context is the question of whether your house is on the *monumentenlijst* (list of monuments). Houses that are protected under *Monumentenzorg* (Monuments Care) are subject to strict regulations and restrictions regarding maintenance, and any changes have to be approved by a commission representing the Association for the Preservation of Monuments. Even seemingly straightforward matters such as the color of paint used often needs approval. It can take months of waiting for approvals, and in the meantime you are prohibited from making any changes. Your contractor likely knows the best way to approach obtaining permission for any changes you wish to make – and how long it will take. They will also be able to give you a fair idea of what you will be allowed to do.

WORKING 'BLACK'

In order to have a guarantee on your work it is best to work *wit met een bonnetje* ('white with a receipt'). Some tradesmen will work *zwart* ('black'); that is, without a receipt and without adding the 21% VAT (BTW), thus reducing your bill – however, this is illegal and constitutes tax fraud. In addition, you forfeit your right to any claims due to shoddy workmanship or incompletion of the project. Nor will insurance companies cover claims resulting from damages incurred by leaking pipes, electrical fires and the likes. Furthermore, you have no proof regarding the services rendered and materials used.

HANDYMAN

Sometimes people will hire in a handyman (*klusjesman*) who works at the going rate of around € 25-35 per hour ('ex BTW', meaning that VAT is still to be added to the total bill). Once again, you can probably find a handyman who

works 'black' (*zwartwerken*), but if they do, they will not be insured, and any liability claims that could arise from accidents (like their falling off your roof while working) will not be covered and a settlement will not be possible.

A NEW INTERIOR

Though the contractor carries out the project, you yourself will have to select the kitchen cabinets, bathtub, closets, tiles, curtains, carpeting, faucets, paint colors, etc. If you want, you can do this with the help of an interior decorator (look online, under *binnenhuisarchitectuur* or *interieurontwerpers*). To do it yourself, look under *woninginrichting* (decorating your home) for carpeting, curtains, but also beds and furniture, *keukens* for kitchens, *sanitaire artikelen* for bathrooms, *verf en lak* for paint. Often, your contractor will have reached an agreement with a local bathroom, kitchen or tile specialist regarding deliveries and quality, so you may wish to wait and see whom they recommend – though you are not obligated to go by their recommendations alone.

GARDEN

If you want to do your own garden, you will find what you need at a garden center – to be found online under *tuincentra* (for plants and other necessities) or *tuinartikelen* (for garden furniture, sheds, ponds, lighting). If you want to enlist the help of a professional, look under *tuinaanleg en -onderhoud* (garden design and maintenance).

Hidden Defects

If it turns out, after you have purchased your house, that there are a number of things that are not in order, you will have to ask yourself what type of 'defect' you are dealing with. In principle, you buy a house 'as is'; this means, including all visible and invisible defects – and the premise is that you, the new owner, are responsible for all that comes with your new home. It is therefore essential that you have a structural survey of the home carried out before deciding to buy it.

If an invisible defect is considered serious, however, it can officially qualify as a 'hidden' defect – and there are situations in which the former owner can be held liable (see further on) for the consequences.

OBLIGATIONS REALTORS

The selling realtor has an obligation to inform you of known defects of the house. For instance, wooden constructions could be infected with wood rot, mold or fungus growth. Or there could be an oil tank in the back yard, or pests; causing you to run up a hefty bill for extermination. If they fail to inform you of these issues, the owner can be held liable.

You may also expect *your* realtor to pay attention and be critical – asking the seller pertinent questions that may arise on the basis of their, or your, observations.

REPORTING A DEFECT

In either a rental or purchase property, any discovered hidden defect will need to be reported within a reasonable time frame from the date of purchase or rental. Case law generally states that this should be within two months. Sometimes this is not enough time to have a good idea of the extent and consequences of the defect; in that case, you report the defect within two months, but state that its extent will be made clear later. For a purchased property, you will have to report any defects or problems to the estate agent who sold you the property and they will negotiate on your behalf with the seller. If the seller is not willing to fix the problem or pay for the damages, you will have to take the matter to the courts. For rentals, see further on.

RESPONSIBILITIES FOR PURCHASED PROPERTY

For the former owner to be held liable, the following conditions must be met:

1. the defect must have been there at the time of the sale and you must be able to prove this
2. you, the buyer, must have inspected the new home. If you *could* have detected the defect during this inspection, but didn't, then this is your responsibility. Some defects occur after the inspection, but before the transfer – the seller will be liable for these
3. the seller did not inform you of the defects that they were aware of (note: the seller may not necessarily aware of the existence of the defect, yet still can be held liable) and that could not be detected or were not easy to detect in the case of a normal inspection. The seller must inform you of the defects even if the extent of the defect is not clear – also if it will not influence a normal use of the house
4. the defect must hinder a 'normal' use of (part of) the house – or, put differently, the house must have the qualities that you could expect based on the sales contract. This is considered a 'serious' defect for which the seller might even be held liable if they were not aware of its existence
5. both seller and buyer had expected that the property could be given a special use, which proves impossible.

Another important factor is the age of the house. The older it is, there more you can be expected to have anticipated certain problems. The sales contract might also include a clause stating that the seller has not been living in the house (the house has been rented out), and that they do not know the exact state of the house. This is done in order to protect the seller. Whether this will be successful depends on the wording of the clause.

If you compare points 3 and 4, they would appear to contradict each other. It is clear that there is a gray area there somewhere, so be sure to obtain expert advice in the case of problems. And keep in mind, while looking at a house, that if anything looks fishy (or rickety); ask, take notes, point it out... Another important point is that the buyer and seller can agree, in writing, that the seller will not be held liable – though the seller will not always be able to invoke this.

NEW PROPERTY

In the case of new property, the contractor is liable for any defects / deficiencies not only until the moment they deliver the property,

notifications that the rental contract will be terminated. Should they be even one day late, the rental contract will be converted into a contract for an indefinite period of time and you will enjoy extensive protection. Rental contracts can, however, be terminated prematurely by the lessor (usually after requesting permission from the court) for specific reasons, such as that you are in arrears in your rent payment, you generate noise pollution, or the lessor urgently needs the home themself (for instance, after a divorce). These latter exceptions cannot be invoked by the time a second or third renter is in the home. If you have agreed to a two-year rental contract, and the lessor wants to terminate it before the end of this period, you can refuse to leave – though you should keep in mind that this will of course not create an atmosphere of goodwill between you and the lessor.

CHECKING OUT / RETURN OF THE DEPOSIT

Preferably on the last day of the lease period, a check-out is done with all parties concerned. The inventory and condition of the lease property are evaluated with the checklist made when checking in. If the state of the property is found to be satisfactory and all bills in connection with the property have been paid, the deposit will be paid back within three months after the check-out date. If necessary, the costs of restoring the rental property back to the required state will be deducted from the deposit in accordance with the bills provided by the lessor. Should the deposit not be enough to cover the expenses, the renter will owe the additional amount.

but also beyond, unless they cannot be held accountable for them. They are to take you on an inspection of the property and you must sign a piece of paper stating that you will accept the property as is. Be sure to have an independent professional inspect the property and make a report before you do this, based on which the contractor will have to make – and bear the cost of – any necessary adaptations. Do not sign a so-called pre-delivery report: new issues might come up that will have to be dealt with. Once the property has been delivered, the contractor has three months in which to fix the issues brought to their attention. This period stretches out to six months – the so-called maintenance period – for any other problems that may occur. Be sure to keep a written record of everything and to inform the contractor as soon as possible. Defects that were impossible to discover earlier are for the responsibility of the constructor until five years after the maintenance period. Serious defects until 20 years after the maintenance period.

YOU FEEL MISLED

You can also hold the seller of the house responsible if you have been misled regarding (certain parts of) the house and its (their) use. For you to be able to do this, the seller must have been aware of your expectations – which may be hard to prove, certainly if there is nothing in writing or if there are no witnesses (such as your realtor). Another example would be if the realtor (purposely) failed to inform you of the impossibility of your intentions or impressions. If you were mistaken – but not actively misinformed – regarding the house then though in theory you may seek compensation, this will not be easy. Particularly if the seller was not aware of your expectations or plans. If you want to use the house for special purposes, be sure to include this in your contract, to avoid miscommunication and to make clear who can be held liable for a hidden defect.

PROBLEMS IN THE NEIGHBORHOOD

The seller also has a duty to report beforehand (*mededelingsplicht*) any knowledge of contaminated ground in the neighborhood, or problems in the area, such as wood rot in the foundation poles under the houses. The buyer has a buyer's responsibility to also check to see if there are problems in the area, or if there are any pre-existing building reports (*bouwkundige keuringen*).

WHAT CAN YOU DEMAND?

If you find a hidden defect in the home you purchased, you can demand that the situation be restored; in other words, either that you receive compensation of the costs you incur in fixing the problem, or else that the former owner fix it themself. In serious cases, you can demand that the purchase be annulled, or that the purchase price be reduced retroactively.

LEGAL AID

If it turns out that you were not adequately informed, you may have to go to court and let the judge decide about compensation for the reparation of damages. Being as how proving conclusively whether or not one can presume that the selling party knowingly withheld vital information can prove rather hard to do, you may need the services of a lawyer if a timely agreement to remedy the situation cannot be reached (see page 148 for more on legal aid).

RESPONSIBILITIES FOR RENTALS

By law, you should have full, quiet enjoyment of your rental. If there are any defects that impede this legal right, your landlord needs to fix these. You are responsible for small repairs that occur in the course of normal daily life, and damages that are not your responsibility can usually be claimed under your household insurance. If you do not have household insurance, keep in mind that you can only hold your landlord liable if they can be held responsible – for instance, if they have carried out sloppy repairs, are behind in their maintenance duties, or have not responded to your complaints, resulting in higher damages.

A general rule of thumb is that anything that is structural is the responsibility of the party letting out the property (*verhuurder*). Any repairs that lie above a certain cost, require certain technical knowledge or that have to be carried out in a hard-to-reach place, should be paid by the owner. The best recourse is to be very clear beforehand as to the division of the responsibilities. If you discover problems after you have moved in, you will need to contact the landlord (and/or the housing agency) to notify them of the problem. Hopefully something can be done to solve the problem right away, however, sometimes this is not the case. You may wind up having to pay for the repairman or the exterminator yourself, and then attempting to be reimbursed. To be on the safe side, you can ask the court permission to carry out the repairs / take the necessary measures. Furthermore, you can ask for a rent deduction over the period in which the landlord is in default, or you can start a so-called defect procedure before the rent assessment committee.

YOU HAVE DECIDED TO BUY

Before embarking on the actual process of finding a house to buy, make sure you first contact a bank or mortgage broker to discuss what types of mortgage there are, whether you will be able to take out a mortgage here, to what amount you can do this and what the related monthly expenses will be. Having clarified these points will allow you to focus on finding a new home, without being faced with unpleasant surprises just when you think you have found one.

After going into the process of buying a house, we will discuss the available mortgages in more detail.

STEP-BY-STEP

First, a short step-by-step plan of the purchasing process. In the remainder of this paragraph and in other parts of this chapter, insofar as they have not been discussed earlier, we will go into these steps in more detail:

- You contact a mortgage provider, to find out exactly how much mortgage you can take out, whereby you take into account additional expenses involved in the purchase of the home (these are discussed further on).
- You select a real estate agent and discuss what you are looking for, what you need and what is realistic. A good realtor will also be able to advise you on a money lender / mortgage broker, if you do not have one.
- If you have any special wishes regarding the property, make sure your real estate agent and the real estate agent of the seller are aware of this. If they are not, and it turns out your home does not meet these wishes, you cannot hold them accountable for it.

- You visit various properties.
- When you have found a home you like, you discuss all issues such as city council regulations, but also issues such as soil contamination.
- If you want this home, you can inform your real estate agent of this verbally.
- Your real estate agent will contact the selling party and relay this message.
- You contact your mortgage broker (or bank) again to start the official mortgage application process (which takes approximately six weeks)
- Have a building inspection carried out. If you fail to do this and there is a problem, more likely than not, you will have lost your right to hold the seller accountable.
- Make the purchase of the house contingent upon its passing the structural survey.
- The initial verbal agreement you reach with the seller is put in writing by the realtor (in Amsterdam, this is done by the civil law notary) in the preliminary purchase contract. A penalty clause is usually included in case the seller or the buyer does not meet their obligations.
- After being signed by all the parties, the preliminary purchase contract is sent to the civil law notary who deals with the transfer of the title of the home.
- A three-day 'cooling-off' period starts the day after the buyer receives a copy of the signed contract. During these three days, the buyer can cancel the deal without any repercussions and without having to state the reason.
- The civil law notary inspects the public registers of the Land Registry regarding mortgages and/or attachments with which the property may be encumbered.
- The transfer of ownership takes place at the civil law notary's office by means of a deed of transfer that is drawn up by the civil law notary and signed by the seller, the buyer and the civil law notary. You will receive a draft of this deed and of the mortgage deed beforehand. Also your agent will receive these and check them.
- The agent will check together with you to see whether the house has been vacated and is in the agreed condition. At this point, the utility meters will also be read. This is called the inspection, or last walk-through.
- The civil law notary takes care of the financial settlement of the transaction and ensures that the deed of transfer is entered in the public registers (Land Registry).
- The transfer then becomes official, and you receive the keys of your new house.

POINTS TO WATCH FOR WHEN BUYING A HOUSE

1. General

When you decide to buy a house, it is doubly advisable to engage an agent, as there are more complicated matters involved than when renting a house. For instance, you need expert advice on matters such as the fluctuation of prices in certain areas, environmental laws, the construction of a house, hidden defects (see page 100), and the issues that need to be taken into account when you buy property on leasehold rather than freehold.

2. Fixtures and Fittings

When you start negotiating, you should keep in mind that the purchase price excludes furniture, carpets, curtains, light fixtures and sometimes kitchen appliances. You must reach a clear agreement with the seller on which goods are included in the purchase, and which should be removed. To this purpose, the seller fills out a list of items, which their real estate agent hands over to you. When you buy the house, the purchase contract will include a so-called questionnaire (vragenlijst), containing detailed information on the house.

3. Deposit

The deposit on the house is generally 10% of the purchase price – due approximately six weeks after the deal has been made – and is arranged by the mortgage advisor or the bank itself by means of a bank guarantee issued by a Dutch banking institution. This deposit is to be paid to a civil law notary and can be part of the financing agreement reached for the purchase of the house. The deposit will be held in an escrow account of the notary until the day of the transfer of the deed.

4. Additional Costs

The purchase transaction will cost you an additional approximately 6-7%. This amount includes a government transfer tax of 2%, land registry expenses, the civil law notary's fees, and the real estate agent's commission and other expenses – see below.

5. Resolutive Conditions

If you need to obtain a mortgage to finance the purchase, any purchase agreement should be made subject to financing. If necessary, other resolutive conditions should be part of the agreement, such as (if applicable) being able to obtain a permit to occupy the real estate, or even more importantly, the option of having a structural survey carried out.

THE ACTUAL HOUSE-HUNTING

It is advisable to make sure the agent is well-informed of your specific wishes prior to the actual house-hunting in order for them to put together a list of properties that meet your requirements. The agent can also help you become acquainted with the different terms and conditions of contracts and procedures, and check if the specifications you have given are in line with price ranges and the kind of housing available. Based on your specific requirements, a selection from the available market supply will be made and a tour of inspection of those residences will be organized. Normally, more tours will follow until a suitable house is found. It is easier to determine which kind of house suits you best after you have visited several different properties. The average search for the right house normally takes a few months, depending on availability, your needs and market circumstances. Last year, houses were being picked up like hot cakes. This year, this is no longer the case; fewer people are looking for houses and overbidding is limited to on average approximately 0.2%, compared to 8% at the start of 2022 – though in some neighborhoods and in the case of renovated homes, it can still be 5-6%. The person who makes the highest bid and offers the best conditions generally 'wins'.

NEGOTIATIONS

Prices and conditions quoted in the listings for sales and rentals are usually negotiable. In close consultation with the agent, these will be negotiated with the agent representing the owner. These negotiations used to consist of several rounds of verbal bidding and counter-bidding – except during periods such as last year, when people were often forced to bring out the highest bid they felt they could make in order to ensure they got the home. Sometimes, other factors are deciding, such as the convenience of the date on which the buyer wishes to purchase the house, how many household items / furniture they want to keep, or simply a personal preference for a particular buyer.

COSTS

As mentioned earlier, as a general rule, the costs of purchasing a house in the Netherlands amount to approximately 6-7% of the price of the house (this is not the same as the 10% down payment!). These expenses include:

- appraisal fee (expense for having the house officially appraised in order to secure a mortgage)
- notary costs mortgage deed (*hypotheekakte*)
- cadastral registration fee mortgage deed
- cadastral investigation fee
- administration fee mortgage deed
- structural survey of the house
- bank guarantee fee
- mortgage commission fee (paid either to the bank or the broker)
- National Mortgage Insurance – *Nationale Hypotheek Garantie* – fee
- transfer tax
- estate agent fee
- notary costs for the transfer deed
- interpreter fees.

On a house of € 350,000, your approximate cost would therefore be an additional more or less € 22,750 over and above the € 350,000 purchase price.

TAX-DEDUCTIBLE COSTS

Of interest to know is that the costs listed below are tax-deductible and can be declared (one-time) on your income tax return:

- notary costs mortgage deed (*hypotheekakte*) (VAT/BTW)
- mortgage commission fee (paid either to the bank or the broker)
- cadastral registration fee
- cadastral investigation fee
- appraisal (*taxatie*) fee
- administration fee (*afsluitprovisie*) mortgage deed
- bank guarantee fee.

PRELIMINARY PURCHASE CONTRACT AND TRANSFER OF OWNERSHIP

The verbal agreement is put in writing in the preliminary purchase contract (*voorlopige koopakte*). A penalty clause is usually included in case the seller or the buyer does not meet their obligations. After being signed by all the parties, the preliminary purchase contract is sent to the civil law notary who will deal with the transfer of the title of the house. A three-day 'cooling-off' period starts the day after the buyer receives a copy of the signed contract. During these three days the buyer can cancel the deal without any repercussions and without having to state the reason.

The buyer usually chooses the civil law notary. Upon receipt of the preliminary purchase contract, the civil law notary inspects the public registers of the Land Registry regarding mortgages and/or attachments with which the property may be encumbered. Both parties and their agents visit the office of the civil law notary together for the signing of the preliminary purchase contract.

The transfer of ownership will take place at the civil law notary's office by means of a deed of transfer to be drawn up by the civil law notary and to be signed by the seller, the buyer and the civil law notary. The civil law notary will first send you a draft of this deed of transfer together with a statement showing the payment due in order to complete the purchase. This statement includes the purchase price, the transfer tax, the cadastral registration fees, notarial fees, the commission on a possible mortgage loan, real estate agent's fees, etc. If there is a mortgage loan, you will receive a draft of the mortgage deed. Your agent will also receive these documents and check them.

Usually on the day of the transfer, the agent will check together with you to see whether the house has been vacated and is in the agreed condition. It is the task of the civil law notary to take care of the financial settlement of the transaction and to ensure that the deed of transfer is entered in the public registers (Land Registry). The transfer then becomes official and the seller turns over the keys to your new house.

INTERPRETER

If your command of the Dutch language is such that you will be needing the assistance of an interpreter when communicating with the civil law notary, then you are legally required to request the assistance of a sworn interpreter. Depending on your language, this will cost you anywhere between € 250 and € 500, excluding VAT.

THE TAX CONSEQUENCES OF RENTING OR BUYING A HOUSE

When moving to a new country, just about the first question you are faced with is; where am I going to live? This decision is, predictably, largely influenced by the decision: am I going to buy a house or am I going to rent one? Many of the issues involved in this choice have been discussed in the preceding paragraphs. However, one important question remains: what are the tax consequences of your decision? This is a complex matter, and we will give a short overview of the topics that will play a role when making your choice.

In some parts, reference will be made to the tax paragraphs which you can find in the chapter on *Legal, Tax and Financial Matters*.

BUYING A HOUSE

Mortgage Expenses Deductible

One of the most important reasons to buy real estate – instead of renting it – is most probably the fact that interest paid on a mortgage is deductible from your taxable income when you use the house as your principal place of residence (as of 2015, the rules on deductibility have slowly changed: the maximum rate of deductibility is now 36.97 (2024). Again: aside from the interest, the one-time expenses related to the mortgage (for example, that part of the civil law notary fee related to the mortgage deed, cadastral registration fee, mortgage advisor fee and appraisal fee) as well as leasehold are also deductible, via your income tax return. Furthermore, to most, investing in real estate through a mortgage is a more financially attractive option than simply spending it on rent, which is high – Amsterdam being the most expensive city to rent in in the EU.

If you decide to take out a higher mortgage than required to finance the purchase of the house itself or for its reconstruction, the related part of the mortgage interest will *not* be deductible, with the exception of investments aimed at making the property more sustainable. Other expenses related to the house (such as insurance premiums and capital repayment) are never deductible.

Specific rules apply when it comes to the deductibility of mortgage interest if you sell a house and buy a new one. As the rules are too complicated to summarize for the purpose of this book, you are advised to consult a specialist (a mortgage advisor or tax consultant) should you find yourself in this situation.

In recent years, the government has been re-evaluating its overall mortgage legislation, resulting not only in a lowering of the maximum rate of deductibility, but also in the following measures: mortgage interest is deductible over a maximum period of 30 years, provided the mortgage provides for monthly redemption payments (straight line or annuity), and the maximum mortgage amount has been reduced to 100% of the purchase price (or 100% of the appraised market value) of the property, since 2018. Consequently, buyers will no longer be able to completely finance the additional expenses related to buying a house by means of the mortgage, and will have to bear these costs themselves.

What Type of Mortgage?

You should seek proper advice on the type of mortgage that is suitable in your situation, particularly in view of the limited period of time during which you may need the mortgage. Do not forget to inform the mortgage advisor if you are benefiting from the 30%-ruling. If the mortgage is linked to a capital insurance, you may be faced with additional tax consequences. Be sure to get expert advice! More on mortgages on page 105.

Deemed Rental Value and WOZ-Value

Those who own a house and use it as their principal place of residence have to report a certain amount – related to the home ownership – on their income tax return. This amount is a percentage of the value of the house, and is called the *eigenwoningforfait* (or deemed rental value). The *eigenwoningforfait* is based on the official value of the house, also known as the WOZ-value, which is determined every year by the municipality and is not the same as the market value. Every year, the owner receives a so-called woz-*beschikking* (woz-decision, see also page 105), 'confirming' the value of the house, which is used as a basis for determining a number of levies and taxes and has been created in order to rule out the possibility of arbitrariness – as owners used to make their own calculation of the value of their house for tax purposes. woz stands for Wet Waardering Onroerende Zaken, or Value of Immovable Property Act. In 2024, a woz-value of up to € 1.2 million will be charged a percentage of 0.35, and above € 1.2 million will be charged € 4,200, plus 2.35% of the woz-value.

The balance of the deemed rental value and the interest can be deducted from your income. You can only deduct your own share in the mortgage. If you are married or if you and your partner are considered fiscal partners (see page 120), you can allocate the mortgage deduction in such a way as to obtain the highest tax relief. If you have no, or very little, mortgage interest to deduct, as a consequence of which your *eigenwoningforfait* exceeds your interest due, you have a right to a deduction called the Hillenaftrek to compensate for this. This measure is slowly being phased out until it reaches 0 in 2048.

If your partner does not live in the Netherlands, then you can generally only deduct your own share in the mortgage. It would be a good idea for both of you to look into whether choosing to be treated as a resident taxpayer would be beneficial in your situation.

Preliminary Tax Refund

You can receive a tax refund on the mortgage interest deduction every month by requesting a preliminary negative tax bill from the tax authorities. This is done by means of a special form. The tax authorities will then deposit the refund directly into your bank account, every month.

Real Estate Owned Abroad

If you are a *resident* taxpayer, you cannot deduct the negative income from real estate that is located outside the Netherlands as it is not your principal place of residence. If you are a *non-resident* taxpayer living abroad in your principal place of residence, you can choose to be treated as a resident taxpayer. In that case, you can deduct the mortgage interest (reduced with the deemed rental value) from your Dutch taxable income. However, keep in mind that this option might have – possibly negative – consequences. We recommend that you approach a specialist for advice specifically geared to your situation.

You Don't Live Here, But Own Real Estate Here

You will have to pay tax on a deemed benefit arising from the ownership of the real estate minus the value of the mortgage (a fixed assumed yield) in box 3. This 'benefit' is set at, for most houses, 6.04% (2024) of the woz-value of the real estate less the debt (the mortgage), which will be taxed at a rate of 36% (2024). If you only own a house in box 3 (and have no other investments, etc.) then a tax-exempt amount of € 57,000 (2024) will be deducted first. Mortgage interest will no longer be deductible. Each partner has to report their own share. If you rent out the real estate, the rental income is free of tax. Any expenses incurred are not tax-deductible.

There are special rules for those who leave the Netherlands only temporarily.

RENTING A HOUSE

Renting a house in the Netherlands is expensive, especially if you need to rent in the western part of the country or close to international schools. There is no tax facility for renting a house whatsoever. With any luck, your employer will choose to compensate you for the housing costs. But in that case, be aware of the tax consequences, see the following paragraphs:

Free Housing Taxable

If you are a resident of the Netherlands (resident taxpayer or partial non-resident taxpayer), any compensation for housing provided by your employer constitutes taxable income. Whether you will have to pay the tax yourself depends on your contract; is it net or gross?

If you are a 'real' non-resident taxpayer, you may benefit from an exemption during a period of two years, under certain conditions.

Special Treatment Under 30%-Ruling

Residents

If you are a resident of the Netherlands (also if you are a partial non-resident taxpayer – an option that will cease to exist in 2025), in principle the full benefit resulting from the fact that your employer is providing you with housing is a taxable benefit.

If you benefit from the 30%-ruling, special rules apply. A part of the rent may be qualified as an 'extraterritorial expense' (you can read more about this on page 124). That part of the rent can be compensated free of tax (thus reducing the amount of the fixed 30%-allowance!)

Non-Residents

If you are a non-resident of the Netherlands, any compensation of double housing expenses is regarded as compensation for extraterritorial expenses: tax-free, but resulting in a reduction of the 30%-allowance.

TAKING OUT A MORTGAGE

If you have decided to buy a house, you are faced with the question of what will be the most appropriate type of mortgage. The recommended mortgage depends on your special tax position and whether you are likely to move again. In these paragraphs we provide a brief explanation of the relevant types of mortgages available in the Netherlands – whereby we point out that if you take out a new mortgage, you will only be allowed to deduct your mortgage interest from your taxable income if you take out a mortgage with straight line redemption or an annuity mortgage. We will also give a few recommendations as to which types are best suited to your specific tax status.

THE RELEVANT TYPES OF MORTGAGES

Usually, a mortgage has a duration of 30 years. Here, we will discuss the three principal types of mortgages and give a brief summary of the mortgages that can no longer be newly taken out.

MORTGAGE WITH STRAIGHT LINE REDEMPTION

The most important characteristic of this mortgage is that the loan is repaid yearly in equal installments (i.e. straight line). As a result of the repayments, the amount of interest payable dimin-

pararius
Searching for a
rental home?
Find it easily yourself!
www.pararius.com
Pararius is the leading rental website in The Netherlands, available in English and five other languages.
Scan to go to our website

Energy Label

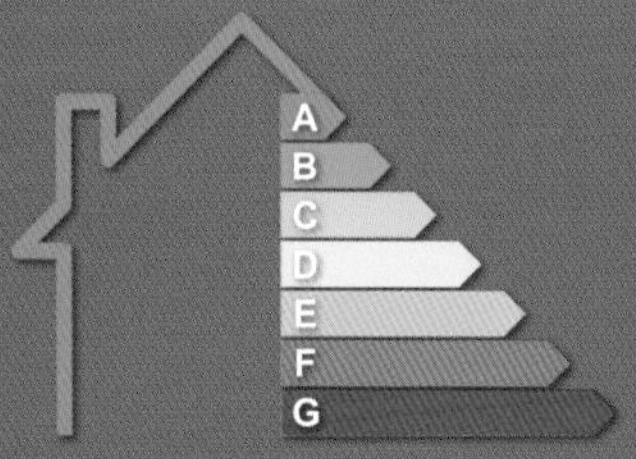

For quite a while now, cars and household equipment have been issued an 'energy label', ranging from A – G, to indicate how energy-efficient they are. A is the most efficient, G the least. All houses / apartments must also carry this same label (also called *energieprestatiecertificaat*), to be issued by a certified advisor, which is valid for a period of ten years and is handed over with the sale or renting out of the house / apartment. If you cannot show this label, you will not be able to sell your house, while renters will owe less rent. This is all part of the government's aim to become one of the cleanest and most energy-efficient countries within Europe. Measures that influence the classification of your house are, for instance: roof insulation, double glazing, and a ventilation system that allows the recuperation of heat. Though you are not obligated to take measures to improve the rating of your house, doing so may contribute to increasing its value, and you might be able to get a more favorable mortgage.

On January 2010, a new type of energy label was introduced, that takes into account the type of house and that provides more information on how energy can be saved, making it easier to compare the energy efficiency of houses, and in 2016, all homeowners in the Netherlands were issued a provisional label, aimed at encouraging them to look into how they could upgrade their energy efficiency. Anyone who wants to sell or rent out their house, will first have to arrange a definitive label – or risk a maximum € 450-fine.

The cost of obtaining the energy label depends on the size and type of house, as well as the available documentation on the house and how much time the advisor will need for their evaluation. In the case of apartment buildings, a rebate may be possible, while, in the case of 'similar houses' an 'example house' of the series may be used as a basis. Nonetheless, a separate certificate must be issued for each house. A certified advisor can be found by visiting www.energielabel.nl/woningen, and following the steps on this site. You will need your DigiD (or digital identity, see page 84) to do this. As the site is in Dutch, you might wish to enlist the assistance of your realtor to arrange theenergy label.

ishes every year. Since the interest expenditure decreases steadily, this mortgage is best suited for borrowers who cannot fully benefit from the tax relief on the interest payments.

ANNUITY MORTGAGE

The chief characteristic of an annuity mortgage is that the yearly total of redemption and interest payments remains the same throughout its duration. Although the total remains the same, the mix of interest and redemption of course changes over the years. Owing to this balance between interest and redemption, the redemption is not on a straight-line basis.

In the first years, the amount paid by the borrower consists mainly of interest payments. Hence there is a large tax relief in the initial years. Consequently, an annuity mortgage is ideal for people who wish to have a large tax relief in the early years and expect to have a sufficiently high income in later years to be able to make the redemption payments that do not qualify for tax relief.

NATIONALE HYPOTHEEKGARANTIE (NHG)

With a Nationale Hypotheek Garantie (National Mortgage Guarantee), the Stichting Waarborgfonds Eigen Woningen (Homeowners' Guarantee Fund) guarantees payment of the mortgage. In return for this you pay the NHG a one-time fee (0.6% for 2024). If you cannot meet your payments, NHG pays them for you – and becomes your creditor for this amount. The advantage to this system for the mortgage provider is that they are guaranteed payment, in return for which they offer a reduction in mortgage interest of anywhere between 0.3 and 0.7% (in some cases, even 1%). The actual reduction depends on the percentage to which you mortgage your home.

An NHG mortgage loan can be taken out to a maximum of € 435,000 (2024), or € 461,100 (an additional 6%) if sustainable measures have been taken to increase the sustainability of the property. This extra amount may only be used to finance energy-expense reducing measures. For further information on conditions, please consult a mortgage advisor.

OTHER MORTGAGES

With the following mortgage types you will no longer be allowed to deduct the related mortgage interest from your taxable income. For this reason, they are basically no longer offered – though they are discussed further on. If you already have one of these mortgages prior to January 2013 and lower your mortgage interest, or change mortgage providers, you can keep it – including the deduction.

Endowment mortgage: No repayments are made during the term of the mortgage. Instead, the whole loan is redeemed in a single lump sum at the end of the term. The redemption is financed by means of a with-profits endowment policy that matures on the expiry date of the mortgage.

Special endowment mortgage (*Spaarhypotheek*): This is a variation on the Endowment Mortgage. It too provides for a lump-sum redemption of the mortgage loan at the end of the term. The distinguishing feature is that the interest rate on the loan is exactly the same as the gross rate of return on the investment under the endowment policy.

Banksparen mortgage (SEW): With this type of mortgage, instead of an endowment policy, a special savings or investment account is linked to the mortgage. This type of mortgage is only possible in the case of immovable property and a related mortgage; at the end of the term, the savings must be used to pay off the mortgage; payments must have been made into the account for a period of at least 15 years, and the highest payment may never exceed ten times the previous payment.

Interest-only mortgage: Here, no redemptions take place during the term of the mortgage. It is usually part of an ordinary

Utilities – Gas and Electricity

Don't you love those cozy winter evenings, when you've taken a warm shower, made yourself a hot cup of tea, turned on the light and crawled into your comfy bed in a nice, warm bedroom? None of that would be possible without the services of a utility company.

So, how do you go about arranging your utilities in this country?

You start out by visiting a site such as www.gaslicht.com or www.independer.nl – which offer an independent overview of all suppliers – or www.energievergelijk.nl/english, which offers the same information in English. On these sites, you generally type in your postal code, your house number and select your current supplier. This list contains all the suppliers in the Netherlands as well as the options *onbekend / anders* (which boils down to 'don't know / different'), *geen i.v.m. verhuizing* ('just moved, don't have one yet') and *verschillend voor gas en stroom* ('different ones for gas and electricity'). At the top of the list of suppliers are the three largest companies at that moment.

Next, you can fill in your annual use, or – as you probably don't know this yet, as you've just moved here – the number of people in your household. You can also indicate whether your house has solar panels. This will give you an approximation of your use; only a year later will you of course know the actual numbers.

On the next web page, you will find an overview of the various offers, plus the option of selecting 100% sustainable ('green'), 50% sustainable or 0% sustainable energy, the duration of the contract and whether you want fixed or variable rates.

Based on your (actual or estimated consumption), you will find a list of offers of monthly (or annual) amounts that you will pay the various companies for the utilities they supply. A number of issues to look at when comparing these offers are:

1. the per-unit cost of gas
2. the per-unit cost of electricity
3. the delivery (administrative) costs of each of these; a low per-unit cost may be neutralized by high delivery costs
4. any introductory ('welcome') rebates the company may have to attract new customers.

On the page with the overview, you can select a number of companies in order to compare their prices. Here you can take a closer look at the items mentioned above: per-unit price, delivery costs, and welcome rebate. Though in 2022 and 2023, due to the situation surrounding the delivery of gas after the invasion of Ukraine, very few companies (if any) were offering contracts for fixed prices, this is changing and contracts at fixed prices are becoming available again.

At the end of the year, you will receive an overview of your actual use. If you exceeded the estimated use, you will owe the additional amount, if you stayed below it, you will receive a refund. The company will also determine what you will owe per month over the next year, which they will base in part on your past use and in part on expected price developments (unless you've opted for a fixed rate). However, you are not held to this amount; online – once you have created an account – you can adjust this monthly amount upwards or downwards. Of course, adjusting it downwards creates the risks of owing the excess amount – should there be one – in one go at the end of the contractual year.

Keep in mind that some of us like to keep it toasty and warm all day long, and throughout the house. Not so the Dutch. Many of them sleep with the windows open at night (even in the winter), and turn off the radiators in certain rooms, or during certain hours. This means that the monthly price quoted for a four-person household will probably be lower than what you will personally end up using. Consequently, you might want to raise your monthly price, or be psychologically prepared to pay a substantial difference at the end of the contractual year.

Don't forget to request a 'smart meter' (*slimme meter*) to be installed in your house. This will allow you to set up your own schedule, depending on your family routine as well as on the rates that they sometimes inform you of beforehand – for instance, on many days,

Endowment Mortgage and can only be taken out for a maximum of 50% of the value of the property or of the purchase price.

DUTCH TAX ISSUES FOR EXPATRIATES

In essence, a mortgage is a tax-driven product. Hence, to determine the most appropriate type of mortgage for you, it is necessary to first consider your tax status. In the Netherlands, the two major tax issues with which an expatriate is faced are the 30%-ruling and the choice between resident (*binnenlands belastingplichtige*) and partial non-resident tax status (*partieel buitenlands belastingplichtige*). A more in-depth explanation can be found on page 120.

The 30%-Ruling

Simply put, the 30%-ruling allows an employer to grant an employee a tax-free allowance of up to 30% of their total remuneration to cover expenses related to their placement abroad that they would not have had had they not been sent abroad – such as, for instance, housing-related expenses. Your total gross remuneration is reduced by 30% and in return you receive a 30% tax-free allowance. The result of the 30%-ruling is a higher net salary. When applying for the 30%-ruling, the employee may choose to have resident or partial non-resident tax status, see the following paragraph (and page 120).

Partial Non-Resident Tax Status

Expatriates who are partial non-residents owe taxes on income derived from certain sources specifically stated in the Dutch income tax legislation. *Once again; this option will cease to exist in 2025, with a transitional measure for those who made use of it in 2023.*

the rates are lower between 11 A.M. and 2 P.M. (provided you have a flexible contract). It will also allow you to monitor your daily use of both gas and electricity, as well as – if you really have time to spare – the amount of electricity certain gadgets use (an electric water boiler for your tea generates an impressive spike!). The services offered by the smart meter depend on the utilities company and it is worthwhile knowing that if you switch to a different utilities company, you might no longer be able to make use of all its features (programming will always be possible), plus you will receive a (modest) monthly invoice for its use from the company that initially installed it.

As for the contract period; you can opt for a one-year, two-year, three-year, four-year or five-year contract – the longer the duration, the lower the price (this is more so when taking out a contract for a fixed price). This makes some people nervous; they would rather pay a little more and be able to switch after one year. Maybe you, being new to the country, would like to take this route too. If you do opt for, say, a three-year contract, then you will owe a fine if you make an early switch (for instance, more than three months before the end of the contract). Often, your new supplier will offer to pay this fine for you, but be careful about making a switch after the winter. The monthly amount you pay is an average, meant to cover the more expensive winter months, and the cheaper summer months. If you switch in March and are more or less halfway your contractual year, then your monthly payments will not cover your actual expenses and you could find yourself paying several hundreds of euros more – which your new supplier will *not* cover. A little tip: if you switch suppliers every year, this will allow you to enjoy the 'welcome' rebate every year too.

You can opt for fixed rates and variable rates, though, as the situation in Ukraine continues, it is hard to predict how the market will develop. Therefore, the following advice is still included in this version of *The Holland Handbook*: It might seem attractive to opt for variable rates (they change every January 1 and July 1) if you are confident prices will go down. Nonetheless, according to the consumer site PriceWise (www.pricewise.nl) it is wiser to go with fixed anyway, as often the prices are actually cheaper, while with a variable contract – if the price is continuously rising – you are locked into this contract for its duration, with the accompanying obligation to go with the rising prices.

If you want to make sure that you contribute to sustainability, the Dutch consumers' association (Consumentenbond) has looked into the various companies offering 'green' energy. They evaluate the companies based on the sustainability of the produced or purchased utilities, how the utilities are delivered to the consumers, and their investment policies. The use of fossil fuels, gas and nuclear energy is 'penalized', while the use of wind energy, solar energy, and (certain types of) biomass is rewarded, as is the (direct or indirect) investment in sustainable production capacities. The most recent overview can be found on www.consumentenbond.nl/energie-vergelijken/de-groenste-energieleverancier.

Partial non-residents are also entitled to tax deductions insofar as they relate to specific income sources, alimony payments and mortgage interest payments for their principal place of residence.

A final important observation regarding partial non-residents is that, contrary to resident taxpayers, their net wealth (i.e. assets minus liabilities, taxed in box 3, over a 'fictitious' yield, at 36%) is not taxed here. Hence, the ideal mortgage for a partial non-resident takes advantage of the fact that the interest payments on the mortgage are tax-deductible and that the investment income is not taxed. The corresponding mortgage is discussed further on.

Resident Tax Status

Unless an expatriate chooses to be treated as a partial non-resident taxpayer, they are viewed as a resident for Dutch tax purposes. They are then taxed just as any ordinary Dutch citizen. Resident taxpayers (as well as partial non-resident taxpayers) are only entitled to mortgage interest relief on the principal place of residence. The value of every other residence is subject to wealth tax (over, in principle, the WOZ-value of the property on January 1 of the year preceding the tax year in question, minus the mortgage loan – over a fictitious yield, at a rate of 36%). Whether this also applies to a house abroad depends on whether this is dealt with in a tax treaty between the Netherlands and the country in which the house is situated.

EXPATRIATES: WHAT MORTGAGES ARE APPROPRIATE?

The recommended mortgage depends on your special tax position and whether you are likely to move again.

The ordinary and the Special Endowment Mortgage are not appropriate for a number of reasons. This has to do with the likely

Do I Need a Dutch Residence Permit to Buy a House?

Each year, companies transfer a sizeable contingent of expats to the Netherlands for a limited period of time. Some stay as little as a year, others stay for three years, and then rotate out to another country. These kinds of expats use temporary rental accommodations, and generally do not even consider buying their own house or apartment in the Low Countries.

Then there are the expats who relocate to the Netherlands because they have fallen in love with the country (or one of its residents), and have decided to make it their home. Can they buy a home here?

Buying a property in the Netherlands can make sense especially if the expat is allowed to legally reside in the Netherlands. The Dutch immigration service decides on that. The result is reflected on the front and on the back of the Dutch residence permit. However, Dutch law does not bar non-Dutch nationals (documented or not) from buying or owning a property in the Netherlands. In essence, they only need to identify themselves at the Dutch *notaris* (civil law notary's) office at the time of the purchase of the property.

When applying for a Dutch mortgage, however, the Dutch banks are usually interested in the financial / employment situation of the expat, and their Dutch residence permit status. The reason is straightforward. These banks want know why the expat is in the Netherlands, and if they can meet their monthly obligations. Banks sometimes ask for proof of permanent residency. With the help of an independent mortgage advisor, most banks can be persuaded to grant a mortgage to an expat buyer, even if they have a temporary Dutch residence permit.

duration of your stay. If you leave within, say, seven years and upon leaving decide to surrender the endowment policy, you may receive back only the total of premiums paid. The reason why there will be hardly any investment return is that insurance companies write off all policy costs during the first years of the insurance. Hence, if you surrender within this write-off period, the investment return will only be marginal.

Most expats opt to pay off the mortgage amount (either through an annuity or straight line mortgage), or to accrue the related amount on a savings account – on a special 'Own Home Bank Savings Account', or SEW, see earlier on – and sometimes they opt for an investment mortgage (investment account linked to a mortgage). The redemption-free mortgage is also a reasonably popular option. Generally speaking, mortgages that are linked to insurances are no longer taken out, especially not by expats. As mentioned above, though, the mortgage interest is not deductible for most of these options (see above).

YOU ARE A RESIDENT TAXPAYER

If you are benefiting from the 30%-ruling, this will mean that you have a high net salary. This will enable you to make repayments. At the same time, income from wealth is tax-free. For that reason, barring special circumstances, repaying the loan will usually not be tax efficient.

YOU ARE A PARTIAL NON-RESIDENT TAXPAYER

In this case you need to find a mortgage which allows you to benefit from the tax-deductibility of the interest payments while at the same time allowing you to benefit from the tax-exempt investment income (since there is no 'wealth / box 3' tax for partial non-resident taxpayers). A special type of mortgage can be found, allowing you to fully benefit from these advantages: a redemption-free mortgage combined with a compulsory savings scheme. Since there are no repayments, you benefit to the full from the tax-deductibility of the interest payments.

And since the investment income on the savings scheme is not taxed, you can use this to generate capital with which all or part of the mortgage can be repaid once your partial non-resident tax status ceases to apply. Because the savings are not taxed, it is better to save than to make repayments: the after-tax effect of the repayments will usually be lower than the tax-free effect of the savings. It follows that it is advisable to borrow as much as possible provided that it can be demonstrated that the funds are used for the acquisition of immovable property in the Netherlands. Finally, as partial non-resident taxpayers benefit from the 30%-ruling; here too this allows you to make savings. However, don't forget that the status of partial non-resident taxpayer will cease to be option over the coming years.

U.S. TAXPAYERS

Special provisions apply to U.S. taxpayers; these are not covered here, but can be discussed with your tax advisor.

LOCAL TAXES

The aim of local taxes is to improve the taxpayers' surroundings, such as maintaining the streets, canals and city gardens, but also in the form of an extra contribution to education. And then there are the fun things, such as sports and recreational activities, art and culture.

Local taxes are levied and collected by the municipality or other government organizations. The majority of the total amount collected is levied through municipal property tax (*Onroerendezaakbelasting* – OZB), waste collection taxes and sewerage charges.

MUNICIPAL PROPERTY TAX

If you own a house, you owe municipal property tax. This is purely an 'owner's tax'; users owe nothing. When determining the amount due, the value of the property, or the WOZ-value, must first be determined. The municipality employs its own valuation surveyors to do this. This value is determined annually and is adjusted each year by applying an inflation rate that differs per municipality. When real estate prices go up, the municipalities generally lower their property tax rates to compensate for this. When they go down, the property tax rates are raised accordingly. Thus, in terms of euros, the height of the municipal property tax assessment is largely independent of the developments in the housing market. The WOZ-value forms the basis for calculating local taxes, such as OZB and the water board assessment, as well as the deemed rental value (*eigenwoningforfait*) for income tax purposes (see page 104).

WASTE COLLECTION TAXES

This tax is levied to cover the costs of collecting and processing household waste. This includes the emptying of the glass, paper, plastics, organic waste and clothing containers that can be found in Dutch towns and cities. Processing waste is an expensive business. Environmental laws are becoming stricter and separating waste is a costly affair.

SEWERAGE CHARGES

These taxes are meant to cover the costs of maintaining the municipal sewerage system. Everyone who makes use of this system, owes sewerage taxes. Only owners of immovable property have to pay it. You might notice that your sewerage charges increase each year, due to the arrears in the maintenance of the city sewerage system.

WATER BOARD ASSESSMENTS

This is money spent for keeping the water level in, among others, rivers, canals, ditches and streams at a certain level and ensuring the quality of the surface water. During the wet season, the water systems are drained. During the dry season, if necessary and possible, more water is brought in. Thus the water boards play an important role in this wet country. Your water board assessment helps to pay for these services.

POLLUTION LEVY

The higher water control corporations, or Waterschappen, collect the pollution levy from all households. This levy is used for maintaining or improving the quality of surface water, while sewerage treatment plants are used for cleaning wastewater.

A COUNTRY OF TAXES

The Netherlands is truly a country of taxes. In order to guarantee or, where necessary, improve our enjoyment, local taxes are expected to continue to rise during the coming years. As they are

Affordable Housing

The Hague has introduced a new measure to safeguard affordable homes for those who cannot afford high rental prices. You need to request an affordable housing permit in order to be permitted to rent property that lies within a certain rental price range or that has a certain number of points. Points are awarded based on a rental property's area, kitchen and bathroom facilities, energy label, location and woz-value (which you can read more about on page 104). If it has 185 points or less, you will need to request an affordable housing permit to rent it, regardless of the rental price. If the rental price is € 763.47 or less a month, you will also need to request a permit. If the rental price lies between € 808.06 and € 1,116.85, a permit will also have to be requested, though the rental property can have more than 185 points. A permit is not required for all other types of rentals. You can request an affordable housing permit online (for which you will need a DigiD), or by downloading the necessary documents. You can find more information on www.denhaag.nl/en/permits-and-exemptions/residential-permits/affordable-housing-permit.htm.

On this site, you will find the conditions for being issued the permit, based on your income, the square meters of the property, the rental amount, the number of people you will be sharing a household with, proof of identity, and your residency status (if you are a non-EU national, you must have a residence permit). Special rules apply to those who are divorced and living with children younger than 18. As for income, you need to be able to supply proof of income; how this can be done is explained on above site.

Note: also Amsterdam and other cities apply these (or similar) rules: www.amsterdam.nl/en/housing/housing-permit/, while a housing permit is required for certain neighborhoods in Rotterdam: https://answers.housinganywhere.com/en/articles/4068359-what-is-an-hvv-housing-permit-and-how-do-you-obtain-it.

levied locally, there are great differences between municipalities in the amounts due. The Consumentenbond (Consumers' Association), a Dutch organization that looks into and informs us on issues of importance to consumers, and Vereniging Eigen Huis (Association for Property Owners) investigate the local tax situation every year, to help ensure that these differences do not become too great. In order to estimate the local taxes due, you can use the following calculation tool: www.coelo.nl (ocale lasten calculator).

These local taxes, as well as the deemed rental value and property transfer tax – along with fees for gas, electricity and water, insurances – can be seen as costs of living. The costs for gas, electricity, water, and insurances, as well as the local taxes, are charged by the municipality, the water boards, privately owned gas / electricity or water providers or the government. The costs for gas, electricity and water amount to at least 30% of the total cost of living, and local taxes; 25%.

DOG TAX

A very special tax is dog tax. Initially, the dog tax was a tax for companies that used dogs to pull carts. Now it is more of an environmental tax and is used to cover the costs of setting aside places for the dogs to run and play, and to clean up after them. Anyone who owns a dog must pay this tax, if they reside in a municipality that still levies it. Nowadays, about 60% of the municipalities have abolished dog tax, and more are to follow. The average dog tax amounts to € 50-120 per dog, per year (in most municipalities you pay less per additional dog).

PAPER SERVICES

Also, we owe tax for the 'paper services' provided by municipalities. Some examples are:

- marriage license
- registration papers
- driver's license
- passport
- residence permit
- parking permit (in the larger cities).

Though municipalities and other government organizations are not allowed to make a profit on these services, they can pass on the costs in their entirety.

DENT

All these levies, added up together, can come to a considerable – and sometimes unexpected – amount and can put quite a dent in your vacation savings! So be sure to reserve a generous amount a year for these taxes.

EXEMPTION FROM CUSTOMS DUTIES

If you transfer goods from a non-EU country to an EU Member State (such as the Netherlands), you are subject to customs duties, VAT and other special taxes (for example excises and a special tax on cars). The taxation incurred upon importation can mean a great financial burden if you regularly change your place of residence for work or for other purposes. A special exemption can provide relief in these circumstances if you meet certain conditions.

EXTENT OF EXEMPTION

All EU Member States provide an exemption if the imported goods form part of your household (personal) effects and they are transported as part of your change of fixed address. Usually, the removal company will ensure that you make use of the exemption and will take care of administrative obligations. Whether you meet the related conditions is a question only the Customs Authorities can answer, however.

PERSONAL EFFECTS

These are effects such as clothing, furniture, linen, kitchen equipment, audio equipment, etc. Used cars, (motor) bikes, pleasure yachts and pleasure aircraft are also deemed to be personal goods. The exemption will be issued in the form of a permit (license). Usually, the Customs Authorities will issue a license for the personal goods and a separate license for the car. To obtain the licenses mentioned above, you will have to fill out an application form. In certain circumstances, a car that is made available to a natural person by an employer, and that is used by that person for both business and private purposes, may be regarded as an item of personal property that is eligible for relief from customs duties.

CONDITIONS

When transferring your place of residence to any of the EU Member States, certain conditions that must be met in order to successfully claim a relief from duties and tax:

- your usual place of residence must be transferred to an EU Member State (in this case, the Netherlands)
- your usual place of residence must have been in a non-EU Member State for at least 12 months
- the goods to be transferred must have been in your personal possession, and must have been in your use during the last six months. In exceptional cases the authorities may grant an exception to this requirement
- you must apply for a permit in the Netherlands
- with the exemption request, you should submit a signed list of household effects and other goods to be moved
- you should fulfill the usual customs requirements upon importation
- the goods must be imported within 12 months of your actual change of residency. The importation may take place in separate transports but in each case there must be a direct link between the change of residency and the importation of the goods
- you must use the goods for the same purpose in the Netherlands and are not allowed to lend, hire out, transfer or otherwise dispose of the goods within a period of 12 months of the acceptance of the customs declaration by the Customs Authorities.

DETERMINING RESIDENCY

As mentioned above, the exemption can be requested if you change your place of permanent / usual residence from a non-EU country to the Netherlands and it will only be granted if you have been a resident of the non-EU country for at least 12 months preceding the move. If you do not have work connections here, or your work and personal connections are in different countries, then your home is considered to be where your personal connections are. It is up to you, when applying for the exemption, to prove the 12-month residency in the non-EU country. If you are deemed to have been resident in more than one country, the country with which your personal connections (family and/or social commitments) are, will prevail. If, for example your family remained in the Netherlands while you stayed in a non-EU country for a period of two years, the Customs Authorities will deem that you remained a resident of the Netherlands. Consequently, your 'return' to the Netherlands will not qualify as a change of residence.

Circumstances that prove personal ties with a particular country are: where your family / other personal relations live; memberships; municipal registration; a fixed home, either owned or rented; other sources of income; and nationality. Also the following issues can play a role: physical presence; other living space; where you carry out your work; financial interests; and your administrative ties with the government and other social institutes. In other words, if your family is not the deciding factor, there are several other circumstances that are also taken into account.

Based on recent case law, one can conclude that the Dutch Customs Authorities have become stricter, which is further supported by rulings issued by the Court of Haarlem and the Court of Justice in Amsterdam.

MOVING FROM AN EU MEMBER STATE TO THE NETHERLANDS

If you import goods from another member state, you will have already paid EU VAT and the exemption will therefore not be of any use. This is different, however, for cars – for more information, see page 171.

REVOCATION OF THE EXEMPTION

After the permit has been granted and you have imported the goods, the exemption will be revoked if you lend, hire out, transfer or otherwise dispose of any of the household effects, including the car, to another party within 12 months. Therefore, if anyone borrows your car, even for a short while, during your first 12 months in the EU, you will be liable for duties and tax immediately. This condition is in effect for 12 months starting on the date on which the Customs Authorities accept the customs declaration.

LARGE SAVINGS ON DUTIES

The exemption for household effects, when you move your permanent place of residence to the Netherlands, is subject to a number of strict conditions, but, when applied, provides worthwhile savings on duties upon importation.

References

CHAPTER 4

A Place to Live

Organizations

NEDERLANDSE VERENIGING VAN MAKELAARS, NVM
Dutch Association of Real Estate Brokers
Fakkelstede 1, 3431 HZ Nieuwegein
P.O. Box 2222, 3430 DC Nieuwegein
Tel.: 030 608 51 85
www.nvm.nl

VERENIGING EIGEN HUIS
Dutch Housing Association
Displayweg 1, 3821 BT Amersfoort
Tel.: 033 450 77 52
www.eigenhuis.nl

CONSUMENTENBOND
Consumer Society
Enthovenplein 1, 2521 DA The Hague
Tel.: 070 445 45 45
www.consumentenbond.nl

KONINKLIJKE NOTARIËLE BEROEPSORGANISATIE, KNB
Royal Dutch Notaries
Spui 184, 2511 BW The Hague
Tel.: 070 330 71 11
www.notaris.nl

DOUANE NEDERLAND
Dutch Customs
Service desk: 0800 0143
www.douane.nl

TAX AND CUSTOMS ADMINISTRATION
Steenvoordelaan 370, 2284 EH Rijswijk
Tel.: 070 372 49 05
www.belastingdienst.nl

Recommended Reading

THE ACCESS GUIDE/HOUSING IN THE NETHERLANDS
Useful information on renting and buying property, valuation and about choosing an agent
www.access-nl.org

THE HAGUE HOUSES & HAPPINESS
By Karola Grünenbaum
www.starkrealestate.nl

Websites

GENERAL HOUSE HUNTING WEBSITES
www.funda.nl
www.huislijn.nl
www.huizenzoeker.nl
www.jaap.nl
www.miljoenhuizen.nl
www.pararius.nl
www.vbo.nl
www.zah.nl

REAL ESTATE AGENTS PORTALS
www.makelaars.net: real estate brokers portal
www.makelaars-nederland.nl: real estate brokers portal
www.mva.nl: Makelaars Vereniging Amsterdam
www.nvm.nl: Nederlandse Vereniging van Makelaars

HOUSING/REAL ESTATE AGENCIES
Amstel Housing: www.amstelhousing.nl
Amsterdamse Maatschappij: www.amsterdamsemaatschappij.nl
Beeuwkes Makelaardij: www.beeuwkes.nl
Bosch & Duyn: www.boschenduyn.nl
Burger van Leeuwen: www.bvl-residential.nl
Buise van Soest Makelaars: www.buisevansoest.nl
Diagonal Makelaardij: www.diagonal-makelaardij.com
De Vries Robbe: www.vriesrobbe.nl
Direct Wonen: www.directwonen.nl
Dutch Real Estate Company: www.dutchrealestatecompany.com
Estata Makelaars: www.estata.nl
Expat Rentals: www.expatrentals.com
Finsens Makelaardij: www.finsensmakelaardij.nl
Gravestate: www.gravestate.com
Haagen & Partners: www.haagen-partners.nl
Holland2Stay: www.holland2stay.com
Holland Home Management: www.hollandhomemanagement.nl
Home in Amsterdam: www.homeinamsterdam.com
HomeRent: www.homerent.nl
Home to Rent: www.hometorent.nl
Housing Agent: www.housingagent.com
Housingonline: www.housingonline.nl
Housingsolutions: www.housingsolutions.nl
Kimmel & Co: www.kimmel.nl
Local Home: www.localhome.nl
Luijckx Makelaardij: www.luijckx-mak.nl
Makelaars Associatie: www.makas.nl
Mie Lan Kok: www.mielankok.nl
Nelisse Makelaars: www.nelisse.nl
Onesta: www.onesta-vastgoed.com
Pararius: www.pararius.nl
Perfect Housing: www.perfecthousing.nl
Plink Adviesgroep: www.plink.nl
Quality Rentals: www.qualityrentals.eu
Stark Real Estate: www.starkrealestate.nl
Stoit Groep: www.stoit.nl
Tettero & Wetters: www.tettero-wetters.nl
The Hague Real Estate Services: www.thehaguerealestate.nl
TVN Real Estate: www.tvnsite.nl
27 House Real Estate: www.27house.nl
Van Dorp Verhoog Makelaars: www.vandorpverhoog.nl
Van Paaschen Makelaardij: www.vanpaaschen.nl
Welp Makelaardij: www.welpmakelaardij.nl
Wobeco Housing: www.wobeco.com
Zeilstra Beheer: www.zeilstrabeheer.nl

TEMPORARY RESIDENCE
Corporate Housing Factory: www.corporatehousingfactory.com
Hotel Residences: www.hotelresidences.nl
Htel Serviced Apartments: www.htel.nl
Prinsenhof: www.prinsenhof.info
Rien vd Broeke Village: www.village.nl
ServicedApartments.nl: www.servicedapartments.nl
Short Stay Citizens: www.shortstaycitizens.com
The Student Hotel: www.thestudenthotel.com

RENTAL FURNITURE
In-Lease Nederland: www.in-lease.com
Home Inspirations: www.home-inspirations.org
Re-Place: www.re-place.nl
Rental FURN: www.rentalfurn.com

MORTGAGES
Hypotheekvisie: www.hypotheekvisie.nl
Expat Mortgages: www.expat-mortgages.nl
Finsens: www.finsens.nl
Huis & Hypotheek: www.huis-hypotheek.nl

Hypotheekshop: www.hypotheekshop.nl
De Hypotheker: www.hypotheker.nl
Independer: www.independer.nl
Mister Mortgage: www.mistermortgage.nl
Oversluiten.nl: www.oversluiten.nl

UTILITIES COMPARISON WEBSITES

Gaslicht: www.gaslicht.com
Independer: www.independer.nl
Keuze.nl: www.keuze.nl
PartnerPete: www.partnerpete.com
Pricewise: www.pricewise.nl
Overstappen: www.overstappen.nl
Utility Provider: www.utility-provider.nl

MAIN ENERGY SUPPLIERS

Overview of licensed energy suppliers: www.energieleveranciers.nl
Budget Energie: www.budgetthuis.nl/energie
Eneco: www.eneco.nl
Energiedirect: www.energiedirect.nl
Engie: www.engie.nl
Essent: www.essent.nl
Greenchoice: www.greenchoice.nl
Nuon: www.nuon.nl
Oxxio: www.oxxio.nl
Pure Energie: www.pure-energie.nl
UnitedConsumers: www.unitedconsumers.com
Vattenfall: www.vattenfall.nl
Vandebron: www.vandebron.nl

HOME IMPROVEMENT DO IT YOURSELF STORES

Fixet: www.fixet.nl
Gamma: www.gamma.com
Hornbach: www.hornbach.nl
Hubo: www.hubo.nl
Karwei: www.karwei.nl
Praxis: www.praxis.nl

This chapter covers the legal, tax and financial information you may need during your stay in the Netherlands, such as: money matters; where much of your hard-earned money goes (the tax man); obtaining permits; getting married in the Netherlands and its legal consequences; what to do when you want a divorce; the rules on inheritance; insurances you need to consider; where to go for legal assistance, and much more.

CHAPTER 5

Legal, Tax and Financial Matters

CONTRIBUTING AUTHORS MONIQUE BEIJERSBERGEN, STEPHANIE DIJKSTRA, ARJAN ENNEMAN, KEES DE GRAAF AND ROBIN SCHALEKAMP

MONEY MATTERS

THE EURO

Since January 2002, the monetary unit of the Netherlands has been the euro (or €), replacing 700 years of the guilder. The euro is also the currency in, Austria, Belgium, Croatia, Cyprus, Estonia, Finland, France, Germany, Greece, Ireland, Italy, Latvia, Lithuania, Luxembourg, Malta, Portugal, Slovakia, Slovenia, and Spain. Denmark and Sweden still make use of their own currency, as do Poland, Romania, Bulgaria, the Czech Republic and Hungary. Montenegro and Kosovo have their own currency, but you can pay with euros there too, while Andorra, Monaco, San Marino and Vatican City use the euro as well as their own coins.

All EMU countries that have introduced the euro have the same bank notes and coins. These coins have two faces: the common euro face and a national face – though these coins look different, they can be used in any of the countries that have introduced the euro. There are seven bank notes: 5, 10, 20, 50, 100, 200 and 500 euros, and eight coins: 1 and 2 euros and 1, 2, 5, 10, 20 and 50 euro cents.

Until January 1, 2032, you can exchange guilder bank notes at De Nederlandsche Bank for euros.

NUMBER PUNCTUATION

The Dutch way of punctuating numbers and decimals is exactly opposite to the English way, so that € 25,25 is 25 euros and 25 eurocents, and € 10.000 is ten thousand euros. Round figures are written with a comma and a dash: e.g. 15 euros is € 15,-.

CHANGING MONEY

The introduction of the euro has made it easier to travel throughout most of Europe: you can go from country to country and use the same currency. However, for all other currencies, the issue of exchange rates is still an important one.

The exchange rate (*wisselkoers*) is fixed every day and will be posted wherever you exchange money. The rate does not vary from one bank to the next, although the charge for exchanging money may differ. The most common place to exchange money is a bank (such as ABN Amro, ING or Rabobank), or a GWK Travelex exchange office. You will find GWK Travelex offices at railway stations, the airport, and places where there are many tourists.

In very heavily-touristed areas you may see other types of exchange offices, but their charges could be higher, so it is best to wait until you see a bank or GWK Travelex office. There is no informal market for currency. Anyone who approaches you on the street with an offer to change money will be a thief or con artist, rather than a money-changer.

OPENING YOUR BANK ACCOUNT

To manage your day-to-day finances, you will need a current account, called a *privérekening*. The former Postbank, which has now merged with the ING, referred to this account as the *girorekening*, so that you might still come across this name in certain documents.

In principle, you can open an account via the app of the bank in question. You take a picture of your ID and of yourself, and you answer a couple of questions. Within minutes to hours, you can often already do online payments. For some banks, you need a Citizen Service Number (*burgerservicenummer*, see page 78) to open a bank account – for others, you don't. Looked at from the point of view of the Dutch tax authorities, if you *pay taxes* here, you will need a *burgerservicenummer* to open a bank account – ask your bank about this, to be on the safe side. You might need to provide some type of proof of a regular income (such as a pay slip).

Most banks do not send statements anymore as almost everyone uses online banking nowadays. If you wish to receive 'paper' statements, you had best communicate this to the bank. With some banks, if you want to be able to overdraw your account ('go into the red'), you must bring proof of a source of regular income, so that you can determine together with the bank employee to what amount you can do this.

If you want to arrange a loan, the bank will check with the BKR (Bureau for Credit Registration) whether you are 'creditworthy'; here they keep records of your credit card and bank history. If the BKR issues a negative advice, the bank can refuse you.

Current accounts pay no interest, but you are charged interest if you overdraw from them: i.e., if you 'go into the red'. Various other types of savings accounts are available for other purposes.

DEBIT CARDS

When you open your account, the bank will offer you options regarding plastic cards. Some banks offer a choice of cards, depending on whether you plan to use them abroad or not, other banks offer 'only' one type of card, all functions included. These cards allow you to withdraw up to several thousand euros a day at the bank or in the stores. For the use of these cards, you pay a nominal annual fee. An account at a commercial bank is functional the same day that (or the day after) you open it. The basic card, or *bankpas, betaalpas* or *europas*, is used for making cash withdrawals from cash dispensers and for paying in stores using a *pinauto-*

maat. If you choose to have one, you will receive by mail, and can follow the included instructions on how to activate it. You will be issued a four-digit *pincode* to be used every time you use the card to withdraw cash or make a payment. Be sure to memorize it, or at least not save it with your card, so that a thief can never steal your card and find out your number at the same time. If you forget the number, you have to get a new card. If you want, you can change your *pincode* into any other four-digit combination you like, at the bank. If you receive a replacement card (for instance, every so many years, you are issued a new card), you activate the card by making a payment in a store, by making a withdrawal from an ATM, or by requesting how much money is in your account through the ATM.

Your basic card will have various symbols on it, indicating its various functions. One symbol matches the one on *pinautomaten* (for paying in stores), and others match symbols on cash dispensers. Most debit cards also work in ATMs abroad, a feature which, in most cases, must be activated online or through the bank. Before going on vacation, make sure this feature has been activated – and make sure it is set to 'worldwide' if you are leaving Europe. This can also be done temporarily.

Some banks offer variations on this basic card, which give it extra functions. They will tell you about these possibilities.

On www.bankenvergelijking.nl/prive-bankrekening/, you will find an overview of what the various banks offer, in terms of online banking, a credit card, mobile banking, etc. (in Dutch).

CREDIT CARDS

A credit card is a separate card. In the Netherlands, the commercial banks mostly have an arrangement with either MasterCard or VISA. The money you spend with your Dutch credit card will be deducted on a monthly basis from your account or you will receive an invoice from the credit card company.

The main difference between your basic debit card and a credit card is that your basic card will refuse to make a transaction if your balance is insufficient, whereas a credit card will always work unless it has been blocked – following theft, for example. This is why banks will give their clients credit cards only after they have known them a while, and have been able to determine, for instance, if the client has a regular source of income – and why the use of a credit card costs more.

Paying by credit card is less common in shops – especially smaller shops and supermarkets – mainly because the shops must pay a percentage of each sale to the credit card company. Restaurants, hotels and department stores generally accept all major cards, however. Look at the window beside the door to see which cards they will take. In some stores, they will ask you to present some form of identification before allowing you to use the credit card. For payments exceeding certain amounts, you may have to insert your credit card's chip through the slot in the machine and enter a four-digit (pin) code. For lesser amounts, you generally hold your card over the machine's reader which then scans it to accept payment.

CASH DISPENSERS (OR AUTOMATED TELLER MACHINES, ATM)

You will find a *geldautomaat* or cash dispenser at every bank (though there are only very few physical offices left), and in railway stations and other public places where people are spending money. Dispensers will accept almost every kind of card, nowadays. You must find a match among the symbols on the dispenser and on your card. Don't forget that, if you type in the wrong *pincode* more than twice, the machine will swallow your card and you will have to go to the bank for a new one.

PAYING IN STORES

Paying with a debit card (*pin*, *pinpas*; the operative word being *pinnen*) has become the most popular way of paying – though, increasingly, stores are starting to accept credit cards.

Shops have a link to the bank system, and the amount due is deducted immediately from your account. You can hold your 'contact-free' debit card against the reader and pay up to a maximum of € 50 without having to enter your pincode. For larger amounts, you insert your card into a reader that looks like an oversized calculator and you type in your own secret four-digit personal identification number (PIN, or *pincode*), sometimes only after saying 'OK' to the amount they are about to deduct. The bank checks whether or not your balance will cover the amount; you verify the amount by pressing *ja* ('yes'), and the transaction is complete. If there isn't enough money in your bank account, you will have to find some other way to pay. In some stores.

Also when goods are delivered to your home – if you have not already paid for them – you pay the delivery person in cash, or, if they have an 'ambulant' pin machine, with your debit card and pincode.

THE COIN ISSUE

In shops, clerks sometimes have trouble making change and will ask you for coins. During the last few years of the guilder, the use of the single cent was unceremoniously abolished and prices got rounded off to the nearest five cents. With the introduction of the euro, came the introduction of not only the one cent-coin but also the two cent-coin, much to the annoyance of shopkeepers and customers. Starting towards the end of 2004, it became common use again to round prices off to the nearest five cents.

BANK TRANSFERS / ACCEPTGIRO

Bills are generally paid by bank transfer, also known as the *giro* system. When bills are sent, they usually have a yellow *acceptgirokaart* attached to them. In the olden days, you filled in your own account number on it, signed your name, and sent it to your bank (either by means of the specially-provided postage-free envelope, or by depositing it in their mail box), which deducted the money from your account. Nowadays, most people pay the bill online, entering the receiver's name and bank account number, as well as the *acceptgiro* number in the required spaces. If you pay through your banking app, you can often scan the bottom of the *acceptgirokaart*, allowing an automatic filling in of the relevant payment data.

For bills that you have to pay on a regular basis, such as your monthly rent, you can go to the bank and fill in a form known as a *machtiging*. This gives the bank permission to transfer a certain amount from your account on a specific day of the month. *Machtigingen* can also be arranged online, if you have opted for online banking. This will continue until you tell them to cancel a payment or to stop altogether.

ONLINE BANKING

Online banking allows you to contact the bank online and – by means of an entry code – recall the amount on your bank account and carry out any payments. Furthermore, you can access an overview of your insurances and investments, and place orders for the buying and selling of shares, options, etc. – also from abroad, of course. Logging in on your computer can be done by opening the bank app on your mobile phone and scanning the QR-code that appears on your laptop / computer screen. Or you can just access the app on your mobile phone. Contact your bank for information on what else they offer through online banking.

When you participate in an Internet savings 'plan', you save money on an account that you can only access online. The amount of interest you receive on this account is relatively high, as the margins can be kept low, due to the fact that you are the one managing the account and executing the moves.

PAYING ONLINE

Now that we do more and more virtual shopping online, we need a virtual purse. In this virtual purse, we of course find our credit card, but there are also alternatives. The two best-known ways of paying online are called PayPal and iDEAL, which deducts the amount from your bank account. For more information, visit their websites. For prepaid payments – so that you need give neither your bank account number nor your credit card details – there is the paysafecard (www.paysafecard.com), or pre-paid credit cards (an overview of the cards available in the Netherlands can be found on www.creditcard.nl/prepaid).

BANKING HOURS

Regular banks are open Monday through Friday, generally from 9 A.M. to 5 P.M. Many also open for a couple of hours on the one evening of the week that shops in the neighborhood stay open. This is usually a Thursday or a Friday. Due to the advent of online banking, there are much fewer bank offices now than just a few years ago.

TAXES

For purposes of application of the tax laws, it is very important to know whether you are a resident of the Netherlands or not. If you are, you are considered a 'resident taxpayer'; if not, a 'non-resident taxpayer' – though so-called qualifying non-residents can also be treated as resident taxpayers. And then there is a fourth option: if you are benefiting from the 30%-ruling, you may opt to be treated as a partial non-resident taxpayer. As it would – not surprisingly – require at least one book to tell you about the tax treatment of these four categories, we have picked out a handful of subjects that could be of interest to you, as an expatriate. These have been divided into the following headings: Income Tax, Wage Tax, and the 30%-ruling.

INCOME TAX

ARE YOU A RESIDENT?

Determining your place of residence is important when assessing where you will be liable for taxes and where you are considered to be living is assessed according to the actual circumstances; civil law and formal criteria (e.g. registration in municipal registers) are decisive.

You are considered a resident of the Netherlands if all circumstances indicate that there is a durable link of a personal nature with the Netherlands. That link need not be stronger than with any other country. Circumstances that may be important in determining a place of residence include the place of residence of the partner, family and social circle. However, as all circumstances count, one should also consider elements such as a gym subscription or membership of an association.

FOUR TAXPAYER OPTIONS

Resident Taxpayers

If you are a resident taxpayer, you owe income tax on your entire, worldwide, income. In principle it makes no difference where in the world you earn your income. Consequently, you may end up owing double taxes, though in most cases this can be prevented (see further on). The main sources of income that constitute taxable income are: business income, employment income, income in the form of periodic benefits and income from savings and investments.

Non-Resident Taxpayers

If you are a non-resident taxpayer, you are only liable to pay income tax on your income from certain sources in the Netherlands, resulting in a limited tax liability. The main sources of income that are considered taxable are: Dutch business income, employment income, income from real estate in the Netherlands and income in the form of periodic benefits (whether in cash or in kind) and a substantial shareholding in a Dutch company. In principle, employment income that you earn while you are physically not in the Netherlands is not taxable here (see further on).

'Qualifying' Non-Residents Treated as Resident Taxpayers

The scheme for qualifying non-resident taxpayer status applies since January 1, 2015. You are a qualifying non-resident taxpayer if you live in an EU country, Liechtenstein, Norway, Iceland, Switzerland, Bonaire, Sint Eustatius or Saba, and pay taxes in the Netherlands on more than 90% of your worldwide income. Do you meet all conditions of this scheme? In that case, you are entitled to the same deductible items, tax credits and tax-free allowances as residents of the Netherlands. The same conditions apply to your partner.

Do you not meet all conditions? For instance, because you pay tax in the Netherlands on less than 90% of your worldwide income? In that case, you may, for example, no longer deduct the interest on the loan for your owner-occupied home on your tax return, nor can you opt for resident taxpayer status.

Partial Non-Resident Taxpayers

You only have the option of being treated as a partial non-resident taxpayer if you benefit from the so-called 30%-ruling (which will be discussed further on). When making use of this option, you are a resident of the Netherlands for income (and deductibles) in box 1, but you are treated – upon your request – as a non-resident in boxes 2 and 3. This option gives you the best tax position you can have in the Netherlands. This rule will cease to apply as of January 1, 2025. It will continue to apply until December 31, 2026, to those who already made use of this option in the last quarter of 2023.

DOUBLE TAXATION

Resident Taxpayers

As a resident of the Netherlands, you have to pay tax on your worldwide income, as a consequence of which you may be faced with double taxation. After all, income earned abroad will often also be subject to taxation there. This situation is covered by the tax treaties that the Netherlands has entered into with many countries. In most of these treaties, income from employment in the Netherlands will be tax-exempt in the Netherlands, provided all the following conditions are satisfied:

- you are present in the Netherlands for a period or periods not exceeding in the aggregate 183 days in any 12-month period or in a fiscal year, and
- the remuneration is paid by or on behalf of an employer who is not a resident of the Netherlands, and
- the remuneration is not borne by a permanent establishment or permanent representative of the employer in the Netherlands.

If the cumulative conditions summarized above are not met, your income from employment will be taxable in the Netherlands.

Please note that if you carry out work in the Netherlands via a foreign employment agency, you cannot always apply the '183-day rule'. The material relationship between you, the foreign employment agency, and the Dutch recipient will also have to be taken into consideration.

Income from a property abroad is taxed in the country in which the property is located. Business income is in principle taxed in the country where the company is based.

For countries with which the Netherlands has not entered into a tax treaty, there is a unilateral arrangement. This will often mean that income earned abroad is exempt from taxation in the Netherlands, although it will be taken into account for the purpose of calculating the (progressive) tax rate applicable to your further income, which is then taxed in keeping with the 'normal' rules.

Non-Resident Taxpayers

As a non-resident taxpayer, you generally owe tax in your country of residence on income earned in the Netherlands, as a consequence of which you may be faced with double taxation. This situation is also covered by tax treaties.

U.S. TAXPAYERS

If you are a U.S. citizen benefiting from the 30%-ruling and you opt for the status of partial non-resident taxpayer, you owe tax in the Netherlands over income earned on working days physically spent in the Netherlands only. Therefore, if you spend a lot of time traveling outside the Netherlands, this could clearly be to your advantage.

A lower tax credit may, of course, have a negative impact on your U.S. tax liability, but this will very likely be outweighed by the benefit. This rule does not apply to statutory directors.

THE TAX SYSTEM

There are different categories of income divided over three boxes, each of which is treated differently for tax purposes and with its own tax rates, deductions and exemptions. Legislation and amounts mentioned shall apply for the year 2024.

Box 1: Income from work and home

This box includes, among others, income from employment, pensions, social security benefits, business income, periodic payments (e.g. alimony received), income from home ownership (*eigenwoningforfait*, if the house is your principal place of residence, see page 104) – less deductibles, for example mortgage interest. The amount of tax due is calculated on the taxable income according to the progressive tax rates. The brackets for those under pensionable age are (other tax brackets apply to those who have reached pensionable age):

2024	INCOME	INCOME TAX + SOCIAL SECURITY
Bracket 1	up to € 75,518	36.97%
Bracket 2	€ 75,518 and more	49.50%

Box 2: Income from substantial shareholding

If you own (possibly together with your partner) at least 5% of the shares in a Dutch company (BV or NV) or in a similar foreign company limited by shares, this income is taxed in box 2 at 24.5% for over the first € 67,000 and 31% over the amount exceeding this (this two-tier system was introduced on January 1, 2024).

Box 3: Taxable income from savings and investments

A notional income from savings and investments is taxed, instead of the actual income. On December 24, 2021, the Supreme Court ruled that the way in which the income in box 3 was being calculated infringed property rights and could therefore no longer be applied. As a result, the legislation regarding box 3 is expected to be amended in 2027 and in the meantime a temporary solution will be introduced, in which the calculation of savings income in particular will be based on a very low percentage. In 2024, this notional income is based on a combined percentage between 0.01 and 6.04% of the value of the assets, depending on the type of asset (saving or investment, whereby an investment is taxed higher) reduced with (part of) the debts and a personal allowance of € 57,000. These planned percentages and amounts may still change. The tax rate is 36%. If you benefit from the 30% ruling, you will not have to declare all your assets in box 3 (see further on, under The 30%-Ruling).

Personal Deduction

Sometimes there are personal circumstances that cause you to incur extra expenses. Some extra expenses may be deducted from the tax due. This is your personal deduction and includes for example paid partner alimony, extraordinary medical expenses and donations.

Rate Correction for Deductions if You Have a Higher Income

Does your income in 2024 exceed € 73,303? Then a lower rate applies to your deductions. A lower rate already applied to deductions for owner-occupied homes. This means that in 2024 you will receive a maximum tax refund of 36.97% on all your deductions in the highest tax bracket – without the rate adjustment, you would have received a maximum tax refund of 49.50%.

It concerns the following deductions:

- personal deductions
- deduction costs of the owner-occupied home
- entrepreneurial facilities.

FISCAL PARTNERS

Fiscal partners can allocate common sources of income and deductible items – such as mortgage interest for the principal

place of residence, medical expenses or study costs – to each other's tax return in such a way that they can reap the maximum benefit from them. Without fiscal partnership, certain items could end up being deducted against lower tax rates (resulting in lower refunds), or certain levy rebates could be reduced.

Married couples and registered couples are automatically considered fiscal partners. Unmarried couples who are living together are only considered fiscal partners if they are registered at the same address with the municipal registration office, and meet one or more of the following conditions. They:

- have a civil partnership agreement drawn by a civil law notary (as of 2012 the contract must also include a mutual care stipulation)
- have a child together
- jointly own their principal residence
- are considered partners in a pension scheme
- were fiscal partners the previous year.

Partners are not free to choose whether or not they wish to become fiscal partners. The law determines whether they are or not.

Retroactive Effect

If one of the aforementioned conditions is fulfilled during the course of the fiscal year, fiscal partnership will automatically apply as of that date. If you are already living together and then buy a house, you will be considered fiscal partners. Those who, during the course of a year, become fiscal partners can choose to have this status for the entire year. Those who were fiscal partners during the preceding year, are automatically fiscal partners as of January 1 of the next fiscal year.

LEVY REBATES

Instead of personal allowances, Dutch tax law contains levy rebates; rebates on tax and on the so-called general insurance contributions. Various levy rebates are available, depending on your personal circumstances. The general levy rebate, which has been created for those who either receive income from (self-)employment or a government benefit (it is taken into account when wage tax is withheld over these payments), is also available if you have no such income, provided you have a fiscal partner who pays taxes in the Netherlands as well as contributions for the national insurance schemes. All you have to do is submit a request with the tax authorities and – as there is nothing to deduct it from – the tax authorities will pay out the amount of the rebate.

TAX REFUND

The tax authorities may invite you to file an income tax return after the tax year is over. The tax year is equal to the calendar year. If you believe you are entitled to a tax refund since you for example didn't work in the Netherlands the whole year or if you can claim certain deductions and you didn't receive an invitation from the tax authorities, it is still possible to file a tax return on your own initiative. You can also contact a qualified tax advisor to assist you.

In order to realize the tax benefit from deductibles (such as your mortgage interest) at an earlier point in time than through the final income tax bill, you can request the tax inspector to pay the tax refund in advance during the current year through a negative preliminary tax bill. The tax refund is then transferred directly by the tax authorities to your bank account, on a monthly basis.

WAGE TAX

PAYROLL DEDUCTION

The term 'wage' is interpreted very widely and includes cash benefits, benefits in kind, and also entitlements (such as pensions, which you can read about further on). In general, your employer is required to deduct the wage tax due from your wages and pay it to the tax authorities. The amount thus deducted can later on be credited with the income tax due. In some cases, no tax bill is imposed and thus the payroll deduction is the final tax due. If you are working for a non-Netherlands employer who does not have a permanent establishment, a deemed permanent establishment or a permanent representative in the Netherlands, your employer must register with the Dutch tax authorities as a foreign withholding agent and set up a payroll administration for the employees who are working in the Netherlands.

COST ALLOWANCES

The Netherlands wage tax law provides the following cost allowances for both resident and non-resident taxpayers:

- cost allowances: allowances for all kinds of expenses, the (non) taxability of which is determined by the business or personal nature of the expenses; the same applies to income in kind. Business expenses cannot be deducted on your personal income tax return, with the exception of (fixed) public transportation costs – subject to certain conditions
- extraterritorial expenses: under certain conditions, if you are an employee and have come to the Netherlands from abroad, extra expenses called 'extraterritorial expenses' can be reimbursed tax-free, either for the amount of the actual expenses or on a notional basis, being a maximum of 30% of your wage. The latter can be done if the Dutch tax authorities have issued you an official approval (the actual 30%-ruling). Your employer can also decide to reimburse your actual extraterritorial expenses instead.

PENSION

The term 'pension' has been strictly defined for tax purposes. A pension scheme that complies with this definition is a 'qualifying pension scheme'. If your pension scheme is indeed a qualifying pension scheme, your contributions are deductible and your employer's contributions are tax-exempt. The related benefits you receive are subject to tax at the time of payment. However, if a pension scheme does not 'qualify', your contributions are not deductible nor are your employer's contributions tax-exempt.

The continuation of a non-Netherlands pension scheme requires particular attention, since it will often not satisfy the Dutch criteria. In order for your pension scheme to be considered a qualifying pension scheme, your employer will have to request the approval of the Dutch tax authorities. If you continue to contribute to a non-Netherlands pension scheme with a non-recognized foreign insurance company, you may receive a so-called 'protective tax bill'. This tax bill will only be 'cashed' if, according to Dutch law, improper use is made of the pension insurance. If you contribute to a (qualifying) Netherlands pension scheme, you may receive a protective tax bill upon emigration. See more on pensions on page 82.

COMPANY CAR

The 'benefit' that you enjoy from the private use of a company car is taxable as income from employment (to be reported through

new perspectives
In the new economy we need to capitalize on market opportunities faster than ever. New rules challenge us to act more business-like. And a new generation is ready to do things differently. Better, smarter, more innovatively. To succeed as an entrepreneur we need to renew ourselves too. Be open to change. And have a broad-minded view of the possibilities that lie before us. New perspectives. That's what BDO wants to offer you. And that's exactly what we do, with our unique combination of local market knowledge and an international network. Personal service and a professional approach. At BDO, we want to help you get a fresh angle on your business. So you can make the right decisions to increase the agility, strength and success of your organisation – whether it is a small or medium-sized enterprise, a family-owned business, a public organisation or an international corporation.
BDO is eager to look ahead with you. Together we will gain new insights and new opportunities in your market. Together we will create new perspectives. Our professional tax consultants can offer you professional advice and have extensive experience in all expat-related issues. To find out more, visit www.bdo.nl or contact Robin Schalekamp or Kees de Graaf +31(0)10 - 242 46 00.
BDO

the payroll administration) whether you are a resident or a non-resident taxpayer. If you drive fewer than 500 kilometers a year for private purposes, it could prove worthwhile to keep a daily log of your private and business kilometers, as the benefit will then not be added to your taxable income. If the benefit related to the use of the car is taxed through your payroll, the 30%-ruling applies to it. A reduced taxable benefit applies to electric cars (battery or hydrogen).

THE 30%-RULING

30%-RULING / EXTRATERRITORIAL EXPENSES

The 30%-ruling is a tax facility that has been created for employees who have been posted from or recruited outside the Netherlands to work in the Netherlands. You do not need to be a resident of the Netherlands and you do not have to (physically) carry out work in the Netherlands for it to apply. The ruling can be found in the Wage Tax Act. The effect of this facility is that your employer can pay you a tax-free allowance of up to 30% of your wage for so-called 'extraterritorial expenses', as a result of which the effective rate of wage tax is reduced.

THE CONDITIONS FOR THE 30%-RULING

Whether you satisfy the conditions for the 30%-ruling or not depends on the circumstances at the start of your employment in the Netherlands as an 'extraterritorial employee'. These conditions are:

- Posted or recruited from abroad: you must have been posted to the Netherlands from another country or recruited abroad. Dutch nationals coming in from abroad may also qualify. The Dutch tax authorities also want to know the date on which you signed the contract, as this could help determine the country you lived in before you accepted the employment position for which the 30%-ruling is being requested.
- Netherlands payroll: for the ruling to apply, there must be a Netherlands withholding entity. This means that your employer must deduct wage tax (and general insurance contributions, if applicable) from any wages paid out to you (in principle including any salary earned abroad that is taxable here) and pay this to the Dutch tax authorities. A non-Netherlands employer can also act as a Netherlands withholding entity.
- Specific expertise / scarcity: you must have 'specific expertise which is not or scarcely available on the Dutch labor market'. The condition that you have specific expertise, will normally be considered to be met if you earn a minimum salary of € 46,107 (excluding the tax-free allowance of the 30%-ruling). If you are younger than 30, have a master's degree and are recruited from abroad, a reduced salary threshold of € 35,048 applies. (When you reach the age of 30, the higher threshold applies.) Academic scientists are exempt from the salary norm. The condition that you have specific skills that are scarce on the Dutch labor market will only be assessed in exceptional cases or if you are part of a group of employees that is brought in.
- 150-kilometer boundary norm: if you lived within 150 km of the Dutch border during two-thirds of a 24-month period before starting your activities in the Netherlands, you are not entitled to the ruling. This can affect you if you come to work here from, for instance, Belgium or Germany. If you had already been

VAT and Refunds

Everyone who purchases goods or services in the Netherlands, pays value added tax (VAT), known here as BTW.

The suppliers of these goods and services charge their clients / customers VAT over and above the price of the goods/services and pay it to the tax authorities – after offsetting it against any VAT they have paid themselves. The price you see on items in stores includes this tax, so that you are not in for a little surprise at the cash register, like you are in some countries. (Please note that in retail stores for businesses, the 'ex-BTW' price is quoted; however, you *do* pay BTW when checking out. You will be allowed to deduct this BTW on your quarterly or annual BTW-tax return, if you have your own business. You can read more about this on page 88). In the case of services, it is always advisable to ask whether the stated price includes VAT or not.

In the Netherlands, most goods and services are taxed at a rate of 21%, but some fall under the 9%-category – such as food, water, pharmaceuticals, books, magazines and newspapers, and services such as fixing a bicycle, repairs to shoes and clothing, and the hairdresser. For information on how much tax is due on online purchases from abroad and what to do if you are overcharged, visit: www.belastingdienst.nl/wps/wcm/connect/nl/internetaankopen/internetaankopen.

Tourists and expatriates can receive a refund on the VAT they have paid. The refund can be arranged through some stores affiliated with a refund group, or by showing the tax receipts at Customs, where they stamp them and then send them back to the retailer with a request for a refund. There are also several organizations (see the reference pages) in the Netherlands that help you arrange your refund. The administration fee varies from 4% to 10% over a minimum expenditure that varies per country of purchase. Note, however, that retailers are not obligated by law to provide this service and therefore in most cases will not cooperate; visit www.vatfree.com/how-to-get-a-refund, or download their app, to find out who does. Vatfree.com charges a certain percentage of the VAT amount, up to a maximum, for their services, if you use their app.

Who can benefit from the services of these organizations?

1. travelers who live outside the European Union and purchase goods in the EU for personal use
2. expats who move back to a country outside of the European Union, on goods they have bought during the last three months preceding the move
3. (Dutch) persons who are emigrating to a non-EU country.

For more on the rules, contact the Dutch Customs Authorities (0800 0143) or the organizations listed at the end of the chapter, or visit their websites.

Tax Issues for U.S. Citizens

Living abroad gives rise to complex tax issues that often confuse expatriates. The following is a brief overview of the main issues affecting U.S. citizens or Green Card holders living in the Netherlands. The first item to note is that, if you are a U.S. citizen or Green Card holder, you are still required to file a U.S. tax return. There are, however, several provisions in the tax code and the tax treaty aimed at reducing your tax liability. Another thing to keep in mind is that your tax return can, and may have to be, extended beyond the original filing deadline.

EXCLUSIONS FROM TAX

The first of these provisions is the foreign earned income exclusion under which you can exempt up to $ 120,000 (2023 – $ 112,000 for 2022). If the president's plans go through, U.S. citizens will owe zero tax on income earned abroad. However, this has not gone through yet.

To qualify for this exclusion, you must meet one of two tests – the Physical Presence Test (PPT) or the Bona Fide Resident test (BFR). To meet the PPT-requirements, you must be out of the country for 330 (not necessarily consecutive) days during any period of 12 consecutive months. It does not matter what the nature or purpose of your stay abroad is (employment as well as brief vacations qualify), the kind of residence you establish, or what your intentions are about returning to the U.S. The nature and purpose of your stay, however, *are* relevant when determining whether you meet the tax home test, which determines the place where you are permanently or indefinitely engaged to work in (self-)employment. (To make matters complicated, however, this 'tax home' is not necessarily your tax home for domicile or tax purposes.) You do not meet the physical presence test if illness, family problems, a long vacation, or your employer's orders cause you to be present in the other country for less than the required amount of time. For this reason, this is considered a riskier ground for requesting a tax exclusion, as missing it by even one day will disqualify you. To qualify for BFR you must be living outside the U.S. 'for an uninterrupted period that includes an entire tax year' – a tax year being from January 1 to December 31. As long as it is clearly your intention to return to this country, brief vacations and other trips will not jeopardize this status. All you have to do is make sure that you are not in the U.S. more than 183 days a year, and that you do not work in the U.S. more than four months a year. In case of 'war, civil unrest, or similar adverse conditions', the minimum time requirements can be waived.

Your tax home is the general area of your main place of business, employment, or post of duty, regardless of where you maintain your family home. It is the place where you are permanently or indefinitely engaged to work as an employee or self-employed individual. Having a 'tax home' in a given location does not necessarily mean that the given location is your residence or domicile for tax purposes. If you do not have a regular or main place of business because of the nature of your work, your tax home may be the place where you regularly live. If you have neither a regular or main place of business nor a place where you regularly live, you are considered an itinerant and your tax home is wherever you work.

Another exclusion available to expatriates who qualify for the PPT or the BFR, is the foreign housing exclusion, under which you can deduct a portion of your housing costs such as rent, certain utilities, and other expenses associated with maintaining a home abroad.

If you are self-employed and work abroad, you can claim the foreign earned income exclusion and the foreign housing deduction. This reduces your regular income tax, but not your self-employment tax. The foreign housing deduction is not the same as the foreign housing exclusion, as the exclusion applies to amounts considered paid for with employer-provided amounts, while the deduction applies only to amounts paid for with earnings from self-employment.

FOREIGN-EARNED INCOME

For the specifics on what and who qualifies and what and who doesn't, visit www.irs.gov/publications and select the Tax Guide for U.S. Citizens and Resident Aliens Abroad (for tax year 2023, this was publication 54).

FOREIGN TAX CREDITS

Another strategy for reducing your U.S. tax liability involves the use of foreign tax credits. Foreign tax credits may be taken whether you qualify for the abovementioned exclusions or not. Dutch income taxes paid on income that is not already excluded can be used as a credit towards your U.S. taxes.

TAX TREATY

As mentioned above, the U.S. has entered into a tax treaty with the Netherlands that may exclude your income from either U.S. or Dutch taxation. Generally, a person on a short business trip to the Netherlands will not have to pay Dutch taxes. Numerous requirements are set forth by the treaty, so caution should be used before applying this broad statement.

FILING FOR EXTENSION

All Americans are familiar with the April 15 filing deadline. If you are living in the Netherlands on April 15, you are automatically granted an extension till June 15. For a variety of situations, your U.S. tax return may be further delayed and can be extended up until October 15. The tax implications of a foreign assignment may seem confusing. The most important things to keep in mind are that there are provisions set up to avoid paying double taxes on the same income and that good record keeping is very important.

granted the 30%-ruling on January 1, 2012, transitional rules apply. If you are a doctoral student, the period of your doctoral research will not be taken into account, as long as you resided outside the 150-kilometer boundary before starting your doctoral research and on the condition that your employment in the Netherlands starts directly after you have completed your doctoral research. The question has been put to court as to whether or not this norm is in conflict with the EU rules on the free movement of workers. The court has stated that this is not the case, unless the 30% reduction of the 30%-ruling is far more than the reimbursement of the actual extraterritorial costs – a decision that is up to the Dutch court to make.

- Request by both employee and employer: you and your employer must jointly file a request for the application of the 30%-ruling. The request must be submitted with the Tax Office for Non-Residents in Heerlen within four months after the start of your employment for the ruling to apply from day one.

THE 150-KILOMETER BOUNDARY NORM EXEMPTION

In practice, the 150-kilometer boundary norm presented a problem for employees who left the Netherlands after having benefitted from the 30%-ruling, and then returned to the Netherlands, applying for the 30%-ruling again. For instance, if the previous employment in the Netherlands had lasted more than eight months of the preceding 24 months, the employee would theoretically not be entitled to the 30%-ruling upon return to the Netherlands. However, an exemption has been created for abovementioned situation. Now (with retroactive effect until January 1, 2012), the date on which the work activities were first carried out in the Netherlands is taken into account when determining whether or not the conditions for 150-kilometer boundary / two-thirds of 24-month norm have been met. The commencement date of the subsequent employment in the Netherlands is therefore not decisive. Please note that the maximum period for the 30%-ruling (see below) should still be taken into account.

CHOICE BETWEEN REIMBURSEMENT OR 30%-RULING

Subject to conditions, employers can choose to either reimburse the actual extraterritorial costs tax-free, or apply the 30%-ruling. Until December 31, 2022, this choice between the two options could be made every month. As of January 1, 2023, it will no longer be possible to switch between the two options within the same calendar year, as a consequence of which this choice will apply to the entire calendar year. An exception will be made during the first four months of the first year of employment.

CAPPING THE 30%-RULING

On Budget Day (*Prinsjesdag*) 2023, the Dutch government passed a tax proposal containing an amendment to the 30%-ruling that boils down to an annual cap of the 30%-ruling to the maximum set in the Standards for Remuneration Acts; the so-called *WNT-norm*. The annual *WNT-norm* in 2024 is € 233,000. As a consequence, once the base for the 30%-ruling exceeds € 233,000, the 30%-ruling will be capped at € 69,000. This measure enters into effect on January 1, 2024. It applies to all who were granted the ruling on or after January 1, 2023. Those who granted it before that, are subject to a transitional arrangement until January 1, 2026.

REDUCTION OF THE 30%-RULING

The government has agreed to a proposal to reduce the 30%-ruling, whereby over the first 20 months, 30% of your income can be paid tax-free; the following 20 months, 20%; and the last 20 months, 10%. The incoming government must comply with the reduction of the 30%-ruling by law, only a new percentage has not yet been set. If the First Chamber agrees to the proposal, the intended effective date would be January 1, 2024. In the proposal it is mentioned that there will be a transitional arrangement for employees who benefited from the 30%-ruling in December 2023. To these employees, the reduction will not apply.

THE 30%-RULING AFTER TERMINATION OF EMPLOYMENT

The 30%-ruling is only applicable till the last day of the wage tax period following the wage tax period in which the employment ended. For instance, if your employment contract ended July 8, 2023, and you receive an additional payment in September 2023, the 30%-ruling will not apply to this payment.

CHANGING EMPLOYERS

If you are benefiting from the 30%-ruling and you switch employers, you will be able to 'take it with you' to your new employment (if a new employer is found within three months and the other conditions are satisfied) though only for the number of months left of the maximum duration of the ruling. The request must be filed within four months of the change.

MAXIMUM PERIOD FIVE YEARS

The ruling applies for a maximum period of 60 months (five years). At some point during the course of the 30%-ruling, your employer will have to check whether the 30%-ruling can continue to apply during the rest of the period. As soon as it becomes clear that the conditions are no longer met, the 30%-ruling will end. You should also keep in mind that previous periods of residence or employment in the Netherlands that ended less than 25 years ago will reduce the period of five years.

EMPLOYMENT AGREEMENT

You may not simply split the gross salary for tax calculation purposes into a taxable part and a tax-free allowance. Your employment contract (or an addendum to it) should clearly indicate a reduced gross salary, any further taxable or tax-free benefits, as well as the fixed 30%-allowance to be paid on top of the salary and benefits. The Ministry of Finance has provided an approved draft that can serve as an addendum to the contract, for those who wish to have a clear idea as to how this can be arranged.

EXTRATERRITORIAL EXPENSES, NO 30%-RULING

If you do not qualify for the 30%-ruling, for whatever reason, your employer can reimburse your actual extraterritorial expenses, without any tax consequences. In this situation, you have to deliver proof of these expenses.

CONSEQUENCES FOR WAGE TAX PURPOSES

Basis for Taxation

Your taxable wage, after having determined the tax-free 30%-allowance, is assessed according to the normal legal wage tax rules, in the same way as they apply to all employees in the Netherlands. This means that your employer may provide tax-exempt allow-

ances for certain expenses in addition to the 30%-allowance. On the other hand, certain allowances for expenses that qualify as extraterritorial will reduce the level of the net 30%-allowance or will be taxable, so that you do not benefit (doubly) from both tax-free opportunities.

School Fees International Schools

Your employer may pay a tax-free allowance for the school fees of children attending an international (primary or secondary) school or pay them directly. School fees that you pay yourself are not tax-deductible. Dutch schools with an international stream do not automatically qualify as international schools for purposes of the 30%-ruling.

Impact on Social Security and Pensionable Base

Employee insurance contributions and pension rights may be accrued on your contractual (lower) gross salary only! In order to avoid a pension gap, ask your employer or seek expert advice; a solution is available.

Partial Non-Resident Taxpayers

If you have been granted the 30%-ruling, then you may choose to be treated as a partial non-resident taxpayer on your Dutch income tax return (see page 120). The choice to be treated as a partial non-resident taxpayer will be made on the application form and can be changed every year. This option will cease to exist as of January 1, 2025. It will continue to apply until December 31, 2026, to those who already made use of this option in the last quarter of 2023.

As a partial non-resident taxpayer, you need not report any investment income on your Dutch income tax return (except for Dutch source income, such as Dutch real estate), but you can still deduct certain personal expenses (i.e. alimony payments, medical expenses, etc.).

PERMITS

SHORT STAY

If your stay in the Netherlands will not exceed three months, then most likely you will not need a visa to enter the Netherlands. In most cases a valid passport will be sufficient. You should check with the Dutch Embassy or Consulate in your home country whether or not a visa is needed. If you do, this type of visa is called a *visum kort verblijf*, or short stay visa.

LONGER STAY

If you will be staying longer than three months, then you might need one of the following permits:

- Provisional residence permit (as the case may be; for highly skilled migrants) (*Machtiging tot Voorlopig Verblijf, or* MVV)
- Residence permit (as the case may be; for highly skilled migrants) (*Verblijfsvergunning*)
- Work permit (*Tewerkstellingsvergunning*) (not required for highly skilled migrants).

HEALTH INSURANCE

All residents of the Netherlands are obligated to arrange private health insurance. To this purpose, they will have to arrange a Citizen Service Number (*burgerservicenummer*) (see page 78) and a residence permit. EU/EEA nationals need a Citizen Service Number (*burgerservicenummer*) and a valid passport to do this.

PROVISIONAL RESIDENCE PERMIT / RESIDENCE PERMIT

EU/EEA AND SWISS NATIONALS

If you are a national of any of the European Union (EU) or European Economic Area (EEA) member states or Switzerland, you will not need a provisional residence permit prior to traveling to the Netherlands. Formally, EU/EEA and Swiss nationals also do not need a residence permit; however, if you intend to stay here longer than four months, you will have to register with the municipality.

Although EU/EEA/Swiss nationals will be entitled to reside and work in the Netherlands without any kind of permit, they will only be entitled to a residence permit – should they want one – if they have sufficient financial means, being at least the minimum social security norm (*bijstandsnorm*).

NON-EU/EEA/SWISS NATIONALS

You are exempted from the need to arrange a provisional residence permit (MVV) if you are from the United States, Canada, Japan, South Korea, Monaco, Vatican City, Australia or New Zealand. Under certain conditions, if you are a family member of an EU/EEA/Swiss national, you also do not have to apply for an MVV (more information can be found on https://ind.nl/en/residence-

permits/family-and-partner/verification-against-eu-law-for-union-citizen-family-members). In all other cases, you need a provisional residence permit prior to traveling to the Netherlands as well as to be able to apply for a residence permit upon arrival. You cannot apply for a residence permit if you entered the Netherlands without making use of this entry visa.

U.K. CITIZENS AND BREXIT

Special (transitional) rules apply to UK citizens since Brexit. These can be found on https://ind.nl/en/living-in-the-netherlands-after-brexit.

ENTRY AND RESIDENCE PROCEDURE (TEV)

In keeping with the Modern Migration Policy, immigrants need not apply separately for a provisional residence permit (MVV) and the residence permit, but instead can use the Admission and Residence procedure (TEV). With the TEV-procedure, you start with applying for the MVV with the Dutch Embassy or Consulate in your home country / country of legal residence – or your prospective employer informs with the IND in the Netherlands as to whether there is any objection against issuing you one. If there is indeed no such objection, the IND sends an MVV-approval to the Dutch embassy in your home country / country of legal residence and immediately issues your residence permit so that you do not need to apply for it separately.

Prior to traveling to the Netherlands, you collect the provisional residence permit at the Dutch Embassy or Consulate in your home country / country of legal residence. Once you have arrived in the Netherlands you collect your residence document in person within two weeks at the IND desk. In order to be able to issue you your residence document, the IND needs your fingerprints, passport photo and signature. Please check with the IND as to how and where you can provide these. An MVV must also be requested for your accompanying family members. Processing time is approximately 90 days.

RESIDENCE PERMIT (VVR-PROCEDURE)

If you are exempted from the need to arrange an MVV (for instance, on the basis of your nationality), you can apply for a residence permit with the IND. Or your prospective employer can apply for the residence permit while you are still living abroad.

REGISTERING WITH THE MUNICIPALITY

If you are planning on staying in the Netherlands longer than four months, you have to report with the municipality (*stadhuis* or *gemeentehuis*) to have yourself entered in the municipal register (*bevolkingsregister*). Please keep in mind that this procedure can only be executed when suitable housing has been arranged.

REQUIRED DOCUMENTS

The documents that you have to submit when registering and/or applying for a residence permit are, among others:

- a legalized certified copy of your birth certificate (also your spouse's or partner's)
- a legalized marriage license, if applicable
- if either you or your partner were previously married, a copy of the legalized divorce decree.

Whatever else you need depends on your circumstances and country of origin. Other documents, such as a passport, work permit and proof of insurance will be required at some later point, check with the IND what these are.

YOUR STAY EXCEEDS FIVE YEARS

If you are a national of an EU/EEA-country or a Swiss national and have legally resided in the Netherlands for a period of five years, you qualify for the residence document 'long-term residence of citizens of the Union'. Please note that you are not obligated to request this.

ECONOMICALLY NON-ACTIVE

If you are an economically non-active EU-citizen, you may come to the Netherlands to, for instance, spend your retirement years. However, you must have health insurance and have sufficient money, being the 'income norm' applicable to you for a minimum of one year (the applicable income norm can be found on the site of the IND), and – if you are not an EU citizen – you must be a long-term EU resident, which should be noted on your EU residence permit. Aforementioned income may also be your spouse's or registered partner's income. Citizens of the new members of the EU need to apply for a residence document for economically inactive persons.

WORK PERMIT

EU/EEA/SWISS-NATIONALS

In principle, if you are a national of an EU/EEA member state or of Switzerland, you may work in the Netherlands without a work permit. Your EU/EEA/Swiss passport is enough proof that you are permitted to work in the Netherlands.

To work here as a self-employed person, you do not need a work permit. For more on the applicable rules, visit the website of the IND.

NON-EU/EEA/SWISS NATIONALS

If you are a non-EU/EEA/Swiss national and wish to work in the Netherlands for fewer than 90 days, you will need a work permit. Your prospective employer can apply for a work permit with the UWV.

If you are a non-EU/EEA/Swiss national and wish to work in the Netherlands for more than 90 days, you will have to apply for a combined residence and work permit (GVVA), also known as the single permit. The employer applies for a single permit with the IND. Please note that the single permit does not apply to:

- seasonal workers
- students
- asylum seekers
- employees of an international company.

For these latter immigrants, the employer still needs to apply for a work permit with the UWV.

To work here as a self-employed person, you do not need a work permit. For more on the applicable rules, visit the website of the IND. Certain other persons also do not need a work permit; an extensive list of these can be found on www.uwv.nl/werkgevers/werkvergunning/welke-werkvergunning-heb-ik-nodig/detail/wanneer-hoef-ik-geen-werkvergunning-aan-te-vragen (in Dutch).

If you already live here on a residence permit, but do not have free access to the labor market, or want to go from self-employment to employment, or want to switch employers, you will also need a work permit (TWV).

REQUIREMENTS

In general, the UWV only issues work permits if the employer has been able to convince them that there are no qualified individuals available on the EU/EEA labor market who can do the job. The employer should therefore submit proof that they have done everything in their capacity to find individuals on the EU/EEA labor market (i.e. by submitting copies of advertisements, statements from recruitment agencies, online postings, etc.). Several months prior to filing the work permit application, the vacancy must be reported with the local UWV. If this condition is not met, a work permit will not be issued. Furthermore, the permit may be granted on the condition that the employer provide retraining opportunities for EU/EEA nationals seeking jobs, insofar as this can reasonably be requested of them.

An easier way to obtain a work permit is on the basis of a so-called inter-company transfer, see *Special Rules for Work Permits*, on page 144.

PROCESSING TIME

Theoretically, processing time for a work permit is five weeks after a complete application – together with the answers to possible additional questions raised by the UWV – has been submitted. The processing time for a so-called single permit is 90 days. During the application process, you will not be allowed to work in the Netherlands. Companies risk high penalties, and their directors even prison, if they break the law on this matter.

PERIOD OF VALIDITY

You will be issued a work permit or a single permit for the duration of one year. This period may be extended. A work permit or single permit is not transferable to another employer or to another position.

REFUSAL

A reason to refuse an work permit is if there is a suspicion that the vacancy will not be filled by people from EU/EEA-countries who are seeking work because the terms and conditions of employment or the working conditions in the business concerned do not comply with the collective labor agreement or the law.

WHO DOES WHAT

The employer takes care of the work permit and single permit application. They can start the application procedure while you are still living abroad.

HIGHLY SKILLED MIGRANTS AND EUROPEAN BLUE CARD

Almost 20 years ago, a policy that allows highly skilled migrants into the Netherlands was introduced. The aim of the policy is to simplify the entry of highly skilled people from outside the EU/EEA into the Netherlands in order to improve the position of the Netherlands as a knowledge economy and to make the Netherlands more attractive as a work location for highly skilled migrants. To this end, the work permit requirement for this category of persons has been abolished and replaced by a residence permit under the restriction of 'highly skilled migrant'.

Only companies that are established in the Netherlands can make use of the highly skilled migrant policy.

PROCEDURE

If your employer wants to bring you here as a highly skilled migrant, they must submit a 'request for advice about issuing a permit for temporary residence for a highly skilled migrant', the so-called TEV-procedure, with the IND. Once positive advice has been issued, your prospective employer will inform you of this and you will be able to pick up your MVV at the Dutch Embassy or Consulate in your country of origin within three weeks. After this, you have three weeks to travel to the Netherlands, after which you collect your residence document at the IND office in person, within two weeks.

If you are a national of a country for which the Netherlands does not require an MVV (provisional residence permit), you may only start working once your residence permit for highly skilled migrants has been issued. To circumvent this wait, you can apply for an 'MVV for a foreign national who is not subject to an MVV requirement'.

DURATION PERMIT

This permit will be issued for a maximum period of five years if you have an employment contract for an indefinite period of time.

If it is a fixed-term contract, the permit will be issued for the duration of the contract.

IND

The Immigration and Naturalization Service (IND) has sole responsibility for implementing the procedures for entry into the Netherlands / the Dutch employment market.

DEFINITION

Highly skilled migrants are defined as contracted employees who earn a minimum gross income of € 5,008 a month (2023; excluding the 8% holiday allowance), to be indexed annually. The annual income includes salary withholding tax, employee and social security contributions, the holiday allowance, and a monthly supplement (which must be guaranteed and paid every month), but excludes bonuses and payments in kind (e.g. company car). Employer charges are also not taken into account.

Since this income requirement is a considerable obstacle for young migrant workers, a lower threshold applies to them; persons under the age of 30 who earn a minimum of € 3,672 gross per month (2023; excluding holiday allowance) can also qualify as highly skilled migrants. Holders of a European Blue Card must earn a salary of € 5,867 (2023; excluding the 8% holiday allowance) to qualify as highly skilled migrants. For recent graduates who have found employment in the Netherlands, the salary norm is adjusted to € 2,631 a month (2023; excluding the 8% holiday allowance). When this *Holland Handbook* went to print, the salary norm for 2024 had not yet been communicated.

STUDENTS

Foreign students who have obtained a bachelor's or a master's degree in the Netherlands and students who have obtained a master's degree or their Ph.D. at a qualifying university abroad, as well as scientific researchers and post-doctoral students, have three years to request a residence permit to dedicate a year to finding work as a highly skilled migrant in the Netherlands, to start a so-called 'innovative company', or to work without a work permit. Until such time as they find work, they are not eligible for a benefit and will therefore have to be able to provide for their own basic needs, nor are they considered highly skilled migrants (yet).

The aim of this Scheme – which was implemented in anticipation of the Modern Migration Policy – is to ensure that foreign ('exceptional') talents, who might represent added economic value, are admitted into the country.

CHANGE OF EMPLOYER

Highly skilled migrants are allowed to change employers while their residence permit is still valid. The IND will test the change to a new employer against the applicable conditions.

If you are dismissed, a reasonable term of three months will be granted to find another position that satisfies the conditions. Should you accept a position that does not satisfy the wage requirement, you will have to apply for a work permit.

PARTNERS AND CHILDREN

Partners and children of highly skilled migrants will initially be granted a residence permit in keeping with the duration of the permit of the highly skilled migrant. Partners of highly skilled migrants can apply for a work permit without having to go

through the labor market assessment described on page 75, under *Protection Labor Market*.

PRACTICAL ISSUES

Companies can enter into a standard contract with the IND, which can be found on www.ind.nl. Once the IND has authorized the company to make use of the regulation, the company will be issued entry codes that will allow them to access the application forms that can be found on the IND website. This will help the IND process applications within two weeks.

ACCELERATED MVV-PROCEDURE

Employers who have been appointed as 'referent' are eligible for using the accelerated MVV-procedure for highly skilled migrants. A decision on such a request will basically be made within two weeks.

Part of the procedure requires that the identity of the highly skilled migrant and their relatives be confirmed on the basis of a passport. Marriage certificates and birth certificates of children will still have to be authenticated to show the family ties. The authentication requirements that apply to citizens of so-called problem countries do not apply.

EUROPEAN BLUE CARD

The European Blue Card has been created for non-EU employees who come to carry out highly qualified work in the EU. The conditions are stricter. They must:

- have an employment contact of at least one year
- earn a gross salary of at least € 5,867 a month (2023)
- have the required professional qualifications
- have followed at least three years of higher education
- have their diplomas valuated by Nuffic (see end of chapter)

- if they wish to carry out the profession of doctor or lawyer: be able to supply proof of the fact that they are legally qualified to carry out their profession
- have the right documents for entering the country
- not necessarily have a sponsor (recognized and registered with the IND), though the procedure will go faster if they do.

Family members, if they meet the general requirements for family reunification, may request to be allowed to enter the country as 'accompaniers' of a holder of a European Blue Card.

MARRIAGE / REGISTERED PARTNERSHIP

THE CEREMONY

Ja, ik wil – Marriage Dutch Style

Imagine this scenario: you spent months arranging your wedding; you've stood up in church and declared 'I do'; you've celebrated with your nearest and dearest; only to discover down the track that your wedding was as valid as Mick Jagger and Jerry Hall's Bali nuptials. In the Netherlands, a church service alone does not satisfy the legal requirements for the state of marriage. A civil service is all that is deemed legally valid. This is actually the case in many countries, the difference being that in some other countries churches are licensed to register marriages. If you want a church wedding in the Netherlands, you will first have to undergo a separate civil service.

CIVIL WEDDING

For most people the term 'civil' conjures up images of a hurried, impersonal service held in an ugly municipal building with couples queuing up for the privilege. In the Netherlands it doesn't need to be like this as there is a great variety of interesting locations available for a civil wedding. The municipality of The Hague alone offers many possible locations. Couples are not restricted to marrying within their own municipality (*gemeente*). They could, for instance, consider any of the following options: a theater in Leidschendam; the Rotterdam Zoo ('Blijdorp'); the Huygensmuseum Hofwijck, in Voorburg; a castle in the countryside; the Commandeurskamer at the Bataviawerf in Lelystad; or the *trouwzaal* of an historic *stadhuis* such as those in The Hague, Delft, Gouda or Middelburg.

A ROOF OVER YOUR HEAD

If you have always dreamed of an outdoor setting for your wedding, and you are brave enough to try such a thing in the Netherlands, then you need to be aware of the fact that for a marriage to be legal it has to take place with a roof above your heads. In effect this means that you could have the ceremony conducted outdoors, but you would need to move inside for the signing of the registrar.

WEEKDAY WEDDINGS

Many foreigners are surprised by the fact that Dutch weddings often take place on weekdays. This may have something to do with the costs involved. A free civil service wedding is possible, but it is usually only available between 9 – 10 A.M. on a Monday or Wednesday morning (hours vary per municipality). Please note that, in the bigger cities, the dates for the free wedding or the registered partnership are often fully booked months ahead of time. It won't be conducted in an atmospheric *trouwzaal*, but in a small room at the *gemeentehuis*. The ceremony lasts 10 minutes; no speech will be given and no music will be played, and only a handful of guests will be allowed. Despite the fact that the service is free, it will still set you back some money as you are required to purchase a *registratieboekje* (a booklet in which your marriage is registered), and to pay for proof of registration with the municipality as well as for witnesses if you can't provide your own.

The costs for a civil wedding service range quite dramatically, starting around € 140 and going up to around € 1,200 – depending on the time and location chosen. Generally speaking Monday to Thursday between 9 A.M. and 4 P.M. is the cheapest time to marry, and (as mentioned earlier) in some municipalities you can get married free of charge on certain weekday mornings. After 4 P.M. weekdays and on weekends, the costs can increase substantially. The cost for marrying on a Saturday is approximately three times as high as a mid-week wedding, making it very attractive to marry on a Friday. For further information regarding times available for weddings, and the relevant costs involved, consult www.bruiloft.nl/gemeente-info.

WHO CAN GET MARRIED HERE?

Anyone of Dutch nationality can get married here, regardless of whether they live here and regardless of the nationality of their intended. Two foreign nationals may marry in the Netherlands on the condition that one of them legally resides in the Netherlands. If both foreign nationals live here and want to marry here, they must both reside here legally. The condition of having the right residence documents does not apply to EU/EEA nationals.

The above also applies to those entering into a registered partnership.

If both of you live outside the Netherlands and would like to get married or enter into a registered partnership in the Netherlands, you will first need to announce this to the Department of National Tasks (Afdeling Landelijke Taken). If neither of you has Dutch nationality and you both reside outside the Netherlands, you cannot get married or enter into a registered partnership here.

Furthermore, below conditions of Dutch law apply to marriages entered into in the Netherlands (but always be sure to check, in case legislative changes have been made):

- you cannot currently be married or be in a registered partnership
- you must be 18 years or older
- you must give notice of your intent to marry at least 14 days before the intended wedding (to a maximum of 12 months)
- same-sex marriages are possible and legal
- blood relatives are not allowed to marry. As of December 2015, this rule applies to nieces / nephews, though there are exceptions (more information can be found on www.government.nl)
- if you are under guardianship, you need to get permission first.

IN CASE OF DOUBT

If one of the partners legally resides in the Netherlands or has Dutch nationality, then the question of whether or not this person is allowed to get married or enter into a registered partnership is answered in accordance with Dutch law. If the marriage is permitted in the Netherlands, then the fact that the national law of the non-Dutch partner does not allow the marriage (for instance, a same-sex marriage) will not influence their ability to get married in the Netherlands. However, this does not guarantee that the marriage / partnership will be recognized in the home country.

Non-Dutch nationals who are not allowed to get married / enter into a registered partnership according to Dutch law, can do this anyway in the Netherlands if they are allowed to do this according to their national law, and provided the marriage / partnership is not in violation of Dutch public order.

NOTIFICATION

Would you like to get married? Then you first need to notify the municipality. This is called *melding voorgenomen huwelijk* – or 'notice of intent to marry'. This notice must be given at least 14 days before the marriage or wedding ceremony at the city office in which you or your spouse-to-be are / is registered. You can arrange this online if both of you are registered with the Municipal Personal Records Database (Basisregistratie Personen – BRP). You need to produce passports (identity cards), birth certificates, witness forms (see next paragraph for more on witnesses), proof of single status and evidence of your Dutch residency. When you notify the municipality of your wish to become married or enter into a registered partnership, those of you who do not have Dutch nationality will be asked to fill out a so-called personal declaration, see the following paragraph. Documents from overseas require the appropriate *apostille* stamp (see International Certificate for an explanation of the *apostille* stamp), or other proof of legalization.

When giving notice, you can indicate on which date and in which municipality you wish to marry or enter into a registered partnership. Your marriage should be officiated within 12 months of filing the notice, otherwise the notice is rendered invalid.

NOT A MARRIAGE OF CONVENIENCE

As of September 1, 2015, a foreigner who is marrying a Dutch national must issue a declaration that this is not a marriage of convenience (former M46-declaration), stating that (a) they have not entered into any other marriage or registered partnership in the world and (b) they do not have the intention to use the marriage to obtain admission to the Netherlands. The declaration is not necessary if both partners have the nationality of an EU-country, Liechtenstein, Norway, Iceland or Switzerland.

WITNESSES

At least two witnesses or a maximum of four witnesses must sign the marriage certificate. All the witnesses must be 18 years or older. The municipality does not provide witnesses. Witnesses can be of any nationality, and you need to provide copies of their passports to the municipality where you are marrying. This is one document you don't need to have stamped with an *apostille*!

INTERNATIONAL CERTIFICATE

A foreigner marrying in the Netherlands can pay a small sum extra to have an international extract of the marriage certificate (*Internationaal Uittreksel uit de Huwelijksakte*) issued. This certificate contains the most important details as well as an explanation in nine languages so it should save many people the cost of having the certificate officially translated for use in another country. However, if the certificate is needed for official use in a country outside the Netherlands then it will need to be endorsed by the Dutch authorities with an *apostille* stamp. An *apostille* stamp is simply an internationally recognized certification of authenticity and is required by all countries on official documents issued in another country. In some cases, the international authorities will want a copy of the full certificate, in which case you will have to obtain a certified translation of the marriage certificate.

AGE, SAME SEX, REGISTERED PARTNERSHIP

Eighteen is the minimum legal age for marriage, although a pregnant female may marry at 16 providing she has proof from her gynecologist and her parents / guardians have granted their permission. The same applies to the 16 or 17-year-old father. Same-sex marriages are also possible (since April 1, 2001).

As touched on earlier, it is also possible for two people of the same or the opposite sex to enter into an arrangement similar to marriage, known as a registered partnership. (Please note that a registered partnership is not the same as a cohabitation agreement.) The consequences of a registered partnership and the marriage between two persons of the same sex are the same as the consequences of an ordinary marriage. If you wish to enter into a registered partnership (see further on, under *Age, Same Sex, Registered Partnership*), then you must also register for this in advance (minimum 14 days, maximum one year) and be able to produce the declaration stating that it is not a partnership of convenience, with the same exceptions as stated above.

If children are born during a same-sex marriage / registered partnership, specific rules apply regarding who becomes the parent.

One of the most important differences between registered partnership and marriage lie in the area of dissolution. A marriage is dissolved in court, while a registered partnership can be dissolved by means of a written statement by a civil law notary or a lawyer (if both parties agree to the dissolution, and provided there are no children under the age of 18 involved). If there is a dispute about the dissolution and/or if minors are involved, the dissolution of a partnership can only be pronounced by the court. The agreement (in case of dissolution without the interference of the court) or decree (in case of a dissolution by the court) will have to be registered in the municipal registry. A registered partnership is legally recognized in 20 EU countries.

LAST NAMES

Once married, couples have a number of choices regarding their last names. In the Netherlands, a partner can take the other's surname after marriage, and vice versa. You can also choose to use your surname followed by your spouse's surname, or the reverse, your spouse's surname followed by your surname. And, a last option, both husband and wife may choose to keep their own surnames. Official documents must show the person's own name.

Children can be given the surname of their father, the mother, or the "duo"-mother as the Dutch say. As of January 1, 2024, you can give your first-born child born on (or after) this date the surnames of both parents. There is also a transitional arrangement for children born on (or after) January 1, 2016. Has your first child's surname been chosen, then the chosen surname will also apply to all subsequent children. Should you fail to choose a surname or to record the choice on time, then the law will determine which surname your child receives. This depends on whether or not you are married or have a registered partnership. Are you married as husband and wife or in a registered partnership, then your child will automatically receive the father's surname. If you want your child to have the mother's surname, then you must register this together at the civil registry before or during the registration of the child's birth. If you are neither married nor registered partners, then your child will automatically receive the mother's surname. If you want your child to have the father's surname, then the father must acknowledge the child. At the time of acknowledgement, you can communicate the choice of name together.

RING FINGERS

If you are used to surreptitiously checking out a person's marital status by the sight of a wedding band on the ring finger of the left hand, be aware that in the Netherlands a wedding ring may be worn on the ring finger of either hand. For a church wedding the tradition in this country is that Catholics wear their wedding ring on their left hand, whilst Protestants wear it on their right hand.

DUTCH LAW ON MATRIMONIAL PROPERTY

COMMUNITY PROPERTY

Until not so long ago, the Dutch legal system determined that if you got married under Dutch law before January 1, 2018 without having drawn up a marriage contract, in principle all property and debts that either of you had before the marriage, became joint property and joint debts once you were married. The same applied to property and debts that you acquired during your marriage, whereby it was irrelevant whether the assets were in both names or in the name of one of the spouses. All assets were considered community property independent of who factually owned certain assets or property. Only a special category of assets that were closely attached to the person of one of the spouses were not included in the community property. This legal system was called general community property.

Gifts and inheritances could be left out of the community property provided this was stipulated in the will of the testator or in the deed of gift.

NEW MARITAL PROPERTY LAW

The regime of general community property has since been replaced by 'limited community property'. This new law affects couples who get married after January 1, 2018, without drawing up a prenuptial agreement. One of the changes is that properties and debts gained before the marriage will no longer become part of the community property. Nor will inheritances or gifts obtained before, or during, the marriage. Only assets and debts that were already jointly owned by the spouses prior to the marriage or assets and debts acquired during the marriage (or registered partnership) fall within the limited community of property. When the marriage ends, only these possessions will be divided on a 50-50 basis. This means, for example, that inheritances or gifts do not need to be shared in the event of a divorce. Similarly, debts incurred by either spouse before marriage are the sole responsibility of the spouse who incurred them.

The new law requires spouses to keep a careful record of their property – personal as well as jointly-owned – during the course of their marriage. If they fail to keep a proper record, it will be very difficult to make a clear distinction between the two. Without proper registration, the property will be assumed to be joint in case of a divorce.

MARRIAGE CONTRACT

You can deviate from the legal system before or after entering into marriage by means of a marriage contract (*huwelijkse voorwaarden*). The spouses can enter into such an agreement at the time of concluding the marriage and during the marriage itself. A pre/postnuptial agreement can hold all sorts of agreements between spouses concerning the financial settlement of matrimonial property. Each and every agreement stands alone and must be reviewed individually. The most common pre/postnuptial agreements according to Dutch law are the ones that determine that there will be no communal assets during and after the marriage – perhaps in accordance with a paragraph detailing what to do in case of divorce or death of one of the spouses, or detailing the arrangement that income that was not spent during the year will, at the end of that year, be divided equally between both the spouses.

The marriage contract has to be drawn up by a civil law notary who enters the deed containing the marriage contract in the public matrimonial property register at the District Court of the district in which you were married. If you were married outside the Netherlands, it is entered in the public matrimonial property register of the District Court in The Hague. This you do, in order to ensure that anyone can find out whether you have a marriage contract and what clauses it contains. The contract can help avoid that debts incurred by you or your spouse can be recovered from the other.

When moving to the Netherlands, if you do not have a marriage contract, it is always wise to seek the advice of a civil law

notary or lawyer on whether unexpected Dutch rules of legislation might affect your matrimonial regime.

REGISTERED PARTNERSHIP

Matrimonial property law also affects partners (also same-sex partners) who choose to become registered as common-law partners in the civil registers, meaning that general community property is the starting point in case of a partnership that was entered into before January 1, 2018, and limited community property in case of a partnership that was entered into after January 1, 2018 – which can be avoided by means of a 'registered partnership agreement' drawn up by a civil law notary.

THE LAW ABROAD AND INTERNATIONAL PRIVATE LAW

International private law determines which legislation is applicable to a marriage with international aspects – for instance in the case you and your spouse were married abroad or do not have the same nationality. Every country has its own rules on matrimonial property and International Private Law and the authorities of a country always apply the country's own rules. This can lead to different, conflicting results. International treaties are meant to avoid such conflicting results. Regarding the law on matrimonial property, the Dutch authorities apply the rules of the Hague Matrimonial Treaty 1978 to all marriages entered into after September 1, 1992, and before January 29, 2019. For marriages and (same-sex) registered partnerships entered into after this date, please read *The EU Regulations on Property Regimes for International Couples, further on.*

THE HAGUE MATRIMONIAL PROPERTY TREATY 1978

At the moment, the convention has only been ratified by the Netherlands, France and Luxembourg, and signed by Austria and Portugal. As such, international divorce cases that take place outside the authority of the convention are not clear-cut. The premise of the treaty is that if you if you entered into marriage on or after September 1, 1992 and have not stated a particular choice of law in a marriage contract, the law of the first country in which you both have your habitual residence after entering into marriage is applicable to the worldwide assets and debts in the case of divorce or death of one of the spouses, and other issues, such as bankruptcy. If you and your spouse have the same nationality, there are some exceptions to aforementioned premise.

EMIGRATION, IMMIGRATION OR NATURALIZATION

Abovementioned treaty determines that during the marriage – due to emigration, immigration or naturalization – the originally applicable law on matrimonial property may be replaced by the law on matrimonial property of a different country. This is only the case if you entered into marriage between September 1, 1992 and January 29, 2019 and did not explicitly state a choice of law in your marriage contract. The replacement of the applicable law can have considerable consequences for, for instance, the extent and the division of the matrimonial property should you get divorced or should either one of you die.

MOVING TO THE NETHERLANDS

If you got married between September 1, 1992, and January 29, 2019, lived abroad at the time of the marriage and subsequently moved to the Netherlands, the matrimonial property system changes after ten years. Ten years after you moved to the Netherlands, if you do not have a marriage contract, you become married according to the Dutch system. If you are both of Dutch nationality at the time of the move, then the Dutch law of matrimonial property becomes applicable as of the moment you settle in the Netherlands.

The change in system of matrimonial property also takes place if you married between September 1, 1992, and January 29, 2019, and both subsequently acquired Dutch nationality while living in the Netherlands. As of the moment you acquire Dutch nationality, the Dutch legal system applies to your matrimonial property regime – unless you have explicitly chosen another applicable law.

CHOOSING AN APPLICABLE LAW

By stipulating which law is to apply, you leave no doubt as to which law of matrimonial property is applicable. Making such a choice is of particular importance if your marriage has international aspects. A choice of law helps to avoid that – due to emigration, immigration or naturalization – a different law becomes applicable. However, beware of the fact that a choice made in the Netherlands does not always have the desired effect in a country that is not a party to the Hague Matrimonial Property Treaty 1978. In order to ensure that other parties are also bound by your choice, you must have this choice registered. Who does this and how this is done, depends on the law that you have chosen. According to Dutch law, the choice must be made in an agreement, drawn up by a civil law notary. The choice, however, is limited; it is only possible to choose:

- the national law of one of the spouses
- the law of the country in which one of the spouses resides
- the law of the first country in which one of the spouses has their marriage domicile right after the marriage.

THE EU REGULATIONS ON THE PROPERTY REGIMES FOR INTERNATIONAL COUPLES

New EU rules apply to the property regimes of all international marriages entered into after January 29, 2019. They aim to clarify the property rights for international couples, whether they are married or in a registered partnership. The EU regulation will help international couples manage their property on a daily basis or divide it in case of death, divorce or separation, and bring an end to parallel and possibly conflicting proceedings in different EU countries.

The EU regulations on the property regimes of international couples apply in 18 EU countries, namely: Austria, Belgium, Bulgaria, Croatia, Cyprus, Czechia, Finland, France, Germany, Greece, Italy, Luxembourg, Malta, the Netherlands, Portugal, Slovenia, Spain and Sweden. These rules determine:

- which EU country court is competent to deal with a case regarding a couple's property regimes
- which law is applicable to the case (it can be the law of an EU country or the law of a non-EU country)
- the rules for the recognition and enforcement in an EU country of a decisions given in another EU country.

The new EU regulation is applicable to marriages and registered partnerships entered in by citizens of (a) EU or (b) non-EU nationality who:

- live in the EU and have different nationalities, or
- live in an EU country that is not their country of origin, or
- do not live in the EU but have assets in an EU country.

COMPETENCE OF THE COURT

In case of a divorce / legal separation or the dissolution of a registered partnership, the competent court to deal with the couple's property regimes will be the court in the EU country:

- of the current usual residence of both spouses / partners, or failing that
- of the last usual residence of both spouses / partners, or failing that
- of the usual residence of the respondent, or failing that
- of the common nationality of spouses / partners, or failing that
- under whose law the registered partnership was registered.

APPLICABLE LAW AND CHOICE-OF-LAW AGREEMENT

As a spouse or registered partner, you can agree with your spouse or partner to draw up a formal choice-of-law agreement (in writing, signed and dated by both parties) to choose the law that will apply to your property regime. A choice-of-law agreement can be drawn up before, on entering or during the marriage or registered partnership. The spouses or partners can choose the law of:

- the country of residence of both or either spouse(s) / partner(s) or,
- the country of nationality of either spouse or partner, or
- the country where your partnership is registered, if you are in a registered partnership.

If you have not made a formal choice-of-law agreement, the applicable law will be the law of the country:

- of the spouses' first common habitual residence following marriage
- of the spouses' common nationality at the time of the marriage
- with which the spouses jointly have the closest connection at the time of the marriage, taking into account all the circumstances
- where your partnership is registered, if you are in a registered partnership.

RECOGNITION AND ENFORCEMENT

The principle of mutual recognition is applicable to matters of matrimonial property regimes. A decision given in a Member State will be recognized in the remaining Member States without any special procedure. Enforceable decisions made in a Member State are likewise enforceable in other Member States when they have been declared enforceable in accordance with the procedure provided for in the Regulation. It should be noted that definite enforceability only exists within the EU. Decisions made pursuant to the Regulation might not be enforceable in a third country.

MAKING THE MATRIMONIAL PROPERTY REGIME KNOWN

Third parties, such as creditors, are not always bound by your matrimonial property regime. If your matrimonial property regime is not governed by Dutch law, a Dutch civil law notary can have the regime entered in the Dutch matrimonial property register at the court, so that the rules of your marriage system are binding for, for instance, creditors in the Netherlands. If this has not been done, a creditor may assume that you have been married according to the Dutch legal system unless they knew or could have known to the contrary. However, both you and your creditor had to have been living in the Netherlands at the time the debt was incurred.

DIVORCE

The sole ground for divorce is the irretrievable breakdown of the marriage. With the introduction of this sole requirement, the Dutch lawmakers let go of the 'guilt question', and the 'need' for a guilty party. In other words, it is not necessary to prove adultery or any other form of neglect of the marital rights and obligations to end a marriage; simply stating the marriage has been broken down irretrievably is enough. Since 1998, the number of divorces has been steadily increasing to approximately 39% of all marriages, though since 2016, this number has been on the decline. This is ascribed to the fact that younger people don't get married at all (and therefore do not get divorced), get married at a later age or opt for a registered partnership. Another factor is the aging population, whereby it has been determined that those who have been together for a long time are less likely to get a divorce.

It has been argued that Dutch law is to be preferred over for instance English or Scottish law – which systems require a legal waiting period before the marriage can end – or other systems known to us that see to a mandatory reconciliation period. Especially to persons who are non-Dutch nationals but who want to end their marriage fairly quickly, Dutch law holds a certain appeal.

A marriage can only be ended in court by mutual request or upon a divorce request submitted by one of the spouses. The proceedings are started by means of a (joint or unilateral) petition. It is dissolved once the court pronounces a divorce and the judgment is entered in the marriage register in the municipality in which the marriage took place.

COMPETENCE OF THE COURTS

The Dutch courts are competent to take cognizance of a petition for divorce if one of the following conditions is met:

- both of you have Dutch nationality
- both of you legally reside in the Netherlands
- both of you legally resided in the Netherlands and one of you still lives here
- one of you legally resides in the Netherlands, and both of you submit a request for divorce
- one of you legally resides in the Netherlands while the other files for divorce here
- the one requesting the divorce is Dutch and has been living here for a period of six months or more
- the non-Dutch spouse requesting the divorce has been living in the Netherlands for at least 12 months.

In all other cases, the Dutch courts are not competent and you cannot file for divorce in the Netherlands.

APPLICABLE LAW

If the Dutch court is competent to decide on the request for the dissolution of the marriage, Dutch law applies to this request. Exceptions can be made if both of you have a common other nationality and:

- you choose to apply the law of your common nationality or one of you makes this choice in the divorce proceedings and the other does not contradict this choice
- one of you chooses to apply the law of your common nationality and both of you have a real social connection with the country of your common nationality.

If the Dutch court is competent to take cognizance of the petition and Dutch law is applicable, the Dutch court can then end the marriage if the marriage has irretrievably broken down.

RECOGNITION

Whether or not the ruling of the Dutch court will be recognized abroad depends on whether your country is a party to the treaty that the Netherlands has entered into on this matter – the Treaty on the Recognition of Divorces – and on your country's national law. Be sure to get solid advice on this matter, particularly on how you can make sure the divorce is recognized in your home country.

UNILATERAL PETITION

Should you be the one filing the unilateral petition, the petition should contain a request on how you would like the four consequences of the divorce (which you will find below) to be arranged. Your spouse can lodge a statement of defense, containing their wishes regarding the consequences.

In a hearing, the court will allow itself to be further informed on these matters and will determine the date on which it will rule on the divorce and its consequences. If the proceedings are likely to take a long time, the court, if asked explicitly, will come up with provisional measures on such pressing matters as child visitation rights, alimony, and child support. If you or your spouse do not agree with the final ruling, you or your spouse can bring an appeal before the Court of Appeals. No appeal can be brought against the provisional measures.

JOINT PETITION

If both of you have come to an agreement regarding the legal consequences of divorce, you can have these drawn up in a settlement. This settlement can be drawn up by two lawyers – if each of you has a lawyer – or by one lawyer, who is then the 'divorce mediator'. This settlement is brought before the court, which rules in keeping with it, requiring no future hearing. Children aged 12 and older are invited to come to court to give their opinion on the care arrangements. However, they can also do this by means of a written statement. A hearing will then not be necessary.

MEDIATION

The purpose of a divorce mediator is to have both of you arrange the consequences of the divorce together, thus promoting the acceptance and durability of the agreement. The idea is that the discussion with the mediator provides you with better insight into the underlying emotional problems, allowing you to better describe your differences and see the merits of the various solutions that the mediator suggests. The settlement is submitted before the court along with the petition and the court rules in keeping with this settlement.

In the case of divorce, there are several reasonably diverse areas that the mediator should be able to advise you on, such as (joint) parental authority, care arrangements, alimony, the division of marital property / the settlement of the prenuptial agreement, and how to deal with the (future) pension payments. If they cannot advise you on all these matters, they will be able to refer you to a specialist who can.

COLLABORATIVE DIVORCE

In order to avoid the uncertain outcome of a divorce court procedure and possible further litigation, a couple who wants to separate can also opt for what is referred to as a collaborative divorce. If this is the case, they work together with their lawyers and, if necessary, other family professionals, towards a settlement that best meets the needs of both parties and their children. To this purpose, they sign a contract (the 'participation agreement'), binding each other to the process and disqualifying their respective lawyer's right to represent either one in any future family-related litigation.

THE LEGAL CONSEQUENCES OF DIVORCE

When people decide to end their marriage, this decision has certain consequences: both legal and practical. An important question is which law is applicable to the various consequences of the divorce. It is for instance possible that different laws are applicable to different consequences (and therefore different outcomes are entirely possible), so it is always wise to check in advance.

1. Children

As long as the children reside in the Netherlands, Dutch law is applicable to the related consequences, regardless of the nationality of the spouses.

Parenting plan. According to Dutch law, parents who are getting a divorce are obligated to draw up a parenting plan. The court will in general not pronounce the divorce requested by one or both of the parties with children under the age of 18 until a parenting plan has been drawn up. At the very least, this plan needs to contain arrangements concerning the following child-related issues: visitation rights, the way in which information will be exchanged, how consultations regarding important matters will take place, and arrangements concerning the costs of care and upbringing. Also, the plan needs to outline the way the parents plan to involve the children when drawing up the plan.

Custody. According to Dutch law, the shared parental authority or joint custody that exists during the marriage remains after the divorce. This means that the parents, even after they are divorced, still have to make certain decisions about the children together. For example, decisions regarding school, medical treatment, emigration or immigration. Only on rare occasions does a Dutch court decide that it is in the best interest of the children that only one of the spouses have parental authority or custody after the divorce.

Place of residence. When you both have custody, you need to agree on with which parent the children will have their main place of residence.

Visitation rights. The parents will have to agree on when the children will be with the one and when they will be with the other parent. If they cannot agree, the court can be asked to decide. The general rule of Dutch law is that children and their parents have a fundamental right to be in contact with each other. How this contact should take place is left up entirely to the parents – and/or the judge in case the parents are unable to reach an agreement.

Child support and care. Child support is based on the idea that the children should be allowed to maintain the same 'standard of living' after the divorce. To determine the amount of financial support required, the court looks at the needs of the children entitled to the support and the financial capacity of the parent who has

The Role of the Civil Law Notary

In the Netherlands, there are several important moments when you will need the help of a so-called civil law notary. For instance, when you buy a house, when you draw up your (pre)nuptial agreement or cohabitation agreement, when you draw up a will and when you establish a corporation. In order for these documents to have legal effect, and to ensure legal certainty, the law states that you need a deed, drawn up by a civil law notary.

The original deed always remains in the files of the notary. Sometimes you are required to enter a copy of the deed in a public register.

Civil law notaries are lawyers who have specific tasks and competencies and who are appointed by the King. They play an impartial role in the drawing up of notarial deeds and can advise the parties in such a way that the interests of all parties are taken into account and that there are no unpleasant surprises. If one of you does not have Dutch nationality, then matters of international law enter the scene. Be sure to seek advice on these!

BUYING A HOUSE

The civil law notary takes care of all the legalities involved in the transfer of the ownership of the house, including the drawing up and execution of the deed of transfer. This can only be done by a civil law notary. They evaluate the transfer and look into the background of the parties involved. If there is anything that seems not quite right, they will immediately freeze the process and – if possible – resolve the situation. Due to new, strict legislation aimed at preventing money laundering and terrorism, the civil law notary will have to be informed – by the buyer – as to the origins of the own money to be used for the purchase.

The civil law notary is the financial spider in the web. They make sure that the bank, the seller and any creditors get the money they are due and that the transfer tax is paid. And it goes without saying that the payment of the house and the transfer take place at the same time; they carry out the payment on your behalf only once they are sure that you will become owner of the house.

It is also the task of the civil law notary to carry out a number of investigations – in the Land Registry, the Bankruptcy Registry, the Matrimonial Property Registry and, as the case may be, the registry of the Chamber of Commerce – to verify that the property is not in any way encumbered. They also consult the Land Registry to check if all the data on the house is correct and whether it is subject to a mortgage and/or attachments. If it is, then in most cases, its ownership cannot be transferred without dealing with these first and they and the owner will have to find a solution. They also check whether there are any impediments or possible servitudes, such as a right of way through the garden.

In the Matrimonial Property Registry, the civil law notary checks whether the seller has been divorced sometime between the purchase and the sale of the house, in which case the former spouse may have ownership rights regarding the house.

Should you take out a loan to finance the house, the civil law notary is responsible for drawing up the mortgage deed.

In principle, you can select whichever civil law notary you want. The real estate agent can draw up the purchase contract for you, but the notary can do that too. Once the contract has been signed, the notary has it entered in the Land Registry. This way, the seller cannot sell the property again to someone else, while it also protects you against possible bankruptcy and/or attachments resulting from any financial problems they may have. Your notary can provide you with more information on these issues.

RELATIONSHIPS

You and your loved one can lay down certain agreements regarding your relationship in a contract. For instance, if you want to live together without getting married, you can draw up a cohabitation contract. Or, if you want to get married, you might want a prenuptial agreement.

These contracts will also have to be drawn up by a civil law notary, who can advise you on their content. As an impartial party, they will draw up a balanced agreement that will take into account all personal circumstances, of both you and your partner / spouse-to-be. Your civil law notary, who should be specialized in international law, will have to take into account the rules that have been put down in the EU regulation on international marital property. This regulation applies as of January 29, 2019.

After talking to both of you, the civil law notary will make a draft of the contract. Once you agree on the content, the final deed will be drawn up and signed by the two of you and the notary. In case of a marriage, this will have to be done before the actual ceremony takes place. Though, of course, you can also arrange a post-nuptial agreement, if you are already married.

INHERITANCE / WILLS

You need a civil law notary if you want to draw up a (living) will. In a personal meeting, you will get together to discuss your wishes. In your will, you can state who your heirs are to be and make detailed legacies regarding leaving specific items or sums of money to specific persons or institutions. Should you wish to appoint an executor or, for instance, a guardian for your child(ren), then this must be included in the will.

Once you have signed the will at the office of the notary, they will enter it in the Central Registry of Wills. This way, the will can always be found.

The notary can also give you advice regarding the validity of a will drawn up abroad and whether or not it will be necessary to draw up a will in the Netherlands. Of note in this context is the fact that, on August 17, 2015, the European Inheritance Law Regulation entered into force. The Regulation has been accepted in all countries of the European Union, except for Ireland and Denmark. The aim of this Regulation is to simplify successions – that have an international context – for European citizens, and to make the settlement of international inheritances within the European Union run smoother. Your civil law notary will be able to advise you as to how to set up your will, taking into account the rules of the Regulation.

the duty to provide financial support. The needs of the children are based on the actual 'costs' that are related to the (ages and number of) children and net family income before the divorce. Once the level of cost has been determined, the next step is to work out how much each parent is able to contribute, based on their ability to pay. The basic principle under Dutch law is that each parent contributes towards the cost of the children's care and upbringing in accordance with their financial means. You can find more information on the financial aspects of divorce in the brochure *Geldwijzer Alimentatie & Co-ouderschap* (Money Guide for Alimony), which you can order from NIBUD (you will find the address at the end of the chapter).

Child support is due until the children reach the age of 21. As of their 18th birthday, the child support is to be paid out directly to the children and, until they reach the age of 21, aims to cover (a portion) of their study costs.

The parent with whom the child(ren) is / are registered will receive the Child Benefit (*kinderbijslag* – see page 212). When both of you are to share an equal part in the raising and maintaining of the children, then – unless you request otherwise – one of you will receive the Child Benefit, but you will be expected to divide it among the two of you. On top of that, there are some other benefits that pay out a monthly allowance but only to parents whose income or wealth lies below a certain maximum.

2. 'Partner' Alimony

Another consequence of a divorce is the obligation of one of the spouses to pay alimony to the spouse who is unable to provide fully in all costs of living for themself. The court will determine whether and to what degree you will have to support each other financially. If the court has not set a time limit, the obligation to provide maintenance shall automatically end upon expiry of a time limit equal to half the duration of the marriage up to a maximum of five years. There are three exceptions to this:

- if, at the time the application for divorce is filed, the duration of the marriage exceeds 15 years and the age of the spouse entitled to maintenance is not more than 10 years below the (pensionable) age pursuant to Article 7a of the General Old Age Pensions Act, the maintenance obligation does not end until the person entitled to maintenance reaches that age
- if, at the time the application for divorce is filed, the duration of the marriage exceeds 15 years and the spouse entitled to maintenance was born on or before 1 January 1970 and their age is more than 10 years below the (pensionable) age referred to in Section 7a of the General Old Age Pensions Act, the obligation shall end after 10 years
- in the case of a child born by marriage who is younger than 12 years of age, the obligation shall not end until the child has reached the age of 12 years. In the event of concurrence, the longest term shall apply.

When calculating the alimony, the court takes the following into account:

a. The needs of the one who has the right to alimony

The court will take into account the standard of living you were accustomed to during your marriage. Also the fact that you could get a job will be taken into account.

b. Financial capacity of the other spouse

Having determined your needs, the court determines the amount that your (former) spouse can contribute, taking into account their income and financial needs.

c. New relationship

If you start living together with another person as if you were married or in a civil partnership, get married or enter into a civil partnership, you lose the right to spousal support.

d. Change of circumstances

If, after determining the amount of alimony you are to receive, you get a job and are capable of providing for yourself, your right to alimony may cease or be reduced to a lower amount. Conversely, should it be agreed that no one owes alimony, after which one of the two partners finds themself in a situation in which they can no longer provide for themself, it can be determined that alimony is due after all.

Alimony paid to former spouses is entirely deductible, the amount of taxes thus saved is added to the amount of income available for partner alimony. The receiving spouse, however, owes the related income tax (taking into account this spouse's tax bracket, which could lead to a difference in income tax deducted and income tax paid – this is also taken into account when calculating the amount of alimony).

3. Division of the Marital Property

The ruling of the court on the divorce should contain instructions on how the marital property is to be divided (taking into account the fact that your marriage is governed by the Dutch rules on community property or that you have a pre or postnuptial agreement, see page 133). Legally, that which is part of the communal property should be divided equally among you, including the debts; however, you can agree otherwise. Be aware of tax complications if the worth is not shared 50/50. Also keep in mind that, if another country's law is applicable, the Dutch court may apply those rules.

4. Pension Rights

Anyone who contributes to a pension scheme builds up entitlement to a retirement or surviving dependents' pension. In the case of divorce, each of you has a right to a portion of the amount of retirement pension accrued by the other during the period of marriage / partnership – provided the pension is covered by Dutch law – to be paid out as of the retirement of the person in whose name the pension has been built up. You can agree otherwise, allowing it to stay entirely with the person who built it up, or agreeing to a different division. The Dutch courts rarely rule on this matter. Either you decide to act in accordance with the law, or you agree not to.

If you are the spouse / partner of the pension receiver, the wisest would be to inform the pension provider of your divorce within two years after the date you are officially divorced; the provider is then obligated to pay out your half to you as soon as the pension receiver retires. The surviving spouse / partner of a formerly married couple is eligible for a surviving dependent's pension after the death of the spouse / partner, unless parties agree otherwise.

SEPARATION IN THE CASE OF REGISTERED PARTNERSCHIP

If you have underage children, your separation must go through the court, and you will have to include a parenting plan. Otherwise, all you need is a lawyer or civil law notary, who will draw up an agreement on issues such as partner alimony and pension to be signed by both parties – it will only go to court if you cannot reach an agreement. Your lawyer / civil law notary will inform the civil registry of the divorce, while you will be charged with notifying your municipality of your separation.

DUTCH INHERITANCE LAW

SUCCESSION BY WILL

In the Netherlands you can determine who your heirs are in a will (succession by will). If there is no will, then the law determines who your heirs are (succession by law / intestate succession). If you make a will in the Netherlands, according to Dutch law, it should be done by means of a deed made up by a Dutch civil law notary.

SUCCESSION BY LAW

Only blood relatives, spouses or registered partners are entitled to the inheritance. The (adopted) children and spouse or registered partner form the first group of heirs, each inheriting an equal share. If a child has predeceased you, their descendants will take their place. The brothers, sisters (and their children) and parents form the second group of heirs. Grandparents and great-grandparents finally form the third and fourth group. If there are no relatives within the first, second or third group respectively, then the relatives within the next group are eligible.

ALLOCATION BY LAW

If the spouse or registered partner, together with one or more children of the deceased, is the heir, then, by intestate succession, they will get all assets and debts of the deceased. The children will only have a monetary claim on them to the amount of their share, claimable at the time they die or go bankrupt. Should the spouse or registered partner remarry, the children are entitled to claim the proprietary rights of assets derived from the inheritance, to avoid that these assets end up with the stepfamily. The spouse or registered partner may retain the usufruct of these assets.

This allocation by law can be set aside in a will so that, for instance, the children also take part in the proprietary rights and liabilities as of the day of the devolution of the estate, instead of just having the monetary claim.

STATUTORY CLAIMS

Children always have a right to a fixed, minimum value of the estate of their parents, also referred to as the statutory claim. Even if, for example, a parent states in a will that a child is not to inherit anything, the child can make this monetary claim on the joint heirs anyway. The statutory claim amounts to half of the value of the portion which the child would have inherited had they not been disinherited. In a will, the parent can state that the statutory claim is not claimable until their spouse, registered partner or partner with whom the parent has a cohabitation agreement, dies.

If the spouse or registered partner is disinherited, they can claim the usufruct of the family dwelling and furniture and even of other assets, insofar as they are in need of this.

FOREIGN INHERITANCE LAW AND INTERNATIONAL PRIVATE LAW

Every country has its own rules on inheritance law and international private law. International private law determines which legislation is applicable to an estate of an international nature – for instance if the deceased did not have Dutch nationality or was not residing in the Netherlands at the time of their death. The authorities of a country always apply the country's own rules of international private law, which can lead to different, conflicting results. International treaties are meant to avoid such conflicting results.

In Europe, the Regulation on inheritance law was introduced in 2015 and applies to 'international' inheritances that came / come to be on or after August 17, 2015.

GENERAL RULES OF THE EUROPEAN INHERITANCE REGULATION

The Regulation applies to the entire European Union – with the exception of Ireland and Denmark – and provides answers to the following questions:

- Which law applies to the inheritance? For instance: who are the heirs; who has a right to what; is there a legitimate portion for certain members of the family; and who is liable for the deceased's debts?
- Which law applies to the settlement and the formalities of the cross-border succession?

The Regulation states that the law of the last country of residence of the deceased applies to the inheritance and its settlement – also to property located in other countries. In short, as of August 2015, one single national law applies to an entire inheritance.

INHERITANCE TAX

The European Inheritance Regulation does not have any fiscal consequences. Each country will continue to apply its own rules regarding the levying of inheritance tax – such as, for instance, the location of the property, the country of residence of the deceased, or their nationality. This can generate considerable complications.

WILL

The Regulation makes it possible to make the law of your country of nationality applicable to your estate instead of that of your last country of residence. Whether or not this is advisable, depends on your personal circumstances, the location of your property and your relocation plans for the future.

Furthermore, you can appoint an executor and/or administrator in your will, as well as make bequests, or make arrangements that deviate from the legal inheritance rules. It can also include arrangements for property that is not located in the European Union, taking into account the laws of the country in which it is located, so as to avoid any complications such as those mentioned in above example.

In international circumstances, it is best to include all arrangements that apply to your entire estate in one single will; if need be, accompanied by clauses regarding specific items or property.

A Dutch civil law notary who specializes in international inheritance law will be able to offer you tailor-made advice on these matters, taking into account your personal circumstances.

TAXES IN THE CASE OF DEATH

Nationality not Important

If you are a resident of the Netherlands when you die, then, in all likelihood, inheritance taxes will be due in the Netherlands. It does not matter what your nationality is: the entire worldwide estate of non-Dutch nationals who die while living in the Netherlands is (also) subject to taxation here. It also does not make a difference where your heirs are living at the time of your death.

Factual Situation

To determine whether you were living in the Netherlands, the factual situation is taken into account. If you had a house in the Netherlands and a family that also lived in the Netherlands for Dutch tax purposes, then you will most probably be considered to have been a resident of the Netherlands (and to have had resident tax liability). Also if you benefited from the so-called 30%-ruling and opted for the status of 'partial non-resident taxpayer' (see page 120) you will still be deemed to have been a resident taxpayer for inheritance tax purposes. In other words, the 30%-ruling has no bearing on this.

Double Taxation

As not every country applies the same taxation principles as the Netherlands, your passing away while living in the Netherlands could lead to double taxation. Some countries apply the principle of nationality of the deceased instead of the principle of residence. Furthermore, most countries levy inheritance tax on any portion of the estate located in that country (for instance immovable property). To avoid double taxation, the Netherlands has entered into tax treaties with a number of countries. In the situation in which there is no treaty, a national ruling aimed at the avoidance of double taxation can be invoked. However, this is no guarantee that double taxation will be completely avoided.

Exemptions

The inheritance tax law contains a few exemptions. The most important ones are (for 2024):

- the spouse/ registered / cohabiting partner has an exemption of € 795,156
- children (also step and foster children) and grandchildren have an exemption of € 25,187
- parents (regardless of whether one parent inherits, or both parents inherit together) have an exemption of € 59,643
- children with an impairment / illness who were largely supported by the deceased or that are not likely to be able to provide for themselves have an exemption of € 75,546
- all other relations: € 2,658
- donations for causes of a religious, life philosophy, charity, cultural, and scientific nature, as well as for causes for the general good are fully exempted
- institutions that serve a social need and that are registered as a co-called ANBI or SBBI pay no inheritance tax.

These exemptions are subject, however, to certain deductions, such as for pensions.

Gifts

These rates, listed above, also apply to gifts. The following exemptions apply:

- (foster) children: € 6,633
- children, for a pre-determined purpose: € 31,813
- children, for study purposes: € 66,268
- grandchildren: € 2,658
- other: € 2,658
- institutions that serve a social need and that are registered as an ANBI or SBBI pay no gift tax.

Rates

Inheritances and gifts that exceed the exemption are subject to various rates. The rates are 'double progressive'. This means that the higher the value of the inheritance or gift, the higher the rate; and the greater the (family) distance to the deceased / gifting relative, the higher the rate. Inheritances are divided into two categories, those that go up to € 152,368 (2024) and those that exceed this amount. Spouses, partners and children (also step and foster) are subject to a rate of 10% for the first category and 20% for the second. Grandchildren and other descendants / receivers owe 18% over the first category and 36% over the second. All others owe 30% over the first category and 40% over the second.

WHAT TYPE OF INSURANCE IS AVAILABLE

Perhaps you have not even thought about insurance at this stage. It is, however, of the utmost importance for a safe and healthy stay abroad. You could fall off your Dutch bicycle, have appendicitis, or have your house broken into. It is, therefore, advisable to arrange your insurance, if possible before you leave your home country or immediately upon your arrival in the Netherlands.

What exactly do you have to insure yourself against? Here is an overview of a few of the standard insurances available in the Netherlands, either through private insurance companies, banks, or your employer. Keep in mind that if you take out all insurances with the same insurance company, they may offer you a rebate on the entire package. You can also arrange your insurances through an insurance broker. You can find more information on brokers' associations and the Dutch insurance situation on the websites listed at the end of the chapter.

MEDICAL

Medical insurance is perhaps the most important insurance you can arrange. The last thing you want to deal with, when you are battling the local flu, is that your visit to the doctor and your medication are not covered.

All residents of the Netherlands are obligated to arrange health insurance in order to be able to legally reside in the Netherlands. To pay for this, everyone pays a fixed contribution starting at € 1,800 (depending on the insurance company and package) and an income-dependent contribution. This income-dependent contribution is compensated by your employer, who pays it directly to the tax authorities. If you are unemployed or self-employed, you receive no such compensation, but the percentage for determining the income-dependent contribution is lower. You receive an annual preliminary assessment for the amount you owe, which is based on what the tax authorities estimate you will be earning that year (in the case of self-employment). If you end up paying too much, you will be reimbursed after the final tax assessment over the year in question. Also if you are receiving a benefit or old age pension, you pay an income-dependent contribution – whether this is compensated, depends on your social security institution or pension plan. Children are covered free of charge and the government offers financial assistance (called *zorgtoeslag*) to persons (also self-employed) whose income lies below a certain level, to help pay the premium. There is a fixed deductible (see further on); by increasing the amount of the deductible, you can decrease the income-independent part of your contribution.

All insurance companies are obligated to accept all applications, regardless of age, gender or health. The cost of a basic insurance is pretty much the same across the board; doing a little comparative shopping becomes worth your while if you are interested in additional coverage – or eliminating certain coverage. However, keep in mind that insurance companies are not obligated to take you on for additional coverage – in other words, they *may* refuse you for an additional health care package. You can change insurance companies every year; visit www.independer.nl, https://zeker.com/verzekeringen/zorgverzekering/#/ or zorgwijzer.nl to compare insurance companies and coverage. English-language information can be found on www.zorgwijzer.nl/zorgvergelijker/english.

Issues that are of interest to look at when doing comparative shopping are: the amount of the deductible (*eigen risico*, or 'own risk'), what the coverage is if you are abroad and fall ill or otherwise require medical care, level of dental care offered, alternative therapies, etc. Another very important issue is described in the next paragraph.

Also; if you are traveling within Europe, ask your insurance company to issue you your European Health Insurance Card, which will allow you to receive free medical care (or at a reduced cost) in any of the other EU/EEA countries and Switzerland, if treatment becomes necessary during your visit or you are suffering from an existing chronic condition. Keep in mind that it has not been created for those who go abroad specifically to receive medical care. Be sure to ask your insurance company what, if any, further conditions apply.

INSURANCE IN KIND OR RESTITUTION

When you are arranging your insurance, you will run into the terms '*natura polis*' or '*restitutie polis*'. If you take out a *natura* policy, your insurance will pay your medical bills directly. However, they will only pay out these bills to medical service providers they have entered into a contract with (you are free to select your own *huisarts*, or GP), which means that you must verify that such a contract exists between the medical care provider you wish to select and your insurance company before you make use of their services – or else run the risk of paying the bill yourself.

The *restitutie* policy is slightly more expensive, but does give you freedom of choice as to whom you wish to turn to for medical assistance. With the restitution policy, you may be requested to pay the bill yourself and then submit it with your insurance company, for restitution.

Some insurance companies offer a combination of the two types of insurances, and with many insurance companies you will find they are not excessively strict about the existence of an actual contract between them and the care provider, provided they are recognized by a professional organization.

DEDUCTIBLE – 'OWN RISK'

For 2024, the deductible amounts to € 385 over the entire year for your total claimed health expenses. The deductible does not apply to children until the age of 18, visits to the GP, visits to the midwife, maternity care (see page 256), care covered by voluntary additional insurance or dental care for children / persons until the age of 21. You can also opt for a voluntary deductible of up to € 885 a year.

EXCEPTIONAL MEDICAL EXPENSES

Long-term medical care

The WLZ (Wet Langdurige Ziektekosten, or Long-Term Medical Care Act) is a national insurance scheme that insures persons against risks that cannot be covered by individual insurance. Everyone who legally resides and works in the Netherlands has a right to coverage by this insurance. You can read more about it on page 82. Its premise is that everyone should be able to stay living at home with the support of their social network or the assistance of the municipality, though it also covers care in an institution. It is meant to cover steep medical expenses that are not covered by a regular health insurance and that are simply not affordable. The same health care insurance company with which you have placed your 'regular' health insurance also takes on your personal coverage by this insurance. You owe a social security contribution to pay for the WLZ, which is calculated over – and withheld from – your salary and some types of benefits. You also owe a contribution for this insurance over income from self-employment.

A special aspect of exceptional medical expenses is the PGB (*persoonsgebonden budget*, or personal budget): you are granted a certain amount of money, which you can use to 'purchase' personal care, care by a nurse or other personal assistance. PGB-WMO helps cover assistance if you want to stay living at home but cannot live fully independently, PGB-WLZ is for long-term care, PGB-jeugdwet is for children (it is used to cover psychological care, for instance), and PGB-ZVW is for medical care at home. A combination of multiple PGB-budgets is possible.

DENTAL CARE

We mention dental care here separately because it is not included in any basic package (with the exception of dental care for children up to the age of 18 and 'specialist' dental care, including dentures). You must take out an additional dental policy to cover standard dental care.

MEDICATION

Also medication deserves special attention: in your policy you are likely to find something along the lines of "we only cover GVS medication". This is a consequence of an arrangement whereby types of medication have been 'clustered', after which a maximum price has been determined for this cluster. If you are prescribed medication, then the cluster-specific maximum price is covered by the insurance. If your medication is more expensive than that, you will have to pay the difference. If this is the case, then you can also discuss with your doctor and/or pharmacist whether a cheaper – and equally as effective – alternative is available. Homeopathic medicine is not covered by the 'GVS'-system, so that you will have to pay for it yourself, unless you arrange additional insurance to cover it.

Check with your insurance company whether you can take out an additional policy to cover these extra costs as well as the cost of homeopathic / alternative medication.

On the website www.medicijnkosten.nl you can check whether your medication is covered by your insurance company. You fill in the name of your medication, then on the next page other specifics (such as g/ml), and then it tells you how much of it will be covered and how much you have to contribute to paying the costs.

PREGNANCY AND CHILDBIRTH

During pregnancy, you visit a midwife with increasing frequency up to and including delivery; this is covered by your insurance. At least two ultrasounds, if they are medically required, are also covered.

In principle, in the Netherlands, a 'normal' childbirth takes place in the home, with the help of a midwife (in actual fact, only about 12% of the deliveries take place at home); this is covered by your insurance. The costs of a hospital delivery are fully covered if your midwife, GP or specialist has determined that, for health and safety reasons, the baby should be delivered in the hospital. This is called a *bevalling op medische indicatie*. If you voluntarily choose to have your baby in the hospital (called a *poliklinische bevalling*), you will have to contribute towards the costs of your hospital delivery – though some insurance companies also cover these costs. You can find more on having a baby on page 253.

Kraamzorg (Maternity Home Care, see page 256) is also covered by the basic insurance package, though you have to pay a contribution towards the costs.

STUDENTS

Students who come to the Netherlands merely to study cannot take out Dutch health insurance. In some cases, your host institution has made sure that you are insured – as everyone is required by law to have health insurance – though you should verify this, of course. Special insurance packages for students are available for those who nonetheless need to arrange insurance here. For more information, see page 143. Furthermore, under certain conditions, if you are insured under the public health care scheme in your home country (EU/EEA/Switzerland), you can request to be issued the European Health Insurance Card, proving that you are covered by this insurance policy. Note: once you take on a job or start an internship in the Netherlands, you may have to arrange health insurance here.

SELF-EMPLOYED PERSONS – DISABILITY

Employees are covered by the employee insurance schemes for the consequences of disability. Self-employed persons are not, and have to arrange private insurance to cover these consequences.

When selecting this type of insurance, you can take the following issues into account: when you wish the payments to cease (for instance, when your pension starts to pay out), your job level (the amount of premium you owe depends on your job level), as of which percentage of disability you want the insurance to start paying out, the degree of disability it is meant to cover (for instance, inability to do the same work, similar work, or any type of work), and whether or not you want the payments indexed over time. The payments will amount to 80% of your average income over the last three years, however, you can insure a lower amount. Some insurance companies offer a lower premium to beginning entrepreneurs.

You should investigate your options carefully when deciding whether you want to take out the standard insurance or the insur-

Special Rules for Work Permits

TEMPORARY WORK

In the case of temporary work, a work permit can be issued for a maximum period of 24 weeks. The work must then be carried out by a non-Dutch national who has lived outside the Netherlands during a period of at least 14 weeks preceding the issuing of the work permit. This type of work permit cannot be extended. These permits are usually issued for seasonal work.

INCIDENTAL WORK

Those who have 'regulated' professions (such as a professor) and want to come to the Netherlands to carry out their work temporarily and/or incidentally, must report this in advance (*verklaring vooraf*). Regulated professions are professions that are carried out by persons who must meet specific legal requirements, such as a university title, a diploma or a certificate of experience. Whether or not their stay is 'temporary or incidental' is evaluated per request, taking into account the length, frequency, regularity and continuity of the work for which this person is coming to the Netherlands.

Temporary and incidental work on the basis of a 'regulated' profession can be carried out in the Netherlands, provided:

- the employee is an EU/EEA/Swiss resident
- the profession is regulated. If it is not, it must have been carried out during at least two years of the ten years preceding the employee's arrival in the Netherlands.

In some cases, an advance verification is carried out; this is the case if the profession is in the areas of national health or public order. When applying for approval, the employee must submit a number of documents, such as proof of nationality, professional qualifications and experience. Other professions might require more papers.

INTER-COMPANY TRANSFER WITHIN A GROUP OF COMPANIES

The inter-company transfer (ICT) directive makes it possible for companies from outside the European Union – that have an entity in an EU-member state – to temporarily second managers, specialists or trainees to their entity in the EU. The ICT-permit is a combined work and residence permit. This permit must be requested in the country in which the employee is expected to stay the longest. The ICT permit will be granted for a maximum period of three years to managers and specialists and for a maximum of one year to trainees. An extension based on the ICT directive is in principle not possible.

The transferee needs to be employed for a period of at least three months with the company outside the EU, and the place of residency of the transferee at the moment of filing the request should be outside the EU as well. Furthermore, it should concern a temporary secondment to one or more group entities within the EU. The employment with the home country company should remain in place (no local contract with the host company). Finally, it is important that the employment conditions be competitive in the local labor market. Please note, there is no salary threshold. The offered salary must be market-competitive according to Dutch standards. According to the IND, for the time being, the salary thresholds that are applicable for the Dutch Highly Skilled Migrant Rule will be applied. These salary thresholds are € 5,008 (excluding holiday allowance) for employees above 30 years, and € 3,672 (excluding holiday allowance) for employees under 30 years (amounts for the year 2023).

One of the benefits of the ICT-permit is the simplification of the short-term mobility of employees to other group entities within the EU. In case of a transfer of an employee, who has qualified under the ICT Directive, to another group entity within the EU for a period of fewer than 90 days within a period of 180 days, only a so-called notification obligation will apply. However, this is only possible if the employee will not be moving their residency to this country. In the Netherlands, this notification should be filed with the UWV (Dutch social security authorities for work). The employee is allowed to start working here straight away. In case of a transfer to another group entity for a period exceeding 90 days, a simplified and shorter request procedure is applicable. In the Netherlands, this request should be

ance with the higher premium / exclusions as the latter may, in fact, turn out to be more attractive, despite its financial drawbacks. And you may simply opt not to insure yourself at all; this particular insurance is not obligatory. The premiums you pay for this insurance are tax-deductible, you will pay taxes over the payments you receive should be you become disabled for work.

If you are considered a high-risk client (due to a chronic disease, or a physical challenge, or health issues in the past), the insurance company you approach may charge a higher premium or refuse to insure you at all. For these people, a so-called alternative insurance (called *vangnetverzekering* – safety net insurance) has been created. To make use of this possibility, you must request this disability insurance within 15 months of starting your own company. More information (in Dutch) can be found on www.aov-zzp.nl/producten/94-vangnetverzekering/1165-vangnetverzekering.

HOUSE

You've finally settled for that beautiful house in the center of Amsterdam or out in the woods. Just putting your key in the lock makes you feel happy. Now you want it insured!

A house insurance generally covers the financial consequences of fire, breaking and entry, as well as unexpected events such as storm, fire, lightning, theft, vandalism, explosions and more.

HOUSEHOLD CONTENTS

And how about that luxurious, expensive couch, or your antique dining room, or Dutch painting? A household contents insurance covers virtually everything you have in your house against fire, theft, water damage, storms and more. For possessions that are especially valuable, such as jewelry, antique musical instruments or your stamp collection, you can take out additional insurance for Valuable Possessions. Some insurance companies offer a 'Home filed with the IND. Also in this case, the employee is allowed to start working immediately.

If the ICT-directive is applicable, it is not possible to apply for the highly skilled migrant ruling.

WORKING VIA AN EMPLOYMENT AGENCY

If an employee is hired via another company or an employment agency, the employer need not arrange the work permit; this must be done by the other company or the employment agency. The employer should, however, ask for and keep a copy of the work permit in their administration.

JOURNALISTS / MUSICIANS

Journalists and musicians do not need a work permit, if their principal place of residence is outside the Netherlands and they come here to work on an incidental basis and stay here for a short period of time (six weeks continuously within a 13-week period).

GUEST LECTURER

Work permits are not required for those who come as guest lecturers to universities, universities of applied sciences (*hogeschool* or HBO), institutions for higher international education, or research institutions that are connected to, or operate in the area of, one of these universities / institutions – under the condition that the lecturer has their principal place of residence outside the Netherlands and works and stays here on an incidental basis.

SCIENTIFIC RESEARCHER / DOCTOR IN TRAINING

Certain scientific researchers, paid or unpaid, do not need a work permit to work here. Unpaid scientific researchers do not need a formal employment agreement, merely a so-called Guest Agreement. Once they receive remuneration for their efforts, however, they do need an employment agreement. Furthermore, certain requirements apply to their academic background, while research must be their main task and their employer / host institution must be registered with the IND, which means that the accelerated procedure is available to them.

Those working on a Ph.D. at a university or research institution and medical doctors in training can come to the Netherlands as highly

skilled migrants; the minimum income does not apply to them, though it may not lie below the minimum wage.

FOREIGN SERVICE PROVIDERS

Foreign service providers from within the EU/EEA/Switzerland do not have to request a work permit when working with non-EU citizens in the Netherlands. For instance, a French service provider does not need a work permit when bringing in an employee from Algeria, assuming the relevant conditions are met. However, the service provider must comply with the rules stated in the Posted Workers Scheme.

ASYLUM SEEKERS

Asylum seekers may work in the Netherlands, provided they are not on the deportation list and have been under the care of COA (Central Organization for Asylum Seekers) or a municipality for at least six months. In 2023, a Dutch Court decided that the rule that had applied till then, limiting their ability to work to 24 weeks a year, can no longer be enforced as it constitutes an unnecessary limitation to an effective access to the labor market. Their employer must request a work permit for them from the UWV. They also need a work permit to work in self-employment, which will only be issued once their request for asylum has been under review for six months.

Electronics' insurance, to ensure coverage of your computer, television and sound installation, among others. The household content insurance can also cover your mobile phone, should you wish to insure it. Be sure to enquire as to what exactly they cover, in case you can find cheaper coverage through a company that offers specific mobile phone insurance.

TRAVEL

You've finally booked that wonderful trip to Singapore, but you are worried about whether your luggage will come back in one piece, or that you might be pickpocketed, or lose your camera! Or maybe you've decided to go skiing instead, but are worried about what type of costs you might incur if you fall and break a leg. In that case, you might want to contribute to your peace of mind (and what else are vacations for?) by taking out travel insurance (which can include cancelation insurance). You might find it economically more interesting, even, to take out year-round travel insurance; it often costs little more than the insurance for a three-week vacation.

CAR

Driving around in the Netherlands can be risky business. Though the Netherlands is considered one of the safest countries when it comes to driving, the Dutch are not the gentlest of people behind the steering wheel. Particularly tailgating and claiming the right of way (which they have when coming from the right, unless indicated otherwise) can lead to some hair-raising situations. In short, if you own a car here, you will want to take out car insurance. Furthermore, car owners are obligated by law to have minimum liability coverage, called a *WA-verzekering*. If you take out car insurance, this will automatically include minimum liability insurance (which can be extended upon for a fee). For the various types of insurances available (for instance, covering damage to your car,

Students

When coming to the Netherlands as a non-EU student, special immigration procedures apply. Which specific requirements are to be met depend on your nationality and the purpose of your stay. Some nationals need an entry visa plus residence permit, while other nationals only need a residence permit. Upon arrival, other procedures must be completed, such as your registration with the municipal population register (BRP/*bevolkingsregister*). For more on this, see page 128.

ENTRY VISA: MVV / SHORT STAY VISA

If you are a national of an EU/EEA member state, Switzerland, Monaco, Canada, the U.S., Japan, Australia, South Korea, New Zealand, or Vatican City you will not need a provisional residence permit (MVV) to study in the Netherlands, though you might need a residence permit (see further on). You may enter the Netherlands without a visa.

If you are from any other country and you intend to stay here longer than three months, you will need a provisional residence permit (MVV) to enter the country. All Dutch educational institutes are required to apply for the MVV on behalf of their foreign students. This means that you, as a student, cannot apply for the MVV yourself. Please contact your Dutch university for more about their MVV application procedure.

If you will be here shorter than 90 days, you may need a 'short stay visa' (*visum kort verblijf*). You can apply for this visa at the Dutch embassy or consulate in your home country.

RESIDENCE PERMIT / REGISTRATION GBA

All Dutch educational institutes are required to apply for the residence permits on behalf of their foreign students, which means that you are not allowed to do this yourself. Upon arrival you will need to pick up your residence permit – as the MVV merely allows you to enter the country and is only valid for 90 days. You will also have to register with the municipality (registration BRP / *bevolkingsregister*).

EU/EEA/Swiss nationals do not need a residence permit, but if they stay here longer than four months, they too need to register with the municipality. Also, once you are a resident of the Netherlands, in principle you are obligated to arrange private health insurance, pursuant to the Health Insurance Act (perhaps your host institution has arranged a collective insurance in which you can participate). In order to be able to do this, you will have to obtain a Citizen Service Number (*burgerservicenummer*, see page 78) and provide proof that you are staying here legally, such as a residence permit or, if you are an EU/EEA citizen, a valid passport. You obtain the Citizen Service Number (BSN) when you register with the municipality. Note: people under the age of 30 who are in the Netherlands solely for the purpose of studying, cannot take out Dutch health care insurance. For instance, if you have an EU Health Insurance Card, which you can get if you are insured under the public health care scheme in your (EU) home country and your stay abroad is temporary, you will be continued to be covered by this insurance policy. It is up to your health insurance provider to determine what constitutes a temporary stay.

REQUIREMENTS FOR ADMISSION TO UNIVERSITY

To be granted a residence permit for study purposes, you must follow a study at a recognized school or university (of applied sciences). It is not enough just to be taking Dutch language lessons. However, if you do not meet all the requirements for admission to a university / program or you need only to pass the language proficiency test, you can stay in the Netherlands for a period of one year to follow a customized preparatory program, to which purpose the university can – and must – request a residence permit for you, if you are a non-EU/EEA/Swiss national.

Many educational institutes offer a year-long 'familiarization and language' course (called a *schakeljaar*, or link-year), created specifically for students from non-European, non-Western countries who come to the Netherlands to follow an education at HBO or university level. You can read more about this in chapter 9. Be careful when googling the word *schakeljaar*; the same term has been introduced for third-year medical master's students who will be entering further training.

theft, joyriding, etc.), contact your insurance company. You can also opt to include legal aid insurance, if you do not already have a general one.

PASSENGER

Other drivers claiming their right of way can be particularly unnerving for passengers. Should anything happen to one of your passengers, this is most often not covered by your regular car insurance and therefore it is advisable to take out this additional insurance. It covers not only the situation in which you are 'rolling', but also when you are on the side of the road because your car has broken down, or when you are filling your gas tank. You will probably have two choices: a 'damages' insurance and an 'accidents to passengers' insurance. The former pays out damages, including a certain amount of emotional damages, the latter pays out a fixed amount in the case of death or permanent disability.

ACCIDENT

This insurance covers any type of accident (not only those on the road), such as falling off the stepladder, or dislocating your arm playing rugby. Those who take out this insurance are paid a lump sum if something goes wrong, to cover any large expenses that may be the consequence of the accident. You can take out individual or family insurance.

LIABILITY FOR PRIVATE PERSONS

Say, the little apples of your eye have decided to play soccer in the front yard after all and have kicked the soccer ball not through your window, but your neighbor's. Or that you drop a can of paint on the car parked next to yours. To cover the expenses related to any of these accidents, you can take out liability insurance for private persons, which will then cover the bills. You can take out individual or family insurance.

INTERNSHIP

If you have a residence permit for studying in the Netherlands, and you have to do an internship here, you do not need an employment permit (*tewerkstellingsvergunning*). However, you do need to arrange the standard internship agreement, which you can find on www.studyinholland.nl. This agreement has to be signed by three parties: yourself, your employer, and the educational institution.

If you are not studying in the Netherlands, and want to come here to do an internship or to acquire work experience, you will need a residence permit and work permit if you are a non-EU/EEA/Swiss national. You must be able to demonstrate that you need this work experience for your job in your country of residence or, as the case may be, as part of your studies, and that you will be resuming your studies once you return to your home country.

A JOB ON THE SIDE

Being enrolled as a student in the Netherlands, you are allowed to work a maximum of 16 hours a week, or full-time during the months of June, July and August. Your employer will need to apply for a work permit. Note that EU/EEA/Swiss students can work as many hours as they like, without the need for a work permit.

GRADUATES

If you are a graduate of a foreign university, you can come to the Netherlands for a period of one year to find work as a highly skilled migrant. You have to apply for the Orientation Year for Highly Educated Persons Residence Permit within three years of graduating. You must have at least a master's degree or a Ph.D. from a qualifying university, and your diploma must be evaluated by Nuffic (see chapter 9). For further conditions, please check the website of the Immigration and Naturalization Services (IND).

If you have graduated from a Dutch higher education institution with either a bachelor's or a master's degree, you have three years to apply for a change in the purpose of your stay from 'study' to 'orientation year for graduates in the Netherlands'. During one year you are free to take up any job, traineeship or placement to gain work experience without the need for a work permit, but after that year you must change your residence, unless you find a job as a highly skilled migrant, start your own company, or get a job and accompanying work permit. The terms for changing it into a permit for a highly skilled migrant are more lenient for recent graduates, as a lower minimum salary requirement applies: € 2,631 (excluding the holiday allowance) gross a month (2023).

It is very important for you, as an employer, to comply with the rules stated in the Act on Employment for Foreigners (WAV) and Aliens Act (VW). If you are convicted of illegal employment or do not comply with the arrangements made with the IND, you might not be able to arrange a residence permit for knowledge migrants or a work permit for your employees in the future. A risk you cannot afford to run if you depend on personnel that you bring in from abroad.

DISABILITY INSURANCE FOR EMPLOYEES

The days that you could count on the government to guarantee you a lifestyle as the one you were used to before you became disabled for work are over.

The government has had to introduce a few changes in its spending pattern too, so that, should you end up with a disability, chances are that your benefit-related income will be far below the level of income you were accustomed to receiving. To help cover this difference, you can take out additional private disability insurance. There is, however, the possibility that your employer has made additional arrangements. Please ask your employer about this before arranging your own additional insurance.

LEGAL AID INSURANCE

You might end up having to deal with the situation in which a person you have held liable will not pay, or your kitchen has not been delivered, or your boss is not sticking to what you agreed to in your employment contract. This can be very tough to cope with and quite time-consuming, especially in another culture, language and legal system – and is hardly something you can deal with without legal aid. To this end, you can take out legal aid insurance, which will not only provide you with the aid you need, but will also cover your legal aid expenses. Family members are often automatically included in this insurance.

Note that the legal aid insurance provider will want you to make use of their own lawyers. Should you have to go to court, then you can select your own lawyer and they will pay for the expenses (up to a maximum). However, should you enlist the aid of a lawyer not provided by them without legally being required to do so, the insurance provider will lower the amount they cover. Also keep in mind that there may be a deductible. The site www.consumentenbond.nl/rechtsbijstandverzekering/vrije-advocaat-keuze provides you with a (Dutch-language) overview of which insurance companies will cover what.

MOTOR AND 'SCOOTER'

Maybe you want to go touring around the country and actually feel the wind in your face. Then you might choose to buy a motorcycle or a moped. For these types of vehicles there is a separate – obligatory – insurance, called the Motor and Scooter Insurance. Also for motorcycles and mopeds, you can take out additional Passenger Insurance. Always be sure you take your proof of insurance with you, for you will be fined if you are caught without this document!

BICYCLE

One of the thriving black markets in the Netherlands is that of stolen bicycles. After a few months of watching those happy Dutch cyclists, you may succumb to the temptation of buying one of those environmentally friendly contraptions yourself, only to have it stolen! Or damaged. It's a good thing you can take out bicycle insurance.

LEGAL PROBLEMS

Legal problems are always on the lure: for example, your rental agreement could be canceled, you could be fired, or your landlord could refuse to make important repairs. You could have problems with the tax authorities or with receiving your benefits. Repairs to your washing machine were not done properly. Your divorce is pending or, following an accident, your damages have not been reimbursed. In other words, since there are many kinds of legal problems, chances are you might have one or two of your own.

You might want some legal advice as well, before making an important decision. For example, before accepting a job, borrowing money or renting a house. In all such cases, it is good to know where you can go for legal advice. More information can be found on: www.rechtspraak.nl/English/Judicial-system-and-legislation.

ADVICE

All legal aid agencies offer advice. These include legal counters, trade unions, lawyers and municipal social service counselors. For more on these, read on.

LEGAL PROCEEDINGS

Civil Law

There is no obligation to have legal representation before the subdistrict sector of the District Court. Cases involving amounts lower than € 25,000, employment law cases, and cases involving rent law, light misdemeanors and consumer credit are to be brought before the subdistrict sector of the District Court and therefore do not require representation by a lawyer. You can choose between representing yourself, or letting yourself be represented by a person with legal training, such as a process-server. On the website of www.rechtspraak.nl, under Naar de rechter, and then Advocaat wel of niet verplicht you can find an overview (in Dutch) of precisely when you will or will not be required to arrange a lawyer.

In all other civil-law situations, the case comes before the District Court and legal representation is mandatory (with the exception of administrative law cases), as it is when you appear before the Court of Appeals and the Netherlands Supreme Court. If you have not arranged it, the magistrates will not accept the case.

Administrative Law

Administrative law applies to governmental decisions, for example relating to building permits or benefit payments. A lawyer is not required for administrative law issues. Also here, you may represent yourself. For more complex matters, however, it would be wise to consult an expert – for example, a lawyer.

Criminal Law

In principle, criminal law does not require legal representation. You, as a defendant, may defend yourself. If you are taken into custody, you are automatically assigned a lawyer. However, you are free to change lawyers if you wish. If you face criminal charges but are not in custody, you can consult a lawyer.

Summary Proceedings

if you initiate a summary proceeding, you will need to use the services of a lawyer. If you are a defendant in such a proceeding, you are not obligated to employ the services of a lawyer, unless you submit a counterclaim.

FEES

There are no flat rates for the services of lawyers. The rates vary not only from one law office to the other but also according to the type of case. Therefore, it is worth the trouble to inquire at several law offices about their (hourly) rates for the type of case, and about the amount of time the lawyer expects to dedicate to the case.

No cure, no pay is not allowed by the code of conduct all lawyers have to abide by.

FINANCIAL ASSISTANCE

For many people, legal fees can be a problem. If you wish to start or are facing legal proceedings but cannot pay for them (entirely), you can ask your lawyer to request government-financed legal aid (*toevoeging*). If it is granted – and this depends, among others, on your income and financial means – the government will pay part of your legal fees. *Toevoeging* is only granted to pay your lawyer's fees – and not related expenses, such as court registry fees, extract fees, process server expenses, etc. (it therefore usually does not cover what is normally charged). It can also be used to help cover the costs of mediation. The income limits in question are fixed and are regularly adjusted (www.rechtsbijstand.nl/mediation-rechtsbijstand/hoeveel-betalen/eigen-bijdrage/).

If your income is high or you have sufficient financial means and do not qualify for government-financed legal aid, you must pay the legal fees yourself. You can, however, take out legal aid insurance to help pay for lawyers' fees. There may be a first risk clause.

INTERPRETERS

The Dutch courts make use of interpreters in the case of (criminal) law proceedings and for asylum seekers – but you can also request the assistance of an interpreter if you feel you need one in any other type of case. You will have to pay for this, but depending on your financial situation, you may be able to request assistance (information can also be found on www.rechtspraak.nl/english, search for interpreter). If the court requests the assistance of an interpreter, the costs are in principle carried either by the state or by the party who is ordered to pay the costs in a civil case. If you need the use of a translator / interpreter, ask your legal aid agency where you can find one and what the costs will be. Beware that price and quality are not always consistent. The Dutch courts are obligated to make use of sworn interpreters that are listed Register of Sworn Interpreters and Translators (Register beëdigde Tolken en Vertalers).

WHERE TO OBTAIN LEGAL AID ASSISTANCE

Juridisch Loket – Legal Counter

The Juridisch Loket has been created to provide you with free legal information and advice on matters regarding employment issues, family issues, social security (benefits), rent and housing law, alien affairs, problems regarding products bought or services rendered (consumer issues), criminal law, neighbor problems, permits and driver's licenses. If you require actual legal assistance, the Juridisch Loket can recommend a lawyer or mediator and can inform you of whether you qualify for subsidized legal aid from either one of these. To find a Juridisch Loket near you, visit www.juridischloket.nl and click on *Vestigingen en openingstijden* (locations and office hours), and fill in where you live or are looking for advice.

Legal Aid Bureaus

For more information on organizations providing subsidized legal aid and/or mediation, and to find one close to you, visit www.rvr.org (Raad voor Rechtsbijstand), or www.rechtsbijstand.nl. More sites can be found at the end of the chapter. The plan is to merge the Raad voor de Rechtsbijstand and the Juridisch Loketten.

Lawyers

It is usually wise to seek advice or legal representation, especially if the other party already has. If you do not qualify for subsidized legal aid, then you will likely turn to a lawyer. Most lawyers specialize in certain types of cases or legal areas. You can approach the Netherlands Bar Association – an organization to which all lawyers in the Netherlands belong – for a recommendation. As mentioned earlier, a Juridisch Loket can sometimes recommend a particular lawyer, depending on your case.

Many lawyers offer free introductory consultations. The first consultation lasts about thirty minutes, during which the lawyer will examine your case and recommend any steps you should take. Be sure to ask in advance whether – and what – the lawyer charges for the first consultation.

Mediators

The option of mediation first noticeably entered the 'conflict scene' in divorce cases, but is now rapidly gaining popularity in other legal areas as well, such as commercial law (including 'business mediation'), family law, labor law, inheritance law and administrative law. It is, of course, an attractive approach that can save you both time and money – as it is more likely to result in a solution that is a viable compromise reached by the parties involved, rather than one that is chosen for you by an emotionally distant judge.

Also once a case has gone to court it is not too late to enlist the help of a mediator: either you and the other party together can decide to go to a mediator or, either before or during the court hearings, the judge can evaluate with you whether employing the services of a mediator might be preferable.

For more information, visit www.gecertificeerdemediators.nl or www.rvr.org.

Fees

No cure, no pay also does not apply if you enlist the help of a mediator: you will owe them their fees and the reimbursement of any expenses they may have incurred. In some cases, the first 2.5 hours of consultation are free. Rest assured, the total costs will almost always be considerably less than what you would end up paying in legal fees if you went to court. In principle, both parties carry an equal share in the expenses, but you may choose to allocate the costs differently. In many cases, a mediator can also request a *toevoeging* for you, allowing your mediation expenses to be subsidized.

Municipal Counselors

Many municipalities have municipal counselors (*Sociaal Raadslieden*) – ask at your municipality whether this is the case where you live. These councilors can answer many questions regarding social security, taxes, legislation, regulations and (semi)governmental institutions. They can also help you write letters, draw up notices of information. To find one, visit www.sociaalwerknederland.nl.

Process-Servers

Also process-servers offer legal aid, particularly, of course, when it comes to collecting your debts, but also with financial questions. As mentioned earlier, there where you are not required to have yourself represented by a lawyer in civil cases, you can nonetheless request the assistance of a process-server.

Unions

All unions have a legal department that you can consult for information and advice if you are a member. They offer assistance in employment law cases and social security cases – all free of charge, if you are a member.

Legal Advice Centers

Anyone can go to a Legal Advice Center, for information and advice. They are usually manned by volunteers, mostly law students.

Other Organizations

There are a number of organizations you can turn to for advice and aid as well, if you are a member. Some of the more useful ones are:

- the Consumers Association (Consumentenbond): this association offers advice on consumer issues, such as the renting or buying of products and/or services. Though they do not offer legal-procedural aid, they can mediate in conflicts with manufacturers or those who provide services.
- ANWB: members of the ANWB are given free legal advice on issues regarding transportation, recreation and tourism. The ANWB offers its members full legal aid in the case of accidents abroad, as well as for personal injury.
- Vereniging Eigen Huis (Homeowners' Association): Vereniging Eigen Huis offers its members advice on issues involving home ownership, such as financing, construction and legal matters.
- If you have taken out legal aid insurance, the organizations that provide the insurance often also offer legal aid.

References

CHAPTER 5

Legal, Tax and Financial Matters

Major Dutch Banks

ABN AMRO BANK
www.abnamro.nl or www.abnamro.com (international)

ASN BANK
www.asnbank.nl

ING BANK
www.ing.nl or www.ing.com (international)

RABO BANK
www.rabobank.nl or www.rabobank.com (international)

SNS BANK
www.sns.nl

TRIODOS BANK
www.triodos.nl

Taxes

BELASTINGDIENST
National Tax Office
Tel.: 0800 05 43 (National Information line for residents)
Tel.: +31 555 385 385 (Information line for non residents)
Central website: www.belastingdienst.nl

INTERNATIONAL TAX OFFICE HEERLEN
Postal address: P.O. Box 2865, 6401 DJ Heerlen
Visiting address: Kloosterweg 22,
6412 CN Heerlen (by appointment only)
Tel.: 0800 05 43 (National Information line for residents)
Tel.: +31 555 385 385 (Information line for non residents)
www.belastingdienst.nl

MINISTERIE VAN FINANCIEN
Ministry of Finance
Korte Voorhout 7, The Hague
P.O. Box 20201, 2500 EE The Hague
Tel.: 070 342 80 00
www.government.nl/ministries/fin

DOUANE
Tax and Customs Administration
Postal address: P.O. Box 3070, 6401 DN Heerlen
Visiting address: Kloosterweg 22,
6412 CN Heerlen (by appointment only)
Tel.: 0800 05 43 (National Information line for residents)
Tel.: +31 555 385 385 (Information line for non residents)
www.belastingdienst.nl

Payroll Service

PAYINGIT INTERNATIONAL
Kabelweg 21, 1014 BA Amsterdam
Tel.: 020 225 25 80
www.payingit-international.com

WEPAYPEOPLE
Donauweg 10, 1043 AJ Amsterdam
Tel.: 020 820 80 40 – www.wepaypeople.com

DUTCH UMBRELLA COMPANY
Donauweg 10, 1043 AJ Amsterdam
Tel.: 020 820 15 60
www.dutchumbrellacompany.com

Immigration/Permits

GENERAL
www.immigratiedienst.nl

IMMIGRATIE EN NATURALISATIE DIENST, IND
Immigration and Naturalization Service
Various locations: www.ind.nl

MINISTERIE VAN BUITENLANDSE ZAKEN
Ministry of Foreign Affairs
Rijnstraat 8, 2515 XP The Hague
Tel.: 070 348 64 86
www.government.nl/ministries/ministry-of-foreign-affairs

DIGID
Digital Identity
To digitally authenticate the identity of a person who applies for a transaction service via www.digid.nl/en

UWV
Tel.: 088 898 92 94
www.uwv.nl

PERMITS FOUNDATION
An international corporate initiative aimed at promoting the improvement of work permit regulations for the spouses of expatriate employees.
www.permitsfoundation.com

WORK PERMITS
www.workpermit.com/netherlands

EXPATRIATE FOUNDATION
An independent interest organization for expatriates and their Dutch based employers.
www.expatriatefoundation.org

Legal

MINISTERIE VAN JUSTITIE EN VEILIGHEID
Ministry of Justice an Security
Turfmarkt 147, 2511 DP The Hague
Tel.: 070 370 79 11
www.government.nl/ministries/ministry-of-justice-and-security

INSTITUTE FOR INTERNATIONAL PRIVATE AND PUBLIC INTERNATIONAL LAW
T.M.C. Asser Instituut
R.J. Schimmelpenninckłaan 20-22,
2517 JN The Hague
Tel.: 070 342 03 00
www.asser.nl

KONINKLIJKE NOTARIËLE BEROEPSORGANISATIE, KNB
Royal Dutch Notaries
Spui 184, 2511 BW The Hague
Tel.: 070 330 71 11 – www.notaris.nl

DE NOTARISTELEFOON
The Notary Helpline
Tel.: 0900 346 93 93 (0.80 € per minute)
www.notaris.nl

NEDERLANDSE ORDE VAN ADVOCATEN
Netherlands Bar Association
Neuhuyskade 94, 2596 XM The Hague
Tel.: 070 335 35 35 – www.advocatenorde.nl

VERENIGING VAN PERSONEN- EN FAMILIERECHT ADVOCATEN
Association of Family Lawyers
Eisenhowerlaan 77 C, 2517 KK The Hague
Tel.: 070 362 62 15 – www.verenigingfas.nl

DE NATIONALE OMBUDSMAN
National Ombudsman
An independent institution that investigates citizens' complaints about improper conduct on the part of government and police authorities and officers
Bezuidenhoutseweg 151, 2594 AG The Hague
Tel.: 0800 335 55 55 (toll free)
www.nationaleombudsman.nl

CONSUMENTENBOND
Consumers Association
www.consumentenbond.nl

RAAD VOOR DE KINDERBESCHERMING
Child Care and Protection Board
www.kinderbescherming.nl

NEDERLANDS MEDIATION INSTITUUT
www.gecertificeerdemediators.nl
and specifically for divorce mediation:
www.vas-scheidingsbemiddeling.nl

THE ROYAL DUTCH TOURING CLUB (ANWB)
Wassenaarseweg 220, 2596 EC The Hague
P.O. Box 93200, 2509 BA The Hague
General tel. no for members: 088 269 22 22
Legal Assistance, tel.: 088 269 72 05
Specially for victims of traffic accidents, tel.: 088 269 77 66 (also for non-members)
www.anwb.nl

Embassies by Country

AUSTRALIA
Carnegielaan 4, 2517 KH The Hague
Tel.: 070 310 82 00
www.netherlands.embassy.gov.au

BELGIUM
Alexanderveld 97, 2585 DB The Hague
Tel.: 070 312 34 56
www.diplomatie.belgium.be

BRAZIL
Mauritskade 19, 2514 HD The Hague
Tel.: 070 302 39 59 – www.brazilianembassy.nl

CANADA
Sophialaan 7, 2514 JP The Hague
Tel.: 070 311 16 00 – www.canada.nl

CHINA
Willem Lodewijklaan 10, 2517 JT The Hague
Tel.: 070 306 50 61
www.nl.china-embassy.org/eng/

DENMARK
Koninginnegracht 30, 2514 AB The Hague
Tel.: 070 302 59 59
www.danishembassy.nl

FINLAND
Groot Hertoginnelaan 16, 2517 EG The Hague
Tel.: 070 346 97 54 – www.finlande.nl

FRANCE
Smidsplein 1, 2514 BT The Hague
Tel.: 070 312 58 00 – www.ambafrance.nl

GERMANY
Groot Hertoginnelaan 18, 2517 EG The Hague
Tel.: 070 342 06 00
www.duitse-ambassade.nl

GHANA
Laan Copus van Cattenburch 70, 2585 GD The Hague
Tel.: 070 338 43 84
www.ghanaembassy.nl

GREECE
Amaliastraat 1, 2514 JC The Hague
Tel.: 070 363 87 00
www.greekembassy.nl

INDIA
Buitenrustweg 2, 2517 KD The Hague
Tel.: 070 346 97 71
www.indianembassy.nl

INDONESIA
Tobias Asserlaan 8, 2517 KC The Hague
Tel.: 070 310 81 00
www.indonesia.nl

IRELAND
Dr. Kuyperstraat 9, 2514 BA The Hague
Tel.: 070 363 09 93
www.irishembassy.nl

ISRAEL
Buitenhof 47, 2513 AH The Hague
Tel.: 070 376 05 00
www.israel.nl

ITALY
Alexanderstraat 12, 2514 JL The Hague
Tel.: 070 302 10 30
www.italy.nl

JAPAN
Tobias Asserlaan 5, 2517 KC The Hague
Tel.: 070 346 95 44
www.nl.emb-japan.go.jp

NEW ZEALAND
Eisenhowerlaan 77, 2517 KK The Hague
Tel.: 070 346 93 24
www.mft.govt.nz

NORWAY
Lange Vijverberg 11, 2513 AC The Hague
Tel.: 070 311 76 11
www.noorwegen.nl

PAKISTAN
Amaliastraat 8, 2517 JC The Hague
Tel.: 070 364 89 48
www.embassyofpakistan.com

PORTUGAL
Zeestraat 74, 2518 AD The Hague
Tel.: 070 328 12 39
www.portugalglobal.pt

RUSSIAN FEDERATION
A. Bickerweg 2, 2517 JP The Hague
Tel.: 070 345 13 00
www.netherlands.mid.ru/ru/

SAUDI ARABIA
Alexanderstraat 19, 2514 JM The Hague
Tel.: 070 361 43 91
www.saudiembassy.nl

SOUTH AFRICA
Wassenaarseweg 40, 2596 CJ The Hague
Tel.: 070 392 45 01
www.zuidafrika.nl

SPAIN
Lange Voorhout 50, 2514 EG The Hague
Tel.: 070 302 49 99
www.exteriores.gob.es

TURKEY
Jan Evertsenstraat 15, 2514 BS The Hague
Tel.: 070 360 49 12
www.turkishembassy.nl

SWEDEN
Burg. van Karnebeeklaan 6a, 2585 DB The Hague
Tel.: 070 412 02 00
www.swedenabroad.se/the-hague

UNITED KINGDOM
Lange Voorhout 10, 2514 CR The Hague
Tel.: 070 427 04 27
www.gov.uk/government/world/organisations/british-embassy-the-hague

UNITED STATES OF AMERICA
John Adams Park 1, 2244 BZ Wassenaar
Tel.: 070 310 22 09
https://nl.usembassy.gov

FOR A COMPLETE LIST OF EMBASSIES AND CONSULATES
www.government.nl/issues/embassies-consulates-and-other-representations

Getting around in the Netherlands is quite simple, the road networks are good and the public transportation system, which includes several airports, is excellent. All you need to know is how the system works. This chapter goes into the public transportation system, how to get a Dutch driver's license, the system of vehicle approval, the idiosyncrasies of Dutch drivers, whether or not you should buy a car here, the fact that you have to pay road tax, the Dutch automobile association, cycling and walking through the country, and last but definitely not least, the Dutch airports.

CHAPTER 6

Getting Around

CONTRIBUTING AUTHORS STEPHANIE DIJKSTRA AND JACOB VOSSESTEIN

THE SPIDER IN THE INTERNATIONAL WEB

In many ways, the Netherlands is like the spider in the web of Europe. Rotterdam is home to one of the busiest seaports in the world, the International Court of Justice is in The Hague, Amsterdam is one of the diamond capitals of the world, and several multinational companies and NGOs have their offices here. Furthermore, there are excellent universities that cater to international students, while world-renowned museums, unique exhibitions, and cultural events of all shapes and sizes lure tens of thousands of visitors to the country every year. A lot of international business is negotiated in this little country, facilitated by the fact that almost everyone here speaks at least one other language – in most cases English. In short, millions of people enter and make their way through the country, either on business, on vacation or to set up home here.

All this requires a lot of traveling and could not be achieved without an excellent infrastructure: Schiphol remains (one of) the busiest airport(s) on the European mainland; the Thalys-train takes you from Amsterdam to Paris in three-and-a-half hours; the Betuwe train-line transports goods to the east (particularly Germany); the public transportation system, including not only trains, but buses, trams and metros, offers an extensive and detailed network; there are several regional airports that also offer international connections; and the roads promise a comfortable cruise to your destination...

AIR TRAVEL

SCHIPHOL

As mentioned earlier, Schiphol is the busiest airport on the European mainland, with roughly 70 million passengers and approximately 1.7 million tons of freight passing through previous to Covid. Post-Covid, the airport quickly started recuperating its activity, creating a challenge for the airport in 2022, due to a shortage in security personnel and luggage handlers. Though it appears to have mostly overcome these challenges over the course of 2023, it still has not reached its pre-Covid peak in terms of passengers.

Aside from its logistic uses, it is also a prime business location, with a World Trade Center, a number of hotels, recreational activities, over 800 companies that employ almost 68,000 people, and, of course, its booming duty-free shopping business. (Though there is no longer such a thing as duty-free shopping in Europe, it still applies to passengers shopping at Schiphol Airport, regardless of their destination, with the restriction that tax-free shopping is not possible for alcohol and tobacco if you are traveling to a destination within the EU, unless you subsequently leave the EU within 24 hours.)

SECURITY

Those who are departing from Amsterdam are advised to arrive three hours in advance in connection with continued security measures after September 11, 2001.

TRAVELING BY TRAIN FROM SCHIPHOL

Amsterdam is 15 minutes away; The Hague and Utrecht 30 minutes; Rotterdam either 30 or 45, depending on which train you catch; Brussels two hours; Cologne and Paris three. The train station is located right underneath the Arrivals Hall, allowing you to easily board the various Intercity and high speed-lines to these, and countless more, destinations.

REGIONAL AIRPORTS

The Netherlands boasts many regional airports, such as Eindhoven, Groningen, Maastricht, and Rotterdam-The Hague, which offer direct flights abroad. The advantages of making use of one of these airports are not hard to think of: often they are closer to your home or office; they are easily accessible by car, taxi or bus; parking is cheap; the walking distances are short; check-in times are brief; and there are sometimes special services for business travelers.

TRAIN TRAVEL

The Netherlands has a dense railway network that offers frequent service, as well as the quickest way to travel between city centers. The carriages are modern and clean and, although many Dutch people complain about delays, the trains usually run on time. (Everything is relative!)

HIGH-SPEED TRAVEL

As mentioned above, you can travel by high-speed train (the Thalys or the TGV) from Amsterdam, Schiphol or Rotterdam to Belgium and – final destination – Paris. If you are going to Germany or Switzerland, you can take the high-speed ICE train, and if you are going to London, there is the Eurostar. These high-speed trains are really only a worthwhile option if you intend to travel all the way

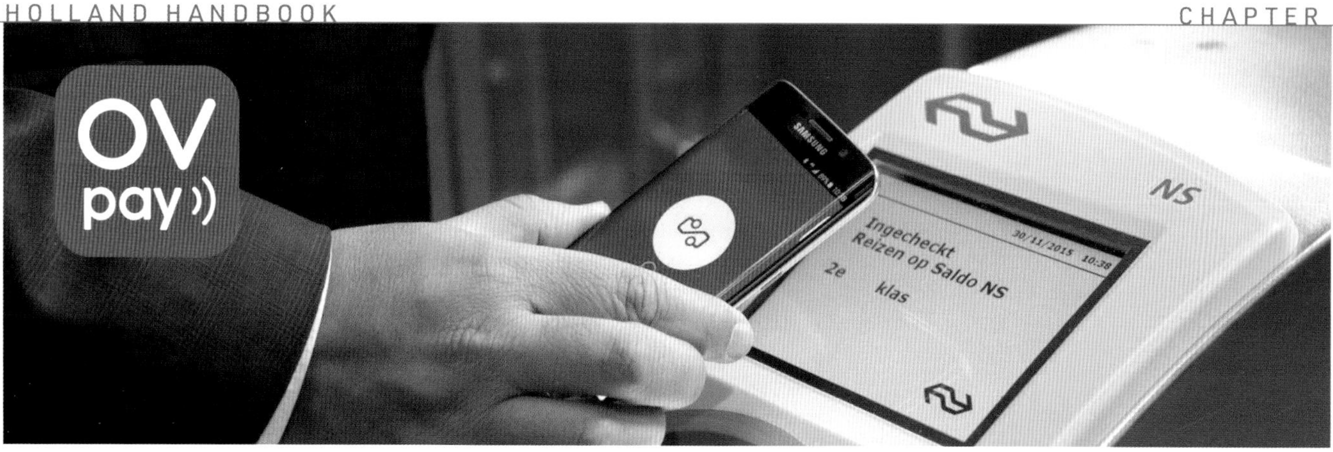

to these far-away destinations as, within the Netherlands, they still travel at a maximum speed of 160 km/h outside the densely populated areas. Only once they pass Brussels, in Belgium, do they pick up speed.

Note, however, that you may only travel on a high-speed train if you have bought a special (more expensive) ticket for this train and have made a reservation. If you inadvertently board the Thalys in Amsterdam to go visit your friend in The Hague and you are caught, you could find yourself paying a nasty fine!

OPTIONS

On the train you have a choice of first or second class, which is indicated with a large 1 or 2 painted on the outside. First class costs about 40% more and gives you a slightly larger seat in a compartment that is less likely to be full. Though smoking and no-smoking compartments may be indicated, this is no longer of relevance as, as you can read further on, you are no longer allowed to smoke on the trains.

TICKETS

Regular train travel is either one-way (*enkele reis*) or round-trip (*retour*). You cannot buy 'paper' tickets anymore, instead you purchase either an *ov-chipkaart* (Public Transportation Card) or a one-time *chipkaart*, which you can buy at a ticket window or at a yellow ticket machine, which you will find either in the main hall of the station or on the platform. The ticket machine – which, at many stations, is starting to replace ticket windows altogether – takes either cash, credit card or debit card. You can read more about the *ov-chipkaart* further on. You can also buy a train ticket through the 9292 or the GoAbout app.

Note: even though you now use the same pass to travel by train, bus and tram (metro), you need to check out of each one before you get on another one! Largely, this does not apply if you switch trains, but it does apply if you go from traveling by train to say, traveling by bus. When does it apply when traveling by train? When you switch companies: to a regional train company, such as for instance Arriva or Connexxion.

OVPAY

You can now also check in using your debit card, credit card or smartphone, without having to buy a ticket or have an *ov-chipkaart* or subscription. For more information, visit https://ovpay.nl/en. Don't forget to check out when you reach your destination!

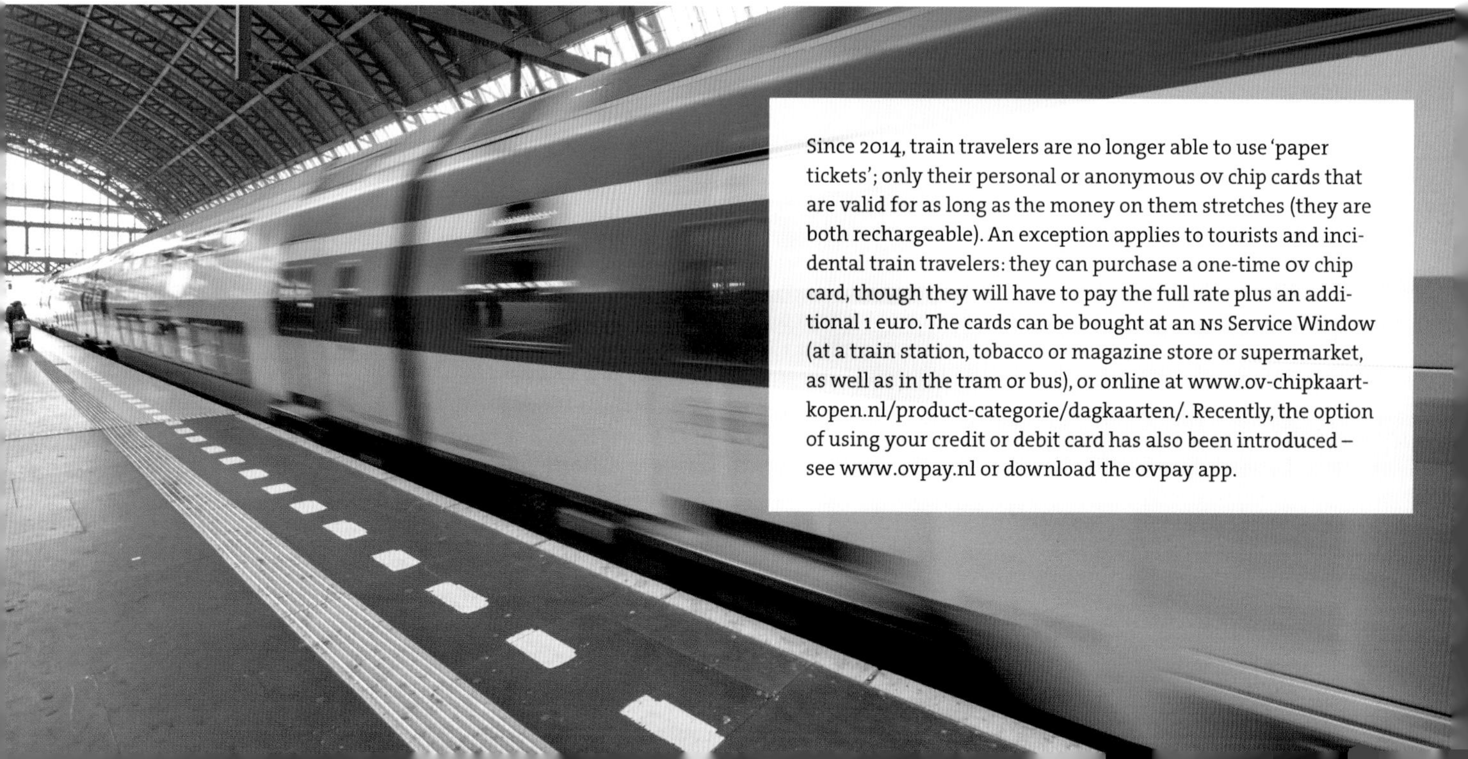

Since 2014, train travelers are no longer able to use 'paper tickets'; only their personal or anonymous ov chip cards that are valid for as long as the money on them stretches (they are both rechargeable). An exception applies to tourists and incidental train travelers: they can purchase a one-time ov chip card, though they will have to pay the full rate plus an additional 1 euro. The cards can be bought at an NS Service Window (at a train station, tobacco or magazine store or supermarket, as well as in the tram or bus), or online at www.ov-chipkaart-kopen.nl/product-categorie/dagkaarten/. Recently, the option of using your credit or debit card has also been introduced – see www.ovpay.nl or download the ovpay app.

PASSES

There are a wide variety of passes and special tickets that can save you money. Which type you choose depends on the kind of traveling you will be doing – frequent or infrequent, long distances or short, alone or in a group, during rush hour or not, and your age. The clerks at the ticket windows, which you can find at the large train stations in the cities, can advise you and will be especially helpful if you choose a time of day when they are not busy. Also one-day *ov-chipkaarten* are available, which can be used for traveling by bus, tram, metro or train.

If you wish to look into your options online, visit www.ov-chipkaart.nl and click on the British flag in the top right-hand corner to enter the English-language section. By clicking on the various card types, you can read more about them and find out which one will best suit your needs. The general public transportation card, or *ov-chipkaart*, can be used on trains, trams, and buses, as well as to arrange – see later on – a public transportation bicycle. For more on how the card works, see *The Public Transportation Card*, on page 156.

Students are issued a public transportation pass for traveling at a reduced price, called the *Studenten ov-chipkaart*. You can choose whether you want to travel for free between Monday morning 4 A.M. and Saturday morning 4 A.M. (and at a reduced price during the weekends, on holidays and during summer break) or for free between noon Fridays and Monday 4 A.M., as well as holidays and summer break, and at a reduced price on weekdays. This choice is marked on the *chipkaart* and is referred to as the *studentenreisproduct*.

INSPECTORS

You will often travel on the train without anyone ever looking at your *ov-chipkaart*. If the conductor catches you without one, however, you will be fined. In the larger cities, the NS railway company is trying to reduce the number of people who hang around at the stations without any particular purpose. For this reason, you might be asked to show your public transportation pass on the platform. In fact, it is increasingly becoming impossible to make your way inside and onto the platform without swiping your card first.

TIMETABLES AND INFORMATION

You can check the complete railway timetable online, by visiting www.ns.nl. This site offers more than just train schedules, it also includes information on how to get to and from the station, in Dutch and in English. Another option is to download the app: 9292.

You can also call the general number for information on public transportation: 0900 9292, or visit www.goabout.com (or download their app) for travel advice that includes bus, tram and metro lines, as well as 'share' bicycles and cars.

SMOKING

You are not allowed to smoke on trains – not even on the balconies. This ban also applies to all areas you might be in while waiting for, or walking to, your train; halls, stairs, flyovers, elevators and covered platforms.

ONCE YOU GET THERE

Once you arrive at your destination station, you have a few options for how to get where you are going from there. These you find in the following paragraphs.

- There are about 23 million bicycles in the Netherlands, making that more than one for every inhabitant
- About 1.1 million new bicycles are sold every year
- The Dutch cycle approximately 1,000 kilometers per year, per person; kids aged 6-23, 800 km; kids aged 23-18, 1,880; and those 75 and older, 830 km
- The percentage of bicycle owners is the highest among those with the highest income
- The country has 2,655 bicycle shops
- There are 37,000 kilometers of bicycle paths and lanes, and 116,500 kilometers of paved roads (including 2,235 kilometers of expressways)
- There are approximately 10.3 million registered cars
- The Netherlands is in the middle when it comes to car density percentages in the whole of the EU: 59%
- In the provinces of Drenthe and Noord-Brabant there are relatively more cars, due to the fact that distances are greater and public transportation is not quite as omnipresent
- Conversely, the number of cars in the bigger cities is relatively low
- Almost 6% of the Dutch households have three or more cars, 50% have one and 25% have none
- In the world, the Netherlands is the eighth safest country to drive in. Within Europe, only Sweden, the U.K. and Switzerland have lower numbers of fatalities. And Monaco, but that might be due to its low population density
- Based on road quality, use of seatbelts, traffic levels and the use of bicycles instead of cars, the Netherlands has come out on top as being the safest country to drive in (according to one study)
- There are 6,300 kilometers of waterways
- There are approximately 400,000 recreational boats
- In Drenthe, there are 1,000 recreational boats, in the provinces of North Holland and South Holland, there are 32,000 each
- There are 3,200 kilometers of standard gauge railways, with appr. 400 train stations, or one every 8.1 km of railroad tracks
- On average, the Dutch travel a little over 30 kilometers a day: 22.5 by car (either as a driver or a passenger), 3 by train and 2.5 by bike
- 8.6 of these kilometers are work-related, 6 are for social purposes (visiting other people's homes), and 5.5 for sports, hobbies or going out.

TIP If a stranger offers to sell you a bicycle for less than € 40, don't buy it. It's probably stolen, and you too are violating the law if you take possession of it.

TAXI SERVICES

Say you want to visit your long-lost cousin in the remote, but picturesque village of Cothen. You find out that you can take a train to Zeist – which you courageously do – but what do you do once you get there? Cothen would constitute a brisk, say, two-hour walk from there. Or perhaps you've agreed to meet your friends in Amsterdam, and need to get from Central Station to the Rijksmuseum within half an hour?

TAXIS

You cannot hail taxis on the street in the Netherlands like you can in many parts of the world. You must either request one by phone, or go to a taxi-stand where taxis wait. All major railway stations have a taxi-stand. Hotels and restaurants are always happy to call a taxi for you if you ask.

The regular Dutch taxis use meters and charge roughly the same rates. When you start, the meter will already show a balance of several euros. This ensures the driver a minimum fare. Only for very long distances is it sometimes possible to negotiate a fare in advance. Otherwise you pay what the meter indicates. It is customary to give taxi drivers a tip, which usually means increasing the amount up to a round figure.

PUBLIC TRANSPORTATION TAXIS

At many train stations, there are special taxi services, offered at a reduced rate as, in most cases, you share these taxis with other passengers. Below, we have included a list of these taxis – which one you will end up using, depends on where you will be requiring its services; the province of North Holland, or Gelderland, or South Holland, or one of the major cities. You can also visit www.ns.nl, click on *In English*, and enter 'taxi' under search.

These taxis are available at almost all train stations in the Netherlands, but not in the biggest cities. As they are useful mostly for reaching the smaller towns, the idea is that you take a train to a location close to your place of destination and arrange to have a public transportation taxi pick you up there. The related phone numbers and sites for information depend on where you will be traveling; there is no central telephone number or site for this service. If you call 0900 9292, they can tell you which number to call for travel within your region or put your call through to the available taxi services in your area.

Types of public transportation taxis:

- OV taxis: You can step into an NS OV Taxi at more than 320 train stations throughout the country. You pay based on the shortest route calculated by a route planner. Reservations are made using the NS app or online on https://ov.taxi, after which you will immediately be informed of the fare via email or text. Payments are done in advance, via IDEAL. Once you have made a reservation, which you do up to 30 minutes in advance, the taxi will be ready at the station, by the taxi stand (the message confirming your booking will tell you where to find it), or will pick you up where you are and take you to the station. You can bring up to three other people on the ride with you.
- Regio taxi: This is a cross between public transportation and taxi services that take you from door to door. Special taxi services are available for persons with physical disabilities. More information, in Dutch, can be found on www.connexxion.nl/nl/onze-routes/vervoersmiddelen/connexxion-taxi/regiotaxi.

SCHIPHOL AIRPORT TAXI

And last, but not least, there are several Schiphol taxi services to take you to and from all Dutch airports, saving you the hassle of arranging long-term parking, dragging your luggage to the connecting bus and worrying about your car while away. For more information visit www.schiphol.nl/nl/pagina/met-de-taxi-van-of-naar-schiphol (click on *EN* for English), or www.connexxion.nl/nl/onze-routes/vervoersmiddelen/connexxion-taxi (in the top right-hand drop-down, select EN).

For travel to and from Schiphol Airport and other airports in the country, visit www.schipholtraveltaxi.nl. Or else, check out the Schiphol Business Taxi (www.schipholbusinesstaxi.nl).

'CORPORATE' TAXIS

For 'top managers and policy makers', Connexxion offers a variety of services, available 24 / 7, visit www.connexxion.nl/nl/onze-routes/vervoersmiddelen/connexxion-taxi/zakelijk-vervoer.

BUSES AND TRAMS

If you are looking to make your way through the larger cities, or from one town to the next, the Dutch transportation companies provide frequent services on buses and trams. Amsterdam and Rotterdam also have a subway (called the metro). Rural communities are linked by bus.

BUS SERVICES

There are two types of buses; city buses and regional buses. Depending on the area they operate in, they go by different names. City buses operate within towns and cities and stop frequently. Regional buses take you from town to town and cover considerable distances between stops once they leave town.

FIGURING IT OUT

Visit www.connexxion.nl to find out which lines operate in your region and to plan your trip. In the top, right-hand corner, you can select either *EN* for English or *DE* for German. On www.connexxion.nl/en/travel-information/apps-on-your-smartphone, you can find an overview of handy travel apps.

In the larger cities, you will find a map of the city – dotted and lined with the bus, tram and subway (metro) lines – at many of the tram stops, allowing you to figure out where you can go and how to get there. Or you can download the 9292-app.

THE PUBLIC TRANSPORTATION CARD – *OV-CHIPKAART*

There two types of public transportation card, or *ov-chipkaart*: the personal *ov-chipkaart* and the so-called anonymous *ov-chipkaart*. The personal *ov-chipkaart* is a plastic credit-card shaped public transportation card with your photograph that contains information on the amount of credit on it, on whether you have a right to certain reductions, and on whether you are traveling on the basis of a public transportation 'subscription', or pass. You can find travel discount products on www.ns.nl/en/nsflex/webshop#/abonnementen/lijst. To make use of these products, you have to have an account first. Special travel products, for persons with disabilities,

Netherlands Railways Network

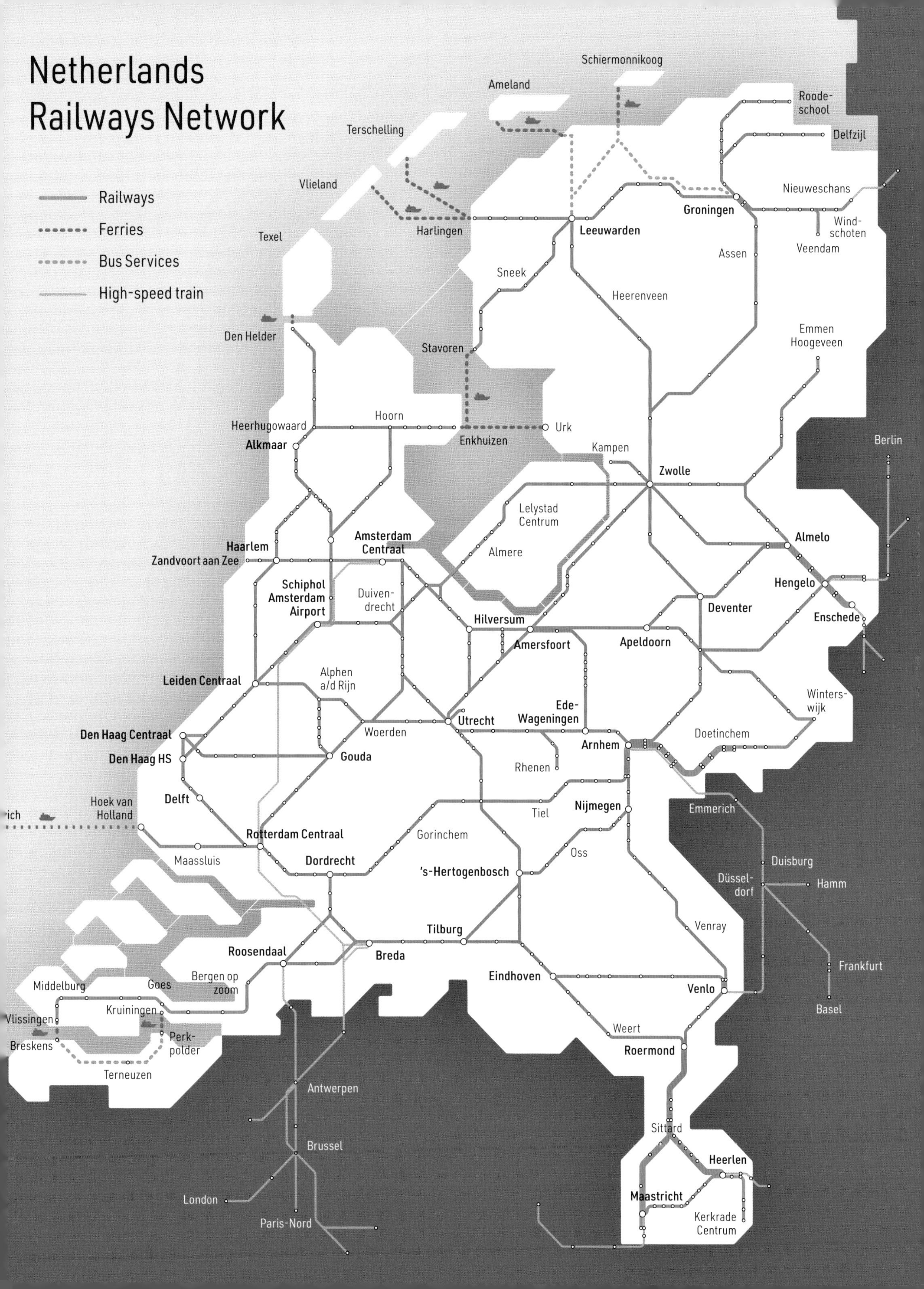

can be found on https://9292.nl/en/extra/accessibility/special-travel-products.

When entering the tram, bus or metro, you hold the card against the card reader. When you leave, you again hold the card against the card reader and it will tell you how much the trip cost and how much credit remains on the card. When traveling by train, you hold the card against the card reader on the platform before entering the train and, upon arrival, before leaving the platform. This way you pay for your travel based on the number of kilometers you travel rather than based on the number of zones you travel through (though the zone system may remain in place in some areas). The 'anonymous' *ov-chipkaart* does not have your photograph and is issued without the option of an automatic 'refill' or the use of subscription or (age-related) reductions. For one-time use, for tourists for instance, there are 'disposable' one-day cards – to be bought from an NS ticket automat or NS service window at the train station – that are only valid 28 hours (from midnight till 4 a.m. the next day) on the day of purchase, and that can also be bought on buses and trams. Students are issued a public transportation pass (see next paragraph).

More information on the *ov-chipkaart* can be found on www.ov-chipkaart.nl. This site also has English-language information and is where you can order your card (and upload your photograph), as well as arrange travel credit and fix things if you forgot to check out at the end of your trip. Travel credit can also be arranged at, for instance, train stations, supermarkets and magazine / bookstores where you will find the yellow automats for transferring money (credit) onto your *ov-chipkaart,* using your debit card. For some or other reason, you cannot buy a train 'ticket' online via this site, however; you *can* buy one via www.ns.nl. You click on In *English*, and then on *Single ticket*. Check out the *Holland* or *Amsterdam (Region) Travel Ticket* while you're at it, if you're planning on going to Amsterdam, or the *Season Tickets*, for more tailor-made options.

OVPAY

As mentioned under Train Travel, you can now also check in using your debit card, credit card or smartphone, without having to buy a ticket or have an *ov-chipkaart* or subscription. For more information, visit https://ovpay.nl/en. Don't forget to check out when you reach your destination!

PASSES

If you will be using the buses and trams four days a week or more, it might be more economical for you to buy a monthly pass. To arrange this pass, visit a Connexxion booth at the bus stations outside the train stations.

Again, students are issued a public transportation pass, called the *Studenten ov-chipkaart*. As a student, you can choose whether you want to travel for free between Monday morning 4 A.M. and Saturday morning 4 A.M. (and at a reduced price during the weekends, on holidays and during summer break) or for free between noon Fridays and Monday 4 A.M., as well as holidays and summer break, and at a reduced price on weekdays.

INSPECTORS

Though you have been given the responsibility of swiping the *ov-chipkaart* yourself – and might find that you can generally elude inspection – sooner or later, a team of inspectors will suddenly appear in the bus or tram, and if you are caught traveling without a swiped *ov-chipkaart*, you will be fined.

SHARE CAR

With more than 2,400 cars – at, among others, more than 130 train stations – in the Netherlands, Greenwheels Share (rental) cars is a convenient option for those who don't have a car of their own. Both individual and shared subscriptions are possible, provided all drivers are at least 18 years of age. Gas is included in the rent, recharging electric cards is included in the mileage rate, and you pay a deposit of € 100 (or € 250 for business subscriptions). There are various types of subscriptions; you can find them on the site, as well as information on what type of driver's license you need to drive a Greenwheels Share Car. NS travelers enjoy a discount.

If you 'subscribe' to a Greenwheels car, this car is parked on a fixed location and is available 24 / 7, though you must not forget to reserve it in advance – something you can do just a few minutes before picking it up, provided the car is available, of course – by visiting their site, using the app or calling their telephone number. Instructions on how to reserve and use a car can be found on Greenwheels.nl, click on *EN* for English. You can also use a Greenwheels fuel pass to fill your tank and instructions for charging an electric car can be found online. Once you return, you log out and the computer automatically registers the time and the kilometers. Visit www.greenwheels.nl for additional information, for instance to see on which non-Dutch driver's licenses you may drive one of their cars. The site is also in English.

Greenwheels cars can also be used by companies who want to make them available to employees. For instance, employees who come to work by public transportation or bicycle, but need a car every now and then to visit a client or attend a meeting at another office.

Other 'share car' options can be found on ritjeweg.nl, though this site is still only in Dutch.

PUBLIC TRANSPORTATION BICYCLE

One final way to get to your destination once you have arrived somewhere by train is by Public Transportation Bicycle (*ov-fiets*). To rent one of these, you pay € 4.45 per 24 hours. To this is added a surcharge of € 5 per 24 hours, once you exceed 72 hours. Handing in the bicycle at a different location comes at an extra charge. You need a so-called season ticket to rent an *ov-fiets*, which costs € 0.01, and which you can link to your public transportation pass (also the *Studenten ov-chipkaart* student pass qualifies). Payments are done after the fact, by means of an automatic payment (*automatische incasso*). Bicycles are available on almost 300 locations throughout the country (approximately 100 towns / cities), including various locations within the bigger cities of Amsterdam, The Hague and Rotterdam. The *nearby* (*in de buurt*) feature of the NS app can help you locate one. For more information, visit www.ns.nl/door-to-door/ov-fiets/.

Other options can be found on www.fietsverhuur.nl.

Cheaper Travel by Public Transportation

Tourists can make use of a public transportation pass, called the Holland Travel Ticket (www.ns.nl/producten/en/onbeperkt-reizen/p/holland-travel-ticket). For either € 70 or € 48, they can use this ticket on the train, bus tram and metro – without limitation (though not on the Thalys train, and – at an extra fee – on ICE and Intercity Direct trains), for an entire day. The cheaper version will allow travel only after morning rush hour is over, and during weekends and public holidays. It can be bought online as a voucher and exchanged at certain train stations, which you will find listed on the website given above.

Tourists visiting the province of South Holland (which includes The Hague and Rotterdam) can buy a Tourist Day Ticket for € 15.50. This can be used on buses, trams, the metro and the waterbus – not the train. When you buy this ticket, you are given a free map with information on places to visit in the region. You can find an overview of where to buy a Tourist Day Ticket, and for what type of public transportation you can use it per region, on https://touristdaytickets.nl.

Visitors of Amsterdam can buy the Amsterdam Travel Ticket (www.ns.nl/producten/en/onbeperkt-reizen/p/amsterdam-travel-ticket), which includes travel by train between Schiphol Airport and any train station in the city, as well as on the Amsterdam Airport Express bus, and unlimited travel on buses, trams, metros and ferries operated by GVB. It costs € 18 for one day, € 24 for two days, and € 30 for three, and comes with a map with highlights of the city. Sales points are: Schiphol Airport, Amsterdam Central Station and various other locations in the city. The Amsterdam & Region Travel Ticket offers unlimited travel in Amsterdam and throughout the region, and costs € 21 for one, € 31.50 for two and € 40.50 for three days. It can be purchased on www.iamsterdam.com/en/plan-your-trip/getting-around/public-transport/amsterdam-region-travel-ticket.

If all you are planning on doing is traveling by train, and you are feeling adventurous, you can also opt for a so-called 'day ticket' (*dagkaart*), which can be bought at certain chain stores and supermarkets (such as *Blokker* or *Hema*) and is often offered in combination with a reduced price for, for instance, a zoo, a museum, a day of wellness, or a special lunch. These are temporary offers and an overview of what is available on a given day can be found on www.treinreiziger.nl. Click on *Treinkaartjes*. On www.ns.nl, you can find the *dagkaart* (day ticket), which offers unlimited travel for a full day for € 58.80 (www.ns.nl/producten/en/onbeperkt-reizen/p/dagkaart).

WATER TRANSPORTATION

If there is one thing that we have in abundance in the Netherlands, it's water. So it would be only logical to expect a public water transportation net – which there is. There is the ferry service between Hoek van Holland and the Maasvlakte (www.ret.nl); a waterbus in the Dordrecht / Rotterdam area (www.waterbus.nl); and a watertaxi / maastaxi in Rotterdam (www.watertaxirotterdam.nl). The former two are very convenient for commuters while the water and maastaxi in Rotterdam offer a much-needed connection between the city's two shores.

There are also plenty of non-public transportation and very picturesque (and cheap) ferries across the many rivers and canals of the Netherlands. Sometimes it could be well worth your while (it could save you time as well as stress!) to get off the highway, out of the traffic jam and take an inland road to a ferry across the river.

DRIVING YOUR CAR

Remember the bumper sticker: 'If you don't like my driving, get off of the sidewalk'? Well, sometimes partaking of the road system here feels that way too. All of a sudden, you are supposed to know that any car *coming from the right* has the right of way, unless specifically indicated otherwise. This means not only developing rightview paranoia, but also rearview paranoia; if you do not take your right of way, you are almost sure to incur the wrath (if not the front bumper) of the car behind you. It is also important to know that the window of opportunity for taking your right of way is about a second-and-a-half, after which you might as well settle for letting the other car go first – in other words, there is lots of potential for upsetting at least one other person!

Also, slowing down to see if this is the street you want to enter – or parking space you wish to take – is almost certain to generate an irritated passing by (either left or right, depending on where there is more space) so that it is best to check before making your definite turn. Since we're on the subject of checking, be sure, before making any turn, that there are no bicycles going straight ahead as they have the right of way over you (even if you 'are' the car).

Other, guaranteed, sources of irritation to Dutch drivers are: lingering in the left-hand lane on the highway if you are only planning on exceeding the speed limit by a mere 10 kilometers, taking more than two seconds to get your car rolling once the light turns green – and driving an obviously very expensive car (but that is a whole other issue).

Having said all these deliciously unkind things about the Dutch drivers, fairness requires us to point out that the Netherlands is statistically one of the safest countries in the world to drive in.

MOTORCYCLE

Everything written in the following paragraphs also applies to having a motorcycle. Only the rules on exchanging a license might vary on certain points; for more information, contact the RDW (see further on).

OWNING A CAR

Once you plan on owning a car, keep the following in mind. You must (these topics will be covered in the subsequent paragraphs):

- arrange the vehicle registration card
- if you import a car: pay BPM
- arrange a periodic check-up of the car (*Vehicle Approval – APK*)
- have a valid driver's license (see *Driver's License*)
- know the rules of the road (you will find a few further on)
- take out car and liability insurance (more on insurances in chapter 5)
- pay road tax (see *Road Tax*).

THE VEHICLE REGISTRATION CARD

When you buy a vehicle, from a private person or a garage, they will give you either the credit-card sized *kentekencard* and code, or the proof of registration (*tenaamstellingsbewijs, deel 1B*) and the proof of transfer (*overschrijvingsbewijs*), which you will take to an RDW-window (or store offering postal services), plus proof of identification and of your address (a driver's license will suffice). There the vehicle will be put in your name and you will be handed a document that will prove that the transaction has taken place, plus the first four digits of the registration code. Within one or two days, the RDW will send you your new *kentekencard*, plus a five-digit code. These five digits, plus the four on the transaction document, are what you will need to sell the car again. They will also issue you a document stating that the vehicle is no longer registered in the name of the seller (*vrijwaringsbewijs*, or warranty against liability); this you give to the seller. It will allow him to prove that he is no longer responsible for the vehicle. When you buy a new car, this is all generally arranged by the car salesperson.

Previously, when you owned a car, you were issued three paper documents, called *deel IA*, *deel IB* and *deel II* (parts IA, IB and II) – which, together, constituted the *kentekenbewijs* (vehicle registration certificate). *Deel IA* contained all the technical information on your car, such as brand, type and number and was called the *voertuigbewijs*. *Deel IB* contained the name and address of the owner of the car and was your proof of ownership / registration. It was called the *tenaamstellingsbewijs*. Whoever was driving the car had to carry *deel IA* and *IB* with him at all times. You could not buy a car from someone who cannot produce this document and you could not sell your car without it. *Deel II* was the proof of transfer, or *overschrijvingsbewijs*. Ownership was transferred, making use of this document, at a store offering post office services. In vehicle registration certificates issued before June 1, 2004, these documents were called *deel I, II* and *III* (corresponding to *deel IA, IB* and *II*, respectively). We mention these, because you might still be confronted with them, even though there is a new system since 2015. If you want, you can exchange the old documents for a *kentekencard*.

THE RDW

If you own a car, you will soon find out about the the Rijksdienst voor Wegverkeer, or RDW. The RDW is the Dutch Road Traffic and Transport Authority. A government-commissioned body, it produces technical and administrative regulations aimed at making Dutch road traffic and transportation as safe and effective as possible. Its vehicle registration system enables the administration of the country's vehicular details, making it possible to quickly locate the owners or holders of vehicles and to call their attention to tax, insurance and APK obligations (see the next paragraph), for instance. This system is also indispensable when following up traffic offenses.

Besides the vehicle registration system and the approval of imported cars, the RDW also manages the Central Driver's License and Moped Certificate Registry, and the exchange of Dutch driver's licenses for those issued outside the Netherlands.

Traffic and Safety

For years, measures implemented by the authorities succeeded in structurally reducing the number of fatal accidents, which went from 1,088 in 2003 to 745 in 2022. It appears that these are largely caused by cyclists as well as senior citizens riding 'scootmobiles' and electric wheelchairs. There were fewer deaths among younger people, though one in five cycling accidents among young people are due to the use of smart phones while cycling. The Ministry points an accusatory finger at the municipal roads as it has observed that the greatest number of victims are to be found within the country's city limits. The VVN (Veilig Verkeer Nederland, or organization for Safe Traffic in the Netherlands) organizes annual theory lessons and practical exams for children in the last two years of elementary school (either fifth grade or sixth grade), as a consequence of which children the age of 11 are already familiarized with important rules regarding the right of way (for buses, pedestrians, horses, cyclists, etc.), traffic signs, using a mobile phone while cycling, and making sure they are seen in traffic.

MOST FREQUENTLY ASKED QUESTIONS FOR THE VVN: WHAT IS THE PERMITTED BLOOD ALCOHOL LEVEL?

The law says 0.5 promille is the limit for all drivers (except for those who have just acquired their license, see further on). This does not translate into a fixed number of glasses of a particular type of alcohol – it depends on weight, age, sex, stomach content, etc. During the first five years after obtaining your driver's license, the permitted blood alcohol level is 0.2 promille. The limit is not only for the drivers of cars, but also of (motor)cycles and mopeds! The limit of 0.2 promille applies to moped and motorized bicycle riders until the age of 24.

On the water, the permitted blood alcohol level is 0.5.

In 2001, the BOB-campaign was introduced, aimed at encouraging partiers to always select one person who will not drink and who will do the driving. This campaign has proven successful: over the course of 15 years, the number of drunk drivers was reduced by almost half – and has more or less remained at this point.

MAY I USE A MOBILE PHONE IN THE CAR?

Not while driving. It is permitted if you are standing still in a traffic jam or at a red light. See page 167. The same applies to moped riders.

SHOULD MY CHILD USE A BICYCLE HELMET?

Though they are not obligatory, there is no doubt that they can help avoid serious head injury, if worn correctly (which also means using the right size). There are many bicycle riders in the Netherlands and every year, there are 26 fatal accidents involving children; 14,000 children end up in the hospital and 23,000 have to see a doctor due to biking accidents.

WHERE SHOULD MOPEDS / SCOOTERS RIDE?

Mopeds ride in the regular car lanes within city limits, unless there is a blue, round sign by the bicycle path with both a bicycle and a moped on it; this sign means that mopeds must ride on the bicycle path. Outside city limits, mopeds must ride on the bicycle paths, unless there isn't one. For further information, we refer you to the road signs and their explanation.

Scooters and motorized bicycles (*snorfiets*) may make use of bicycle lanes. Helmets are not required for motorized bicycles, but they are for scooters. Drivers of these vehicles must have passed a theoretical traffic exam and must have taken out insurance.

WHAT ABOUT CAR LIGHTS?

During the day, if you cannot see clearly, and after dark, you use regular headlights. In the case of fog, snow or rain, you should use your fog lights front and back. If you are stopped by the police because one of your car lights is not working, you must have reserve bulbs with you so that you can replace the broken one. If you don't have any with you, you will be fined € 150.

For more information, visit: www.vvn.nl

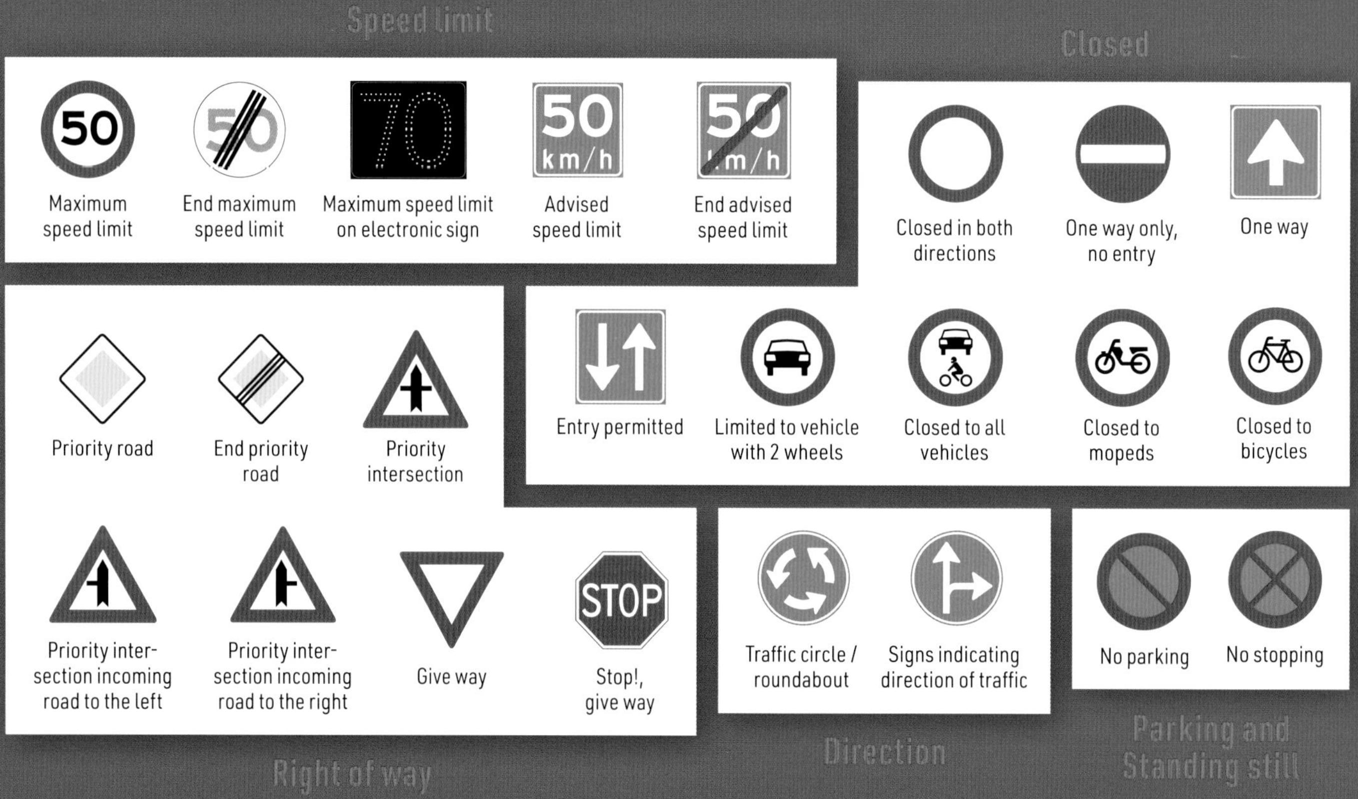

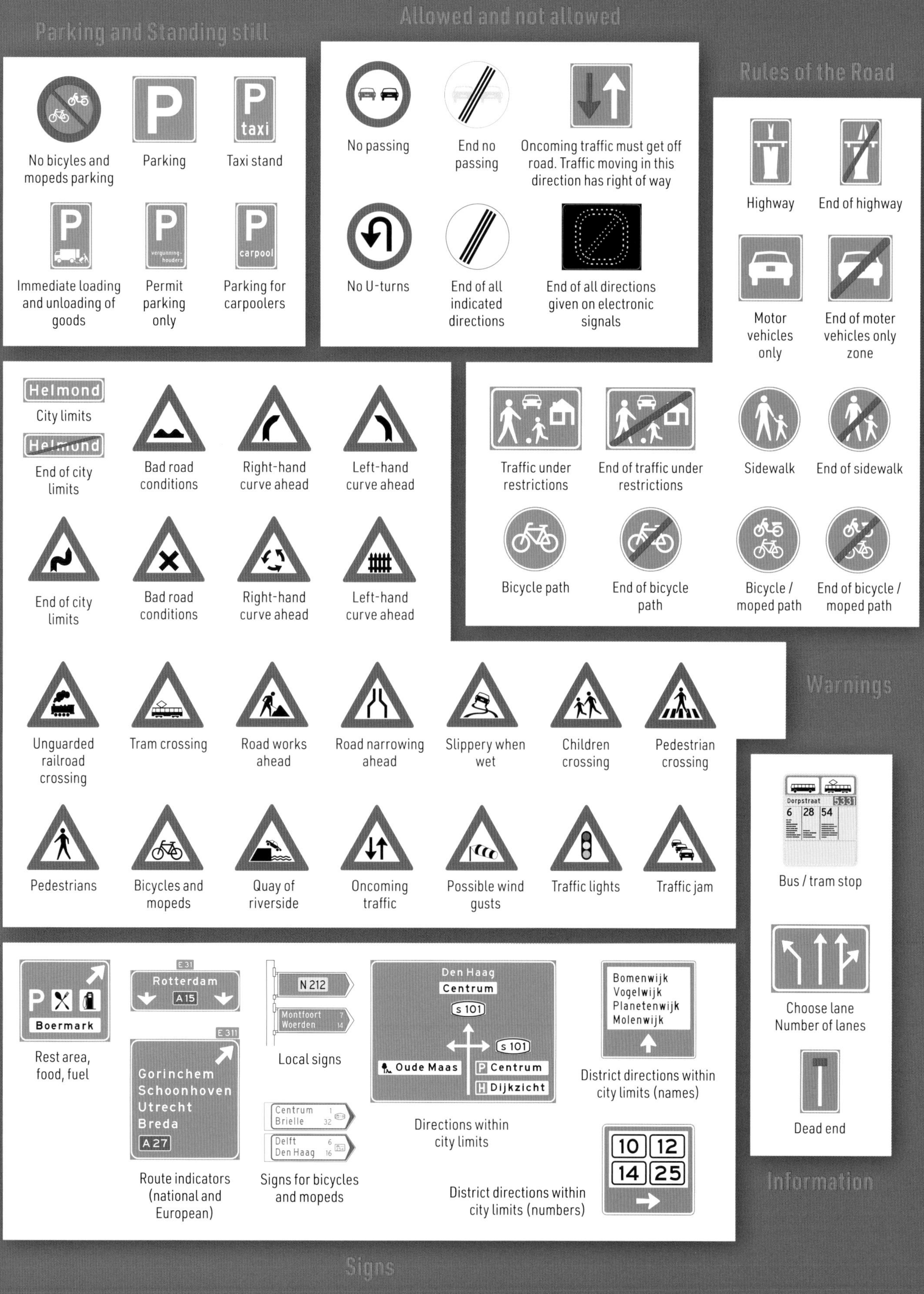

Parking and Standing still
No bicyles and mopeds parking
P
Parking
P
taxi
Taxi stand
P
Immediate loading and unloading of goods
P
vergunning-houders
Permit parking only
P
carpool
Parking for carpoolers
Allowed and not allowed
No passing
End no passing
Oncoming traffic must get off road. Traffic moving in this direction has right of way
No U-turns
End of all indicated directions
End of all directions given on electronic signals
Rules of the Road
Highway
End of highway
Motor vehicles only
End of moter vehicles only zone
Helmond
City limits
Helmond
End of city limits
Bad road conditions
Right-hand curve ahead
Left-hand curve ahead
End of city limits
Bad road conditions
Right-hand curve ahead
Left-hand curve ahead
Traffic under restrictions
End of traffic under restrictions
Sidewalk
End of sidewalk
Bicycle path
End of bicycle path
Bicycle / moped path
End of bicycle / moped path
Warnings
Unguarded railroad crossing
Tram crossing
Road works ahead
Road narrowing ahead
Slippery when wet
Children crossing
Pedestrian crossing
Pedestrians
Bicycles and mopeds
Quay of riverside
Oncoming traffic
Possible wind gusts
Traffic lights
Traffic jam
Dorpstraat
5331
6
28
54
Bus / tram stop
Choose lane
Number of lanes
Dead end
Information
P
Boermark
Rest area, food, fuel
E 31
Rotterdam
A15
E 311
Gorinchem
Schoonhoven
Utrecht
Breda
A 27
Route indicators (national and European)
N 212
Montfoort 7
Woerden 14
Local signs
Centrum 1
Brielle 32
Delft 6
Den Haag 16
Signs for bicycles and mopeds
Den Haag
Centrum
s 101
s 101
Oude Maas
P Centrum
H Dijkzicht
Directions within city limits
Bomenwijk
Vogelwijk
Planetenwijk
Molenwijk
District directions within city limits (names)
10
12
14
25
District directions within city limits (numbers)
Signs

The ANWB

Almost all Dutch drivers are members of the ANWB, the Royal Dutch Touring Club. As befits this country of bicycle riders, the ANWB started – in 1883 – as an organization for cyclists. Though they still offer, for instance, recreational maps for the original target group and hikers, they were clever enough to expand their services to include car and motor cycle drivers. Members of the ANWB are offered the following:

ROAD SERVICES – WEGENWACHT

The ANWB Road Services offer members of the ANWB 24-hour breakdown assistance (called Wegenwacht) on the Dutch roads (and for an extra fee: in your driveway), and even European roads (the level of help depends on the package you select). Help usually arrives within 30 minutes, though this of course depends on road, traffic and weather conditions, as well as the number of breakdowns on the route. If the repair service cannot repair your vehicle on the spot, ANWB offers free transportation of your vehicle and the passengers. Furthermore, members who make use of Road Services also have the option of the Car Replacement Service and a replacement driver in case of illness or accident, depending on the assistance package you select. With this service you are loaned a car if yours cannot be repaired within the hour. It offers two levels of service; the second level includes legal assistance in certain circumstances. Membership fees are cheaper for those younger than 24 and for those whose partner is already a member.

SERVICES WHEN TRAVELING ABROAD

When traveling abroad, ANWB membership (Wegenwacht Europa Service) also offers you certain benefits, such as an internationally-recognized credit card to give you access to cash in the case of an emergency, legal help, car replacement, assistance from foreign road services organizations, and more – such as, for instance, a replacement driver should you fall ill or become injured. Fees vary, according to the level of service, so be sure to check the website. Even when traveling outside Europe, you can call the ANWB for assistance and for roadside help (be sure to check in which countries this is the case).

LEGAL SERVICE

The ANWB legal services department provides its members with advice and information by phone, including mediation should problems arise concerning travel insurance or in case of

VEHICLE APPROVAL – APK

Before a vehicle is allowed onto the Dutch roads, and at intervals during its use, the RDW (Vehicle Technology and Information Center) ensures that the vehicle meets environmental, safety and economic demands. This work includes providing vehicle type approvals, carrying out certain independent tests, and supervising the Dutch *Algemene Periodieke Keuring*, or APK (annual general technical test), after which you are issued the Individual Approval Certificate. For cars that run on gasoline and that were manufactured more than four years ago, an APK is carried out once every two years until the car is eight years old – after which it is carried out annually. Cars that run on any other type of fuel require an annual APK once they have been manufactured more than three years ago. This can be done by specialized centers, called *keuringsstations*, or by a local garage that has been recognized by the RDW. There is no fixed price for this test, and prices vary greatly. If you do not agree with the outcome of the test, you can submit a request for a renewed test with the RDW.

Though the RDW will often send you a reminder, it is your responsibility to remember to have the APK done (beware that they have been known to carry out random tests and that you are obligated to cooperate!). As an extra service, your garage may send you a letter of reminder. When your car has been APK-tested, the garage notifies the RDW of this and of the outcome. If the RDW receives no such notification, because you failed to have your car tested on time, they will send you an invoice with a fine. If you are not sure when you have to have your APK carried out, you can visit ovi.rdw.nl, and fill in your license plate number. This site provides you with the technical information on your car, too, should you be in need of this.

If you want to import a car that was manufactured more than three / four years ago (depending on the type of fuel), then it must be APK-approved. A car that is imported from outside the EU or the EEA (see inset on page 170) will have to meet stricter codes. Which these are, depends on the year of manufacture. In some cases, the certificate of conformity will suffice (you can read more about this in the following paragraphs).

IMPORTING A CAR

In the following paragraphs you can read about the steps you must take to obtain a registration card for your car.

VEHICLE TAX – BPM

BPM is a vehicle tax that is due by the first person to register a particular car or motorcycle in their name in the Netherlands. If you buy a car in the Netherlands, the official car importer takes care of it (the tax is included in the price). If you bring your car / motorcycle in from abroad, convert a non-passenger car into a passenger car, or drive a car / motorcycle with foreign license plates in the Netherlands, then you have to take care of it yourself. See the following paragraphs.

The amount of BPM you owe depends on the CO_2 emission of your car. This is determined by the RDW. They issue you a form stating your car's CO_2 emission, which is based on the European Type Approval of your car. Should no such form be available, a fixed emission rate is determined based on the type of fuel you use. If you want, you can have an individual test carried out on your car, to determine its emission rate.

APPROVAL RDW

To register your car for the BPM, you must have your car approved by the RDW (see page 161). To this purpose, you visit an RDW-vehicle approval center (call 0900 0739 to find the one nearest you), bringing:

- the vehicle
- proof of identity (passport, ID card or Dutch driver's license)

an accident. Their legal assistance also includes assistance if things go wrong with a second-hand car that you've bought, provided it was purchased from a recognized garage. If you have a (legal) question, you can contact the Legal Department of the ANWB via e-mail or by phone, and they will let you know whether and how they can help you.

INSURANCE

You can take out a variety of insurances with the ANWB, such as, among others, travel insurance, cancelation insurance, car, bicycle, motorcycle, house, household content, and boat insurance.

STORES AND PUBLICATIONS

Members of the ANWB are issued membership cards which offer them special discounts on books, maps, guides, and other items sold at the special ANWB stores – including travel pouches, car seats for children and outdoor clothing.

MEMBERSHIP CARD

Showing your ANWB-membership card will also provide you with a discount on entrance fees to amusement parks and museums; on hotel and shop prices; and on fees for rental cars.

- foreign vehicle registration certificate
- the Individual Approval Certificate (APK-rapport)
- the Certificate of Conformity.

You can set up an appointment online. In that case, be sure to have your vehicle identification number (VIN) ready. For more information on importing a car from an EU/EEA country, visit www.rdw.nl/en/import-export-transit/importing-a-car-from-a-eu-or-efta-country. If you want it to undergo an APK-test while you're there (the general technical test), you can have the RDW carry this out simultaneously. If you already have a foreign APK, this can be adopted – but be sure to verify this upon arrival for your appointment. On the day of your appointment, you bring the items listed above. The RDW will then determine whether the car can be registered. A Certificate of Conformity (*Certificaat van Overeenstemming*) lists all specifics related to the car and you can request it from the manufacturer of the car or their representative in the Netherlands.

If you import a car from outside above countries, you cannot have the approval and APK carried out at an RDW approval center; you will have to go to the RDW test center in Lelystad, for which you will have to make an appointment. A tip given by the RDW themselves is to go to a garage and have them do an APK check, to make sure you meet all the requirements for APK approval when you visit the RDW. Visit www.rdw.nl/en/import-export-transit/moving-to-the-netherlands-and-taking-your-vehicle-with-you to check the procedure for importing a car as part of your household goods.

In principle, a vehicle that was registered in an EU-country, Andorra, Monaco, San Marino, Vatican City, Switzerland, Norway, Liechtenstein or Iceland, or that forms part of your moving inventory will be allowed into the country, provided it meets the APK-requirements (see page 164). For importing cars from outside the EU / EEA (also from England, Scotland, Wales and Northern Ireland), visit www.rdw.nl/en/import-export-transit/importing-a-vehicle-from-a-country-outside-the-eu-or-efta.

Registration

If the RDW approves your car, you will have to pay BPM tax, which you arrange through the Tax Office – more information can be found on www.belastingdienst.nl. Depending in the situation, it will have to be accompanied by a number of additional forms – please be sure to contact the Tax Office to ask which these are. You can also mail it all in to the Tax Office of your district; you can find the addresses on the site of the Tax Office (www.belastingdienst.nl), or by calling them.

The Tax Office / Customs Authorities will determine how much BPM you owe and send you a payment notice. Once you have paid this, the Customs Authorities will send proof of payment to the RDW, after which the RDW will send you your vehicle registration card within four weekdays, and the car will have been registered in your name.

Exceptions

Under certain conditions, you do not owe BPM. The most important one is covered in *Should You Keep Your Car?*, further on. Other exceptions include if you will be here temporarily, if you import your car from within the EU as part of your household goods, or certain conditions subject to which you may continue driving with your foreign license plates. If you export your car, you can, subject to conditions, request a restitution of the BPM you paid for your car. More information can be found on the website of the tax authorities: www.belastingdienst.nl/wps/wcm/connect/bldcontenten/belastingdienst/individuals/cars/bpm/exemption/.

License Plates and Insurance
You have now successfully imported your car, but first you need to arrange license plates – ask with the RDW where you can have this done. Don't forget to arrange insurance! You will need to arrange minimum (statutory liability) insurance, as well as any other type of voluntary insurance you wish to arrange. For more on this, see page 145. Until you have received your new license plates, you will not be allowed to drive your car, so you will have to store it. You will be issued a one-day plate, allowing you to drive your car home.

OTHER TAXES
When importing a car or motorcycle, you owe the customs department import duties and VAT. No VAT is due for a car that has driven more than 6,000 km, or whose license plates were issued more than six months ago and no customs duties are due over cars bought in the EU. See page 171 on possible exemptions from these taxes and the BPM. And do not forget about Road Tax, on page 174.

BUYING A (SECOND-HAND) CAR
If you buy a car, either second-hand or new, in the Netherlands, all that has been described above has been taken care of – all you need to do is have the car's registration card put in your name. Every vehicle, car, motorcycle or trailer weighing more than 750 Kg must be registered with the RDW. Though under certain circumstances this can be done on behalf of the owner, in principle it is the owner / buyer who must do this. Registration takes place at an authorized RDW dealer or RDW location. To register a car or motorcycle, the new owner must be 18 years or older and a resident of the Netherlands. You can also register your new vehicle if you only have a foreign driver's license. Not every car dealer knows how to register a car in this situation, but there are car dealers who do (we refer you to the *References* at the end of the chapter). The only difference is that the registration must take place at an RDW administration office, which you can find at various locations across the Netherlands. You can find out more about this on www.rdw.nl.

If you are buying a second-hand car from a previous owner – or from a non-authorized dealer – you (and, as the case may be, the former owner) can go to a store offering post office services. At the store / dealer's office / RDW office, they enter your information into the system, provide you with written proof of the transaction and issue you a four-digit code. You will receive your *kentekencard* in the mail one or two days later, as well as the second part of the nine-digit code (mentioned under *The Vehicle Registration Card*), which you will need in order to sell your car when the time comes. For a more in-depth explanation of this process, see *Road Tax – Declaration and Payment*.) This process can also be done online, by visiting www.rdw.nl and following the instructions. It's a six-step process, fully in Dutch – so it might not be the most practical solution for you if you don't speak the language.

RULES OF THE ROAD

Before you take place behind your steering wheel, in order to avoid unpleasant surprises, a few main traffic rules for cars:

- traffic coming from the right has the right of way (unless you are driving on a priority road, indicated by an orange diamond for you and 'shark's teeth' for the incoming roads)
- cars turning off a road must give right of way to cyclists and pedestrians who are continuing straight ahead
- traffic entering a roundabout (traffic circle) has the right of way unless indicated otherwise
- the speed limits, unless otherwise marked, are 50 kilometers an hour in cities and towns, 60 or 80 on secondary roads, and 100 or 120/130 on the motorways
- until the age of 18, children who are not taller than 1 meter 35 must use a booster seat when sitting in the passenger seat or in the back
- when crossing railroad tracks: as soon as the bells start ringing and the lights start flashing, get off. You may only proceed across the tracks once the lights have stopped flashing
- seat belts are mandatory.

A CHILD IN THE CAR

Everyone traveling by car must use a seat belt. Children who are not yet 1 meter 35 tall, are legally obligated to make use of a car (booster) seat. If they are taller than 1 meter 35, they have to make use of a seat belt and, if possible, a booster seat. For children younger than 12 months, or who weigh less than 13 kg, or have not yet reached 83 cm, you must use a baby seat (in most cases, these are referred to as a Maxi Cosi). Children who weigh between 9 and 18 kg are to be put in a car seat that has back support for more protection, and that is secured in the car by means of the seat belt and that has a five-point belt to secure the child. Children who weigh between 22 and 36 kg should make use of a booster seat (other official sites say between 15 and 36 kg). Both the car seats and the booster seats must be approved, which can be verified by checking a sticker placed on the seat, stating ECE R44/03 or ECE R44/04, or else that the seat meets the R129 / i-Size norm. The sticker also indicates the weight category for which the seat has been created. An important advice is to transport babies facing backwards whenever possible. This way, in case of a collision, they are pushed back into the baby seat, rather than flung forwards. When transporting a baby in a baby seat in the front seat, the airbag must be switched off. More information can be found on https://business.gov.nl/regulation/child-car-seats/.

There are no approved seats for children who weigh more than 36 kilos. These children are expected to use a seat belt, and, if they are not yet 1 meter 50 tall (the same applies to adults), a seat belt clip to ensure that the seat belt runs across their shoulder and not their neck – or a booster seat.

You may not transport more passengers than there are seats and seatbelts. The only exception to the obligation to use a booster seat (aside from traveling by taxi or bus) is if you pick up your children at school and are taking home a playmate, or are taking children to a party or to participate in a sports event; in that case, you must put your own child in the car seat and may transport the other child (using a seat belt) for a maximum distance of 50 km. Also, if you already have two car seats in the back and are transporting a third child while there is no space for a third car seat, you can use a seat belt for this child. You may never transport a child under the age of 3 if you do not have a seatbelt for it. There are also exemptions for children / persons who, for medical reasons, cannot comply with the rules.

If transporting a child / adult in front who is not yet 1 meter 50, make sure you deactivate the airbag on the passenger side, as your passenger might suffocate if it inflates. If you have no other recourse, put the seat as far back as possible or, preferably, use a booster seat or have the child / adult sit in the back seat. You should not travel in the front seat with a child on your lap.

USING A MOBILE PHONE

Drivers / riders of motorized vehicles, mopeds and vehicles for people with disabilities may not call or receive calls on their mobile phones without an aid, such as a headset or car kit. Nor may they send or read text messages, e-mails or WAP messages. If you need to talk, you must stop your vehicle, though you may briefly make use of your phone while waiting at a traffic light or standing still in a traffic jam.

Violation of this prohibition carries a minimum fine of € 350 (€ 260, if you are riding a moped) – though fines are expected to go up to € 380 for cars soon (2024). In addition, your mobile phone may be confiscated. The cost of arranging hands-free calling is less than the fine, so it is a smart move to just do about it. In all likelihood, what with radios that have Bluetooth, the ability to make hands-free calls has already been taken care of.

As of 2019, this also applies to cyclists – if you are caught you will be issued a € 150 fine. This legislation does not apply to horse riders and driving instructors in passenger seats. Other types of behavior, such as eating while driving, can also lead to a fine or prosecution if they contribute to an accident or a (potentially) dangerous situation in traffic.

TRAFFIC SIGNS

In general, blue signs tell you what is permitted, and red signs warn you of a restriction. A red circle indicates that something is forbidden, and a red triangle tells you something about the road conditions. A yellow or orange diamond indicates that you are on a road with priority (in which case, cars coming from the right do not have the right of way). An English-language explanation of the Dutch traffic signs and regulations can be found on www.universiteitleiden.nl, which is a university site, but just as useful!

PARKING

Parking regulations vary from city to city, so you should ask a local what they do about parking. A local map will have carparks marked with a blue symbol and a P. Carparks with controlled entry have various payment systems.

Sometimes streets and carparks look as though you can park in them for free, but in fact there is a ticket dispenser (it will have a blue sign with a white P on it) nearby. Look for signs that say *betaald parkeren* (paid parking), and *parkeerautomaat*. During certain hours, which are posted on the dispenser, you must pay enough (using your debit card and pincode) to cover the period you will be parked. You then place the ticket that comes out of the dispenser of your car so that the parking inspectors can read it. In some cases, you are not given a ticket, but instead enter your license plate number in the dispenser. You can also download the ANWB or Yellowbrick app (the ANWB and Yellowbrick work together on this). Once you have registered with them, the police can verify whether you have paid for you parking spot, by running a check on your license plate. Through the app, you enter the zone code (which you find on the parking automat) and then press 'start'. When you return, you press 'stop' – your charges are automatically deducted from the bank account you have linked to the app. They also provide you with a Q-Park card, which you use when entering a Q-Park parking garage and once again when leaving it. Another option is to download the parkmobile app.

Also beware, particularly in the inner cities, of signs saying *Parkeren voor vergunninghouders*. These are placed few and far between, but usually indicate that the entire area, if not neighborhood, is reserved for car owners holding a parking permit. If you live in this area, you can get one of these permits at the *gemeentehuis* or the local *Dienst Parkeerzaken* (parking department). Prices vary per city. Sometimes you can 'park & pay' in these areas; this is indicated by one of those blue signs with a white P, with an automat underneath. Whether you can get a permit if you work in one of these areas, depends on the city's rules.

In some of the smaller towns, you will see blue lines painted along where you park. This means that you need to place a *parkeerschijf* (parking disc) on your dashboard, indicating your time of arrival. On signs along the street (usually at the beginning) you will see how long you may remain parked there (the sign will say, for instance, 'max. 30 min.' or 'max. 2 uur'). You can buy a *parkeerschijf* at newspaper stores, gas stations and automobile accessory stores.

Parking violations are punished rather severely. Fines start at € 110, but what can make it seriously costly is the fact that, in some places, the inspectors will attach a wheel clamp or tow away your car, generating a nasty bill for you.

IF YOUR CAR BREAKS DOWN

There are a variety of services available for those of you who need roadside assistance in the case of a car breakdown. For 60 years, the ANWB (see page 164) held the monopoly on offering road-side car-breakdown services, under the name of Wegenwacht. Recent years saw the introduction of a number of competitors to the market, such as Blij dat ik rij, Allianz-Assistance, AA, as well as individual insurance companies that offer cheaper membership – while still providing help within 30 minutes, as well as assistance abroad. The difference in price lies in the variety of services; you can find their websites at the end of the chapter for more information. RoadGuard offers roadside help without the need for a subscription. You can contact them through their app.

An overview of car services is available on www.pechhulpvergelijker.nl, where you can browse roadside assistance in the Netherlands, assistance abroad and assistance in combination with an insurance company.

EXPORTING YOUR CAR

If you are moving out of the Netherlands and want to take your car with you, you must de-register it with the RDW. To do this, you visit the RDW, bringing along proof of identity (passport or Dutch driver's license, or a valid travel document), the license plates, and the *kentekencard* plus the nine-digit code – or, if you still have one of these; proof of registration (*tenaamstellingsbewijs*; *deel 1B* of the registration certificates), the transfer certificate (*overschrijvingsbewijs*; *deel II* of the certificates), and the most recently issued license plates of the car.

The RDW will give you a *vrijwaringsbewijs* (proof that the vehicle is no longer registered with the RDW), and return to you the *kentekencard*, with a corner cut off or (if you still have one of these) your old proof of registration (*tenaamstellingsbewijs*; *deel 1B* of the registration certificates), and the so-called *kentekenbewijs deel II*, which you will use together with your old *kentekencard* or *deel 1B*, to register the vehicle abroad. They will keep the license plates.

Once exportation has been accepted by the RDW, you can drive your car in the Netherlands for a period of 14 days, provided you arrange insurance, the APK is still valid, and that you have arranged white license plates with black letters and numbers. If you no longer plan on using the car, you can terminate the insurance. The road tax payments will stop automatically.

For more information, contact the RDW. They can also provide you with more information if you wish to export a car that is already physically located abroad and tell you about additional rules regarding exporting your car to a country outside the EU. More information can be found on www.rdw.nl/en/import-export-transit/exporting-a-vehicle.

DRIVER'S LICENSE

Residents of the Netherlands are required to have a Dutch driver's license in order to drive a motor vehicle. You are a resident if you spend at least 185 days per calendar year in the Netherlands. There are, however, a number of exceptions to this rule. If you have a driver's license that was issued in the countries listed on page 170, you are entitled to drive in the Netherlands on your foreign license for 15 years after it was issued, unless it expires earlier, in which case you can use it until that date (other rules apply to truck and bus driver's licenses). For further rules and exceptions, consult www.rijbewijs.nl. After this period, you will have to get a Dutch driver's license – to which purpose you can exchange it. You can also opt to exchange it for a Dutch license straight away. If you are issued a driver's license in one of these countries while you are already registered as living in the Netherlands, you cannot use it.

If you have a driver's license that has been issued in any other country, you may drive in the Netherlands on your foreign license for a period of six months (185 days) after registering as a Dutch resident. During this period, you have to take a driving test in the Netherlands to acquire a Dutch driver's license. Also for some of these countries it has been determined that you do not have to take the test and can simply exchange your license; in the following paragraph you can see for which countries this is the case.

Special rules apply to those who have been accorded diplomatic or consular staff status, as well their families. Contact the RDW (Dutch Road Traffic and Transport Authority – see the end of the chapter) or the Ministry of Foreign Affairs, Protocol Department, for more information. Special rules also apply to those who benefit from the 30%-ruling, see further on. More information can be found on www.rdw.nl/en/.

Furthermore, you must be at least 18 years of age to drive a car, unaccompanied, in the Netherlands.

OBTAINING YOUR LICENSE

As of the age of 16, you can do your theoretical exam, while as of the age of 16-and-a-half you may start taking driving lessons. When you are 17, you can take the road test. If you pass before the age of 18, you will be allowed to drive, but only if you are accompa-

nied by an adult who must be registered as an 'accompanier' (*begeleider*). You will be issued a *begeleiderspas* (accompanier's document) along with your driver's license, both of which you must always have with you. Plus the adult, of course.

EXCHANGING A FOREIGN DRIVER'S LICENSE

As mentioned earlier, if you live in the Netherlands and possess valid residential status you may trade in a valid driver's license issued by the countries listed in the inset on page 170.

Driver's licenses issued in the following countries can only be exchanged if they cover the categories listed here: Great Britain, Northern Ireland, Guernsey, and Jersey (all categories); Gibraltar (all categories); Taiwan, B (passenger car); Israel, B (passenger car); Japan, IB (passenger cars and motorcycles of more than 400cc); Singapore, Class 2 (motorcycles of more than 400cc) and Class 3 (passenger car), Andorra (license for passenger cars); South Korea, second class ordinary license; the Quebec and Alberta provinces of Canada, Class 5; and all categories of licenses from the former Netherlands Antilles, Isle of Man, and Monaco. If you had a Dutch driver's license that was valid after June 30, 1985, then in most cases you can exchange your foreign driver's license, no matter which country issued it, for a new Dutch license.

You cannot exchange a so-called international driver's license for a Dutch license, as it is merely considered to be a translation of the national driver's license.

The driver's license must also have been issued in a one-year period during which the holder resided at least 185 days in the issuing country.

More information can be found on www.rdw.nl/en/.

The 30%-Ruling

If you are benefiting from the 30% tax ruling, you and the other member(s) of your family can simply exchange your license, no matter where you are from. Ask for an exchange form for your foreign driver's license at your local municipal office (www.rdw.nl/en/driving-licence/foreign-driving-license/exchanging-a-foreign-driving-licence, under You are in the Netherlands for work).

License Verification

As so many different types of driver's licenses from various countries are submitted for exchange, the validity or authenticity of every document has to be verified. The RDW may therefore ask you to have the validity and significance of certain information confirmed by the Consulate or Embassy of the country that issued the foreign driver's license. You may also be required to have the content of the foreign driver's license translated by an approved interpreter / translator. For Japanese, Taiwanese and Chinese licenses, this is obligatory.

The Procedure

In order to exchange your foreign driver's license, you must go to your local municipal office, taking:

- one recent color passport photograph
- the original, valid foreign driver's license (EU/EEA licenses that have expired may be exchanged – in the case of a license from Liechtenstein, Iceland and Switzerland you need a statement issued by the relevant authority abroad that there is no objection against exchanging the license)
- non EU/EEA licenses can be exchanged if you can demonstrate that you lived in the issuing country during at least 185 days in the year in which it was issued

- valid proof of identity
- if you still have a Dutch driver's license that has expired but was valid after June 30, 1985 – this driver's license
- proof of registration as a resident with the BRP (Basisregistratie Personen)
- for non-EU/EEA citizens: a residence permit
- for students: proof of registration with institute of education
- for non-EU/EEA citizens: a health certificate, stating that you are physically and mentally capable of driving
- (if you are benefiting from the 30%-ruling:) a copy of a statement issued by the Tax Office in Heerlen proving that you or the other member(s) of your family are benefiting from the 30% tax-ruling
- in some cases, see the next paragraph, a health certificate.

As soon as the municipal fees have been paid, the municipal office issues you a certified copy of your license and proof of receipt. It then sends the entire application, your original license, and the papers, to the RDW, who evaluate the request and – if they grant it – send you a notice within 5-15 days (depending on your municipality) stating that you can pick up your Dutch driver's license at the municipal offices. If they require more information first, they will inform you by letter. You are not allowed to drive using only the certified copy; you have to wait for your new license.

You cannot exchange your driver's license if you do not live in the Netherlands. Other rules can be found on www.rdw.nl/en/driving-licence/foreign-driving-license/driving-with-a-foreign-driving-licence.

Health Certificate / Medical Check-Up

If you are from an EU/EEA country or Switzerland, then you will not need a Health Certificate unless your license has been issued for a shorter period of validity than usual (for the country issuing the license), you are older than 75, or if it contains annotations that are not recognized within the EU. Nationals of all other countries need a Certificate of Fitness and, as the case may be, a medical check-up (note: the rules are often subject to change, so it is always best to check – on www.rdw.nl/en/driving-licence/renewing-a-dutch-driving-licence/medical-exam – which rules currently apply, to be on the safe side). A medical check-up is required:

- when trading in a license issued by certain countries
- when certain medical issues are involved
- when the license has been issued for a shorter period of validity than usual (for the country issuing the license)
- when you are older than 70 and your license expires the day (after) you turn 75
- if you are older than 75
- when it contains unrecognized limitations
- when the license concerns certain categories
- when the validity of the license in the Netherlands has expired or you have driven on it for a longer period than permitted
- if the license has not been registered and you have been here longer than one year.

This process starts with the *eigen verklaring* (Statement of Health) which you fill in via www.cbr.nl, using your DigiD – so be sure you have one (see page 84). Based on what you fill in, the CBR might request additional information, of they might send you an email confirming that you may drive. If they feel it is necessary, they will ask you to visit a specialist for further check-up. Depending on the outcome of this visit, the medical advisor of the CBR will decide whether or not you will be allowed to drive. For more information, you can approach the CBR or the RDW.

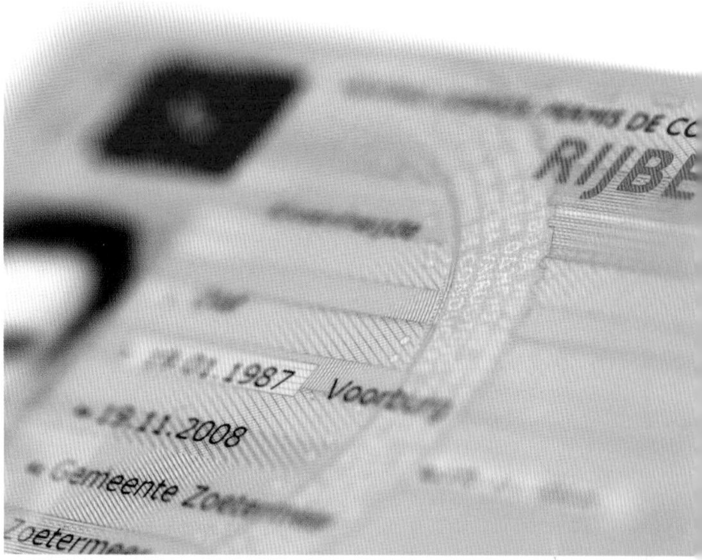

Countries on whose license you are allowed to drive in the Netherlands for a period of 15 years after issuance (or, if it is valid for a shorter period of time, until the expiration date): Austria, Belgium, Bulgaria, Croatia, (the Greek part of) Cyprus, Czech Republic, Denmark, Estonia, Finland, France, Germany, Greece, Hungary, Iceland, Ireland, Italy, Latvia, Liechtenstein, Lithuania, Luxembourg, Malta, Norway, Poland, Portugal, Rumania, Slovakia, Slovenia, Spain, Sweden, and Switzerland. If the license was issued more than 15 years ago when you move here, but still valid, you can use it for two years. On a license issued in any other country, you are allowed to drive during a period of 6 months. Check www.rdw.nl/en/driving-licence/foreign-driving-license.

Return of Your Original Driver's License

The original driver's license will be returned to the embassy or country of origin of the license. Depending on the legislation of the country that has issued the license, you can then have it returned to you.

RETAKING THE TEST

If your driver's license cannot be traded in, you will have to take a theory test and a road test at the Central Road Aptitude Bureau (Centraal Bureau Rijvaardigheid, or CBR). More information on this subject can be obtained by calling the RDW (0900 0739). If you visit www.rdw.nl and click on Go to *English site* at the bottom of the page, you can read about exchanging your license; however, when this issue of *The Holland Handbook* went to print, you could not find any information on taking the test on these sites, or the option of taking it in English – which *is* possible.

You register for the theory test by visiting cbr.nl, and clicking on *Theorie-examen auto*. In order to continue, you will have to create an account with the CBR, for which you will need a DigiD (digital identity code, see page 84), or by downloading the form *Aanvraagformulier Theorie-examen*, which you send to the address listed at the bottom of the form. On this form, you will have to fill in your BSN (*burgerservicenummer*, or Citizen Service Number), which you are issued when you register to live in a municipality (see page 78). The test consists of questions on traffic rules and questions on the recognition of dangerous situations (and how to act). Unless you take the test in English – an option which is available when you make your online reservation – or Dutch, you have to arrange an interpreter at least two weeks in advance. Though you can arrange the theory exam by visiting the site of the CBR and selecting a location and time, the road test has to be booked for you by a driving school, you *cannot* do this yourself. You do have to authorize them to do this, which you do on the CBR-site as well. On www.traffictrainer.nl you can take theoretical practice exams in English.

Once you have passed the theoretical exam, you have approximately three months to go to your municipal offices (starting the next day) and request the license. You can then pick it up within five days. Should you decide to drive without having arranged and picked up your license, you can be fined and will not be insured.

SHOULD YOU KEEP YOUR CAR?

When moving to another country there is always the question of what to do with your car. Should you keep your old car, buy a new one in the country you are leaving or buy a new one in the country you are going to? All these options have their own merits for tax purposes. And, when returning to your native country, the same questions arise.

In these paragraphs you will find a brief overview of some of the issues you should be aware of. These paragraphs are based on the premise that the Netherlands is your new country of residence, however the same principles are applicable in every country of the European Union. In the Netherlands the taxes involved when importing a car are the Value Added Tax (VAT/BTW), the *Bijzondere Verbruiksbelasting van Personenauto's* (BPM – see page 164) and import duties.

COMING INTO THE NETHERLANDS

From a European Union Member State

When it comes to taxes, if you are coming from another member state there are no special requirements for bringing your old car with you.

If you are considering buying a new car, you should be aware that the taxes levied on a new car in the Netherlands are extremely high. They can amount to up to 45% of the list price. In view of the fact that there is hardly any country in the European Union that levies the same amount of taxes on new cars, you might therefore want to buy your new car in the country you are coming from. Keep in mind that if your car is less than six months or 6,000 km old, or its license plates have been issued within the last six months, you will have to pay VAT in the Netherlands. Check whether you can get a (partial) refund of the VAT/BTW paid when the car was delivered to you in the country where you bought it.

For the rules on importing a car, read the first paragraphs under *Driving Your Car*.

From a Non-European Union Member State

If goods are imported into an EU-member state, customs duties are due. However, for your household effects – this includes cars – there can be an exemption from customs duties (see page 112). Some of the conditions to be met are that you must have lived in a non-EU member state for a period of at least 12 months and that you must have had the car in your possession for at least six months.

We will look at these two requirements in the following two paragraphs.

WHERE DO YOU LIVE?

Your usual place of residence is the place where you normally live for at least 185 days of each calendar year for personal and professional reasons. If there are no professional reasons, evidence must be produced proving that personal commitments lead to close ties between yourself and your place of residence. If you are living in a country in order to carry out an assignment, the usual place of residence is the country where you have your personal commitments. Personal commitments mean family and/or social commitments, such as:

- the place of residence of your family, your children or other people with whom you have a personal relationship
- the place with which you have social ties (e.g. cultural activities societies, sports clubs, committees).

POSSESSION FOR A PERIOD OF SIX MONTHS

You must have had the car in your possession for at least six months and you must have used it in the non-EU member state from which you are moving. This condition is very important. Generally speaking, if your employer has put a car at your disposal, the customs authorities are of the point of view that the car has not been in your possession. The same applies if you have leased a car in the country from which you are moving. In these cases, the exemption from customs duties is not granted for your car.

CONDITIONS AFTER THE EXEMPTION IS GRANTED

After the customs authorities have granted an exemption and you have imported the car, you may not lend out, hire out or sell your car within a period of 12 months after the customs have accepted your customs declaration. In short, you should keep the full power of use of the car for 12 months.

If the twelve month-condition is not met, you will be liable to pay taxes immediately and even be fined for misuse of the rules. Even if the car is stolen or badly damaged and the insurance company sells the wreckage, the exemption will be revoked. In those cases you will have to pay duties for a car you do not and could not own anymore!

LEAVING THE NETHERLANDS

When leaving the Netherlands, the first question of importance is: am I going to another member state of the European Union, or am I leaving the European Union altogether.

Going to Another Member State

When you are going to another member state there are also no special requirements for taking your old car with you. Via the website of the Dutch tax authorities, you can request a (partial) refund of the BPM – visit the site for more information. As you read earlier, the taxes levied on a new car in the Netherlands are

Bicycles, the Heart of Dutch Culture

BY JACOB VOSSESTEIN

Ah, the bike, the Dutch bike, *de fiets*. Pity it wasn't invented in the Netherlands, for wouldn't it be a far better symbol of this nation than the tulip or the wooden shoe? It conjures up the very essence of Dutch culture, and I will tell you why.

Not all immigrants / expats appreciate Dutch bikers, whichever background they may have. Foreign visitors find their behavior unpredictable, dangerous, and anarchistic – with bikers suddenly popping up when you least expect them. And I agree, it is all true, but let me take you along another line of thought which may be worth considering too...

To my idea, the Dutch bike – the simple, sturdy, run-of-the-mill black bike, omnipresent in Dutch cities – reflects several traditional Dutch characteristics.

Obviously, in a flat and very crowded country, it is a pragmatic means of transportation that gets you everywhere in no time, certainly when you ignore traffic signs and other silly official obstructions which, as a tax-paying citizen, you may question and toss aside. In applying a riding style that foreigners tend to describe as 'suicidal', a Dutch city biker will reach his / her destination far sooner than when using the tram, let alone a car.

Another plus: everyone can afford a bike, be it new or second-hand. Not generally employed in any status games, it is a very egalitarian means of transportation. As bikers are exposed to rain and wind and the laws of gravity on steep bridges, any difference in status or social stature between them is soon eradicated, revealing the essence of life: a body struggling against the forces of nature. Office clerk, bricklayer, human resources manager or secretary of state, all bikers have to bow to the elements. And toiling against gale force 8 on an unsheltered dike road or a straight-as-a-ruler suburban street will encourage modesty in anyone, making him equal to his fellow human beings who suffer likewise. Well, theoretically, that is.

The bike also satisfies the Dutch inclination to not waste any resources. It is not only a cheap means of transportation, it also improves one's general shape, thus reducing medical expenses. On a slightly more abstract level, bikers can also congratulate themselves on the fact that their effort is for the good of the planet as a whole: no fumes, no noise, no use of exhaustible resources, no great amount of unnaturally paved space needed. What could be more satisfying than a good conscience combined with excellent health and a well-filled wallet?

But that is not all. Riding a bike could be seen as having a touch of philosophy to it, even spirituality. It teaches the rider balance, and we're not only talking about physical balance. Riding along during rush hour at about 20 km/h among scores of other bikers doing likewise, all – well, most of them – waiting for the red light to turn green, trying to find a clear section of road to cross, cycling through the pouring rain... Things like that produce a certain equilibrium with your fellow bikers, peace of mind almost, to quote a Hindu term. It makes you realize the true size of your ego: just a small flame among many, hardly more than that of a match, nothing special really.

Besides balance, biking teaches you alertness. Though the race may not be about winning, it's challenging nonetheless: avoiding the carefully parking truck, calculating whether you can still pass just in front of that car that has no right whatsoever to be going so fast, racing for a minute to catch the bridge just before it closes (or is it: opens?) for a ship, catching the orange light nanoseconds before it turns red and when this fails, scanning the surroundings for any signs of police presence.

So with eyes on all sides and ears open to the sounds of car tires, tram bells, moped noises and of course each other's ringing bells, bikers wind their way through the ever-changing river of traffic where they may physically be the weaker party but morally speaking are superior by far: unpretentious, silent, un-polluting, utterly democratic, going with the flow and yet self-willed. This feeling of modest self-righteousness gets stronger when the bike is used for the transportation of items such as the daily shopping, the two children, a dog, or a pile of wood for some do-it-yourself job.

There are a thousand and one subtle effects and conditions which become part of your delicate existence when you bike. In a densely-populated nation, give and take are essential, and biking may be a good preparation for the bigger podium of life. Royalty, prime ministers and captains of industry have preceded you, so what's keeping you from joining the steel-framed army when going to work, school or the supermarket? If you can't beat us, join us. See you at the traffic light!

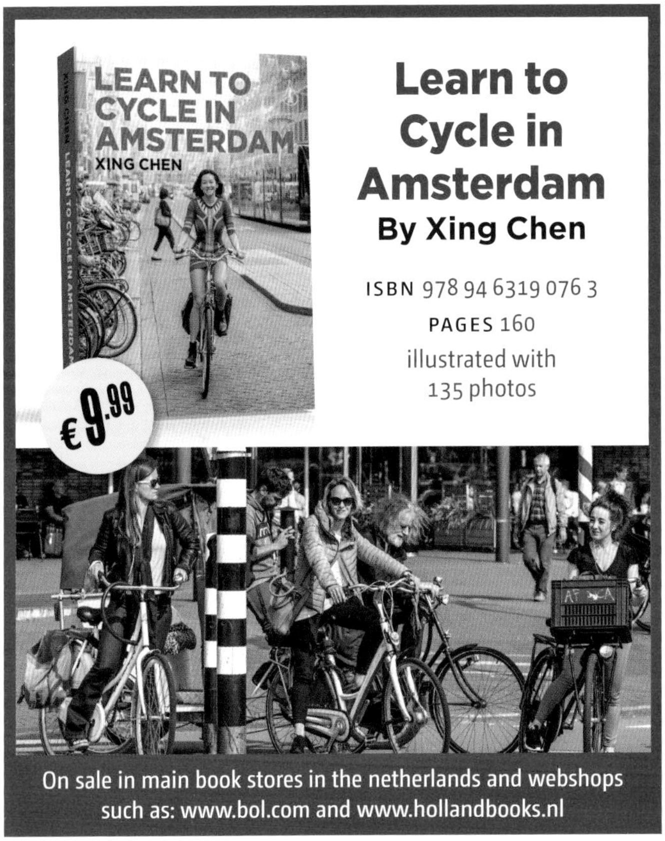
LEARN TO CYCLE IN AMSTERDAM
XING CHEN
€ 9.99
Learn to Cycle in Amsterdam
By Xing Chen
ISBN 978 94 6319 076 3
PAGES 160
illustrated with 135 photos
On sale in main book stores in the netherlands and webshops such as: www.bol.com and www.hollandbooks.nl

The Little Orange Handbook 2.0
The Netherlands for Newcomers
€ 14.95
The Little Orange Handbook 2.0
The Netherlands for Newcomers
208 pages • Paperback
2ND COMPLETELY REVISED EDITION
AVAILABLE AT WWW.HOLLANDBOOKS.NL

Welcome to Cycling Paradise the Netherlands!
The Netherlands
THE CYCLING Paradise
Including bike routes & places to stay
€ 17.50
With more than 200 photos and 10 amazing bike routes, this book is an absolute ode to the Dutch bicycle culture
Now available at www.hollandbooks.nl, www.bol.com and main book stores in the Netherlands

How to Be Dutch The Quiz
The questions that SHOULD be on the Dutch citizenship exam
HOW TO BE DUTCH
The Quiz
Greg Shapiro
the American Netherlander
XPAT Scriptum Publishers
€ 17.99
On sale in main book stores in the netherlands and webshops such as: www.bol.com and www.hollandbooks.nl

extremely high, amounting up to 45% of the list price, and there won't be any refund of these taxes either. In view of the fact that there is hardly any country in the European Union that levies the same amount of taxes on new cars as in the Netherlands, it is advisable to buy your new car in the country you are going to.

Another option would be to buy it in the Netherlands when you are already living in the other country. In that case you might even be cheaper off altogether, because then you do not have to pay VAT/BTW and BPM in the Netherlands, but only the taxes in the country you are then living in and the list prices here are relatively cheap. If you live in the United Kingdom, for instance, this could lead to a price difference of € 2,300 and more – *and* you can easily arrange for the steering wheel to be placed on the right-hand side.

Mind you, when your car is less than six months or 6,000 km old, you will have to pay VAT in the member state you are going to. On the other hand, you can get a (partial) refund of the VAT/BTW paid when the car was delivered to you.

Leaving the European Union

When leaving the European Union altogether there also are no special requirements for taking your old car with you. However, you can request a (partial) refund of the BPM – see the website of the tax authorities. When you buy a new car in the Netherlands and it is exported within 30 days, you can buy the car duty-free. In effect it is the same procedure as described before for buying a car in the Netherlands whilst living in another member state. You have to be able to prove that the car actually left the European Union within 30 days. The tax authorities can demand that you produce evidence of the importation and the car duties paid in your new country.

Of course the country you are moving to might levy import duties on your car. However, in general they will grant you an exemption if you have owned the car for more than six months. Clearly, it is vital that you get detailed information on the applicable rules before you move.

TAKE CARE OF BUSINESS BEFORE YOU MOVE

There are plenty of possibilities for reducing the tax burden on your car when you are leaving or returning to a country. Because of the detailed rules on this issue, you should take care of business before you actually move. Preferably you should seek professional assistance at least six months before moving. That will give you the opportunity to use the rules to your advantage and save money.

ROAD TAX

As mentioned earlier, if you own a car, delivery van or motorcycle in the Netherlands, you must pay road tax. Cars are 'vehicles with three or more wheels, designed for transporting a maximum of eight persons, excluding the driver'. A delivery van is a vehicle with cargo space and also a maximum permitted loaded weight of 3,500 kg. Other regulations apply to vehicles with cargo space and a higher maximum permitted loaded weight.

WHEN DO YOU HAVE TO PAY?

You have to pay road tax from the time your name is transferred to the vehicle registration card (*kentekencard*, see page 161). Regardless of whether you are temporarily unable or unwilling to use your vehicle, you are always required to pay road tax. You pay for possession of a vehicle, even if it remains parked on private premises. (See further on, for suspension options.)

If you are a resident of the Netherlands, but driving a car that is registered abroad, you still have to pay road tax and vehicle tax (BPM) – unless you use the car fewer than two weeks – see the exceptions regarding BPM on page 165. For those two weeks you will still have to request an exemption from the RDW.

DECLARATION AND PAYMENT

When you buy a car, once your name is transferred to the registration certificate, this also serves as a road tax declaration. You must indicate whether you want to pay for each three-month period separately or for four consecutive periods at once. Soon afterwards, you will automatically be sent a bill and *giro* payment slip (*acceptgiro*) for the road tax for which you are liable (if, for some or other reason you don't receive one, contact the Central Tax Office). Thereafter, the bills will be posted to you on a periodic basis. The period for which you must pay road tax is stated on the bill, as is the due date.

You can also arrange to have the bills paid automatically by means of a *machtiging* (authorization). However, in order to effectuate these automatic payments, you must request permission to do this from the Tax Office / Central Administration. If you send in a *machtigingsformulier* (authorization form, authorizing the Tax Office to automatically deduct the periodic payments), which you will receive along with your first *acceptgiro*, this is considered a request for permission. If granted, the payments will be collected automatically. This option is available for quarterly and monthly payments.

ROAD TAX RATES

The amount of road tax you pay depends on the following:

- the type of vehicle (i.e. passenger car, delivery van, motorcycle)
- for passenger cars and delivery vans: tare weight. This is stated on the registration certificate (under *massa ledig voertuig*)
- for passenger cars: the fuel used (gasoline, diesel, LPG or a combination of gasoline / LPG)
- the province in which you live
- the amount of CO_2-emission of your car
- in the case of an old-timer: its age, fuel and use
- whether your car is (semi-) electric or a hybrid
- whether your car has been adapted to transport a wheelchair
- whether your car has foreign license plates – in some cases, you will not owe road tax
- whether you have a physical disability. Contact the tax authorities for more information.

You do not have to pay additional road tax for a caravan (camper), collapsible caravan or static caravan, even if their maximum permitted loaded weight exceeds 750 kg. For campers that are not pulled by a car, but that can be driven independently, you owe road tax; however, in principle, you owe only a quarter of the amount of road tax due. For cars with 0 CO_2-emission, the amount of road tax you owe depends on additional conditions that can be found on the site of the tax authorities (www.belastingdienst.nl).

You can always inquire at any store offering post office services or the Tax Department offices of the Central Office for Motor Vehicle Taxes, if you want to know precisely how much road tax you have to pay for your vehicle. (You can also calculate how much you will owe if you visit www.belastingdienst.nl/rekenhulpen/motorrijtuigenbelasting.)

VEHICLE MODIFICATIONS

You may have to pay more, or less, road tax if you modify your vehicle. For example if:

- modification of your vehicle results in a change in its tare weight. As a result, your vehicle may then fall under a different weight category
- you change the type of fuel you use in your passenger car. If you modify your vehicle in this way, you must have your registration certificate adjusted. For this, contact the RDW Centrum voor Voertuigtechniek en Informatie (0900 0739). They will inform the Tax Department of the change
- you have made any vehicle conversions: for instance, from van to camper or to regular car.

If you have made these changes, you also must have the vehicle re-inspected by the RDW. If the changes lead to a change in weight or fuel, you must have your *kentekencard* (see page 161, under *Vehicle Registration Card*) adjusted accordingly by the RDW. The vehicle does not need to be re-inspected by the RDW if the car has been converted to run on gas by a recognized garage. They will also arrange the new registration papers for you.

As of the next road tax period, you will owe the new amount, for which you will automatically be billed. If you paid road tax for a full year in advance, you will receive an additional assessment or a reimbursement, depending on the situation.

MOVING WITHIN THE COUNTRY

If you move within the Netherlands, you register with your (new) municipality. They will pass on the new address to the Tax Office, who will send the bills to your new address.

SALE OF YOUR VEHICLE

When you sell your vehicle, you must pay road tax over the period during which it was sold, but you can be reimbursed. If you have yet to receive a bill for the tax, you will be sent one for a lesser amount. Automatic payments will be stopped automatically.

You deliver proof of the sale of your vehicle by means of the *vrijwaringsbewijs* (warranty against liability), which you will either receive from the dealer to whom you sell it, or from the buyer, who is issued this document when he registers the car in his name at a store offering post office services. If you transfer ownership of your vehicle online, the buyer will receive this *vrijwaringsbewijs*, which they pass on to you.

GOING ABROAD TEMPORARILY

If you temporarily go abroad, you are still required to pay road tax on time for the duration of your absence, regardless of whether you take your vehicle with you (however, see following paragraph on *Suspension*). There are three ways to ensure that the road tax is paid on time. You can:

- pay the bill(s) for the duration of your stay abroad in advance. For this, contact the Central Office for Motor Vehicle Taxes
- authorize someone to pay the bill(s) for you
- arrange a *machtiging*, allowing the Tax Office to collect the payments automatically. To do this, you contact the Tax Office / Central Administration.

SUSPENSION

If you will not be using your vehicle for an extended period of time (for instance because you are going abroad), you can apply for suspension of the registration certificate at a store offering post office services – for a fee. To this purpose, you must bring along proof of identification and your *kentekencard*. You will not owe road tax as of the date of suspension (provided the period of suspension lasts at least a month) and will automatically be reimbursed for amounts already paid. If you end the suspension before the month has passed, then you will owe road tax over the entire month. Suspension is granted for a period of one to three years and you will receive a reminder four to five weeks before it ends. During the period of suspension you will not be allowed to drive your vehicle on a public highway and you must inform the Tax Office of its physical whereabouts during this period. If you wish to extend the period of extension, this is also possible.

You can also arrange the suspension (and its extension) online, on the website of the RDW. To this purpose, you must have a DigiD (digital identification code), which you can read more about on page 84.

SUSPENSION AND APK

While your road tax payments are suspended, your car might still have to undergo the APK-test to make sure it is APK-approved before you start driving it again. In that case, an exception is made to the rule that you may not drive your car out on the road. You must, however, request a one-day dispensation from the tax authorities before you do this. And make sure that your car is insured! Call 0800 0749 (the Central Office for Motor Vehicle Taxes) to enquire as to what your best course of action is under the circumstances.

SUSPENSION AND INSURANCE

Once you have suspended the payment of road tax, you can use proof of this suspension to suspend your car insurance are well. It might be useful to continue to insure it against theft and damage, however.

REACTIVATING THE PAYMENTS

If you want to start using your car again, after a period of suspension, you go back to the store offering post office services with the same papers to reverse the situation. Regardless of whether you had a paper proof of registration (*tenaamstellingsbewijs*) or *kentekencard*, you will be sent a new *kentekencard* by the RDW. If the full 12 months have gone by, the suspension ends of its own accord and the RDW will automatically send you your new proof of registration. As mentioned above, if you want to extend the suspension, you have to go back to store offering post office services to arrange this. You can also do all of this online, via www.rdw.nl.

YOUR VEHICLE LEAVES THE COUNTRY PERMANENTLY

If your vehicle leaves the country permanently, you must arrange its deregistration with the RDW (see page 168). Once you have taken care of these formalities, you will automatically receive a road tax reimbursement for the period during which your car is no longer in the Netherlands. If you paid road tax for four consecutive periods at once, you will also receive a tax reimbursement for the periods that have not yet taken effect.

FREQUENT CHECKS
The Central Office for Motor Vehicle Taxes closely monitors the payment of road tax. Photographs, customs data and police information, such as fines and records, are also utilized. If it is discovered that you have not paid road tax, or have paid too little, you will receive an increased assessment.

BICYCLES AND MOPEDS

THE BEST WAY TO GET AROUND
If you really want to sample Dutch life, and get around quickly and easily, buy yourself a bicycle – Dutch-style: a sturdy, no-nonsense bike, preferably not too expensive so that if it gets stolen you won't feel too bad. Fancy, 10-speed bicycles are relatively rare, and used only for recreational cycling.

A new bicycle, made by one of the better-known manufacturers and sold at a bicycle shop, costs between € 275 and € 500. A discount store will sell you a new, imported bike for as little as € 175, but you must examine it to make sure the quality is alright.

BUYING A SECOND-HAND BICYCLE
Most students (and foreign visitors) buy second-hand bicycles (*tweedehands fietsen* or *tweedehands rijwielen*). A reasonable one will cost you between € 75 and € 175. You can find them at (second-hand) bicycle shops, at the bicycle parking facilities near railway stations or on www.marktplaats.nl. They will also be advertised in the small ads at the back of the local newspaper under *Rijwielen*, or on the notice board at the supermarket or anywhere students congregate. (A women's bike is a *damesfiets* and a men's bike is a *herenfiets*. Dutch men are not embarrassed to ride women's bicycles – and vice versa.)

Since the second-hand bicycle market is different in different towns, you should ask a local for advice. They may know of an especially good place, and, if you're lucky, may even help you pick your bicycle and negotiate the price.

When you buy a bicycle, make sure that its lights work and that it has a sturdy lock (*slot*). Even better is to buy a chain and padlock so you can fasten your bicycle to something when you park it. Secure parking for bicycles is available at most railway stations and in some city centers. Look for the signs for *rijwielstalling* or *fietsenstalling*).

TOURING THE COUNTRY
The Netherlands is one of the most cyclist-friendly countries in the world. Crisscrossing the country are well-kept cycling paths, running straight through areas that are not accessible to anything with an engine, offering you the beautiful, quiet enjoyment of Dutch nature, unhindered by anything other than fellow nature lovers and nature itself. You can pick up great guide books and maps at the VVV or the ANWB and plan long or short trips anywhere you like. Or you can visit www.fietsnetwerk.nl/knooppuntenroute or nederlandfietsland.nl for more information on cycling tours, including recommendations on where to make a quick stop, what to look for and where to stop for a bite to eat – supported by the Fietsknooppunten app. Trains have special bicycle compartments, so that you can travel wherever you want within the country and then take off from there. For a cheap, pleasant and cozy place to spend the night, visit www.vriendenopdefiets.nl.

RENTING A BICYCLE
You can also rent bicycles by the day from the parking facility at many railway stations, under payment of a deposit. It is wise to telephone in advance to make a reservation. Ask at the railway station for the free booklet. In certain places, such as Veluwe National Park, bicycles are available, free of charge, to roam the beautiful woods at your leisure. In many cities, you will see cyclists riding a bicycle with a blue front tire; these are called Swapfiets, or Swap Bicycle, and are available for rent at affordable prices – and a further discount for students, plus they offer repair services. There are two types of contracts for these bikes, you can find more information on https://swapfiets.nl.

For more on renting a bicycle and on the Public Transportation Bicycle, see page 158.

TRAFFIC RULES FOR CYCLISTS
As a cyclist, you too must obey the traffic signs and rules, and stay in the bicycle lanes marked on the street. As a rule, cars that are turning across your path are supposed to stop for you, but it is wise to watch out. And don't forget to signal with your arm if you are planning to turn – AND if you are planning on going straight on a traffic circle. You can be fined for riding at night without lights, and for drunken cycling as well as for reckless endangerment when using your mobile phone while on the bike. Contrary to the situation in many countries, you may *not* ride your bicycle on the sidewalk.

MOPEDS
Anyone riding a moped (*brommer* or *bromfiets*), motorized bicycle (*snorfiets*), light vehicle (*brommobiel*) or quad (*vierwielige brommobiel*) needs a moped license, called the AM-license. If you have a driver's license for automobiles or motorcycles, you do not need to get a separate AM-license. You can take the theoretical exam as of age 15-and-a-half and the practical exam as of age 16. If, for medical reasons, your driver's license is no longer valid, you can still obtain or retain an AM-license for purposes of driving a light vehicle.

You take the exam at one of the CBR (Centraal Bureau voor Rijvaardigheid, Road Aptitude Bureau or www.cbr.nl) 'theory centers'. Once you have passed the theoretical exam, you can go to the municipality – bringing along a passport photograph, proof of identity and the required payment – and request them to issue you the so-called AM-license. They will check with the CBR whether you have indeed passed your exam, which will remain valid for a period of six months. Within five days, you can go pick up your license, bringing along proof that you paid for the license.

When riding a moped, keep in mind that you must always wear a (suitable) helmet (fine; € 100), and carry with you your moped certificate / license and proof of insurance. Failure to do either of these will result in a fine of € 150. Riding without having obtained a license will cost you € 270, and without having arranged insurance; € 450. Mopeds must also have a license plate. The process of arranging this is comparable to the process for a car; it takes place via the RDW. For more information, please check page 166, on how to go about this and whom to contact. And, as with a car, you may not make any 'hand-held' calls on your mobile phone while riding your moped; the fine will be € 260.

BEING A PEDESTRIAN

Tourists have been known to take a seat in the window of a café at a busy Amsterdam intersection just to watch the show of Dutch traffic interaction. All pedestrians jaywalk, none of the bicycle riders pay any attention to the color of their traffic light, trams trundle along and stop within an inch of all cars' lives (be they Mercedes or Toyota), buses wheeze their asthmatic way through this all with an inch to spare, and cars ... well, cars take whatever space everyone else deigns to grant them.

In all this mess, being a pedestrian is by far the most convenient. Riding a bike is faster, but pedestrians can squeeze through, around or over any obstacle and, if it starts to rain, they can hop on a tram or bus and get out of there high and dry.

BLIND PEDESTRIANS

Luckily, this does not mean that those of us who cannot see had best stay home. In many cities and towns, there is a whole intricate system in place to help the blind navigate their way. For instance, the pedestrian lights produce a variety of ticking sounds, depending on whether they signal *walk* or *don't walk*. Also, hidden among the regular sidewalk tiles, are special ribbed or rubber tiles (also in place at railroad stations), indicating where the sidewalks end. And fellow-pedestrians, but also other road users, have an eye out for the special white sticks with red rims, used by the blind – and often take the time to lend a helping hand.

TOURING THE COUNTRY

Just as is the case for cyclists, there is a great network of pedestrian paths running across the entire country. Visit any VVV or ANWB-store to pick up a guide book on walking routes and local sites of interest to visit.

RULES

Jaywalking may be quicker, but, if you want to make sure you make it across in one piece, it's nice to know that cars must yield to pedestrians on zebra crossings (but don't be naïve; car drivers are not naturally inclined to yield to anyone who isn't at least half-way across – they expect you to 'wait your turn'). Cars making a turn on a green light must yield to pedestrians going straight ahead on a zebra crossing. Don't expect them to wait till you have made it all the way across, though; just out of their way gives them plenty of room to proceed, as far as the Dutch drivers are concerned.

Also make sure that you don't mistake a bicycle path (*fietspad*) for a pedestrian path, they often look very much the same and at times run parallel. Generally speaking, the path closest to the road is the bicycle path.

Trams have priority over everyone, no matter where they are coming from.

References

CHAPTER 6

Getting Around

General

MINISTERIE VAN INFRASTRUCTUUR EN WATERSTAAT
Ministry of Infrastructure and Water Management
Rijnstraat 8, 2515 XP The Hague
P.O. Box 20901, 2500 EX The Hague
Tel.: 070 456 00 00
www.government.nl/ministries/ministry-of-infrastructure-and-water-management

DOUANE
Dutch Customs
www.douane.nl

Public Transportation

GENERAL
Prices, departure and arrival times
Tel.: 0900 92 92
www.9292ov.nl
9292ov app: available at the App Store

OV CHIPCARD
www.ov-chipkaart.nl

NEDERLANDSE SPOORWEGEN, NS
Dutch Railways
Prices, departure, arrival times and travel planner
www.ns.nl
Reisplanner app: available at the App Store

NS INTERNATIONAL
www.nsinternational.nl

PLAN YOUR JOURNEY
http://9292.nl/en#
9292 app: available at the App Store

Driver's License

GENERAL ENGLISH-LANGUAGE INFO
www.rdw.nl: search for driving license

CENTRAL OFFICE FOR MOTOR VEHICLE DRIVING TESTING, CBR
CBR Examencentrum Rijswijk
Head office, Lange Kleiweg 30,
2288 GK Rijswijk
Tel.: 088 227 7700
www.cbr.nl

DRIVER'S LICENSE INFORMATION FOR PERSONS HOLDING DIPLOMATIC OR CONSULAR STAFF STATUS
Ministry of Foreign Affairs, Protocol Department
Tel.: 070 348 64 86
www.government.nl/ministries/bz

Traffic Rules

GENERAL
www.veiligverkeernederland.nl

Road Tax

CENTRAAL BUREAU MOTORRIJTUIGEN-BELASTING
Central Office for Motor Vehicle Taxes
Tel.: 0800 0749 – From outside NL call +31 55 538 53 74
P.O. Box 9047, 7300 GJ Apeldoorn
www.belastingdienst.nl

RIJKSDIENST VOOR HET WEGVERKEER
(National Traffic Authority) Vehicle technology and information center
Head office: Europaweg 205, 2711 ER Zoetermeer
Tel.: 088 008 7447
www.rdw.nl

THE ROYAL DUTCH TOURING CLUB (ANWB)
Wassenaarseweg 220, 2596 EC The Hague
General tel. no for members: 088 269 22 22
To become a member: www.anwb.nl/lidmaatschap
Roadside Assistance Service (Wegenwacht), tel.: 088 269 28 88/+31 70 314 14 14
Legal assistance, tel.: 088 269 72 05
Specially for victims of traffic accidents, tel.: 088 269 77 66
Traffic information, tel.: 0900 96 22
General website: www.anwb.nl
Route Planner: http://route.anwb.nl/routeplanner
General information: www.anwb.nl
ANWB traffic app: available at the App Store

Roadside Assistance Service Providers

AA Team: www.aa-team.nl
ANWB: www.anwb.nl/wegenwacht
Allianz Assistance: www.allianz-assistance.nl
Eurocross: www.eurocross.nl
Routemobiel: www.routemobiel.nl

Car Rental

Auto Europe: www.autoeurope.nl
Avis: www.avis.nl
Budget: www.budget.nl
Europcar: www.europcar.nl
Hertz: www.hertz.nl
Sixt: www.sixt.nl

Second-Hand Cars

Bynco: www.bynco.com/nl
ANWB: www.anwb.nl
Autotrader: www.autotrader.nl
Autotrack: www.autotrack.nl

Cycling

THE CYCLING PARADISE
By Peter de Lange
Published by XPat Media
An ode to the unique Dutch cycling culture. Including 10 stunning bike routes & places to stay
To order: www.hollandbooks.nl

LEARN TO CYCLE IN AMSTERDAM
By Xing Chen
Published by XPat Media
This book will ease you through the process of learning to cycle amidst the hustle and bustle of this small but dynamic city, covering topics such as road etiquette, traffic regulations, cycling technique, and the weather
To order: www.hollandbooks.nl

IN THE CITY OF BIKES

The story of the Amsterdam Cyclist
By Pete Jordan
Published by Harper Collins
A funny, engaging and exhaustively tribute to Amsterdam's unique biking history
www.cityofbikes.com

CYCLING TOURS IN THE NETHERLANDS

www.anwb.nl/fietsroutes
www.bike-netherlands.com
www.cycletours.nl
www.fietsen.123.nl
www.fietsknoop.nl
www.fietspad.nl
www.holland-cycling.com
www.nederlandfietsland.nl
www.route.nl
www.totzo.org
www.tulipcycling.com
Fiets! app: available at the App Store

BICYCLE AND PUBLIC TRANSPORTATION

www.ov-fiets.nl
www.nsfiets.nl

BIKE RENTAL

www.bikecity.nl
www.macbike.nl
www.orangebike.nl
www.rentabike.nl
www.tulipcycling.com
www.yellowbike.nl

SHOPS TO BUY DUTCH STYLE BICYCLES

www.bakfiets-en-meer.nl
www.dutchbicyclegroup.nl
www.fietswinkel.nl
www.workcycles.nl

BICYCLE INSURANCE

www.anwb.nl/verzekeringen/fietsverzekering
www.allianz-assistance.nl
www.unive.nl/fietsverzekering
www.unigarant.nl/verzekeringen/fietsverzekering/

Airports

SCHIPHOL AMSTERDAM AIRPORT

Evert van de Beekstraat, 1118 CP Schiphol
Tel.: 0900 0141, from outside NL 020 794 0800
www.schiphol.nl
Schiphol app: available at the App Store
Schiphol flight information app: available at the App Store

ROTTERDAM THE HAGUE AIRPORT

Rotterdam Airportplein 60, 3045 AP Rotterdam
Tel.: 010 446 34 44
www.rotterdamthehagueairport.nl

MAASTRICHT AACHEN AIRPORT

Vliegveldweg 17, 6191 SB Beek
Tel.: 043 358 98 98 – www.maa.nl

EINDHOVEN AIRPORT

Luchthavenweg 25, 5657 EA Eindhoven
Tel.: 040 291 98 18
www.eindhovenairport.nl

GRONINGEN AIRPORT EELDE

Machlaan 14, 9761 TK Eelde
Tel.: 050 308 08 50
www.groningenairport.nl

LELYSTAD AIRPORT

Tel.: 0320 284 770
Arendweg 7, 8218 PE Lelystad
www.lelystad-airport.nl

Flight Booking

www.cheaptickets.nl
www.ebookers.nl
www.expedia.nl
www.skyscanner.nl
www.vliegtickets.nl
www.vliegwinkel.nl

Once you have solved the more pressing matters, there are many other things you will need to know about living in the Netherlands, such as shopping hours and customs, how to arrange household help, safety, taking care of your pets, Dutch gardens and family life, utilities and Internet Service Providers – not necessarily in that order. You will find answers to such 'pressing' questions as 'Why do the Dutch leave their curtains open?', but also on how to get your telephone service started and whether the Netherlands is a safe country to live in.

CHAPTER 7

Daily Life

CONTRIBUTING AUTHORS STEPHANIE DIJKSTRA AND CONNIE MOSER

SHOPPING

OPENING HOURS

Shopping hours in the Netherlands for a long time were based on the idea that people who work in shops should be able to live according to much the same pattern as other people. Nearly all shops were therefore closed on Sundays and in the evenings. This started to change during the '90s and in 1996 the government made it official by extending the number of hours shops are allowed to stay open. The pattern has therefore become much more variable, in order to meet the shopping needs of the many double-income households.

In general, shops in the Netherlands are open Monday through Saturday from 9 A.M. to 6 P.M., with the following most common exceptions:

- many shops (at least in the smaller villages) are closed on Monday mornings to enable shopkeepers to stock the shelves and do their administration
- in villages, small shops often close an hour or two early on Saturdays
- one evening each week, all shops in an area will either stay open until 9 P.M., or open again from 7 – 9 P.M. This is called *koopavond*, and is usually on a Thursday in cities and a Friday in towns and villages
- the bigger supermarkets open an hour earlier and stay open a few hours longer in the evening, and many of them now also open on Sundays
- all stores in an area may decide to open their doors on Sundays, particularly in the bigger cities
- in the big cities you might be able to find a small grocery shop that is open late in the evenings and on Sundays. This is called an *avondwinkel*, and its prices will be higher than prices elsewhere
- mini-markets carrying a small selection of goods can be found at some gas stations, larger train stations and at Schiphol Airport.

THE OPEN-AIR MARKET

Once or twice a week, each town or district will have an open-air market, often in the central market square. This starts around 8 / 9 A.M. or 1 P.M. and closes between 4 and 6 P.M. Here you can buy fruit and vegetables, fish, sweets, bakery products, fabric, clothing, bedding, cosmetics and many other items. Excellent bargains can be found, but you must have a critical eye for quality.

Especially in the big city markets, products are available from all across the world in stalls that cater to the tastes of customers from, among others, the Caribbean and Mediterranean regions.

Keep in mind that the rules regarding starting and finishing hours can be applied so strictly that a market salesman will refuse to sell you his goods 15 minutes before 'opening time', even though it is pouring rain and you have a cantankerous baby with you and chances are absolutely nil that you will return at any other point during the day.

APPLIANCES

The current used in the Netherlands is 220 volt, so – unless you are inclined to import a shipload of converters or are moving here from another 220-volt country – you are most likely going to be looking for a small army of appliances when you move here.

The good news is that there are several chains for buying household appliances. They usually sell all that you need in one place: refrigerators, washing machines, dryers, dishwashers, vacuum cleaners, toasters, coffee machines, air-fryers, televisions, radios, heaters – that sort of stuff. Prices among these chains can vary considerably, so have a good look around before you spend a whole lot of unnecessary euros.

One tip is that little stores that reek of exclusivity – in towns filled with expats and other high-spenders – are bound to have a nice little margin on top of the purchasing price. On the other hand, they are also more likely to have someone who is willing to come over and help you install it all and to offer service with a smile, during your appliances' lifetime. This is worth looking into and may even be worth that margin.

Another thought is that, as expats often move on to other countries where the current is different again, you could try the various clubs and your (partner's) employer's Intranet-bulletins for second-hand goods.

The most common place in the Netherlands to go for second-hand goods nowadays is www.marktplaats.nl, or the marktplaats app.

COMPUTERS AND SOFTWARE

Computers, laptops and tablets can be bought at larger and smaller computer, electronics and appliance (chain) stores, or via the Internet.

On rare occasions, certain supermarkets or large drugstore chains will offer a computer (or printer, or small electronic device) bargain. There's no way to predict the likelihood of this, so it is a matter of chance – and luck – whether you will run into such an offer just as you are looking for a computer – or printer, or small electronic device.

For buying a (mobile) telephone, see further on, in *Being Connected*.

FURNITURE, BEDS

Furniture can be bought in any number of places, from tiny, exclusive little shops to big well-known chains. The Netherlands has two names for its furniture conglomerates, being either *meubelboulevards* or *woonboulevards* (furniture or living boulevards). Some are huge indoor malls with stores of all levels of exclusivity, some are geographic locations where a sizeable collection of larger stores are all located. There are also *brocante*-stores (where they sell furniture and other more decorative items that do not yet quite deserve the name antique, but are already in the 'nostalgic'-category) as well as, of course, antique stores (see more about these in Chapter 11, under *For Antique Lovers Only*). In Chapter 9, under *Living On a Shoestring*, you will find more on low-budget spending.

Beds can be bought at either certain furniture chains or stores as well as in specialized stores.

BOOKS

With the exception of the bookstores in possibly the littler towns, they almost all carry a selection of English-language books. In the bigger cities, there are specialized English-language bookstores such as the *American Book Center* or *Waterstone's* – and then there are the large bookstores that carry not only English-language books, but also, for instance, French, German and Spanish.

A CLEAN HOME AND SELF

Detergents, floor polishers, carpet cleaners and the like can be bought both in supermarkets (again, prices can vary considerably, so if you have a tight budget, shop around!), but also at the drugstore (*drogisterij*) – where you will also find drain de-cloggers, stain removers, mold removers and some of the more chemical products.

Soaps, shampoos, toothbrushes, toothpaste, shaving cream, hand cream and sanitary items can also be bought at supermarkets and *drogisterijen* – while at the latter you will also find make-up, homeopathic medicines, dietary supplements, bubble baths, some toys, travel kits, mosquito repellent and a range of massage oils, for starters.

Baby necessities, including food and formula, can also be bought at either type of store.

SHOPPING ETIQUETTE

Take one or more shopping bags with you when you go to buy groceries. Even in the supermarket, you must pack your groceries yourself. While you already paid for the sturdier plastic bags at the supermarket, as of 2016, shops must charge you for the smaller bags they pack your groceries in, too. This way, the government hopes to make consumers more aware of plastic pollution and to thereby protect the environment. The really thin bags for meats, fruits and vegetables will remain free, the rest can cost anywhere between two and 25 cents. All supermarkets have shopping carts handy at the entrance, but in most supermarkets they are interlocked with chains and it takes a 50-cent or one euro coin to unlock the connection. You get your coin back when you re-connect the cart.

Payments can be made with cash, but shops also accept PIN or bank debit cards. In the supermarket, pay attention to the line you join, for sometimes it will be a 'pin-only' cash register. If you want to pay cash, you join a line at a different register. At self-scan registers, you can only pay using your debit card.

GETTING SERVED

The Dutch do not queue, as you will soon notice. You must learn the art of gently but firmly pushing your way into the bus or train, for example. You must also learn the art of getting served in a shop. Look first to see if there is a system by which people take numbers

- the Dutch consume an average of 8.4 kilograms of coffee per person per year. This makes the Dutch the fifth biggest coffee drinkers in the world, after Finland, Norway, Iceland and Denmark
- this comes down to 18.6 billion cups of coffee a year, with black and cappuccino being the most popular
- the Dutch drink an average of 79.3 liters of beer per person per year
- there are 1.57 million milk cows in the Netherlands. They produce 14.2 billion kg (not liters) of milk
- 60% of all the milk produced in the Netherlands is turned into cheese
- the Netherlands is in the world's top 5 when it comes to the exportation of milk products
- Dutch exports of milk and dairy products total approximately € 7.5 billion
- the Netherlands exports 1.1 billion kilos of tomatoes, or 61.8 kilos per person
- 21.7% of the Dutch smoke; 25.4% of men and 18.1% of women
- 3.2% of 12-16-year-olds have occasionally smoked, and 21.1% of 16-20-year-olds
- Dutch libraries lend out 38 million books a year; approximately 43 million books are sold
- the Netherlands has the highest percentage of left-handed people in the world: 13.23%
- 22% of the Dutch population do not drink alcohol, and 41.5% drink no more than 1 glass a day (this percentage includes the teetotalers)
- the higher the level of education, the more likely the Dutch are to drink more than one glass a day
- 77.4% of those between the ages of 12-16 have never tried alcohol
- when the Dutch have food delivered, the most popular kitchens are American, Chinese, Indian, Italian and Japanese
- home-delivered vegetarian and vegan food is increasing in popularity and went up 57% in 2021.

from a small dispenser at the entrance. This makes it easy; you need only watch for your number to come up. Otherwise you are expected to keep track of who was waiting before you and to speak up when it is your turn. A trick, used by many Dutch, is to enquire: '*Wie was de laatste?*' (Who came in last?), this way, you only have to keep an eye on this person to know when your turn is. This takes practice (and patience).

BARGAINING

This is not customary. You are expected to pay the price that is marked, especially for new items. If you are buying something second-hand – at a flea market, for example, or on the marktplaats app – you can try making an offer. The answer will be an angry 'no', however, if you drop the price by more than about 25%.

EYE CONTACT AND GREETINGS

When Dutch people enter and leave a small shop, they generally greet the shopkeeper ('*Goede dag*' – good day – is always a friendly greeting). It is important in any case to acknowledge the shopkeeper's presence by at least establishing eye contact.

FOOD

The Netherlands is a former shipping and colonial power that had interests in Indonesia, South Africa and the Caribbean. Many people from these countries eventually came to live in the Netherlands. They were later joined by guest workers from the Mediterranean countries and by international businessmen and women and their families as the Netherlands became the hub of their business interests in Europe. Thus, from a culinary perspective, the Netherlands is a truly international country and it is relatively easy to find supermarkets and delicatessen / gourmet food shops that cater to most palates.

DUTCH WAY OF EATING

The Dutch usually only eat one hot meal a day; it can be served for lunch or dinner, but it is generally served as the evening meal. Breakfast may consist of bakery-fresh breads, open-faced sandwiches, or Dutch rusks (*beschuit*), rolls, or croissants, topped with butter, jams or jellies, cheese, sausages or cold cuts. Lunch is usually more of the same, but it might include a small cup of hot soup (this does not qualify as a hot meal), fruit, a *kroket* (croquettes – *kroketten* are shaped like a fat hot dog, but are made with a soft, meat-based filling, covered in bread crumbs and fried), a mixed salad, or an *uitsmijter* (two fried eggs on a layer of ham, roast beef and/or cheese, on two slices of bread). The meal is accompanied by milk, coffee or tea. There are coffee and/or tea breaks in the mornings and afternoons that are sacred in the Netherlands (also in the offices) and the piping hot beverages are served with cookies – or pastries or cakes, if there is a special occasion. In the evening, there might be a *borrel* or drink consisting of, in most cases, beer, and a snack such as *bitterballen* (little round croquettes) before dinner – though, again, this is most often saved for a special occasion. Dinner is heartier with vegetables, meat and a healthy serving of the ubiquitous potato side dish like *patat frites* (French fries) or merely potatoes that are boiled or steamed. Sometimes, the vegetables and potatoes are mashed together to create the traditional Dutch *stamppot* dishes (see next paragraph), which are served with some delicious *rookworst* (smoked sausage) or *draadjesvlees* (simmered beef). There is also some kind of dessert, usually yogurt that comes in a variety of tastes, or *vla* (custard), fruit or sometimes cheese. To accompany the meals, the Dutch usually stick to water or milk or maybe soft drinks – wine is more often saved for special occasions.

When the Dutch eat out, they will eat the foods they don't cook at home, in other words, Indonesian, Italian, French, and Chinese, among others.

TYPICAL DUTCH FOODS

While the local cuisine is rich in variety due to the inclusion of many recipes that criss-cross international borders, there is a basic Dutch cuisine that is best described as 'home cooking'. It is the 'comfort food' that most Dutchmen crave when away from home for prolonged periods or after a summer of light meals.

If you were to ask a Dutchman to name one national dish, he would probably mention *erwtensoep* (pea soup). Next would come the *stamppot* dishes of *boerenkool met worst* (curly kale with sausage), *hachée* (beef and onion stew), *zuurkool met worst* (sauerkraut with sausage) and *witlof met ham en kaas* (Belgian endives with ham and cheese sauce). In May and June, everyone eats *asperges met ham en eieren* (asparagus with ham and eggs).

Other goodies that are generally the first to be consumed by the Dutch who have been away for a while are: a *boterham met hagelslag* or *vlokken* (sandwich with chocolate sprinkles or flakes), *bitterballen* or *kroketten*, *stroopwafels* (fine waffles, filled with syrup) and raw herring with chopped onions.

INDONESIAN / CHINESE FOOD & SPICES

At last count, there were over 900 Chinese / Indonesian shops in the Netherlands. Thus it is safe to say that virtually everyone in the Netherlands eats Indonesian food in what has become known as the Indonesian *rijsttafel*, where rice is the central dish with any number of side dishes. These may include three different types of rice, several fish, meat, poultry and vegetables dishes, and condiments. The *rijsttafel* may be prepared at home, eaten at restaurants or carried home from Indonesian or Chinese / Indonesian takeouts.

If you are thinking of preparing some of these dishes yourself, then it is good to know that since the 16th century, when the Dutch explorers started to return from the orient with exotic spices, these spices have had an important place in the Dutch kitchen cabinet. Most are available in the supermarkets. If you don't find what you are looking for there, almost all of the herbs and spices known to man are sold in Indonesian shops or *tokos*, and Chinese supermarkets.

ETHNIC SHOPS

Also in the big cities you will find shops specializing in foods and other products for specific ethnic groups, such as a *Turkse slager* (a *slager* is a butcher) or a *Turkse winkel*, where they sell products from Turkey and the eastern Mediterranean. You can buy meat that is *halal* at an *Islamitische slager*. In Amsterdam you can find kosher (Jewish) meat markets, and in Amsterdam, Rotterdam and The Hague there is a small Chinatown. And there are more possibilities: Moroccan, Japanese, Indian, etc. Also available are the Tex / Mex dishes popular in America; most supermarkets have a small Tex / Mex department.

If you are looking for something from a specific culinary / geographic area, check the Internet.

SUPERMARKETS

Dutch supermarkets carry the basic groceries, such as baking and cooking ingredients, dairy products (including cheese), herbs and spices, bakery goods, some health foods, 'exotic foods' (such as Japanese, Moroccan, Tex / Mex, Indian and Indonesian), fruits and vegetables, meats, fish and poultry, baby foods and pet foods, along with daily house and kitchen supplies (such as detergent, toilet paper and cleaning supplies). The selection of frozen foods is proportionate to the capacity of the store; the larger the supermarket, the more goods there are on offer.

At the supermarkets you can browse at your leisure while getting acquainted with the local products, and buy the basics to stock your pantry. If you feel shy or awkward about the language, contact can be kept to a minimum. The check-out system is relatively simple – in fact, the number of self-check-out stations is increasing – and not all that different from the systems in other countries. However, there will come a time when you will overcome your fears and be lured by the sights and smells of the neighborhood specialty shops, or stalls at open markets.

DAIRY PRODUCTS

Of all of the wonderful foodstuffs produced in the Netherlands, the Dutch are probably most proud of their milk and milk products. The ubiquitous purveyor of this life-sustaining substance, the Holstein Frisian cow, grazes everywhere. The Gouda and Edam cheeses are so well-known around the globe that wherever cheese is sold, Gouda and/or Edam are always present.

While the supermarkets offer a good selection of fresh and processed cheese, serious cheese lovers and connoisseurs shop at their local cheese specialist or *kaasspecialist*. They not only have the largest selection of cheeses, but they age their Dutch cheeses naturally to obtain the optimum taste and perfection, and their cheeses never hit the shelves until they are least two months old. And, since most Dutch cheeses are classified according to age, they keep a watchful eye on the aging process. The cheese shops and supermarket cheese departments are also well-stocked with imported cheeses from, among others, France, Italy, Spain, Belgium and England.

Generally, the place to buy your milk and other dairy products is in the supermarket; however, you might also consider buying directly from the cheese farms that sell fresh farmer's milk, buttermilk, eggs and cheese – and of course from the cheese specialist.

DRUG TOURISM

For a short while, the government had introduced a law stating that, if you were planning on getting a taste of the mellow side of Dutch life and joining the crowd in a coffee shop for a little recreational consumption, you had to become member of the shop – including a membership card, only available to those who could demonstrate that they were living in the municipality in which the coffee shop is established. This is no longer the case. Now, theoretically, all you have to do is prove you are a legal resident – but already several municipalities have announced that they will not be enforcing this rule. After all, a substantial percentage of their income is generated by 'drug tourists' – a source they are not keen to lose. Coffee shop owners, meanwhile, are expected to destroy their 'membership' lists.

Drugs and Alcohol Use

SALE OF LIQUOR

From the age of 18 onwards you may legally buy beer, wine and liquor. Alcoholic beverages are for sale in liquor stores and supermarkets, though supermarkets only sell beer, wine and alcoholic beverages with an alcohol percentage up to 12 or 13%.

Bartenders, liquor dealers and cashiers must ask youngsters who are buying alcohol from them to submit proof of their age, such as a passport, ID-card or driver's license. If either of these cannot be supplied, they are not allowed to sell it to them.

DRINKING AND DRIVING

You may not drive if you are over the 0.5-blood alcohol level or, during the first five years after you have been issued a driver's license, 0.2. This latter limit also applies to drivers of mopeds and motorized bicycles until the age of 24. Driving under the influence is a criminal offense and applies to driving a car and riding a motorcycle, scooter, moped or bicycle. You risk a fine running from € 300 to € 650 (and a four-month driving ban, if you are a novice driver), depending on your blood alcohol level, plus a possible ban on driving of up to almost a year and possible incarceration. In some cases (for instance, if your blood alcohol level is between 1.3 and 1.8, or as a 'beginning' driver, over 0.8), you may be required to take a two-halfday (€ 683) or four-halfday (€ 1,075) course (to be paid for by you), which, if you do not take it (from start to finish) could lead to the loss of your driver's license. If your blood alcohol level exceeds 1.8, you may also be required to take an (expensive) alcohol dependency test. Also drunk cyclists can expect a fine of € 200, if their blood alcohol level exceeds 0.54, while drunk scooter drivers can expect a fine between € 125 and € 225.

If you are caught driving under the influence of soft or hard drugs, you run the risk of one year of incarceration, having your driver's license suspended for up to five years, or a fine of up to € 21,750. If it is decided that you must be examined by a doctor, this will cost you € 1,200.

DRUG USE

For the record, trafficking in (importing or exporting), selling, producing and processing either hard or soft drugs are offenses in the Netherlands. The possession of soft drugs (up to 5 grams) or hard drugs (0.5 grams) for personal use is a summary, non-indictable offense. Anyone under the age of 18 caught with 5 grams of soft drugs will have to hand them in, pay a fine of € 60 and do 12 hours of community service. If they have between 6 and 30 grams, the fine goes up to € 75-100, while they have to do 16-30 hours of community service. Those older than 18 pay a fine of € 75. For various pills, heroin and cocaine, you pay a fine of up to € 100-200, while if you are younger than 18 you will have to do 20-40 hours of community service. First offenders pay lower fines. An up-to-date overview can be found on https://boetebase.om.nl, under Drugs.

COFFEE SHOPS

Coffee shops can sell soft drugs without being prosecuted, provided they observe strict rules. The aim of this policy is to prevent users of soft drugs from becoming marginalized or being exposed to more harmful drugs.

A coffee shop can best be described as a café that does not sell alcoholic beverages (except in Amsterdam, where some do), and in which, subject to certain restrictions, soft drugs may be sold. Although the sale of soft drugs is an offense, low priority is given to the prosecution of coffee shop owners, provided they sell small quantities only and meet the following conditions:

- no more than five grams per person may be sold in any one transaction
- the stock may not exceed 500 grams
- no alcohol is served
- no hard drugs may be sold
- drugs may not be advertised
- the coffee shop must not cause any nuisance
- the coffee shop may not be in the vicinity of a school
- no drugs may be sold to persons under the age of 18, nor may minors be admitted onto the premises.

Municipalities may set up extra rules, for instance regarding the presence of informational material and the required physical presence of the proprietor. Agreements are made with the local police regarding routine checks and the mayor of a city has the authority to close coffee shops that do not meet these conditions.

For those of you who think coffee shops can only be found in the bigger cities: there are somewhere in the vicinity of 565 coffee shops, spread over 100-plus municipalities (more than 160 are in Amsterdam). As this is more than 25% of all Dutch municipalities and only a handful of these are 'big' cities, don't be surprised if your sleepy little village has one too. On the other hand, almost 300 municipalities have a so-called zero policy, meaning they will not allow any coffee shops within their municipal limits. Incidentally, three-quarters of the cannabis sold here is of the home-grown variety (referred to as 'nederwiet').

LEGAL GYMNASTICS

The Dutch government has to perform legal gymnastics in order to make the sale of soft drugs in 'coffee shops' possible. First of all, clearly, the sale of soft drugs is not allowed. Secondly, nor is the culturing of soft drugs. To nonetheless make the existence of coffee shops possible, two terms have been introduced: 'gedoogbeleid' (policy of tolerance) and 'lage opsporingsbeleid' (policy of low investigational priority). The sale of soft drugs in coffee shops is tolerated and, provided the conditions are met, the culturing of soft drugs to be sold via coffee shops will not be prosecuted. If is often remarked that the words 'tolerance' and 'flexibility' well describe the Dutch mentality – and there is no better example than this, some might say. Another interesting observation is that, though shop owners may not charge VAT over their sales, they do owe income tax over their income; generating a calculated pleasant € 400 million a year for the state coffers.

Conversions

Dimensions

American	Metric
0.03937 in	1 millimeter [mm]
0.3937 in	1 centimeter [cm]
39.37 in / 1.094 yard	1 meter [m]
0.621 mi / 3281.5 ft	1 kilometer [km]

American	Metric
1 inch	2.54 cm
1 foot	0.3048 m
1 yard	0.9144 m
1 mile	1609 m

Dry measures

American	Metric
1 ounce	30 grams
1/2 pound	225 grams
1 pound	450 grams
2.2 pounds	1 kilogram

American	Dutch
31/2 ounces	1 ons = 100 gram
1.1 pounds	5 ons = 500 gram = 1 pond
2.2 pounds	10 ons = 2 pond = 1 kg
1/2 cup + 1 T	1 kopje
1 T	1 eetlepel [el] = 15 gram
1/2 t	1 theelepel [tl] = een lepeltje

Liquid measures

American	Dutch
quart + 3 T	1 liter
3 T + 1 t	1/2 deciliter [dl]
6 T + 1 t	1 deciliter = 1/10 liter
1/2 c + 2 t	2 deciliter
3/4 c + 2 t	21/2 deciliter
11/3 c	3 deciliter

Temperature

Fahrenheit to Celsius	Celsius to Fahrenheit
Substract 32 and multiply by 5, then divide by 9	Multiply by 9, divide by 5 and add 32
Example: 68°F: 68-32=36, 36x5=180, 180/9=20°C	Example: 20°C: 20x9=180, 180/5=36, 36+32=68°F

Oven temperature

Fahrenheit	Celsius
300	150
350	180
400	205
450	230
500	260

BAKERY – *BAKKERIJ*

The shops that probably delight foreign residents most are the bakeries (*bakkerijen*) that turn out those mouth-watering fresh breads, rolls, cookies, pastries and creamy bon-bons. At Christmastime they have a full range of seasonal breads and cookies, then at Easter-time they outdo themselves with a stunning array of brilliant, foil-wrapped chocolate bunnies, bon-bons, marzipan animals and fruits, and cakes decorated for the season.

The bakeries often also offer breads baked according to French, Italian and Middle Eastern tradition. Bread is baked fresh daily and is often still hot when you get home from your shopping.

THE FISH SHOP – *VISHANDEL*

Although not the great seafaring nation it once was, the Netherlands still retains its reputation for being a purveyor of fine seafood. The quality and quantity available here are excellent. Supermarkets may carry a small variety of fish and seafood but the seafood specialists in the shops called *vishandel* offer by far the largest selection. Not every village has one, so look in the larger towns for the best selection.

Much of what is on sale is cold water fish but occasionally you will see some excellent fish from the Mediterranean. In addition to the fish you buy to prepare at home, the fishmonger will have some pre-fried haddock and codpieces (*kibbeling*), raw and pickled herring and some excellent prepared dishes such as fish salads, jambalaya and paella. The fishmonger will also cut or fillet your fish to your specifications.

THE CHICKEN OR POULTRY SPECIALIST – *POELIER*

While most supermarkets and butcher shops and some stalls at open markets carry whole chickens, chicken parts and eggs, there are also shops that specialize in all kinds of poultry and eggs and, in the late autumn and winter months, game birds and game. The signs outside their establishments either read *kip specialist* or *poelier – wild en gevogelte* (venison and fowl). Most of these shops have a selection of chicken and turkey parts, rolled roasts, ground chicken and turkey, and prepared foods such as chicken *saté* and grilled chicken, as well as (prepared) rice and vegetable dishes – and, as the case may be, (roe) deer, hare, pheasant, duck, wild boar, goose, guinea fowl, etc.

GREENGROCERY – *GROENTEBOER*

Dutch farmers provide this country with a stunning variety of fruits and vegetables. There is a large concentration of apple, pear and cherry orchards in the Betuwe region while vegetable gardens and greenhouses dot the landscape. To supplement these locally grown products, fruits and vegetables are imported from as far away as China and South America.

Vegetables play a central role in the Dutch meal, so you can expect them to be fresh and tasty. Supermarkets all have a fruit and vegetable department, but for the best selection and personal service, you might want to try the independent greengrocer known as *groenteboer* and their shop, called the *groentewinkel*, while often the local Turkish / Moroccan store will also carry an excellent selection of fresh fruit and vegetables. Many greengrocers also offer prepared *rauwkost* (cut fruits or salad material ready for mixed salads), soups, stews and casseroles. In the late autumn and winter months, they sell packets of pre-cut vegetables for the famous Dutch pea soup and *stamppot* dishes.

THE BUTCHER'S – *SLAGER*

Dutch farmers produce very fine beef, pork, lamb, veal and poultry. However, if you have been raised on succulent marbled steaks and roasts carved from grain-fed beef cattle, the local beef may be disappointing; it is lean – but it *does* have a fuller flavor than its grain-fed cousins. Thus, a good butcher is invaluable. You will find them behind the butcher counter in butcher shops and supermarkets. They are called a *slager* and their business is called a *slagerij*. Visit them on a quiet day and they will usually be willing to give advice on how to cook the Dutch meats. Notice the singular way they trim and present their meats. Almost all fat and bones are removed from the beef and if you want the bones for soups and stews, you will have to pay extra.

A good, innovative butcher prepares the meats for barbecues, fondues and snacks and sells prepared salads and sauces as accompaniments. They might also have some delicatessen dishes such as quiches and savory meat pies. They most certainly offer some delicious locally made sausages and cold cuts from all across Europe.

CHILDREN'S FOODS

Everything is in place for raising healthy babies in the Netherlands. Supermarkets, drugstores (*drogisterijen*) and pharmacies (*apotheken*) all carry baby foods in jars, as well as vitamins and infant formulas. Your *huisarts* (GP) or the doctor at the *Consultatiebureau* (Well-Baby Clinic, see page 256) can also recommend foods for your baby and will refer you to a specialist if required.

HEALTH AND VEGETARIAN FOODS

The Dutch are very aware of the benefits of eating well and there are health food departments in every supermarket. There are also health food stores (*reformhuizen* or *reformwinkels, or biologische winkels*) in most cities and villages. Theirs are natural products, with no chemicals added, that are made from organically grown, or *biologische,* materials. Many greengrocers also sell prepared vegetarian foods and organically grown or eco foods. At least one health food company offers boxes that are delivered to your home, together with recipes, saving you the effort of planning and shopping for dinner. These are also available from non health-food affiliated stores / supermarkets / businesses.

QUANTITIES TO BUY

Food sold in bulk is advertised by the piece (*per stuk*) or by weight:

- kilo = 1,000 grams = 2.2 (US) pounds
- pond = 500 grams = 1.1 (US) pounds
- ons = 100 grams = approx. 3.5 ounces

HOUSEHOLD HELP

Quite a few Dutch households make use of a household help / cleaning lady, most often referred to as *hulp in het huishouden* – literally 'household help' – or a *werkster*. Cleaning ladies are very hard to find, but there are a few ways in which you can go about this: you can hang a little card on the notice board of your local supermarket (while you're at it, check and see if someone hasn't hung up a card, offering their services) or you can place an ad in the local newspaper. Most newspapers have an item called *Kleintjes*, which means 'little ones', that has been created specifically for short notices and ads. The card or ad should state: *hulp in het huishouden gezocht* and you might want to add the fact that it would be helpful if (he or) she spoke English – or some other common language. A third, and probably best, way to find household help is through friends, neighbors and other acquaintances, as this way you are more likely to find a reliable, dependable and honest one.

The per-hour price for household help is usually around € 12-17, plus sometimes their public transportation fare. If you hire household help, you are not expected to withhold wage tax and social insurance contributions on the wages you pay out to them – provided they do not work for you more than three days a week. They are expected to declare their earnings on their own income tax return (though many of them don't). Once they work for you more than three days a week, you are expected to withhold wage tax and social insurance contributions – though special rules apply. In this type of situation, make sure you have yourself informed by a tax specialist, before you tread on slippery ground!

In the bigger cities, you will find commercial cleaning companies for businesses that offer an on-the-side service of household help. Their hourly rate is a bit higher, as the company pays their taxes and contributions. To find one of these companies, you can check online under *Schoonmaakbedrijven*, and see if one of them offers *Huishoudelijk werk*. Or else just select one of the bigger-looking companies and call and ask. Beware of the fact that they may have long waiting lists! On the Internet, you might wish to give www.ikzoekeenwittewerkster.nl a try – with 'wit' (white), they mean that your household help owes (and pays) taxes over their earnings!

SAFETY

The Netherlands is a safe country to live in. Your children can safely ride their bikes to school (the impatience of the average Dutch driver being the greatest threat) and you can safely go out to dinner – even in the 'big' cities and even after dark. In the smaller towns, this is even more so.

Drug-related crime, murder and other forms of human aggression are at a low level here. But let's remain realistic: they do, of course, take place and you must always keep your eyes and senses (particularly your common sense) open. Do not go walking in deserted (woody) areas after dark. Do not use the cash dispenser, when the only other person around is a nervous, strung out-looking individual. When walking alone, search for well-lit areas. Keep your eye on your child. And no matter where you are, do not leave your mobile phone, computer or other obvious valuables behind in the car, where everyone can see them.

BEING IN THE BIG CITIES

It goes without saying that, as in any big city, you should keep your eye on your purse, bags, cameras and whatever else you might have on you. And that you should not wander alone into a dark alleyway. And that if you do not like the looks of certain characters hanging around the street you want to go into, you should walk down the next, if you have that option. It also goes without saying that it is always better to have the look of a worldly-wise, undaunted cosmopolitan – rather than a frightened, hunted deer. It is human nature for con artists, thieves and other unpleasant folk to zero in on those who look especially vulnerable. But that goes for walking around in Atlanta, Santiago, Seville and Singapore too.

A MYTH OR TWO

Now that we are talking about the big cities, this is a good opportunity to deal with a myth or two about the Netherlands. Yes, the government hands out drugs – for free – to so-called 'incurable' drug addicts. As you might know, the Dutch are big on helping the underdog, and assistance is given to drug addicts to promote their rehabilitation, and to improve their physical and mental condition as well as their social circumstances. However, when 'free' drugs are handed out, this is not so much to make life easier for the drug users, but rather to decrease crime in the streets. Instead of having desperate junkies roaming the streets, looking for someone to mug, the government has chosen to hand out drugs, which they do in fixed places in the big cities – away from the crowds – where the addicts know where to find them.

And yes, there are areas in the cities where prostitution is condoned. One of these areas, the so-called red-light district in Amsterdam, is famous for it. It might interest you to know that this can be considered one of the safest areas of Amsterdam: it is always well-lit, well-patrolled by the police and never deserted, as the prostitution industry is one that operates 24 hours a day – particularly at night, of course. However, should you wish to visit the area, a daytime visit may be a better idea as this will reduce the risk of being targeted by the nevertheless ever-present pickpockets or other questionable characters with dubious intentions. If there is ever any problem, you can rest assured that there is nothing the police hasn't seen or dealt with – so don't hesitate to enlist their help.

REPORTING A CRIME

Should you become a victim of crime, locate the nearest police officer or police station to report it. The police will take your statement, give advice on canceling credit cards and provide you with helpful phone numbers and addresses. Be sure to give a description of the culprit and the location. In the Netherlands, good citizens turn in found wallets or purses to the police. Thieves remove the cash, debit cards and credit cards and toss the rest.

Confirm the loss or theft in writing to your insurance company, including a copy of the police report. It is always a good idea to

Obligation to Carry ID

Everyone over the age of 13 must carry some form of legal ID at all times; this being a passport / ID (for EU nationals) or a valid aliens document (for non-EU nationals). Dutch nationals may show either a driver's license, a passport, or an identity card. Photocopies are not allowed, nor is inviting the police officer to your home to check your documents. Children over the age of 13 must have their own papers; inclusion in their parents' passport is not enough.

Who is authorized to ask you to show your papers? The police are, as well as parking inspectors, officers of the Health and Safety Inspectorate, inspectors from the Building Control Department, tax inspectors, customs inspectors, forest rangers (whom you will meet while walking your dog), school inspectors, etc. And, of course, but this is a totally different type of situation, you show your ID when opening a bank account, requesting a government benefit, starting a new job, etc. – AND when attending a soccer game...

The purpose of this obligation is to help combat crime and you may only be requested to show your documents if there is a valid reason for this – for instance, if you have committed a (traffic) offense or crime, are using public transportation without having paid for it, or if the police need your assistance, for instance to help solve a crime, or to maintain public order. The request must be in keeping with the position of the person asking you for your ID. In other words, a tax inspector cannot detain you for this purpose in connection with running a red light.

If you refuse to comply, you may be taken to the police station for identification and run the risk of owing a € 50 fine, for those younger than 16, and € 100 for those aged 16 and older.

Store and building security officers may ask you for your ID, but you do not have to show it. However, they are then allowed to deny you entry or to escort you out of the building.

have copies of your travel documents and/or important papers in case something unfortunate does happen.

LOCK YOUR DOOR

Streets are generally well-lit in the cities and towns in the Netherlands, so that you can safely let out your dog in the evening, run to the supermarket or walk to your friends' house a couple of streets away. When you leave the house, however, it is always best to lock the door, particularly if you live in a reasonably well-to-do neighborhood. There is always the chance that there is a certain individual out there, waiting for you to leave the house.

Make sure you have good locks on your doors and windows. Double locks on doors, or dead bolts, can offer additional protection. A *dievenklauw* is a special lock that prevents entry. A locksmith can install these for you, or you can purchase the locks at a hardware or do-it-yourself store and install them yourself.

A SAFE HOME

Although it is customary for the Dutch to leave their curtains open, it is generally not a good idea to show off too many possessions. Having expensive television, stereo and computer equipment out in full view might prove to be too tempting. Likewise leaving a pocketbook or wallet on the table, or jewelry you have removed from your person, could pique the interest of a potential thief.

There are security systems companies (*beveiligingsbedrijven*) with specialists who can install security systems for you. They can help you with alarm systems, video cameras, fences, electronic eyes, movement detectors, lighting, etc.

In order to ascertain that you are dealing with a reputable agency for your security needs, look for the *Preventiecertificaat* or *Politiekeurmerk* registration. Not only does this guarantee the reliability of their personnel and the quality of the work, it is also recognized by insurance companies, so that you may be entitled to discounts on your personal property and home owners' insurance (*inboedel* and *opstal verzekering*). A list of companies with these certifications can be found on https://hetccv.nl/keurmerken/zakelijk/digitale-veiligheid/ccv-keurmerk-pentesten/vakman/. Always ask if a company has this certification before doing business with them.

If you would prefer not to leave behind an empty house, but can't find anyone who'd be willing to watch over it for while, you could always try to find someone via a house-sitter organization. One such organization is Holiday Link, which you can find on www.holidaysitting.nl/nl/ (click on *Vakantieoppas*), while there is also www.huisoppasser.nl or www.homecareoppas.nl. House-sitters will even take care of your pets, if you want.

FIRE PROTECTION

All homes should have smoke alarms, and they are easily installed. If you are renting, ask your landlord to do it. If they are unwilling, you can do it yourself. Smoke alarms can be bought at do-it-yourself / hardware stores or department stores. Small fire extinguishers can also be purchased at do-it-yourself / hardware stores, while fire blankets for kitchens and powder extinguishers are also available.

OCCUPANT IDENTIFICATION CARD

You can also create an identification card listing the names of all of the occupants of the house (including pets) and hang this up somewhere logical, such as your meter closet (*meterkast*) in the hallway, or by the telephone. In the event of an emergency, or a fire, the police and fire department will first look here for any information on the inhabitants of the house. Cards are available at your local police bureau.

EMERGENCY!

Should you have an emergency and need the police, the fire department or an ambulance, the national number for all services in Holland is: 1-1-2.

You can stick a 1-1-2 sticker on your phone and let all family members know this is the number to call if a serious emergency arises. The operator will send the services you need, or all three if required.

If there is a problem that does not constitute an emergency, 0900 8844 will connect you to your local police.

RECYCLING AND WASTE MANAGEMENT

In general, the Netherlands is considered to be a very 'green' country; not just for its wide-open fields, but also for the mentality of the Dutch in protecting their environment. The vast majority of the population takes part in various recycling efforts. From the organic waste, which is collected separately, compost is made which is then reused in gardens and agriculture. Of the more than two million tons of paper and glass collected, close to 90% is recycled and used for new products.

The Ministry of Infrastructure and Environment (Ministerie van Infrastructuur en Milieu) works in close cooperation with international and domestic partners on improving the living environment of this country. There are many organizations working to monitor issues such as living space, respect for nature, space and raw materials and over 4,000 people are concerned with issues of living space, housing and environment. An additional task is to plan, conduct and supervise the building of projects in government housing, and to develop a sustainable environmental policy. There are also numerous programs and activities that citizens can get involved in aimed at helping to preserve and improve the environment.

To foreigners coming to live in the Netherlands, the rules and regulations may seem to be bewildering in their detail, so here is a basic guideline to the most common recycling practices.

1. Recycling tax: upon purchasing new electronic and household equipment, you will automatically be charged a recycling tax or removal tax known as *verwijderingsbijdrage*, regardless of whether you are handing in an old appliance or not. The assumption is that, for each new appliance purchased, the old one will have to be environmentally disposed of or recycled at some point in time. A list of rates is available from the store.

2. Household waste: outside of Amsterdam, households are usually furnished with two, or sometimes three, separate waste containers (a green *groenbak* for garden, fruit and vegetable waste, a gray *grijs container* for all remaining waste, and, as the case may be, a third container for paper). As of 2015, many municipalities have issued their inhabitants yet another container: for plastics, metal, and drink packaging (PMD), encouraging consumers to separate these *before* they are taken to the waste separation facilities. These containers are emptied on alternating weeks. Pay attention – if you place the wrong container at the curbside it will not be emptied. In some cities the city provides a multi-purpose waste container, a so-called *duobak*. This is one container with a separation inside. The smaller part in the back is intended for 'green' waste, the larger part in the front for all other waste. If you feel the container(s) provided is/are not sufficient, you can always contact the city council for an additional one. This will entail an additional yearly contribution, as the additional waste also needs to be disposed of. Make sure you do not leave your containers on the street at the end of the day. You can be fined for not returning them to your property. There are a few municipalities where glass and paper are also collected curbside, usually in wealthier suburban areas.

3. Groenbak: cat litter and used baby diapers are not considered organic waste for the *groenbak* and should be placed in the gray container. Milk packages, plastic bags, large pieces of wood and thick tree branches, the ashes from your fireplace, sand, dog and cat hair and the contents of your vacuum cleaner are also NOT to be placed in the green container. 'Green waste' is vegetable, fruit, and potato peels, leftover cooked food, fish and meat leftovers with bones (wrapped in newspaper in the summer months), nut shells and eggshells, hardened cooking fat, tea bags, coffee filters with coffee grains, small garden trimmings, mowed grass and leaves, weeds, flowers and houseplants, straw and the contents of your hamster or rabbit cages.

In some cities, due to the lack of space, there unfortunately is no separation of waste, other than what a private individual brings to the separate waste disposal stations and/or containers. Most towns publish a calendar, distributed around November (regarding the following year) to each household, of contact addresses for properly disposing of all types of waste, as well as pick-up dates for waste containers and locations for *chemokars* (chemical cars – see further on, under chemical waste). If you don't have one of these calendars, you can request one from your *gemeentereinigingsdienst* (sanitation department) or download it from your municipality's website.

4. Refunds on bottles: most glass soft drink bottles, the large acrylic plastic *euroflessen* and some small glass bottles or jars have a deposit that is paid upon buying them. The word *statiegeld* (deposit) and an amount will be listed on the label. Once you return these to the store for recycling (there are special bottle stations for these at most supermarkets), the deposit is returned to you by way of a *bonnetje*, or paper receipt, after you have placed the bottles into the bottle return machine. This receipt can be redeemed when you pay for your groceries or at the *klantenservice* (customer service).

5. Glass: all glass that does not have a deposit can be dropped in special containers which are usually placed at convenient locations throughout the town (such as in the supermarket parking area). There is often a symbol on the label showing a hand with a bottle and the word *glasbak*. These 'glass collectors' (*glasbakken*) are often, but not always, yellow. Some cities allow for the separation of white, green and brown glass. The containers will stipulate *bont* (white), *groen* (green), or *bruin* (brown). Since this effort was started, the Dutch have come to recycle more than 89% of their glass.

6. Paper: often placed near to the glass recycling containers you will find the blue paper collectors (*papierbakken*). Again, most of the paper in the Netherlands is recycled. You may recycle newspapers, magazines, junk mail, envelopes, paper packaging, and wrappers. Don't forget to remove all plastic first. As mentioned earlier, in a number of municipalities, houses are provided with a separate paper container.

7. Batteries: most supermarkets and some stores and schools have special containers for collecting old batteries. Often these are located by the bottle recycling station at the grocery store or at the checkout counter of stores; the *batterijenbak* is usually red or blue. If none are available close by, you can ask at the supermarket or inquire with the city council where the nearest collection points are (batteries can also be handed in with other chemical waste – see next point).

8. Chemical waste (paint and painting materials, toners, printer cartridges, batteries, oil, turpentine, nail polish, and caustic cleaning agents, etc.): many cities have a special car (*chemokar*) that comes by every three months to collect chemical waste. You can check with the city council on collection dates and times or request the calendar listing all relevant contact information for the year.

   Alternatively, you can dispose of these materials, as other large pieces of rubbish (construction waste, car tires, etc.), at the waste separation and recycling station that is available in nearly every city and town.

9. Medicines: outdated prescriptions and any overdue non-prescription medicine can be handed in at most pharmacies for proper disposal. Pills, cough syrup, suppositories, antibiotic ointments, etc. should all be disposed of via the pharmacy.

10. Clothing and bedding: some cities and towns have a large container for clothes and shoes, generally placed by local organizations, and most often located close to a shopping area. During the year there are often also special initiatives by schools or

churches to collect clothes for specific charities. Aside from the Salvation Army (*Leger des Heils*) you can contact the following organization to get information on addresses to hand in clothes: Sympany, or www.sympany.nl.

11. Large waste (*grof vuil*): any furniture (if not recycled through second-hand shops) and large household debris can be collected by special appointment through the city's waste collection department. Within certain volume limitations, this waste will be collected free of charge, but it has to comply with certain regulations, e.g. wooden parts have to be gathered and tied with rope. Anything outside city regulations is best brought to the municipal waste separation and recycling station (*afvalscheidingsstation*, see next point) or, alternatively, one could order a private container to collect and dispose of all waste. This *puinbak* waste container (generally used during construction for large amounts of debris) can be ordered for a fee covering the delivery and removal. Contact your town hall and ask for *gemeentereiniging grof vuil*.

12. *Afvalscheidingsstation* (waste separation and recycling station): anything that is too large or specific (e.g. chemical waste) to be put in your regular waste container can be taken to a waste disposal station. For private individuals the rules here are pretty lax, as opposed to business disposal of waste, which usually comes at a price. You will usually be questioned upon entering the station as to what kind of waste you want to discard and will be directed to the right locations. There are, for instance, separate containers for wood, cardboard, tires, stones and construction rubbish, and chemical waste.

    It bears to be kept in mind that any soil and earth removed when redoing a garden is generally not accepted unless a special government inspection (at a price) has taken place to ensure that it is not polluted by contaminants such as oil, lead or chemicals.

13. Computers, printers and scanners: if you need to dispose of ICT equipment in working order you can contact IT Recycling, or www.it-recycling.nl, and ask about *grijsgoed* (gray goods) recycling.

If you wish to become involved in a local environmental group, contact your municipality. There are 'eco-teams' in many neighborhoods who work to increase awareness of the necessity to recycle and to protect the environment that carry out local projects.

PETS

DOG TAX

If you have been living in the Netherlands for a while, you have undoubtedly taken a slip over *hondenpoep* – dog poop. Rather than enjoying the beautiful architecture of the Dutch cities, you find yourself staring at the sidewalks, navigating your way around the deposits of our furry friends. How can it be that this nation of clean, hygienic, well-educated people can live with sidewalks pockmarked with *hondenpoep*? If we had an answer, we'd tell you. There is, however, an ongoing campaign to have dog owners train their dogs to leave their mess in the roadside gutters (watch out

when stepping out of the car!) and, as you can read elsewhere in this book, dog owners pay taxes for their hounds. This tax used to be a 'corporate' tax, but is now levied on private dog owners, the proceeds of which are used to create areas within the cities and towns that can be considered public dog toilets or to place dog-poop baggy dispensers and trash cans at regular intervals throughout the municipality and keep these well-stocked. This is the only pet-related tax there is, so maybe there is some justice after all.

FAVORITE PETS

And then there is a whole array of other favorite pets: cats, canaries, parrots and fish, for instance. Also rabbits, guinea pigs and hamsters are very popular. In some gardens, you will find the occasional goat, miniature pony or pot-bellied swine and in some children's bedrooms; rats, snakes, spiders, turtles, and the occasional bat.

PET CARE

Pets have a position in Dutch households that is very similar to that of the children. Some are served the best cut of the rarest beef, others are given the best chair, with the best view of the TV – and, naturally, access to the accompanying snacks. And the care provided is top-notch: the veterinary services (a vet is called a *dierenarts*) are excellent in the Netherlands, and include animal hospitals, ambulances and even crematoriums. There are also dog-walking services (*hondenuitlaatservice*) for those who can't imagine life without Whoofy, but unfortunately have to spend the whole day in the office. And last but not least, the pet stores in the Netherlands offer a colorful array of toys, cushions, cages, leashes, snacks, top-of-the-line food, and... pets, of course.

FINDING A PET

If you want to buy a dog, however, it is always better to do this via a recognized breeder rather than through a pet store. Breeders can be found through the Raad van Beheer op Kynologische Gebied in Nederland, the phone number for which you will find at the end of the chapter. For any other type of animal (other than the household rodent type – for which the pet store, or the petting farm, called *kinderboerderij*, will do fine) – you can best ask the local vet where you can find one. If you are looking to save an unwanted cat or dog, there are kennels, called *dierenasiel,* where 'lost and found' or otherwise homeless animals are brought. These kennels are well-run and most of the time have a good profile of the animals they are trying to place. Often, they have to find a new home for the pets of families who have to go abroad, or who have family member who is allergic to animals, and find it greatly rewarding to have found such a loving pet a new home. There are also similar organizations that place abandoned dogs found abroad in the Netherlands, after a thorough medical check-up.

RELOCATING YOUR PET

The family pet has relocation needs as well. Each year, more than 750,000 animals are transported around the world. For admittance to the Netherlands, cats and dogs must have a health certificate in Dutch, English, French or German, legalized by the Veterinary Service in the country of origin, stating a complete description of the animal (genus, age, breed, color, hair, marks – this part must be laminated in passports issued after December 12, 2014), the name of the owner, and that a complete vaccination against rabies has taken place with the date, type of vaccine used, expiry date, batch number and manufacturer, which must have taken place at least 21 days before entry into the Netherlands. As puppies, kittens and baby ferrets must be at least 12 weeks old to receive this vaccination, this means that they must be at least 15 weeks old when they enter the country. The maximum amount of time that is allowed to pass between a vaccination and your pet's entry into the country depends on the make of the vaccination and can be read in its information leaflet. Animals must be dewormed and checked for ticks. Some countries have quarantine regulations. It is best to check with the Dutch Consulate well in advance as to what the requirements are, so that you can make sure you meet them (see the website at the end of the chapter).

Furthermore, when transporting dogs, cats and ferrets (yes, ferrets...) within Europe; you must arrange a European-style animal passport, arrange a rabies vaccination and make sure they have identification (a chip / microtransponder – tattoos are not accepted for animals coming from outside the EU / EEA). At the moment, the European Commission is working on a veterinary certificate for other pets, but as this has not yet been finalized, rabbits, small rodents, birds, fish, amphibians and reptiles usually only need a declaration of health issued by a vet. For more information, visit the (Dutch-language) website of the Landelijk Informatiecentrum voor Gezelschapsdieren (National Information Center for Pets) at www.licg.nl. Click on *Reizen en vakantie*, *Invoereisen per land – Europa*, then on *Een dier meenemen naar Nederland (Bringing an animal to the Netherlands).* On this page, you can click on www.nvwa.nl/onderwerpen/huisdieren-en-reizen, for step-by-step advice on importing your pet (in Dutch).

ADVICE ON ANIMAL TRANSFER

A professional organization such as KLM Cargo, specialists in animal transfer, can inform you on all regulations, provide you with helpful travel tips for your pet and arrange suitable transportation for your animal. They also operate a 24 hour-a-day animal hotel at the Schiphol Airport (their website and phone number can be found at the end of the chapter). KLM Cargo transports a wide variety of animals and if you have an animal they don't transport, they will likely be able to inform on you whom to contact for the transportation of other animals. Else contact the airline you will be traveling with. Or visit www.klm.com, click on *Information*, and then on *Travelling with Pets*.

IDENTIFICATION AND REGISTRATION

In order to simplify the identification and registration of pets in case of loss or theft, identification microchips can be easily implanted by a veterinarian. The site www.stichtingchip.nl (which also has English-language pages) makes it possible to find information on where the lost animal is. The sites ndg.nl, www.chipjedier and www.licg can provide you with more information.

ANIMAL BOARDING

Though you love your animals and have brought them all the way here, traveling back and forth may not be something you wish to subject them to on too regular a basis. Should you be leaving the country on vacation (or for work) you might wish them the same comfort and care that you hope to enjoy during your trip. Look online under *dierenpension* to find a list of 'animal hotels' (a *hondenpension* is specifically for dogs, a *kattenpension* for cats). There is no surefire way to find out whether you can expect your family pet to be happy there – the best you can do is visit the place itself to discuss your (animal's) needs, check out the conditions and see whether you have a good feeling about the place and the owner in general. Maybe a trial run over a weekend will give you some peace of mind.

GARDENS AND CURTAINS

Ask the Belgians what they find typical of the homes of their Northern Neighbors and they will mention two things. One is their gardens, and the other is their curtains. In Belgium, family life is for the family: there are virtually no front yards (the garden is in the back) and huge, no-nonsense blinds go down as soon as the first lights go on inside the house.

Not so the Dutch. The Dutch are very proud of their gardens, be they postage stamp-size or park-size – particularly their front yards, as these are what everyone sees. They love a cozy (*gezellig*) neighborhood with flowers, flowering bushes, little rock gardens and – yes – the occasional garden gnome or even windmill. It is not without reason that Dutch flower bulbs are exported all across the world and that the hub of the world's flower industry is near Schiphol Airport: the Netherlands is where the flowering heart of the world beats.

The neighborhoods in the Netherlands can look very prim and proper: there are special rules about not building too many different types of houses in one street (this is of course different in the very expensive areas, where the houses are so far apart – if they are even visible – that no one really cares). So what you get is a row of well-kept, dime-a-dozen houses, with picture-perfect front yards and... uncurtained windows.

If you take an evening stroll after sunset, you get a chance to admire family life, Dutch style. Grandma and Grandpa are sitting behind a steaming cup of coffee, savoring their evening ration of one cookie. Or the parents are reading a magazine, with one of their teenage children surreptitiously eyeing the TV over their homework. Or the living room is empty and upstairs you see one parent dressing baby on the dressing table, while the other is chasing their three-year-old from room to room. Later in the evening, Moms and Dads will settle down to their well-deserved cup of coffee – still to be admired through open curtains. Only once they go to bed, will the curtains downstairs be closed. For those of you who were wondering: bedroom curtains are always closed once the lights go on.

The Dutch do not feel self-conscious about what goes on behind their front door and feel comfortable with their curtains open. The rule of Dutch behavior is *doe maar gewoon, dan doe je gek genoeg* – act normal and you will be acting crazy enough. What this boils down to, basically, is modesty. Act modest, live modestly: do not buy expensive cars, do not have any airs, decorate your home simply, and don't do anything I wouldn't do. If you close your curtains, you probably have something to hide. Which is why many Dutch families leave their curtains open: so that everyone can see for themselves; look, we are 'normal'.

THE MEDIA

THE PRINTED MEDIA

In the Netherlands, there are 30 daily newspapers – nine nationwide and 21 regional – each with its own editorial staff and amounting to a daily total of 4 million papers. The six major *nationwide* newspapers (there are a few regional newspapers whose number of subscribers exceeds those of some of the larger nationwide papers) in the Netherlands are *De Telegraaf*, *De Volkskrant*, the AD, *NRC Handelsblad* (*NRC* also has a morning paper, *NRC.Next*, for a younger public), *Trouw*, and the Protestant *Reformatorisch Dagblad*. Popular among those who are active in the business world is the *Financieele Dagblad*, which has economic news and stock market analyses. These numbers do not include online subscriptions (you can find the websites at the end of the chapter), which are usually the number of subscribers multiplied by five and which are growing quickly. Almost 11 million people over the age of 13 (occasionally or regularly) read a newspaper in the Netherlands; 76% of them only a printed version and 4% only digital – the rest read both. Investing on average 30 minutes in reading one on weekdays and 45 minutes per day in the weekend, 56% of readers read more than three-quarters of the paper, whereby the *AD*, *De Telegragf*, and De *Volkskrant* receive the most attention, and the older age group reads more. Most newspapers go to the age group 35-64 (50%), followed by those age 65 and more (28%) and those age 13-34 (22%).

As mentioned above, there are many regional newspapers, which can provide you with important information on what is going on in your region. And if you want to know what is going on in your town, you can take out a subscription to the local town paper. The Netherlands also has many magazines (distribution approximately 9.5 million); for art lovers, computer fanatics, travelers, feminists, men, children, animal lovers, garden lovers and just about any other type of hobby. Do not despair, however, that you will have to wait until you speak Dutch before you can read about what is going on in the world, as sometimes even in the smallest towns you will find such magazines as *Newsweek*, *Time Magazine*, *The Economist*, *The Financial Times* as well as the newspapers *El País*, *The International New York Times*, and more (such as German, Italian, Turkish, French magazines and newspapers, to name a few).

The subscription-free newspaper, *Metro*, no longer makes printed editions, but the website still exists.

TELEVISION AND RADIO

Dutch television will also not present much of a problem as it is subtitled, leaving all foreign movies, series and other programs in their original language. The Netherlands has a plethora of television channels to choose from available through cable, including British, Belgian, French, Spanish, German, Italian and Turkish television as well as CNN (news) and MTV (music) – but keep in mind that the cable package available depends on where you live.

The main Dutch broadcasting companies are: TROS (general), VARA (social-democratic), AVRO (general), NCRV (Protestant), KRO (Catholic), VPRO (progressive), BNN (general, young audience), Talpa (which owns companies such as SBS6 and Veronica) and EO (evangelical Christian) who all work together in the NOS (Nether-

Post Offices a Thing of the Past

This country's last remaining post offices closed in 2012. Mail services are now carried out under the banner of PostNL and are offered through post office ticket windows in regular stores, such as bookstores, tobacco stores, and supermarkets. These services also include paperwork services, such as the issuing of fishing licenses, vehicle registration cards, and recharging your public transportation pass. Full-time mail delivery jobs no longer exist either; the work is now carried out by a team of cheaper flex workers. For more information, for instance to find out where you can buy stamps near you, visit www.postnl.nl.

In order to cut costs, PostNL has also removed more than half of the existing mailboxes, leaving 8,700 across the country. The number of stores offering mail services is being brought back from 2,500 to 1,000.

lands Broadcasting Corporation). The fact that these companies have a certain denomination does not mean that you will watch solely Catholic programs on the KRO, or social-democratic programs on the VARA: these denominations are to be considered from where the broadcasting company originated and dictate only a percentage of the types of program you will see (with the exception of the EO, whose character is most clearly noticeable in the type of programs it broadcasts). In fact, some of them have merged to form KRO-NCRV, AVROTROS, and BNN-VARA. The broadcasting companies share broadcasting time on NPO 1, 2 and 3, but there are more Dutch channels, such as RTL 4, RTL 5, RTL 7, RTL 8, RTL Z, Net 5, SBS 6, SBS 9, Veronica/Disney, and FOX, which mainly broadcast popular (often U.S. or U.K.-purchased) programs. For more viewing pleasure there is Discovery Channel, National Geographic, Animal Planet, MTV, CNN and EuroSport, as well as the international channels mentioned above. Children's programming is available daily from 7 A.M. on several of the Dutch channels as well as on Nickelodeon, Ketnet / Canvas (Belgium) and on BBC 2. For an overview of what's on, go to www.tvgids.nl. If 60 channels is not enough, or you cannot be connected to the cable lines because you bought a farm house way out in the middle of nowhere, then, of course, you can solve this problem by purchasing a satellite dish or digitenne (for both, see further on). Satellite TV will bring you many more international channels, as well as movie channels – though increasingly these are becoming available through cable TV as well.

Furthermore, the Netherlands has several national and regional radio stations, but the fun thing is, of course, that certainly when it comes to radio, you can listen to broadcasts from just about anywhere in the world.

KIJKWIJZER

The NICAM or Netherlands Institute for the Classification of Audiovisual Media has developed the *kijkwijzer* (whose principle is *weet wat je ziet* or know what you see), a system using pictograms to rate the content of films, DVDs, television programs, and computer games. The picture symbols indicate violence, sex, fear, discrimination, drug and alcohol misuse, and rough language. Also shown are age limit recommendations of AL (all ages), MG6 (watch with children under 6), 12 (not younger) and 16 (not younger). Any media items (including games) with a 16 year-advice should not be sold to minors under 16, and movie theaters may refuse entrance to those who appear to fall outside the age category.

For more information, visit www.kijkwijzer.nl and view the icons or pictograms.

AL	All ages		Fear
6	Caution with children under 6		Sex
12	Caution with children under 12		Discrimination
16	Caution with children under 16		Drugs and alcohol abuse
	Violence		Coarse Language

BEING CONNECTED

STARTING YOUR TELEPHONE SERVICE

With mobile phones solidly planted in our hands, facilitating automatic debits and habits, the number of people using fixed telephone lines has been steadily decreasing. At the start of 2022, there were 23.9 million mobile phone connections, through which 11.4 billion call minutes were placed, and 5 million landline connections, through which 1.7 billion call minutes were placed. Many households don't even have landlines anymore, making the distinction between fixed-line telephony and mobile telephony feel somewhat archaic. However, for purposes of this *Holland Handbook*, we will nonetheless focus on the two topics separately, as – for instance – some of the cheap calling options only work through a fixed line.

SUBSCRIPTION

Almost all telephone companies offer a combination of a fixed phone line, Internet and TV – KPN is the only one that offers the option of choosing a fixed line-only subscriptions. Generally speaking, you have two options for a fixed-line subscription; either you pay – at the end of the month – for the actual amount of time you called, or you pay a fixed amount for unlimited calling, within the Netherlands or within the EU. The former option includes a fixed charge per (mobile of landline) call, plus the number of seconds, whereby they charge more for calls made to mobile phones. The latter option does not include a charge per call, but might seem more expensive – and with some companies, the fixed rate only includes calls made to landlines.

To arrange payment of your bills, you can provide the company with your bank account number and they will automatically deduct the payment every month.

OTHER CHEAP CALLING OPTIONS

0900 Access Numbers: One option is to make use of 0900 access numbers: for instance, you dial 0900, followed by the country's so-called service number. Once you have connected to this number, you dial the country code, followed by the person's telephone number. You do not have to register to make use of this option, but you should verify that you have not blocked the use of 0900-numbers (which some people do, as they also provide access to more dubious – and expensive – options). The costs of making this type of call are a connection rate and a per-minute fee, or really per second, as minutes are not rounded off. Before being put through to the person you are calling, you will automatically be informed of the rate for this call – a service for which you are not charged. Visit www.televergelijk.nl for up-to-date information on the most attractive 0900-providers per country that you want to call. You can also make use of the Bel0900-app for mobile phones.

Other access numbers: You can also dial a local number, for which you are charged a local rate (or, if you have taken out a subscription that allows unlimited calling within the Netherlands for a fixed fee per month; the call is included in the fee). Once you have dialed this number, you enter your personal code, after which they tell you how many cents you will be paying for the connection (just a few cents). Once you have completed this process, you dial the number you want to dial abroad. This service is not available for all countries, but if it is, this means the entire call, no mat-

ter how long, will cost you no more than the connection fee of a few cents.

Carrier (Pre)Select: With Carrier PreSelect, you dial 16xy (representing the two digits of the carrier) and then the number of the person you want to call. You then call via a fixed (not mobile) KPN line, but the calls are put through and charged by another carrier, which offers you cheaper rates. With Select, your call is immediately made through the other carrier – you do, however, still make use of the KPN lines, dialing 16xy first. More information can be found on www.bellen.com/veelgestelde-vragen/carrier-preselect-goedkoper-bellen.

Call cards: These cards can be purchased at supermarkets, kiosks, telephone stores, and online. You scratch off a protective layer from the card to reveal your access code, which you enter after calling a computer free or at local rates, followed by the number you want to call. More information can be found (in Dutch) on www.prepaidsimkaart.net/telefoonkaart.

MORE CHEAP CALLING

In some places, it is possible to make phone calls over the wireless WiFi-net, while retaining your own number and telephone. This way you can call anywhere in the Netherlands at local rates and in the rest of the world at *very* cheap rates. Or, you just call over Whatsapp or FaceTime, using your mobile phone – for free.

Furthermore, Skype and VoipBuster allow you to make free telephone calls to another Skype, etc.-user (also abroad), via your computer – or, for a small fee, to a fixed or mobile telephone (visit www.skype.com or www.voipbuster.com for more information or to download the software needed). For more information on calling via the Internet, visit www.bellen.com. Be sure to also check out those carriers that offer VoIP calling: for more information, visit www.voipkiezen.nl.

SOCIAL MEDIA

Ninety-six percent of those living in the Netherlands makes use of social media. The following user numbers illustrate the use of social media in 2023, in the Netherlands:

- Whatsapp: 13.3 million
- Facebook: 9.9 million
- Youtube: 9.9 million
- Instagram: 7.8 million
- LinkedIn: 5 million
- Pinterest: 4.6 million
- TikTok: 4 million
- Snapchat: 3.9 million
- X: 3.1 million
- BeReal 0.8 million.

The increase in the use of social media has particularly been given a boost by the 65+ age category. There are even several social media enthusiasts in the 80+ age group, 59% of whom use Facebook (probably to see what's going on in their grandchildren's lives in an unobtrusive way) – though Facebook is no longer very popular among the younger generations. Also Whatsapp is consistently gaining in popularity among those aged 65 and older; free phone calls are always attractive.

MOBILE TELEPHONES

Despite its relatively modest size, the Netherlands has a high number of mobile operators, with four major players, and several smaller ones. This makes the mobile phone market highly fluid and sometimes a bit confusing, what with the numerous special promotions and mobile telephone options. Only KPN, Odido and Vodafone have their own network; all other companies use one of these three networks.

CHOOSING A MOBILE PHONE SERVICE

There are several criteria that are important to consider when choosing a mobile phone service. The total number of minutes per month that you use, the amount of data you will need to satisfy your mobile Internet needs, and the need for additional services such as voicemail, SMS text messages, calling long distance, and using the mobile phone when abroad. Depending on your needs, you will use one of the following three possibilities:

- subscription services with a contract, which includes a certain number of minutes that you can call, text messages you can send, and data. You receive a monthly bill (for the subscription and, if you have exceeded your contractual number of minutes, a fee for these minutes). Subscription services will charge an initial connection fee, but there are many special offers available aimed at attracting new customers – so shop around
- a pre-pay service based on buying a card with call units and no subscription fee. You can read more about this below.
- sim-only; you buy your own mobile phone (make sure it's simlock-free; *simlock-vrij!*) and take out a 'sim-only' subscription, which means that you are sent a sim-card, without an accompanying mobile phone. This can be a financially quite attractive option. To compare rates, visit www.bellen.com/vergelijken/sim-only.

Virtually all the mobile phone operators cover the entire country. For an overview of these providers, and to help you make your choice, we advise you to visit www.bellen.com. Be sure not to miss the smaller, less-profiled companies that offer financially attractive pre-pay and/or subscription services. You will also find a list of websites at the end of the chapter.

Most consumers make use of the service providers of these network operators, however, there is also Ortel Mobile, where you can obtain a pre-paid sim-card without needing a contract, allowing you to make use of the KPN-network.

PRE-PAID CALLING

This is a popular choice among Dutch users, particularly young people. One reason is that the pre-pay phone allows users to pay for their calls in advance, and thus avoid subscription fees and hefty unexpected bills. They are cheap, convenient and provide enough coverage for most Dutch users in the Netherlands.

Each pre-pay phone will only be suitable for that particular network, for example, if you buy an Odido phone, you are restricted to using that phone and buying call units for the Odido network. However, the networks are so extensive and so many agreements have been reached with other companies (abroad), that you will likely experience very little hinder in making local calls, or receiving calls from, abroad – see further on in *Free to Roam?*

Pre-pay cards can be bought at a variety of locations, such as supermarkets and drugstores, as well as the brand-specific stores. For more on the various packages offered by the mobile phone companies, visit their websites, as they are continually subject to change.

BUYING A MOBILE PHONE

If you are buying a (subscription, pre-pay or sim-lock free) mobile phone, you can do this at the larger department stores, electronic

chains, brand stores, non-brand telephone (subscription) stores, or, simply, via the Internet. It is always worth your while to shop around, as both the brand stores and the non-brand stores may offer certain reductions and other special promotions. Most mobile phone companies include a 'free' mobile phone in their subscription package. For more expensive models, you can choose between buying a mobile phone outright through the phone company, or spreading the payment of the mobile phone over the term of the subscription. When opting for the latter, you can choose which amount you wish to pay straight away for the phone and which amount you want to pay in installments.

Be sure to bring your passport / driver's license and proof (such as a bank statement) of your most current address (and sometimes income) if you are planning on buying a mobile phone with a subscription in a store.

SWITCHING

Once you have chosen a particular mobile phone company for your phone with subscription, you are not stuck for life. You can switch companies and even keep your own phone number. Check with your company to see what the rules are (on giving notice and over what period), if you are not yet sure which one to go for. The same goes for pre-pay phones, whereby you can also switch from pre-pay to subscription and vice versa. In most cases, the phone company that you are planning on switching to, arranges the switch. You wait for a message from them that they have completed the switch and they terminate your contract with your former provider.

FREE TO ROAM?

From the expat's perspective, perhaps the most important issue is being able to make and receive calls in other countries. Through international 'roaming' agreements, cellular operators allow foreign operators to use their networks so that they have broader international coverage. Also, mobile telephone companies increasingly have their own international network, allowing you to call from wherever you are, simply using their network, whether it be by pre-pay or subscription. Unsurprisingly, the cost of using a mobile for international and overseas calling can be high – though this is no longer the case within the EU. Any call made – while abroad – on an EU mobile phone subscription to another EU country, will cost the same as a local call. However, any call made abroad from the country where the subscription has been taken out, still comes at a stiff margin. In other words, if you have a Dutch subscription, it is cheaper to call Holland from Spain, than Spain from Holland.

Whereas before, travelers were challenged by the incompatibility of mobile phones and networks, this is largely no longer an issue. If you are faced with this problem, keep in mind that some mobile phone companies offer the possibility of placing the SIM-card (containing your phone's memory, including your own phone number) of your Dutch mobile phone in a phone that will work in the other country – this can be done at the Airport Telecom at Schiphol Airport (www.airporttelecom.nl, also for satellite phones) or you can visit www.onesimcard.com. Visit these sites for other options as well.

If you want to keep things simple, you can also just buy or rent a cheap pre-pay phone in your country of destination if you travel frequently to a particular country, while many cell phone companies offer e-sim cards for those who have a double-sim cell phone. Via www.airporttelecom.nl you can also order a prepaid sim-card, which you can use in the Netherlands, or one that you can use in the Netherlands and the rest of Europe. Prepaid (data) sim cards are also available. This is particularly convenient for family and friends, who will be staying with you for a while.

MOBILE PHONE TECHNOLOGIES

As the technology and the possibilities offered by the various mobile telephone companies are continuously changing, we recommend that you visit the various mobile phone company websites to see what they have to offer.

MOBILE PHONE USE IN THE CAR

You may not use a mobile phone while driving unless you are using a hands-free device. Nor can you use on while riding a bicycle. You can read more about this on page 167.

INTERNET SERVICE PROVIDERS AND CONNECTIVITY

As mentioned earlier, the number of fixed telephone lines in the Netherlands is decreasing, while 93% of Dutch people have a smart phone. Almost 98.7% of all Dutch people had either a desktop or a laptop as well as access to the Internet, whereby an increasing amount of connections to the Internet takes place via a laptop or some other device (such as a tablet or mobile phone; in fact 82% of those who access the Internet use a laptop and 64% of them a tablet). In the 12-25 age category, 99.8% have access to Internet, in the age category 65 or older, this is 86.4%.

In short, the Netherlands is connected: 96% of the Dutch population is active on social media, whereby the numbers are increasing even among those older than 80. Internet is used for obtaining information, for joining political / societal discussions and for communicating – 95% of all communication via the Internet involves e-mail. So it is only logical that all companies offering television and telephony services focus on offering Internet services as well – or else they would be missing out on a lot of the action! At least the four largest Dutch cable companies offer digital TV and high-speed Internet services to their subscribers now and have considerably expanded services, including discounted telephony. Also certain telephone companies offer Internet, television and telephone services via cable – please check their websites, or visit www.prijsvergelijken.nl, www.providercheck.nl, or www.breed-

bandwinkel.nl for more information. One of the more interesting services they offer is that of being able to create your own website and/or customized e-mail addresses – so if that is something that is of interest to you, be sure to check out what is on offer.

TELEVISION

DENSELY CABLED / DIGITAL

The Dutch watch an average of 160 minutes of TV a day – though more and more do this on a tablet or their phone and more and more make use of the option of watching a program at a different moment than the actual broadcast. In fact, while among those age 65 and older, the average number of TV minutes is 270 and among those younger than 20, this is less than an hour, this trend is reversed when it comes to online and on-demand (video and TV) watching. Nonetheless, though more than 3 million people watch TV online, the use of Netflix, YouTube and social media still does not exceed 'regular' TV.

The number of TV connections via digital cable is going down, due to the introduction of glass fiber and the increased popularity of broadband internet. Caiway, Delta, Ziggo, KPN, Online.nl, and Odido are the largest providers, though not necessarily the cheapest – so *do* do some online shopping before making any choices, as also mobile subscription providers such as Odido and Telfort offer TV packages, online.

For only approximately € 35 a month, you can already watch 60 digital channels (though there are 290 on offer in the Netherlands!), making access is so cheap that you probably won't even know that you're paying for it. If you opt for Internet and TV, you pay anywhere between € 30 and € 55, depending on the options you choose: watching missed programs, TV on your tablet, being able to pause your program, multiple TVs, On Demand Films, etc. An excellent overview of the various providers and their packages can be found on www.prijsvergelijken.nl and clicking on *Internet pakketten*.

While consumers may assume that this means they have no choice if they are not happy with their service and that they are at the whim of the cable companies, this is not the case; consumers are protected by heavy regulations.

DIGITAL TV

Currently, there are five ways to receive a digital TV signal; via cable, ether, the Internet (IP, it requires an ADSL-connection), via satellite or via "free digital internet" (the latter is explained in more detail on www.internetten.nl). The option of receiving your signal via the ether (digitenne – https://digitenne.kpn.com) allows you to place a simple receiver in your windowsill, tent, or car, and watch TV anywhere you like.

For more on who is on the market, what they are offering, and what is available where you live, visit www.overstappen.nl/internet or www.prijsvergelijken.nl.

EXPANDED SERVICES

Over the years, the standard number of channels available to the cable TV subscriber has jumped to around 60. As mentioned earlier, there are now ready-made interactive capabilities and expanded channel options available through digital TV, as well as high-speed Internet and local and long-distance telephony. For more channels, you might want to consider installing a satellite on your roof; see further on.

ADSL AND BROADBAND

The providers of ADSL high-speed Internet can be found on www.breedbandwinkel.nl (type in your postal code, and it will tell you what is available in your area).

The list of those offering high-speed capabilities is ever-changing, so rather than list the ones that can be found at the time of typing this contribution, we recommend that you visit above site.

FAST-MOVING INDUSTRY

Once again; this is a fast-moving industry and, as this book appears only once a year, we have found ourselves limited to describing the situation as it was in the fourth quarter of 2023. For more up-to-date information, we advise you to call the cable net-companies or visit their websites, which you will find at the end of the chapter.

THE ALTERNATIVE: SATELLITE TV / IPTV

If you do not have cable (by choice or because you live in a remote area) or want to see channels not available through cable, you can opt for satellite TV. This involves finding an electronics store or other distributor who sells satellite dishes, and arranging for its installation. Canaldigitaal offers an impressive range of channels (more than 400), which you can receive by making use of a special decoder. For an additional charge, you can choose from several other packages (Basis, Family, Entertainment, etc.).

Visit www.canaldigitaal.nl for more information on – and to order – the equipment necessary for hooking up to them.

An IPtv allows you to watch up to 1,000 different channels, without the need for a satellite – more information can be found on www.mediaboxkopen.nl/iptv-kopen/.

References

CHAPTER 7
Daily Life

Safety

NATIONAL EMERGENCY NUMBER: 112

TO CONTACT THE POLICE
Emergencies, tel.: 112
Central National Police Information Number, tel.: 0900 8844
Report Crime Anonymously, tel.: 0800 7000 (free of charge)
www.politie.nl

TO CONTACT THE FIRE DEPARTMENT
Emergencies, tel.: 112
No emergency, tel.: 0900 0904
Amsterdam, tel.: 020 555 66 66
Rotterdam, tel.: 088 877 9000
The Hague, tel.: 088 886 8000
Utrecht, tel.: 088 878 1000
General website: www.brandweer.nl

AMBULANCE
Emergencies, tel.: 112

News in Dutch

MAIN DUTCH NEWSPAPERS
Algemeen Dagblad: www.ad.nl
De Telegraaf: www.detelegraaf.nl
De Volkskrant: www.volkskrant.nl
NRC Handelsblad: www.nrc.nl
Het Parool: www.parool.nl
Trouw: www.trouw.nl

MAIN DUTCH NEWS WEBSITES
www.nieuws.nl
www.nu.nl
http://nos.nl/nieuws

Dutch News in English

Dutchnews.nl
English-language daily news from business and politics to sport. Plus features, opinion and debate
www.dutchnews.nl

Dutchreview
www.dutchreview.com

Net In Nederland
Dutch tv-programs all subtitled In Dutch, English and Arabic
www.netinnederland.nl

Telecom

MAIN MOBILE TELEPHONE SERVICE PROVIDERS
Ben: www.ben.nl
Hollandsnieuwe: www.hollandsnieuwe.nl
KPN Mobile: www.kpn.com
Odido: www.odido.nl
Vodafone: www.vodafone.nl
Lebara: www.mobile.lebara.com
Youfone: www.youfone.nl
Simyo: www.simyo.nl

MOBILE PHONE COMPARISON WEBSITES
Bellen.com: www.bellen.com
Consumentenbond:
www.consumentenbond.nl
Prijsvergelijken.nl: www.prijsvergelijken.nl

MAIN INTERNET PROVIDERS
Budget Thuis: www.budgetthuis.nl
KPN: www.kpn.com
Odido: www.odido.nl
Online: www.online.nl
Tele 2: www.tele2.nl
XS4ALL: www.xs4all.nl
Ziggo: www.ziggo.nl

INTERNET / CABLE TV / TELEPHONE COMPARISON WEBSITES
Breedbandwinkel.nl:
www.breedbandwinkel.nl
Internetvergelijk.nl: www.internetvergelijk.nl
Pricewise.nl: www.pricewise.nl/internet/providers
Prijsvergelijken.nl: www.prijsvergelijken.nl
Telecomproviders.nl:
www.telecomproviders.nl

Pets

ANIMAL AMBULANCE
www.dierenambulance.nl
Tel.: 0900 0245

LOST PETS
To report lost animals
www.amivedi.nl
Tel.: 0900 264 83 34

TO (CHIP)REGISTRATE PETS
Nederlandse Databank Gezelschapsdieren (NDG)
Tel.: 0900 404 04 56
www.ndg.nl

EUROPEAN PET NETWORK
www.europetnet.com

PET MOVING SERVICES
Air Animal: www.airanimal.com
Air Pets Oceanic: www.airpets.com
Animal Transport Europe:
www.animaltransporteurope.com
Animals to Fly: www.animalstofly.com
Flying Dutch Pets: www.flyingdutchpets.com
International Pet and Animal Transportation Association: www.ipata.org
Zoologistics: www.zoologistics.com

Shops for Products from Home

KELLY'S EXPAT SHOPPING
Ferdinand Bolstraat 139, 1072 LG Amsterdam
Tel.: 020 773 12 77
Zoutmanstraat 22a, 2518 GP The Hague
Tel.: 070 346 97 53
Luifelbaan 50, 2242 KV Wassenaar
Tel.: 070 511 87 29
Nachtegaalstraat 9 HJ, 3581 AA Utrecht
Tel.: 030 2687917
Pannekoekstraat 72-74, 3011 LK Rotterdam
Tel.: 06 255 46 907

www.kellys-expat-shopping.nl

Online Shops for Products from Home

British Cornershop:
www.britishcornershop.co.uk
The English Shop: www.english-shop.com
Kelly's Expat Shop:
www.kellys-expat-shopping.nl

Typical Dutch Products

Typical Dutch Stuff:
www.typicaldutchstuff.com
Dutch Expat Shop: www.dutchexpatshop.com
Holland For You: www.hollandforyou.com
Holland Food Shop: www.hollandfood.shop

Dutch Selling and Buying Websites

Marktplaats: www.marktplaats.nl
Facebook Marktplaats: https://nl-nl.facebook.com/Marktplaats

Recommended Reading

DUTCH COOKBOOK
By Laura de Grave
Published by Uitgeverij Brandt
If you think that the Netherlands is the ultimate underdog when it comes to all things culinary, think again!
www.bol.com

DUTCH DELIGHT
Text by Sylvia Pessiron
Photography by Jurjen Drenth & friends
Published by Nilsson & Lamm
Learn what the Dutch eat and drink, graze through their eating habits and recipes, and when you're done, try them.
www.dutchshop.nl

STUFF DUTCH PEOPLE EAT
By Colleen Geske
A comprehensive celebration of Dutch cuisine
www.stuffdutchpeoplelike.com

THE NEW DUTCH CUISINE
Text by Albert Kooy
Photography by Pieter Ouddeken
Published by KM Publishers
This basic cookbook offers possible guidelines for the contemporary cook.
www.kmuitgevers.nl

ONLINE BOOKSHOPS
www.abc.nl
www.amazon.nl
www.bol.com
www.hollandbooks.nl
www.libris.nl

Bookstores for English-Language Books

THE AMERICAN BOOK CENTER
Spui 12, 1012 XA Amsterdam
Tel.: 020 625 55 37
Lange Poten 23, 2511 CM The Hague
Tel.: 070 364 27 42
www.abc.nl

BESTSELLER
with 4 shops in Amsterdam
Clercqstraat 46
Kinkerstraat 135
Ferdinand Bolstraat 115
Amstelveenseweg 212
www. bestselleronline.nl

WATERSTONES BOOKSELLERS
Kalverstraat 152, 1012 XE Amsterdam
Tel.: 020 638 38 21
www.waterstones.com

THE ENGLISH BOOKSTORE
Passage 24, 2511 AD The Hague
Tel.: 070 302 81 10
www.devriesvanstockum.nl/nl/english-bookstore-den-haag

NEW ENGLISH BOOKSTORE
Kalverstraat 223, 1012 XC Amsterdam

Public Libraries

General: www.bibliotheek.nl
Rotterdam: www.bibliotheek.rotterdam.nl
Amsterdam: www.oba.nl
The Hague: www.bibliotheekdenhaag.nl
Utrecht: www.bibliotheek-utrecht.nl

Children are very important members of the expat population, as the success of a placement abroad depends largely on whether the children (the family as a whole) manage to feel at home in their new country. Luckily, the Netherlands is probably one of the smoothest countries to ease into. There are a lot of fun attractions, parks, activities and other sources of entertainment, several child-friendly festivities and plenty to stimulate the curious mind of the child, and perhaps one of the most charming aspects; children still come together to play outdoors here. Read on through this chapter to learn about day care, the Child Benefit, parental leave, birthday parties, Sinterklaas, shopping, general entertainment and a host of other subjects.

CHAPTER 8

Kids

CONTRIBUTING AUTHORS STEPHANIE DIJKSTRA

DAY CARE

The Dutch government is keen on keeping women in the work force, yet the demand for day care far outweighs availability, particularly in the western part of the country. Though the number of children going to day care has been decreasing (fewer births, other alternatives), waiting lists remain long in certain areas, and the average waiting time is three months, so we advise you to register early on (preferably as soon as you are pregnant) if you live in one of the bigger cities.

Kinderopvang is the general term used in Dutch to cover child care. In the following paragraphs, you will find a brief description of the various options available to you as a (working) parent. Each type of *opvang* has its own approach, yet it might be reassuring to know that every municipality has a legal obligation to ensure that minimum rules regarding the following issues are implemented: hygiene, safety, size of groups, sleeping space, toys, insurance, and sick children (they must stay home).

KINDERDAGVERBLIJF

Kinderdagverblijf, or *crèche*, is a cross between a day care center and nursery school and is available for children between the ages of 0 and 4 (infants as of six weeks). Over 1 million children currently make use of the various types of day care available in the Netherlands, though with the rising prices of *kinderopvang*, parents are increasingly going in search of cheaper alternatives – all of which are listed in this chapter as well. Drop-off time is between 8 and 8:30 A.M., pick-up time between 5:30 and 6 P.M., while some centers offer more flexible hours; even 24 hours non-stop. You can place your child there for a number of mornings and/or afternoons a week (called *dagdelen*; day portions) or for a full week, if necessary. Some of the *kinderdagverblijven* also have arrangements for older children (until the age of 12) for pre and after-school hours and school holidays.

Finding a Kinderdagverblijf

One of the largest day care organizations in the Netherlands, Partou (www.partou.nl), offers more than 300 day care centers across the country and – for your convenience – has English-language web pages.

Cost

Fees vary from municipality to municipality, from one day care center to another and of course depending on whether you receive a subsidized spot. On average, you pay approximately € 988 per two full days per month. The maximum government subsidy (*kinderopvangtoeslag*, see further on) you will receive is € 10.25 per hour (2024), for a maximum of 230 hours per month, per child. The actual amount depends on your income. If you earn € 100,000 a year, you will end up paying € 522 yourself; if you earn € 25,000, you will end up paying € 148 yourself. Any hours exceeding the 230-hour maximum will be paid for fully by you.

See the following paragraph on government subsidy. Visit www.rekentoolkinderopvang.nl or www.partou.nl to calculate what your approximate expenses and subsidy will be.

Regulations and Subsidy

Parents who place their children in day care, receive an income-independent and an income-dependent contribution, the amount of which also depends on the number of children and the actual costs of the day care or after-school care for elementary-aged children. The amount you receive is determined by the number of months the parent who worked the least, worked – presumably based on the assumption that this parent will be home to take care of the children the rest of the time. The employer is obligated to contribute in the costs of the income-independent portion, but you *receive* the contribution from the tax authorities. Parents receive the income-dependent contribution from the government. Together, this is referred to as *kinderopvangtoeslag*.

To arrange it, you visit www.toeslagen.nl, click on *kinderopvangtoeslag* and follow the instructions. If you have already arranged the *toeslag*, it will automatically be extended. If there are any changes in your situation – moving in together, marriage, divorce, more or fewer children in day care, a change in income or in bank account number, etc. – you have to notify the tax authorities on this same site. Check the website of the tax authorities (www.belastingdienst.nl): subject to conditions, you can receive *kinderopvangtoeslag* if you live abroad (under *Toeslagen, Kinderopvangtoeslag*, Wonen of werken in het buitenland (living or working abroad).

To qualify for *kinderopvangtoeslag*, you and your partner must meet the following requirements (always check for legislative changes and additional options):

- you have Dutch nationality, or legally reside in the Netherlands
- you have one or more children registered at your address for whom you receive *kinderbijslag* (see page 212), a foster parent contribution, or whom you largely support financially
- the day care center your child attends (be it day care, after school care, or a host family) is registered with the municipality in which it is located as an acknowledged organization, to which purpose it must be meet certain criteria. If they are indeed regis-

tered, they will have been issued a statement saying so – so be sure to ask to see it. You can also visit the website of the National Register for *kinderopvang* (www.landelijkregisterkinderopvang.nl) to verify whether the day care center is registered there
- you have entered into a written agreement with the facility offering *kinderopvang*
- the child does not yet attend middle or high school
- you or your partner pay(s) for the day care; you have to be able to demonstrate this
- you, and your partner if you have one, earn income from (self-) employment and pay tax over this income (some exceptions allowed), or
- you receive a benefit that includes the right to a contribution by the municipality towards the day care payments. This is the case, for instance, if you are: rejoining the labor market after a long period of time (combined with either a benefit or a registration with the Center for Work and Income); a student; (as above) following a cultural familiarization course (*inburgeringscursus*), etc.

Under certain conditions, you might still receive kinderopvangtoeslag when you're not working: visit www.belastingdienst.nl, and look under *Toeslagen, Kinderopvangtoeslag*, Kan ik kinderopvangtoeslag krijgen als ik niet werk? (Can I receive kinderopvangtoeslag if I don't have a job?).

PEUTERSPEELZALEN (TODDLER GROUPS)

Peuterspeelzalen are toddler groups for children age 2 – 4 and are usually open in the mornings although some municipalities now offer afternoon programs. Technically speaking, the *peuterspeelzaal* is not a day care facility and should be seen more as a preschool facility, especially since opening hours are limited. Often, they are liaised with (and on the same premises as) a primary school, which allows an easy transition from the *speelzaal* to the school. There are approximately 15 children in a group to two teachers. Typically, children are accepted two or three fixed mornings per week. You will find *peuterspeelzalen* in the (online) *gemeentegids* – a guide published by your municipality with useful addresses – or by searching online.

Cost

The cost of sending your child to a *peuterspeelzaal* may be income-indexed. Expect to pay anywhere from € 190 to € 300 per month for two mornings a week. The maximum *kinderopvangtoeslag* for this is also € 10.25 per hour (2024), for a maximum of 230 hours per month, per child. The rules as described above for *kinderdagverblijf* apply to *peuterspeelzaal* care too.

Recognized and registered *peuterspeelzalen* also qualify for employer or government contributions, see the rules explained above.

BUITENSCHOOLSE / NASCHOOLSE OPVANG (AFTER-SCHOOL DAY CARE)

Both the *buitenschoolse opvang* (BSO) as well as the *naschoolse opvang* provide day care during after-school hours and holidays to children between the ages of 4 and 12. The BSO also offers an additional service during pre-school hours. These services are, as you can imagine, in great demand. To find out who provides 'non-school-hour care' near you, visit www.landelijkregisterkinderopvang.nl and fill in the type of care you are looking for under *Kenmerk*. Additional options include: day and night care (single parents with night shifts might benefit from this), and 'teen'-care. Your municipal guide or municipal website will provide you with more information on these options.

Elementary schools are obligated to arrange BSO for their pupils, either on or off-premise. They also offer so-called *tussenschoolse opvang*, or between-school care. This is a fancy word for lunch break. There is no subsidy available to help cover any related costs for this type of care.

Cost

The fee structure is much the same as for the *kinderdagverblijf*. We refer you to our explanation under *Regulations and Subsidy*, on page 205, regarding employer and government contributions. Also here, the rule applies that the organization providing the *buitenschoolse opvang* and *naschoolse opvang* must be registered as an acknowledged organization. This maximum amount of government contribution you can request is € 9.12 (2024) per hour.

GASTOUDER (HOST PARENT) / TEACHER AT HOME

A host parent usually has children of their own and cares for up to six children at their home. In some cases, the *gastouder* will come to your house. Another option is to have a *leidster* (preschool teacher) or *oppas* (sitter, who must meet certain requirements) come to your house.

There appears to be a growing demand for this type of day care. Check online or your (online) *gemeentegids* (municipal guide) under *kinderopvang* to find a *gastouder / leidster / oppas* in your neighborhood. We have included a number of websites at the end of the chapter through which you can arrange a *gastouder / leidster / oppas*; these sites also help you arrange the government contribution to help cover the costs. Word-of-mouth is also a good source of sitters of either type; plenty of excellent sitters are not officially registered, but rely on the mommy network. Also the website www.sitly.nl/en (for English) is a very helpful site, providing you with the opportunity to find other parents in your vicinity to connect and find a child care solution together, or else you can visit www.gastouderland.nl, or www.gobmare.nl.

Cost

The *gastouderbureau / kinderopvang aan huis* maintains strict guidelines regarding fees and responsibilities. The cost of making use of these options is usually income-indexed and currently ranges around € 5.50 to € 13 per hour, depending on the number of children, whether the person in question has experience and whether you expect her (him) to do some (light) household work. Parents can only request a maximum of € 7.53 (2024) government subsidy and this only for *gastouders* who have been entered in a national registry, and they cannot make the payments directly; this has to take place via a *gastouderbureau*. If you want to provide *gastouder* care yourself, visit https://ondernemersplein.kvk.nl/stappenplan-gastouderbureau-starten for tips.

Note!: Sending your child to a *gastouder* or making use of a *leidster / oppas* is also covered by the legislation regarding employer and government contributions as described on page 205. In order for you to qualify for a government contribution, the *gastouder(-bureau) / leidster / oppas* must be officially registered. If you already have a favorite child-sitter, then in order for this person to qualify, he or she has to register with the National Register for *kinderopvang*. To do this, they have to meet the following conditions:

- they must be 18 years of age or older
- they, and anyone they share the home with who is 18 years of age or older, must have a valid Statement of Good Behavior
- they must have a valid EHBO (first aid) for children diploma
- they (and any adults who live on location) must be registered Personenregister Kinderopvang (Registry of persons)
- they must be registered with a bureau that is listed by the Landelijk Register Kinderopvang (Registry of organizations)
- they must follow the *gastouder* bureau's rules on a child psychology, safety & health, and the reporting of domestic violence and child abuse
- they must have a recognized degree or one of the diplomas listed on the Ministry of Education's site (under *diploma's gastouderopvang*). Foreign diplomas must be verified
- they must have a risk inventory carried out for their home.

These, and possible further, conditions can also be found on www.gastouderland.nl.

PARENT PARTICIPATION DAY CARE

Another option is the Parent Participation Day Care (*ouderparticipatiecrèche*); whereby the children rotate among the parents of the group. This is an accepted form of day care according to the day care laws described earlier in this chapter, which means that the parents qualify for government support in the costs, provided the group is registered, recognized and meets certain legal requirements.

Cost

It's hard to predict what the costs will be of this type of care, as it will likely depend on the agreement the parents reach among themselves. The fact that it qualifies for subsidy will probably influence what the parents ultimately agree upon. In order to ensure quality child care, the government has created stricter rules regarding this type of care, such as regarding the type of (child care) diploma the parents have (see above, where the conditions are listed). If these requirements are not met, this type of care will not qualify for subsidy.

AU PAIR

Au pairs in the Netherlands receive room and board and, in exchange, their primary responsibility is child care. In addition, the au pair may be required to help with light housekeeping duties. They must be between 18 and 25 years of age at the time they are invited, be unmarried and not they cannot have any (foster) children. The host family must be made up of at least two persons who are either Dutch or have a valid residence permit for the Netherlands. EU/EEU au pairs do not need a visa, work permit or residence permit. Au pairs from all other countries need a residence permit that will be valid for a maximum of one year and that must be requested by an au pair agency that has been recognized by the IND (Immigration and Naturalization Services). On the IND website, you will find a list of recognized au pair agencies. Further conditions for coming here as an au pair can be found on https://ind.nl/nl/verblijfsvergunningen/au-pair-en-uitwisseling/verblijfsvergunning-au-pair.

Cost

Au pairs receive approximately € 300 – € 350 per month, while the host family is also responsible for covering visa, permit and insurance expenses. Furthermore, you will pay the au pair organization a one-time interview, registration and placement fee. Some organizations also charge a monthly management fee, so be sure to check out several organizations (see the list at the end of the chapter) before signing on the dotted line.

OPPAS (BABY-SITTER)

Planning a quiet evening out with your partner? A neighborhood high school or university student is probably your best bet. Although some communities maintain an *Oppascentrale* (central listing of local baby-sitters and telephone numbers – check online), often the best way to locate a reliable sitter is through your local network or by word-of-mouth, or on www.sitly.nl/en.

Cost

Depending on age, experience and geographic region, fees can range from € 3.50 to € 11 per hour (depending on the age of the sitter and also on the number of children). Other rates apply should you decide to employ a baby-sitter on a permanent basis in your home. In this case, an hourly fee of around € 5 to € 11 is paid for basic childcare responsibilities. Another fee schedule applies if housekeeping duties are also required (approximately € 7 to € 18 per hour).

LESS RUN-OF-THE-MILL OPTIONS

1. *Flexibel Kinderopvang / Kinderdagverblijf (Flexible Child Center)*: This is a type of child care center that is open 24 hours a day, 7 days a week. Some of them qualify for government support. You will find them in the larger cities in the Netherlands. To find one, check your (online) *gemeentegids*. The cost depends entirely on the center, and the number of days / hours that you place your child(ren) there. One full day (7 A.M. – 6:30 P.M. costs approximately € 115, based on a charge of approximately € 11.50 an hour. You can find more information on www.kinderopvang.org/blog/wat-is-flexibele-opvang-kinderdagverblijf/.

2. *Nanny*: Visit www.care.com, www.nannyzoeken.nl, or www.topnanny.nl – for instance.

3. *International (Women's) Clubs*: Many international (women's) clubs have their own Moms and Tots Groups and will be happy to have you join the group. Although this is not, per se, a day care option, it is a great way to meet other parents and to net-

work. For a list of (women's) clubs, see page 276. ACCESS also maintains a list of non-Dutch day care options (toddler playgroups, pre-schools, international day care centers, etc.). You can find their number at the end of the chapter.

PARTY TIME

Life is a party! Here are a few festivities in honor of children:

KRAAMBEZOEK

(Visiting the New-Born Child)
In the Netherlands, when a child is born, you send out announcements (called *geboortekaarten*, or birth cards) to just about anyone you know: 90-year-old aunts, colleagues you haven't seen in five years, uncles you never really liked, your best friend from nursery school. And they all respond! You might end up sending out 150 announcements – but beware! The Dutch interpret this is an invitation to come and admire the little tyke; so be sure you stock up on some *beschuit met muisjes* (rusks covered with sugared aniseeds – pink aniseeds for a girl and blue aniseeds for a boy) as your 90-year-old aunt, ex-colleagues, unpleasant uncle and best friend from nursery school will be arriving shortly (that is, assuming you have any of these people 'on supply' in the Netherlands). This is why so many birth announcements contain the short sentence: *Moeder en kind rusten van 13.00 – 15.00 en ná 20.00 uur*, (Mother and child will be resting ...) or *Bezoek is welkom, maar bel even* (Visitors are welcome, but please call in advance).

Often the question is asked: 'How so rusks with aniseed?' – well; eating aniseeds will do the mother a lot of good as tradition has it that they stimulate her milk production. That explains why mommy is eating them, but not why everybody else has to...

VERJAARDAG (BIRTHDAY)

Kids' birthdays are, of course, Very Important Events. Luckily, the Dutch think so too. So, how do they celebrate them? On the day of the birthday, the birthday boy or girl gets to *trakteren* at school. This means that at some point in the morning, he or she hands out little items of food to his or her classmates. There are about 30 children per class; consequently this happens, on average, two or three times a month. For this reason, many teachers prefer that you bring something other than sweets, such as tangerines, cheese or *worst* (slices of sausage) on a toothpick, an apple or maybe even little boxes of raisins. Some parents put a lot of effort into making these packages look fun: they make bugs or boats or dolls by arranging the cheese, pickles or carrots just so.

Dutch children also get to give birthday parties, to which they invite a couple of their best friends from school and/or the neighborhood. Interestingly, kids often have *two* birthday parties: one with fun and games for the kids from school and the neighborhood and one for the extended family and other grown-ups (including *their* kids). The latter is usually without organized fun and games and mostly involves the receiving of gifts, the eating of cake and cookies and putting up with aunts and uncles saying how much everybody has *grown* since the last time they saw them. What you organize for the former (more official) party more or less depends on your budget and your imagination (a visit from a clown, a treasure hunt, dressing up and making a movie, visiting a circus, a farm, a puppet theater, you name it). Ask other parents about what is popular among the children in your child's age group.

If your kid is invited to a Dutch birthday party, the invitation will state when and where it is taking place and what to bring in terms of, for instance, a bathing suit or a dress-up costume. The Dutch are not into big expensive gifts: generally speaking something in the price range between € 7.50 and € 15 will suffice. If you bring something more expensive, they might feel a little embarrassed. And of course: do not forget to arrive ON TIME. This is Holland, remember? Plus, chances are the actual party will be somewhere else (like the pool, or the woods), so coming late means your child might miss out on all the fun – for everyone generally comes together at the birthday boy's or girl's house first and leaves from there!

SINTERKLAAS (SAINT NICHOLAS)

You will find more about Sinterklaas on page 50, however, he is definitely worth mentioning here as he is *the* children's friend in the Netherlands.

St. Nicholas, or Sinterklaas, is considered the patron saint of children. Every year on December 5th, in honor of his birthday, he makes children happy by giving them lots of gifts. Contrary to Christmas, the festivities surrounding this important event are not limited to one single day. Somewhere halfway November already, Sinterklaas arrives on his steamboat from Spain, accompanied by his helpers, Roet Pieten. The Roet Pieten (Soot Petes) are his helpers, colorfully dressed and made up with soot-stained faces, funny wigs and white, ruffled collars. (A little note: due to the upheaval surrounding the political incorrectness of the concept of 'Black Pete', they now go by the name of Kleur (Color) Piet, or Roet (Soot) Piet, or other names. You can read more about this matter in chapter 2. Their appearance has therefore changed, going from completely black hair and faces to the sooty faces and variety of wigs you see now.) Sinterklaas has one major arrival date and point in the Netherlands that is covered extensively on television. However, after this day, he makes a grand entry into almost all towns and cities, parading down the main street with his energetic Roet Pieten and waving royally at his little fans.

The Roet Pieten are the ones who know who's been good and who's been bad and who have the sooty task of climbing down the household chimney to deliver gifts to those who have been good. Again, contrary to Christmas, these gifts are not delivered merely on December 5th. Any time between Sinterklaas's arrival in November and his departure in December, he and his helpers may decide to pay a kid's home a surprise visit at night. In order to limit the excitement, parents usually compromise to having him visit twice a week, say on Tuesday night and Saturday night, in order not to be dragged out of bed at 6 o'clock *every* morning to see if there are any surprises. During these weeks, Sinterklaas also pays a visit to offices, schools, day care centers, old age homes, department stores and private homes, bringing little gifts, cookies (*pepernoten* and *kruidnoten*; ginger and cinnamon cookies), candies (*schuimpjes* – sugary cushions) and chocolate coins, which are handed out to the attending crowd.

When the children are told they can anticipate a nighttime visit from their friend, they place a shoe by the chimney, often with a little note in it, explaining what they hope to receive or thanking Sinterklaas for their previous gift, plus a little present for Sinterklaas or Roet Piet and sometimes a carrot for Sinterklaas's white horse, Amerigo. And then they sing a little song, aiming the notes

Fertile Storks

During the 17th century, there was no such thing as the sexual revolution. Babies and the conception thereof were shrouded in mystery. In order to answer the painful question 'Where do babies come from?' the Dutch came up with the following, absolutely plausible, explanation: babies were brought by the stork. If this failed to impress the children, other, equally plausible, explanations were available: babies were found among the beets, or they were found in wells or in hollow trees.

Why, of all birds, did the stork get to be the one to deliver this precious freight? In the Netherlands, storks were always considered harbingers of good luck. Therefore, it was only logical that they would be the ones to bring proof of the fact that the mother was fertile, the marriage fruitful and the father a real man.

Nowadays, if you pass a front yard with a stork in it, you can be sure that this is the announcement of the birth of a new world citizen. The use of storks is also very popular on birth announcements.

up the chimney. It is a heart-warming, Norman-Rockwell-type of moment that makes your heart sing too.

The festivities change, as the children get older, or if Sinterklaas is celebrated among only grown-ups – because, yes, this is something the grown-ups enjoy doing long after they've stopped believing in fairytales. The older age group arranges a type of lottery, in which they each draw one other person in the group to make a gift for, and a poem. 'Make' a gift being the operative word here, because in most cases, the real gift is disguised, hidden or incorporated into a much bigger playful contraption, designed and created by the giver. Also the poem has its specific elements; in particular, humor and a little bit of leg-pulling, often listing memorable moments of the past year including, preferably, a few of the receiver's more embarrassing adventures. The reader has to be able to abandon taking him or herself too seriously for the occasion, though the poems are ultimately written with much affection.

Most families try to have the main celebration on December 5 itself, regardless of the day of week. On this day, called *pakjesavond* (or gift evening), families and friends get together for the exchanging of gifts. In the case of families with littler children, the parents often arrange either a personal visit from Sinterklaas, or else for a big bag of gifts to be deposited at the front door by a friendly neighbor, who will then bang on the door and the windows as a cue for the parents to exclaim: "Oh, there's Roet Piet! Quick, let's see whether he's left us any gifts!" – and run away quickly before the ever-vigilant kids catch them in the act.

The rest of the evening is spent enjoying this unique Dutch family tradition (most schools start an hour later the next day, to allow the children to catch up on the sleep they inevitably missed due to the excitement of *pakjesavond*).

KERSTMIS (CHRISTMAS)

Does all this mean that there is no Christmas in the Netherlands? Not at all. Though the celebration of Christmas, as many know it, is based on the Dutch tradition of Sinterklaas (and is therefore really a 'repeat' just three weeks later), this does not mean that, come December 25, everyone will be going about their daily routine. Kerstmis is definitely a time of *gezelligheid* (a unique Dutch word for what can best be described as coziness) when friends and family get together to enjoy each other's company and a good meal, and companies organize Christmas celebrations for the entire staff. Increasingly, the Dutch are taking to whipping out all sorts of outdoor decorations to lighten up the dreary December days, and, while they are at it, buying each other gifts to put under the tree – though some Dutch purists limit the gift-giving to only Sinterklaas. And so, even among the most die-hard purist families, Christmas remains a very important day on the kiddie calendar, with families traveling across the country to visit grandma and grandpa and all the favorite aunts and uncles – who can seldom resist the temptation to give a little something to the children.

LEGAL ISSUES

ZWANGERSCHAPSVERKLARING – 'STATEMENT OF PREGNANCY'

If you are pregnant, currently working and plan to do so following delivery, you will need to obtain a *zwangerschapsverklaring* (or 'statement of pregnancy') from your midwife or gynecologist. This document confirms your estimated due date and will be used to determine when you will be eligible for *zwangerschapsverlof* (pregnancy leave), which you can read about in the next paragraph.

ZWANGERSCHAPSVERLOF AND BEVALLINGSVERLOF – PREGNANCY LEAVE AND BIRTH LEAVE

In the Netherlands, women have a right to 16 weeks' paid leave, divided into 4-6 weeks of pregnancy leave and 10 weeks of birth leave. Pregnancy leave may be initiated between 4-6 weeks prior to the estimated due date, but no later than that, as Dutch law states that you may not work from 4 weeks before, until 6 weeks after, delivery. *When* you take up your leave should be determined

together with your employer. If you are expecting twins (or more) you will get 20 weeks' leave and it will have to start at least 8 weeks before your due date.You can go back to work after the legally required 6 weeks have ended, and spread the remaining 4 weeks of birth leave over a maximum period of 30 weeks. If you lose your baby after more than 24 weeks of pregnancy, you also have a right to pregnancy and birth leave.

During pregnancy leave you receive 100% of your normal wages – either directly from the Social Security Institution or via your employer – up to a maximum of € 274.44 (the so-called daily wage) a day, though some employers pay out the gap between this and your full last-earned salary. Should the baby arrive early, you still have a right to the full 16 weeks. If it is late, and you have used up the 6 weeks beforehand, you still have the right to a 10-week leave (birth leave) following the baby's birth. If your child has to stay in the hospital for an extended period of time, then you have a right to a maximum of 10 additional weeks of birth leave to take care of your child once you come home.

If, prior to the start of your pregnancy leave, you are unable to work due to a pregnancy-related illness and must stay at home, then you have a right to 100% of the official daily wage. If you are unable to *return* to work due to medical reasons secondary to pregnancy and/or delivery, then you also have a right to up to 104 weeks of benefits at 100% of the daily wage. Both of these benefits are based on the Sickness Benefits Act and not on the Pregnancy Leave-regulation. If you become ill more than six weeks before your due date, then your pregnancy leave officially starts six weeks before your due date, regardless of any agreement you have reached with your employer. During the days preceding the official leave, if the illness is not due to pregnancy, you will receive at least 70% of your personal wage.

Would you like to take more than the government-stipulated 16-week leave? In order to do so you need to apply for a voluntary *Ziektewet*-insurance at your Social Security Institution (UWV) within four weeks of discontinuing your work activities.

Pregnancy Leave for Self-Employed Mothers

The Zelfstandig en Zwangerregeling (Self-Employed and Pregnant Regulation) gives self-employed mothers a right to 16 weeks of pregnancy leave. It starts between 6 and 4 weeks before the due date, but if you are expecting twins, it starts between 10 and 8 weeks before the due date and you have a right to 20 weeks of leave. Once the baby is born, you have a right to 6 weeks of birth leave. If the baby was born early (before you used up the 6 weeks of pregnancy leave), you can add the remaining days of pregnancy leave to your birth leave. In the case of pregnancy-related illness, you will have to have arranged voluntary insurance in order to receive anything during this period. If your baby has to stay in the hospital after birth, and this lasts longer than 7 days, you have a right to a maximum of 10 additional weeks of leave. If you lose your baby after more than 24 weeks of pregnancy, you also have a right to pregnancy and birth leave.

How much you receive depends on the number of hours you worked in self-employment the previous year. If you worked 1,225 hours or more, then you will receive a benefit equal to the minimum wage. If you worked fewer than 1,225 hours, then your benefit will be less and will depend on your profits / income over the previous year. You also have a right to this benefit if you work for your partner's / spouse's company. If you are both employed and self-employed, you receive a benefit from both sources, to a total of no more than your normal earnings, and no more than the minimum wage.

You request this benefit by contacting the Social Security Institution (UWV).

If you have arranged a voluntary disability insurance, it will also often pay out during your pregnancy / birth period. Though this will not reduce your government benefit, the fact that you receive the government benefit might reduce your disability payments. Be sure to check this beforehand.

Pregnancy Leave if You Are Receiving a Benefit
If you are receiving the unemployment benefit (WW), Sickness Benefit (ZW), or a benefit due to disability for work, then the pregnancy leave payments will temporarily replace these payments. You should arrange this yourself with the UWV (Social Security Institution).

YOUR RIGHTS AS A PREGNANT EMPLOYEE

You are not obligated to tell a prospective employer that you are (or wish to become) pregnant (even if they ask about this), but if you choose to do so, they may not turn you down for this reason. You *do* have an obligation to tell your current employer that you are pregnant, however – at the latest three weeks before your pregnancy leave is due to start. You may not be fired during pregnancy or within 12 weeks following the birth of your child. Only under very special circumstances, for example in the case of bankruptcy, may your employment be terminated. Should your contract end during pregnancy, for instance, at the end of a contract for a limited period of time, you have the right to unemployment (WW) and sickness benefits – and therefore also pregnancy leave. Should you quit your job and your baby is due or born within ten weeks, then you have a right to pregnancy leave as well.

During pregnancy, your employer is obligated to protect your safety and health, and you are eligible for certain additional rights. Discuss these with your employer. If you do not tell your employer that you are pregnant, you cannot exercise these rights. A few examples of your rights are: the right to regular working and resting hours, extra breaks and a suitable, closed-off space to rest (and where you can lie down). You are under no obligation to work overtime or at night. These rights are applicable up until six months after delivery. You also have the right to other working hours or other work if your current work is unsafe or hazardous to your health. If neither option is available, you have the right to be exempted from work. There are also special regulations regarding nursing, hard physical labor, stress, chemicals, radiation, risk of infection, noise, extreme vibrations, extreme heat or cold, etc. Check the website of the FNV (Federation of the Dutch Labor Movement): www.fnv.nl/werk-inkomen/zwanger-ouderschap/brochure-werk-en-zwangerschap and download the brochure for details.

'DELIVERY LEAVE' AND CALAMITY LEAVE

Partners have a right to stand by their wife / partner while she gives birth, amounting to, in total, the number of hours worked in a week. During this period, the employer continues to pay wages. It is up to the partner to decide when they will do this, though it must be taken up within four weeks of the child's birth. In July 2020, an additional (subsequent) leave was introduced of five weeks of leave, during which the partner receives 70% of their wages, to a maximum of 70% of the maximum daily wage (€ 274.44). You have six months in which to request this leave and you must request it at least four weeks in advance. This paid leave is not available for self-employed persons. Under the fascinatingly misnomered banner of 'calamity leave', partners may also take time off to register the birth of their child – not a full day, but for however much time is needed to do this, provided this is something that cannot be done during their free time.

REGISTRATION

Within three working days (not including the day of birth) your baby has to be registered at the *gemeentehuis* (town hall), though it can also be done online by either the mother or the father, depending on where the child was born. This must take place at the town hall of the municipality in which your baby was born – not your home town, if different. The partner usually performs this task. If this is not possible, then it must be done by someone who was present during the birth of the baby, the person who owned the house the baby was born in, or someone who works for the institution where the baby was born – or, of course, by the birth mother. Necessary to register the baby are; valid proof of identity of the person registering the birth, statement of birth issued by the hospital the baby was born in or the attending midwife, proof of recognition of the baby (if applicable), and a certificate containing the choice of the last name of the child (if applicable). In order to avoid undue hassle, check with the *gemeentehuis* in question prior to registration as to what is needed, as requirements may vary from one municipality to another. Also ask for an International Birth Certificate (for an additional fee) at this time. This document will come in handy when registering your baby with your embassy or consulate and when applying for a passport. Being born in the Netherlands does not give your baby the right to a Dutch passport – that is unless one, or both, of the parents is/are Dutch (see the following paragraph, however!).

LEGALLY RECOGNIZING BABY

If you and your partner are not married or registered partners, your partner (man or woman) may choose to legally recognize the baby either prior to birth, at the time of registration at the town hall or at a later date. The birth mother must give permission for this. If the child is older than 12, recognition can only take place with the child's permission in addition to that of the mother. After the age of 16, the birth mother's permission is no longer required. Recognition takes place in the town hall where you reside – not where you register the birth (unless of course this is one and the same). Check with your municipal offices or lawyer to verify which documents are necessary and what other possible requirements there may be. If the mother is not Dutch, while the recognizing partner is, the baby will acquire Dutch nationality if they are recognized before birth or before the child reaches the age of 7. Children are considered legally recognized if they are adopted.

If you wish to choose a particular last name for the baby, you can do this either before the child is born or when registering the baby's birth. You must do this in person – both parents – by visiting the town hall. If one of you will be recognizing the child, the name choice can be made when doing this, by visiting the Civil Registry. A choice of name can also be made in case of adoption or in case a court appoints a person to be a child's parent.

If the partner legally recognizes the baby, then this determines that there is a family relationship between this partner and the child, a duty to support the child and a right for the child in the inheritance, should the partner pass away. Since January 1, 2023, it also means that the recognizing partner obtains parental authority. Upon recognition (depending on the national law of the parent in question) the child acquires the recognizing parent's nationality. The Dutch rules can be found on www.rijksoverheid.nl/onderwerpen/erkenning-kind/vraag-en-antwoord/kind-erkennen-gevolgen.

If the partner does not have Dutch nationality, then the civil servant of the municipality will have to check whether recognition is possible. Make sure you are well-informed of the consequences of recognition for the baby's nationality, name and military duties (at a later age), as well as the partner's obligation to support it.

KINDERBIJSLAG – CHILD BENEFIT

If you are living in the Netherlands and/or are employed and pay Dutch wage taxes, then you are entitled to *kinderbijslag*. This holds true not only for your own (adopted) children, but also for step and foster children and other children you raise and care for as if they were your own. Following the registration of your child's birth, the municipal offices forward your data to the Sociale Verzekeringsbank (the Social Insurance Bank). Within a few days you receive a registration form for the benefit. Payment is made on a quarterly basis directly into your bank account up until your child is 18 years of age. The amount paid out is based on the age of your child and is currently set at € 279.47 for children between the ages of 0-5, € 289.38 for children between the ages of 6-11, and € 340.45 for children aged 12-17 (2024 – these amounts might still be subject to change). Children age 16 and 17 must still be going to school (either HAVO, VWO or MBO – for more on these acronyms, see chapter 9). For more information, visit www.svb.nl.

If you already have children when you move here, you can request the *kinderbijslag* by contacting the SVB (Sociale Verzekeringsbank).

CHILD ALLOWANCE

The *kindgebonden budget*, or Child Allowance, is paid out by the tax authorities. The amount depends on the parents' income, the number of children in the family, and whether the parent is a single parent. The amounts run from a maximum of € 2,436 per year, per child, with an additional € 3,480 per year for single parents (2024). Additional amounts are available for children who reach the age of 12 (€ 694) and, once again, as of the age of 16 (€ 924). To qualify, parents must either have Dutch nationality or a valid residence permit, and receive *kinderbijslag* for their child (unless they are 16 or 17 and no longer attend school and therefore no longer receives *kinderbijslag*, in which case parents might still get the *kindgebonden budget*). The *kindgebonden budget* does not affect the payment of the *kinderbijslag* (see above), which is an income-independent allowance. If you, your partner or your child live abroad, you might still qualify for the kindgebonden budget, though it might be reduced, taking into account the cost of living in the other country, while benefits paid out in this country are also taken into account.

OUDERSCHAPSVERLOF – PARENTAL LEAVE

The law stipulates that both working parents have the right to take an unpaid leave of absence to care for a child (adoption, step or foster child included) as of their first day of employment (it used to be that they had to have been in employment for at least one year). Leave may be taken either by both parents together or one after the other, at any time during the first seven years of the child's life. Parents can decide for themselves when and how they take up this leave. A request for leave must be submitted at least two months before the intended first day of leave. In the case of twins, leave is available for each child. The legal amount of time allotted is based on the number of contractual hours per week that you work, times 26 – and the standard rule is that you will work 50% during a period of one year. For instance, if you work 32 hours a week, this means you can work 16 hours a week during a period of one year. As the rules are not always practical – for either the employee or employer – other conditions may be agreed upon, such as taking up 100% leave over a period of six months, working at 75% of your normal working hours over a period of two years, or spreading your leave over six periods. Check whether a collective labor agreement applies to you, in which there may be further, more beneficial, rules on parental leave. Although not required by law, some employers continue to pay up to 75% of the wages during parental leave. If you become sick during this leave, your employer must pay wages over the hours during which you would otherwise have worked. If you switch jobs, you can take your remaining parental-leave days with you to your new employer.

As of August 2022, employed parents have a right to an additional partially paid (70% of their wages, to a maximum of 70% of the daily wage) leave of nine weeks, to be taken before the child reaches the age of 1. This can be taken up in one go, or spread across time. Double leave is available for twins. Also in case of adopted or recognized children, you have this leave per child. For adopted and foster children, this leave must be taken before the child turns 8 and within a year of their becoming a member of the family. The leave of nine weeks must be taken up in one go for foster and stepchildren.

During the period of unpaid leave, you might experience financial hardship. Single parent families can request government support during this period based on the *Bijstand* (welfare) regulations, via the Sociale Verzekeringsbank (SVB), as well as rent subsidy, health care insurance subsidy and child care subsidy. Two-parent families are expected to be able to solve this by means of an income earned by the other parent, though this rule may be subject to change.

BORSTVOEDING – BREAST-FEEDING

Employers must provide breast-feeding employees with a quiet area in which to breast-feed or express – not the restroom! If this is not feasible, then the employer must allow the employee to find an appropriate spot or to go to the baby in order to do this. Feeding / expressing time is considered work time and may therefore not lead to a reduction in your wages. A maximum of one quarter of normal working hours may be used for this purpose, up until the child is nine months old. Discuss the various options with your employer prior to initiating pregnancy leave.

ADOPTION / FOSTER LEAVE

If you adopt a child, you and your partner individually have a right to six consecutive weeks' adoption leave surrounding the arrival of the child (if you adopt more than one child at once, the period of leave is still six weeks). This leave may be taken up anywhere between four weeks before the arrival of the child and 22 weeks after their arrival and can be spread out over these 26 weeks. During the period of leave, your employer receives a benefit from the government, which they use to pay you 100% of your wage during this period, up to a maximum of the daily wage € 274.44). Self-employed persons do not have a right to a benefit in connection with unpaid leave for adoption.

Under certain conditions, this same leave is available to persons taking in a foster child.

KORTDUREND ZORGVERLOF – SHORT CARE LEAVE

By law, a full-time employee has the right – per year – to take a maximum of two times the number of hours they work in a week, in order to care for a sick (foster) child, partner or parent (if you work 36 hours a week, you have a right to 72 hours, with 32 hours you have a right to 64 hours, and so on, to a maximum of 10 days) – also if this person lives abroad. There are two conditions for this: one is that the care is really necessary and two is that you are the one who must provide this care. Your employer may ask for proof of this and they may only refuse to grant you this leave on substantial company grounds. This type of leave does not have to be taken up in one go. The employer is obligated to continue to pay at least 70% of your wages during this period, but no less than the minimum wage. Your industry's CAO (Collective Labor Agreement) or the company's regulations may contain additional rules, so be sure to check what these may be.

If your child / partner / parent suddenly falls ill and you have to leave your work immediately, this first day is covered by the rules on Calamity Leave. Short Care Leave starts the next day.

LANGDUREND ZORGVERLOF – LONG CARE LEAVE

You have an annual right to take up leave to care for a terminally ill, long-term ill or long-term disabled (foster) child, partner or parent for a longer period of time. You can also use this leave to care for grandparents, grandchildren, siblings, other people living with you (such as an uncle), and people with whom you have a social relationship who rely on you for help (such as a neighbor or a friend). Also if this person is abroad. The state of the person needing your help need not be critical: 'simply' being ill or in need of your help is sufficient. The right amounts to – in total, per year – six times the number of hours you work per week. If you work 40 hours a week, this means that you have a right to 240 hours of long care leave per year. You cannot take up leave for more than 12 consecutive weeks. You can reach an agreement with your employer based on which you take up a full 100% leave over six weeks, or you take up your leave in 'chunks'. Again, this can only be refused on substantial company grounds, and you must inform your employer of your intention to make use of this leave at least two weeks in advance – and they must reply at least one week in advance. In principle, you have no income over the hours you don't work, unless this has been specified otherwise, for instance in a collective labor agreement (CAO), which can also contain other – different – rules regarding this leave. You might, however, qualify for rent subsidy, child care subsidy and health care insurance subsidy.

CALAMITY LEAVE / SHORT LEAVE

Calamity leave has been created for unforeseen situations in which you have to act immediately and personally, for instance, to find a baby-sitter for your suddenly sick child, to fulfill certain legal obligations, to find a plumber if the water pipes have burst, in the case of sudden death in the family or, as mentioned above, to register the birth of your newborn child. In principle, this leave is granted for a couple of hours, though it could be extended to a couple of days, during which period your employer is to continue 100% payment of your salary. There is no maximum to the number of hours / days that you take up this kind of leave. If the circumstances are such that they qualify for Short Care Leave, your leave will automatically be converted into this type of leave after 24 hours. For the rules on this type of leave, see above.

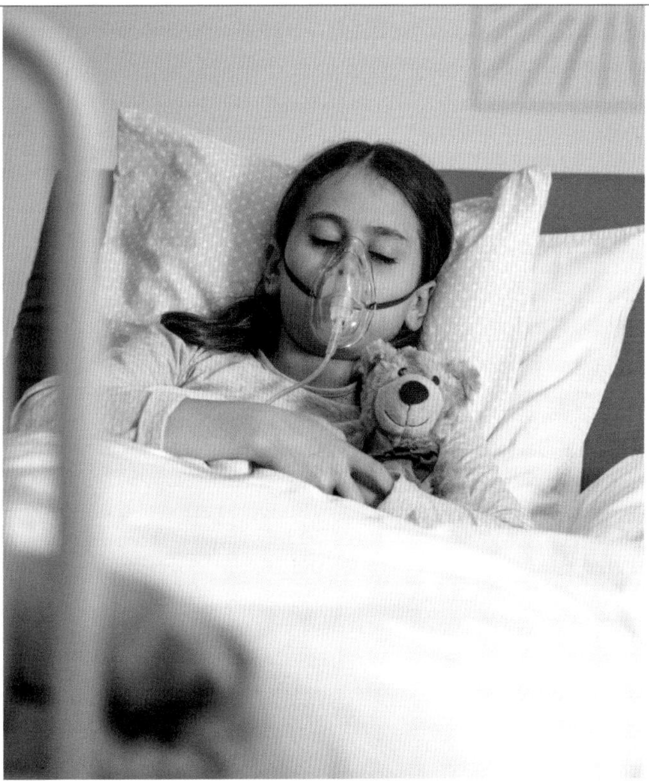

UNPAID LEAVE – SOCIAL SECURITY AND PENSION

Before taking up any kind of unpaid leave, be sure to inform yourself about the consequences for your build-up of social security benefits and your pension.

TAKING CARE OF A HANDICAPPED CHILD

Parents who have a (mentally or physically) handicapped (foster) child between the ages of 3 and 17 living at home receive double *kinderbijslag*, depending on conditions set by the Social Insurance Bank (SVB – www.svb.nl) – for instance to help cover expenses due to the fact that the child cannot live at home unattended. Subject to conditions, an extra amount over and above this double payment may be available.

Children who, before they reached the age of 18, or while following a higher education, have become sick or disabled in such a way that they are permanently disabled for work, receive the Wajong-benefit independently. If a child is partially disabled for work, they have a right to assistance from the municipality in finding work and to the welfare benefit (*Bijstand*).

LAST WILL AND TESTAMENT

Preparing a will is probably one of the most important steps you will take to ensure the future well-being of your newborn. Although not common knowledge, not all foreign wills are valid in the Netherlands. This depends, among others, on your country of origin (what are the requirements for a valid will there?), how the will has been drawn up and whether the Netherlands has entered into a treaty on the matter with your country of origin.

If something were to happen to both parents, the courts will appoint a guardian; most often the person mentioned in the will. If the will states nothing on this matter, a relative in the country of origin will be appointed. In order to guarantee that the *voogdij* (guardianship) of your child is given to the person of your choosing, it would be best to have a testament drawn up, or at least checked, by a Dutch *notaris* (civil law notary) – to be on the safe side. Check online or get a referral from a friend for the name of a civil law notary in your area.

VACATION

According to Dutch law, all children as of the age of 5 are *leerplichtig* and must attend school (unless they are sick). Exceptions may be made for children of parents who are required to work during standard school holidays and vacations, generally up to a maximum of 10 days. Extraordinary family situations such as special birthdays, anniversaries, illness or death are other exceptions. Dutch schools are very strict about this (the fines are € 100 per day per child and they even threaten a suspended sentence if you repeatedly take your children out of school for an extended period of time on non-vacation days) and a formal request in writing is required prior to taking your child out of school. International schools may have their own set of regulations – so when in doubt, ask!

SHOPPING

BABY FOOD AND FORMULA

Baby food (*babyvoeding*) can be purchased at all supermarkets and most *drogisterijen* (drugstores) and *apotheken* (pharmacies). You can also find formula (*opvolgmelk*, treated milk for babies) in these stores, though the very specialized types of formula for babies with allergies (soy-based products) are often only available through the *apotheek*. Also health food stores (*reformhuizen* or *reformwinkels*) carry their own baby foods and formula.

You will be advised as to what kind of formula to try by the *Consultatiebureau* (Well Baby Clinic, see page 256).

BABY CARE PRODUCTS

(Popular) baby care products – baby shampoos, soaps, ointments, etc. – can be found at the *drogist* (drugstore), while a smaller selection is available in supermarkets. Brand name and own label diapers are available at the *drogist* and the supermarket.

CLOTHES

Clothes for babies and children can be found in the larger department stores, certain brand stores and, of course, stores specializing in baby and children's items. Virtually every main shopping street in every little town has a store that carries a large variety of children's clothing. Children's shoes can be bought at almost any shoe store. At the end of the chapter you will find a list of shops.

MATERNITY CLOTHES

Maternity clothes are called *positiekleding* or *zwangerschapskleding*. Many department stores carry maternity clothes, as do the specialty shops listed at the end of the chapter. You can also purchase very stylish 'oversize clothes' at an Extra Size (*grote maten*) woman's shop or in the XL larger sizes sections of most clothing stores. Many second-hand clothing shops (*tweedehandswinkels*) have a selection of maternity clothes, too. *Zwangerschapszwempakken* (swim suits) can best be purchased at a specialty shop.

FURNITURE

There are large chains of stores as well as smaller shops, all across the Netherlands, that carry or specialize in baby furniture. Here you can also find cribs, strollers, car seats, highchairs, lamps, bottles, baths, clothes, toys, the works. Check online under *Babyartikelen* and check the list at the end of the chapter.

TOYS & GAMES

Speelgoedwinkels are toy stores carrying a wide selection of toys and games, but toys and games can also be found in department stores and even in a few of the household chains. Second-hand children's shops carry playthings as well as children's books. Often they (and supermarkets) will have a message board where you can post larger items for sale such as carriages, cribs, furniture, etc. Furthermore, there are splendid toy stores all across the country that do not belong to any chain and that sell some of the more old-fashioned variety of (wooden) toys.

FUN THINGS TO DO

EXTRACURRICULAR ACTIVITIES

Some of you may be used to extracurricular activities arranged by the school, but, unfortunately, most Dutch schools do not have such a program. On the other hand, tuition is free if you send your child to a local school, so this may have something to do with it. Yet this does not mean that your child has to twiddle their thumbs all day, once school is out. In almost all municipalities you will find an organization or private persons that offer all sorts of activities, such as carpentry, painting, music, dancing, art, cooking, etc. Just ask around, go online or give your municipality a call. And, perhaps even the best fun of all is simply being able to go out and play with the kids in the neighborhood – something that is still very popular here.

Furthermore, there are several sports organizations; the more popular ones being for tennis, field hockey and gymnastics – though there is also judo, basketball, baseball, soccer, dancing, horseback-riding, cycling (of course) and much, much more.

SWIMMING

One very important extracurricular activity (that is sometimes arranged through schools) is swimming, which should come as no surprise in this country of canals, rivers, lakes and the sea. Though your child does not *have* to take swimming lessons, there is a well-regulated system of classes to take and diplomas to aspire to – a program that virtually every child follows and takes pride in completing.

SCOUTS AND OTHER CAMPS

Boy and Girl Scouts (called *scouting*) clubs are very popular here. The kids get together almost every Saturday afternoon, and engage in fun and educational activities. Occasionally, the groups go camping for an entire weekend, while they organize week-long summer camps during summer vacation. Check online or check your (online) *gemeentegids* for the local chapter, or visit www.scouting.nl.

Other popular camps are for horseback-riding and sailing and you could of course also ask among the international schools whether they are arranging anything for the summer (or know of someone who is). Some municipalities arrange a day-camp during the summer vacations with a full program of activities for the children; drop-off time early in the morning, pick-up time late afternoon. Once again, your (online) *gemeentegids* or someone at the municipal offices should be able to tell you whether there's something like that going on in your town or one nearby.

FILLING YOUR DAYS

A very popular item of entertainment for younger kids in the Netherlands is the petting farm, to be found in almost every town and city. They usually have goats, sheep, rabbits, guinea pigs, chickens, ducks, pigs, a pony, some cats and the occasional donkey. Kids love it, and often learn a thing or two about the animals while they are there. Also, if you are looking for a rabbit for the family, this is a place to go and have a look as they tend to have a few extra hopping around that they are willing to sell. Aside from the petting farm, you'll be surprised to find that many towns also have a so-called *hertenkamp* (there are more than 200 in the Netherlands); an enclosed area with deer who peacefully graze their way through life, and who happily welcome a handful of leftover bread should you and the kids care to pay them a visit. It is not quite clear what the origin of these deer "camps" is; are they a reminder of the days when deer roamed around freely? Or were they once the private parks of the well-to-do at a time when it was the thing to do to populate these parks with something a little more dainty than a woolly sheep? The answer to this question remains a little elusive, but the sight of these elegant animals is nonetheless a pleasant one – and they are quite friendly.

Playgrounds are also to be found on various locations in towns and cities, with swings, slides, seesaws, a sand box, and more. And, of course, most zoos also have *great* (and large) playgrounds for your children to let off steam, while you sit and enjoy a well-deserved cup of coffee. You can find more on zoos a little further on in this chapter.

Another staple activity of Dutch summertime are the traveling circuses and fairs (*kermis*), whose arrival is announced well in advance so that you can set aside time for a fun day out with the kids. You buy an admission ticket to the circuses. The fairs sometimes charge an entry fee, but mostly you pay for the rides and attractions you choose to enter.

For rainy days (of which there will be plenty), there are the covered playgrounds – called Ballorig, Monkey Town, or Kidzcity – which are huge covered areas with a great variety of things to enjoy: humongous slides, intricate rope-climbing structures, merry-go-rounds, trains, you name it. In some of the bigger cities you will find activity centers, where children learn to build tree houses, floats and other complicated contraptions. A valuable source of information on these activities and centers is: www.uitmetkinderen.nl (a day out with kids), where you can search for museums, amusement parks, pools, zoos, playgrounds, etc. according to age, postal code, price range, and alphabet.

AMUSEMENT PARKS AND MUSEUMS

The Netherlands has some great amusement parks and museums, such as:

- De Efteling: a huge park offering several days' worth of entertainment in fantasyland, with fairytale woods, wild rides on rollercoasters, castles, fairytale figures and more.
  Europalaan 1, Kaatsheuvel (near Tilburg)
  www.efteling.com.
- Corpus: a journey through the human body during which the visitor can see, feel and hear how the human body works and what roles healthy food, a healthy life and exercise play. It offers education and entertainment, as well as a vast number of permanent and temporary exhibitions.
  Willem Einthovenstraat 1, Oegstgeest
  www.corpusexperience.nl
- The Open Air Museums (Openluchtmuseum): where you can make a trip through time. There are many, including, among others:
  - *Nederlands Openluchtmuseum* (daily life in the Netherlands between 1600 and 1970).
    Schelmseweg 89, Arnhem
    www.openluchtmuseum.nl
  - *Orientalis* (Open Air Museum, for a glimpse of the world 2,000 years ago in the Middle East, focusing on Judaism, Christianity and Islam).
    Profetenlaan 2, Heilig Landstichting
    www.museumparkorientalis.nl
  - *Zuiderzeemuseum* (life in a fishing village around 1900).
    Wierdijk 12-22, Enkhuizen
    www.zuiderzeemuseum.nl
- NEMO Science Museum: a scientifically oriented play / educational center; offering a discovery trip through fantasy and reality.
  Oosterdok 2, Amsterdam
  www.nemosciencemuseum.nl

- Safari Park Beekse Bergen: a place where you can take a drive (or walk) among more than 100 wild animals, a trip that could take more than a day!
  Beekse Bergen 1, Hilvarenbeek (near Tilburg)
  www.beeksebergen.nl or www.safaripark.nl
- Duinrell: a fantastic water festival, with attractions, a ski valley, a wild pool and lots of entertainment.
  Duinrell 1, Wassenaar
  www.duinrell.com

- Pony Park Slagharen: a place where you can experience life in the Red Bandits Adventure, with an amusement park, a shopping street, Wigwam World and lots of entertainment.
  Zwarte Dijk 37, Slagharen
  www.slagharen.com
- Planetarium Franeker, where, more than 200 years ago, Eise Eisinga made a scale model of the solar system in his living room, with a mechanism that keeps planets and pointers in motion and that works to this day.
  Eise Eisingastraat 3, Franeker
  www.eisinga-planetarium.nl
- Children's Museum at The Tropical Institute (Koninklijk Instituut voor de Tropen), where contemporary non-Western cultures are brought to life for children between the ages of 6 and 12. Also available for children's parties.
  Linnaeusstraat 2, Amsterdam
  www.kit.nl
- Walibi World: a huge outdoor swimming and water paradise, with more than 50 attractions and shows, offering entertainment and adventure.
  Spijkweg 30, Biddinghuizen
  www.walibi.nl
- Louwman Museum: the national automobile museum. For anyone who is car crazy and interested in the history of automobiles from the first horseless carriages through subsequent models of motorized, steam and electric vehicles.
  Leidsestraatweg 57, The Hague
  www.louwmanmuseum.nl
- Madurodam: a miniature version of the Netherlands, including Schiphol Airport, the Delta works, the center of Amsterdam and more.
  George Maduroplein 1, The Hague
  www.madurodam.nl

This is but a small selection (see Chapter 11 for more tourist attractions). Ask around among other parents or at the vvv (Tourist Information Office; you will find a list of vvvs at the end of chapter 11) what other tips they may have.

ZOOS

Animals are always a great success with children and what makes the Netherlands such a wonderful 'zoo country' is that there are so many of them, and that a lot of effort is put into recreating the natural habitats of the animals – so that both we and they can enjoy their stay here. As mentioned earlier, the zoos all have extensive playgrounds, for when your kids need to blow off steam, as well as indoor facilities for rainy days, and child-friendly cafeterias.

- Amersfoort Zoo: This large zoo near Amersfoort has provided its animals with increasingly spacious and comfortable habitats, bringing it on a par with all the other large zoos in the Netherlands. It has a Savannah, encircled all the way around, allowing you to circumnavigate the area and enjoy the animals as they graze and drink peacefully; use its app to plan your day or find your favorite animal.
  DierenPark Amersfoort, Barchman Wuytierslaan 224, Amersfoort
  www.dierenparkamersfoort.nl
- Apenheul: Apenheul has 35 species of apes, monkeys and prosimians – many of which are allowed to roam free (monkey-proof bags recommended)! Their group areas are extensive and imaginative, providing them with familiar surroundings and all manner of activities to keep them occupied. But monkeys and apes are not the only animals you will meet at Apenheul. The 'zoo' also provides a home to other animals that can be found in the monkeys' / apes' natural habitats. Note: Apenheul closes during winter, but may allow groups on pre-arranged dates.
  Apenheul, J.C. Wilslaan 21, Apeldoorn
  www.apenheul.nl
- Artis Zoo: Artis was founded more than 180 years ago, and its winding paths, majestic trees and the monumental historical buildings still give it a special, 19th-century atmosphere. There are 750 different types of animals in the zoo (down from 1,600 – in order to create more space for those present), as well as the Planetarium, a magnificent, recently renovated Aquarium, and Micropia: the only microbe-museum in the world.
  Artis, Plantage Kerklaan 38, Amsterdam
  www.artis.nl/en
- Avifauna: Avifauna is one of the largest bird parks in the world. The birds originate from anywhere between the tropics to the cold Northern Hemisphere. There are more than 250 species of birds, in beautiful settings, which are expertly and lovingly taken care of. Avifauna is not only a bird 'zoo', it is actively involved in endangered species breeding programs and bird protection activities, and educates children on nature protection programs. It also has a special Madagascar and an oriental garden, as well as an Argentine Cerrado and a Cuban water swamp.
  Vogelpark Hotel Rederij Avifauna, Hoorn 65, Alphen aan den Rijn
  www.avifauna.nl/en
- Blijdorp Zoo: At Rotterdam Zoo you can walk from continent to continent, meeting fascinating animals that feel perfectly at home in the surroundings that emulate their natural habitat. The covered facilities, in case of rain, include Taman Indah,

Amazonica (temporarily closed), Biotopia, Oceanium, with sharks, king penguins, sea lions and jellyfish, while you can also visit the Asian Corridors, the African Jungle and Plains, the Caribbean Coast, and the Himalayan Peaks.
Rotterdam Zoo / Blijdorp, Blijdorplaan 8, Rotterdam
www.rotterdamzoo.nl or www.diergaardeblijdorp.nl/en

- Burgers' Zoo: Burgers' Zoo is a modern, but genuine jungle! This zoo, located near Arnhem, covers more than 45 hectares and houses more than 3,000 animals. It has a spectacular tropical rain forest, a living desert and a large animal population, such as bighorns and red lynxes, to be admired in their natural surroundings. Furthermore, a large number of hoofed animals and birds live with the lions in the 'Safari Park' and there is a wonderful indoor water world.
  Burgers' Zoo, Antoon van Hooffplein 1, Arnhem
  www.burgerszoo.com
- National Park Veluwe: 5,500 hectares of grassland, heaths and woods, and home to the Big Four of the area: deer, roe deer, wild boars and mouflon, as well as badgers, foxes, pine marten, almost 100 species of birds, and countless amphibians and reptiles – and, since a few years, wolves. If horseback-riding is your thing, there are 500 km worth of horse-riding trails, and at the entrance to the park you can pick up your white bicycle for free and explore the 40 km of cycling paths – or else put on your hiking boots and take off into the woods, with or without a guide. For children, there are countless activities, including the Museonder – the museum that shows you what happens underneath our feet – and children's safaris (also at night!) with a forest ranger. For adults, there is the Kröller-Müller Museum, with works by the likes of Monet, Mondriaan, Picasso and Seurat, as well as a constantly changing exhibition of the museum's almost 90 paintings and more than 180 sketches by Van Gogh.
  Nationaal Park De Hoge Veluwe, as it has more than 20 information points, we refer you to the website for information: www.visitveluwe.com
- Emmen Zoo or Wildlands: Emmen Zoo is famous for the manner in which the park's habitats reflect the continents of the world. The animals reside in that part of the world where they belong. The zoo has a very spacious feel about it and all the animals enjoy a great amount of freedom in their enclosures, allowing them to behave as naturally as possible. You can spend hours enjoying the Jungola jungle, the Serenga Savannah, or the cold rocks of Nortica.
  Noorder Dierenpark Emmen, Hoofdstraat 18, Emmen
  www.wildlands.nl
- Naturalis: At Naturalis, nature is exhibited in all its colors and diversity. The museum is a combination of natural history and high-tech multi-media in a modern, artistic and technologically advanced setting, representing but a selection of two centuries' worth of collecting animal and plant specimens, fossils, stones and minerals. Exhibition rooms have seven permanent displays (including a walk through the Ice Age, with dinosaurs), while Naturalis hosts many fascinating temporary displays as well. There is also a Nature Information Center where amateur researchers can search through a wide range of books, magazines, slides, photographs, videotapes, computer files and reference collections.
  Naturalis, National Museum of Natural History, Darwinweg 2, Leiden. Museum entrance: Pesthuislaan 7, Leiden
  www.naturalis.nl/en
- Ouwehands Dierenpark in Rhenen: This is a wonderful family zoo, close to Arnhem, but off the beaten track. It was established more than 90 years ago and has retained that early-20th century cozy feel. It has a bear habitat with rescued circus bears, and a polar bear pool, where kids can press their noses up against the glass and be inches away from these huge white animals, a seal show, and much more. Extra-special is its huge, indoor, all-wood-mulch-and-sand playground for children (RavotAapia), with rope-bridges, sand games, waterplay, huts, caves and slides – at no extra charge. Even if the weather doesn't clear up all day, making it impossible to see the animals, you can still spend a full day in this indoor children's habitat and have the children begging you to go back soon!
  Ouwehands Dierenpark, Grebbeweg 111, Rhenen
  www.ouwehand.nl

References

CHAPTER 8
Kids

Recommended Reading

THE ACCESS GUIDE/FAQ SHEET ON HAVING A BABY IN THE NETHERLANDS
Information for expectant parents, parents of babies and toddlers. Topics include pregnancy, child health and safety, insurances, support groups, childcare services
www.access-nl.org

HOW TO BE A GLOBAL GRANDPARENT
Living With the Separation
By Anne Huscroft and Peter Gosling
Published by Zodiac Publishing
www.amazon.com

THIRD CULTURE KIDS
The Experience of Growing up Among Worlds
By David C. Pollock and Ruth E. Van Reken
www.nicholasbrealey.com
www.bol.com

RAISING GLOBAL NOMADS
Parenting in an On-Demand World
Published by Expatriate Press
By Robin Pascoe
With contributions from Barbara F. Schaetti, PhD and Lois J. Bushong, MS, LMFT
www.expatexpert.com

KIDS LIKE ME
Voices of the Immigrant Experience
Published by Intercultural Press
By Judith M. Blohm and Terri Lapinsky
www.nicholasbrealey.com

THE MOBILE LIFE – 2ND REVISED EDITION
Published by XPat Media
By Diane Lemieux & Anne Parker
Master the challenge of moving somewhere new
Also available as e-book
www.themobilelife.eu
www.hollandbooks.nl

Financial Issues

NIBUD
National Budget Institute
P.O. Box 19250, 3501 DG Utrecht
Tel.: 030 23 91 350
www.nibud.nl

SOCIALE VERZEKERINGSBANK
Social Insurance Bank
For the Child Benefit (*kinderbijslag*)
Tel.: 071 512 90 00 – www.svb.nl

Day Care

ACCESS
Provides a free guide/FAQ sheet "Your Child" on issues relating to day-care options for expats
www.access-nl.org

KINDEROPVANG, AFTER-SCHOOL HOURS CARE
www.afterscool.nl
www.eigenoppas.nl
www.gastouderservice.nl
www.regeltante.nl

10FORKIDS
Paulus Buijsstraat 51, 2582 CH The Hague
Tel.: 06 109 366 80
www.10forkids.nl

COMPANANNY
English-language day care for children 0 to 4 years, and after school care for children 4 to 12 years
Several locations in Amsterdam, The Hague, Rotterdam, Oegstgeest and more
Tel.: 020 417 01 17
www.compananny.nl

COMME A LA MAISON
International day care for children 0 to 6 years
Duinweg 1, 2585 JT The Hague
Tel.: 070 404 97 50
www.commealamaison.nl

BIG BEN KIDS
Leeghwaterplein 45, 2521 DB The Hague
Tel.: 070 219 25 70
www.bigbenkids.com

PARTOU KINDEROPVANG
Servicekantoor Partou, Sportlaan 1, 4131 NN Vianen
Tel.: 088 235 75 50
www.partou.nl

TRUE COLORS
Part of the Stichting Rijswijkse Kinderopvang with 25 locations in Rijswijk and Ypenburg
Karel Doormanlaan 1, 2283 AG Rijswijk
Tel.: 070 792 01 04
www.truecolorschildcare.eu

VILLA BLOOM
Loosduinse Hoofdstraat 536, 2552 AP The Hague
Tel.: 070 820 05 42
www.villabloom.nl

HUMANKIND
Has over 470 *kinderdagverblijven* in the Netherlands as well as *gastouder* centers.
Headoffice: Meezenbroekerweg 1a, 6412 VK Heerlen
Tel.: 0900 5 10 15 20
www.kinderopvanghumanitas.nl

STICHTING KINDEROPVANG CENTRAAL NEDERLAND (SKCN)
Has a national network for *kinderopvang, naschoolse opvang* and *buitenschoolse opvang*
Head office: Energieweg 15a, 4143 HK Leerdam
Tel.: 0345 639 555
www.skcn.nl

TRIODUS KINDEROPVANG
Has approximately 60 *kinderdagverblijven* in The Hague
Koninginnegracht 10, 2501 ED The Hague
Tel.: 070 312 00 10
www.triodus.nl

ZEIN INTERNATIONAL CHILDCARE
7 locations in The Hague Region and 1 in Amsterdam
Head office: Jozef Israelsplein 36, 2596 AV The Hague
Tel.: 070 200 2374
www.zeinchildcare.nl

ZO KINDEROPVANG & BSO VARIOUS LOCATIONS IN THE HAGUE
Head office: Leeghwaterplein 45, The Hague, Nederland
Tel.: 070 345 85 63
www.zokinderopvang.nl

BIG BEN KIDS WASSENAAR
Hallekenstraat 28A, 2242 VD Wassenaar
Tel.: 070 514 67 38
www. bigbenkids.com

THE CLOWN CLUB
Johan de Wittstraat 33, 2242 LA Wassenaar
Tel.: 07 514 09 81
www.theclownclub.com

KINDERGARDEN NEDERLAND
Herengracht 250, 1016 BV Amsterdam
Tel.: 020 423 54 22
www.kindergarden.nl

Au Pairs/Nannies

WORLD WIDE AU PAIR AND NANNY SEARCH
www.findaupair.com

AU PAIR NEDERLAND
Maashegeweg 79a, 5804 AB Venray
Tel.: 085 222 4812
www.aupair-nederland.nl

AUPAIR AGENCY MONDIAL
Schipperstraat 145, 4871 KK Etten-Leur
Tel.: 076 532 96 24
www.aupair-agency.nl

AUPAIR INTERNATIONAL
Hoge Traan 22, 9351 VV Leek
Tel.: 050 502 00 05
www. aupairinternational.nl

Special-Needs Children

AUTISM ASSOCIATION FOR OVERSEAS FAMILIES (NL)
Parents and professionals working together for children with autism
www.aaof.info

LIGHTHOUSE SPECIAL EDUCATION (PRIMARY)
Individual SEN-program taught in English
Van Heutszstraat 12, 2593 PJ The Hague
Tel.: 070 335 56 98
www.lighthousese.nl

DOWN SYNDROME FOUNDATION
Industrieweg 5, 7944 HT Meppel
Tel.: 0522 281 337
www.downsyndroom.nl

Things To Do

AMSTERDAM MAMAS
Community of mothers in Amsterdam organizing all kinds of activities
www.amsterdam-mamas.nl

DELFT MAMA
Connecting International Families
www.delftmama.nl

LITTLE STAR FITNESS
Sport, circus, fitness, aerial silks & dance for children between the ages of 2-12
Jan van Eijckstraat 47, 1077 LH Amsterdam
Tel.: 06 110 76 992
www.littlestarfitness.com

VINEA
Summer camp activities for children age 7-20
Tel.: 030 22 70 680 – www.vinea.nl

SNOWWORLD
www.snowworld.com

SUMMER CAMPS HOLLAND
Gildeweg 7, 7074 AR Braamt
Tel.: 0314 68 06 88
www.summercamps.nl

Swimming Lessons

SWIMKIDS
English and Dutch spoken swimming lessons for children from 4 to 12 years and adults
www.swimkids.eu

ZWEMSCHOOL MAX, THE HAGUE
Klatteweg 109, 2597 KA The Hague
Tel.: 070 354 93 28
www.maxzwemschool.nl

The first part of this chapter has been written for parents of either elementary or secondary-school children. It goes into the types of international education available, preparing for university, fees and taxes. Then it describes the Dutch school system, including for children with special needs. The second part has been written with university-level students in mind. It describes the types of university – research-oriented 'traditional' universities and 'universities of applied sciences' – as well as the international programs and courses available in the Netherlands. Here you will also find information on qualifications for entering a university program, the credit system and the type of degree students obtain. Next, this second part goes into student life in the Netherlands; eating out, socializing, sports, as well as finding suitable housing, a job on the side and arranging a student grant. The final part describes 'Life on a Shoestring'; how to survive on little while either studying or otherwise living in the Netherlands on a modest income.

CHAPTER 9

Education

CONTRIBUTING AUTHORS ANNEBET VAN MAMEREN, STEPHANIE DIJKSTRA, WILLEMIJN VAN OPPEN AND NUFFIC

SENDING YOUR CHILDREN TO SCHOOL

WHAT SCHOOL SHOULD I CHOOSE?

When moving from one country to another, there are several issues that come to mind when trying to decide on what type of school to send your children to. Not only do you want to make the transition a smooth one, you also want to ensure that should your children decide to go to university, they have the right diplomas, or you might need take into account your child's special needs. And, last but not least, you want to keep your children's emotional well-being in mind.

There are several factors you can take into account when choosing your children's new school, such as language, your child(ren)'s age, culture, curriculum and, of course, what's available. If your children are young and you intend to stay in the Netherlands for a longer period of time, you might consider a Dutch national school. If your children are older, or will stay here temporarily, an international school might be a better option. A word on all these matters in the following paragraphs.

INTERNATIONAL EDUCATION OPTIONS

In the Netherlands, you will find private international schools, as well as subsidized international education at the so-called 'Dutch International Schools' (DIS). The latter schools are spread throughout the country and feature an international curriculum taught in English according to the international standards, at a relatively low, but mandatory, fee. An overview of these schools can be found on www.dutchinternationalschools.nl. The Dutch International Schools are part of the Dutch school system and thus bound by ministry rules, while other international (or foreign national) schools are privately operated.

The subsidy provided by the Dutch Ministry of Education makes it possible for these schools to offer a good quality international education at a reasonable fee. The fees range from € 4,500 to € 8,500 for primary schools and from € 6,000 to € 11,000 for secondary schools and are non-negotiable (although extra fees may be charged for, for example, projects or field trips). Fees at private international schools can go up to € 27,000 a year.

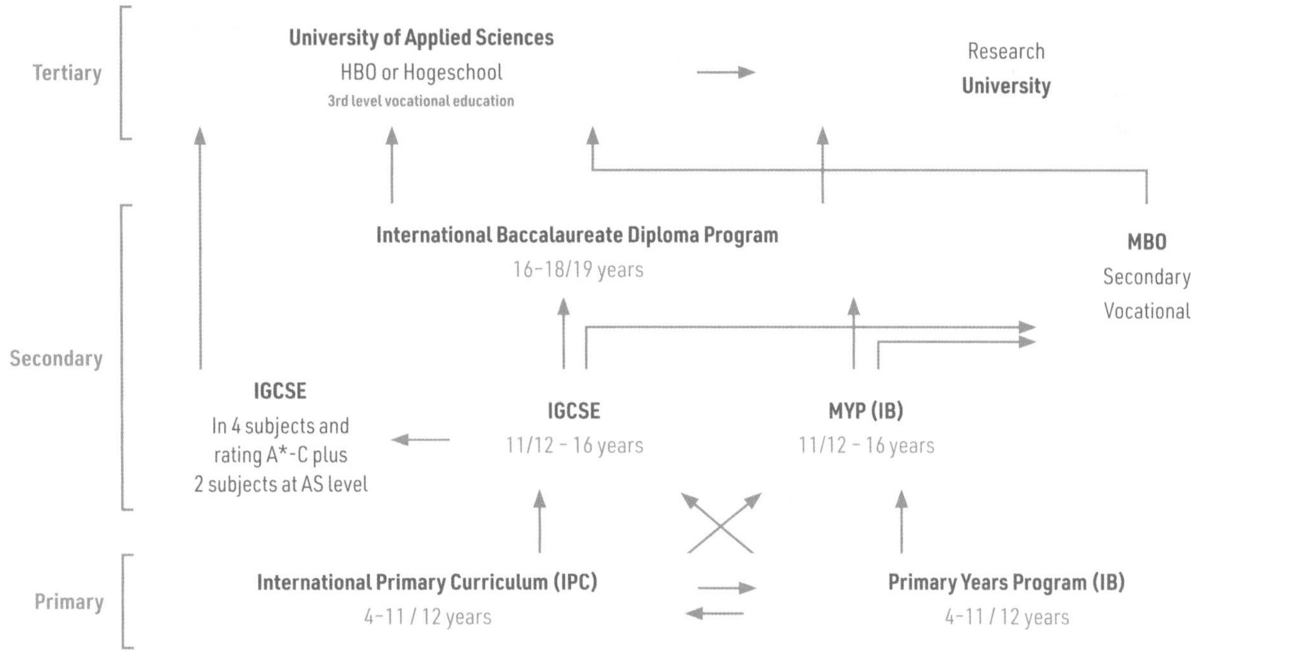

Table by Willemijn van Oppen, Educaide

QUALIFICATION FOR ADMISSION

The qualifications for admission to DIS schools are set by the Dutch Ministry of Education, Culture and Science. The following students may be admitted to these schools:

- children from a non-Dutch family with an expatriate status that will be staying in the Netherlands for a limited period of time (max. 2-3 years)
- children from an internationally mobile Dutch family, who have largely been educated abroad, and for whom an international education will be more advisable in order to ensure continuity
- children with Dutch nationality, whose parent(s) / legal guardian(s) (with whom the student will be living) will be stationed abroad within two years for at least two years.

Parents are asked about their future plans upon admission; pupils may stay at the school when their plans have changed overtime and they have surpassed the initial 2-3 years.

There is one exception; students with Dutch nationality are eligible to follow the two-year IB-diploma program at one of the Dutch international secondary schools, instead of the VWO 5&6 program, with Dutch A-higher as a mandatory subject. The same financial conditions apply as to international students.

In general, subsidized and private international schools only offer English-language education, though the so-called 'Foreign National Schools', such as the French, German, Indonesian and Japanese schools, teach their national curricula in their native tongue. As do the American and British schools, be it that they also offer the International Baccalaureate Diploma Program in the final two years next to the national diploma programs, with the exception of the British School in Amsterdam, which only offers the A-levels.

PRIMARY INTERNATIONAL EDUCATION

International primary education starts at the age of 4 and continues up until the age of 11 or 12. The Dutch International Primary Schools and the private international schools use either the International Primary Curriculum (IPC) or the International Baccalaureate Primary Years Program (IBPYP). For international children with special educational needs, there is Lighthouse Special Education school in The Hague. For more information, we refer you to page 230 and to our reference page at the end of the chapter.

SECONDARY INTERNATIONAL EDUCATION

During the first four to five years of international secondary education, the Dutch International Secondary Schools prepare their students for either the International Baccalaureate Middle Years Program (IBMYP) or the International General Certificate of Secondary Education (IGCSE). The IGCSE is the globally recognized equivalent of the British GCSE. If at least four (I)GCSE subjects with marks ranging from A*-C plus a GCE in two subjects at AS level are obtained, the Dutch Ministry of Education validates it at the same level as the Dutch HAVO, which entitles a student to an entry ticket to the universities of applied sciences.

Students who have successfully completed the IBMYP can be admitted to the two-year International Baccalaureate Diploma Program (IBDP). The IB-diploma is widely recognized as providing a well-balanced pre-university education. It is an accepted entrance qualification for top universities around the world, which also applies to the British A-level Diploma, following the (I) GSCE Program.

Private so-called foreign national schools may have different curricula for both junior and senior secondary school.

SECONDARY LEVEL VOCATIONAL SCHOOLS

If a student has successfully completed the IGCSE or IBMYP (Middle School) but is not admitted to the IB-Diploma Program, then either the MBO or the IBCP might be a good option. MBO offers 3-4 years of secondary vocational training; students can take several English-language programs in, for instance, Business and Hospitality studies, but also in Agriculture (www.mboraad.nl/english). With an MBO-4 diploma, a student can be admitted to a university of applied sciences (HBO).

The IB Organization has developed a new curriculum for the final two high school years, as an alternative to the IBDP; the IBCP (International Baccalaureate Career-Related Program). It offers secondary general and vocational education, and the diploma has been validated by the Dutch authorities to be comparable to at least a Dutch HAVO-diploma with vocational subjects. The IBCP incorporates the IB-principles in a program created for students who want to focus on career-related learning, thus providing them with both an academic and practical foundation. Currently, the British School in the Netherlands (BSN), the International School of The Hague (ISH) and AICS in Amsterdam offer the IBCP track.

EUROPEAN BACCALAUREATE

For children of staff of the European Union, 13 European schools have been created, offering the European Baccalaureate, which is taken at the end of the seventh year of secondary education. The EB is not the same as the International Baccalaureate or the various national Baccalaureates. It supports a rounded knowledge of all subjects and allows students – who must have strong skills in at least three European languages as well – to specialize in individual fields. Classes and examinations are offered in multiple European languages.

Currently there are two European Schools in the Netherlands, one in Bergen (near Alkmaar, Noord-Holland), and one Accredited European School in The Hague (the latter school is not listed on the official site, but does award the European Baccalaureate). The European Union pays the school fees for the children of their employees. For a fee of € 5,545 for primary and around € 7,561 for secondary, the European School in Bergen is also accessible to children whose parents are not employed by the European Union. Contrary to most other schools, they also give a substantial sibling discount. Within a few years, this school will move to a new location nearby the Alkmaar Noord train station.

BILINGUAL EDUCATION

Primary Schools

In August 2014, 12 Dutch Primary Schools joined a national pilot offering bilingual primary education. In the meantime, some schools have been added to the list, and others have quit, bringing the current total to 17. This pilot ended in August 2023.

In the national bilingual pilot primary schools, lessons are taught in another language 30 to 50% of the time – most often English. These schools also have a strong focus on internationalization. For example, pupils at these schools write letters to pen pals across the world, take part in charity projects, and discuss cultural differences. Some of these schools follow the theme-based International Primary Curriculum, which is still pretty unique for Dutch schools. A few other schools have come up with their own form of teaching some classes in English. As they are not official pilot schools, they are more restricted. Usually, classes are given in English about 15 to 20% of the time, and they do not receive the extra resources and support the 'official' bilingual schools receive.

The intermediate results of the pilot schools have been positive, and the students of bilingual schools have a greater English vocabulary than children at non-bilingual schools, while their level of Dutch doesn't seem to drop. In the near future, it is expected that more schools will become bilingual.

Many international parents see bilingual schools as an ideal in-between solution, somewhere between a Dutch and an international school, which seemingly complements their family dynamics very well. However, this might not always be the best option if their child speaks little Dutch, if any at all. First of all, it is important to note that the bilingual schools are *Dutch* schools, where English is offered in addition to the Dutch curriculum. Since the end tests of bilingual primary schools (be it a CITO test or another type of test) are the same as fully Dutch schools, pupils at bilingual schools need to master the Dutch language at (near) native level to take them, and some of these schools require that at least one of the parents speaks fluent Dutch.

A child who doesn't speak Dutch at home is largely dependent on what the school provides in terms of learning the language; will this child learn enough Dutch while being taught in this language only half of the time? And since the (often not-native) English teachers target their classes to mainly native Dutch children, how well would your native English speaker learn English at school? It would be good to ask the principal in advance about how the school deals with these issues.

The situation becomes even more complicated when a child doesn't speak either Dutch *or* English at home, as they would then have to study in two foreign languages at the same time.

Usually, these schools can't accommodate children who are 6 or older and don't speak Dutch yet. Consequently, these children are normally required to follow a one-year Dutch immersion program at a newcomer class first. You can read more about this further on.

Secondary Schools

An increasing number of Dutch Secondary Schools (HAVO and VWO, and also a couple of VMBO and MBO-schools) also offer TTO; *tweetalig onderwijs*, or bilingual education, in which some of the courses are offered in Dutch and others in English. This is, of course, only an option if your child has a sufficient command of the Dutch language, because all exams at these schools are in Dutch. Usually, classes are increasingly taught in Dutch as students approach the pre-exam years, in preparation for the Dutch-language final exams. Many of these schools offer either an IB-certificate English A-2 upon graduation, or the CAE (Cambridge Advanced English) certificate, or even the CPE-diploma (Certificate of Proficiency in English). TTO-students can also opt to follow the IB-diploma program at one of the subsidized Dutch international secondary schools instead of the 'standard' VWO 5 & 6, subject to the same financial conditions that are applicable to the international students, which are non-negotiable.

To explain the acronyms HAVO and VWO: HAVO (which lasts five years) is an equivalent of General Secondary Education. It prepares students for either the MBO (2nd level vocational education) or the University of Applied Sciences (HBO, 3rd level vocational education), or the last two years of VWO. VWO, which stands for pre-university education, lasts six years and leads to either the university of applied sciences or (academic) university. More information on this topic can be found on page 228.

The third type of secondary education, VMBO (1st level vocational education), lasts four years and prepares students either for senior secondary vocational education and training (MBO, *middelbaar beroepsonderwijs*), or the last two years of HAVO.

A Year of Immersion Before Going Dutch

Children who are 6 or older and don't speak Dutch are usually sent to a Dutch immersion (newcomer) class first. Maybe contrary to your expectations, this applies to the bilingual schools as well. At the newcomer class, all children follow their tailor-made program, which usually takes around one year, depending on their progress. Most schools don't have their own immersion class, which means that your child will have to start their education in the Netherlands at a separate, specialized school.

There are newcomer classes for younger children aged 6-12 (sometimes they start at age 4), and others for high school children aged 12-18 (called ISK). Normally there are around 15 children per class. Due to the small size of the newcomer class, the children get a lot of personal attention. They all get a tailor-made program, and their progress is regularly measured. The teachers are specialized in teaching Dutch to non-Dutch speaking children, and usually have a good understanding of the various cultures, languages, and socio-economic backgrounds represented by their pupils.

In this class, the children not only learn the Dutch language, but also about the culture, history and geography of the Netherlands, while they also take gym, swimming, music, and arts & crafts lessons, for which they use a broad vocabulary. The teachers offer the newly acquired words in different contexts, so the pupils truly understand how to use them. They go shopping together, and interview Dutch speakers about their jobs and hobbies. They also do math, which in the Netherlands – perhaps unlike to what you are used to – is very language-based. Often students are presented with numerical problems hidden in a story. In order to give the right answer to the math question, they first have to unravel the words that explain the problem.

Every newcomer learns at their own pace. Once they are really confident at speaking Dutch, they transfer to a regular school. On average this process takes one year. The exact duration really depends on a lot of different factors: the pupil's talent for languages, the closeness of their home language(s) to Dutch, the educational background of their parents, their emotional well-being, and the stability of their home situation, to name but a few.

Every city has organized the policy for newcomer children in their own way. In some places there is one big, dedicated newcomer school. After finishing their tailor-made program at this school, the students transfer to a regular school, usually to the same class as their peers, which means they don't 'lose' a year. In some cities you can find regular schools which have one or two internal newcomer classes, also with a maximum of 15 children per class. This type of school is especially favored by families with two or more children, where one child will go to the newcomer class, and the younger sibling can go to their regular class, depending on their age (and thus need for fluency). For these families, this means fewer transitions and less complicated logistics.

Usually, the advantage of the dedicated schools is that, because of their bigger scale, they are more experienced, knowledgeable and specialized than a regular school with a newcomer class. Another difference is that, in regular schools, children of different ages are combined in the same newcomer class, so a 6-year-old may have the overwhelming prospect of being in the same class as a 12-year-old. At the dedicated newcomer schools, on the other hand, a pupil's classmates are all children of the same age.

And what about the population of these newcomer schools? Well, it often reflects the neighborhood of the school. Some newcomer schools have a regional function, and so you'll find children from almost all imaginable backgrounds together.

For the majority of these students, it means that they have only one common language, Dutch, which gives them an extra opportunity to practice the language. On the other hand, in areas like Amstelveen, most children in the local newcomer class are native English speakers, to such an extent that some parents are worried their children won't ever learn enough Dutch there. In short, it is wise to look into how the particular school operates, and then decide if that would be a good option for your family.

Where to Start

A large number of parents want to send their child(ren) to an international school first, and once they become more adjusted to the country, move them to a Dutch school. In most cases this isn't a good idea, though. While at the international school they will learn some Dutch, it usually isn't enough to be able to follow the classes at a fully Dutch school.

Furthermore, immersion classes only get subsidies for children who have lived in the Netherlands for less than one year. Which means that, after one year or more at an international school, this subsidy will not be available for your child. Dedicated newcomer schools are often only able to admit a few children for whom they don't get a subsidy. And for regular schools with only one newcomer class of 15 children, an unsubsidized pupil is completely unaffordable. In this case the parents often end up hiring a private Dutch tutor, or leaving their children at the international school after all.

PREPARING FOR UNIVERSITY

If it is likely that your child is planning on going to university abroad after graduating from high school, then your best bet would be to find out whether there are any national schools from that country here. If there are no such schools, you should find out what the additional requirements are to be admitted with either a Dutch VWO diploma, or an A-level, IB or EB diploma to the university / universities of your preference, before your child starts with the final two years of high school. As there are so many different types of international and nationality-based schools in the Netherlands, it is impossible to provide you with information on each and every one of them. We therefore advise you to contact the various international schools directly for more information on their program. For a list of all international schools in the Netherlands, visit the following websites: https://new2nl.com/international-schools-in-the-netherlands, or www.educaide.nl. You can also find their addresses through the websites listed at the end of this chapter.

If there are no schools that offer the national program of your home country, or if you are going to be moving to another country later on, check whether the school you are considering for your child offers the IB (International Baccalaureate)-Diploma Program, as almost all universities accept the IB-diploma. The IB-program is offered at all international secondary schools in the Netherlands as well as at the American Schools and British schools in The Hague.

A lot of universities in the Netherlands offer their courses in English. For EEA-residents, university costs € 2,530 for 2024-2025. First-year students, as well as first and second-year students who were training to become a teacher, paid half, but this will be abolished as of September 1, 2024. There are some possibilities for student loans and scholarships. More info you can find on the www.studyinnl.org website and further on in this chapter.

FEES AND TAXES

It must be noted that the fees of the various non-Dutch schools vary considerably. In order to obtain information on these fees, please contact the schools in question. Many companies pay or reimburse the tuition fees for expat children, and the payments and reimbursements are often exempted from income tax. Tuition fees and taxes are a complicated issue, as there is also the 30%-reimbursement ruling, under which most tuition fees are deductible, to be taken into account. To be brought entirely up-to-date on this issue, we advise you to contact your tax consultant.

WAITING LIST

As many schools (Dutch and international) may have a waiting list, you are strongly advised to register your child with the school of your liking well in advance, if possible. In most cases, you don't need to have an address, nor a BSN (*burgerservicenummer*, or citizen service number) in order to apply for a school. Directly contact the school(s) of your interest to make sure of this.

THE NATIONAL EDUCATION SYSTEM

In these paragraphs, you will find a description of the Dutch primary and secondary school system.

PRIMARY EDUCATION

In the Netherlands, most children start primary school (*basisschool*) the day after their fourth birthday, whenever that is throughout the year. The *leerplicht* or compulsory education age applies as of the age of five, meaning that – as of that age – you cannot keep children out of school and take them back to your home country for extended periods of time, outside of school vacations, without the school principal's / inspector's permission. For a maximum of ten days, you need the principal's permission – for more; the school inspector's. It also means that home-schooling is only rarely permitted – and under strict conditions. Children may also take time off on days that their parents' religious or 'life' convictions require that the children stay home from school. For special family celebrations and emergencies, you can also get a few days off. Parents always need to ask permission in advance, and submit proof of the event.

Primary education lasts eight years (including two years of kindergarten), usually until the age of 12. Most schools combine groups 1&2 (ages 4 through just 6), where the pupils learn through play, and gradually prepare for reading and writing. 'Real' reading, writing and math start in 'group 3', at age 6. In the final year ('group 8'), pupils are advised as to the type of secondary education they should pursue. This advice is based largely on the *leerlingvolgsysteem* (pupil monitoring system) which is used to register the achievements of the pupils during their entire elementary school time, and an aptitude test (of which the CITO-*toets is the best-known*). In this test – which is not an exam that the students can either pass or fail – children answer questions in the areas of

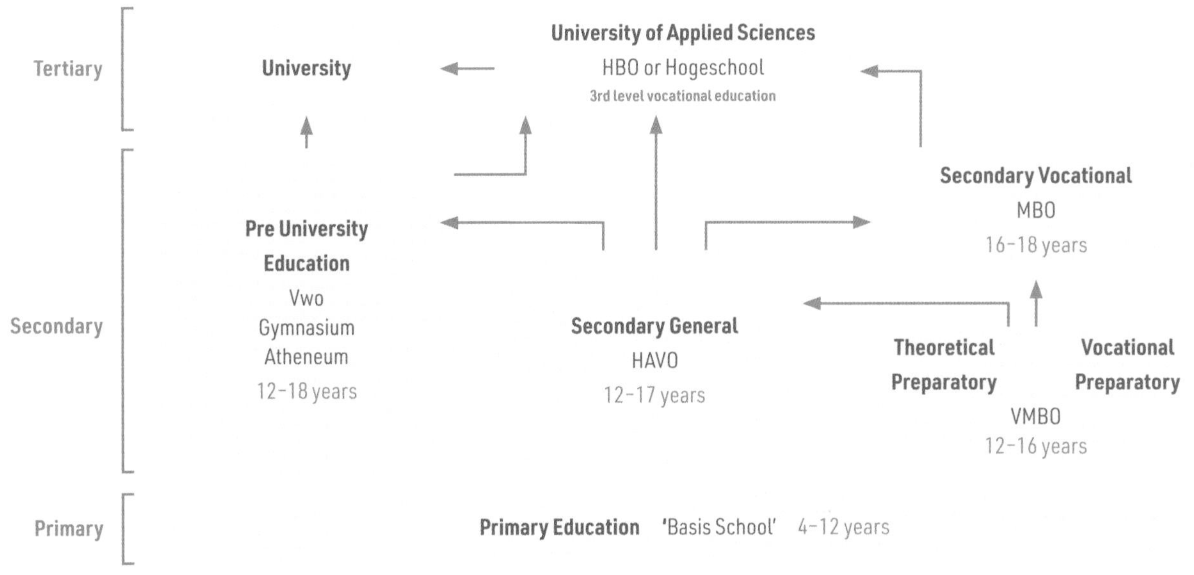

Table by Willemijn van Oppen, Educaide

Dutch language (e.g., spelling, grammar, comprehensive reading) and math. Since the 2014/2015 school year, all Dutch schools are obligated to administer one of the six transition tests that have been approved by the Ministry of Education, Culture and Science (OCW). Also since then, the teacher's recommendation for high school is leading. The teachers base their advice on the above-mentioned pupil monitoring system, as well as other characteristics, such as the pupil's eagerness to learn, attitude, interests, motivation, intelligence, and level of maturity. The transition test comes after the teacher's preliminary advice, and has become more of a second opinion. If the test scores come out higher than the teacher's recommendation, the pupil might be able to go to a higher level of high school education. If the test results are lower, the teacher's recommendation stands. In the near future, the end test and the teacher's recommendation will most likely take place at the same time. Before April 1st of the school year, all group 8 pupils in the Netherlands need to apply for secondary school, based on their final advice.

In the Netherlands, approximately 1.4 million children attend a primary school. The following three types of Primary Education are subsidized by the Ministry of Education, Culture and Science:

- Approximately one-third of the children goes to an *openbare school*, or 'public' school. These schools are usually run by an independent foundation which has originally been set up by the municipality and are not based on any particular religion or conviction, though they do teach about all world religions in a 'neutral' way. For more information on these schools, you can contact the Association for Public Education (Vereniging voor Openbaar Onderwijs); see the telephone number at the end of the chapter.
- Approximately two thirds of the children go to a *bijzondere*, or 'special', school. These schools are run by their own board, which is usually a group of parents or a foundation. They often reflect a particular denomination, such as Roman Catholic or Protestant. Other options are: Jewish, Islamic, Hindustani, or Humanistic schools.
- Some other 'special' schools are based on a particular educational philosophy, such as Montessori, Jenaplan, Dalton, Freinet, and so-called Waldorf schools (or *Vrije* schools, as they are called here). Combinations of denominational schools with an educational philosophy can also be found, as well as *openbare* schools that follow a philosophy.

FOREIGN LANGUAGE TEACHING IN DUTCH PRIMARY SCHOOLS

By law, all Dutch schools are obligated to start teaching English as a subject by the time the children are in group 7 (about age 10) at the latest. An increasing number of schools have decided to start with English earlier; sometimes even starting in group 1 (kindergarten). You'll also find a few primary schools that teach French, German, or Spanish. The schools that offer early foreign languages as a subject are called VVTO (Vroeg Vreemde Talen Onderwijs) schools. You can find a list of all participating schools (currently over 1,150) and some more useful information on: www.nuffic.nl/onderwerpen/vroeg-vreemdetalenonderwijs/vroeg-vreemdetalenonderwijs-vvto. The International Primary Curriculum (IPC) has been translated into the Dutch language too, so that, by now, there are more than 400 Dutch primary schools that teach this theme-based curriculum (more information can be found on https://ipc-nederland.nl).

Primary and Secondary School Vacations

Spring 2024
Northern and Middle Regions: February 17-25
Southern Region: February 10-18

May 2024
All regions: April 27-May 5

Summer 2024
Northern Region: July 20 - September 1
Middle Region: July 13 - August 25
Southern Region: July 6 - August 18

Fall 2024
Northern region: October 26 - November 3
Middle and Southern Regions: October 19-27

Christmas 2024
All Regions:
December 21 - January 5, 2025

Note: The dates for the short holidays may differ from one school to another. For further information concerning holidays, you should consult the school your child is attending

CHILDREN REQUIRING SPECIAL CARE

In the Netherlands, in principle all primary schools are 'inclusive' – meaning that children with mild special needs such as e.g. dyslexia will be admitted to a regular primary school. For children who need additional special care and attention, there are dedicated special needs schools, for instance for children with physical disabilities, children who are sick for a long period of time, and children with more severe learning or behavioral issues. These schools typically have smaller classes, offer more personal attention and employ in-house specialists and therapists.

DUTCH TRANSITION CLASS

In Dutch schools, the language of instruction is Dutch. Non-Dutch-speaking four and five-year-olds usually ease in pretty smoothly, though some cities require that children follow Dutch immersion class starting in group 1 (age four). If your child is six years or older, and doesn't speak Dutch, you could still enroll him or her in a Dutch school. However, many schools will require attendance of a Dutch transition class (called *schakelklas* or *nieuwkomersklas*) first. For more on this, see earlier, under *A Year of Immersion Before Going Dutch*, on page 224. Also at secondary level there are Dutch immersion classes, also called *internationale schakelklas (ISK)*.

Some cities also offer a *kopklas*. This intensive language class is meant for highly motivated children who have finished primary school with high grades for math, but much lower ones for the Dutch language. The aim is for these pupils to move on to a higher level of secondary education compared to their initial high school advice, after one year of *kopklas*.

GOVERNMENT FUNDING

Most schools are funded by the government. Each child costs the government approximately € 7,200 per year (more in the case of special needs schools). Parents are only asked to pay a contribution for extras such as field trips and festivities. The amount of the parent contribution varies per school and lies between approximately € 40 to € 700 per year, with most parents paying less than € 100. The government gives extra money to schools that have many newcomers, and school that are located in underprivileged neighborhoods.

PRIVATE DUTCH SCHOOLS

In the Netherlands, there are also a few private (non-government funded) primary and secondary schools, attended by less than 1% of the student population. These schools typically have smaller classes compared to the regular schools, and are often experienced in supporting pupils with minor behavioral issues, learning difficulties like dyslexia or dyscalculia, and gifted children. The fees of these schools start at € 15,500 – € 39,500 per year. Many of the private schools are international.

SECONDARY EDUCATION

In the Netherlands, after a child has completed primary school, the parents and child together choose what type of secondary school the child will go to. This decision is based, for the most part, on the recommendation given by the primary school during the final year (see the information provided in the previous section).

There are three types of secondary school pupils can choose from and they go by the following acronyms: VMBO, HAVO and VWO. All three start with a sort of 'basic package' – adapted to the level of education, see further on – that usually lasts two years and consists of subjects that generally all students follow. At the end of the first year (called the *brugklas*, or 'bridge class'), a final decision is usually made regarding the type and level of secondary education in which the student will continue until graduation. Many secondary schools offer a mixed *brugklas* (VMBO / HAVO or HAVO / VWO), giving the pupils one year to make up their minds and to demonstrate the level at which they are capable of performing. In some secondary schools, this decision is made after two or three years. In the third year of secondary education, the three types of schools become considerably different, see the following paragraphs.

For children requiring a less academic type of secondary education there is a so-called 'vocational' learning path, focused on practical skills and the competencies necessary for employment.

GENERAL SECONDARY EDUCATION: HAVO AND VWO

The two programs of secondary education that grant admission to higher education are HAVO, which lasts five years, and VWO, which lasts six years. Pupils are enrolled according to their ability, and VWO is considered more rigorous. The VWO curriculum prepares pupils for (research) university (also known as WO), while the HAVO-diploma prepares students for admission to a university of applied sciences, also known as HBO, or *Hogeschool*.

The last two (for HAVO) or three (for VWO) years are referred to as the exam preparation phase, or upper secondary education. During these years, pupils focus on one of four subject clusters (*profielen*), each of which emphasizes a certain field of study in addition to satisfying general education requirements and allowing them to take a number of electives. A pupil enrolled in VWO or HAVO can choose one the following subject clusters: 1) Science and Technology (*Natuur en Techniek*); 2) Science and Health (*Natuur en Gezondheid*); 3) Economics and Society (*Economie en Maatschappij*), and; 4) Culture and Society (*Cultuur en Maatschappij*). With a HAVO diploma, a student may move onto the 5th and then 6th year of VWO, and then to research university, if they want. Or they can opt to do an HBO bachelor's program, followed by a master's at a research university, while some HBO studies also offer a master's program.

As mentioned earlier under International Education Options, an increasing number of Dutch secondary schools also offer TTO; *tweetalig onderwijs*, or bilingual education, in which some of the courses are offered in Dutch and others in English. It is important to be aware that all final exams at these schools are in Dutch, though. Also many of these schools award an IB-certificate English A-2 upon graduation. Some schools also offer the Cambridge Certificate in English, either the CAE or the CPE. This additional diploma offers proof of proficiency in reading, writing, listening, speaking and "English in Use" (idiom and grammar). This certificate is well appreciated by schools of further education and future employers, and is considered sufficient to allow entry into an English-language university (both research and applied sciences) program.

VOCATIONAL SECONDARY EDUCATION: VMBO / MBO

VMBO lasts four years and offers a choice of four 'learning paths' (or 'routes' as the Dutch call them): theoretical, mixed, vocational and basic profession-oriented – each of which offers a choice out of four further sectors: Economics, Technology, Social Sciences (including Biology), and Green / Agriculture. Also a number of VMBO-schools now offer the option of a bilingual program.

Students who have completed VMBO have the option of either going on to the 4th (and then 5th) year of HAVO (if they have completed the theoretical or the mixed 'route') or senior secondary vocational education and training (MBO, *middelbaar beroepsonderwijs*). MBO students may choose from ten study profiles, including economics, hospitality, technology, services, social welfare and agriculture. MBO programs vary in length from one to four years as well as in level (1 to 4). Completion of a level-4 MBO program qualifies pupils for access to HBO (university of applied sciences).

TYPES OF SCHOOLS

As is the case for primary schools, the majority of secondary schools are government-funded and can be divided into 'public' schools and schools based on a particular denomination (for instance, Roman-Catholic, Protestant, Jewish or Islamic) or educational philosophy (for instance, Montessori, Waldorf or Dalton). Of course, there are also secondary schools for students requiring special needs support, see further on.

COMPULSORY EDUCATION AND GOVERNMENT FUNDING

Education is compulsory until a student reaches the age of 18, or has obtained the so-called *startkwalificatie* (basically a VWO, HAVO or MBO level 2 diploma). This obligation to pursue an education is referred to as the child's *leerplicht*, or period of compulsory attendance.

As mentioned earlier, leerplicht starts at the age of five and, until the age of 16, children are fully *leerplichtig*. After that, the obligation focuses not so much on attending school full-time as on obtaining a secondary-school diploma. This is also referred to as their *kwalificatieplicht* (until the age of 23), during which time they are allowed to combine school and work.

Secondary education is government-funded and each child costs the government approximately € 7,300 per year. Parents can also be asked to make a contribution to the school, but this is a voluntary contribution and is meant to cover 'extras', such as festivities and excursions. If you send your child to TTO, or bilingual education, you have to pay an additional amount of € 100 to € 500, depending on the school – though some schools charge up to € 800.

SPECIAL NEEDS EDUCATION

In August 2014, the current 'Inclusive Education' (*Passend Onderwijs*) Act took effect. This act dictates that all schools are responsible for providing a suitable learning place for every child, with the idea that children with and without special needs should be able to go together to the same schools.

Parents first register their preschooler with a mainstream school, which is obligated to investigate whether they can provide the (external) support this child may need. Regional alliances (*samenwerkingsverbanden*) consisting of both mainstream schools and Special Education Needs (SEN) schools receive their own budgets for educational support.

However, not all mainstream schools are equally equipped for, or experienced in, teaching non-Dutch children with special needs, so parents should select the school very carefully. You should ask the school in advance about their previous experiences with providing the specific support your child needs, and how they would handle your specific situation. Also ask for their formal support plan (*ondersteuningsplan*), which describes their procedures for special needs support, and keep in mind that additional, external support is often limited to a few hours per week.

If your child already attends a mainstream school, and you suspect they need more learning support, your first point of contact in the school is the IB'er, who is the member of staff who performs the role of care coordinator. They can carry out some additional tests or ask for help from an external specialist.

TYPES OF SPECIAL NEEDS EDUCATION

If the support required turns out to be too specialized or intensive, the child might be referred to a dedicated special needs school. There are three main types of special needs education: *speciaal basisonderwijs* (SBO), and *speciaal onderwijs,* at both primary (SO) and secondary (VSO) levels.

At SBO schools, the pupils follow the same program and have the same government-set core objectives as regular primary schools. However, the classes at these schools are smaller, which ensures that the children receive more personal attention and tailor-made support. They also get more time to complete primary school (till age 14, instead of age 12). This type of education especially caters for children who have more serious learning difficulties, a lower IQ, or behavioral challenges.

At the dedicated special needs schools (*speciaal onderwijs*), there are four cluster schools based on the type of special needs. Also here, class sizes are smaller than at regular schools, and the children receive more tailor-made and specialized support and therapies focused on their specific needs. The teachers teach at different levels in the class, and most children follow the regular curriculum.

The *speciaal onderwijs* schools are divided into the following clusters:

- cluster 1 schools are meant for children who are visually impaired or blind
- cluster 2 is for children who have serious communication problems (hard of hearing, speech disorder, etc.)
- cluster 3 schools welcome children who have cognitive or physical disabilities, or a chronic illness that makes going to school difficult
- cluster 4 schools are for children with psychiatric or serious behavioral issues (autism, ADHD, PDD-NOS, ODD, CD, etc.).

These cluster schools often work together in order to provide the most suitable support. Some complications could arise, though, if a child doesn't fit precisely into one of the clusters. Some extra tests, interviews, and meetings with the parents might then be required. When a pupil makes enough progress at the special needs school, they may transfer to a regular (primary or secondary) school.

SECONDARY SCHOOL

After a special needs primary school, a child can go to either a regular secondary school (with extra support, if needed), or a special needs school at secondary level (VSO). A special needs school at secondary level needs to make an educational plan with the child and guide them towards a suitable career.

If your child grows up in the Netherlands, their development will be routinely monitored by the *Consultatiebureau* (GGD/OKC), a health clinic for babies and toddlers. In case of any irregularities, they may refer you to a specialist. If needed, this specialist can help you apply for additional support at a mainstream school, or for a special needs school.

Curiosity
We are curious, compassionate and connected.
www.isutrecht.nl
Governed by NUOVO Scholen and SPO Utrecht
We are
a learning
community.
International
School
Utrecht

International education
with a Dutch touch
• Offering IB Middle Years and Diploma Programmes
• Encouraging students to become creative, critical and reflective learners
• Exploring global challenges in a culturally diverse environment
• Broad and balanced IB curriculum prepares for Universities worldwide
• Near Leiden - between Amsterdam and The Hague
Visit our
website
Discover your talent
International School
Rijnlands Lyceum
Oegstgeest

In order for your child to be accepted into a special needs school, they should first get a referral, which is issued by the regional alliance in your place of residence. This referral is called a *toelaatbaarheidsverklaring* (TLV) – which, literarily translated, means 'admissibility statement'.

Your child will have to go through several observations and tests, and – as their parent – you will be interviewed. It is often a long and tiring process.

SUPPORT FOR INTERNATIONAL PARENTS OF SEN CHILDREN

Support for international parents is available at local and national levels. A specialized educational consultant (*onderwijsconsulent*) can assist your family in this process. An *onderwijsconsulent* is an independent educational specialist who has a lot of experience with SEN children. Parents don't need to pay for the help of this consultant.

At the end of this chapter, there is a list of some more organizations and support groups that can help you through the process.

If you are arriving in the Netherlands with a child who has already had special needs support, you need to register this with the municipality (*gemeente*) during the registration process, so that the appropriate steps can be taken to put adequate support in place. You can try and speed up this lengthy process by arranging as many things as possible prior to your arrival.

SPECIAL NEEDS SUPPORT IN INTERNATIONAL SCHOOLS

Most international schools in the Netherlands (both state-funded and private) work with SEN teachers. Usually, they can only accommodate a limited number of SEN-children a year. You may have to pay extra for a teaching assistant. Please make sure you look into how this works beforehand, to make the process more manageable.

In the Netherlands, there is only one international special needs school: Lighthouse Special Education, located in The Hague. They specialize in complex behavioral and/or developmental problems, and are a private (fee-paying) school.

SCHOOLS FOR GIFTED PUPILS

There is another type of special needs school; the Leonardo schools for gifted children. Usually, they are regular schools that have a dedicated department for gifted children who are offered extra cognitive challenges and subjects. These schools have their own admission criteria.

GOING TO UNIVERSITY

The higher education system in the Netherlands is based on a two-cycle degree system, consisting of a bachelor's, master's (with the option of obtaining a Ph.D. degree upon completing a master's degree). It is offered at two types of institutions: research universities (WO / *Universiteiten*) and universities of applied sciences (HBO / *hogescholen*). Whereas research universities are primarily responsible for offering research-oriented programs in an academic setting, universities of applied sciences are primarily responsible for offering programs of higher professional education, preparing students for specific professions. These tend to be more practice-oriented than the programs offered by research universities. On www.studyinnl.org/dutch-education you can find more information on the Dutch higher education system.

Approximately 53% (2021) of the Dutch population between the ages of 30 and 35 has a higher education degree – either a bachelor's degree or a master's degree – 58% of women and 49% of men.

RESEARCH UNIVERSITIES

Academic education (in Dutch: wetenschappelijk onderwijs) at university is accessible to students with an IB Diploma or the Dutch VWO – or their equivalent – and offered by research universities in Maastricht, Eindhoven, Tilburg, Nijmegen, Wageningen, Enschede, Groningen, Utrecht, Amsterdam, Leiden, Delft, Heerlen, Breukelen and Rotterdam. Some of these universities also have faculties / departments in other cities. Universities typically set a minimum qualification requirement for admission to their program. If you know which diploma is required for the program of your choice, you can check how your own diploma compares to this on the Nuffic website.

The university degree programs are organized around a bachelor's or undergraduate phase that lasts three years and a master's or graduate phase that lasts one to three years. These universities (including the Open University) are primarily responsible for offering research-oriented programs (*Wetenschappelijk Onderwijs*, WO) and the opportunity to conduct research in a wide range of disciplines: language and culture, behavior and society, economics, law, medical and health sciences, natural sciences, mathematics, engineering, and agriculture. All research universities also offer Ph.D.-programs.

As many Dutch universities have partner institutions in other countries, students can follow part of their degree program course abroad. Your university can provide information about the exchange agreements it has with other universities.

HOGESCHOLEN OR 'UNIVERSITIES OF APPLIED SCIENCES'

Higher professional education (*Hoger Beroepsonderwijs*, HBO) is accessible for students with an IB diploma, an MBO-diploma (level 4), the HAVO *diploma* or the VWO diploma. Universities of applied sciences offer higher professional education, which focuses on applied arts and sciences in one of the seven HBO sectors: agriculture, technology, economics, health care, art, education, and social and community work. Once again: universities typically set a minimum qualification requirement for admission to their program. If you know which diploma is required for the program of your choice, you can check how your own diploma compares to this on the Nuffic website.

The universities of applied sciences offer three or four-year bachelor's degree programs as well as master's programs lasting one to two years. All degree programs focus on preparing students for particular professions. They tend to be more practically oriented than programs offered by research universities. In addition to lectures, seminars, projects and independent study, students are often required to complete an internship or work placement (*stage*) which normally takes up part of the third year of study, as well as a final project or a major paper in the fourth year.

INSTITUTES FOR INTERNATIONAL EDUCATION

Institutes for international education (IE) in the Netherlands offer advanced training courses across a variety of fields. Many of these institutes are affiliated with research universities. These institutes offer various types of education, including short courses, master's programs and sometimes Ph.D. programs. More details about IE

institutes can be found on the Study in NL website: Institutes for International Education | Study in NL. The courses are taught in English, and are originally designed for people from developing countries whose jobs require highly specialized knowledge, focusing on courses relevant to developing countries.

STUDYING IN ANOTHER LANGUAGE / COUNTRY

Across the country, the Dutch higher education institutions offer an extensive number of courses in English, both specialized courses as well as entire bachelor's, master's and Ph.D.-programs. Many courses are taught entirely in English; in fact, 70% of all master's courses and 20% of all bachelor's degrees are offered in English. Just wandering across university campuses, you will find that you are surrounded by a very international community, where people speak a variety of languages.

The site www.studyinnl.org/dutch-education/studies offers international students an independent and reliable overview of English-taught study programs offered by Dutch higher education institutions, ranging from short or summer courses to full-fledged bachelor's and master's degree programs.

As Europe's higher education market is becoming more and more unified, European students are increasingly investigating their study options across national borders. At the same time, Europe is becoming more attractive for students from overseas as well. Unfortunately, most information resources still focus on the national level so that students are often not aware of what their options are. The sites https://education.ec.europa.eu/study-in-europe, www.bachelorsportal.com, www.mastersportal.com and www.phdportal.com fill this information vacuum for the different degrees and help students find and choose an equivalent study program across Europe. On www.scholarshipportal.com you will find an overview of the financial support available from many different sources for those who want to study in Europe, while www.shortcoursesportal.com lists the options for short-term programs in Europe, such as summer and winter schools, and www.distancelearningportal.com lists learning courses to be followed in other parts of the world. Together, these portals are the European study choice platform, listing over 20,000 study options in almost 40 European countries and more than 1,000 scholarships – aimed towards stimulating student mobility and promoting European Higher education. More information on scholarships in the Netherlands can also be found on www.studyinnl.org/finances.

Even though there are many degree programs taught entirely in English, you may want to take on the challenge and do a study program in Dutch. If you are looking for a program or course conducted in Dutch, you can check the following websites: www.studyinnl.org/dutch-education/study-programmes-in-dutch, www.studiekeuze123.nl and www.duo.nl. A number of university centers offer Dutch-as-a-second-language courses. The courses are specially designed for international students who have otherwise qualified for admission to Dutch higher education, but must first prove that they have mastered the language sufficiently.

REQUIREMENTS FOR ADMISSION TO HIGHER EDUCATION

As mentioned earlier, for access to WO bachelor's programs, students are required to have an IB diploma, a VWO diploma or an equivalent foreign diploma. In some cases, having completed the first year (60 ECTS, see further on) of an HBO program may also be accepted. The minimum entry requirement for HBO is an IB diploma (and, in some cases, the IGCSE diploma with two additional subjects at GCE-level), the Dutch HAVO / VWO diploma, a level-4 MBO-diploma, or an equivalent foreign diploma. Students with four GCSEs with marks ranging from A*-C, plus two GCEs at A/S level are also eligible for admission. When applying for WO or HBO, students are required to have completed at least one of the subject clusters (in Dutch: *profielen*) that fulfils the requirements for the higher education program in question.

Certain programs apply a quota, or *numerus fixus*, for access – primarily in the health sector. N*umerus fixus* programs have a fixed number of students that will be accepted; in order to be admitted, you need to complete a selection procedure. The only access requirement for the Open University is that applicants be at least 18 years of age.

To determine whether your diploma qualifies for access to Dutch higher education, you need to get your diploma evaluated by your prospective educational institution.

Institutions may have additional admission requirements. To begin, select a study program and then review its specific admission requirements. On www.studyinnl.org/dutch-education/studies you can search all English-taught degree programs in the Netherlands. It is essential that you speak, read and write English well, and you will be required to show that you have passed an English language test. IELTS (International English Language Testing System) and TOEFL (Test of English as a Foreign Language) are commonly accepted, but institutions may accept other tests as well, such as Cambridge English (CAE, CPE).

The required scores are at least 550 (paper-based) or 213 (Internet-based) for TOEFL. For IELTS, a score of at least 6 is required. On www.studyinnl.org/plan-your-stay/admission-requirements you can find more information on admission requirements at higher education institutions in the Netherlands.

DEADLINES

If you want to study in the Netherlands, keep an eye out for the application deadlines. For numerus fixus programs, the deadline is January 15. For other programs, the deadline is usually May 1st. These are general deadlines; the actual deadlines may vary per institution and study program. You also have the option of visiting the universities' open days (online and offline), to get a feel for the campus, the people and the program, and to ask any questions you might have. An even more in-depth familiarization option are the *meeloop-dagen*, which you can sign up for online. During those days, you join a student on their day at university, attending classes and experiencing the day-to-day feel of going to this university. Make sure to visit the website of the higher education institution where you would like to study to check for any upcoming open days or *meeloop-dagen* listed on their calendar.

DEGREES / BSA

Bachelor's degrees are awarded by universities and universities of applied sciences. An HBO bachelor's degree program requires three or four years of study to complete, at the end of which graduates obtain the degree Bachelor of Arts, Bachelor of Science, or Bachelor of Laws. Students graduating from programs in business administration, social work, education and music may obtain a BBA/BSW/BED or BM, respectively. A WO bachelor's degree requires three years of study to complete, and graduates are awarded the degree Bachelor of Science, Bachelor of Arts, or Bachelor of Laws. The same master's degree titles are awarded by research universities and universities of applied sciences.

In the Netherlands, a propedeuse is a diploma you can get after completing your first year of studies. To earn a propedeuse, you need to successfully finish all the subjects and requirements in your first year, obtaining 60 credits. It's important to note that the propedeuse is not an official degree and does not have value outside the Dutch education system. Once you have your HBO-*propedeuse*, you have a choice: you can either continue in the bachelor's program at the university of applied sciences, or you can begin in the first year of a WO (research university) program – though this is usually only the case for related programs. This is a way for HAVO-students, who are not qualified to enter a WO university program, to enter one after all, after 'investing' a year in obtaining an HBO *propedeuse*. Students following a higher education program in the Netherlands will receive a 'binding recommendation' (*Bindend studie advies*, or BSA) at the end of the first year. To do this, they will have to have obtained a determined minimum of ECTS during their first year, on the basis of which they are allowed to continue on to their second year. In principle, without a BSA, you must quit this study, though exceptions for personal circumstances are allowed.

Upon earning a WO-bachelor's degree at a particular university, the student is automatically eligible to pursue a master's program. This can also be at a different university – in the Netherlands or in a foreign country.

Associate's Degree

The associate's degree (it goes by the same name in Dutch) is offered at universities of applied sciences. This degree enables students to obtain a professional qualification in a shorter period of time (two years, 120 ECTS) and can help them learn the skills and competencies needed to improve their chances on the job market. It is more practically oriented than an HBO program and usually focuses on professions that are in demand. The theory is linked to practice: the students learn to map and solve problems during practical assignments / internships at companies, municipalities, or organizations. Access requirements to an associate's degree program are HAVO, VWO or MBO level 4, though there may be extra skills and/or requirements. Once they have obtained an associate's degree, graduates can seek employment or go on to an HBO-program to obtain a bachelor's degree, which usually only requires another two years of study.

International Secondary Vocational Education and Training

Within the Netherlands, MBO-schools (secondary Vocational Education and Training, or VET) are diversifying in terms of available MBO degrees. For example, there are MBO/VET schools that offer not only the Dutch MBO-4 diploma, but also an additional BTEC level 3 diploma or EBBD (European Business Baccalaureate Diploma) program. The BTEC diploma (www.ivs-alliance.nl) is composed of several units with themes such as Accounting, Marketing, and Management, and focuses on the future profession of the student. Within the chosen direction, 18 units need to be completed successfully. The program is bilingual for now, meaning that students must master both Dutch and English. The EBBD program focuses on students and adult learners wishing to acquire a label of excellence in the field of business administration. For more information about the EBBD program, you can visit https://ebbd.eu or go to the next sub-heading.

The following courses are offered at BTEC 3 level: Business and Fashion, Hospitality, Horticulture, Aviation, Tourism and an Extended Diploma in Business. Within the BTEC International Branch, the IVS-Alliance is the largest player in the Netherlands with 10 MBO /VET schools. All members of the IVS Alliance work with different courses of BTEC (e.g., Business, Engineering, Fashion, Hospitality, etc.) at their schools. For more information regarding this topic and participating schools, you can visit www.ivs-alliance.nl. There are also MBO/VET schools that offer the BTEC3 in combination with the Dutch MBO4, that are not members of the IVS alliance. In all cases, the BTEC3 diploma is internationally recognized, and offers plenty of opportunities to study and/or work abroad. It is issued by the British organization Pearson Edexcel, the largest UK awarding organization.

Graduates with a BTEC extended diploma can follow an accelerated program within the third level vocational schools (university of applied sciences or HBO) in the Netherlands and also abroad. There are good partnerships between the MBO-schools and other third level vocational schools that offer, among others, courses in International Business & Management Studies (IBMS), Small Business, Asian studies and International Business & Language (IBL).

As the BTEC diploma program is not subsidized, it needs to be financed by (the parents of) the student.

There is a network of bilingual MBO/VET courses in the Netherlands, currently consisting of 43 MBO/VET courses. At a bilingual MBO/VET school, 50% of the curriculum is taught in English. Students who graduate with a bilingual MBO/VET diploma are obligated to obtain an internationally acknowledged diploma or certificate such as BTEC, VTCT, Linguaskill, Cambridge, Anglia, or Goethe (German). Another important part of bilingual education is the focus on international awareness in the curriculum, for instance through international internships or projects. At the moment, there are a few MBO/VET schools that offer full degrees in English, like ROC Mondriaan (The Hague) and the Summa College (Eindhoven). Other schools in the Netherlands are extending their curricula with international courses, like ROC Amsterdam/Flevoland, where students can follow an intensive one-year international course in denim development.

European Business Baccalaureate Diploma

Recently, a new program has been developed: the European Business Baccalaureate Diploma (EBBD), which is recognized all across Europe. The program focuses on business competence and soft skills in an international environment, for professions in the area of business administration. In the Netherlands, the Albeda College in Rotterdam, Summa College in Eindhoven, Koning Willem I College in Den Bosch, Rijn IJssel in Arnhem, ROC Noorderport in Groningen, ROC Midden Nederland in Amersfoort, and ROC Midden Nederland in Utrecht offer this program. For more information check https://ebbd.eu.

Schakeljaar Foundation Year

Refugees, asylum seekers and other non-Dutch nationals who come to study in the Netherlands often go through a period of cultural and language adjustment that conceivably prevents them from getting everything they can out of their studies – or giving it all they have. For this reason, a number of institutes of higher education and schools offering MBO now offer a so-called *schakeljaar* (foundation year), created specifically for non-European, non-Western students, who are planning on following a study at a Dutch university (of applied sciences).

The course helps you study independently, work on projects and group assignments, give presentations, and work together with a professor. At the end of the year, you speak Dutch level NT2-II and are well-prepared for the Dutch university education system, including – as mentioned earlier – style of classes, giving presentations and working in groups. The course is offered by UAF, More information on UAF can be found on www.uaf.nl/en/about-us/.

Schakeljaren are offered in several locations, including, a.o. Amsterdam, Utrecht, Groningen, and Tilburg. For more information, visit https://www.uaf.nl/en/ondersteuning/ik-wil-studeren/schakeljaar/. Also check out https://www.uaf.nl/en/partners/onderwijs/.

What the costs of the ***schakeljaar*** are, depend on your personal situation, as well as any agreements reached between your university and the municipality on financing and whether you have a right to the *studiefinanciering*-loan. For more information, approach your university.

NOTE: when googling ***schakeljaar***, pay attention; the same name is used for the third and final year of the master's degree in medicine – being the year in which a specialization is chosen. The best way to avoid possible confusion, is to type in the entire UAF URLs mentioned above.

CREDIT SYSTEM

The European Credit Transfer and Accumulation System (ECTS) credit system is used by all higher education institutions in the Netherlands. A WO bachelor's program requires the completion of 180 credits (3 years), an HBO bachelor's program requires the completion of 180 credits (3 years) or 240 credits (4 years). An associate degree requires the completion of 120 credits.

In most cases, a WO master's program requires the completion of 60 to 120 credits (1 or 2 years). In engineering, agriculture, dentistry, math, and the natural sciences, 120 credits are always required. For medicine, veterinary medicine and pharmacy, 180 credits are required. An HBO master's program requires the completion of 60 to 120 credits.

DOCTORATE

The third cycle of higher education, leading to a Ph.D degree, is awarded only by research universities. All research universities in the Netherlands are entitled to award the country's highest academic degree, the *doctoraat* or Ph.D., which entitles a person to use the title *doctor*, abbreviated to *dr.* The process by which a doctorate is obtained is referred to as the *promotie*. The doctorate is primarily a research degree, for which a dissertation based on original research must be written and publicly defended. The minimum amount of time required to complete a doctorate is four years.

Most students working on doctorates are in fact paid employees rather than students. They apply for positions as AIOs, or research assistants. These positions are advertised in the same way jobs are, and candidates approach the supervisor directly. Candidates with foreign qualifications may apply for these positions and ask for permission to write their dissertation in another language. Candidates may also contact a university faculty / department independently, and write their own research proposal. Sometimes the research for a dissertation can be conducted in the candidate's own country.

It is not necessary to take on a position as an AIO in order to get a Ph.D.; it merely enables candidates to have a source of income while working on their Ph.D. More information can be found at www.studyinnl.org/dutch-education/phd.

GRADING

The grading system has been the same for many decades: the scale is from 1 (very poor) to 10 (outstanding). The minimum passing grade is 5.5; 10s and 9s are seldom awarded, and grades 1-3 are hardly ever granted.

CHOOSING A UNIVERSITY (OF APPLIED SCIENCES)

The Dutch system of quality control guarantees that the education offered at all the institutions meets the same high standards. When Dutch students choose where they want to study, they are not thinking of which research university or university of applied sciences is best, but instead are looking at which specializations are offered and which emphasis or academic tradition is featured. Each institution has its own atmosphere and style. They distinguish themselves in this way, and not through any absolute measure of quality. For these reasons, employers in the Netherlands look first at the degree a person has earned. Where this degree was earned is not so important.

On www.studyinnl.org/dutch-education/studies you can search and compare study programs taught in the English language based on the criteria that matter to you. This can be the city where the institution is located or the study subjects that are taught.

QUALITY CONTROL

How do you know for sure that your course or program is of the right quality? Find out whether it has been accredited by the Accreditation Organization of the Netherlands and Flanders (Nederlands Vlaamse Accreditatie Organisatie, www.nvao.net), which has been appointed by the Dutch and Flemish government for the purpose of monitoring the quality of the higher education courses and programs on offer. Institutions that offer English-language education must sign a special Code of Conduct, for their non-EU students to be granted a residence permit to study here. This code sets out standards for the Dutch higher education institutions in their dealings with international students. By signing the Code of Conduct, the institutions guarantee international students that they will adhere to rules regarding the quality of programs, student recruitment policy, selection, and counseling procedures. All Dutch higher institutions that you will find on www.studyinnl.org/dutch-education/studies have signed the Code of Conduct. Find out more about which institutions have signed the Code of Conduct on www.internationalstudy.nl.

LANGUAGE

To enroll in a program or course that is conducted in English, you must have the appropriate level of command of the English language. To determine this, you must take an English language test, such as TOEFL (Test of English as a Foreign Language, see www.ets.org) or IELTS (International English Language Testing System, see www.ielts.org). At most universities, a CPE/CAE diploma that is less than two years old is also accepted. Additional language requirements can be found by visiting the database of international courses that can be found on www.studyinnl.org/dutch-education/studies.

MAKING THE TRANSITION

In principle, if you want to come to the Netherlands as a student, you can only come here to follow a particular course (or full study program) and you must meet all requirements. There are, however, three exceptions to this. The first is: if you meet all requirements for studying in the Netherlands, you are allowed to come here for a year to study Dutch first. The second is: if you do not meet all requirements, you can come here for a year to follow a preparatory program for the particular study of your choice. More information on the conditions can be found on https://ind.nl/en/residence-permits/study/student-residence-permit-for-university-or-higher-professional-education. The third option, which you can read more about on page 236, is the so-called foundation year (*schakeljaar*); a transitional year that has been created for specifically for non-European, non-Western students to help them prepare for their studies here.

TUITION

There are two types of institutions that offer higher education in the Netherlands: government-funded and government-approved. The statutory tuitions fees at a government-funded institution are € 2,530 a year (2024-2025), for EU/EEA/Swiss/Surinam-students, students who are related to an EU citizen who lives in the Netherlands, and students who have a residence permit that gives them a right to *studiefinanciering* (see further on). As of September 2024, first-year students, starting a bachelor's or associate degree program, no longer pay half (€ 1,157), nor do students in teacher training programs. You can read more about the fees on www.studyinnl.org/finances/tuition-fees. Students of all other nationalities and students who enroll in a government-approved institution pay higher fees; the average tuition fee for bachelor's programs being between € 6,000 and € 15,000, and for a master's program between € 8,000 and € 20,000. Tuition for theology studies is lower.

The Dutch government no longer funds study placements occupied by non-EU/EEA/Swiss students. Nonetheless, tuition fees in the Netherlands can be considered reasonable, compared to international education options in other countries, while the level of education is excellent. Furthermore, there are grants available, which you can read about further on. EU/EEA/Swiss students can apply for the *studiefinanciering*-loan, see https://duo.nl/particulier/international-visitor/.

You can find more about student grants further on www.studyinnl.org/finances, or by visiting www.scholarshipportal.com.

PERMITS

For more information about permits, such as residence permits and visas, see page 146 for the rules when coming to the Netherlands to study.

COSTS OF DAILY LIVING

If you come to study in the Netherlands, you will need to take into account such issues as tuition, rent and daily expenses, as well as basic health insurance, obtaining a permit, transportation (though, if you qualify for the study loan – *studiefinanciering* – you are offered a public transportation pass), books, notebooks and perhaps membership fees for student (sports) organizations. You can expect all this to amount to approximately € 800 – € 1,100 a month, excluding tuition. Housing will cost you between € 300 and € 600 a month. For more information on this, visit www.studyinnl.org/finances/daily-student-expenses-and-cost-of-living-in-holland.

PROOF OF SUFFICIENT FINANCIAL MEANS

Foreign students from outside the EU – in order to be issued a (provisional) residence permit – must prove that they have sufficient financial means to cover the study expenses and to provide for themselves. This means that you must have access to a monthly amount that has been determined in the *Studiefinanciering* Act 2000, and depends on what you will be studying. For universities (of applied sciences) studies, this is approximately € 958 (excluding tuition fees) per month. You must either have this amount in your bank account (multiplied by 12, proving that you can afford living here for a year), or you must deliver proof of the fact that you have arranged a bank loan or found a financier in the Netherlands. This financier must also prove that he or she can provide for you (and your family, if there is one) and their own family. The actual amounts can be found on https://ind.nl/en/required-amounts-income-requirements.

STUDENT GRANTS

In many cases, you will qualify for a loan for your tuition fees, if you don't qualify for the *studiefinanciering*-loan. For more on student grants, tuition fee restitution, as well as financial assistance for refugees and asylum seekers, see page 241. Also contact your university (of applied sciences) to see whether they offer any grants.

ORIENTATION YEAR HIGHLY EDUCATED PERSONS – SEARCH YEAR

As mentioned in chapter 5, non-EU students who have obtained a bachelor's or a master's degree in the Netherlands and students who have obtained a master's degree or their Ph.D. at a qualifying university abroad, as well as scientific researchers and post-doctoral students, have three years to request a residence permit to dedicate a year to finding work as a highly skilled migrant in the Netherlands – during this year, graduates are free to work anywhere or do an internship.

The aim of the orientation year for highly educated people is to attract and retain talent and scarce skills. More information can be found on https://ind.nl/en/residence-permits/work/residence-permit-for-orientation-year. There are also other options for staying in the Netherlands after you graduate, such as the start-up visa or a self-employment permit.

STUDENT LIFE

TYPES OF STUDY UNIVERSITY TOWNS

During the academic year 2023-2024, there were almost 822,500 registered students in the Netherlands, 15% of whom are international students. To recap, the term 'students' covers two types: those who attend a research university (referred to as *Wetenschappelijk Onderwijs* or WO – 42%) and those who attend a university of applied sciences (referred to as *Hoger Beroeps Onderwijs, hogeschool* or HBO – 58%).

As mentioned earlier, there are 12 cities in the Netherlands that have a research university: Amsterdam, Rotterdam, Delft, Leiden, Utrecht, Wageningen, Groningen, Enschede, Nijmegen, Tilburg, Eindhoven, Breukelen, Heerlen and Maastricht. Some of these universities are very old, with ancient jails, court houses and convents acting as university buildings – which are naturally also filled with the required amenities for modern-day students.

There are more than 35 universities of applied sciences. They haven't been around as long as the classical universities, but because of the sheer numbers of their students, they generate the feel of a student town in many of their home locations. Universities of applied sciences, incidentally, often share a city or town with a classical research university, while other cities house only universities of applied sciences, such as Arnhem, Leeuwarden, 's-Hertogenbosch, Sittard, Breda, Diemen, Alkmaar and Haarlem. Almost all the student towns have a genuine student atmosphere; student cafés, restaurants, etc., making it easy to have a 'cheap' night out on the town.

HOUSING

Most student towns share one problem: it is hard to find proper housing. It is already hard enough for Dutch students, let alone for international students who do not have their own network and who will not be staying here long. If you are participating in an exchange program or are enrolled in an international course, it is quite possible that housing has been arranged for you by the institution. You should consider accepting it immediately, or you might regret it later. If your institution has not actually arranged housing for you, they often have special departments for foreign students that help them find a suitable place to live. Almost every institute of higher education has an international office where you can go for questions related to course enrolment, (international) student life and housing. The best thing to do would be to contact your faculty / department and/or to visit the university's / faculty's website, which you can find at the end of the chapter.

A few websites where you can look for more on housing are: www.studyinnl.org/plan-your-stay/finding-a-place-to-live, www.kamernet.nl (available in English), www.housinganywhere.com (in English), and www.huurwoningen.nl (where you click on the town or city in which you are looking for a place to live). Though the information may be in Dutch, they are fairly simple to navigate. Housing is *huisvesting*, *huur* means rent, and anything with the word *kamers* – meaning 'rooms' – also refers to housing.

Make sure you read your rental contract carefully before signing it. Check what you are allowed to do in your room, but also carefully check the room itself, and do not sign any contract if you have not seen the room. If you have a complaint about your accommodation, first speak to your housing provider. If you need help, ask the housing officer at your institution. If that is not enough, you can also contact the Housing Hotline (https://dutchstudentunion.nl/housinghotline/). They will assist you and use the information anonymously to improve the overall housing situation of international students.

Once you have found a place to live, what can you expect? In the Netherlands, students usually have their own room. You might have to share the shower, toilet, kitchen and living room with other students, and it is common for men and women to live together in a shared house. If this is a problem for you, you should make this known as soon as possible. Given the shortage of good accommodation, you may find the room you are offered rather small and below the standard you expected. Usually, there is not much you can do about this, as most institutions are glad to have found accommodation for their students at all. You can find more information on housing for students in the Netherlands on abovementioned site www.studyinnl.org/plan-your-stay/finding-a-place-to-live.

STUDENT ORGANIZATIONS

Not many Dutch institutions of higher education have a campus whose atmosphere is dominated by the local fraternities / sororities and student organizations, though an increasing number of universities do have campuses where classes and other facilities (such as sports halls) are clustered – particularly the so-called Science Parks. This does not mean to say, however, that student life does not influence the atmosphere in these student towns. The cities are not very big and the student population is always relatively large enough to allow its presence be felt when downtown, or in certain neighborhoods. And though there may not be large campuses, every student town has a number of student organizations that do or do not have their own 'club houses', and that have their own traditions, rules, atmosphere and culture which can also be felt outside their walls. The advantage of joining one of these organizations is that you meet many new people in a short period of time and that their club houses provide a regular place to meet up with your friends when going out. Young students become a member of these organizations to find a network for having fun now – and for their career later on.

Becoming a member does, however, often include going through hazing. If you are studying here for just a short period of time, you might prefer to check out the smaller student organizations that do not have any hazing traditions, or only a short one. Many student organizations have been founded by the institutions of higher education themselves, but there are also organizations that are organized around a sport, religion or other common interest. It would be virtually impossible to list them all here, but you can visit the following website: www.mijnstudentenleven.nl/studentenverenigingen/, or https://studiegids.nl/studentenverenigingen/, which will give you an overview of all the student organizations per city and most international student organizations. And of course, you can ask anyone at your institute of higher education what they recommend.

Aside from the so-called free time organizations (*gezelligheidsverenigingen*) there are the faculty organizations (*studieverenigingen*). Also these organize many activities, but then related to the subject of your studies. They organize lectures, workshops and, for instance, the sale of textbooks at a reduced price. These organizations are faculty-based and can be found via the university (of applied sciences). They are definitely worth visiting, as they allow you to meet many people who can help with and advise you on your study and other important student life issues. Check with your institution for an up-to-date overview of the *studieverenigingen* (usually to be found on the faculty page of your program) or visit https://studiegids.nl/studieverenigingen/. You can also find a list on, of all places, Wikipedia (in Dutch), also for universities of applied sciences.

And last but not least, there are a few national and international student organizations that can help you find internships, work placements and temporary jobs as well as fun and interesting activities. The most important ones are AEGEE and AIESEC. AEGEE is a general European student organization, while AIESEC helps students find international internships in a global learning environment. Their websites are https://.aiesec.org and www.aegee.org, respectively.

ALUMNI

Until recently, as an international student, you could join the NL Alumni network. This network for international graduates has been discontinued, however there is the Career Ambassadors Network on After Your Studies | Study in NL. Most Dutch educational institutions will continue to maintain data on their international alumni and after graduation you will be able to join your host's alumni community. Some Dutch embassies also play a role in gathering and maintaining alumni data and running local networks. You can contact the Netherlands embassy in your country for more information. We encourage you to stay connected with fellow alumni and with the Netherlands. If you attended one of the capacity building programs, you can keep in touch by following www.linkedin.com/company/nuffic-gd.

SPORTS FOR STUDENTS

All student towns have facilities for the more popular sports, which are sometimes a part of a regular sports organization, but are sometimes affiliated with the institute of higher education – in many cities they are, in fact, on-campus. The Dutch student sports organizations are about sporting together rather than about competition. Membership is often quite affordable, especially as most organizations offer a student discount.

One of the most important and more competitive student sports in the Netherlands is rowing. Most Dutch rowing clubs are student clubs, either affiliated with the larger student organizations, or independent. Many students take up this sport during their first year and stop after graduating. Its main event is the Varsity, a huge rowing tournament to which the larger student rowing clubs send their best teams to compete. While all the competing is going on, thousands of students sit and stand by the water to watch, picnic, drink and party – a party which continues until deep in the night on the premises of the student organization of the winning team of the so-called Old Four Race.

However, rowing is not all there is. There is soccer, hockey, rugby, tennis, and more – most of which have their own organization. You can find out more about these at your university / faculty or you can visit the website of Studentensport Nederland (SSN), at https://studentensportnederland.com (in Dutch).

A NIGHT OUT ON THE TOWN

Where to go for fun and socializing? Some of the Dutch student towns are also the largest towns / cities in the Netherlands and have enough to offer in terms of cafés, restaurants, dance clubs and other places. The answer to the question of where to go is obvious: wherever you want. Still, the most fun would be to go where you find other students and where things are not too expensive. Luckily,

there are many student cafés and restaurants and designated student cafeterias, where, at little cost, you can buy a meal. But don't overlook the so-called 'eet-cafés', which have a pleasant atmosphere and cheap food. Go out and investigate, and ask others what they recommend. This search alone is already half the fun.

If you are looking for a cultural night out on the town, you might be interested in obtaining a CJP (pronounced say-yay-pay: *cultureel jongeren paspoort*, or cultural youth pass). The CJP is the Dutch equivalent of the Euro <26 card, and costs € 17.50 per year for those under 30. The CJP can be bought via www.cjp.nl. With this you not only obtain reductions on tickets for theater and concert events, but also on the entrance fee for exhibitions and films. You can also download their app. The card is part of EYCA (European Youth Card Network, https://eyca.org), meaning that students can benefit from discounts at restaurants, cinemas and shops around the world. Other student cards that offer discounts are ISIC (International Student Identity Card, www.isic.org or www.isic.nl) and Knaek (see www.knaek.nl).

FINANCES

The word alone is intimidating, because who wouldn't want more spending money? And how do you avoid huge student debts? Here is some advice on arranging a loan, taking out insurance, finding a job, and on applying for grants and scholarships.

Banks

Most banks will probably be willing to support you financially and to answer any finance-related questions you may have. Ask about their loans. Several Dutch, but also international, banks have special programs for students in the Netherlands. To open a Dutch bank account, you will need a valid ID (for non-EU students; a passport), a Dutch address, and proof of enrollment at a Dutch university (at most banks; for at least one semester). Generally speaking, you will also need a Citizen Service Number or BSN (see page 78), though not all banks require one for students.

Several banks (certainly in the cities where there is a substantial international student population) understand the situation of international students and are quite flexible about working out an arrangement that will help you cover your costs and pay back your loan once you have completed your studies and have a job. The banks will certainly ask to see your student registration and for you to find a guarantor.

Insurance

Students under the age of 30 who are in the Netherlands solely for study purposes (and are not in a part-time job or paid internship, and you earn at least the Dutch minimum wage) are exempt from the general requirement to take out Dutch public health care insurance; however, they will have to make alternative arrangements. Perhaps you are covered under a public health care insurance plan at home. If this is the case, make sure this provides adequate coverage during your stay in the Netherlands. If you are from an EU-country, your insurance company can provide you with an EU Health Insurance Card (EHIC) – proof of your insurance. See the Zorgwijzer website for further information on EHIC: www.zorgwijzer.nl/faq/european-health-insurance-card. Otherwise, you will have to make other arrangements, for example by taking out a private insurance policy. There are private packages on the market, created especially for international students, visit AON (www.students-insurance.eu/students/en), whose packages also include liability insurance, household content insurance, legal advice, etc.

You can find more about insurances in the insurance section on www.studyinnl.org/plan-your-stay/insurance. It covers situations such as internships, having a job and working in self-employment while a student.

Jobs

If you would like to take on a paid job alongside your studies, you are allowed to do so – however, keep in mind that to do this you will need a residence permit and a *burgerservicenummer* (BSN, or Citizen Service Number)! You can read more about these on pages 78 and 127. For more on working here as an international student, go to page 146. Depending on your nationality, you can only work for a limited number of hours per week and only if your employer has applied for a work permit for you – always make sure you check the applicable regulations. This can be either full-time seasonal work in June, July and August, or part-time work of no more than 16 hours a week outside the summer period. Though your Dutch employer will have to apply for a work permit for you, this process will be relatively uncomplicated as your employer will not need to prove that there are no EU/EEA/Swiss nationals capable of doing the job. EU/EEA and Swiss nationals are free to work as many hours as they like, alongside their studies. Do not forget that you will have to arrange Dutch health care insurance if you take on a job, see above paragraph. You can find more about working during your studies at www.studyinnl.org/life-in-holland/working-while-studying.

Many students have on-the-side jobs in cafés and restaurants. However, you can also go to one of the employment agencies you will find listed at the end of chapter 3. Of course, you can also try to find a job without their help. If you feel your Dutch is not up to snuff then you can certainly try the bigger multinational companies in the Netherlands: they often have international projects that can be carried out without having to speak any (or faultless) Dutch. You can find these companies on www.intermediair.nl. Two other sites to visit, though you mostly will be required to be able to speak at least some Dutch, are www.youngcapital.nl/ (in Dutch, but it also has jobs for English-speaking students) and https://recruitastudent.nl/jobs (has a page in English).

As of January 1, 2024, if you are receiving the *studiefinanciering* loan and are in a higher education degree program, there is no limit on how much you are allowed to earn while receiving this grant.

A CAREER IN THE NETHERLANDS AFTER GRADUATION

If you are considering starting your career in the Netherlands after graduating from your Dutch institution, visit www.studyinnl.org/after-your-studies and find all the information you need. As mentioned earlier and in chapter 5, international students who have obtained a bachelor's or a master's degree in the Netherlands and students that have obtained a master's degree or their Ph.D. at a qualifying university abroad, as well as scientific researchers and post-doctoral students, have three years to request a residence permit to dedicate a year to finding work as a highly skilled migrant in the Netherlands. You can also use this time to start a so-called 'innovative company' or to work without a work permit. Until such time as you find work, you are not eligible for a benefit and will therefore have to be able to provide for your own basic needs.

GRANTS

Scholarships

A lot is already taken care of for EU-students who come to the Netherlands as part of an EU exchange program, such as acceptance at the education institution, funding and often housing too. To find out more about this, you can look into the Erasmus program (www.erasmusprogramme.com).

To find out more about scholarships, also for non-EU students, and whether you qualify, visit www.studyinnl.org/finances. If you search for programs in the database of English-taught programs on www.studyinnl.org/dutch-education/studies, you can also see which scholarships are available for each program. Also check www.scholarshipportal.com or contact your university (of applied sciences) in the Netherlands to find out whether it has a grant for international students, as some have their own grant programs.

Refugees and Asylum Seekers

Those who have refugee status or are asylum seekers and are starting a higher education, can approach Stichting UAF Steunpunt (www.uaf.nl) for more information on the possibilities of a grant. On their website, click on the little British flag in the top right-hand corner to access a leaflet listing the conditions you must meet.

Studiefinanciering

As mentioned earlier, there are government-funded and government-approved institutions; tuition fees at the former amount to € 2,530 a year (2024-2025 – no reduction anymore for first-year students as of September, 2024), at the latter, they amount to more. Based on *studiefinanciering* rules, students can take out a tuition fee loan to cover these fees, as well as the basisbeurs (basic grant), a loan and an additional grant – all paid out in monthly installments. The tuition fee loan that is paid out is equal to the amount of tuition charged by the university – in the case of the more expensive government-approved universities, this is capped at five times the legal tuition fee of € 2,530 (for 2024). As of September 2024, this amounts to € 210.83 a month. The basisbeurs – which will be converted from a loan into a gift, provided you get your degree within 10 years – will amount to € 121.33 (if you are living at home) or € 302.39 (if you are living independently). For MBO students, it starts paying out during the quarter after which they turn 18. As for the loan; you can determine how high you want your loan to be, to a maximum of € 293.67. The additional grant is for those whose parents are of limited financial means, and amounts to a maximum of € 457.60 a month, which will be converted into a gift if you obtain your diploma within ten years (for students at a university, a university of applied sciences or MBO 3 or 4). The maximum combined grant and loans is € 1,264.49 (2024) a month, for students living independently, and € 1,083.43 for students living at home. You will have 15 years in which to pay off the loan (those who start in, or after, the 2018-2019 academic year will have 35 years to pay off the loan). As of January 2024, there are no limits as to the amount of money you are allowed to earn while receiving the *studiefinanciering* loan (but *do* verify the latest rules on this). If you entered a Dutch research university between 2015-2019 and 2018-2019, and obtained your master's degree, you will be issued a € 2,000-voucher for further studies. You also receive it if you obtained a bachelor's degree at a university of applied sciences. Students following secondary vocational education (MBO) receive slightly lower amounts. All amounts listed above are for the academic year starting in September 2024.

If you have a right to the *studiefinanciering*-loan, you also have a right to the *Studenten ov-chipkaart*, with which you can travel by public transportation for free either during the weekend or on weekdays (your choice) and at reduced rates during the other days. This public transportation pass is also subject to the condition that you complete your studies within ten years, six years if you are following a two-year master's degree, seven years if you are following a three-year master's degree. If you do not, then, retroactively, you owe a monthly amount for the possession of this card. You are granted a *Studenten ov-chipkaart* during a maximum of five years. If you do not wish to take out a loan, you can still make use of the free *Studenten ov-chipkaart*.

Visit www.duo.nl and click on *International Visitor* for more on study grants, the restitution of tuition fees and other information. Note: be sure to arrange a DigiD (see page 84), in order to arrange your *studiefinanciering* / tuition fee loan online!

Studiefinanciering for Non-Dutch Nationals

If you are a non-Dutch national, legally residing in the Netherlands, you can apply for the *studiefinanciering*-loan if:

- you are enrolled in a recognized, full-time or dual course of at least one year
- you are an EU/EEA/Swiss national and lived in the Netherlands for five consecutive years
- you are, or your parent or partner is, a EU/EEA/Swiss national and a migrant worker – additional qualifying conditions, include having come to the Netherlands to work for 32 hours a month (under certain conditions; 24) or more and a minimum monthly income
- UK citizens: you have a residence permit Article 50 and have been living in the Netherlands for at least 5 consecutive years, or are a migrant worker
- UK citizens: your parent or partner is an EU/EEA/Swiss national and a migrant worker – additional qualifying conditions include having come to the Netherlands to work for 32 hours a month (under certain conditions; 24) or more and a minimum monthly income
- UK citizens: your British partner / parent has a residence permit Article 50 and is or was a migrant worker, subject to the conditions regarding income and hours mentioned above
- you have a type I (temporary) residence permit issued on a variety of grounds (for an overview, please visit the DUO site)
- you have a type II (permanent) residence permit
- you have a type III (temporary) residence permit or type IV (permanent) residence permit, for asylum seekers
- you have a type V residence permit (EU residence permit for long-term residents).

The latest information, condition and exceptions can be found on https://duo.nl/particulier/student-finance/eligibility. DUO strongly advises international EU-students (if you have not been living in the Netherlands for five consecutive years or more) to contact one of their support offices. They can provide you with further information. Also visit https://duo.nl/particulier/student-finance/.

EU/EEA/Swiss nationals who do not qualify for the *studiefinanciering*-loan, can, however, apply for a tuition fee loan, to be repaid upon completing their studies, see the following paragraph.

Loan Tuition Fees

If you are an EU/EEA/Swiss national (listed below), but do not qualify for the *studiefinanciering*-loan, you can receive a loan to cover your tuition fees. In the case of legal tuition fees paid in connection with a government-funded institute of higher education, the total annual amount of the loan is € 2,530 (academic year of 2024-2025). In the case of tuition fees paid in connection with a non-government-funded institute of higher education, you can apply for a loan for the total amount of fees, up to a maximum of five times the so-called legal tuition fees.

To qualify for this, you must meet the following conditions (for up-to-date information, visit https://duo.nl/particulier/student-finance/tuition-fee-loan.jsp):

- you are between the ages of 18 and 30
- you are from: Austria, Belgium, Bulgaria, Croatia, Cyprus, the Czech Republic, Denmark, Estonia, Finland, France, Germany, Greece, Hungary, Iceland, Ireland, Italy, Latvia, Liechtenstein, Lithuania, Luxembourg, Malta, Norway, Poland, Portugal, Rumania, Slovakia, Slovenia, Spain, Sweden, or Switzerland
- you are from the U.K. and have an article 50 residence permit
- you are enrolled as a full-time student in an accredited course at a funded or recognized institute of higher education or university, senior vocational education (MBO), or secondary vocational education for adults (VAVO)
- you pay tuition fees in the Netherlands
- you would have qualified for *studiefinanciering*, were it not for your nationality or residency status
- you have a *burgerservicenummer* (see page 78).

Forms can be downloaded from www.duo.nl, for HBO students, this is www.duo.nl/forms. You apply for restitution during the college year of the study for which you are requesting it, in other words, before August 31 (this date sometimes changes, so be sure to double-check). For MBO and VAVO students, a contribution towards course fees is also available; https://duo.nl/particulier/student-finance/tuition-fee-loan.jsp.

Lifelong Learning Credit

If you don't qualify for either the *studiefinanciering*-loan or the loan tuition fees, you can apply for the lifelong learning credit, subject to the following conditions:

- you are a full-time, dual or part-time student at a university of applied sciences or research university (also for modular and work-study programs) or you are a full-time student in an MBO BOL (more theory-focused) learning program
- your study program is officially recognized in the Netherlands (listed in the CROHO register)
- your coursework is carried out in the Netherlands (not the Dutch Caribbean)
- you are an EU/EEA/Swiss national (as yet, no particular rules have been stated on the website regarding UK nationals, other than stating that they are no longer EEA nationals)
- you have a residence permit type II, III, IV or V
- you have a type I residence permit, in which case you should visit the DUO-site to see whether you qualify
- you are older than 30 and younger than 56
- if you are younger than 30, you can apply for this if you already have a bachelor's or master's degree and are following a second full or part-time study at a university (of applied sciences)

- you are not being reimbursed in full for your tuition fees, by for instance an employer, your parents or your home government
- in case of partial reimbursement, you can request this credit for the remaining amount.

You get the credit for four years – in 2024-2025: € 2,530 a year for university (of applied sciences) and approximately the same for MBO programs (students younger than 18 do not pay tuition fees and therefore do not receive compensation for them) – and must request it every year. It is used to pay tuition fees (*instellingscollegegeld*) for your university (of applied sciences) or course fees (*cursusgeld*) for MBO. To follow a study at a government-approved institution, as with *studiefinanciering*, the loan is capped at five times the tuition fee for government-funded institutions. Ask your school to fill out the form Verklaring collegegeld/lesgeld and send it in along with your application. More information can be found on https://duo.nl/particulier/lifelong-learning-credit, for instance, regarding conditions. You have 15 years to pay back the loan.

Five Years of Legal Residence
To prove that you have been living here for at least five years (with a maximum interruption of six months), you must be able to submit the document 'long-term residence of citizens of the Union' or else your history of registration in the various municipalities that you have lived in.

Going Abroad
If you have a right to the *studiefinanciering*-loan, in principle you can take this right abroad with you, provided you have 'demonstrable' ties with the Netherlands. This could be because you legally resided in the Netherlands during three of the preceding six years (there are other ties, as well as exceptions to the need to have lived here three of the preceding six years, so be sure to visit the DUO-website to find the exact conditions), do not receive a grant abroad, and follow a study abroad that is considered of 'sufficient quality'. This can be for a temporary period abroad or for a full study program. If you are going abroad on an exchange semester, you also keep your *studiefinanciering*. Be sure to contact DUO to get the most up-to-date information. You cannot use your ov-studentenkaart abroad; instead, you will have to cancel it and will receive a public transportation reimbursement (ov-vergoeding). Students who received a basisbeurs for students living at home, can request that this be changed to a basisbeurs for students living independently for the duration of their studies abroad.

LIVING ON A SHOESTRING

WELL-FED AND WELL-DRESSED

It would be nicest, if your employer were to send you to the Netherlands within the context of a jointly agreed career move in order to hone and show your professional talents at a local branch. Then, you would be welcomed by the Human Resource Department who would probably arrange suitable housing for you and help you with your accommodation expenses. However, most of you who come to the Netherlands will not enjoy such luxuries. You might have come here, driven by ambition; to study, or to find a job. Or possibly to seek protection from persecution. Or because your multinational employer has not yet caught on to your talents. Your income will lie somewhere between € 600 and € 1,200 a month, sometimes less. This will indeed quite likely be the case if you have come here as a student.

If this is your situation, how do you deal with it?

FOOD
Most Dutch people shop for their daily needs at supermarkets, many of which target a wide segment of the consumer market that has relatively little spending money. The quality of the products will be comparable, as the Netherlands has a very strict and effective Inspectorate for Consumer Goods.

In the store, always be on the look-out for the word *aanbieding*. And check whether the supermarket sells goods under its own label, as these are usually cheaper. The quality will almost always be the same; only the packaging will be cheaper. Pay attention if there is a reduction for buying more than one package (*2 halen, 1 betalen* – buy two, pay for one).

When buying food, pay attention to the 'best before'-date: *tenminste houdbaar tot*, sometimes merely *t.h.t.*

But don't limit yourself to the supermarkets; the local street markets, which are organized once or twice a week, have plenty to offer. There are two main segments at the market: food and textile (but also flowers and plants – to buy those, you should go at the end of the day, when the vendors want to 'get rid' of their stuff and sell it at greatly reduced prices). You can also buy quite a decent wardrobe at the street market.

A third, excellent, source of supplies is the local 'exotic' food stores. Already since a long time, this country has had a good supply of *tokos* (Indonesian) and Chinese stores and supermarkets. Since it has become even more multi-cultural, the smaller shopkeepers –especially those from the Middle and Far East – have taken on the challenge of opening small butcher stores, bakeries and grocery stores, with success. With the added advantage that they often sell goods and spices that cannot be found in the traditional supermarkets (but can sometimes also be found at the street markets).

GOING OUT TO EAT

If you decide to go out, focus on *eet-café's* rather than restaurants and check out the price of their *dagschotel* (meal of the day), which should not be more than € 17. They are served on a large plate and are sufficiently filling and nutritious. Even cheaper are the Surinam take-outs, which you can find in most big cities, and their Turkish and Moroccan competitors, who mostly advertise their *shoarma*. Or you can go to the traditional Dutch *patatzaak*, for French Fries and other local goodies.

CAR

Buy a car only if you really need it, as taxes are high (both on the purchase price and on fuel) and the road tax (which is unavoidable) is considerable. The amount of road tax you pay depends on where you live, and the weight and fuel of your car. If you live in a city, be prepared to walk long distances as you can seldom park near your destination (or home), and keep in mind that parking is expensive. If you want a car anyway, check out the used cars market: www.gaspedaal.nl.

TRANSPORTATION

Don't forget that students who qualify for the *studiefinanciering*-loan receive a public transportation pass. See more on page 242.

DURABLE GOODS

A popular source of 'pre-owned' goods is www.marktplaats.nl, where you type in the brand name or simply the item you are searching for, indicate in which area of the Netherlands (if necessary all of the Netherlands) you wish to find it, and wait for the results. Keep a dictionary at hand, as it is in Dutch and you will not find anything in the category 'couch', but will have more success looking under *zitbanken*.

In all cities and many towns you can find many stores for used items, including clothing, though you should always check the quality. And there are the so-called recycle-centers (thrift shops), called *kringloopwinkels*, for just about anything ranging from clothes to furniture, to sports equipment, to bicycles – where you can also take stuff you no longer want, but someone else might.

BEWARE OF VERY CHEAP PRICES

One final word of warning: there are quite a few stolen goods on the market, such as electronic ware, scooters and bicycles – and their prices are very attractive. But beware of the fact that there are often well-concealed registration numbers on these items and that if the police find such a number (corresponding to a stolen good) on your purchase, then you have a problem. *The buyer of stolen goods is worse than the thief*, is their motto and they – nor the judge – will be much impressed by your defense that you bought the item in good faith. They operate on the principle that if an item has been sold at a 'ridiculously' low price, then you should have known better and cannot have been acting in good faith.

HEALTH INSURANCE

In order to register in the Netherlands, you have to show that you have a valid health insurance, which is not always cheap. You pay a nominal contribution and an income-dependent contribution, however, if your income is below a certain level, you can request government support (called *zorgtoeslag*) to help pay for the nominal contribution. If you are employed or receiving a government benefit then, in most cases, your employer or social security institution will pay the income-dependent portion. Students who are here only for the purpose of studying cannot take out health insurance in the Netherlands. They need to take one out in their home country. Students from EU/EEA countries can most likely request a European Health Insurance card from their insurance company. Once they take on a job, they must arrange health insurance, however; see page 240.

You can read more about insurances on page 141. For more on the *zorgtoeslag*, visit www.toeslagen.nl.

PAYING THE RENT

If you are 18 years or older (subject to conditions, you can be younger than 18) and reside here legally (the same applies to anyone you are sharing a house with; partner, roommates), you have right to rent subsidy (*huurtoeslag*) if you don't pay too much rent, don't earn too much, and rent 'independent' accommodation – for further conditions, check the site of the tax authorities or www.toeslagen.nl.

STUDENT LOANS

If you have come here as a foreign student, keep in mind that you can approach many of the larger banks for (low interest) loans and a student insurance package (if your educational institution has not already arranged one for you).

LEGAL AID

If you are in need of (cheap) legal advice, you can approach a so-called *Juridisch Loket*, which offers free consultation on elementary issues that can be dealt with in less than an hour, or else answers legal questions and then sets you up with legal aid. You can read more about the *Juridisch Loket*, and financial aid when dealing with legal issues, on page 148.

References

CHAPTER 9
Education

Websites

STUDY IN NL
Study in NL, your official starting point to studying in the Netherlands: www.studyinNl.nl

HOUSING FOR STUDENTS
DUWO: www.duwo.nl
EasyRoommate: www.easy-apartments-to-rent.com
Housinganywhere: www.housinganywhere.com
Kamernet: www.kamernet.nl
Nestpick: www.nestpick.com
Pararius: www.pararius.com
SSH Student Housing: www.sshxl.nl
The Student Hotel: www.thestudenthotel.com
Uniplaces: www.uniplaces.com

International Education Support

Educaide: www.educaide.nl
Edufax: www.edufax.nl
New2NL: www.new2nl.com

International Student Organizations

AIESEC
Enables contact between students and companies to do an international internship in over 120 countries.
AIESEC is located in 10 main university cities in the Netherlands: www.aiesec.nl

AEGEE
A network of 253 student organizations in 160 cities with over 17,000 members.
www.aegee.nl

ASVA
ASVA offers several services for students such as housing mediation and cheap bikes.
www.asva.nl

ESN (ERASMUS STUDENT NETWORK AMSTERDAM)
ESN is a student-run non-profit organisation dedicated to helping international students studying in Amsterdam.
www.isnamsterdam.nl

FULBRIGHT CENTER
Netherlands America Commission for Educational Exchange
Nieuwezijds Voorburgwal 19,
1012 RC Amsterdam
Tel.: 020 531 59 30 – www.fulbright.nl

International Vocational Education

MBO RAAD
Organization of secondary vocational education
For more information on English Language MBO programs that are offered in your region check: www.mboraad.nl

IVETA
International Vocational Education And Training Association
www.iveta.org

International Higher Education

VERENIGING HOGESCHOLEN
For a complete overview of government funded universities of applied sciences in the Netherlands
Prinsessegracht 21, 2514 AP The Hague
Tel.: 070 312 21 21
www.verenigingghogescholen.nl

UNIVERSITEITEN VAN NEDERLAND (VSNU)
For a complete overview of government funded research universities in the Netherlands
Lange Houtstraat 2, 2511 CW The Hague
Tel.: 070 302 14 00
www.universiteitenvannederland.nl

NUFFIC, THE NETHERLANDS ORGANIZATION FOR INTERNATIONAL COOPERATION IN HIGHER EDUCATION
For information on internationalization in higher education
Kortenaerkade 11, 2518 AX The Hague
Tel.: 070 426 02 60
www.nuffic.nl
www.studyinNl.nl

EUROPEAN ASSOCIATION OF INTERNATIONAL EDUCATION
A non-profit organization whose main aim is the stimulation and facilitation of the internationalization of higher education in Europe and around the world
P.O. Box 11189, 1001 GD Amsterdam
www.eaie.org

Dutch Research Universities

Delft University of Technology: www.tudelft.nl
Eindhoven University of Technology: www.tue.nl
Erasmus University Rotterdam: www.eur.nl
Eindhoven University of Technology: www.tue.nl
Leiden University: www.leiden.edu
Maastricht University: www.maastrichtuniversity.nl
Nyenrode Business Universiteit: www.nyenrode.nl
Radboud University Nijmegen: www.ru.nl
Open University: www.ou.nl
The Protestant Theological University: www.pthu.nl
TiasNimbas Business School: www.tias.edu
Tilburg University: www.tilburguniversity.edu
University of Amsterdam: www.uva.nl/en
University of Groningen: www.rug.nl
University of Twente: www.utwente.nl
Utrecht University: www.uu.nl/EN
VU University Amsterdam: www.vu.nl
Wageningen University: www.wageningenuniversity.nl

Universities of Applied Sciences

Universities of applied sciences offering international degree programs and short courses: www.studyinnl.org/dutch-education/universities-of-applied-sciences

International Schools

For a complete current listing of international schools visit:
www.dutchinternationschools.nl and
www.educaide.nl

ALMERE
International Primary School Almere
Roland Holststraat 58, 1321 RX Almere
Tel.: 036 536 72 40 – www.ipsalmere.nl
International School Almere (Secondary)
Heliumweg 61, 1362 JA Almere-Poort
Tel.: 036 760 07 50
www.internationalschoolalmere.nl

AMERSFOORT
Amersfoort International School
Noordewierweg 235, 3812 DH Amersfoort
Tel.: 06 57 25 70 60
www.amersfoortinternationalschool.nl

AMSTERDAM/AMSTELVEEN
Amsterdam International Community School
Main Campus: Prinses Irenestraat 59,
1077 WV Amsterdam – Tel.: 020 577 12 40
Satellite Campus: A J Ernststraat 130,
1082 LP Amsterdam – Tel.: 020 723 48 30
South-East Campus: Darlingstraat 2,
1102 MX Amsterdam (South East)
www.aics.espritscholen.nl – Tel.: 020 723 52 80
The British School of Amsterdam
Havenstraat 6, 1075 PR Amsterdam
Tel.: 020 679 78 40
www.britishschool.amsterdam
The Japanese School of Amsterdam
Karel Klinkenbergstraat 137, 1061 AL Amsterdam
Tel.: 020 611 8136 – www.jsa.nl
Annexe du Lycée Français Vincent van Gogh
Rustenburgerstraat 246, 1073 GK Amsterdam
Tel.: 020 644 65 07 – www.lfvvg.com
Florencius International School (Primary)
De Savornin Lohmanlaan 2,
1181 XM Amstelveen
Tel.: 020 640 81 18
www.florenciusinternationalschool.nl
International School of Amsterdam
Sportlaan 45, 1185 TB Amstelveen
Tel.: 020 347 11 11 – www.isa.nl
Amity International School Amsterdam
Amsterdamseweg 204, 1182 HL Amstelveen
Tel.: 020 345 44 81 – www.amityschool.nl
Amstelland International School (primary)
Asserring 93, 1187 SM Amstelveen
Tel.: 020 820 9091
www.amstelland-international-school.nl

ARNHEM
Rivers International School Arnhem
Parnassusstraat 20, 6846 RB Arnhem
Tel.: 026 320 28 40
www.riversarnhem.org

BERGEN
The European School
Molenweidtje 5, 1862 BC Bergen NH
Tel.: 072 589 01 09
www.esbergen.eu

BREDA
International School Breda
Mozartlaan 27, 4837 EH Breda
Tel.: 076 560 78 70
www.internationalschoolbreda.nl

BRUNSSUM (LIMBURG)
Afnorth International School
Ferdinand Bolstraat 1, 6445 EE Brunssum
Tel.: 045 527 82 21
www.afnorth-is.com

DELFT
International School Delft
Primary School at Jaffalaan 9, 2628 BX Delft
Tel.: 015 285 00 38 -www.isdelft.com
Secondary School at Colijnlaan 2, 2613 VZ Delft
Tel.: 015 820 02 08
www.internationalschooldelft.org

EERDE
Eerde International Boarding School
Kasteellaan 1, 7731 PJ Ommen
Tel.: 0529 451 4 52
www.eerde.nl

EINDHOVEN
International School Eindhoven
Oirschotsedijk 14B, 5651 GC Eindhoven
Tel.: 040 251 94 37 – www.isecampus.nl

ENSCHEDE
International School Twente (IST)
Primary Dept. at Prinseschool:
Johannes Ter Horststraat 30, 7513 ZH Enschede
053 206 80 35
Secondary Dept. at the Stedelijk College
Tiemeister 20, 7541 WG
Tel.: 053 482 11 00 – www.istwente.com

GRONINGEN
International Schools Groningen
Primary Dept. at Groningse Schoolvereniging
Sweelincklaan 4, 9722 JV Groningen
Tel.: 050 527 08 18 – www.g-s-v.nl
Secondary Dept. at IS Groningen: Rijksstraatweg 24, 9752 AE Haren – Tel.: 050 534 00 84
www.isgroningen.nl

THE HAGUE AREA
HSV International Primary Schools
Nassaulaan 26, 2514 JT The Hague
Tel.: 070 318 49 50
Koningin Sophielaan 24a, 2595 TG The Hague
Tel.: 070 324 34 53
Van Nijenrodestraat 16, 2597 RM The Hague
Tel.: 070 328 14 41
Van Heutszstraat 12, 2593 PJ The Hague
Tel.: 070 385 76 85
Admissions: Tel.: 070 324 34 53
www.hsvdenhaag.nl
Lighthouse Special Education (Primary)
Curriculum: Individual SEN-program taught in English
Van Heutszstraat 12, 2593 PJ The Hague
Tel.: 070 335 56 98
www.lighthousese.nl
International Primary Waldorfschool The Hague
2e Messstraat 31 2586 XA The Hague
Tel.: 070 783 00 30
www.internationalwaldorfschool.nl
International School of The Hague
Wijndaelerduin 1, 2554 BX The Hague
Tel.: 070 328 14 50 – www.ishthehague.nl
The European School of The Hague
Primary Campus: Houtrustweg 2,
2566 HA The Hague
Secondary Campus: Oostduinlaan 50,
2596 JP The Hague
Tel.: 070 700 16 00 – www.eshthehague.nl
Deutsche Internationale Schule (German School)
Van Bleiswijkstraat 125, 2582 LB The Hague
Tel.: 070 354 94 54 – www.disdh.nl
Le Lycée Français Vincent van Gogh
Scheveningseweg 237, 2584 AA The Hague
Tel.: 070 306 69 20- www.lfvvg.com
American School of The Hague
Rijksstraatweg 200, 2241 BX Wassenaar
070 512 10 60 – www.ash.nl
The British School in the Netherlands (BSN)
(also IBDP and IBCP in Business and Hospitality)
Admissions and Enquiries: Tel.: 070 315 40 77
www.britishschool.nl
Junior Schools BSN: Age range 3-11 Vlaskamp 19, 2592 AA The Hague
Diamanthorst 16, 2592 GH The Hague
Vrouw Avenweg 640, 2493 WZ Den Haag-Leidschenveen

Senior Schools BSN, Jan van Hooflaan 3, 2252 BG Voorschoten – Tel.: 071 560 22 22
Vrouw Avenweg 640, 2493 WZ Den Haag-Leidschenveen
Tel.: 070 315 40 50
www.britishschool.nl
International School Wassenaar – Rijnlands Lyceum
Backershagenlaan 5, 2243 AB Wassenaar
Tel.: 070 512 18 00
www.internationalschoolwassenaar.nl
The Indonesian Embassy School in the Netherlands
Rijksstraatweg 679, 2245 CB Wassenaar
Tel.: 070 517 88 75
www.sekolahindonesia.nl

HAARLEM
International School Haarlem
Primary dept. : Schreveliusstraat 27, 2014 XP Haarlem
Secondary dept. and sr primary: Oorkondelaan 65, 2033 MN Haarlem
Tel.: 023 220 00 01
www.internationalschoolhaarlem.nl
Florencius International School (Primary)
Florapark 1, 2012 HK Haarlem
Tel.: 023 767 60 49
www.florenciusinternationalschool.nl

HOOFDDORP
Optimist International School
Waddenweg 87 2134 XL Hoofddorp
Tel.: 023 303 59 24
www.optimist-international-school.nl

HILVERSUM
International Primary School Hilversum
Rembrandtlaan 30, 1213 BH Hilversum
Frans Halslaan 57A, 1213 BK Hilversum
Minckelersstraat 36, 1221 KH Hilversum
Tel.: 035 621 60 53
www.ipshilversum.nl
International School Hilversum
(Primary & Secondary school)
Emmastraat 56, 1213 AL Hilversum
Tel.: 035 672 99 31
www.ishilversum.nl

LAREN
Florencius International School (Primary)
Leemzeulder 29, 1251 AM Laren
Tel.: 035 691 2525
www.florenciusinternationalschool.nl
International School Laren (Sec)
Langsakker 4, 1251 GB Laren
Tel.: 035 539 54 22
www.islaren.nl

LEIDERDORP
Leiden International Primary School
Klimopzoom 41, 2353 RE Leiderdorp
Tel.: 071 589 29 45
www.elckerlyc-international.nl

OEGSTGEEST
International secondary dept. at Het Rijnlands Lyceum
Apollolaan 1, 2341 BA Oegstgeest
Tel.: 071 519 35 55
www.isrlo.nl

MAASTRICHT
United World College Maastricht
Discusworp 65, 6225 XP MAastricht
Tel.: 043 241 04 10
www.uwcmaastricht.nl

ROTTERDAM
De Blijberg International Primary Dept.
Graaf Florisstraat 56, 3021 CJ Rotterdam
Tel.: 010 448 22 66
www.international.blijberg.nl
Rotterdam International Secondary School
Junior Campus: Bentincklaan 294, 3039 Rotterdam
Senior Campus: Schimmelpenninckstraat 23, 3039 KS Rotterdam
Tel.: 010 890 77 49
www.riss.wolfert.nl
Nord Anglia International School of Rotterdam
Verhulstlaan 21, 3055 WJ Rotterdam
Tel.: 010 422 53 51
www.nordangliaeducation.com
The Japanese School of Rotterdam
Verhulstlaan 19, 3055 WJ Rotterdam
Tel.: 010 422 12 11
www.jsrotte.nl

UTRECHT
International School Utrecht
Van Bijnkershoeklaan 8, 3527 XL Utrecht
Tel.: 030 870 04 00
www.isutrecht.nl

Listings of Bilingual Schools

Bilingual primary schools: www.nuffic.nl/onderwerpen/tweetalige-basisscholen
Bilingual secondary schools: www.ikkiestto.nl/informatie-voor-ouders

Special Needs Education

Information from the government about special needs education: www.rijksoverheid.nl/onderwerpen/passend-onderwijs
Specialized educational consultants: www.onderwijsconsulenten.nl
Independent educational consultant for international families in the Netherlands: www.new2nl.com

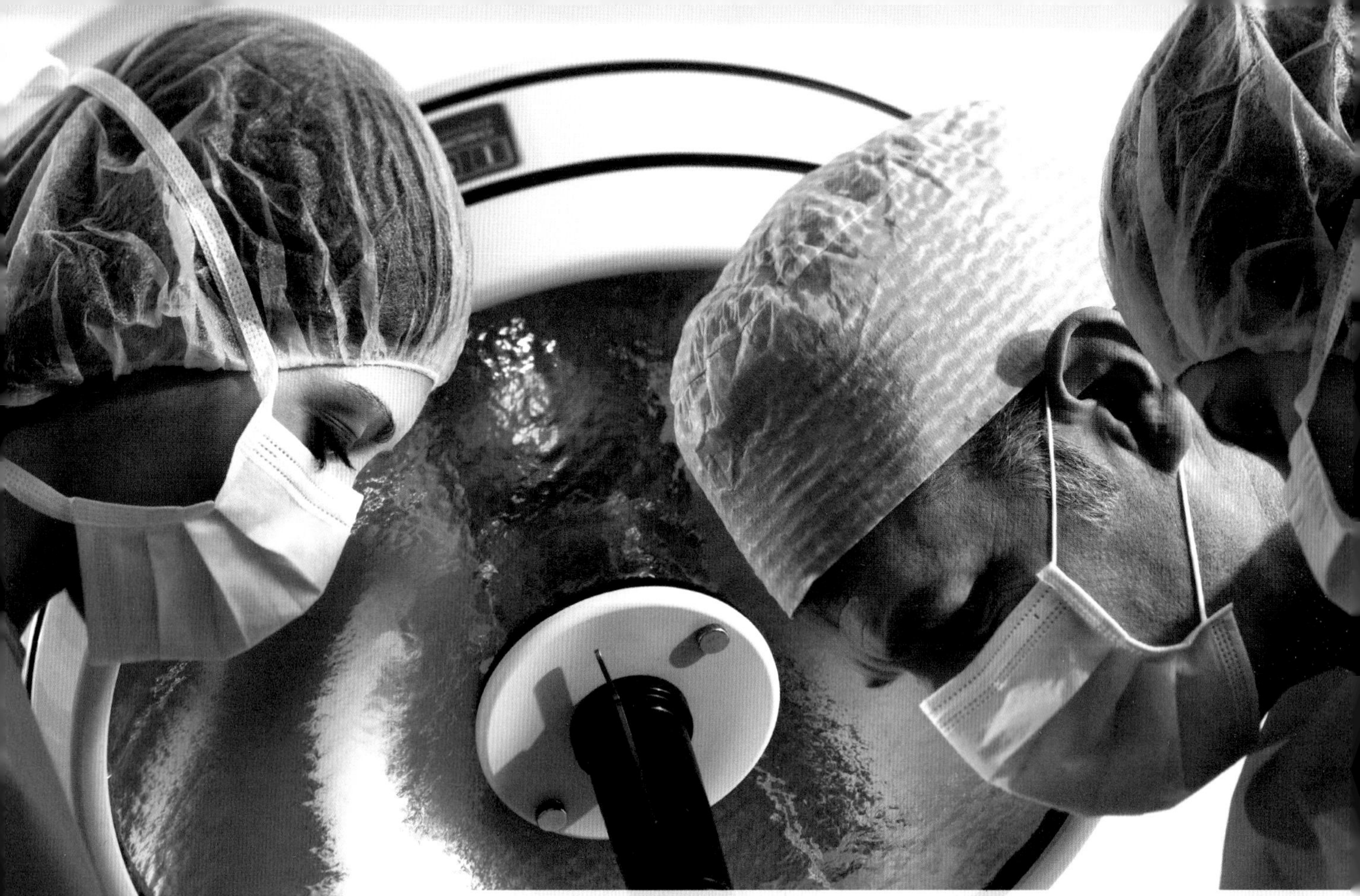

Few things are more distressing than becoming sick abroad. Do the doctors have the same wealth of knowledge as they do in your home country? Will you be able to communicate with them? What are the health facilities? It is undeniably hard to qualify medical care, as it depends on so many factors, but the general consensus – though there will always be someone who has a different opinion or experience – is that, whether you have the common cold, a serious illness or are expecting a baby, you are in good hands in the Netherlands. There are, of course, differences, as this is a different culture. For this reason, we have selected a number of relevant topics (finding a family doctor, going to the hospital, having a baby and other medical issues) to help familiarize you with the careful, caring, though nonetheless Dutch approach to health care. And what always helps: (almost) all doctors here speak English.

CHAPTER 10

Health Care and the Medical System

CONTRIBUTING AUTHORS STEPHANIE DIJKSTRA

THE FAMILY DOCTOR

HUISARTS – FAMILY DOCTOR, OR GP

The Dutch word for family doctor or GP is *huisarts* – which literally translates into 'house doctor'. This does not mean that they will come to your house if you are sick; you are expected to make an appointment and go see them. *Huisartsen* do make house calls in the case of emergencies; either after hours or during specifically allotted hours in their schedule. The name 'neighborhood doctor' would have been closer to the truth, as most people in the Netherlands go to a GP in their neighborhood. Many doctors share an office location and take turns covering after-hours and weekends. Some of these offices are located near (or even in) a hospital, for your convenience.

FINDING A GP

The best place to start looking for a GP is in fact in your neighborhood – and one way to find out which doctor lives in your neighborhood is to visit your *gemeentehuis*, or city / town hall. There you can ask for a *gemeentegids* (a booklet issued by your municipality containing information on just about everything relevant to the town or city you live in, such as doctors, schools, lawyers, health clubs, day care, churches, etc.), which will have a list of all the local GPs. If you feel a bit hesitant about leafing through this booklet and finding your way unassisted, someone at the *gemeentehuis* will probably be glad to help you out. Of course, you can also simply ask those living in your neighborhood or other expats which doctor they go to. Or you can check online (and your online *gemeentegids*) for *Artsen – huisartsen*.

In no way are you *obligated* to go to the GP who lives nearest to you. Nor can you expect them to accept you, should you approach them. Some GPs have more patients than they can handle and find themselves forced to turn down new ones, at least for a while. Once you have settled on a GP, ask them if you can meet to discuss your needs and expectations and to establish compatibility – especially as you are from abroad and might have different expectations. You must register in advance with a GP, as otherwise you may have difficulty finding someone who can see you on short notice, should you become ill.

SPREEKUUR – VISITING HOURS

If you have any medical or psychological questions, ailments, or if you need help, your GP will be the first one you call. Some GPs have walk-in consultation hours, usually early in the morning; you simply go to the GP's office, sit down in the waiting room with the other patients, and await your turn. Other doctors only see you by appointment. You call in, make an appointment for the same or the next day – and come at the agreed hour. Unless the doctor has been called out on an emergency, you will probably not have to wait more than 15 minutes. Sometimes you can only call to make an appointment in the morning, the window for which might fill up quickly. However, if you are taken miserably ill in the afternoon, it is best to simply be persistent about wanting to at least make an appointment already for the next day. If you are scheduling your appointment, you have the opportunity to request a double slot. You will need to explain this to the *receptionist* (assistant) who answers the phone. A double appointment means the GP will have 20 minutes to spend with you, instead of the usual 10. The extra time is often useful, given the differences in culture, language, and expectations, and will help both you and the GP feel less rushed.

For simple questions, most doctors have a *telefonische spreekuur*, whereby you can call in and speak to the doctor (or, at times, their assistant, who has followed special training) with your question or request.

Speaking of questions, most GPs do not necessarily volunteer any extra information. They like to keep things short. If you are feeling a little insecure about your illness, or would like some background information, do not hesitate to ask your questions, as this is likely the only way you will be getting any extended answers. The Dutch GPs are also less likely to (refer you to a specialist to) run a battery of tests 'just in case'; if you have decided you want to rule something out then you should mention this. Unless you happen to have a cranky one (which could happen in any country and, in which case, you are free to go in search of a different doctor), the GPs here are quite understanding of your fears. And they are well aware of the fact that most of us do a little preliminary googling before making our appointment – so they are (reluctantly) resigning themselves to the fact that you will have several questions, as well as a pretty clear idea of what you want to have tested.

IF YOU NEED TO SEE A SPECIALIST

The GP, if they think you need more specialized expertise (or if you think you do), will refer you to a specialist. Most often, this will be someone at the nearest hospital. They will give you a referral notice (containing, among others, a history of your ailment) for the hospital and specialist they feel you should see – you can read more about the referral notice further on. This does not mean that you do not have a say in what (type of) specialist you get to see or which hospital you would like to go to. Most GPs are quite flexible and all you have to do is say what (or who) it is you want.

Keep in mind that, for your insurer to cover the expenses involved in your visit to the specialist, they will want to see a copy of the referral notice (see page 251) – so you have no choice but to visit your GP first! If you want to see a specialist without a referral, this is possible, but it might be more difficult to schedule an appointment and you might need to cover the costs yourself. International insurance policies (rather than local Dutch ones) may have different rules regarding specialist referrals, so consult your specific policy to be sure of what to expect.

EMERGENCIES

Should you have a medical emergency of the type that requires first aid, you can go straight to the hospital to the SEH (*Spoedeisende Hulp*), or in some hospitals that have not yet updated to the current term, EHBO (*Eerste Hulp bij Ongelukken* – First Aid) for assistance. Nowadays, certain regional hospitals no longer offer first aid services. They expect you go to your GP who will do the stitching up or – in case of procedure they cannot perform, such as putting on a cast – will send you to a hospital that *does* do this. In the case of other types of emergencies, you can either dial 1-1-2 (the emergency telephone line), or you can call your GP, who – if they feel you should indeed head straight for the hospital – will call ahead to the hospital and make sure someone is aware of the problem and is ready to receive you.

IF YOUR DOCTOR IS AWAY

If your GP is away on a skiing vacation in the Austrian Alps or is out for an evening at the opera, they will leave a taped message in Dutch giving you the number of an on-duty doctor. The taped message might also give you the number of the emergency line, the *doktersdienst*. The actual name of the *doktersdienst* depends on where you live, as does the telephone number. Once you dial this number, they will ask what your problem is and where you live, after which they will give you the telephone number of a doctor on duty near you, or have a doctor call you.

THE REGIONAL DOCTOR'S OFFICE

Another alternative is the so-called *Regionale Huisartsenpost*. Often, (most of) the GPs in a particular regional area have joined forces to cover the evenings, nights and weekends. To consult a doctor outside of office hours, all you need to do is call one central number. The phone will be answered by a doctor's assistant or GP, and together you can determine whether you need to see a doctor. In that case, you can visit the *Huisartsenpost* or, if this is not possible, a doctor will visit you.

MEDICATION

The GP can recommend medication and give you a prescription (*recept*). If you live in a country where you leave the doctor's office with a prescription for at least three types of medicine no matter what you have, then you had best be prepared. Chances are, your doctor will recommend that you simply go home and go to bed with some toast and a cup of hot tea, which is the Dutch panacea for most minor illnesses. They probably will not prescribe antibiotics, as Dutch doctors take into account the fact that the more frequently you take them, the less effective they become. Furthermore, if truth be told, the thought that suppressing the symptoms (with other types of medication) might bring you more comfort is not something that occurs to most of them.

If you would very much like to be given medication, the best thing is for you to say so. Your doctor might not be in complete agreement, and might make you feel like a bit of a wimp, but to clear away any misunderstandings, you can explain that this is the treatment you receive in your home country and that it makes you feel more secure (or better!).

For medication refills, simply call your GP. In most cases, their assistant will be able to write out the prescription and will forward your request to the pharmacy of your choice. You can also choose to pick up the prescription at the doctor's office. Some doctors charge (a portion of) the consultation fee for this service. Many doctor's offices have a special voice mail or separate phone number for requesting refills, or offer the option of requesting one online.

Medications available in Netherlands are regulated via a central, national, service. In some cases, this means that the medication you are accustomed to may not be available in Netherlands (sometimes it is, but is just not what the doctor is used to prescribing, so be sure to ask about it). A substitute medication will be available, but in some cases special procedures have to be followed to obtain the medication that works best for you – and these are often complex and time-consuming, so it is best to be prepared for that, should special medication be needed.

CHECK-UPS

Another thing to be aware of is that general medical check-ups are, on the whole, not carried out in the Netherlands. There are no annual blood pressure, cholesterol, or blood-sugar tests. You can request them, if you like, but you would have to list exactly what you want – and sometimes even argue your case. This may be surprising, but rather than expending your energy on being frustrated, you might as well do the practical thing: either persist, or have these tests carried out while you are visiting your home country.

In the bigger cities, you may perhaps be able to find (an international) medical center that does offer these tests.

A routine check-up that does take place among residents of the Netherlands, is the so-called *bevolkingsonderzoek*; or population

Covid-19

All measures regarding Covid-19 have been lifted. Should you be at increased risk if you are exposed to the virus, you can visit www.planjeprik.nl in order to schedule a vaccination. On this site, you can make an appointment, using your DigiD. If you do not have a DigiD, you can call the number listed on the site, or find where you can go without having to make an online appointment.

For more (up-to-date) information, call 0800 1351, or visit www.rijksoverheid.nl/onderwerpen/coronavirus-covid-19 (in Dutch), www.rivm.nl/en (in English). The site www.government.nl/topics/coronavirus-covid-19/tackling-new-coronavirus-in-the-netherlands will tell you about the latest measures issued by the government aimed at curbing the spread of the virus.

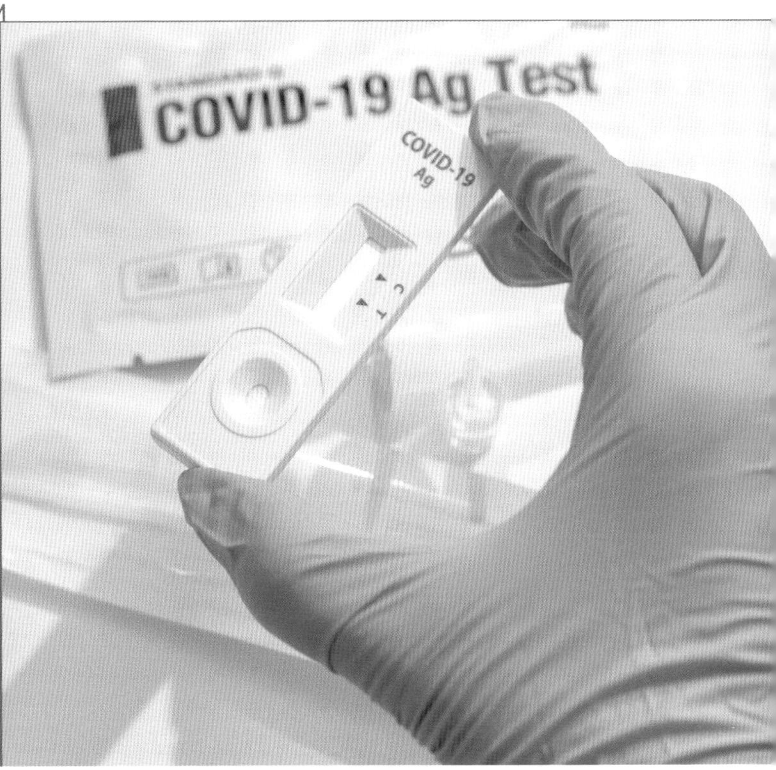

check-up. Once you reach a certain age, you are sent an invitation for mammograms, PAP smears and stool tests, paid for by the government. Depending on the outcome, you are either directly scheduled for a follow-up appointment or are expected to make one yourself.

PAYMENT

You have a choice between taking out health care insurance 'in kind' (*natura*) or based on 'restitution' (*restitutie*). In the latter case, you will have to pay your medical bills yourself and then ask you insurance company for a restitution, in the former, the insurance company will pay your medical bills directly. Be aware that Dutch insurance policies always include an amount – annual, not per incident – that you will need to pay yourself, in addition to your monthly or yearly premium (a deductible, called *eigen risico*). The specific amount changes every year, though it has remained the same for several years now. For more on this, see page 142.

OTHER SERVICES

If you need to see a dentist, eye doctor, physical therapist, need help with physical disabilities, or advice on your sexual health, ask your GP for recommendations. See more about these topics further on.

THE SPECIALIST

If you have been given a referral from your GP to see a specialist, you will then have to make an appointment. Usually, your GP will have written down the relevant phone number on the referral notice. Increasingly, the GP's assistant sends one directly, via e-mail or Zorgmail, to the specialist that you have agreed upon with your GP – and e-mails you a copy of the referral notice. Depending on the type of specialist you need to see and the urgency of your condition, you can see them the same day or only months hence (there has been great dissatisfaction in the Netherlands regarding waiting lists and considerable effort has been put into reducing these, so with any luck, the wait will be reasonable).

MAKING AN APPOINTMENT

Though your GP's assistant will have emailed the specialist / hospital your referral notice, you will have to make an appointment yourself. In order to do this, you need a so-called ZorgDomein number. You will find this number either on the copy of the referral notice or in a separate email sent to you by the assistant. This is to double-check that you are indeed one and the same as the patient who was referred by the GP.

Some hospitals, since Covid, now do their 'intake' interviews by telephone – covering topics such as medication, symptoms, procedure, expectation, side effects of either the medication or the procedure, preparation and after-care. Others have gone back to the system they had before.

THE REFERRAL NOTICE – VERWIJSBRIEF

As mentioned under *The Family Doctor*, do keep in mind that, for your insurer to cover the expenses involved in your visit to the specialist, they will want to see a copy of the referral notice (proving that your doctor thought it was necessary for you to see the specialist) – which they may or may not already have received via e-mail / ZorgMail. Often, the hospital keeps your referral notice – which you hand in to the specialist's assistant when you come in for your appointment – and forwards a copy to the insurer along with the bill they submit on your behalf. If, however, you declare your own expenses with the insurer (either after paying them yourself, or along with a request for your insurer to pay the bill), then you will probably have to send (a copy of) the referral notice yourself, which you will likely also have received via email / Zorgmail. Without this referral, the insurer will likely not pay the bill.

POLIKLINIEK AND PONSPLAATJE

In the Netherlands, most specialists work out of hospitals and not private clinics. When you visit them at the hospital, you look for the sign *Poliklinieken*, and the correct department. If this is your first visit to the hospital, you register at the front desk. There you will be asked a few initial questions (your name, address, insurer, GP, and a few other questions). This information will go into the computer and also onto a little credit card-sized plastic card, called a *ponsplaatje*, which you must bring with you every time you go to the hospital as it is used, among others, to find your records, mark forms, send your bills to your insurance company, and to print out labels for lab tests.

Many hospitals are in the process of replacing the *ponsplaatje* with an electronic card, called the *elektronische patiëntenpas*. This card contains all medical data on the patient in question. Some hospitals have neither and simply refer to the information they have on you in the system – so it is best to inform about this at the information desk the first time you go to the hospital.

ASSISTANT

Once you arrive at the hospital for your appointment, as mentioned earlier, you give the referral notice and an envelope containing a short description of your ailment to the specialist's assistant – unless they already received it electronically from your GP's assistant.

YOUR VISIT WITH THE SPECIALIST

When you visit the specialist, they will read the note provided (as the case may be; via e-mail) by your GP, discuss your situation with you, arrange the necessary tests and prescribe a possible treatment. In most cases, you will not be filling out four pages of your own (and your entire family's) medical history before the visit – but this really depends on the medical problem at hand. If there is anything potentially of importance, be sure to mention it – such as former illnesses, hereditary afflictions and allergies to medication – as the history taken is often minimal. And, as with the GP, if you have any questions, ask. Or, if you expect a particular treatment or medicine, discuss this. Dutch doctors are not circumspect out of orneriness; they simply believe that the patient will ask what they want to know.

Be aware that although you have been referred to a specialist, in many cases the doctor you see at least initially will be an assistant doctor (either one in-training or one just working as an assistant in the practice, without specialty training). Usually, you will not know this unless you ask, so don't feel rude about enquiring. It is often better for you, as the patient, to know with whom you are speaking and what their level of expertise is.

Depending on the seriousness of your illness and the urgency of your lab tests, you may be referred to an emergency room of the hospital or be sent straight to the laboratories for blood tests.

ARRANGING HOSPITALIZATION

If your illness requires immediate hospitalization, the specialist calls ahead and makes the appropriate arrangements, ensuring that the doctors on duty will be waiting for you. If they are of the opinion that they will want to see you again, that you need to see a different specialist or that you require hospitalization at some point in the future, they will send you to either their secretary or the central appointment office to make your next appointment. If you have been admitted to hospital, in addition to the hospital doctors, your GP might check on you from time to time, though they might wait till you have come home from the hospital and pay you a house call.

HOSPITALS

GENERAL

There are many hospitals – eight of them are university hospitals and the others are run by the community or religious organizations. Once you are referred to a specialist or hospital, be sure to ask your GP whether there is a hospital that specializes in your condition.

Though waiting lists are being worked away, keep in mind that for some surgeries there might be a long waiting period.

BEING ADMITTED TO THE HOSPITAL

We mentioned earlier that you should not expect to go through your entire medical history when visiting the specialist. This *does* happen, though, when you are admitted to a hospital, particularly if you are going to be operated on. You may even find yourself going through your whole history three times: with the admitting doctor, with the anesthesiologist and with the doctor who will be operating you. Anything vital, such as allergies to medication, is definitely worth repeating each time. In some hospitals, there is a central office where they set you up sometime before the operation, allowing you to log onto their system and fill out these answers online, so that they can add the information to your records.

ROOMS

Don't expect a private room during your hospital stay. You might be offered a double room but also be prepared for a room for six. The rooms here can also be co-educational so don't be surprised if they ask you if you object to sharing a room with patients of the opposite sex.

Take your pajamas, toothbrush, toothpaste and other toiletries that you might need for any overnight or weekend stay. Also take along your prescription medicines.

Most, if not all, hospitals allow you to have your own telephone line and have a television set hanging over your bed. If you choose to use these, you are charged a daily fee (and given headphones for the television). In most cases, however, patients have their own mobile phones and tablets for their entertainment.

Dutch hospital roommates can be quite chatty so that, if you are fond of your privacy and want your curtains closed all the time, they might be a bit disappointed. This could particularly be the case if they find out you are a foreigner, as they are naturally curious to start with and even more so when they find out you are from another country. They not only want to know more about where you're from, they also want to be sure that you appreciate what a fine country you have come to live in.

CHILDREN'S HOSPITALS

While all hospitals have children's wards, there are also several excellent children's hospitals throughout the country. You can give your GP your preference. Don't forget to take your records

along (unless they have been forwarded electronically) that describe the child's previous illnesses and a list of immunizations given. Children's hospitals put a lot of effort into keeping the children entertained and many offer long-term patients the opportunity to keep up with school, if need be.

LODGING FOR THE RELATIVES

Some hospitals, but particularly children's hospitals, have lodging possibilities if you or your relatives want to be nearby. This is of particular importance if you are still nursing a baby that is being hospitalized. There are also Ronald McDonald houses (for parents of sick children) in the larger cities.

VISITING HOURS

Do not forget to check the visiting hours, as they are different in every hospital. Some hospitals can be very strict about enforcing these hours. Please do check of there are still rules in place for visiting patients, in connection with Covid – or other diseases, such as MRSA.

HAVING A BABY

SAFE

Many newcomers to the Netherlands are taken aback by the non-interventionist approach to perinatal care and are often told that everyone delivers at home with the help of a midwife. In fact, only about 12% of deliveries take place at home; the rest take place in a hospital under the guidance of a midwife or gynecologist. Mothers-to-be are monitored regularly throughout pregnancy, labor and delivery as well as during the postpartum period – as are their babies.

Despite the fact that, in general, mothers are satisfied about perinatal care in the Netherlands, note has been made of the incidence of complications surrounding birth here, particularly compared to other EU-countries. How can this be explained? According to the Dutch medical world, this is not due to the quality of the medical care provided here, but rather to the risks inherent in having your baby *at home*. With their 12%-rate of home births (which was still 29% a decade ago), the Dutch are still outliers in the home-birth statistics, presenting a sometimes risky delay when it comes to the urgent need for medical intervention when things are not going as they should. The Dutch often say: 'Having a baby is not a disease'. And they are right. Yet, everyone knows that the hours or minutes during which a child chooses to enter the world can be critical. And having the full spectrum of medical care available straight away is crucial. Also the fact that expectant mothers only visit a midwife – who generally speaking does not perform ultrasounds – during pregnancy contributes to the risk of infant death, according to Dutch medical specialists. Visiting a specialist and having at least one ultrasound carried out would allow the timely detection of growth deficiencies, heart problems and other potential threats to the babies' health while still in utero – all of which the Dutch specialists are more than equipped to deal with. Therefore, if you opt to go be monitored by midwife – who no doubt will be qualified and experienced – but want to minimize the risks, visit the gynecologist at least once, and have your baby in the hospital, where you are assured of the correct, and complete, medical care. In many cases, your own midwife will come in and assist with the delivery.

In the following paragraphs, you will find a description of the system in the Netherlands.

SO YOU'RE PREGNANT...

Congratulations! The first step is to make an appointment with your local *verloskundige* (midwife) or gynecologist. Make sure to call by week 8-10 as most practices are quite busy. Look online under *verloskundigen* or confer with your GP to find either a midwife or a gynecologist. Although you do not officially need a referral to visit a midwife, your GP will be able point you in the right direction. If you go straight to a gynecologist, you do need a referral for the costs to be covered by your insurance.

PRENATAL CARE

The Midwife

A midwife is an independent practitioner who can legally practice obstetrics without the supervision of a medical doctor. And unless complications arise or there is a previous medical problem – in which case you will be referred to a gynecologist – once you have opted for a midwife, they will be your sole health care provider during pregnancy, labor, delivery (also when you have your baby in the hospital: see page 255, *Where Will You Have Your Baby?* for more on this) and the initial postpartum period. Midwives work alone or in a group practice, in which case you will be seen by different midwives during routine check-ups. One word of advice: as the Dutch feel that pregnancy and childbirth are very normal, natural occurrences, they might not anticipate your need for information or reassurance. Make sure you have a list of questions ready and don't let yourself be thrown by what might appear to be a casual approach to and/or dismissal of your concerns. If need be, explain that there is more (hospital) guidance in your country, and stand your ground.

As mentioned earlier, it is advisable to visit a gynecologist at least once to make sure the baby is healthy and growing – discuss this with your GP and/or midwife so that you can obtain a referral notice to send to your insurance company.

The Gynecologist

Although it is not standard Dutch practice, should you prefer to be cared for by a *gynaecoloog* (gynecologist) from day 1 (or starting early on during your pregnancy), then this can be arranged, but you will need a referral from your midwife or GP in order for the costs to be covered by your insurance. It may not be standard practice, but it is not very likely that they will refuse to give you one.

If at any time your midwife feels that you or the baby are at medical risk, they will also refer you to a gynecologist, under whose treatment you will, if necessary, be for the remainder of the pregnancy. In that case, this will be fully covered by your insurance.

The GP

Though it is very rare, an expectant mother is sometimes cared for by her GP. This holds true in small villages where there is no midwifery practice. The GP, in effect, takes over the midwife's normal responsibilities.

ROUTINE CHECK-UPS

Your first visit to the gynecologist / midwife will take place around week 12. They will note your and your partner's medical history as well as that of your respective families. Your weight and blood pressure as well as fetal growth, position and heartbeat will be monitored. Blood iron levels will also be checked and you will discuss whether you plan to have a *thuisbevalling* (home birth) or a *ziekenhuisbevalling* (hospital birth). You will visit the midwife / gynecologist approximately 12 times during pregnancy and, except for the first visit which should last about half an hour, most visits will be no longer than a quarter of an hour. As most midwives do not have ultrasound equipment, you will be referred on to a hospital should an ultrasound prove necessary or, as mentioned earlier, upon your request. It is also possible to have a so-called *pret-echo* (an ultrasound for fun) or video made of your baby *in utero*. Enquire about this option during your routine visit.

It is important that you feel at ease and free to communicate your needs to your practitioner – whether this be a *verloskundige*, GP or gynecologist. Should you feel that your best interests are not being met, move on. There are other midwives and other doctors.

PRENATAL TESTING

Prenatal testing and genetic screening are not performed on a routine basis in the Netherlands. Genetic screening, for example, is generally conducted only when the pregnant woman is found to be in a high-risk category for fetal chromosomal defects such as Down Syndrome, Patau Syndrome, Edwards Syndrome, Cystic Fibrosis, Spina Bifida or Muscular Dystrophy. In the Netherlands, a pregnant woman is considered at high risk if she is 35 years or older, if she has previously had a child with a congenital defect or if there is a history of chromosomal problems in either her or her partner's family. Should you not fit into one of the above categories but have personal concerns, discuss this matter with you midwife or gynecologist.

There are a variety of prenatal tests available (over time, some of these tests have been combined, and might therefore be known under a different joint name). Your midwife / GP / gynecologist will be able to provide you with information on options such as: Blood Test; Ultrasound (*Echoscopie*); Double (Combination) Test; Triple (Screen) Test, Chorionic Villi Sampling (*Vlokkentest*); Amniocentesis (*Vruchtwaterpuntie*); Neck Fold Measurement (*Nekplooimeting*); NIPT-test; Doptone (Fetal Heart Monitor); Fetoscopy; and Cordocentesis, or Percutaneous Umbilical Cord Blood Sampling.

ZWANGERSCHAPSCURSUSSEN (CHILDBIRTH PREPARATION CLASSES)

The Netherlands offers several types of prenatal exercise and birthing classes. Here is a list of the most common approaches to preparing for childbirth:

- *Zwangerschapsgymnastiek (Childbirth Gym)*: This 8-10 week class is given by a physical therapist and is usually offered through your local *Thuiszorg* organization (for more information on this organization see *Home Care / Institutional Care*), but also by other organizations. A combination of exercises, breathing and relaxation techniques and informal lectures is used to help you prepare you for the big day. One of the classes is a 'partner' evening where spouses / birthing coaches can learn hands-on techniques useful during labor and delivery. Classes start in the last trimester.
- *Yoga*: The emphasis of this course is on mastering simple yoga positions, increasing body awareness and learning breathing techniques to promote relaxation in order to better deal with labor pain. (Coaching) partners can also attend a number of sessions. This course is usually offered as of the second trimester.
- *Lamaze / Psychoprofylaxis*: Lamaze focuses primarily on your mind rather than your body, and on how you can learn to deal with (your fear of) pain. It can be taken separately or as part of the course *Samen Bevallen*.
- *Samen Bevallen ('Delivering Together')*: This nine-week course helps couples prepare for labor and delivery. The role of the partner as well as breathing and relaxation techniques are covered.
- *Haptonomie (Haptonomy)*: Haptonomy is the art of touching and

feeling. Through stroking and rocking, couples learn to make contact with their baby in utero. Breathing and relaxation techniques are also taught in order to better cope with labor pain. These private lessons usually start in the fourth or fifth month and are given by a physical therapist specialized in Haptonomy.

- *Mensendieck / Cesar*: This group class focuses on exercising muscle groups stressed during pregnancy and delivery. Emphasis is placed on improving postural awareness and movement in order to avoid discomfort or pain which may occur during pregnancy. Breathing and relaxation techniques are also thoroughly covered. This course is made up of 8-10 lessons with one partner evening and one postpartum session and is usually initiated by the sixth month. Cesar is similar to Mensendieck, but pays additional attention to the delivery itself, in particular its emotional aspects, and can be continued after having given birth.
- *Zwangerschapszwemmen (Swimming)*: Most local pools offer special classes for expectant mothers. The water temperature is usually warmer, which promotes general relaxation.

English-language childbirth preparation classes are offered through ACCESS (see the information section at the end of the chapter).

WHERE WILL YOU HAVE YOUR BABY?

As previously mentioned, there are two options available when giving birth in the Netherlands: you can do this either at home under the guidance of a midwife (or, very rarely, your GP), or in the hospital, assisted by either a midwife or gynecologist.

At Home

Keep in mind that if you decide to have your baby at home, this is not irreversible. You have the right to change your mind at any point during pregnancy or delivery, although the latter may be more difficult to execute. You will be taken to the hospital by ambulance should the midwife detect any complications during delivery.

At the Hospital

If you have been under specialist (hospital) supervision during your entire pregnancy, then you will most likely deliver your baby at the hospital. If you have been under non-hospital *verloskundige* supervision, you will only deliver in the hospital if there are complications (detected either prior to or during delivery). However, you can also opt for what the Dutch call a *poliklinische bevalling* (out-patient hospital delivery) attended either by a midwife or a gynecologist. You then voluntarily have a hospital delivery, but are in and out of the hospital within 24 hours – barring complications. You will be required to stay longer in the case of medical complications or a (planned) Caesarean section.

As mentioned earlier, for a hospital delivery to be covered by your insurance, there must have been a medical reason for the baby to be born there, which arose either during pregnancy or delivery. If you opt for a voluntary *poliklinische bevalling*, the insurance company will cover a portion and you will be expected to pay a contribution. Sometimes the insurance covers all costs – so be sure to ask. If, in the case of a *poliklinische bevalling*, you have to stay on longer, due to medical complications or the need for a Caesarean, this will always be covered by your insurance. Home deliveries are fully covered by the insurance policy.

ZWANGERSCHAPSVERLOF (PREGNANCY AND PARTNER LEAVE)

If you are currently working and plan to do so following delivery, you will need to obtain a *zwangerschapsverklaring* ('pregnancy statement') from your midwife or gynecologist. This document confirms your estimated due date and is used to determine when you are eligible for *zwangerschapsverlof*. In the Netherlands, women have the right to 16 weeks' paid leave (20 weeks if you are expecting twins or more). In August 2022, this was extended with an additional nine weeks of (partially) paid leave. This may be initiated between 4-6 weeks prior to the estimated due date. The law states that you may not work from four weeks before, until six weeks after delivery. In the case of twins or more, this is eight to ten weeks. Should the baby arrive early, you still have a right to the full 16 weeks. If it is late, and you have used up the six weeks beforehand, you still have the right to a ten-week leave following the baby's birth. And, if your baby has to stay in the hospital after birth, and this lasts longer than 7 days, you still have a right to those 10 weeks of leave after getting home (the first week in the hospital is part of the official 10 weeks). A similar leave exists for pregnant self-employed mothers.

You can read more about pregnancy leave on page 209.

And don't forget, partners also have their own *verlof* (leave). The law stipulates that they are entitled to be by their partner's / spouse's side while she gives birth during a total of the number of hours they work per week (see page 212). This is paid leave and does not all have to be taken up at once; they have four weeks after the child's birth to do this. Since August 2022, partners also have an additional 15 weeks of leave, during which they receive 70% of their wages, up to a maximum of 70% of the maximum daily wage (€ 274.44). This is not paid by their employer, but rather by the UWV (Employee Insurance Agency). They have a year to take it up. This paid leave is not available for self-employed persons. For more on long-term Parental Leave, see further on (and page 212).

THE BIG DAY HAS COME!

Call the midwife or hospital once your waters have broken and/or your contractions have reached a certain frequency. In the case of a *thuisbevalling* (delivery at home), the midwife will either come right over or within a few hours, depending on the stage of labor you are in. They will stay with you throughout the delivery, and once the baby is born, will examine the baby and perform the APGAR-test. During delivery, the midwife is assisted by a *kraamverzorgster* (maternity aid – see further on). Generally speaking, the midwife will leave your house within an hour of the delivery. The *kraamverzorgster*, on the other hand, will stay on to dress and care for the baby, prepare the crib, help the mother take a shower, and clean up the house a bit. If the baby was born during the night, they will take care of mother and baby and leave a list of instructions and their phone number – urging you to call if you have any questions. (See section *Kraamzorg* for more details).

If it has been determined that you are to give birth in the hospital (*bevalling op medische indicatie*) or if you have opted for a *poliklinische bevalling* (out-patient hospital delivery), then you will have to phone either your midwife or the hospital directly – depending on the situation or what has been agreed upon. The hospital will discuss with you whether or not you should come in straight away. Once in the hospital, you will be given a birthing room and they will palpate and examine you to determine how much you are dilated. The heartbeat of the baby will also be monitored. Depending on how busy it is, and how your delivery is going, be prepared to spend much of the time on your own with your (coaching) partner – another reason to take a childbirth class to prepare both of you for this period of waiting and coping with contractions. You will of course be checked on regularly, but it is usually not until the actual delivery – attended by either an in-house midwife, your own midwife, or a gynecologist – that you will have full-time supervision. And keep in mind that you may be assisted by the midwife or gynecologist on duty, and not the practitioner who followed you throughout your pregnancy.

PAIN MEDICATION DURING DELIVERY

As mentioned earlier, the Dutch have a rather 'level-headed' attitude towards pregnancy and delivery and feel that it is a natural process that should not be interfered with. Consequently, pain medication is not offered during a home birth and only rarely during delivery in a hospital. Midwives, on the whole, are not even allowed to administer pain medication. To avoid unpleasant surprises, be sure to discuss with your doctor or midwife what types of medication or pain relief options are available. Be tactful, but persistent! If need be, explain your concerns and let them know that labor and delivery are handled differently in your home country.

Learning to deal and cope with pain is one of the keys to a successful labor and delivery. Research has shown that the more you know about labor and delivery, the better you are able to deal with both pain and any complications that may occur. So sign up for a childbirth preparation class early on – and take your partner along!

Other so-called 'alternative' pain relief options are hypnosis, acupuncture and TENS (Transcutaneous Electrical Nerve Stimulation). Ask your doctor or midwife or call the phone numbers at the end of the chapter for details.

KRAAMZORG (MATERNITY HOME CARE)

The Netherlands provides wonderful maternity home care subsequent to either a home birth or hospital delivery. It is, in fact, obligatory, so if you are from a culture in which you do not expect strangers in your home just after delivering, it can be a bit of a (hopefully pleasant) shock.

You are entitled to a total of 24 to 49 hours of home care provided by a *kraamverzorgster* (maternity aid), which – as of 2024 – can be spread over six weeks. Under circumstances, this can go up to 80 hours. This is covered by your insurance company (in 2024, you pay a contribution of € 5.10 per hour or, if you voluntarily give birth in the hospital; € 40 per day for mother and child), but make sure that there is a contract between your insurance company and the *kraamzorg* organization; if there is not, your insurance might not pay for it (see page 141 on the different types of insurance). If you have spent a considerable amount of time in the hospital, this is considered *kraamzorg* and your hours of home *kraamzorg* will be reduced. At seven months' pregnancy, at the start of your *kraamzorg*, and half-way your *kraamzorg* period, an assessment will be made of how many hours of *kraamzorg* you will actually need, taking into account your and your baby's health, your family situation – are you a single mother? – and whether there are complications and/or extra guidance is needed.

The maternity aid will visit daily to assess the health status of both mother and child. Part or full-time care is available (spreading the total number of hours over several days, for instance; 2 – 8 hours per day) although full-time care is becoming more and more difficult to book due to a shortage of *kraamverzorgsters*. Check online for *kraamzorg* or with friends and/or your midwife or gynecologist for a list of organizations in your area. Should there be a shortage of maternity aids, then, under circumstances, you can hire private assistance and have this covered by your insurance company. And be sure to apply during the first trimester – you certainly do not want to miss out on this unique care.

The *kraamverzorgster* teaches parents / caregivers how to bathe, change and care for the baby. They will also assist with breastfeeding and will, depending on how many hours per day they have been contracted for, tend to housekeeping, cooking, shopping and caring for the other members of the family.

An excellent source of (Dutch-language) information and websites is www.kraamzorg.nl.

BABY IN THE HOSPITAL

If your baby needs to stay in the hospital for a while, check with your hospital what options are available in terms of lodging for you. Also check with your insurance provider what is covered. Many hospitals have some type of maternity lodging option whereby you do not officially take up a hospital bed but still can spend the night – and nurse / be there with your baby.

THE FIRST WEEK AFTER BIRTH

During the first week at home you will be visited 2-3 times by your midwife and/or GP to check on the health status of you and your baby. They will also confer with the *kraamverzorgster*. You must arrange for this service prior to delivery, especially if you are planning to give birth in a hospital – the gynecologist does not make house calls!

Within the first week, the *Consultatiebureau* (Well Baby Clinic, see next section) will send a *wijkverpleegkundige* (neighborhood nurse) to your home to check on the baby, and carry out the 'heel stick' (in Dutch; hielprik) test and a hearing screening. Depending on where you live, the *hielprik* (for more on this, see the next paragraph) may be performed by your midwife or GP. The hearing screening is to ensure the baby hears enough, which is important if the baby is to learn to speak later on, and to be able to take the necessary measures if not.

As you can see, you will have quite a full house that first week: the *kraamverzorgster*, the *verloskundige*, the GP, the *wijkverpleegster* and last but not least, the *kraamvisite* (visitors). And believe me, they will come in droves! In the Netherlands, once a baby is born, everyone comes to admire your new family member: neighbors, colleagues, friends, relatives...

THE CONSULTATIEBUREAU (WELL BABY CLINIC)

Whereas in most countries, routine check-ups are carried out by a GP or *kinderarts* (pediatrician), in the Netherlands this service is provided by the local *Consultatiebureau* up until a child is 4 years of age. The *Consultatiebureau* is a community-based, country-wide network of clinics providing preventative health care to infants and toddlers. Through screening – motor and cognitive development, speech, hearing and sight – abnormalities can be detected early on and monitored. However, the *Consutatiebureau* doctor may not treat your child; if need be, your child will be referred to your GP who, in turn, will refer you to a specialist when appropriate. One of the more important responsibilities of the

Consultatiebureau is carrying out The Ministry of Health, Welfare and Sports' vaccination program. Although it is not mandatory, 95% of all parents do indeed opt to have the clinic perform this service.

Your first contact with the *Consultatiebureau* will take place by phone when they call you to set up an appointment. This should be done soon after delivery. The local office will follow up by sending a *wijkverpleegkundige* (neighborhood nurse) to your home within a week after delivery. During this initial visit the nurse will observe your baby, discuss with you your initial experiences with (breast)feeding and schedule the first check-up at your local *Consultatiebureau* clinic. They will also administer the *hielprik* ('heel prick' or Guthrie test) to check for several metabolic and thyroid diseases – though this is sometimes done by the midwife – and perform a hearing test. You will also be given a *Groeiboek* (Grow Book), which you should take with you to each appointment at the *Consultatiebureau*. An English-language version is available, so be sure to ask for one at the time of registration. During the first year, you will visit the *Consultatiebureau* approximately eight times, and you will be seen by the *Consultatiebureau* doctor and/or the nurse, who will – among others – weigh and measure your infant. You will also have sufficient time during these visits to discuss any other issues of concern (nutrition, parenting issues, etc.). In some municipalities, you can ask for someone from the *Consultatiebureau to visit you at home to discuss certain issues.*

After that initial year, you and your child will visit the *Consultatiebureau* on a yearly basis until it reaches the age of 4 (twice during their second year). Prior to each visit you may be asked to complete a questionnaire regarding your child's health, living situation, development and behavior. The results are discussed during your visit with both the doctor and the nurse.

SCHOOL-AGE CHILDREN
Once your child has reached school age, this health service (including the carrying out of the vaccination program) is transferred to the local health office of the *Gemeentelijke Gezondheidsdienst*, better known as the GGD (Municipal Health Service). In 2009, they introduced the (voluntary) vaccination against cervical cancer for girls, to be administered in the year in which they turn 13. In 2022, it was introduced for buys as well. Both the *Consultatiebureau* and the GGD-services are offered free of charge.

REGISTERING YOUR BABY
Your baby needs to be registered within three working days after birth at the *gemeentehuis* (town hall) in the city or town where the baby was born – not where the baby lives, unless this is the same. You can read more about this on page 211.

POSTPARTUM CLASSES
Postpartum exercise classes to get you back in shape are available through your physical therapist or other organizations. Your best bet is to ask around – through friends, neighbors, your GP or your physical therapist – to find out what is available in your neighborhood.

SIX-WEEK CHECK-UP
You will go back to either your midwife or gynecologist for a check-up around six weeks postpartum. They will examine the position of your uterus, the healing of any ruptures or exterior incisions and – if you had any medical complications – discuss your general recovery. This is a good time to bring up any particular issues of concern such as postpartum blues and contraception, although these may also be discussed with your GP.

OUDERSCHAPSVERLOF (PARENTAL LEAVE)
The law stipulates that both working parents have the right to take a non-paid leave of absence to care for a child (step, adoption or foster child included). You can read more about this on page 212. There are also several types of care leave available, which you will also find in chapter 8.

HOME CARE / INSTITUTIONAL CARE

THUISZORG (HOME CARE) ORGANIZATION
Thuiszorg (literally meaning: home care, also known as wijkverpleging, or neighborhood care) has been created to help inform, care for and prevent complications among those who require assistance at home, such as the elderly, people who are chronically ill, people who have just come home from the hospital and people with physical or mental disabilities. Caring for them at home allows home care providers to reach people who might otherwise not have the opportunity to ask for information or advice. They also offer support to those who are taking care of a sick or disabled relative. Annually, approximately 600,000 people make use of these services. If you require any of these services, including those leading up to the birth of your baby and for follow-up care (*kraamzorg*), check out your local *Thuiszorg* organization.

Among the services *Thuiszorg* offers, aside from the prenatal and postpartum courses we already mentioned, are:

- rental of *bedklossen* (metal frames that raise the bed; required for home birth / first week following delivery) and baby scales
- home care following a serious illness or accident
- home care for the elderly or handicapped
- meal services
- rental of crutches, wheelchairs, special beds, bed pans and lifting devices (these will be brought to your house and installed if necessary)
- household help, if due to illness or handicap you are no longer able to do your housekeeping yourself
- personal care (showering, shaving, eating)
- wound care and application of medication
- dietary and nutritional advice
- courses related to health and well-being.

The *Thuiszorg* system is divided into geographic regions, with services and costs differing from one organization to another. In most regions the *Consultatiebureau* falls under the responsibility of the *Ouder en Kind* (parent and child) department of the *Thuiszorg* organization. To find your local *Thuiszorg* office, look online or ask your GP or midwife, or visit www.zorgkaartnederland.nl/thuiszorg (see also the listing at the end of this chapter). Keep in mind that, whereas some courses are offered to the general public free of charge, others must be paid for. More information on *Thuiszorg* kan be found on https://zorghulpatlas.nl/medische-zorg/thuiszorg/ (in Dutch).

Dental Care in the Netherlands

In the Netherlands, dental care is provided by university-educated dentists, all of whom are government-registered. The quality of the care provided, compared to other countries, is without a doubt, excellent. Of course there are exceptions in both directions but, this being the Netherlands, these are never very extreme.

The Dutch visit their dentist on a regular basis – approximately 85% go once or twice a year – so you won't see many people with poorly cared-for teeth.

TYPES OF PRACTICES

Almost all dental practices in the Netherlands are private, and there are no state practices. Most of them (about 65%) are modest undertakings, with one dentist and one assistant. In the larger cities, there are larger groups, including dentists, assistants, and so-called mouth (dental) hygienists (*mond hygienisten*), who check the state of your teeth and gums and refer you to the dentist if necessary. This allows the practice to diversify its services. In the larger cities there are also separate dental hygienist practices. You can visit these without a referral from your dentist.

RATES

The government determines the rate for services rendered, which makes these rates, generally speaking, lower than in most wealthy countries. All dentists who work in the Netherlands must adhere to these codes. Anything they do is described in uniform (so-called UPT) codes that allow the insurance company to determine the related costs.

INSURANCE

Dentistry is privatized in the Netherlands, meaning that you are responsible for paying for the related costs and not your insurance company. Your insurance company will fully carry the costs of dentistry *for your children* until the age of 18, as well as approximately 75% of their orthodontic care, and dental surgery for adults. All other dental care (the majority of the care you receive!) can only be insured by taking out additional insurance at a fee. Whether or not visits to the dental hygienist are covered by dental insurance, depends on your policy.

SPECIALIZATIONS

In Netherlands, you can find all regular dental specializations. The best-known are dental surgeons, who are usually affiliated with a hospital, and orthodontists, who usually have a private practice, though the number of paradontologists (who specialize in gums),

ARRANGING INSURANCE COVERAGE

Depending on the type of care you require, either the municipality will fund the care you receive, or your insurance policy (this is covered by the WLZ – Long-Term Care Act). In order to receive this care, you need a so-called *indicatie*, stating that you are in need of it. You, or your GP, can submit a request for an *indicatie* with the Center for Care Indication (Centrum Indicatiestelling Zorg, or CIZ). If you want help figuring this out, your municipality is obligated to help you out. You also need an *indicatie* if you need to live in a nursing home, a home for people with physical impairments, or a GGZ home (home for people with psychological or addiction issues). You will, in most cases, have to contribute in the expenses; check with your insurance company whether you can arrange additional insurance to cover this. More on this can be found on page 141.

MEDICATION

THE PHARMACY AND THE DRUGSTORE

Prescription drugs are filled at an *apotheek* (pharmacy or apothecary). They computerize your prescriptions and keep a close watch on the drugs you are taking in order to avoid drug interaction. Many bill your insurance company directly for the costs of prescription medicine.

Opening hours are much the same time as for other establishments, but there is always an *apotheek* open in the evenings and on weekends. The name of the nearest *apotheek* that is open during after-hours is posted on your *apotheek*'s door, in the local newspaper, or you can obtain a copy of their schedule at any local pharmacy. On www.apotheek.nl, you can enter your postal code to see which pharmacy near you is open.

Pharmacies also carry over-the-counter (non-prescription) drugs, vitamins, homeopathic medicines, infant formulas and some baby foods as well as medical supplies such as bandages and thermometers. Drugstores, on the other hand, do not carry prescription drugs, but handle over-the-counter remedies such as throat lozenges, syrups, homeopathic medicines, and pain relievers, as well as toiletries, cosmetics, cleaning supplies and baby formulas and foods.

ALTERNATIVE MEDICINE

Alternative medicine such as acupuncture and homeopathy are also very popular in the Netherlands. For more information, get in touch with the *Alternatieve Geneeswijzen Infolijn* (www.infolijn-ag.nl) or look online for *Alternatieve Geneeswijzen*. More sites can be found at the end of the chapter.

Homeopathic medicines can be purchased at either an *apotheek*, *drogisterij*, a *reformhuis / biologische winkel* (health food store) or online. For more on the insurance coverage of medication, we refer you to page 142.

endodontologists (root canal specialists), implantologists and children's dentists is increasing. You can only visit one of these if you have been referred to them by a regular dentist.

OTHER ISSUES OF INTEREST

All dentists in the Netherlands must comply with the rules set by the Dutch government on hygiene – you will have little to worry about there. Most dentists will give you a local anesthetic before a painful treatment. Laughing gas is seldom used and, if so, only by a limited number of specialized dentists.

FINDING A DENTIST

Most practices have a website. Make sure to do some comparison shopping before you decide on one. Issues to take into consideration are: philosophy of the dentist / practice, opening hours, is there a dental hygienist, do they remain abreast of new developments, what do they specialize in, does the staff speak English, etc.

This having been said, all Dutch dentists follow a thorough training, make use of modern equipment and run a clean shop. If the Netherlands turns out to be your new location, dental care should be the least of your worries.

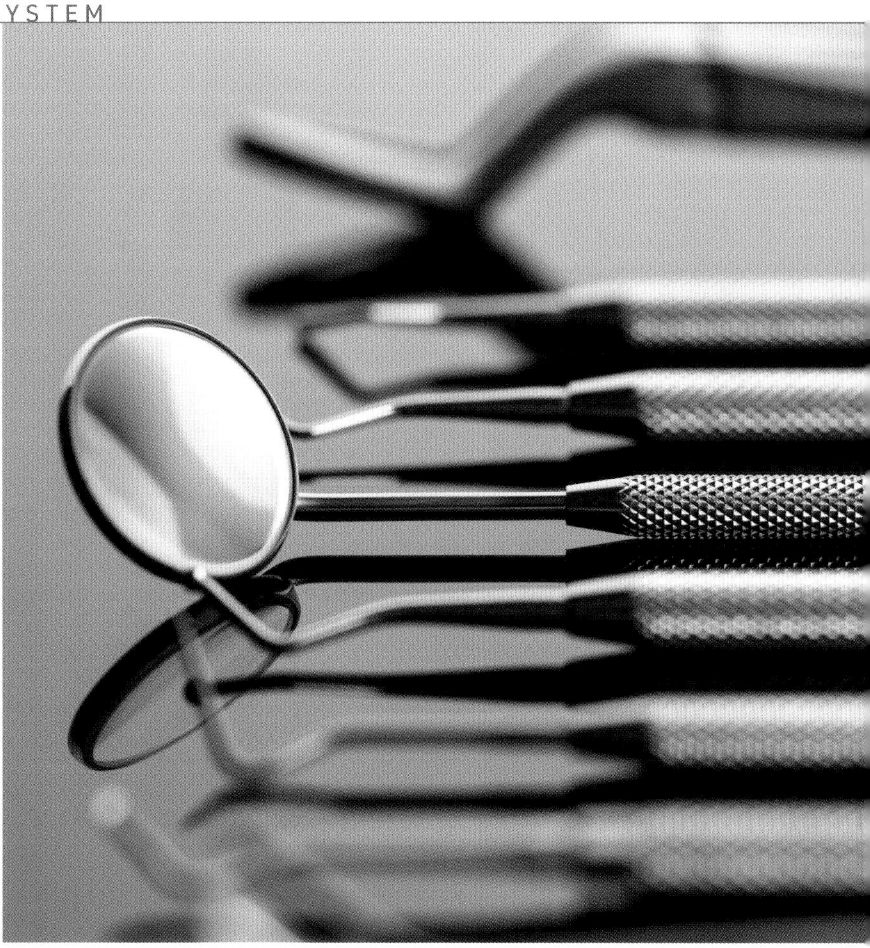

OTHER MEDICAL ISSUES

DENTIST

Many expats save their visits to the dentist for when they go back 'home'. However, also dental emergencies cannot be predicted and it is better to know whom you want to call *before* your gums have decided to call it quits. As when looking for a GP, the (online) *gemeentegids* is a good source of addresses. However, now that you have a GP, you can also simply ask them to recommend you a dentist. Other sources are online, under *Tandartsen*, or colleagues, friends or neighbors. Online, you will also find orthodontists (*specialisten orthodontie*) and dentists specializing in surgery and other mouth afflictions (*specialisten mondziekten en kaakchirurgie*).

As is the case with your GP, if you have an emergency after hours (evening, night, weekend), simply call your dentist and you will hear a recording telling you which dentist in your neighborhood is on duty. Dental care is not covered by the basic insurance you take out in the Netherlands. Children's dental care, however, is covered – free – until they reach the age of 18. In fact, no premium is due at all for children's health insurance. Please check page 142 and see the insert on page 258 for more on dental care.

PHYSICAL THERAPY / ALTERNATIVE THERAPY

For physical therapy, manual therapy, haptonomy, chiropractics, cranial-sacral therapy and more, check online for *Fysiotherapeuten (manueel therapeuten, haptonomie*, etc.), or ask your GP. Alternative medical care is not covered by the basic insurance policy (see page 141 for more on this subject). You have to take out additional insurance to cover this type of care – and while arranging this, you should check whether you are taking out a *natura* or *restitutie* policy. This in connection with the fact that, in the case of a *natura* policy, you have to make use of a(n) (alternative) medical care provider with whom your insurance company has reached an agreement, in which case the insurance company will pay your bills directly. You are free to select your own medical care provider in the case of a *restitutie* policy, but then you will often have to pay your own bills first and request a restitution from your insurance company (see page 142). Also keep in mind that there is a cap on how much they are willing to compensate per session and per year – which you can adapt to a certain degree by increasing your premium.

If you have an existing insurance policy, or are participating in a collective (company or educational institute) policy, make sure you check with your insurance company whether they cover your particular health cost needs and have a contract with the medical care provider of your choice. And do not forget that they often require that you hand in a referral notice from your GP (which they may already have received via ZorgMail), stating that you need this type of therapy, before they are willing to cover the costs (see page 251).

PHYSICAL DISABILITIES

The Netherlands has an impressive record when it comes to assisting individuals with physical disabilities. If you are in this posi-

tion and require special help, contact the city hall (*gemeentehuis*) to see what they can do for you. For instance, depending on your situation or disability, they can help you finance the adaptation of your home to meet your needs. There are also many ways in which other organizations in the Netherlands, such as *Home Care / Institutional Care* (or *Thuiszorg*, see earlier on), can assist. All you have to do is ask.

As for insurance coverage when it comes to physical disabilities, check not only with your insurance company, but also look into what the municipality covers, as they help cover non-medical expenses, such as assisted living, protected living and occupational activities. More information on adapting your home can be found on www.rijksoverheid.nl/onderwerpen/zorg-en-ondersteuning-thuis/vraag-en-antwoord/vergoeding-voor-woningaanpassing.

PUBLIC AND SEXUAL HEALTH

If you are traveling to Third World countries and need injections before you go, you will get them at the city clinics / Municipal Health Service (referred to as the GGD – *Gemeentelijke Gezondheidsdienst* – or GG&GD – *Gemeentelijke Gezondheid & Geneeskundige Dienst*). They will advise on what is required / recommended plus they are responsible for advising the community at large on PAP smears, mammograms, sexually transmitted diseases and vaccinations for babies and older children, as well as the Covid vaccination program. You can also visit the Travel Clinic in several of the bigger cities or the KLM Travel Clinic at various locations for information on traveling to Third World Countries – you can find their websites at the end of the chapter.

For information on sexual health and birth control, you can contact the Rutgers Foundation, which has branches in several of the bigger cities across the Netherlands and has an international, English-language website (https://rutgers.international). For information on AIDS and STDs, you can contact SOAAIDS (www.soaaids.nl), we also refer you to our list of resources at the end of the chapter. SOA is the Dutch acronym for STD, or sexually transmitted diseases.

For more information on the public health program of the Netherlands, including the immunization program for children, visit www.rivm.nl and click on *English*.

MENTAL HEALTH CARE AND ADDICTIONS

Mental health care is available for children and young people, adults, the elderly, addicts, and so-called forensic-psychiatric patients. For more information on the services available, you can contact the Regional Institutions for Ambulatory Mental Health Care (RIAGG). They have several offices in the Netherlands; check online to see if it has a listing where you live, or ask your GP. If you wish to see a private psychologist or psychiatrist, you can also ask your GP to refer you to one, or you can find one yourself that feels right to you. Don't forget to ask for a referral notice! Since 2016, psychotherapy for children is no longer covered by their insurance policy, but is paid out by the municipality through a PGB (see page 142). They reimburse a portion of the costs, through the Social Insurance Bank. It is all very complicated, so should the need for psychotherapy for your child arise, then be sure to have yourself informed on the exact procedure.

For problems with addictions, there are also several options: there are ambulant centers for alcohol and drugs (CAD – Consultatiebureau voor Alcohol en Drugs), institutions for social work that focus on offering care to people with drug problems, clinics for treatment, and outpatient clinics with special departments for addicts. Other options are the Lievegoed Zorggroep, which has an anthropological basis and is for both mental health care, physical disabilities and addictions, or the Jellinek Clinic. Ask your GP for more information.

DEATH

In case of death in the family or a visiting friend, it is best to call your GP, who can certify the death. They can walk you through what is required in the Netherlands. Then you will have to call the embassy or consulate of the country of which the deceased is a passport holder. They will help take care of the required formalities of their country and help notify the next of kin, if necessary.

References

CHAPTER 10

Health Care and the Medical System

Emergencies

In case of an emergency, call the national emergency number 112.
State whether you need an ambulance, the police or the fire department and they will connect you with the right department

General

MINISTERIE VAN VOLKSGEZONDHEID, WELZIJN EN SPORT
Ministry of Health, Welfare and Sport
Parnassusplein 5, 2511 VX The Hague
P.O. Box 20350, 2500 EJ The Hague
Tel.: 070 340 79 11
www.government.nl/ministries/vws

HEALTH COUNCIL OF THE NETHERLANDS
Independent scientific advisory body for government and parliament
www.healthcouncil.nl

THE ACCESS GUIDE/FAQ SHEET ON HEALTH CARE IN THE NETHERLANDS
This publication concisely covers a wide range of health topics from birth to death, insurance to legal rights, home care to hospitals, and special services to social services
www.access-nl.org

International Health Centers

EXPAT MEDICAL CENTRE
Bloemgracht 112, 1015 TN Amsterdam
Tel.: 020 427 50 11
www.expatmc.net

BRONOVO HOSPITAL
Bronovolaan 5, 2597 AX The Hague
Tel.: 070 312 41 41
www.bronovo.nl

HEALTHCARE FOR INTERNATIONALS
Gebouw Strijp-Z.
Tilburgseweg-West 100, 5652 NP Eindhoven
www.h4i.nl

INTERNATIONAL HEALTH CENTRE THE HAGUE
Jan van Nassaustraat 125, 2596 BS The Hague
Tel.: 070 306 51 11
www.ihch.nl

INTERNATIONAL HEALTH CENTRE ROTTERDAM
Gerdesiaweg 488, 3061 RA Rotterdam
Tel.: 010 466 95 73
www.ihcr.nl

INTERNATIONAL PATIENT CENTER THE NETHERLANDS
Dr. Molewaterplein 40, 3015 GD Rotterdam
Tel.: 06 125 29 047
www.ipc.nl

SGE INTERNATIONAL
Gebouw Strijp-Z.
Tournallee 20, 5617 BC Eindhoven
www.sgeinternational.nl

WASSENAAR HEALTH CENTRE
Hofcampweg 65, 2241 KE Wassenaar
Tel.: 088 979 72 00
www.haaglandenmc.nl

Health Services for Travelers

LANDELIJK COÖRDINATIECENTRUM REIZIGERSADVISERING (LCR)
National Coordination Center for Traveler's Advice
The central organization in the Netherlands that occupies itself with the prevention of disease among travelers
www.lcr.nl

KLM HEALTH SERVICES
Stationsplein N.O. 236, 1117 CJ Schiphol-Oost
Gebouw 133
Tel.: 020 649 43 34
www.klmhealthservices.com

TRAVEL CLINIC ERASMUS MC
Zimmermanweg 7, 3015 CP Rotterdam
Tel.: 010 704 5050
ww.travelclinic.com

AMSTERDAM UMC
Tropengeneeskunde for vaccinations and medical examinations
Meibergdreef 9, Amsterdam
Tel.: 020 566 91 11
www.amc.nl

DEREISDOKTER.NL
medical information for travelers:
www.dereisdokter.nl

REISPRIK.NL
Travel advice and vaccinations:
www.reisprik.nl

Huisartsen (GP) Search Engines

www.huisartsen.nl
www.huisarts-gids.com
www.independer.nl/huisarts
www.zorgkaartnederland.nl

Having a Baby

THE ACCESS GUIDE/FAQ SHEET ON HAVING A BABY IN THE NETHERLANDS
Information for expectant parents, parents of babies and toddlers. Topics include pregnancy, child health and safety, insurances, support groups, childcare services
www.access-nl.org

AMSTERDAM MAMAS
Hygïeastraat 8A, 1076 RM Amsterdam
www.amsterdam-mamas.nl

INTERNATIONAL CONFEDERATION OF MIDWIVES
Supports the interests of pregnant women, mothers and midwives
Koninginnegracht 60. 2514 AE The Hague
Tel.: 070 306 05 20
www.internationalmidwives.org

STICHTING KNOV
Midwifery in the Netherlands
Mercatorlaan 1200, 3528 BL Utrecht
Tel.: 030 282 31 00
www.knov.nl

MIDWIFE PRACTICES IN NL
www.zorgkaartnederland.nl/verloskun-depraktijk

ZWANGERSCHAPSYOGA
Pregnancy Yoga
Central Registration of yoga-teachers qualified to teach pregnancy course Samsara
www.yoga-nl.nu

Acupuncture

NEDERLANDSE VERENIGING VOOR ACUPUNCTUUR, N.V.A.
Dutch Association for Acupuncture
Van Persijnstraat 17, 3811 LS Amersfoort
Tel.: 033 461 61 41
www.acupunctuur.nl

Medication

APOTHEEK
Pharmacies per location
www.apotheek.nl

CONSUMED
www.consumed.nl

TO ORDER MEDICINES ONLINE
www.dokteronline.com
www.medicijnen.nl
www.thuisarts.nl

Alternative Medicine

NEDERLANDSE VERENIGING VAN KLASSIEK HOMEOPATHEN
Dutch Association for Classic Homeopathy
P.O. Box 710, 2400 AS Alphen aan den Rijn
Tel.: 0172 49 96 95
www.nvkh.nl

VERENIGING VOOR NATUURKUNDIG THERAPEUTEN
Association for Natural Therapists
Liendertseweg 112-2, 3815 BJ Amersfoort
Tel.: 033 472 60 03
www.vnt-nederland.nl

ALTERATIVE MEDICINE/CARE
www.infolijn-ag.nl

Dutch health insurance companies

FBTO: www.fbto.nl/zorgverzekering
Health Insurance Information Centre: www.zorgverzekering.org/eng
Independer: www.independer.nl
OHRA: www.ohra.nl
ONVZ: ww.onvz.nl
Stad Holland: www.stadholland.nl
UnitedConsumers: www.unitedconsumers.com
Zilveren Kruis: www.zilverenkruis.nl
Zorgverzekeraars Nederland: www.zn.nl

Sexual Health

SOAAIDS FOUNDATION
Keizersgracht 390-394, 1016 GB Amsterdam
Tel.: 020 626 26 69
www.soaaids.nl
www.aidsfonds.nl

RUTGERS INTERNATIONAL
Arthur van Schendelstraat 696, 3511 MJ Utrecht
Tel.: 030 410 07 00
www. rutgers.international

Diet

NEDERLANDSE VERENIGING VAN DIËTISTEN
Dutch Association for Dieticians
De Molen 93, 3995 AW Houten
Tel.: 030 634 62 22
www.nvdietist.nl

VOEDINGSCENTRUM
The Netherlands Nutrition Centre
www.voedingscentrum.nl

Mental Health

NEDERLANDS INSTITUUT VOOR PSYCHOLOGEN
Dutch Institute for Psychologists
Arthur van Schendelstraat 650, 3511 MJ Utrecht
Tel.: 030 820 15 00
www.psynip.nl

NEDERLANDSE VERENIGING VOOR PSYCHIATRIE
Dutch Association for Psychiatry
Mercatorlaan 1200, 3528 BL Utrecht
Tel.: 030 288 84 00
www.nvvp.net

PSYQ
Tel.: 088 357 44 00
www.psyq.nl

KÜHLER & TROOSTER INTERNATIONAL MENTAL HEALTH
Koningslaan 35, 1075 AB Amsterdam
Nassaulaan 5, 2514 JS The Hague
Tel.: 085 066 05 00
www.internationalmentalhealth.nl

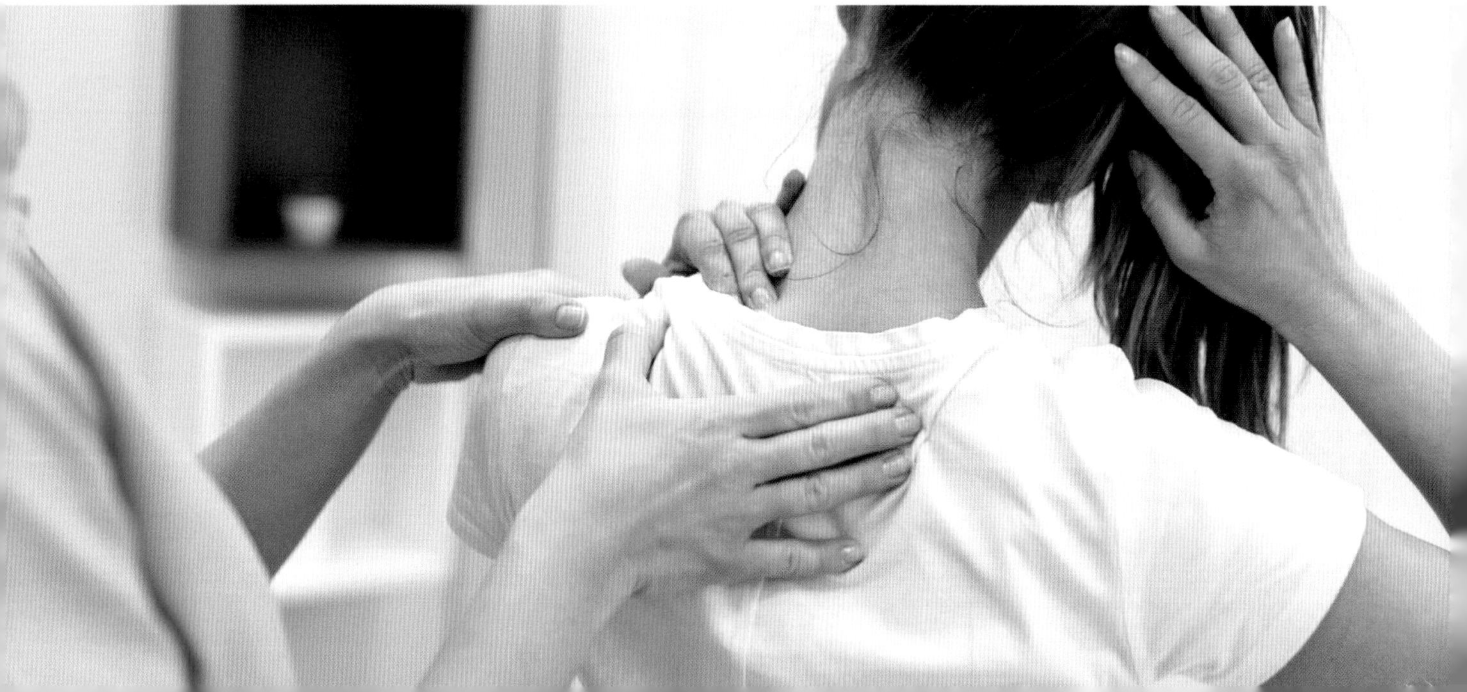

PARNASSIA
Psycho medical centers in the Hague and Noord Holland region
Tel.: 088 357 57 57
www.parnassia.nl

U CENTER
Julianastraat 23a, 6285 AH Epen
De Horst 1, 3971 KR Driebergen
www.u-center.nl

Addiction

ADDICTION AND MENTAL HEALTH
Trimbos Instituut
Da Costakade 45, 3521 VS Utrecht
Tel.: 030 297 11 00
www.trimbos.nl

ALCOHOLICS ANONYMOUS (AA)
Statenweg 207, 3039 HP Rotterdam
Tel.: 010 243 01 75
www.aa-nederland.nl

NATIONAL DRUG INFORMATION
www.drugsinfo.nl

Autism

AUTISM ASSOCIATION FOR OVERSEAS FAMILIES (NL)
Parents and professionals working together for children with autism.
www.aaof.eseng.nl

LIGHT HOUSE SPECIAL EDUCATION
Van Heutszstraat 12, 2593 PJ The Hague
Tel.: 070 335 56 98
www.lighthousese.nl

Physiotherapy

KNGF DE FYSIOTHERAPEUT
Stadsring 159b, 3817 BA Amersfoort
Tel.: 033 467 29 00
www.fysionet.nl

DUTCH ASSOCIATION FOR MANUAL THERAPY, NVMT
Orthopedic Manipulative Therapy
Stadsring 159b, 3817 BA Amersfoort
Tel.: 033 467 29 00
www.fysionet.nl

Dental Care

www.tandarts.nl
www.tandarts.pagina.nl
www.tandartsplein.nl

Dentists

DENTAL CARE ROTTERDAM
Avenue Concordia 99a, 3062 LE Rotterdam
Tel.: 010 892 01 21
www.dentalcarerotterdam.nl

DENTAL CLINICS, LOCATION ROTTERDAM
Berglustlaan 16, 3054 BH Rotterdam
Tel.: 010 418 81 31
www.dentalclinics.nl

DENTAL CARE UTRECHT
Van Hogendorpstraat 1, 3581 KA Utrecht
Tel.: 030 252 03 59
www.dentalcareutrecht.nl

EXPAT DENTAL
Westduinweg 232s, 2584 VW The Hague
Tel.: 070 737 06 30
www.expatdental.nl

LASSUS DENTAL PRACTICE
Lassusstraat 9, 1075 GV Amsterdam
Tel.: 020 471 31 37
Keizersgracht 132, 1015 CW Amsterdam
Tel.: 020 422 19 12
Stadionsplein 125, 1076 CK Amsterdam
Tel.: 020 210 40 07
www.lassustandartsen.nl

MALIEKWARTIER TANDARTSEN
Maliebaan 67, 3581 CE Utrecht
Tel.: 030 760 12 67
www.tandartsutrecht.nl

TANDARTS JORDAAN
Westerstraat 176, 1059 XB Amsterdam
Tel.: 020 612 12 43
www.tandartsjordaan.nl

TANDARTSPRAKTIJK DE LIEFDE
Rietwijkerstraat 52 1015 MR Amsterdam
Tel.: 020 614 00 53
www.tandartspraktijkdliefde.nl

THE HAGUE DENTAL CARE
Muzenplein 91, 2511 GD The Hague
Tel.: 070 200 01 93
www.thehaguedentalcare.nl

TANDHEELKUNDIG CENTRUM WASSENAAR
Kloosterland 1, 2242 JS Wassenaar
Tel.: 070 511 55 35
www.tandheelkundigcentrum-wassenaar.nl

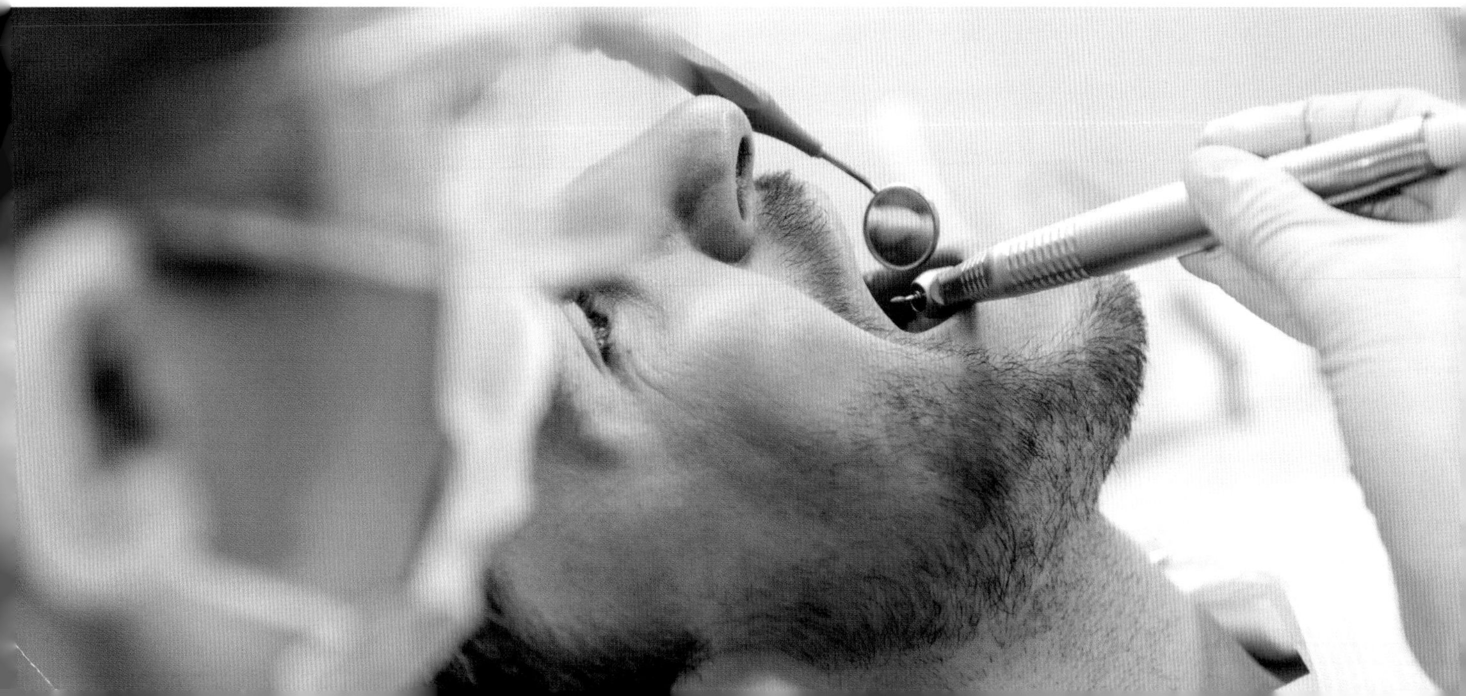

From world-famous museums to an ice-skating extravaganza equaled by none, the Netherlands is one of the best-kept travel secrets and, now that you're living here, it's all right at your doorstep. Considering that the entire country is only 310 kilometers at its longest stretch, you should have no excuse for not exploring this rich cultural realm from top to bottom. This chapter will set you on your way with an up-to-date selection of events for 2024 and beyond, the top ten tourist attractions, an exclusive list of extra haunts favored by the Dutch themselves, plus a special section for outdoor-lovers.

Veel plezier ! (Enjoy!)

CHAPTER 11

Things to Do in Your Free Time

CONTRIBUTING AUTHORS SHIRLEY AGUDO, STEPHANIE DIJKSTRA, CONNIE MOSER AND STEVEN STUPP

CULTURAL LIFE

Small on land but big on culture, the Netherlands is filled to the brim with a rich blend of visual and performing arts steeped in history. Home to almost 1,000 museums, the most famous of which are the Rijksmuseum and the Vincent van Gogh Museum in Amsterdam, the Kröller-Müller Museum in Otterlo, and Boijmans van Beuningen and the Kunsthal in Rotterdam, the Netherlands offers a cultural pick-me-up just waiting for you to imbibe. With such a rich history of Golden Age painters and other artists, including Rembrandt, Vermeer, Van Gogh, Jan Steen, Frans Hals, M.C. Escher, Karel Appel and Piet Mondriaan, Dutch museums are bulging with homegrown legacies. Even the small Mauritshuis Museum in The Hague, which is known for, among others, the famous 'Vermeer' and 'Rembrandt by Himself' exhibitions, has made a name for itself.

From the artist's palette to the architect's drawing table, the Netherlands is home to no less than 55,000 historic monuments and buildings officially protected by preservation laws. These ancient buildings, some several centuries old, can be found not only in the larger inner cities of Amsterdam, Leiden, The Hague and Delft, but virtually everywhere. At the other extreme, the Netherlands is also renowned for its modern architecture, and there are many modern-day architects such as Rem Koolhaas, Herman Hertzberger, Aldo van Eyck and Jo Coenen, whose designs are admired by architecture aficionados the world over.

Performing arts venues, such as various theater groups, both 'mainstream' and experimental, are active all year round in theaters, parks and on the streets. Dance groups that are invited to perform across the globe include the Nederlands Dans Theater, Scapino Ballet and the Nationale Opera & Ballet. Every year, The Hague hosts the CaDance Festival and Utrecht hosts the Spring Festival. Every other year, you will also find the Holland Dance Festival in The Hague. An overview of dance festivals can be found on https://theaterfestival.info/nederlandse-dansdagen.

Throughout the whole month of June, you can visit the Holland Festival in Amsterdam, combining all of the performing arts, while the Early Music Festival in Utrecht is famous for its medieval, renaissance and baroque music. All the major cities have concert halls (such as the Concertgebouw in Amsterdam), where you can enjoy classical concerts and operas. And then there is Pinkpop, Paaspop and Parkpop, all three for popular music, and last, but definitely not least, the wild and woolly North Sea Jazz Festival.

And for movie buffs who want to see more than just the commercial blockbusters, there are film festivals, such as the International Film Festival Rotterdam in February, the Dutch Film Festival in September, the Kaboom Animation Festival in April, and the International Documentary Film Festival in November.

And while you're on the 'expat' trail, be sure to catch a glimpse of one of the busiest seaports on earth in Rotterdam. Nearly destroyed in World War II, the city's modern splendor is a striking testimony to Dutch ingenuity.

GETTING IN

Information about what is happening in the Netherlands is available on a variety of websites and English-language print media, a list of which is available in the reference section at the end of this chapter. Tickets for most entertainment and cultural events are available through the network of local information offices (VVVs) throughout the country, or through www.ticketmaster.nl (beware of non-bonafide sites offering tickets to concerts, festivals, etc.!). A list of these organizations can also be found at the end of this chapter. Tickets can also be purchased at the respective theaters. For the more popular shows you should reserve tickets long in advance. For movies, you can find an overview for the whole of the Netherlands on www.filmladder.nl.

If you are particularly interested in museums, you might want to buy a *museumkaart* (museum pass), which is available at all participating museums (or via their website, www.museum.nl/nl/museumkaart – also in English and German). This card gives you either free or discounted admission to 400 museums throughout the country, plus, in most cases, it allows you to cut the line. If you are older than 19, it will cost you € 75. A youth pass (under 19) costs € 39 – with a special kids' pass through age 12 as well. There is a € 4.95 administration cost the first year you buy the card.

In order to encourage younger people – ages 12 through 30 – to take an interest in culture, the *cultureel jongeren paspoort* (CJP – Cultural Youth Pass) has been introduced. It costs € 17.50 and can be bought at several locations including the Uitburos, the VVV offices and through their website (www.cjp.nl – click on *Word lid!*). The CJP offers you considerable reductions for many of the events listed above, and on their website you will find an overview of what is happening on the cultural scene. There is also the CJP Cultuurkaart, which offers you reduced entry at participating museums and attraction parks (approximately 240); visit https://whichmuseum.nl to find out where you can use your CJP to get in for free (or at a reduced price).

SELECTED CULTURAL EVENTS IN 2024

One of the major advantages of expat life in the Netherlands is the number of cultural activities that non-Dutch speakers can enjoy. The following selected cultural events for 2024 are sure to please everyone regardless of their linguistic abilities. For more up-to-date information as the actual calendar dates approach, you can always consult the websites provided in these paragraphs.

INTERNATIONAL FILM FESTIVAL ROTTERDAM

Dates: Jan. 25-Feb. 4, 2024
International film festival with non-commercial films from all across the world, amounting to approximately 200 movies, documentaries, short films and videos.
Center of Rotterdam
www.iffr.com

TEFAF MAASTRICHT

Date: Mar. 9-14, 2024
In the very southeast corner of the Netherlands in the city of Maastricht, The European Fine Art Fair (TEFAF) is an annual blockbuster event drawing more than 74,000 visitors from around the world. A paradise for antique buffs and buyers, the TEFAF is one of the world's most prestigious arts and antiques fairs, and a trendsetter in the field. The works presented by approximately 275 art and antiques dealers from around the world are museum-quality and unrivaled anywhere in scale and diversity, representing 7,000 years of art history.
MECC, Maastricht
www.tefaf.com

NATIONAL MUSEUM WEEK

Dates: Apr. 1-7, 2024
This is a weekend in which many museums open their doors to the public. There are more than 100 organized excursions. Furthermore, there are free films, slide shows, extra tours, a look behind the scenes, demonstrations, workshops and treasure hunts for children. You can recognize the participating museums by the special red-white-and-blue flags of the Museum Week.
Across the country, various museums
https://www.museum.nl/nl/museumweek

TONG TONG FAIR

Dates: May/Jun. 2024, exact dates to be announced
For 11 days, the Eurasian cultures and their global contexts are put in the spotlight on a 20,000 m2 festival site in The Hague. It is a combination of music festival and large indoor market, and includes 3 food halls, 5 stages, presentations, workshops and artists from Asia and Europe. As of 2025, the date and location of this fair will probably be subject to change.
The Hague, Malieveld
www.tongtongfair.nl

HOLLAND FESTIVAL
Dates: Jun. 4-23, 2024 (dates are tentative)
Innovative stage performances in Amsterdam. The world's most celebrated artists perform one whole month in, among others, the Stadsschouwburg, the Muziektheater and the Concertgebouw. Visitors can enjoy opera, theater, music, dance and film.
Various theaters in Amsterdam
www.hollandfestival.nl

OEROL FESTIVAL
Dates: Jun. 7-16, 2024
10 days of theater on location: street theater, world music and visual arts.
Various locations on Terschelling (one of the Wadden Islands, north of the Netherlands),
www.oerol.nl

NORTH SEA JAZZ FESTIVAL
Dates: Jul. 12-14, 2024
One of the largest and best-known international jazz festivals in the world which has, in its decades-long history, enjoyed performances by virtually all the jazz and contemporary music heroes of all time. More than 8 hours of music on 15 stages per day, with contributions by more than 1,300 jazz musicians.
Ahoy Rotterdam
www.northseajazz.com

FESTIVAL CLASSIQUE
Dates: Jun. 13-16, 2024
5 days of classical concerts for all ages and tastes.
Various locations: Scheveningen
www.festivalclassique.nl

PINKPOP
Dates: Jun. 21-23, 2024
This year is the 52nd edition of what is touted as the world's oldest pop music festival. It is a pleasant, if packed, international open-air affair with various pop artists performing their hits.
Landgraaf Megaland
www.pinkpop.nl

SUMMER CARNIVAL
Dates: Jul. 26-27, 2024
An exotic music, dance and float parade, which turns the inner city of Rotterdam upside down. Dancers in fantastic costumes and swinging orchestras on decorated floats are followed by thousands of dancing visitors. Includes the queen election, the Battle of Drums and the street parade itself. (Note: in previous years, the queen election was held two weeks earlier, so check closer to the date whether the information offered on the site has changed.)
Center of Rotterdam
www.rotterdamunlimited.com/zomercarnaval

DELFT CHAMBER MUSIC FESTIVAL
Dates: Jul. 26 – Aug. 2, 2024
A unique chamber music festival with a variety of concerts.
Museum Het Prinsenhof, Delft
www.delftmusicfestival.nl

CANAL GAY PARADE
Date: Aug. 3, 2024
Amsterdam's celebration of all things Gay, Lesbian, Bi, and Transgender, which has grown into one of the world's premier Pride parades.
Amsterdam canals
www.canalparade.nl

LOWLANDS
Dates: Aug. 16-18, 2024
Lowlands is Holland's biggest and most adventurous outdoor music festival. It offers a choice of the best alternative music, theater, film, stand-up comedy, visual arts, literature and more.
Walibi World, Biddinghuizen
www.lowlands.nl

PREUVENEMINT
Dates: approx. Aug. 29-Sep. 1, 2024 (dates are tentative)
Four-day culinary event, with approximately 30 stands acting as restaurants. Beer and soft drinks available at separate stands. Live music on a permanent open-air stage.
Vrijthof Square, Maastricht
www.preuvenemint.nl

DE OPENING
Dates: Aug. 30 – Sep. 1, 2024
Every year, a different city will host the opening of the new cultural season with shows on indoor and outdoor stages.
Location to be announced
Website to be created

SPOTLIGHT FESTIVAL
Date: Aug. 29-Sep. 1, 2024, exact dates could be subject to change
At this festival, music ensembles, dance companies, orchestras and theater groups give you a taste of what is to come in the new season in The Hague. The performances are held on various stages of the theaters on the Spui and there is a literary, cultural, theater and information market.
Lange Voorhout and Spuiplein, The Hague
https://spotlightfestivaldenhaag.nl

WORLD PORT DAYS
Dates: Sep. 6-8, 2024
Experience daily life in one of the biggest harbors in the world. This festival is all about maritime, educational and cultural activities in which the harbor of Rotterdam and its industrial area are the main feature.
Harbor of Rotterdam
www.wereldhavendagen.nl

CROSSING BORDER FESTIVAL
Dates: Nov. 2024, exact dates to be announced
A refreshing look at poetry, writing and music, with approximately 120 performances on various stages by poets, writers and musicians.
Koninklijke Schouwburg and Het Nationale Toneelgebouw in The Hague
www.crossingborder.nl

PAN AMSTERDAM
Date: Nov. 2024, exact dates to be announced
Known as the best national arts and antiques fair with prominent dealers and gallery owners from the Netherlands and Flanders, PAN Amsterdam is regarded as the most important fair in the world for Dutch glass and silver, though there are plenty of other art forms as well. Equally attractive is its reputation for an excellent price / quality ratio, in other words, good value for your money.
RAI, Amsterdam
www.pan.nl

INTERNATIONAL DOCUMENTARY FILM FESTIVAL (IDFA)
Dates: Nov. 2024 (exact dates to be announced)
One of the biggest documentary film festivals in the world, with more than 150 documentaries and an extensive workshop program.
In and around Pathé Tuschinsky and Pathé de Munt Theaters, Amsterdam
www.idfa.nl

PLACES UNDISCOVERED BY THE MASSES

Expatriates and tourists are not the only ones who like to enjoy the sights in the Netherlands. The following are places recommended by the Dutch themselves. (Be sure to check the websites or call for opening times, as some places are closed, for example, on Mondays.)

TEYLER'S MUSEUM IN HAARLEM
Aside from being the very first museum in the Netherlands, Teyler's Museum was the third museum in Europe, following in the footsteps of the Oxford Ashmolean and the British Museum. It was once a living theater; a place to discuss, with colleagues, the inventions of the times, to hear speakers and to chew over the discoveries of science and art, as well as a laboratory for experiments and demonstrations. Today we can peer into the past through the collection of microscopes and telescopes, Newtonian measuring equipment, fossils, rocks and gems and, of course, paintings, drawings, etches and sketches, or visit its library with its Travel and Important Documents such as the Diderot Encyclopedia (the first in Europe), James Cook's travel journals, Darwin's scribbles and the works of others of world-renown.
Spaarne 16, Haarlem
www.teylersmuseum.nl

BIESBOSCH NATIONAL PARK
7,000 hectares of winding gullies, deep creeks and fields of rushes. The park was created in 1421 when the St. Elizabeth flood washed away 16 villages and turned a prosperous agricultural region into a

Outdoor Activities

Once you've expanded your cultural horizons, you will need to save some of your spare time to improve your physical well-being while living in the Netherlands. This may be one of the most populated countries on the planet, but there is still plenty of space and activity for the outdoor enthusiast, including cycling, running, hiking, wave and kite surfing, wall climbing, horseback riding, parachuting, mini-golf, archery, bird watching, camping or aerobics. This country being as small as it is, the majority of these activities will not make the outing much more than a day trip...

Leisure time can be filled with easy-access activities such as cycling along the 37,000 kilometers of bicycle paths in the country, either as a slow-going family activity or on a race bike for a real workout. The ANWB and VVV sell useful and detailed maps of the whole country as seen from the cyclist's and the hiker's needs. They – and the site www.recreatienoordholland.nl – can also provide you with information on a whole host of recreational activities in and around the Dutch coast, such as in-line skating, mountain-biking, kite-flying, horseback riding, wind surfing, canoeing, sailing, and off-shore fishing, to name a few.

For the intrepid walker, flower parks and gardens are popular, as are walks through castle gardens, sand dunes, mud flats and the numerous parks in the country. Visit www.natuurlijkwandelen.nl for inspiration on beautiful walks through the Dutch countryside. The pinnacle of the walking frenzy is probably the ***Vierdaagse*** in Nijmegen where more than 45,000 hikers converge for a four-day-long hike in July (see www.4daagse.nl/en for information and registration in English). Also Holland.com is a good site for ideas and the VVV offices also offer detailed information, guides and maps.

For the avid golfer there is a large selection of golf courses in the country (see the reference pages at the end of the chapter for more information), however do not forget that, for most Dutch courses, you must have a golfing permit, called Handicap 54 (also known as the GVB, or ***Golfvaardigheidsbewijs*** – see www.golf.nl/beginnen-met-golf/alles-over-golf/rentree-in-golfsport), a registered handicap, or a course permit (***baanpermissie***; permission to play on a specific course, issued by the course itself, subject to conditions). For more information, check www.ngf.nl for the Netherlands Golf Federation. For those looking for something a little spicier on the course, Farmersgolf is the latest variation on the classic game of golf. Played on pastures, over ditches, through forests and amongst the cows, the game was invented in the Netherlands on the pastures of the Weenink Cheese Farm in Lievelde. For more information, see www.boerengolf.nl/en/.

Below are two intrinsically Dutch outdoor activities, popular among young and old, that allow you to explore a part of the country that not many people take the time to see, but that none of those who do ever forget:

NORTH TO SOUTH ON FOOT: THE PIETERPAD ROUTE

Bicycling is not the only cross-country sport in the Netherlands; walking on a well-laid-out path is another – 490 kilometers worth of walk-

ing, that is, from Pieterburen in the northern province of Groningen to the Pieterberg (Pieter Mountain) in Maastricht in the southernmost province of Limburg. Objective: to experience all that the Netherlands has to offer under one low sky and, of course, to commune with nature while getting a hearty dose of exercise. Different routes are detailed in a guidebook, a prerequisite for your journey and available at the VVV or ANWB offices. If you are feeling really ambitious, an extension of the trail continues on through Belgium and France all the way to the Mediterranean Sea.

The Pieterpad has been divided into a number of *etappes*, 26 in total. The distance of each *etappe* varies anywhere from 15 to 20 kilometers and can easily be covered in one day (even by inexperienced walkers). You can walk the *etappes* in two directions, as in from North to South or from South to North; the guide book describes both options.

There are actually two guide books; the first, *Pieterpad Deel I*, maps out the 13 different *etappes* from Pieterburen to Vorden (somewhere in the middle of Holland); the second, *Pieterpad Deel II*, maps out the next 13 *etappes* from Vorden to St. Pietersberg. Unfortunately, these guides have not yet been translated into other languages, nonetheless, the maps are pretty self-explanatory – in fact, essential. On the website www.pieterpad.nl, you can find these guides, a map, accommodation and places to stop for a bite to eat for each etappe.

Keep in mind that you will presumably be walking from point A to point B. This requires parking your car at the end and using public transportation to get to the start – or to get back to where you parked your car after you have completed the walk.

For more information, visit the sites at the end of the chapter.

THE ULTIMATE ADVENTURE: MUD-FLAT WALKING TO THE ISLANDS

To the north of the Netherlands lie the five *Wadden Islands*: Texel, Vlieland, Terschelling, Ameland and Schiermonnikoog. Between these islands lie the famous Wadden, the sea-beds of the Wadden Sea – together with the German and the Danish section, this is one of the UNESCO World Heritage sites, measuring 11,500 km2 in total. Twice a day, thousands of cubic liters of North Sea water stream through the Wadden, accounting for the tremendous riches of sea life present here.

During low tide, it is possible to walk across the sea-bed and experience the abundance of mussels and oysters and clams, amongst other life forms residing here. This is the famous 'Wadlopen', which is commonly translated into 'mud-flat walking' – not to be confused with mud-walking which takes place in the Northern tip of Friesland.

The algorithm of high and low tides are best not left to the uninitiated: visitors are advised to never venture off into the rich life of the Wadden unattended, as it may cost you your life. The tide has been known to rise within minutes, leaving you to the torrents of the seas without warning. Fortunately for us city, or other, folk, there are many guides who have lived their whole lives on these wet planes and who can safely let you in on the treasures of the Wadden Sea bottoms.

Wadlopen takes place from mid-March to early October. To arrange a tour, visit the sites at the end of the chapter.

The Top Ten Places that Draw the Most Foreign Visitors

Tourists and expatriates alike come to the Netherlands to admire its cultural heritage, with lyrical windmills, spectacular fields of tulips and renowned Dutch artists such as Van Gogh, Rembrandt, Vermeer, Hals and Steen completing the picture.

Here you will find the ten most popular sites frequented by visitors. While Amsterdam remains the biggest draw with its rock-and-roll reputation, some of the best-kept travel secrets lie well beyond this hub, and there's much more to see within a very short reach.

To locate these attractions, simply refer to the map on this page. For the main zoos and other children's attractions, see Chapter 8.

1 Van Gogh Museum

Amsterdam's top tourist attraction is devoted almost entirely to the work of one of the most popular artists the world has ever known, spanning his early years in South Holland, through his Impressionist years in Paris, to his last years in St. Rémy. This museum is the perfect size for those short on time.

Paulus Potterstraat 7, Amsterdam

www.vangoghmuseum.nl

2 Anne Frank House

Possibly the most deserving of all the Netherlands' major tourist attractions, the Anne Frank House provides fascinating insight into the Frank family's life in hiding from 1942 until 1944, during the Nazi occupation. The museum also provides information on the plight of the 100,000 Dutch Jews who were killed in the Holocaust and hosts a variety of other exhibitions, focusing on such issues as persecution and the repression of freedom of expression, both past and present. Note: entrance tickets are bought online!

Prinsengracht 267, Amsterdam

www.annefrank.org

3 Rijksmuseum Amsterdam

This largest museum in the Netherlands, which recently reopened its doors after a complete renovation, houses an internationally renowned collection with paintings from the 17th-century Dutch Republic, the 'Golden Age', including works by Rembrandt (the most famous of which is the imposing *Night Watch*), Johannes Vermeer, Frans Hals and Jan Steen. Silver, delftware, doll's houses, prints, drawings, Asiatic art and Dutch history are also featured.

Museumstraat 1, Amsterdam **www.rijksmuseum.nl**

(In inimitable Dutch style, the Rijksmuseum, in conjunction with Amsterdam Airport Schiphol, has opened the world's first, permanent airport museum exhibition center. A fly-through peek at Dutch art history features exhibits by the masters themselves, including Jan van Goyen, Willem van de Velde II, Abraham Mignon and Michiel van Mierevelt. Entrance is free to this 'art on tap' situated behind passport control on the 'Holland Boulevard', the corridor between Lounge 2 and 3.

4 Keukenhof

From late March till mid-May, visitors come in droves to see the display of over 7,000,000 flowers in the famous Keukenhof Gardens. The 70-acre gardens offer a breathtaking, immaculate display of tulips, hyacinths, daffodils and amaryllis planted by the Netherlands' leading flower growers. Not to be missed.

Open: Mar. 24–May 5 **Stationsweg 166a, Lisse**

www.keukenhof.nl

5 Delft

Famous for its distinctive blue and white porcelain, Delft continues to charm visitors – and shoppers. Once home to Dutch artist Vermeer, it has an abundance of beautifully-preserved 17th-century buildings (including the imposing Town Hall and the Old Church), requisite tree-lined canals and a daunting array of porcelain shops.

www.delft.nl/en

www.delft.com

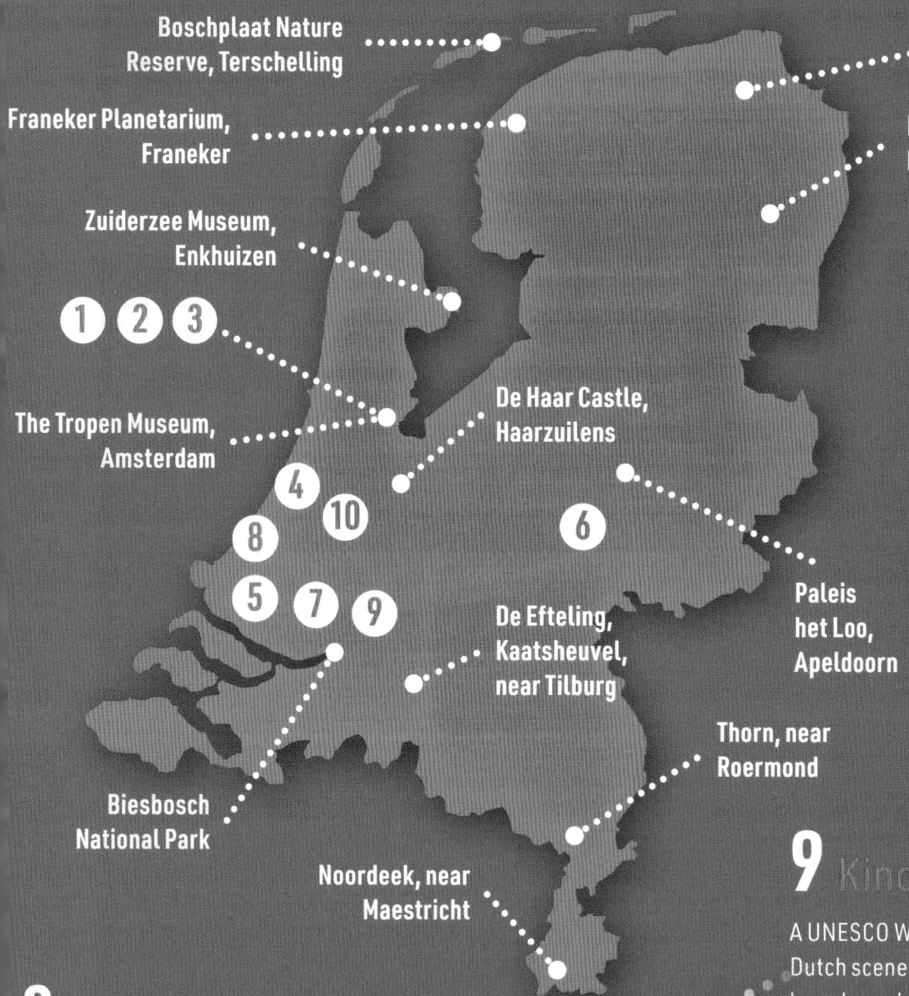

10 The Archeon

This archaeological theme park in Alphen aan de Rijn in South Holland is world-renowned among history buffs. There are reconstructions of villages from three major time periods: Prehistory, the Roman Period, and the Middle Ages. It is a 'live' museum where people in period dress live and work, and is therefore a pleasantly participatory way to see and learn about history.

Archeonlaan 1, Alphen a/d Rijn

www.archeon.nl

9 Kinderdijk

A UNESCO World Heritage Site and the most archetypal of all Dutch scenes, with 19 windmills idyllically situated along a broad canal, where you can take a canal cruise. During July and August the mills are put into action on Saturdays (In 2023, the National Windmill Days, when most windmills across the country are open to the public, will be on May l 13 and 14)

By the Lek River, southeast of Rotterdam

www.kinderdijk.com

8 Madurodam

'All Netherlands in a day' is how to best describe this miniature scale-model town where you can see all of the Netherlands' major cities and landmarks up close and personal, with many mechanized exhibits, including busy motorways and sailing ships.

George Maduroplein 1, The Hague

www.madurodam.nl

7 Delfshaven / Port of Rotterdam

Delfshaven is where the Pilgrim Fathers departed for the New World in 1620. The tiny harbor has been preserved to look much as it did in centuries past, with the addition of some trendy waterfront restaurants. Across the road at the Spido Landing Stage, tours by boat offer unique insight into modern life in one of the world's busiest seaports.

Delfshaven/Spido Cruises: www.spido.nl

www.rotterdamhistorischdelfshaven.nl

Historisch Museum Rotterdam,
Korte Hoogstraat 31, Rotterdam

https://museumrotterdam.nl

6 The Kröller-Müller Museum

When visiting the wooded parkland of De Hoge Veluwe National Park, you can either drive your car or borrow the white bicycles available at the park gates, free of charge, to travel the couple of kilometers to this museum, which ranks as the third most important collection of art in the Netherlands. Over almost 90 paintings and over 180 drawings by Van Gogh (roughly 50 of which are on display at any given time) and other artists such as Seurat, Monet and Picasso are featured, including a Sculpture Garden second to none and worth the trip in itself.

Houtkampweg 6, Otterlo

www.kmm.nl or www.krollermuller.nl

freshwater tidal area. Today, visitors can explore the park on foot or by boat and observe a unique range of plants, animals and birds.
near Dordrecht
www.np-debiesbosch.nl

SINGER LAREN
Laren (near Hilversum in the province of North Holland) became fashionable with painters in the 1870s, notably those of the Impressionist Hague School. The Singers, an American couple who moved to Laren in 1901, collected the paintings of visiting artists, and this delightful museum – situated in the residential area of a very chic town – is based on their collection. Upscale local shops complete the experience.
Oude Drift 1, Laren
www.singerlaren.nl

FRANEKER PLANETARIUM
In 1774, Eise Eisinga, an amateur scientist, built a planetarium in his living room in order to calm the villagers' fears about the end of the world. Despite his limited knowledge about the conjunction of the planets, the planetarium is a masterpiece of engineering that still functions perfectly after 200-some years, making it the oldest in the world.
Eise Eisingastraat 3, Franeker (Friesland)
www.eisinga-planetarium.nl

RECREATIONAL AREA SPAARNWOUDE
In 1969, the government, five municipalities and the province of North Holland decided to keep the area between Amsterdam and Haarlem 'green'. Thus the recreational area 'Spaarnwoude' was launched, covering a total landmass of over 6,178 acres. Located just outside Haarlem, Spaarnwoude has become one of the most popular recreational areas in North Holland. It is considered a pocket of peace and tranquility, offering its visitors the opportunity to hike, cycle and inline skate, while taking in the area's natural beauty. But that is not all: other activities / attractions include parks, play areas, a golf course, a scaling wall, an educational farm, canoe courses, horseback riding and... the opportunity to go skiing at SnowWorld.
just outside Haarlem.
www.spaarnwoudepark.nl

THORN
A favorite subject for posters advertising the province of Limburg, but a village relatively undiscovered by foreign visitors. Thorn is a wonderfully picturesque town with cobbled streets and whitewashed houses and farms that intrude right into the main or 'high' street, giving the town a calmly rural atmosphere. The local abbey was founded towards the end of the 10th century.
Thorn, near Roermond.
www.hartvanlimburg.nl/nl/locatie/vvv-thorn

PANORAMA MESDAG
Panorama Mesdag is a cylindrical painting, more than 14 meters high and 120 meters in circumference. The vista of the sea, the dunes and Scheveningen village was painted by one of the most famous painters of the Hague School, Hendrik Willem Mesdag. It is the oldest 19th-century panorama in the world in its original site, and a unique cultural heritage.
Zeestraat 65, The Hague
www.panorama-mesdag.nl

BOSCHPLAAT NATURE RESERVE (ISLAND OF TERSCHELLING)
Situated on the marshy land of the southern shore of Terschelling, one of the five 'Wadden' islands, this is where thousands of waterfowl and migrating birds gather. Nearby you'll also find lovely beaches where the sand is golden and the water clean.
Terschelling
www.natuurlijkwandelen.nl/boschplaat

THE TROPEN MUSEUM
Not as crowded as Amsterdam's other large museums, here you can discover the culture of Suriname (for kids); learn about art, culture and colonialism; travel through Africa and South-East Asia; or

visit Latin America and the Caribbean, discovering a world apart. An excellent restaurant serves international dishes, and there are also temporary exhibits. The adjacent Tropentheater presents a mind-boggling selection of cultural performances from around the world.
Linnaeusstraat 2, Amsterdam
www.tropenmuseum.nl

WATERLAND NEELTJE JANS (THE DELTA PROJECT)
In a fascinating exhibition and tour, find out about Zeeland's endless fight against the threat of floods and the pragmatic Dutch response – a massive dam and flood barrier that literally closed off the sea. From April-October you can visit a dolphin station and make a round-trip on the Oosterschelde (a portion of the sea that once stretched into the province of Zeeland, but that now, due to the dikes, has become brackish water and a unique nature area). Don't miss the hurricane simulator!
Island of Neeltje Jans, Faelweg 5, Vrouwenpolder
www.neeltjejans.nl/en

ZUIDERZEE MUSEUM
This living museum of 130 buildings built on the banks of the IJsselmeer provides a snapshot of life between 1880 and 1932. The original houses, school, church and shops have been transported from 39 locations in the IJsselmeer region.
Wierdijk 12-22, Enkhuizen
www.zuiderzeemuseum.nl

OPEN AIR MUSEUM (NEDERLANDS OPENLUCHT MUSEUM) – ARNHEM
A 44-acre park representing a time capsule of Dutch provincial life with all the inherent customs and traditions in a living history setting, complete with a cross-section of real historic buildings and houses literally transported from their original location. Windmills, fully furnished thatched-roof farmhouses and craft shops complete the melting pot.
Schelmseweg 89, Arnhem
www.openluchtmuseum.nl

NOORBEEK
Popular with Dutch hikers, this tiny village nestles cozily in a valley (yes, they do exist) in Limburg and still retains its authentic atmosphere with tractors chugging down the high street to deposit hay in the lofts above the farms.
Noorbeek near Maastricht
www.noorbeek.nl

FOAM FOTOGRAFIE MUSEUM – AMSTERDAM
FOAM aims to inform and inspire the audience by presenting all facets of contemporary photography and exhibits world-famous photographers alongside emerging artists, ranging from historical to contemporary work. Includes major exhibitions and discussion forums.
Keizersgracht 609, Amsterdam
www.foam.org

EYE FILM INSTITUTE NETHERLANDS
EYE Film Institute is completely dedicated to film and the moving image. Film is exhibited as art, entertainment, cultural heritage, and a conveyor of information. It offers exhibitions, programs, films for children, educational programs and activities for all ages.
IJpromenade, Amsterdam
www.eyefilm.nl/en

GRONINGER MUSEUM – GRONINGEN
This eclectic museum juts out into the canal and defies description, with exhibits ranging from arts and crafts to fashion. If the drawbridge entrance happens to be raised for a passing boat, be sure to look at the tongue-in-cheek tiles underneath. A zany place through and through.
Museumeiland 1, Groningen
www.groningermuseum.nl/en

HUNEBEDDEN (DOLMENS)
One of the largest concentrations of Stone Age boulder formations exists in the idyllic province of Drenthe in the northeast, where 54 dolmen configurations, one with a capstone weighing an incredible 20,000 kilos, are scattered throughout the countryside, and are believed to be the megalithic skeletons of burial tombs used by farmers in this most ancient area of the Netherlands. Amazingly, these Fred-Flintstone-like structures are almost 2,000 years older than the famous Stonehenge in England, and 1,000 years older than the pyramids in Egypt.

Even more amazing is how they were transported and lifted into place. The Nationaal Hunebedden Informatiecentrum (National Dolmen Information Center) in Borger, where you can also see the largest hunebed, is the perfect place to get the lowdown on theories.
Information center: Hunebedstraat 27, Borger (between Assen and Emmen)
www.hunebedcentrum.eu/en

INTERNATIONAL CLUBS

The real estate agents have found you the ideal place to live, the movers have brought over your possessions from another part of the world, an acquaintance or two at work has shown you the places around town, and you think you are on the road to settling in – but not quite! For those who like the company of others, either occasionally or often, it's the circle of like-minded friends that one needs in order to be able to enjoy the fairly long blustery winters of the Netherlands. Social clubs are a great place to meet other expatriates who have recently arrived, as well as those 'expats' and other members who have been around for a while – as well as locals, of course.

In the Netherlands, those looking for a place to network are sure to find something that will meet their needs: for professional women, there is PWN (Professional Women's Network) in Amsterdam that provides women with a forum for meeting, networking, and getting down to business, and, along similar lines, Connecting Women, in The Hague as well as Women's Business Initiative International. Then, of course, there are International Rotary Clubs, for both men and women. For those who are looking for a nationality-based club, there are plenty on offer, as well as clubs based on a particular hobby, such as dance, drama or art. For those who are simply looking for a group of friends, or a source of fun family outings, there are also several clubs to join, in places as diverse as Eindhoven, Maastricht, Breda, Dordrecht, Enschede, Groningen, and more – and, of course, the cities of Amsterdam, The Hague, Rotterdam and Utrecht. For more information on clubs in the Netherlands, check the reference pages at the end of the chapter.

SPORTS CLUBS

As you'll quickly realize, the hardy Dutch are avid sports enthusiasts with well-organized leagues and clean, modern facilities. Whether it's a bike touring group or a competitive, high-profile sport that you fancy, there's something for everyone here. As an expat, you'll have no excuse not to be fit during your sojourn in this country.

WHY JOIN A SPORTS CLUB?

Sports clubs offer a great outlet for meeting new people, staying (or getting) in shape, practicing the Dutch language and, in many cases, providing an indoor venue when the weather outside is frightful. The question is: what's the best way to find a sports club in your area that suits your interests and budget?

HOW DO I FIND THE RIGHT CLUB?

Depending on where you live:

- find out if your community publishes a(n online) guide titled *stadsgids* or *gemeentegids*, or visit the local city hall, *gemeentehuis*. The sports clubs will be listed under *sportverenigingen*. Most of the titles should be understandable, but you may have to use your dictionary. Call or e-mail the club's chairperson, secretary or contact person. Chances are good that they will speak English if your Dutch is not yet up to speed
- contact ACCESS, www.access-nl.org
- search online
- drop in on the sports facilities or gym in your area to pick up some information
- visit www.sport.nl to find a sports club near you.

Once you have found one or more clubs in the sport you like and have made contact, ask if you can try out the training sessions a couple of times before you become a member. There is no harm in shopping around if the community you live in has more than one club offering a particular sport. Once you join, you are usually committed financially for a year.

COMPETITIONS

Dutch sports are unified into national 'bonds' or governing sports bodies, and competitions follow international rules and regulations.

JUST FOR KIDS

In the Netherlands, sports are not really as much part of the Dutch school curriculum as they are in many other countries. If students want to be active in sports, they must find a venue outside of school – the most popular ones being for hockey, soccer and tennis. International and American schools in the Netherlands, however, generally provide more opportunities. Additionally, this being a country where most people live below sea level, children are (informally) required to earn a swimming diploma. Many clubs and pools offer such a program. A good source of information on sports clubs (for kids) is the *gemeentegids* (or *stadsgids*), which you can pick up at your town hall (*gemeentehuis*), or read online.

AMERICAN BASEBALL FOUNDATION

For nostalgic Americans and all those interested in 'batting up', the American Baseball Foundation has its own clubhouse and has even branched out to feature soccer and baseball. For more information, see the reference pages. Or visit ABF International Sports Club, www.abfsport.nl. Baseball is also gaining in popularity across the Netherlands, among kids and adults; visit www.knbsb.nl for more information.

STUDENTS

For more information on sports activities for students, see page 239.

WEBSITES

More sports sites can be found on the reference pages at the end of the chapter.

SELECTED SPORTS EVENTS IN 2024

JUMPING AMSTERDAM

One of the largest international equestrian events in the Netherlands, that attracts approximately 50,000 visitors a year and includes a.o. dressage, jumping, ponies, juniors, and driving – as well as entertainment.
Jan. 25-28, 2024
Amsterdam RAI
www.jumpingamsterdam.nl

ABN AMRO TENNIS TOURNAMENT

An increasingly famous tournament, which has become one of the 13 worldwide '500 points tournaments', allowing the players to accumulate more ranking points.
Feb. 10-18, 2024
Rotterdam Ahoy
www.abnamro-open.nl

NN CPC LOOP

An international city-pier-city half-marathon that takes place annually in The Hague, attracting over 42,000 participants every year, for all the different races. The course is flat, fast and traffic-free. The race begins in the city center, heads out to the pier at the coastal resort of Scheveningen and then returns to where it started. There is also a 10km fun run and other recreational walking and running events varying in distance – also two for kids.
Mar. 12, 2024
The Hague / Scheveningen
www.nncpcloopdenhaag.com (on this site you will also find other running events)

ROTTERDAM MARATHON

Thanks to the three World records that have been established on this course, the Rotterdam marathon has attained (inter)national fame. The NN Marathon Rotterdam has become the biggest marathon in the Netherlands. The course is fast, the crowds are great and the atmosphere on the Coolsingel is unique.
Apr. 13-14, 2024 – when this issue went to print, the date had not yet been announced
Rotterdam
www.nnmarathonrotterdam.org

SNEEKWEEK

An annually recurring sailing event that spans an entire week. It originated in 1814, when the people of Sneek went out sailing to celebrate the fact that a local hero had deserted the French army and made it home safely. There are sailing races every day, in various categories, as well as festivities and a fair.
Aug. 2-8, 2024
Sneekermeer, Sneek
www.sneekweek.nl

SKÛTSJESILEN

Skûtjesilen is the name for sailing races involving old freight ships, or flat-bottom boats, that were used towards the turn of the 19th century to transport turf, fertilizer and other goods to isolated farms. Their bottoms were flat, allowing them to navigate the shallow waters when approaching their destination. These boats are a sight to behold; beautiful, old-fashioned, lovingly-constructed wooden testaments to a practical, sea-faring nation.
Aug. 3-16, 2024
Frisian Lakes
www.skutsjesilen.nl

FORMULA 1 HEINEKEN DUTCH GRAND PRIX

A weekend at the legendary circuit of Zandvoort with practice rounds, qualification races and the race for the 2024 Dutch Grand Prix.
Aug. 25, 2024
Circuit Park Zandvoort
www.circuitzandvoort.nl/en

DAM TO DAM LOOP

A 16km-course from Dam Square to the center of Zaandam through the IJ-tunnel. In total 70,000 athletes from across the world signed up last year, of which 50,000 sign up for the official Dam tot Dam Loop. Participants are encouraged to run in support of a charity; these charities are given extra publicity preceding the Run. There are bands and small orchestras lining the course, along with hundreds of thousands of spectators, creating a festive atmosphere. Don't forget the evening 8km run in Zaandam!
Sep. 21-22, 2024
Amsterdam
www.damloop.nl

Sports in the Netherlands

Small as it is, with almost 18 million inhabitants, the Netherlands scores well in the international world of sports. It has fantastic skaters, field hockey players, (track) cyclists, sailors, swimmers, soccer players and athletes who can regularly be found on some or other podium, receiving their medals.

During the Tokyo Summer Olympics of 2021, the Netherlands came in 7th in number of medals – outranking countries such as Germany, France and Italy, while at the Beijing 2023 Winter Olympics, it came in 6th. Looking at the last five Summer and Winter Olympics, you can see that the Netherlands consistently finds itself in the top ten of best sports countries in the world. It is therefore also the primary aim of the NOC*NSF, the Dutch umbrella organization for sports, for this country to retain this position.

Just think of the number of Dutch athletes who belong to the absolute top in the world; people such as Max Verstappen (Formula 1), Mathieu van der Poel (cycling), Suzanne Schulting (short track), Sifan Hassan (running), Harrie Lavreysen (track cycling), Kiran Badloe (wind surfing) and Lieke Martens (soccer).

Normally, the Dutch are not openly proud of their nationality. However, on the day of a great game or tournament, an explosion of pride takes place in the form of the royal color orange on cheeks, flags, balloons, shirts and hats. When Max Verstappen became Formula One world champion in December 2021, not only the orange-clad crowds on the stands of the Abu Dhabi circuit erupted, but so did 5 million Dutch people sitting in front of their televisions. And again in 2022. And again in 2023. A similar type of orange hysteria takes place when the Dutch national soccer team reaches the finals in the FIFA Worldcup Championships, such as in Qatar in 2022.

And if the temperature sinks to freezing, the so-called *Elfstedentocht* fever (the *Elfstedentocht* is a 125-mile ice-skating race across the frozen lakes and canals of Friesland) reaches its boiling point. Old heroes from way back when are invited to a variety of talk shows in order to once again share their experiences and expectations. Fortunately, the orange clutter disappears just as quickly once an event is over. And unfortunately, the most recent Elfstedentocht took place way back in 1997.

Whereas, in the U.S., sporting events are family events where fights are few and far between, the situation is quite different in the Netherlands. The supporters' riots that take place at a soccer match no longer surprise anyone. Even though the perpetrators represent a very small minority of the Dutch population, they do make themselves known. Only the British and German hooligans exceed the Dutch in terms of reputation when it comes to violence. The consequence is a huge presence of police, that is somewhat reminiscent of a large military operation. They help maintain the peace during the matches. This includes the Mobiele Eenheid ('Mobile Unit'), the bad dudes of the normally pleasant Dutch police force; the riot police. In the meantime, the fans, who are busy partying and belting out their teams' battle songs, seem to be singularly undeterred by any of this. The collective atmosphere is unusual, to say the least; it has all the appearances of a festival that is making its way through an armed camp. If you think about it, it's odd what people get used to.

The Netherlands has countless local sports clubs and associations where members of all ages and talents can engage in their favorite hobby or simply come together and enjoy each other's company. Sports connect people and bring them together. They help foster understanding and respect for each other, and thereby contribute to a better balance in society, something that proved of even more importance during the pandemic with all its lockdowns. Participating in a sport also means participating in society. The more people 'work out', the healthier the Netherlands becomes, says NOC*NSF, whose aim it is to get 10% more people actively engaged in sports over the years to come. This is important for everyone – whether they be long-term or short-term residents!

And then there is also the Dutch national pastime; cycling! The Netherlands is filled with picturesque routes – through woods, as well as along the coast, rivers and canals – that almost beg to be cycled down. Another favorite pastime is hiking, whether this be the aforementioned mudflat walking across the *wadden* seabeds along the North Sea coast or Nijmegen's annual four-day walking event, called the *Vierdaagse*. Visit https://www.fietsenwandelweb.nl for unique hiking and cycling routes throughout the Netherlands!

Red Bull
RACING

ABBOTT
WORLD
MARATHON
MAJORS
2:18:36
TAGHeuer
balance
tcs
HASSAN
new balance

Step Into a Time Machine

'CUTE AND QUAINT VILLAGE' DESTINATIONS

While there are plenty of picturesque villages or *dorpjes* throughout the country, *The Holland Handbook* award goes first and foremost to five in the northern and heartland provinces: Sloten and Hindeloopen in Friesland, Giethoorn and Staphorst in Overijssel, and Bronckhorst in Gelderland. SLOTEN, about the size of a panoramic snapshot, is the epitome of charm with its gabled houses along a central canal. HINDELOOPEN is famed for its ornately hand-painted furniture and interiors, as well as its ice-skating museum glorifying the *Elfstedentocht* race (a race course that runs along the canals and lakes that connect 11 towns – known as 'cities', or *steden*, by the proud Frisians – in the province of Friesland which can only be held when weather permits). The town clings to the IJsselmeer, cut off and preserved from its sailing prosperity by the construction of the *Afsluitdijk*, or Enclosing Dike, in 1932. GIETHOORN, the 'Venice of the North' where transportation is limited to boats and bikes in the old part, is a punter's paradise and one of the most stunning thatched-roof villages in all of the Netherlands, despite the yearly onslaught of camera-happy gawkers. STAPHORST, where locals still don their traditional garb, wins the time warp prize of the bunch for its fierce adherence to Calvinistic ways. (Be wary of pointing your camera at the traditionally outfitted residents here though, as they consider it a serious invasion of privacy.) BRONCKHORST, officially the smallest town in the Netherlands, is a precious mix of cobblestone streets, farmhouses and local artisans, accented, oddly enough, with a museum devoted to Charles Dickens, and a Christmas festival bar none.

Other prizewinners in this category include Veere, in the southwest province of Zeeland, and the previously mentioned Thorn, in the southeast province of Limburg. VEERE was a former sailing port of major significance, although it's now blocked off from the sea by a dike and sits ever-so-quietly but elegantly on the shore of the Veerse Meer, one of the largest lakes in the Netherlands. THORN, in contrast, is a rural haven known as the 'white village' for its abundance of white-washed, 18th-century houses. It makes for a pleasant respite on your journey either into or out of the bustling metropolis of Maastricht.

And for the quintessential daytrip, offering a combination of village charm and infusion of art, don't miss the glorious studio and gallery of destined-for-eternal-fame, Dutch still-life artist Henk Helmantel. His spectacular, 13th-century parsonage home in WESTEREMDEN lies in the northern province of Groningen. Open to the public on certain afternoons only from late April through October (and by appointment throughout the year), the Helmantel gallery is a work of art in itself (www.helmantel.nl). His home is open to the public (during which a tour of the premises is given) every Thursday, Friday and Saturday afternoon, May through October. Groups can also make appointments for other dates.

For more information on all of the above villages, contact the pertinent VVVs (whose phone numbers you can obtain from your local VVV or via 0900 8008).

TOURING THE LAND OF CASTLES

In a country as rich in history as the Netherlands, it shouldn't surprise you that there are a multitude of castles to visit and explore; in fact there are over 300 castles, manors and estates. Wander into one of these impressive structures and, without even having to close your eyes, you can imagine yourself transported to the times of princes, knights and damsels in distress. Or, at least, in love.

Below, four of the best-known castles – but keep in mind, there are at least 296 more!

One of the most famous castles that are open to the public is the MUIDERSLOT, in Muiden, built in 1280 by Count Floris, a man who was, to use a Dutch expression 'stone rich', which meant that he could afford to build a castle of stone, rather than using the wood that poorer people used to build their houses. The furniture, objects and paintings that are now found in the castle stem from the 17th century, the time when the famous Dutch poet and writer P.C. Hooft lived there. Check the website https://muiderslot.nl for exhibitions and other events.

Also well worth a visit is PALACE HET LOO, in Apeldoorn, which, for three centuries, was the summer palace of the Dutch Royal Family and has since been converted into a museum, illustrating life as it was lived by the royals over the centuries. Particularly the gardens of this palace are famous and have attracted countless visitors.

CASTLE DE HAAR, in Haarzuilens, is the Netherlands' fairytale castle; built in the 14th century and surrounded by a park, water fountains and a garden reminiscent of Versailles, as well as boasting an interior filled with richly colored Flemish tapestries and delicate paintings depicting religious themes, it is a place where weddings are held, as well as children's parties – dressed up as knights and princesses, they make their fantasy come true.

LOEVESTEIN CASTLE, built around 1368, is located strategically in the heart of the Netherlands. In 1673, it became part of the Dutch Water Line, created to protect the Netherlands against Louis XIV's French troops. The concept was simple, but extremely effective; by flooding a 3-5 km stretch of land, the Water Line successfully kept the troops from advancing any further. In fact, in times of floods, the only access road to the castle still becomes untraversable.

Would you like to immerse yourself in the world of kings and dragons? Wake up in a room that held queens and princesses, whose ladies-in-waiting were standing at attention with corsets in hand? Visit https://origineelovernachten.nl/thema/kasteel for an overview of castles that have chosen to continue the age-honored tradition of hospitality, in style.

References

CHAPTER 11
Things to Do in Your Free Time

Websites

OFFICIAL HOLLAND TOURISM WEBSITES
NL Netherlands: www.holland.com: the official website of the Netherlands Board of Tourism
www.lekkerweg.nl: Dutch-language website on tourism and recreation in the Netherlands

EXPAT WEBSITES WITH NATIONAL EVENT DIARIES IN ENGLISH
www.expatica.com
www.iamexpat.nl

ONLINE TICKET SALES
www.ticketmaster.nl
www.ticketsales.com
www.ticketswap.com

MUSEUM WEBSITES
www.museum.nl: an overview of all the museums in the Netherlands
www.museumserver.nl: portal website for museums in the Netherlands

AUCTIONS
Christie's Amsterdam: www.christies.com
Sotheby's Amsterdam: www.sothebys.com
Venduehuis The Hague:
www.venduehuis.com
Veilinghuis Onder de Boompjes, Leiden:
www.onderdeboompjes.nl

CASTLES
www.kastelen.startpagina.nl
www.kasteleninnederland.nl
www.kasteel.nl

OUTDOOR ACTIVITIES
Search for activities at: www.viator.com
Cycling Tours: www.dutch-biketours.nl
De Keukenhof: www.keukenhof.nl/en
Mud flat walking: www.wadlopen.org
National Park De Biesbosch:
www.biesbosch.org
Nederlands Openlucht Museum:
www.openluchtmuseum.nl
Recreational Area Spaarnwoude:
www.spaarnwoude.nl
South Limburg: www.noorbeek.nl
The Groene Hart (Green Heart):
www.vvvhetgroenehart.nl
The Pieterpad: www.pieterpad.nl
The Veluwe: www.develuwe.nl
Wetlands Safaris close to Amsterdam:
www.wetlandssafari.nl
Windmills of Kinderdijk:
www.kinderdijk.com

Dining Out

THE FORK
Offers an up-to-date and objective restaurant survey for the Netherlands
www.thefork.com

TRIPADVISOR
The best restaurants in the Netherlands
www.tripadvisor.nl/Restaurants

Recommended Reading

THE NETHERLANDS
By Jeremy Gray & Reuben Acciano
Published by Lonely Planet Publications
For curious and independent travelers
www.lonelyplanet.com

THE NETHERLANDS – THE ROUGH GUIDE
By Martin Dunford and Phil Lee
Published by Rough Guides
Distributed by Penguin Travel Guide
www.roughguides.nl

THE NETHERLANDS – EYEWITNESS TRAVEL GUIDE
By Gerard Harmans.
Published by Dorling Kindersley.
www.traveldk.com

NL365 – A YEAR IN THE NETHERLANDS
Photography: Frans Lemmens
This extensive photobook is a feast for the eyes and an ode to a special and beautiful country.
www.franslemmens.com or
www.hollandbooks.nl

AMSTERDAM CITY GUIDE
Published by Lonely Planet Publications
By Jeremy Gray
A smart, stylish and streetwise guide which helps to connect with the real Amsterdam
www.lonelyplanet.com

ATLAS OF AMSTERDAM
Published by Noordhoff Uitgevers
The atlas tells you everything you always wanted to know about Amsterdam, and everything you never knew you wanted to know too.
www.bosatlas.nl
To order: www.hollandbooks.nl

THE CYCLING PARADISE
By Peter de Lange
Published by XPat Media
An ode to the unique Dutch cycling culture. Including 10 stunning bike routes & places to stay.
To order: www.hollandbooks.nl

HOLLAND BOOKS
Features a wide range of books and travel guides on Holland: www.hollandbooks.nl

International Social Clubs

ENGLISH-LANGUAGE GROUPS AND CLUBS
ACCESS: www.access-nl.org
American Women's Club Amsterdam:
www.awca.nl
American Women's Club The Hague:
www.awcthehague.org
Andrew's Society of the Netherlands:
www.standrews.nl
British Club The Hague:
www.britishclubthehague.nl
British Society: www.britsoc.nl
CADS (Commercial Anglo Dutch Society):
www.cads-amsterdam.org
Club of Amsterdam:
www.clubofamsterdam.com
Connect International, Groningen:
www.connect-int.org
Connecting Women, The Hague:
www.connectingwomen.nl
Expat Republic: www.expatrepublic.com
ExpatsHaarlem: www.expatshaarlem.nl
International Almere:
www.internationalalmere.com
The International Rotaract Club in Amsterdam: www.rotaract.nl
International Women's Contact The Hague:
www.iwcthehague.nl

International Women's Contact Amsterdam: www.iwcamsterdam.nl
International Women's Contact Breda: www.iwcbreda.nl
International Women's Contact Utrecht/Amersfoort: www.iwcu.nl
International Women's Club Eindhoven: www.iwce.nl
International Women's Club of South Limburg: www.iwc-sl.nl
The Irish Club-Netherlands: www.irishclub.nl
Rotterdam Japan Club: www.rotterdamjapanclub.nl
Toastmasters in the Netherlands: www.toastmasters.nl
The Hague Online Social Club: www.thehagueonline.com
Women's Business Initiative International: www.womensbusinessinitiative.net

FRENCH-SPEAKING CLUBS

Accueil des Francophones de La Haye: www.accueillahaye.com
Alliance Française: www.alliance-francaise.nl
Alliance Française La Haye: www.aflahaye.nl
Institute Français: www.institutfrancais.nl
Union des Français à l'Étranger: www.ufepaysbas.nl

GERMAN-SPEAKING CLUBS

Deutscher Internationaler Klub: www.deutscher-internationaler-klub.org
Deutsch-Niederländischer Verein: www.deutsch-nl-verein.nl

SPANISH-SPEAKING CLUB

Asociación Hispánica De La Haya: www.asoha.nl

Cultural Institutes

The John Adams Institute, Amsterdam,
Herenmarkt 95a, 1013 EC Amsterdam
Tel.: 020 624 72 80
www.john-adams.nl

Goethe-Institut Amsterdam
Herengracht 470, 1017 CA Amsterdam
Tel.: 020 531 2900
www.goethe.de

Goethe-Institut Rotterdam
Westersingel 9, 3014 GM Rotterdam
Tel.: 010 209 20 90
www.goethe.de

Art Clubs

The Arts Society The Hague
Kerkstraat 75, 2242 HE Wassenaar
www.theartssociety.org/the-hague

International Art Club
Weimarstraat 23, 2562 GN The Hague
www.iacdenhaag.nl

Images International Photo Club
English speaking photography club of The Hague
www.imagesphotoclub.com

Studio Jean
Drawing and painting lessons
Thomsonlaan 65, 2565 HX The Hague
Tel.: 070 392 16 72
www.studiojean.nl

Marcello's Art Factory
Drawing and painting lessons, clinics and events
Kon. Emmakade 148, 2518 JK The Hague
Tel.: 070 204 35 40
www.marcellos.nl

The British Choir of The Hague
Tel.: 070 328 28 03
www.cecilia-choir.com

Academy of Vocal Arts
Singing together
Tel.: 070 324 97 78
www.acva.nl

ENGLISH-SPEAKING THEATER GROUPS

The In-Players International Drama Group, Amsterdam
Tel.: 020 770 49 84
www.inplayers.org

International Drama Group of English Speaking Associates (I.D.E.A)
www.idea-panto.nl

Stichting The English Theatre (STET)
Saturnusstraat 9, 2516 AD The Hague
Tel.: 06 38 934 593
www.theenglishtheatre.nl

Anglo-American Theater Group (AATG)
P.O. Box 10239, The Hague
www.aatg.nl

Leiden English-speaking Theater (LEST)
Oude Singel 290, 2312 RK Leiden
www.leidenenglishtheatre.nl

ENGLISH-SPEAKING COMEDY

Boom Chicago
Not cabaret, and not stand-up, Boom Chicago is a mix of sketches and pure improvisation.
Rozengracht 117, 1016 LV Amsterdam
Tel.: 020 217 04 00
www.boomchicago.nl

Comedy Café
Comedy, food, cocktails
IJdok 89, 1013 MM Amsterdam
Tel.: 020 722 08 27
www.comedycafe.nl

The Comedy Embassy
Tel.: 06 14 467 750
www.comedyembassy.com

Toomler (Comedytrain)
Breitnerstraat 2, 1077 BL Amsterdam
www.comedytrain.nl

Sports

ENGLISH-SPEAKING SPORTS CLUBS

ABF International Sports Club
Ammonslaantje 1, 2241 BP Wassenaar
www.abfsport.nl

The Hague Hash House Harriers
www.haguehash.nl

The Hague Road Runners
Groenendaal 11, 2244 BK Wassenaar
Tel.: 070 328 10 25
www.hagueroadrunners.nl

Gaelic Football: www.denhaaggaa.com

CRICKET

CC Qui Vive
Sportpark de Eendracht
Bok de Korverweg 20 1067 HR Amsterdam
www.quivivecc.com

De Kieviten Cricket Club, The Hague
Dr. Mansveltkade 11, 2242 TZ Wassenaar
Tel.: 070 514 24 30
www.kieviten.nl/cricket

Voorburg Cricket Club, Voorburg
Tel.: 070 386 26 78
Groene Zoom 20, 2491 EH The Hague
www.voorburgcc.nl

General info and clubs in the Netherlands
www.cricket.nl

GOLF
Nederlandse Golf Federatie
Orteliuslaan 1041, 3528 BE Utrecht
Tel.: 030 242 63 70
www.ngf.nl

Amsterdamse Golf Club
Bauduinlaan 35, 1047 HK Amsterdam
Tel.: 020 497 78 66
www.amsterdamsegolfclub.nl

For more golf clubs in the Netherlands: www.golf.nl

ROWING
Rowing Center Berlagebrug
Weesperzijde 1094, 1097 DS Amsterdam
Tel.: 020 468 32 41
www.amsterdam.toprow.com

TopRow Haarlem
Noord Schalkwijkerweg 101, 2034 JA Haarlem
wwwhaarlem.toprow.com

TopRow The Hague
Cruquiuskade 10, 2521 EA The Hague
www.denhaag.toprow.com

RUGBY
Rugby Nederland
Bok de Korverweg 6, 1067 HR Amsterdam
www.rugby.nl/organisatie

Haagsche Rugby Club
Theo Mann-Bouwmeesterlaan 800,
2597 HM The Hague
www.haagscherugbyclub.nl

Amstelveense RC
Sportlaan 25a, Amstelveen
Tel.: 020 643 89 79
www.arcrugby.nl

AFL Netherlands (Australian Football)
www.aflnetherlands.org

Rugby Club 't Gooi
Sportpark Naarden
Amersfoortsestraatweg 14, 1411 HC Naarden
Tel.: 035 694 68 19
www.rugbyclub-gooi.nl

SAILING
Watersports Center Sloterplas
Christoffel Plantijngracht 4, 1065 DA Amsterdam
Tel.: 020 617 58 39
www.watersportcentrumsloterplas.nl

Holland Sail
To book sailing trips In the Netherlands
Stationsplein 3, 1601 EN Enkhuizen
Tel.: 228 31 21 33
www.hollandsail.com

Zeezeilschool Scheveningen
RYA Training Center. All RYA classes are in English.
Dr. Lelykade 22, 2593 CM Scheveningen
Tel.: 070 351 48 58
www.zeezeilschool.nl

Kust Zeil Vereniging Scheveningen (KZVS)
Zwarte Pad, Noorderstrand Scheveningen
Tel.: 070 358 95 86
www.kzvs.nl

Kust Zeilvereniging Wassenaar (KZVW)
Strand Wassenaar
Tel.: 06 412 191 81
www.kzvw.nl

KITE SURFING
Kite Surfing School Holland
Monster, Kijkduin, Scheveningen
Tel.: 06 40 80 88 00
www.kiteboardschool.nl
Kitesurfschool.nl
Kijkduin/Scheveningen, Oostvoorne, Hoorn/Schellinkhout
Tel.: 070 358 48 00
www.kitesurfschool.nl

TENNIS
Berg en Dal
Daal en Bergselaan 13, 2565 AB The Hague
Tel.: 070 325 13 33
www.htvbergendal.nl

De Uithof
Jaap Edenweg 10, 2544 NL The Hague
Tel.: 070 404 44 59
www.tcdeuithof.nl

Mets Tennisbanen
Berkenbosch Blokstraat 20, 2586 HG The Hague
Tel.: 070 355 98 49
www.demetselaars.nl

Haagsche Lawn Tennis Club Leimonias
Klatteweg 103, 2597 KA The Hague
Tel.: 070 355 76 76
www.leimonias.nl

Westvliet Fitness & Racquet Club
Westvlietweg 55, 2267 AC Leidschendam
Tel.: 070 386 44 44
www.westvliet.nl

Tennis Club Amsterdam
Nieuwe Kalfjeslaan 19A, 1182 AA Amstelveen
www.tcamsterdam.net

VVV Tourist Info

Tourist Information Office
General – www.vvv.nl

VVV AMSTERDAM
Stationsplein 10, 1012 AB Amsterdam
Tel.: 0900 400 40 40
www.vvvamsterdam.nl

VVV THE HAGUE
Hofweg 1, 2511 AA The Hague
Tel.: 0900 340 35 05
www.vvvdenhaag.nl

VVV MAASTRICHT
Kleine Staat 1, 6122 ED Maastricht
Tel.: 043 325 21 21
www.vvvmaastricht.nl

VVV ROTTERDAM
Coolsingel 67, 3012 AC Rotterdam
Tel.: 0900 403 40 65
www.vvvrotterdam.nl

VVV UTRECHT
Vredenburg 90, 3511 BD Utrecht
Tel.: 0900 128 87 32
www.utrechtyourway.nl

City Info

AMSTERDAM
www.amsterdamsuitburo.nl: outings and events in Amsterdam
www.amsterdam.com: offers an overview of museums, restaurants, hotels, events and shops in Amsterdam
www.amsterdam.nl: is in Dutch and English and provides everything you need to know about Amsterdam
www.amsterdam.info: informative website on Amsterdam in more than 20 languages
www.iamsterdam.com: a portal website on Amsterdam, Almere, Amstelveen and Haarlemmermeer
www.internationallocals.nl: website for internationals living and working in Amsterdam with events, services and places to go

ARNHEM
www.visitarnhem.com

GRONINGEN
www.visitgroningen.nl/en: explore Groningen Province and Groningen City

MAASTRICHT
www.bezoekmaastricht.nl

ROTTERDAM
www.rotterdamsuitburo.nl: outings and events in Rotterdam
www.rotterdam.info: event calendar with events, exhibitions, festivals, general information, tips etc.

THE HAGUE
www.haagsuitburo.nl: outings and events in The Hague
www.thehague.com: The Hague City Council official website offers city news, events and information in English
www.thehagueonline.com: local daily news a weekly calendar of events in the The Hague area

UTRECHT
www.visit-utrecht.com: explore Utrecht
www.visit-utrecht.com/event-calendar: with an event Calendar in English

WE'D LIKE TO THANK THE FOLLOWING COMPANIES AND ORGANIZATIONS FOR THEIR INVALUABLE CONTRIBUTIONS TO THIS BOOK

BDO Accountants & Adviseurs
Robin Schalekamp, Kees de Graaf
Weena 764, 3014 DA Rotterdam
Tel.: 010 242 46 00
E-mail: robin.schalekamp@bdo.nl
www.bdo.nl

Doso! Coaching & Counseling
Dorota Klop-Sowinska
Van Eeghenlaan 27, 1071 EN Amsterdam
Tel.: 06 13 253 655
E-mail: dorota@dosocoaching.com
www.dosocoaching.com

Educaide
your international education solution house
Willemijn van Oppen-Stuyt
P.O.Box 96911, 2509 JH The Hague
Tel.: 06 559 88 998
E-mail: info@educaide.nl
www.educaide.nl

Expatax / Activpayroll
Arjan Enneman
De Bouw 107, 3991 SZ Houten
Tel.: 030 246 85 36
E-mail: arjan.enneman@activpayroll.com
www.expatax.nl

Expat Mortgages
Richardo Cruz Fortes
Barbara Strozzilaan 101, 1083 HN Amsterdam
Tel.: 020 717 39 08
E-mail: info@expatmortgages.nl
www.expatmortgages.nl

Expertise in Labour Mobility
Nannette Ripmeester
Mathenesserlaan 255, 3021 HD Rotterdam
Tel.: 010 477 68 16
E-mail: info@labourmobility.com
www.labourmobility.com

New2NL
Annebet van Mameren
Tel.: 06 2909 39 33
E-mail: annebet@new2nl.com
www.new2nl.com

Nuffic
The Dutch organisation for internationalisation in education
P.O. Box 29777, 2502 LT The Hague
Kortenaerkade 11, 2518 AX The Hague
Tel.: 070 426 0260
www.studyinNl.nl
www.nuffic.nl

Harveybloom Attorneys
Attorneys and Mediators
Monique Beijersbergen
Zuid Hollandlaan 7, 2596 AL The Hague
Tel.: 088 210 2290
E-mail: monique@harveybloomadvocaten.nl
www.harveybloomadvocaten.nl

Annette de Vreede
Punt 13, 4332 AB Middelburg
Tel.: 06 546 873 78
E-mail: annette.de.vreede@outlook.com

Stark Real Estate
Karola Grünenbaum
Breitnerlaan 318, 2596 HH Den Haag
Tel.: 070 326 22 87
E-mail: home@starkrealestate.nl
www.starkrealestate.nl

Védévé Legal
Liane van de Vrugt
Startbaan 6, 1185 XR Amstelveen
P.O. Box 87250, 1080 JG Amsterdam
Tel.: 020 772 23 34
E-mail: lvdvrugt@vedeve.com
www.vedeve.com

Rovers & Moffat
Patrick Rovers
Tenby Place, 102 Selby Road, West Bridgford, Nottingham, Great Britain, NG2 7BA
Tel.: +44 20 70976693
E-mail: patrick@roversmoffat.com
www.roversmoffat.com

ADVERTISERS' INDEX

PHOTO INDEX